INTERNATIONAL HANDBOOK OF JEWISH EDUCATION

International Handbooks of Religion and Education

VOLUME 5

Aims & Scope

The *International Handbooks of Religion and Education* series aims to provide easily accessible, practical, yet scholarly, sources of information about a broad range of topics and issues in religion and education. Each Handbook presents the research and professional practice of scholars who are daily engaged in the consideration of these religious dimensions in education. The accessible style and the consistent illumination of theory by practice make the series very valuable to a broad spectrum of users. Its scale and scope bring a substantive contribution to our understanding of the discipline and, in so doing, provide an agenda for the future.

For further volumes:
http://www.springer.com/series/7477

International Handbook of Jewish Education

Part One

Edited by

Helena Miller
UJIA, London, UK

Lisa D. Grant
Hebrew Union College-Jewish Institute of Religion, New York, NY, USA

and

Alex Pomson
Hebrew University, Jerusalem, Israel

Editors
Helena Miller
United Jewish Israel Appeal (UJIA)
37 Kentish Town Road
NW1 8NX London
United Kingdom
helena.miller@ujia.org

Prof. Lisa D. Grant
Hebrew Union College
Jewish Institute of Religion
Brookdale Center
1 West 4th St.
10012 New York
NY
USA
lgrant54@gmail.com

Prof. Alex Pomson
Hebrew University of Jerusalem
Melton Centre for Jewish Education
Mount Scopus
Jerusalem
Israel
apomson@mscc.huji.ac.il

ISSN 1874-0049   e-ISSN 1874-0057
Printed in 2 parts
ISBN 978-94-007-0353-7   e-ISBN 978-94-007-0354-4
DOI 10.1007/978-94-007-0354-4
Springer Dordrecht Heidelberg London New York

Library of Congress Control Number: 2011922526

© Springer Science+Business Media B.V. 2011
No part of this work may be reproduced, stored in a retrieval system, or transmitted in any form or by any means, electronic, mechanical, photocopying, microfilming, recording or otherwise, without written permission from the Publisher, with the exception of any material supplied specifically for the purpose of being entered and executed on a computer system, for exclusive use by the purchaser of the work.

Printed on acid-free paper

Springer is part of Springer Science+Business Media (www.springer.com)

Preface

This *International Handbook of Jewish Education* represents a major step in the maturation of a field of human endeavor that stretches back thousands of years yet is entirely contemporary. The editors of these volumes are to be congratulated for assembling a broad and deep series of papers that examine Jewish education from every conceivable perspective in every venue in which it is practised. And for the first time in a volume of this sort, they have gone beyond the United States and Israel, the two major Jewish communities of today, to explore Jewish education as a global phenomenon.

For readers with little familiarity with Jewish education, the chapters in this Handbook provide an introduction to the present moment in this ancient yet modern field of human activity. They will learn about issues facing Jewish schools and about the many and varied settings in which formal and informal Jewish education take place. For readers with an interest in religious education in other faith traditions, this volume provides insights that transcend Jewish education and shed light on the transmission of religious culture more broadly. These readers will read about the philosophical questions confronting Jewish education, and they will learn about organizational structures and perspectives on curriculum and planning that have implications for education in their own faith traditions. And for readers familiar with Jewish education from personal or professional experience, this volume provides a "state of the art hologram" of Jewish education by studying the field from every conceivable angle. By looking at questions of content, at issues in various national contexts, and at persistent challenges facing Jewish education, they can transcend the knowledge they have from their own experience and move to a much deeper, more textured and holistic understanding of Jewish education. All of these readers hold in their hands a gift designed by the editors and crafted by the scholars and practitioners who share their knowledge and wisdom in this Handbook.

Jewish education, the focus of this Handbook, is an enterprise that is as old as the Jewish people and yet entirely contemporary in its forms and functions. The Torah, the Five Books of Moses, is replete with dicta to "teach your children diligently" about the mores of the Jewish people and to "tell your child" the historic narrative of the Jewish people. As a result, Jewish education has topped the agenda of Jews whenever and wherever they lived. Since the destruction of the Second Temple in the time of the Romans, the Jewish academy, first in Yavneh, later in Babylonia and throughout the Jewish world, became the premier Jewish institution. While other cultures valued philosophers and kings, Jewish culture valued scholars.

In modern times, too, Jewish life has centered around Jewish learning. Emancipation and enlightenment vaulted Jews into modernity and opened secular learning to them in ways rarely possible in earlier times. And yet, Jewish learning remained central to Jewish culture and to the Jewish people. Zionism, the national movement to establish a Jewish homeland in the ancient land of the Jewish people, was propelled by writers steeped in Jewish learning. Reform, the religious movement to modernize and universalize Judaism, was led by thinkers with deep Jewish learning. Modern Orthodoxy, Conservative Judaism and other modernist movements were also guided by Jews for whom Jewish learning was of paramount importance in their lives and their very beings. Even in the Ghettos and camps of occupied Europe during World War II and the Holocaust, Jewish learning continued.

Following the destruction of European Jewry, Jewish communities throughout the world renewed their interest in Jewish learning. In Israel, the new state developed both secular and religious national educational systems. In the United States, American Jews moved to the suburbs and created new educational systems in the congregations they were creating for the new post-War Jewish community. And in the rest of the world, Jewish communities struggled to remake their educational systems in the wake of the two watershed events of the twentieth century, the Holocaust and the founding of the State of Israel.

New forms of Jewish education flourished in the latter half of the twentieth century: Day schools expanded beyond the Orthodox world and established a foothold as an alternative form of schooling to the predominant Sunday Schools and afternoon Hebrew Schools; Jewish camping took its place alongside Jewish schooling as a valued means of educating the young; Jewish studies programs became widespread in universities everywhere; Jewish museums, many but certainly not all devoted to the Holocaust, sprung up in cities throughout the world; and travel to Israel and other sites of Jewish life, history, and culture were offered to teens, young adults, families, and seniors. At the dawn of the twenty-first century, new forms of Jewish education abound within existing organizational structures, in new community-based venues outside the structures of the organized Jewish community, and as entrepreneurial startups founded by enterprising individuals expressing their passions. The inventive spirit behind this flourishing of new forms of Jewish education has barely been tampered by the economic downturn of recent years.

As the institutional forms of Jewish education have multiplied, so too have the tasks assigned to Jewish education. Whereas in earlier times, Jewish schools could focus on the study of the Jewish textual tradition, by the latter half of the twentieth century schools took on many of the functions previously fulfilled by families, neighborhoods, and other community agencies. The main focus of Jewish education—even in schools but certainly in informal programs—shifted from content learning to the development of Jewish identity. Since the family often did not have the tools to support what children were learning and how they were developing in Jewish schools, schools began to re-envision themselves as places for Jewish learning and growing for the whole family. Since children often did not have other opportunities to celebrate Jewish holidays or experience Jewish prayer, schools took on these roles, too. Since children were saturated by values from the broader culture, schools began to see themselves as places where Jewish values could be experienced and transmitted, even when—and perhaps especially when—those values ran counter to the values of the dominant culture.

Amid this increasingly complex environment comes the current volume. Its breadth is stunning: It addresses the contemporary realities facing Jewish education in all its complexity. Using the tools of a multiplicity of academic disciplines, exploring Jewish education in a wide range of national, religious, and institutional contexts, and addressing a wide variety of elements of the Jewish educational enterprise, these volumes bring together many of the leading scholars and practitioners of Jewish education to illuminate the contemporary state of thought and action in the field.

These volumes ask—and frequently answer—the most provocative questions about Jewish education at the beginning of the twenty-first century. While it might have been tempting for the editors to categorize those questions by academic discipline (e.g., history, philosophy, sociology) or by educational venue (day school, congregational school, camp) or by area of educational activity (e.g., curriculum, teaching, administration), they have rejected easy categorization in favor of a more nuanced approach. In the opening section of the Handbook, they have placed together questions about the relationship of schools to their communities, the ways in which education affects identity and spirituality, how curriculum can be created, the ways in which Jewish thought can affect educational practice, and how understanding history can enrich our understanding of the present. By reading this opening chapter, the reader can develop a textured understanding of some of the major contextual factors that can enrich the ways in which educators conceptualize their work.

The section on teaching and learning which follows raises questions about the teaching of a wide variety of disciplines in Jewish settings. Questions about the teaching of various genres in the canon of the Jewish textual tradition (Bible and rabbinics) form the core of this chapter, and these chapters provide advances in the thinking about these time-honored curricular areas. This section also addresses questions about other content areas not rooted in a single genre of text: Holocaust, Israel, history, and Hebrew language. This section also raises provocative questions about other curricular areas, some like the arts which have been part of Jewish education for at least a century, but others which are quite new curricular topics: environmentalism, travel, and Jewish peoplehood, and digital media.

The third section of the Handbook boldly makes the statement implicit in other sections but quite explicit here: Schooling is not synonymous with education. In American education, a parallel notion is often referred to as the "Bailyn-Cremin" hypothesis. Drawing on the work of noted historians Bernard Bailyn and Lawrence Cremin, this view suggests that many institutions of society, notably the media, family, neighborhoods, and churches and synagogues, participate in the education of children even though they are not part of the apparatus of schooling. This section of the Handbook presents a variation on the theme in Jewish education: Jewish schools for children and adolescents are joined in the Jewish educational enterprise by a variety of other institutions including early childhood education programs for children younger than school age, universities and adult learning programs for Jews who are beyond school age, programs for parents of school-aged children, and a whole host of venues of "informal education." And Jewish education takes also place in one-on-one mentoring and in special community-wide programs. Of particular note is that Jewish education addresses special issues related to gender and intermarriage as well as the unique needs of special needs learners. The Jewish day school, in its Orthodox and liberal manifestations, is also presented here as a form of Jewish education that goes beyond the norm of Jewish education in the congregational setting. This section makes a major contribution by focusing also on the education of educators, from the "pre-service" stage to ongoing professional development. (Of particular note here is the inclusion of rabbis as part of the education profession.)

Finally, the Handbook concludes with a section devoted to the global character of the Jewish people and, therefore, of Jewish education. While not neglecting the United States and Israel, the Handbook widens its lens by examining Jewish education in Europe, Australia, Canada, Latin America, and the Former Soviet Union. This section is a warning against provincialism to everyone interested in Jewish education.

Readers of this *International Handbook of Jewish Education* will be well rewarded for investing their time exploring the riches it offers. They will be informed about the triumphs and challenges facing Jewish education. They will be stimulated to think about Jewish education in new ways. And most important, they will be inspired by the possibilities Jewish education offers for enhancing the lives of individuals, strengthening the vitality of the Jewish community, and stimulating value-based actions to improve the state of the world we share with the rest of humanity.

Michael Zeldin

Contents of Part One

Introduction 1
Helena Miller, Lisa D. Grant, and Alex Pomson

Section One: Vision and Practice

**Analytic Philosophy of Education and Jewish Education:
The Road Not Taken** 11
Barry Chazan

**Community Engagement: The Challenge of Connecting Jewish
Schools to the Wider Community** 29
Helena Miller

Culture: Restoring Culture to Jewish Cultural Education 47
Zvi Bekerman and Sue Rosenfeld

**Curriculum Development: What We Can Learn
from International Curricula** 63
Roberta Louis Goodman and Jan Katzew

**Curriculum Integration in Jewish Day Schools: The Search
for Coherence** 83
Mitchel Malkus

Gender and Jewish Education: "Why Doesn't This Feel So Good?" .. 99
Tova Hartman and Tamar Miller

**Historiography of American Jewish Education:
A Case for Guarded Optimism** 117
Jonathan Krasner

Janush Korczak's Life and Legacy for Jewish Education 143
Marc Silverman

Jewish Identities: Educating for Multiple and Moving Targets 163
Stuart Charmé and Tali Zelkowicz

Jewish Identity and Jewish Education: The Jewish Identity
Space and Its Contribution to Research and Practice 183
Gabriel Horenczyk and Hagit Hacohen Wolf

Jewish Identity: Who You Knew Affects How You
Jew—The Impact of Jewish Networks in Childhood
upon Adult Jewish Identity 203
Steven M. Cohen and Judith Veinstein

Jewish Thought for Jewish Education: Sources and Resources 219
Jonathan A. Cohen

Philosophy of Jewish Education: Some Thoughts 237
Michael Rosenak

Planning for Jewish Education in the Twenty-First Century:
Toward a New Praxis 247
Jonathan S. Woocher

Pluralism in Jewish Education 267
Bryan Conyer

Post Modernism Paradoxes: After Enlightenment – Jewish
Education and the Paradoxes of Post Modernism 285
Hanan Alexander

Spirituality: The Spiritual Child and Jewish Childhood 301
Michael J. Shire

Visions in Jewish Education 319
Daniel Pekarsky

Section Two: Teaching and Learning

Art: Educating with Art Without Ruining It 339
Robbie Gringras

Arts and Jewish Day School Education in North America 355
Ofra A. Backenroth

Bible: Teaching the Bible in Our Times 373
Barry W. Holtz

Environment: Jewish Education as if the Planet Mattered 389
Eilon Schwartz

Havruta: What Do We Know and What Can We Hope to Learn
from Studying in Havruta? 407
Elie Holzer and Orit Kent

Hebrew Language in Israel and the Diaspora 419
Nava Nevo

History: Issues in the Teaching and Learning of Jewish History 441
Benjamin M. Jacobs and Yona Shem-Tov

Holocaust Education 461
Simone Schweber

Israel Education: Purposes and Practices 479
Alick Isaacs

Israel Travel Education 497
Scott Copeland

Jewish Peoplehood Education 515
David Mittelberg

Life Cycle Education: The Power of Tradition, Ritual, and Transition . 541
Howard Deitcher

Other Religions in Jewish Education 561
Michael Gillis

Talmud: Making a Case for Talmud Pedagogy—The Talmud as an Educational Model 581
Marjorie Lehman and Jane Kanarek

Technology: The Digital Revolution That Is Shaping Twenty-First-Century Jewish Education—A Fleeting Snapshot from the First Decade 597
Brian Amkraut

Travel as a Jewish Educational Tool 615
Erik H. Cohen

Travel: 'Location Location Location' – A Practitioner's Perspectives on Diaspora Jewish Travel 633
Jeremy Leigh

Contents of Part Two

Section Three: Applications

Academic Jewish Studies in North America 657
Judith R. Baskin

Adult Jewish Learning: The Landscape 669
Lisa D. Grant and Diane Tickton Schuster

Congregational Schools 691
Isa Aron

**Day Schools in the Liberal Sector: Challenges and Opportunities
at the Intersection of Two Traditions of Jewish Schooling** 713
Alex Pomson

Day Schools in the Orthodox Sector – A Shifting Landscape 729
Shani Bechhofer

Early Childhood Education 749
Michael Ben-Avie, Ilene Vogelstein, Roberta Louis Goodman,
Eli Schaap, and Pat Bidol-Padva

Experiential Jewish Education: Reaching the Tipping Point 767
David Bryfman

**Gender: Shifting from "Evading" to "Engaging"—Gender
Issues and Jewish Adolescents** 785
Shira D. Epstein

**Informal Education: The Decisive Decade – How Informal
Jewish Education Was Transformed in Its Relationship
with Jewish Philanthropy** 805
Joseph Reimer

Intermarriage: Connection, Commitment, and Community 825
Evie Levy Rotstein

Learning Organisations: Learning to Learn – The Learning Organisation in Theory and Practice 843
Susan L. Shevitz

Limmud: A Unique Model of Transformative Jewish Learning 861
Raymond Simonson

Mentoring: Ideological Encounters – Mentoring Teachers in Jewish Education 879
Michal Muszkat-Barkan

Parents and Jewish Educational Settings 901
Jeffrey S. Kress

Practitioner Enquiry and Its Role in Jewish Education 917
Alex Sinclair

Preparing Teachers for Jewish Schools: Enduring Issues in Changing Contexts 937
Sharon Feiman-Nemser

Professional Development of Teachers in Jewish Education 959
Gail Zaiman Dorph

Professional Development: *Vini, Vidi, Vici*? Short-Term Jewish Educators Trips to Israel as Professional-Development Programs 981
Shelley Kedar

Rabbis as Educators: Their Professional Training and Identity Formation 1001
Lisa D. Grant and Michal Muszkat-Barkan

Special Education: "And You Shall Do That Which Is Right and Good . . ." Jewish Special Education in North America: From Exclusion to Inclusion 1021
Rona Milch Novick and Jeffrey Glanz

Teacher Education: Ensuring a Cadre of Well-Qualified Educational Personnel for Jewish Schools 1041
Leora Isaacs, Kate O'Brien, and Shira Rosenblatt

Ultra-Orthodox/Haredi Education 1063
Yoel Finkelman

Section Four: Geographical

American-Jewish Education in an Age of Choice and Pluralism 1087
Jack Wertheimer

Anglo-Jewish Education: Day Schools, State Funding and Religious Education in State Schools 1105
David Mendelsson

Australia: The Jewel in the Crown of Jewish Education 1125
Paul Forgasz and Miriam Munz

Canada: Jewish Education in Canada 1141
Michael Brown

Europe: Education of Adult Jewish Leaders in a Pan-European Perspective 1155
Barbara Lerner Spectre

Europe: Something from (Almost) Nothing – The Challenges of Education in European Communities – A Personal Perspective ... 1167
Steve Israel

Former Soviet Union: Jewish Education 1183
Olga Markus and Michael Farbman

France: Jewish Education in France 1203
Ami Bouganim

Israel: State Religious Education in Israel 1219
Zehavit Gross

Israel: Innovations in Secular Schooling in Israel 1235
Yehuda Bar Shalom and Tamar Ascher Shai

Latin America – Jewish Education in Latin America: Challenges, Trends and Processes 1253
Yossi Goldstein and Drori Ganiel

Netherlands – Social Integration and Religious Identity 1271
Henny van het Hoofd

Author Index 1289

Subject Index 1295

About the Editors

Helena Miller is the Director of Research and Evaluation at the UJIA, London. She has a PhD in Jewish Education from London University, and has taught in schools and higher education for many years. Previously, she was the Director of Education at Leo Baeck College, London. She oversees the inspection of Jewish schools in the UK. Publications include "Changing the Landscape: Pluralist Jewish Education in the UK", Tel Aviv University 2011, "Supplementary Jewish Education in the UK: Facts and Issues of the Cheder System", *International Journal of Jewish Educational Research*, February 2010, *Accountability through Inspection: Monitoring and Evaluating Jewish Schools* London: Board of Deputies of British Jews and Meeting the Challenge: the Jewish Schooling Phenomenon in the UK, *The Oxford Review of Education*, December 2001, as well as books on teaching visual arts, *Craft in Action* (Stenor Books 1986) and *The Magic Box* (Torah Aura 1992).

Helena is currently co-chair of Limmud International, on the Advisory Board of the Institute of Jewish Policy Research, and an associate editor of the Journal of Jewish Education.

Lisa D. Grant is Associate Professor of Jewish Education at the Hebrew Union College—Jewish Institute of Religion, New York. She has a PhD in Jewish Education from the Jewish Theological Seminary of America. Her research and teaching focus on adult Jewish learning, the professional development of rabbi-educators, and the place of Israel in American Jewish life. She has published widely in a range of academic journals, books, and teaching guides. She is lead author of *A Journey of Heart and Mind: Transformational Learning in Adulthood* (JTS Press, 2004) with Diane Schuster, Meredith Woocher and Steven M Cohen, and author of *Aytz Hayim Hi, a two year curriculum guide for Adult Bat Mitzvah* (Women's League of Conservative Judaism, 2001).

Lisa is immediate past chair of the Network for Research in Jewish Education and serves on the executive committee of the Israel Association for Research in Jewish Education. She is currently working on a book on Israel Engagement for 21st Century North American Jews.

Alex Pomson is a senior researcher at the Melton Centre for Jewish Education at the Hebrew University, Jerusalem. He trained in History at the University of Cambridge and received his PhD in Religious education from the University of London in 1994. He was founding head of Jewish Studies at King Solomon High School, London. From 1996 to 2004. He served as an associate professor of Jewish Teacher Education at York University, Toronto, where he coordinated York's Jewish Teacher Education Programme. He is past Chair of the Network for Research in Jewish Education.

He completed a longitudinal study funded by the Social Sciences and Humanities Research Council of the Canadian Government, published in 2008, as a co-authored book, *Back to School: Jewish day school in the lives of adult Jews*. His most recent book, published by the Littman Library of Jewish Civilisation, is a co-edited volume, *Jewish schools, Jewish communities: A reconsideration*.

About the Authors

Hanan Alexander is Professor of Education at the University of Haifa where he heads the Center for Jewish Education. He is also the Goldman Visiting Professor of Education at the University of California, Berkeley.

Brian Amkraut is Provost and Professor of Judaic Studies at Siegal College of Judaic Studies, in Cleveland, Ohio. His areas of expertise include twentieth-century Germany, Zionism, and contemporary American Jewry.

Isa Aron is Professor of Jewish Education at HUC-JIR, Los Angeles, founding director of the Experiment in Congregational Education and co-author of *Sacred Strategies: How Functional Congregations Become Visionary* (Alban Press, 2010).

Tamar Ascher Shai is a lecturer at David Yellin Teacher's College in Jerusalem and holds a PhD dealing with belief systems in teaching and teacher training.

Ofra A. Backenroth, Ed.D is the associate dean of the William Davidson Graduate School of Jewish Education at the Jewish Theological Seminary in New York, and an adjunct assistant professor of Jewish Education.

Yehuda Bar Shalom serves as Chair of Education at the David Yellin College in Jerusalem. His research work deals mainly with multicultural education and innovative educational models.

Judith R. Baskin is Knight Professor of Humanities and Associate Dean, College of Arts and Sciences, University of Oregon, and was President of the Association for Jewish Studies between 2006 and 2008.

Shani Bechhofer, PhD is an assistant professor at the Azrieli Graduate School of Jewish Education & Administration, and a Senior Fellow of the Institute for University-School Partnership, Yeshiva University.

Zvi Bekerman teaches anthropology of education at the School of Education and the Melton Center, Hebrew University. His research interests are in the study of cultural, ethnic, and national identity, including identity processes and negotiation during intercultural encounters and in formal/informal learning contexts.

Michael Ben-Avie, PhD is a recognized expert on education and research as co-editor, with colleagues at the Yale Child Study Center, of six books on educational change and child development.

Pat Bidol-Padva is the Executive Director of the Jewish Early Childhood Initiative (JECEI) and a core faculty member of the American University—NTL's Organisation Development and Change Master's Program.

Ami Bouganim is a writer and philosopher, publishing mainly in French. He has been involved in Jewish education as a researcher, planner, and teacher, mainly in Israel and France.

Michael Brown is Professor Emeritus of History, Humanities, and Hebrew, the former director of the Centre for Jewish Studies and a founder of the Jewish Teacher Education Programme at York University in Toronto.

David Bryfman is the Director of the new Center for Collaborative Leadership at the Jewish Education project in New York. He has written various articles, blog entries and twitter feeds on Jewish adolescents, Israel education, technology and experiential Jewish Education.

Stuart Charmé is Professor of Religion at Rutgers University (Camden). He is currently completing a book on Jewish identity and cultural authenticity.

Barry Chazan is Professor of Education Emeritus at the Hebrew University of Jerusalem. He is founding International Director of Education of Birthright Israel and Professor of Education at Spertus College.

Erik H. Cohen, PhD, is a researcher, educational policy advisor, and senior lecturer at the School of Education at Bar-Ilan University in Israel. He works on education, Jewish identity, youth culture, tourism and migration, in an international comparative approach.

Jonathan A Cohen is currently Chair of the Department of Education at the Hebrew University of Jerusalem. He also teaches at the Melton Center and the Mandel Leadership Institute.

Steven M. Cohen is Research Professor of Jewish Social Policy at HUC-JIR, and Director of the Berman Jewish Policy Archive @ NYU Wagner (www.BJPA.org).

Bryan Conyer is currently serving as Deputy Principal of Jewish Life, Emanuel School, Sydney, Australia. He has completed a PhD at the University of Sydney, focusing upon pluralism in Jewish Education.

Scott Copeland is an Israeli educator and tour guide. He is Director of Israel Travel Education at MAKOM—the Israel Engagement Network sponsored by the Jewish Agency for Israel.

Howard Deitcher is a Senior Lecturer at the Melton Centre for Jewish Education at the Hebrew University of Jerusalem, and its previous director.

Gail Zaiman Dorph is the director of the Mandel Teacher Educator Initiative, a program to develop educational leaders who can design and implement high-quality professional development for teachers, principals, and other educational professionals.

Shira D. Epstein, Ed.D is an Assistant Professor of Jewish Education at the Jewish Theological Seminary.

Michael Farbman currently serves Temple Emanuel of Greater New Haven, CT. His previous positions include West London Synagogue, St. Petersburg, Russia and Washington Hebrew Congregation in Washington DC.

Sharon Feiman Nemser is the Mandel Professor of Jewish Education at Brandeis University and the director of the Mandel Center for Studies in Jewish Education.

Yoel Finkelman is a lecturer in the Interdisciplinary Graduate Program in Contemporary Jewry at Bar Ilan University, and teaches Talmud and Jewish Thought in numerous contexts around Jerusalem.

Paul Forgasz teaches Jewish history at Monash University's Australian Centre for Jewish Civilisation and also lectures in school leadership and in Jewish education at the university's Faculty of Education.

Drori Ganiel is the head of educational, welfare and community services in the city of Eilat, Israel. He served for a number of years as the head of human resources in the education department of the Jewish Agency for Israel.

Michael Gillis is a senior lecturer and director of academic programs at the Melton Centre for Jewish Education at the Hebrew University of Jerusalem.

Jeffrey Glanz holds the Stanley and Raine Silverstein Chair in Professional Ethics and Values in Jewish Education at the Azrieli Graduate School of Jewish Education and Administration at Yeshiva University.

Yossi Goldstein is a teacher and tutor at the Melton Center for Jewish Education, Hebrew University of Jerusalem, and a lecturer at the Yad Vashem Institute on Holocaust Studies and Education.

Roberta Louis Goodman is Director of Research and Standards for JECEI (Jewish Early Childhood Education Initiative) and an Adjunct Associate Professor of Jewish Education at Siegal College of Judaic Studies in Cleveland, Ohio.

Lisa D. Grant is Associate Professor of Jewish Education at the Hebrew Union College-Jewish Institute of Religion, New York. Her research and teaching focus on adult Jewish learning and the place of Israel in American Jewish life.

Robbie Gringras is a British-Israeli writer, performer, and educator who works as an artist-in-residence with Makom in Jerusalem.

Zehavit Gross is a senior lecturer and the head of graduate program of Policy and Leadership in Informal Education Systems in the School of Education, Bar-Ilan

University, Israel. Her main area of specialization is Socialization Processes among adolescents.

Tova Hartman teaches gender studies and education at Bar Ilan University. Her writings include articles on gender, religion, and education. She is the author of *Appropriately subversive: Modern mothers in traditional religions*, 2002, and *Feminism encounters traditional Judaism: Resistance and accommodation*, 2007.

Barry W. Holtz is Dean of the William Davidson Graduate School of Jewish Education and the Theodore and Florence Baumritter Professor of Jewish Education at the Jewish Theological Seminary, New York.

Elie Holzer serves as an assistant professor of education at Bar Ilan University and as a senior research associate at the Mandel Center for Studies in Jewish Education at Brandeis University. He has published a series of research articles related to havruta text study.

Gabriel Horenczyk is Associate Professor at the School of Education, and the Director of the Melton Centre for Jewish Education, the Hebrew University of Jerusalem.

Alick Isaacs teaches at the Melton Centre for Jewish Education at the Hebrew University and at the Hebrew University's Rothberg School for Overseas Students. He also is a research fellow at the Hartman Institute's Kogod Centre for Contemporary Jewish Thought.

Leora Isaacs, PhD, is Vice-President for Programs and Organizational Learning and Director of the Learnings and Consultation Center at JESNA in New York.

Steve Israel is a Jewish educator living in Jerusalem. He teaches and trains in Israel and in different Diaspora communities.

Benjamin M. Jacobs is assistant professor of social studies education and assistant director of the Programs in Education and Jewish Studies at New York University's Steinhardt School of Culture, Education, and Human Development.

Jane Kanarek is Assistant Professor of Rabbinics in the Rabbinical School of Hebrew College, where she teaches Talmud, Midrash, and halakhah.

Jan Katzew, PhD, works at the Union for Reform Judaism in New York where he has guided and supported curricular initiatives for congregational schools, early childhood programs, day schools, camps, and adult learning institutes.

Shelley Kedar, MA, is Director of the School for Jewish Peoplehood Studies within Beit Hatfutsot. She served as Director of Professional Development at the Leo Baeck Education Center and as a Jewish educational *emissary* in the UK.

Orit Kent is a Senior Research Associate at the Mandel Center for Studies in Jewish Education, where she directs the Beit Midrash Research Project and lectures in the DeLeT/MAT program at Brandeis University, Massachusetts.

Jonathan Krasner is Assistant Professor of the American Jewish Experience at HUC-JIR in New York, and author of the book *The Benderly Boys and the Making of American Jewish Education* (UPNE, 2011).

Jeffrey S. Kress is Assistant Professor and Chair of the Department of Jewish Education at the Jewish Theological Seminary of America.

Marjorie Lehman is Assistant Professor of Talmud and Rabbinics at the Jewish Theological Seminary, New York. She writes extensively about the *Ein Yaakov*, a sixteenth-century collection of Talmudic aggadah, Gender and Jewish Studies and about Talmudic Pedagogy.

Jeremy Leigh is Director of 'Jewish Journeys' (Initiatives in Jewish Travel); author of various books on this topic; and a lecturer at the Hebrew Union College in Jerusalem.

Mitch Malkus serves as Head of School of the Rabbi Jacob Pressman Academy of Temple Beth Am in Los Angeles, California.

Olga Markus holds an MA in Religious Education; she served as Senior Educator at West London Synagogue, WUPJ in Russia, and most recently as Educator-in-residence at Washington Hebrew Congregation in Washington, DC.

David Mendelsson was born and raised in London. His book *Jewish Education in England* 1944–1988 will be published by Peter Lang in 2011. He is on the faculty of Hebrew Union College (Jerusalem Campus) and the Rothberg International School of the Hebrew University of Jerusalem.

Helena Miller is Director of Research and Evaluation at UJIA, London. She oversees the inspection of Jewish education in Jewish schools in the UK and has published on Jewish art education, the history of Jewish education in the UK and pluralism in Jewish schools.

Tamar Miller is a consultant to the Fetzer Institute's department of Religious and Spiritual Pathways in Kalamazoo, Michigan, USA. She manages the Albert E. Marks Charitable Trust for Social Justice and Peace-building, and creates training programs for Track II: An Institute for Citizen Diplomacy in San Francisco.

David Mittelberg is Senior Lecturer, Graduate Faculty, Oranim, Academic College of Education in Israel, and has published articles on ethnicity, migration, gender, tourism, kibbutz education, and the sociology of American and Australian Jewry.

Miriam Munz, PhD, is a research associate at Monash University in Melbourne and has worked in Australian Jewish schools for a period of 20 years.

Michal Muszkat-Barkan, PhD, is Head of the Department of Education and Professional Development at Hebrew Union College-Jerusalem, and of the MA program in Pluralistic Jewish Education, in partnership with the Melton Center of the Hebrew University of Jerusalem.

Nava Nevo is a lecturer at the Melton Centre for Jewish Education and the Department of Teacher Education, the Hebrew University of Jerusalem. Her expertise is in Hebrew as a second language, sociolinguistics, and student achievements assessment.

Rona Milch Novick is the associate professor at the Azrieli school at Yeshiva University and director of its Fanya Gottesfeld Heller division of Doctoral Studies.

Kate O'Brien, MA, is Senior Research Writer at the Berman Center for Research and Evaluation at JESNA in New York.

Daniel Pekarsky is a professor in both Educational Policy Studies and Jewish Studies at the University of Wisconsin-Madison, and is a continuing consultant on Jewish education to the Mandel Foundation.

Alex Pomson is a Senior Researcher at the Melton Centre for Jewish Education at the Hebrew University of Jerusalem.

Joseph Reimer is Associate Professor of Jewish Education and Director of the Institute for Informal Jewish Education at Brandeis University, Massachusetts.

Michael Rosenak is Mandel Professor of Jewish Education at the Hebrew University (emeritus).

Shira Rosenblatt, PhD, is Associate Director of the Berman Center for Research and Evaluation at JESNA in New York.

Sue Rosenfeld, a teacher at the Michlala Jerusalem College for Women and Hebrew University's Melton Center for Jewish Education, is interested in the processes of learning and identity.

Evie Levy Rotstein is Director of the Leadership Institute for Congregational Educators, an interdenominational project jointly sponsored by Hebrew Union College-Jewish Institute of Research and the Jewish Theological Seminary. She is also an adjunct professor at the HUC New York School of Education.

Eli Schaap is Program Officer for Education and Research at the Steinhardt Foundation for Jewish Life, USA. His current main focus is on early Jewish childhood and Hebrew language charter schools.

Diane Tickton Schuster is a Visiting Senior Research Fellow at HUC-Los Angeles. Her research focuses on adult and experiential Jewish learning. She is currently writing about Jewish choral singers and conductors.

Simone Schweber is the Goodman Professor of Education and Jewish Studies at the University of Wisconsin-Madison. Her research focuses on Holocaust education in different kinds of schooling environments.

Yona Shem-Tov, a Wexner Graduate Fellowship Alumna, is a doctoral candidate at New York University where she is writing about citizenship education in Jewish and Muslim American schools.

Susan L Shevitz, professor (emeritus) at Brandeis University in Jewish Education, Boston, MA, USA, consults to many organizations, teaches rabbinic students and educators, and conducts research at the intersection of Jewish education, leadership and organizational behavior.

Michael Shire is the Vice-Principal of Leo Baeck College, London, and Director of the Department of Jewish Education. He has a PhD in Jewish Education from the Hebrew Union College, Los Angeles.

Eilon Schwartz is a faculty member at the Melton Centre for Jewish Education of Hebrew University of Jerusalem, and the Director of the Heschel Center for Environmental Learning and Leadership, in Tel Aviv.

Marc Silverman PhD, Melton Centre for Jewish Education academic faculty member, Hebrew University of Jerusalem, specializing in progressive, radical, and moral educational thought, Janush Korczak's legacy and Jewish cultural-educational ideologies today.

Raymond Simonson has a BA (Hons) in Jewish Studies, an MA in Applied Anthropology and Community and Youth Work, and has held key roles in Informal Jewish Education for the Jewish Agency, UJIA and Limmud.

Alex Sinclair, PhD, is lead researcher for Makom, the Israel engagement think tank at the Jewish Agency for Israel, and an adjunct assistant professor in Jewish Education at the Jewish Theological Seminary.

Barbara Lerner Spectre is founding director of Paideia, the European Institute for Jewish Studies in Sweden. Previously, she taught Jewish Thought at the Sholom Hartman Institute, David Yellin College, and the Melton Center for Jewish Education at the Hebrew University of Jerusalem.

Henny van het Hoofd is Director of the Educational Department of NIK, international Coordinator of the JELED program for supplementary schools and teacher of Judaism at the Vrije Universiteit, Amsterdam.

Judith Veinstein is a social psychologist whose research concentrates on American Jewish identity.

Ilene Vogelstein is the facilitator of the Alliance for Jewish Early Education, a national network for organizations addressing early childhood Jewish education and issues facing families with young children.

Jack Wertheimer is professor of American Jewish History at the Jewish Theological Seminary. He has published extensively on trends in American Jewish religious and communal life since World War II.

Hagit Hacohen Wolf is a lecturer and the Director of the Evaluation Research Unit at the Melton Centre for Jewish Education, the Hebrew University of Jerusalem.

Jonathan S. Woocher is Chief Ideas Officer of JESNA and heads its Lippman Kanfer Institute: An Action-oriented Think Tank for Innovation in Jewish Learning and Engagement.

Michael Zeldin is Professor of Jewish Education at Hebrew Union College-Jewish Institute of Religion in Los Angeles and Director of the Rhea Hirsch School of Education. He is also Senior Editor of the *Journal of Jewish Education.*

Tali Zelkowicz, a sociologist of education who studies the role of dissonance in Jewish identity formation, is Assistant Professor of Jewish Education at Hebrew Union College in Los Angeles.

Introduction

Helena Miller, Lisa D. Grant, and Alex Pomson

Jewish teaching and learning have been essential components of Jewish tradition since the earliest of times. The imperative to "teach your children" first appeared in the *Book of Deuteronomy* as part of what later became the *shema*—the most central of Jewish prayers. Rabbinic literature is filled with references to schools and schooling, and to teaching and learning taking place at all levels, and for all ages from the youngest children through adulthood. Indeed, according to the *midrash* (commentary) on Genesis, the first thing that the House of Jacob did, on leaving their home in Canaan, was to establish schools (Genesis Rabbah, 95). It is no accident that Jews are often known as "The People of the Book". Jewish life is lived according to texts, and interpretation of those texts. The varied methods of teaching those texts include the didactic and the experiential, argument and discussion.

The Babylonian Talmud (Kiddushin 29a) spells out the father's obligation to teach his children Torah (Jewish texts), and also to teach them a trade or craft. From this, it can be inferred that in order for the child to develop into an independent adult, secular learning must also be a priority. As the centuries passed, and as Jewish communities around the world interacted with their surrounding environments and increasingly integrated with the modern world, most Jews embraced secular learning and established themselves as among the most highly educated in their respective communities. The story of Jewish education in the twenty-first century is far more complex and diverse depending on a range of historical, geographic, sociological and cultural factors. Indeed, it is these factors and the complexity of the landscape of Jewish education today that provide the rationale for this handbook.

The *International Handbook of Jewish Education* adds to a growing list of substantial volumes that inform and debate issues within religious education traditions and frameworks. The starting point for this book was a conversation in 2007 with Professor Gerald Grace, of London University's Institute of Education, who was then editing *The International Handbook of Catholic Education* (Grace, 2007).

H. Miller (✉)
United Jewish Israel Appeal (UJIA), London, UK
e-mail: helena.miller@ujia.org

It seemed that a sister publication for and by the Jewish education community would be a meaningful addition to this family of Springer publications. This volume would complement other faith-based education handbooks that Springer had already published, notably *The International Handbook of Islamic Education* (Daun & Arjmaud, 2005) and *The International Handbook of the Religious, Moral and Spiritual Dimensions in Education* (De Souza, Engebretson, Durka, Jackson, & McGrady, 2006).

The purpose of *The International Handbook of Jewish Education* is to interrogate thoroughly the field that is known as "Jewish Education". As can be seen from almost all of our chapters, particularly when browsing the bibliographies, there is much that is universal in any discussion of education and much that Jewish educators owe to the considerable body of writing that explores the general, non-religiously focused educational world.

The work of those authors from general education serves to inform, and in some cases to scaffold, the aspects of Jewish education being explored by our authors. What then gives this book its' Jewish focus? Surely chapters on early childhood education, visions of education, the place of parents within education and a host of other topics find their places as comfortably in a general volume on education? The answer is of course in the particular context and content that this *International Handbook of Jewish Education* brings. This publication is both inward looking and outward exploring. It examines issues that are particular to the Jewish community, analyses educational content that is specific to the development of Jewish identities and explores contexts that are embedded in the fabric of a Jewish life. It also acknowledges the impact of the general educational world. As with the other religion-specific and culturally focused Springer publications, the chapters in this book speak directly to the researchers and practitioners engaged in a niche market—in this case the Jewish community.

The *International Handbook of Jewish Education* adds an important voice to the conversations begun in a number of recent publications which have brought together themes and topics within the field of Jewish education, for example the philosophical *Visions of Jewish Education* (Fox, Scheffler, & Marom, 2003), the sociological *Jewish Day Schools, Jewish Communities* (Pomson & Deitcher, 2009) and the more practical *What We Know About Jewish Education* (Kelman, 1992) as well as *What We Now Know About Jewish Education* (Goodman, Flexner, & Bloomberg, 2008). In this handbook, we examine the full diversity of the current state of Jewish education, from both academic and practitioner perspectives. Our authors, all leading educators within their chosen chapter topics, were asked to overview their fields, comment on the successes and challenges they face, and raise research questions for the future. We also asked our authors, where possible, to add an international dimension to their chapters, to make each chapter globally relevant without losing the integrity of the arguments discussed.

The resulting book acknowledges the broad range of theorists, academics, practitioners and policy makers currently working in the field of Jewish education. Our authors span multiple generations. We have been able to include authors who have made influential contributions to the field, as well as newer and younger voices, adding to the richness of the material within these pages. A look at some of the chapter bibliographies will show where our experienced authors have influenced the work of up and coming colleagues in the field. A wide variety of authors has also meant a wide variety of styles of writing, and different treatments of subject matter. While broadly keeping within our guidelines, this has resulted in a compelling tapestry of richness. Our authors also span the Jewish denominational spectrum; thus the notion of pluralism, mentioned by many of our authors, is played out in the variety of Jewish backgrounds and expression of the contributors to this publication. We are pleased at the even gender balance of our authors, but sadly, our wide variety of authors is not so well reflected in the diversity of their geographical location. Similar to the demographic composition of Jewry worldwide, more than 80% of all the authors in this publication are based in North America or Israel. One of our hopes is that this book promotes a growing interest in research into, and publication of, high-quality papers and chapters on issues within Jewish education internationally.

The book is organised into two parts and within each part, sections that cluster themes of Jewish education and its processes into a logical format. Our intent is to ensure the internal integrity of each part, as well as to give overall coherence to the wider overview of the entire book. Some of the chapters tackle enduring topics, for example the chapters on Jewish identity, day schools, and informal education. Others reflect timely and pressing issues in the world of Jewish education at the end of the first decade of the twenty-first century, for example, a focus on the environment and technology. These are also chapters that explore issues of global concern through the lens of Jewish education. We recognise that even in a publication of this size, not every topic could possibly be covered. For example, we would have liked to have included chapters within our geographical section on other centres of Jewish life around the world, in addition to the ones we were able to gather here. We know that despite our best efforts, we did not reach all potential authors who have something important to say on topics of Jewish education not covered within these pages. For these reasons, and because Jewish education is neither static nor complete, we hope that in time, further publications will appear that further develop our themes and explore issues that are missing here.

Section One, "Vision and Practice", sets the scene and underpins the parts that follow. The articulations of vision in this section, as related to practice, form the rationale for what takes place throughout the educative process. The 18 chapters in this section move from the philosophical to the practical, from theory to policy and from policy to practice. The educational endeavour, which is the core, has encouraged our authors to question and reflect, to research and analyse.

In Section Two, which we have called "Teaching and Learning", 17 chapters focus on aspects of curriculum, instruction and learner engagement. This section explores both subject matter and the transmission of subject matter, formal and informal curricular opportunities, the cognitive and the affective, and both traditional and contemporary areas of teaching and learning.

Section Three is called "Applications" and the 21 chapters here address the settings and audiences served through Jewish education in its broadest sense, as well as the trends in the professional development of the educators who serve these sites. As a compilation, these chapters provide the reader with a broad and rich portrait of the wide range of applications for Jewish education by setting, context, mode and audience. Chapters acknowledge that learning takes place in formal and informal settings, and at different ages and stages of life. In each of these contexts, the professional development of the educator is a crucial element for success.

Section Four, which we term "Geographical", reveals to us the extent to which Jewish education emerges at an intersection between the global and local. The 12 chapters in this section provide an opportunity to explore ultimate questions in the social scientific study of Jewry regarding the influence of the local context on the norms, modalities and goals of Jewish education. We conclude from this section that while Jewish education is an international enterprise, in the final analysis it is a local endeavour. Despite the international references throughout many of the chapters in the three Handbook section that precede this one, it is clear that in both its form and content, Jewish education is fundamentally and indelibly shaped by where it is located.

This publication includes 69 chapters and in total 89 contributors. The number of co-authored chapters is particularly pleasing and reflects a commitment to collaboration between colleagues that is quite typical in the field of Jewish educational research. The enthusiasm for honestly presenting and rigorously debating the multitude of issues within Jewish education presented here is a credit to all the contributing authors. For this, we, the editors, owe each of them a debt of enormous gratitude. For us all, the creation of this book has been a journey—the development of our own educational vision—from idea to reality. We set out to produce a record of the state of Jewish education in its widest number of contexts and forms at a particular moment in time. We hope that the resulting book will find its place in the libraries and learning centres, the universities and schools, the agencies and communities across the international Jewish community and in other places where there is interest in how Jews engage with Jewish education. We hope that it sparks debate, makes connections and provides some answers. More than that, we hope to stimulate further questions. We cannot predict the future. An international handbook of the next generation may wrestle with very different pressing issues and concerns. These will reflect the state of the Jewish world of the next generation. What we can hope is that this *International Handbook of Jewish Education* makes some small impact on present generations of teachers and learners.

References

Daun, H., & Arjmaud, R. (2005). *The international handbook of Islamic education*. Netherlands: Springer.
De Souza, M., Engebretson, K., Durka, G., Jackson, R., & McGrady, A. (2006). *The international handbook of the religious, moral and spiritual dimensions*. Netherlands: Springer.
Fox, S., Scheffler, I., & Marom, D. (Eds.) (2003). *Visions of Jewish education*. Cambridge, UK: Cambridge University Press.

Goodman, R. L., Flexner, P. A., & Bloomberg, L. D. (2008). *What we now know about Jewish education*. Los Angeles: Torah Aura.
Grace, G. (2007). *The international handbook of Catholic education*. Netherlands: Springer.
Kelman, S. L. (1992). *What we know about Jewish education*. Los Angeles: Torah Aura.
Pomson, A., & Deitcher, H. (2009). *Jewish day schools, Jewish communities*. Portland: Littman Library of Jewish Civilization.

Section One: Vision and Practice

Introduction

The concept and content of educational vision has been a key component in thinking about knowledge and the imparting of that knowledge through time. This section of the Handbook includes chapters that explore educational thinkers and thinking that have had the greatest global influence on Jewish educational thought and practice. Vision is of utmost importance within a volume that not only reviews the current state of Jewish education and education research, but also looks to the future. But vision on its' own, whilst it sets the scene and provides an underpinning for the ends and means of a Jewish education, is not enough. The articulation of vision has to relate to practice – it forms the rationale for what takes place within the educative process. This section of the Handbook contains, therefore, a third strand which connects the two elements of vision and practice, and that is policy. Together with planning, policy is a process for guiding change towards desired ends. In the chapters that follow, we see how educational development and change have had impact on current practice and has implications for the future.

In his chapter, Michael Rosenak explores basic distinctions in the philosophy of education, and concludes by surveying some of the key questions asked by philosophers of Jewish educators, namely What? How? Why? The influence of Rosenak's writings goes far beyond the content of his chapter in this Handbook. Within the bibliographies of those who contributed to this section, as well as throughout the rest of this publication, Rosenak features repeatedly, reinforcing his position as one of the most influential Jewish educational thinkers of his generation.

Daniel Pekarsky develops themes concerned with the advancement of educational practice and thinking in which vision is central. He considers what kinds of research might most meaningfully influence practice in Jewish education. He suggests why attention to these matters has been important for the advancement of Jewish life and education and indicates some obstacles that have attended the effort to advance vision-guided Jewish education. He places special emphasis on the ways in which the language of vision, as currently employed, has itself sometimes ill-served those who have sought to communicate its very importance.

A further characteristic of the chapter bibliographies within this section is their emphasis on both Jewish and non-Jewish visions and philosophies. Hanan Alexander, in his chapter, which explores contemporary Jewish education from a post-modern perspective, draws upon, amongst others, Scheffler, Buber, Levinas, Oakeshott and Kant. Buber and Levinas are two of a range of philosophers whose ideas are applied by Jonathan Cohen in his chapter on Jewish thought. Cohen illustrates how insights from modern Jewish thought can enrich discourse and reflection on issues of principle in Jewish education. His focus on education for spirituality should be read together with the chapter by Michael Shire who reviews the research in to the spiritual lives of children. Shire's interest is in exploring how faith can be formed in children by means of a Jewish religious education. This interest leads Shire to identify important questions of purpose and practice for Jewish educators hoping to incorporate visions of the child as a spiritual being.

The role of the analytic philosopher is taken up by Barry Chazan, who argues that the field of contemporary Jewish education needs the voices of Scheffler, Soltis and Bernfeld to restrain it from what he characterizes as its fantasising, illusions and sloganeering. For Chazan, it is clear talking and thinking, of the kind provided by the analytical philosopher, that can help lead to creative innovative efforts and also rein in the excessive, obsessive and exaggerated language and mission with which Jewish educators are bombarded and to which they in turn contribute.

Clarity of thought and voice is a feature of those chapters within this section which explore various aspects of Jewish identity. Gaby Horenczyk and Hagit Hacohen Woolf examine the basic assumption that Jewish education is widely perceived as one of the major means for strengthening Jewish identity and identification. They suggest that a multifaceted approach to the mapping of Jewish attitudes and behaviour – mapping what Jewish identity might mean – can help better define the goals of Jewish education. Stuart Charme and Tali Hyman Zelkowicz also approach Jewish identity formation from multifaceted and multiple process formulations in their chapter, in which they argue for a shift in thinking towards conceiving of identities as being multiple and shifting.

Steven Cohen and Judith Veinstein's chapter on Jewish identity shifts the focus of the discussion on to policy and practice. Their chapter examines the impact of Jewish social networks on identity outcomes. The authors argue for educators and policy makers to recognize and value the nurture of Jewish friendship networks as an explicit act of Jewish education. With social-scientific research having repeatedly demonstrated that well-connected individuals exert more influence on others than do social isolates, the challenge for educators and policy makers is to locate such influential youngsters (and others) and mobilize them on behalf of Jewish interests and Jewish engagement – both for their own benefit, and for that of their surrounding circles of contacts and intimates.

Policy and planning is, as Jonathan Woocher writes in his chapter, typically seen as a rational process for guiding change towards desired ends. He argues that this is an unsatisfactory process with regards to Jewish Education. He introduces the reader to what he terms 'praxis planning', in other words planning that is embedded in action and is both highly improvisational and reflective. Helena Miller's chapter, which focuses on the changing nature of how Jewish schools relate to, and integrate with, their local and wider communities, takes a different view of policy and planning. She highlights how the prescriptive policies of government and education agencies can strongly influence educational practice. Miller's chapter, which is one of the few in the Handbook to use Britain and British schools as the lens through which to explore Jewish-educational issues, should be read in conjunction with David Mendelsson's chapter on Anglo-Jewish education, found in Section IV of this book (Part II).

In this first section of the Handbook, policy and planning provide a bridge to a series of chapters which look at the practice of education. Roberta Louis Goodman and Jan Katzew explore what they call the 'sacred' practice of curriculum development. At its best a work in *process*, their view is that curriculum development is also a work in *progress*. With curriculum development efforts increasingly being evaluated, often at the behest of funding partners, they propose that research should make these evaluations part of the public domain so that their impact can be magnified. Knowledge is more powerful when it is shared, they say, and we have yet to harness the potential of Jewish-educational assessment – of individuals, institutions and curricular resources.

Mitch Malkus looks at curriculum through the lens of 'integration', a set of ideas and practices that have had great influence on the contemporary Jewish day school. Drawing on research and on his experience as a school head, Malkus explores the factors that contribute to or mitigate the implementation of an integrated curriculum. His chapter, together with Goodman and Katzew's, provides much of the philosophical underpinning for the chapters on aspects of teaching and learning that follow in the next section of the *International Handbook*.

Our relationship to ancient texts is pivotal in so many ways to a survey of Jewish education and three chapters in this section tackle different aspects of this phenomenon. Tova Hartman and Tamar Miller look through a feminist lens at gender and Jewish education, engaging in a study of texts from the biblical and Talmudic periods that focus on narratives of gender and sexuality. They ask questions related to the covering and uncovering of these texts within the education of younger and older students. Jonathan Krasner, in his chapter on historiography, argues that Talmudic and other texts can provide the teacher with an array of opportunities to assess the manner in which they can develop critical thinking in the classroom. Zvi Beckerman and Sue Rosenfeld argue that philosophical and textual perspectives have too long influenced the field of Jewish education. Understanding these perspectives is important, they recognize, but they call for alternative disciplinary perspectives, such as cultural criticism and anthropology, that might shift the focus of Jewish education from the individual to the production of vital cultural contexts.

Janush Korczak, who is well-known for his heroic stand against Nazism during the Holocaust, left a lasting legacy to Jewish and general education. In his chapter, Marc Silverman explores Korczak's legacy to Jewish education. This legacy, he shows, is deeply connected to the concerns of religious, civic, moral and cultural education. Silverman's chapter, whilst seemingly distinct from the foci of other chapters in this section, complements many of them, for example Beckerman and

Rosenfeld's, with its focus on culture, as well as those chapters that explore aspects of Jewish identity.

The language with which we refer to elements in Jewish education often determines, and can help to elucidate, some of the ambiguity of the discourse and research into the subject. Hartman and Miller argue against some of language in the texts they highlight and Bryan Conyer, in his chapter on pluralism unravels some of the controversy and lack of clarity surrounding the term 'pluralism'. He provides a philosophical framework to help both policy makers and educators determine what pluralism could mean in the contexts of their own Jewish-educational organisations. He provides a stimulus to help bridge the gap between theory and praxis. We recommend reading Conyer's chapter in parallel with Woocher's chapter on planning, to add a layer of understanding to how change can be embedded in action.

Of all four sections in this Handbook, the 18 chapters in this section form the least obviously coherent grouping. There is, however, a logical gathering of these topics, whose themes overlap and entwine, sometimes quite unexpectedly. This section moves from the philosophical to the practical, from theory to policy and from policy to practice. The centre is the educational endeavour, which pulls and pushes and encourages our authors to question and reflect, to research and analyse. This section provides both a solid foundation and a springboard for what follows, which is where we delve deeply into teaching and learning, and the applications and geographical contexts of Jewish education in the twenty-first century.

Helena Miller
Lisa D. Grant
Alex Pomson

Analytic Philosophy of Education and Jewish Education: The Road Not Taken

Barry Chazan

Analytic Philosophy of Education

In the early to middle of the twentieth century a sub-field of philosophy known as analytic philosophy emerged mainly in the English-speaking world, spearheaded by such figures as Bertrand Russell, G.E. Moore, Ludwig Wittgenstein, J.L. Austin, and Gilbert Ryle (Glock, 2008; Stroll, 2000). The term "analytic philosophy" assumed multiple meanings including the following: (1) a tradition of doing philosophy which emphasized clarity using logic and focusing mainly on analysis of ordinary language, (2) reservations about the creation of sweeping philosophic systems as the main goal of philosophy, and (3) great attention to how words and phrases are used in ordinary language. The original focus on formal logic and even mathematical-like precision which characterized analytic philosophy at its inception, morphed in mid-century into great emphasis on how words, phrases, and sentences are used in ordinary language (hence it was often known as "ordinary language analysis").

It was this emphasis that attracted a group of British and American philosophers of education who became known as "the analytic philosophers of education." This group was interested in precision concerning specific educational concepts and terms and it resisted imprecise or ambiguous discussions of broad educational topics. In later iterations, analytic philosophy of education (as implemented by such figures as Peters, Flew, Kai Nelson and D.Z. Phillips among others) encompassed topics which heretofore had been treated somewhat gingerly in this approach, e.g. ethics and religion, but they remained loyal to their credo to analyze and not prescribe.

The two shaping figures in twentieth-century analytic philosophy of education are R.S. Peters at the Institute of Education of the University of London and Israel Scheffler at the Harvard Graduate School of Education. These two institutions, together with Teachers College, Columbia University where Jonas Soltis, one of Scheffler's central students served for many years, became major venues of this

B. Chazan (✉)
Spertus College, Chicago, IL, USA; Hebrew University, Jerusalem, Israel
e-mail: barrytaglit@yahoo.com

"movement." They spawned a generation of students who included I. Snook, J.P. White, Paul Hirst, and others. This "movement" occupied prominent places in universities and professional societies for over two decades in the mid-twentieth century. However, by the 1980s they were a waning force as a movement. While students of the founding fathers continue to serve as professors of philosophy of education in specific universities and contributed to journals, the movement qua movement lost its collective force in appointments, journals and professional societies. Today while many individuals utilize tools and techniques honed by this group, it is doubtful that anyone identifies with the movement as a movement, and the field of philosophy of education has taken significantly different directions in the last decades of the past century and the first decade of this century.

This Chapter

This chapter focuses on the analytic philosophy of education and twentieth-century philosophy of Jewish education. The chapter has four sections: (1) a brief review of the essentials of analytic philosophy of education through an overview of two classics by Soltis and Scheffler; (2) a look at the one overtly self-defined volume in analytic philosophy of Jewish education, Barry Chazan's *The Language of Jewish Education*; (3) a look at the route Jewish educational thinking took instead of the analytic route; and (4) an argument for the importance of analytic philosophy of Jewish education for today.

Israel Scheffler: *The Language of Education*

As noted, Israel Scheffler was the father of analytic philosophy of education in the United States. He edited an influential reader entitled *Philosophy and Education* in 1957 (Scheffler, 1957) and in 1960 wrote his path-breaking volume *The Language of Education* (Scheffler, 1960). In the Preface he concisely states: "The purpose of this book is through an application of philosophical methods, to clarify pervasive features of educational thought and argument" (p. vii). In the Introduction he distinguishes between two approaches to philosophy of education. The first refers to inquiry into educational questions by the use of philosophic methods. This type of philosophy of education focuses on philosophic method applied to educational issues. The second meaning of philosophy of education refers to the historical study of what has been concluded by inquirers into philosophic questions related to education or by users of philosophic methods to argue what education is.

A third usage he does not cite, but which was rampant in educational studies at that time was philosophy of education as prescribing a systematic, comprehensive set of principles and practices that it regarded as logical, reasonable, objective, and correct.

Scheffler indicates that his work and this book are reflective of the first approach—inquiry into educational questions by utilizing philosophic methods, and this book is the ground breaker for this new approach. In Chapter One he uncovers the complexity and frequently misleading nature of definitions of education. He speaks of three types of "definitions." "Stipulative definitions" are "pieces of terminological legislation that do not purport to reflect previously accepted uses of the defined term, but rather legislate (or 'stipulate') a certain way a term will be used in a discourse, discussion or book so as to enable a discussion to proceed." For example, a stipulative definition might work as follows: "For the sake of this discussion, we will understand the word 'a Jew' to mean anyone who self-identifies as a 'Jew.'" Such an approach enables discussions to proceed without getting hung up on complex or ambiguous terms every time they surface. "Descriptive definitions," on the other hand, purport to explain or "define" terms by giving an account of their prior usage or accepted meaning. They come to "describe" the way the term has been used by most people. Thus, a descriptive definition might say, "While there have been diverse definitions of the term a 'Jew', many rabbinical authorities have understood a 'Jew' to be someone born to a Jewish mother and who has not opted out of being Jewish by his/her choice." Whereas stipulative definitions are sort of abbreviations adopted for convenience which purport to economize and enable continued discussion, descriptive definitions purport to present definitive explanatory accounts of meaning. The third type of definition in education is the "programmatic." It purports to propose, suggest, and/or require certain educational practices, methodologies, or programs. Such definitions are neither linguistic devices like stipulative definitions nor explanatory devices like descriptive definitions, but rather they are practical prescriptions for action presented in a definitive fashion.

Scheffler's argument is that much of educational discourse is a confusion of these three types and by analyzing such terms as "teaching" and "telling," "educational slogans," and "educational metaphors" he shows how educational discourse often loses much of its clarity and precision or common understanding. Confused talking leads to confused action and analytic philosophy of education believes that clear talking is critical for decision-making. It is not against decision-making or value positions, but it believes such activities can only happen where there is precision of language, commonality of understanding, and clarity of the issues. The unique contribution of this volume is exemplifying the approach by the careful analysis of some critical confused educational terms. (The British philosopher Gilbert Ryle (1949) had already made contributions in this direction by focusing on the term "knowing" which surfaces in this book.)

Jonas Soltis: *An Introduction to the Analysis of Educational Concepts*

Jonas Soltis completed his doctorate at the Harvard Graduate School of Education and was one of Scheffler's prize students. He was appointed professor of philosophy of education at Teachers College Columbia University. Soltis had an important teaching and methodological influence on scores of students at Teachers College for several decades. In 1968 he published a brief primer of 117 pages entitled *An*

Introduction to the Analysis of Educational Concepts (a second edition was published in 1978) that turned out to be a minor classic in analytic philosophy of education. The book evolved from his classes on "Introduction to Philosophy of Education" at Teachers College which was a required course for non-philosophers coming from a broad range of fields—curriculum, comparative education, psychology, and nursing—and the book was aimed at providing them with a clear understanding of tools of philosophy which they could apply to their work in education in their diverse spheres. The volume shares Scheffler's core analytic approach and language. It differs in being more focused on tools and techniques rather than the concepts per se being analyzed.

The second edition had seven chapters: (1) Education and Analysis, (2) the Disciplines and Subject Matter, (3) Types of Knowledge and Teaching, (4) Learning, Explaining and Understanding, (5) Teaching Re-visited, (6) Analysis: Its Limits and Uses, and (7) Epilogue: The Pedagogy of Analytic-Skills Development. Soltis' Introduction succinctly summarizes his intent:

> This is a book about education and how to bring clarity to our thoughts ... philosophical thinking isn't making the world over to agree with one's own values or views about things, nor is it just the spinning out of a lot of ideas. Philosophical thinking is careful and controlled thinking directed at clarifying how we think and what we thing about (pp. 1 and 2).

The book was clearly an attempt to make the twentieth-century revolution in philosophy, which placed emphasis on clarifying concepts rather than promulgating worldviews, accessible to a broad range of students pursuing graduate studies in education. It was aimed at getting non-philosophers who care for education to learn a series of skills that will help them better elucidate and explicate concepts and ideas central to whatever work they would do in education. In Soltis' metaphor, it was to give people "the tools" to build a birdhouse rather than to focus on the finished product in itself (p. 3).

The book patiently leads the novice through the analysis of some core concepts of education, e.g., "teaching," "learning," "knowing," "aims of education," and "subject matter" by utilizing some basic tools of philosophy that are essential to explicating the meanings of words we use in everyday life in an often unclear, careless, or polemic manner. The main tools that Soltis' book presents and practices with the novice student include the following:

- Asking prior questions—probing a word or concept by asking questions that uncovers meanings that the word presupposes (e.g., "What assumptions does describing teaching as 'transmission' imply about how people learn?").
- Making distinctions—showing the difference between the meaning of the word in diverse phrases or context (e.g., "the good life" as opposed to "a good meal").
- The use of counter examples—sharpening an idea by pointing to examples that test and refine our concepts by negative instances ("When is a car not a car?").

He introduces three core "strategies" of analyzing educational terms:

1. "Generic analysis" refers to a means of explication that clarifies a concept by identifying its key characteristics. It essentially asks, what features must an X have to be called an X. The answer comprises the "generic" features of X (as in "generic drugs")
2. "Differentiation type analysis" asks what are the basic diverse meanings of X? It charts diverse meanings of commonly used terms such as "good," "to teach," "to learn," and helps us understand what usage others or we are employing in a sentence, speech, or educational program.
3. "Conditions-type analysis" asks what are the context requirements that govern the use of X? This approach attempts to isolate the components that are necessary for us to call something an X, e.g., what conditions are necessary to say that "teaching" has taken place?

Thus, this book basically is a guidebook for the novice to learn to use these tools (basic philosophic techniques) to explicate some educational terms that were very common in those days. Papers written for Soltis' courses were not about "What is the nature of the good life?" or "What are the goals of education?" But, rather "discuss some diverse meanings of the word 'good'" or "describe how different people have understood what the goals of education are."

Soltis engaged in this enterprise both in this book and in his career because he was impressed by the "no-nonsense" of such philosophizing and by the stringent demands it made for clarity and precision in dealing with traditional philosophical ideas (Soltis, 1968, p. xi). He believed that such clarity would enhance the talking, the thinking, and ultimately the practice of educators working in the field.

These two teachers had impact on scores of students in the 1950s–1980s because of the positions they held at two distinguished and geographically well-placed schools of education and also, I believe, because their methodologies were engaging and persuasive to many educators. These two books (and other books they wrote) were in my opinion landmarks. These philosophers and others of their ilk shaped the Philosophy of Education Society for 30 years. Today the books are out of print. There are a few copies available on Amazon and some copies cost $70–100. There are likely few or no departments of education in which these books are used and I suspect that few are the people who even know their names.

The Language of Jewish Education

In 1978 I published a book entitled *The Language of Jewish Education*. The title (used with the permission of Israel Scheffler) was clearly intended to signify the presentation of an analytic philosophic approach as framed by Scheffler to issues in Jewish education.

The book opens with a bombastic statement (quite foreign to the spirit of analytic philosophy of education) that "Jewish education is the great failure of Jewish life" (p. 15). It then delineates three kinds of problems that characterize Jewish education: problems of fact, problems of action, and problems of understanding. The third category of problems is the subject of this book and the core hypothesis is that it is time to stop searching for simple, recipe-like answers and instead to delineate a clear picture of the problems of understanding as a prelude to a thorough therapy (p. 14). "Problems of understanding refer to the lack of clear thinking about practical problems in Jewish education whose solution is dependent on careful analysis" (p. 17). The book is devoted specifically to four "problems of understanding": (1) aims in Jewish education, (2) indoctrination and Jewish education, (3) is Jewish education moral or religious Jewish education?, and (4) Israel and Jewish education. Methodologically the book is rooted in analytic philosophy of education and one of its supplementary concerns is to show how analytic techniques and research can be applied to a philosophy of Jewish education.

Chapter 1 builds on the Schefflerian taxonomy of diverse usages and misuses of the phrase "philosophy of Jewish education" using examples from a survey of the existing literature of Jewish education. The lack of an analytic philosophy of Jewish education is bemoaned and the book proposes its potential role in ameliorating the field.

Chapter 2 analyzes diverse and confused usages of the term "goals" in Jewish educational theory and practice, attempting to show how people tend to not be talking to each other while seemingly utilizing the same terms. The last brief section of the chapter breaks with the analytic approach when it offers "A normative goal for Jewish education:"

> Jewish education should deal with the confrontation of the Jewish child with Jewish education to enable him ultimately to make a rational and autonomous decision whether to accept or reject that tradition (p. 55).

Chapter 3 is an adaptation of a paper I published in the journal *Religious Education* dealing with Indoctrination and Religious Education (Chazan, 1972). This paper draws heavily on a rich tradition in general philosophy of education (Atkinson, 1965; Gregory & Woods, 1970; Snook, 1972) which had presented a detailed discussion and debate of diverse usages of the word and meanings of the phenomenon of "indoctrination." This chapter led to one of the only two ongoing analytic debates that I am familiar with in contemporary Jewish education (the other exercise of this sort was the Chazan, Reimer, Bryfman debates concerning the term "informal education" (Chazan, 1981, 1991, 2002, 2007; Reimer, 2007, Reimer & Bryfman, 2008)). Rosenak wrote a cogent response to and critique of my approach (Rosenak, 1989), and Alexander wrote an even more intelligent and cogent response to both essays (Alexander, 1989). Once again, this chapter ends with a non-analytic section on what a non-indoctrinary Jewish education would look like (pp. 73–75). Chapters 3 and 4 follow the same pattern by first carefully analyzing the phrases "moral education" and "religious education" and "teaching Israel" and then concluding with a brief normative statement as to what each of these phrases should be or do.

This volume is a clear attempt to adapt Scheffler's and Soiltis' approach and apply it to Jewish educational terms and literature. It comes both to present a methodology and also to zero in on four very important topics in Jewish education. It is to the best of my knowledge the only volume to ever attempt this specific task. At the same time, even this purportedly analytic book feels obligated to cross-over into the normative realm, ending each chapter with a credo or normative philosophy. (This "normative" quality is subconsciously implied by the dust jacket of the book which shows a schoolbook turned down and up and which is sub-titled "Crisis and Hope in the Jewish School." Such art work and sub-titling is distinctively foreign to the covers and sub-titles of the analytic literature.)

While in further writings I went on to apply this notion of the analytic to other terms (e.g., "informal education") and continued to be focused on educational thinking, I did not pursue a rigid pre-occupation with championing the analysis on educational concepts as my exclusive or even main pre-occupation in the subsequent decades. It may have been a technique I used, but it was not the essential cause that was my mission.

With this volume the story of analytic philosophy of Jewish education pretty much ends. Since Israel Scheffler was a known and distinguished philosopher of education and also a knowledgeable and committed Jew overtly identified with his Jewishness, he involved himself in important Jewish educational ventures mainly by applying his razor sharp mind and methodology to the theory and practice of Jewish education. Moreover, he did supervise several theses on Jewish education (Ron Kronish on Dewey and Jewish education; the late Edy Rauch on day schools; and the late Bennett Solomon on curricular integration in day schools). However, as noted, to the best of my knowledge, the aforementioned volume is the only venture overtly purporting to be analytic philosophy of Jewish education.

Critiques of Analytic Philosophy of Education

As noted, the analytic approach to philosophy of education peaked after a few decades. Its decline is connected to many factors, some related to the norms and culture of academic life, and others related to substantive critiques which influenced its longevity (Chambliss, 1996).

Some critics (professionals and students) argued that analytic philosophy of education quickly degenerates into rather simple word games whereby academics choose a few examples of usages of words and then write detailed essays that focus on words rather than the essential larger questions of education implied in the words. The critique says that this field became an in-house closed network of essays, responses, papers at conferences, and publications for tenure that didn't really address itself to real educational concerns.

This critique was linked to the complexities of teaching the subject which is notoriously difficult. It requires a very talented interactive teacher ideally working with small groups and requiring and then reading many written exercises. Many of those teaching this approach were trained in its philosophic methodology but didn't develop the pedagogy of teaching it. Frequently, philosophy of education classes at graduate schools were large-lecture classes of heterogeneous students from diverse departments, which was not at all conducive to this pedagogic approach.

Another apparently small but not insignificant-related factor is that students come to philosophy of education classes and/or to schools of education seeking both knowledge and also inspiration. They want to learn and also to be touched and inspired by great ideas, visions, and principles. This is not the domain of analytic philosophy of education. Students in these classes were often engaged in hours of focusing on the differences between "knowing how" and "knowing that" when they were hungry for discussions of big ideas and principles.

In the changing cultural climate of the 1960s, radical students in England and other venues began to feel that Peters and his colleagues and this approach in general was not radical enough (Phillips, 2008). Their complaint was that stogy male Anglo-Saxon academics were hiding from making significant changes in education by focusing on how words are used, whereas what really matters is how practices are changed. This point is perhaps exemplified in a famous phrase that R.M. Hare, one of the most influential analytic philosophers would use to describe a cogent argument: it is one with which "any sane or sensible person" would agree (Hare, 1964). This kind of argument, particularly in the era when post-modernism was beginning to be heard, was a kind of proof that British dons had set their own pseudo-rational criteria of who is sane and sensible which excluded many important minorities such as non-Caucasians, women, and gays and lesbians. The troops of post-modernism and critical theory were approaching the cathedrals of analytic philosophy (Grenz, 1996). Finally, while analytic philosophy of education was nurtured by notions of emotive meaning, Janus faced words, and connotative and denotative meanings, its analyses tended to focus on the objective, rational, and cognitive. Books like C. S. Stevenson's *Ethics and Language* or his *Facts and Values* were influential, but analysts often lost the literary touch and the epistemological breadth of such literary-influenced works when analyzing terms, and analytic philosophy seemed to isolate itself in a kind of in-house very cognitive cocoon (Stevenson, 1944, 1963).

Where Jewish Educational Thinking Went

While analytic philosophy of education was in its years of influence, one might well ask why philosophy of Jewish education wasn't more influenced by this zeitgeist of general education between the 1950s and 1980s. That question is an interesting historical topic related to overall currents in the academic and practical world of Jewish education, and well-worthy of a detailed study. One reason was clear then and remains clear today: Jewish education is driven from within and without by the search for answers, praxis, programs, and solutions. It is a defensive activity forever seeking to ameliorate, and pressured to do so quickly with observable results.

It is easier to point to where Jewish educational thinking did go in the middle to last decades of the last century. The first major thrust of Jewish educational thinking was curriculum, and the major general forces were emergent from the University of Chicago school centrally influenced by the curricular focus of the Tyler-Schwab nexus (Westbury & Wilkof, 1978). The Tyler-Schwab rationale was a powerful curriculum theory focus that was co-opted by one of Schwab's important students, Seymour Fox, who implemented a Herculean program of curricular reflection over many decades, first at the Jewish Theological Seminary's Melton Center, then at the Hebrew University's Melton Centre for Jewish Education, and then at the Mandel Center in Jerusalem (Nisan & Schremer, 2005). A significant generation of students throughout the world became focused on curriculum—and particularly Schwab's insightful series of essays on "the practical" which became a "Jewish educational bible" and centerfold of Jewish educational thinking.

The second direction that Jewish education took was normative theologizing and normative philosophizing. I use both the words "theologizing" and "philosophizing" because much but not all of this normative writing was rooted in the theological belief that Jewish education should be religious education. I use the adjective "normative" because while some of this work utilized rigorous philosophic methods, it mainly focused on prescriptive presentations aimed at convincing people of what they ought to do rather than explication per se. Once again, led by "the Jerusalem school" shaped by Fox and particularly by Michael Rosenak, the emphasis on Jewish educational thinking focused on setting goals, visioning, and looking to Jewish sources and scholars for direction (Rosenak, 1987, 1995). The most overt statement of this direction is the 2003 volume and project *Visions of Jewish* Education, published by Cambridge University Press, and edited by Seymour Fox, Israel Scheffler, and Daniel Marom (2003). The heart of this volume is six original essays (the products of a multi-year seminar series) by four Judaic scholars, Isador Twersky, Menachem Brinker, Moshe Greenberg, and Michael Meyer with two educational essays by Michael Rosenak and Israel Scheffler. The four Jewish academic figures, each of great repute in their particular Jewish fields, present their normative theories of a traditional, secular, and liberal vision of the educated Jew. Rosenak and Scheffler propose to then translate this into implications for an overall notion of "the educated Jew" (Fox et al., 2003; Pekarsky, 2008).

A third direction in Jewish educational thinking has been teaching and teacher training. This field covers a broad range of interests that include theories of teaching and learning, teacher training, and methodologies of teaching subjects. This direction has clearly been advanced by the work of Sharon-Feinman Nemser both in the years as a general educationist at Michigan State University and her full-time entry into Jewish education as professor and shaping figure of the Mandel Center of Jewish education at Brandeis University (Feinman-Nemser, 2008). Her work is related to the overall influence of Professor Lee Schulman previously of Stamford University, former head of Carnegie Foundation, and shaping figure of the teacher training field in the last decades of the twentieth century. Like Scheffler, Schulman is a general educationist who also cares about Jewish education and has contributed to it.

While there have been other books and essays in philosophy of Jewish education (one of the noteworthy figures being Hanan Alexander), they generally are the works of individuals and do not constitute a "school" or overall corpus of works. It is telling that the comprehensive volume on *What We Now Know about Jewish*

Education (2008) has only one essay—Perkarsky's referred-to-essay on vision-guided education—that in any way approaches what might be called "philosophy of Jewish education." The focus on curriculum, normative philosophizing and theologizing, and teaching and teacher training has pervaded Jewish education in North America as in Israel for several decades.

Do We Need an Analytic Philosophy of Jewish Education?

Much has happened in the world of Jewish education in the current era. We are witness to many more academic positions in departments and schools of Jewish education that already existed as well as the emergence of new positions at Jewish and general universities. A vibrant research network and journal exists. Jewish educational academics present papers at general education conferences and at conferences of Jewish studies. Moreover, the overall interest in Jewish education by the Jewish community and philanthropists has grown significantly (See the chapter "Informal Education: The Decisive Decade – How Informal Jewish Education was Transformed in its Relationship with Jewish Philanthropy", by J. Reimer, this volume).

Perhaps we should end this essay here, marking this brief chapter as nothing more than an episode in the history of the academics of Jewish education. I should like to argue otherwise. The same needs that gave rise to an analytic philosophy of education in the last century exist today in Jewish education today and indeed one might well argue that increased contemporary interest in Jewish education makes the implementation of an analytic methodology even more important today. At a time when Jewish life may be taking Jewish education more seriously, it behooves us even more to create a way of thinking, talking, and writing that is clear, non-jargoned, and which comes to establish conceptual clarity. This is not to deny the ongoing role of normative thinking in Jewish education (indeed, such thinking is probably indigenous to the very work of Jewish education because of the word "Jewish" in the phrase). But no less important at this time would be a twenty-first century analytic philosophy of Jewish education.

Such an analytic philosophy of Jewish education could not simply pick up from where the general movement left off in the 1980s. A contemporary analytic philosophy of Jewish education should continue to focus on the "language of Jewish education"—i.e., the way people talk about "Jewish education." But the words "people" and "Jewish education" need much broader understandings today. "People" should include the discourses and usages of teachers, principals, lay leaders, rabbis, academics, and general educators. "Language" should include a broad range of usages and understandings of Jewish educational terminology. It should pay greater attention to emotive and affective meanings of terms and the reasons for their emotive impact (the most immediate example and probably first topic for analysis is the painfully negative emotive meanings of the term "Hebrew school" or the very phrase "Jewish education"). The analysis of the language of Jewish education can be enhanced by reference to both contemporary Hebrew and classical Hebrew and Jewish pedagogic language. For example, classical Hebrew words used for "knowing" are very instructive for understanding Jewish perspectives on the aims of education (e.g., *la-da'at*). Contemporary Israeli Hebrew pedagogic terms such as *hinuch, hora'ah, marzeh, moreh,* and *l'ha'aver chomer* each have nuanced and important distinctive meanings which encompass prior assumptions. Furthermore, an analytic philosophy would enhance its value by focusing simply not only on words or phrases but also on issues and topics. We need clear thinking not just about words or sentences, but about types of discourse and categories of problems. Finally, an analytic philosophy of education today would be more effective if it were to work in harmony with aligned fields—social psychology of Jewish identity development, sociology of the Jews, history of Jewish education—rather than if it existed exclusively as an isolated sphere.

The contribution such an enterprise could make is to provide a broad array of practitioners, planners, teachers, policy makers, and philanthropists with clear exposition and delineation of concepts, terms, and ideas so as to enable them to act in a thoughtful manner. Let me give a brief example to illustrate. I recently attended a conference of a talented group of some 30 Jewish educators to deal with the very complex issue of evaluation and "experiential Jewish education." One-day deliberations like this can go many routes and their efficacy is often at a priori risk because of the complexity of the subjects and the diverse languages the various participants bring to the table. The moderator of the day (not an analytic philosopher but an astute university trained academic/practitioner) artfully devoted just enough—but not too much—time at the outset to enabling the various "languages" to be placed on the table before he smoothly obtained agreement on a stipulative definition of "experiential education" which would enable the planners to proceed with what was their main agenda question. In his terms, he was able to put a very controversial term–"experiential education"—in what he called "the parking lot" and utilize an agreed-upon stipulation so as to avoid "road blocks" that might have derailed the day. This is less an example of conceptual clarity and more an example of analytic methodology to advance productive educational discussion.

The value of analytic clarity and methodology is particularly important in the new age of a Jewish education characterized by diverse forms of education, many new ways of talking about Jewish education, and a significant body of philanthropists who have invested great effort and considerable resources into the amelioration of Jewish education. This new world very much needs "clear think" and "clear talk."

Some Concepts to Analyze

It is useful to point to some terms and concepts that are prominent in Jewish educational discourse that are in need of clarification, both to exemplify the case I am trying to make and to begin to set an agenda.

The first term that needs analysis is "Jewish education," since the very term remains ambiguous. Let us look at some of the ways it is understood.

For many people in North America, "Jewish education" immediately implies "Hebrew" or "supplementary" or "religious" school for elementary school children. It has supplementary, religious, and age-defined (usually 8–13) connotations.

For most Latin American, British, Australian, and South African Jews, "Jewish education" refers to all-day educational institutions in which children study both Jewish and general studies.

There are those who do not understand the phrase as aged-defined at all and rather adapt the Maimonidean definition that Jewish education (Maimonides used the words *Talmud Torah*) is life-long studying by Jews of all ages (Kraemer, 2008; Rosenak, 1995; Twersky, 1972).

For an increasing number of people, "Jewish education" is less and less related to schools and more and more associated with out-of-school activities: Birthright Israel, Jewish summer camps, retreats, experiential or informal education American-Jewish World Service or Hillel social action travel programs.

Thus, for some, "Jewish education" refers to an institution, a building, or an age group and for others it is a process, a vision, or an approach not limited by age, geography, or venue.

We could not end this brief discussion of the phrase "Jewish education" without indicating that for many—especially young people—"Jewish education" does not denote anything. Rather it is an alternative linguistic device for expressing the emotional expressions: "boring;" "a waste of time;" "my parents are afraid I'll marry a non-Jew;" or "what you have to do for a bar or bat-mitzvah." According to this pattern of analysis, it is not even a definitional term, but rather an emotive verbalization much like a grunt, sigh, or whine.

So how shall we even begin a discussion of Jewish education? How do we prevent the clear traffic jam that lies ahead of any discussion of the subject without a good conceptual "policeman?" Enter the analytic philosopher of Jewish education.

The second term I would propose for an agenda of analytic philosophy of Jewish education is the phrase "Jewish identity." For well over 50 years now this phrase has become the catch-all phrase for "being Jewish" (sometimes the phrase "Jewish survival" is also used). It has generally replaced such more traditional terms as "*Yiddishkeit*," "*mitzvot*," "*orach hayim yehudi*," "Torah- true Judaism," and "*halacha*" as the end goals of Jewish education. It is interesting that we have replaced classical non-English phrases with either "identity," a purely psychological term (very much influenced by the central psychologist of identity Erik Erikson) or "survival," a biological or sociological term very much influenced by the scientist Charles Darwin and the sociologist Emile Durkheim.

The term "Jewish identity" remains ambivalent even after five decades of discussion and research. There have been some attempts to distinguish between "Jewish identity" and "Jewish identification" (Simon Herman, 1989) as well as some first steps to suggest models of Jewish identity development (Chazan & London, 1990).

Some have defined "Jewish identity" by a list of behavioral actions that a Jew does and attitudes he/she holds; i.e., Jewish identity is activities and beliefs such as attending synagogue services, being a member of a Jewish organization, supporting Israel, believing the Holocaust was a central moment in Jewish history, believing in core Jewish values.

Others have suggested that this "definition" misses a critical internal dimension which is related to a sense of inner self or definition which has been characterized by the notion of "the Jew within" (Cohen & Eisen, 2000). According to this line of thinking, identity is a subjective internal state very much defined by personal feelings, affect, and meaning.

A third approach to the subject is doubtful of the efficacy of the entire notion of "identity." Building on the idea that we live in an age of the saturated self (Gergen, 1991), this approach doubts the very value of the term "an identity" and argues "against identity" (Wiseltier, 1996), opting instead either for an idea of multiple identities or diverse selves that describe who we are.

Thus, this still popular term and apparent goal remains notoriously (and sometimes one wonders if not very consciously) ambivalent. This state is very problematic for educators who do better the more their goal is clearly defined (even if as an end-in-view). It also complicates and even paralyzes researchers of identity who need agreed-upon parameters so as to develop instruments that can measure the intended outcomes. A small sector of Jewish life has quite explicit notions of Jewish identity, e.g., the Orthodox Jewish educational world and the Zionist youth movements. However, the majority of contemporary Jews do not fall into either of these two camps, and therefore the question of what is identity is central to their worlds. Enter the analytic philosopher of education.

A third subject for analysis is the Jewish educational slogan. As Scheffler argued in *The Language of Education*, educational slogans are different than definitions in a number of ways (Scheffler, 1960). They are unsystematic, popular, and usually intended to elicit emotions rather than to induce pondering. Definitions come to clarify; slogans come to arouse.

The field of education seems to be fertile ground for short, pithy, generalizations that evolve into popular "truths" which is what Scheffler meant by "educational slogans." These slogans often become very powerful, but in reality they often are subject to little careful or critical analysis. They somehow swiftly slip into the jargon of common usage as gospel.

It is that very popular and rousing dimension of slogans that suggests the need for a close and critical analysis of them. Because of their power and potential impact, it is important to have a reflective and analytic look at what they are saying. This is not to deny their role; it is rather to monitor their potential misuse.

Jewish educational slogans have blossomed in recent decades. This probably can be attributed to the new attention Jewish education has received in Jewish life and also because of the entry of philanthropists who often come from a world of business, marketing, and finance where the lingua franca of discourse is different from traditional educational language. In that sense, analytic philosophy of education has an important new role to play in contemporary Jewish life.

Let me illustrate this point by analyzing one of the prominent contemporary slogans: "Education is the key to Jewish survival." This slogan appears in rabbis' sermons, federations' campaign materials, foundations' annual reports, and institutions' requests to funding agencies.

The role of the analytic philosopher in such cases differs from linguistic analysis of concepts. In the case of slogans, the task is primarily to determine what kind of statement the slogan actually is, what type of evidence might answer it, and whether there is any definitive veracity to the statement.

At first glance, the "educational is the key to Jewish survival" slogan would seem to be an historical statement asserting that schools or other educational frameworks established by Jewish communities were the *key* factor in the *survival* of the Jews. One respected historian suggests that this theme has actually not been studied in depth by his field (Chazan, R., 2005) and this would lead one to question whether the statement has historical basis. Periodically, Jewish historians and others have cited factors they consider key to Jewish survival, such as theological beliefs, behaviors, the impact non-Jewish world, social and economic factors, or the Land of Israel. But there does not seem (yet at least) to be a definitive historical study or consensus about the historicity of this slogan.

A second possibility about this slogan is that it is sociological; i.e., it comes to verify that the key to maintaining Jewish existence today is education. This too is unclear and not easily verifiable. The importance of day schools, camps, and Israel trips to adult Jewish identity is often cited as proof of this claim, and there have been several attempts to study correlations and causations between these educational frameworks and adult Jewish identity. But the often assumed "definitive study" that Jewish day schools or other educational frameworks guarantee Jewish survival does not in fact exist. Indeed, Jews seem to have survived precisely in a century of lessened commitment and participation in Jewish education. Thus, while there are some studies which support the slogan, it is questionable whether there is enough validity or reliability to justify categorizing this statement as an authoritative sociological statement.

So what kind of statement in fact is "education is the key to Jewish survival?" A close look at the words of this slogan ultimately suggests that it is neither an historical nor sociological sentence, but rather a normative plaint. The sentence "Jewish education is the key to Jewish survival" is best translated as:

> I (or we) who are making the statement believe and want to convince you that if you really care about the continued Jewishness of your children or the future existence of the Jewish community we believe that you should seriously consider sending them to a day school or to a Jewish summer camp or on an Israel trip and/or you should contribute hefty resources to institutions that implement such programs.

The slogan is actually a normative belief or expression of personal conviction probably aimed at rousing interest, emotion, and support under the guise of a verifiable historical or sociological statement. Normative beliefs are very important in life, but they are no more than that—important beliefs. In themselves they carry no a priori validity or reliability. To use such slogans as fact statements might be good for Jewish causes, but it also might be inaccurate or deceptive. It is the job of the analytic philosopher of education to guard against such frivolity, confusion, or out and out deception.

In an age of increased interest and resources for Jewish education, slogan analysis is not simply word-games; it has important practical implications. We need to be really sure that a sentence on the basis of which great effort and resources are invested has veracity and is not simply a sales slogan. In the age of Twitter, Facebook, and streaming news on TV screens, life is particularly susceptible to a new language system comprised of a series of slogans. The goodwill of philanthropists and the practice of Jewish education are too important and binding to be guided by unexamined slogans. Even when we might be forced to question some of the most basic slogans (such as whether Jewish education really is the key to Jewish survival), it is out of faith and belief—not cynicism or scepticism—that we are required to do so. It is precisely at such moments of great passion and emotion that we need the detached pondering of the analytic philosopher of education.

A Road To Be Taken

Freud once suggested that education is one of the "impossible professions" (Britzman, 2009; Freud, 1925; Gay, 1988). For Freud, this reflected his deep suspicions about the role of social institutions in general and especially those which purport to "help people" (Freud, 1926). But I have to believe he also said it in the sense that I intend it: working with people and proposing to change them is one of the more complicated occupations there is. This argument is presented in a most interesting fashion by one of Freud's early followers, Siegfried Bernfeld (Bernfeld, 1973), who also was for a time a very involved educator, Jewish educator, Jewish youth leader, and pro-Zionist. In his book *Sisyphus or the Limits of Education*, Bernfeld argues that education has to exist but there is a sense in which its very existence contradicts what it presumes to do and limits its chances of success.

> For the plain fact is that educational theory does not meet the expectations people set on it ... it gives no clear unambiguous directions, its methods rarely assure success. Its prognosis – often false and never reliable – points to a remote, incalculable future (Bernfeld, 4).

Moreover, educational philosophers of the type who promulgate normative theories "Do their utmost to becloud these plain and simple facts by insisting that teachers not merely instruct but also educate" (p. 5).

Yet, the Bernfeld who wrote this book was a believer in education and for several years a Jewish and educational activist. Indeed, his theory is a fascinating amalgam of contradictory views: belief in youth; doubts about education's efficacy; commitment to ideology; suspicion about education's role; distrust of schools; and commitment to creating better schools. One presumes that it was these beliefs that led him to his general and Jewish pursuits in his earlier years. It was also his commitment to humankind that led him to be the guardian against inaccurate, exaggerated, and sloganistic psychological and educational thinking.

The field of contemporary Jewish education needs the voices of Scheffler, Soltis, and Bernfeld to rein it in from its fantasizing, illusions, and sloganeering. We need clear talking and clear thinking which might help lead to creative innovative efforts and at the same time rein in the excessive, obsessive, and exaggerated language and mission being deposited on the doorsteps of Jewish education. Indeed, Jewish education *is* an impossible profession, and an analytic approach might contribute to extracting some possibilities from an impossible profession. The good news is that the future will always remain remote and incalculable.

References

Alexander, H. (1989). Recent trends in philosophy of Jewish education: Chazan, Rosenak, and beyond. In A. Shkedi (Ed.), *Studies in Jewish education (Volume IX)*. Jerusalem: Magnes Press.
Atkinson, R. F. (1965). Instruction and indoctrination. In R. Archambault (Ed.), *Philosophic analysis and education*. London: Routledge and Kegan Paul.
Bernfeld, S. (1973). *Sisyphus or the limits of education*. Berkeley, CA: University of California Press.
Britzman, D. (2009). *The very thought of education: Psychoanalysis and the impossible professions*. Albany, NY: State University of New York Press.
Chambliss, J. (Ed.) (1996). *Philosophy of education: An encyclopedia*. Oxford: Blackwell.
Chazan, B. (1972). Indoctrination and religious education. *Religious Education, 67*(4), 243–252.
Chazan, B. (1978). *The language of Jewish education*. New York: Hartmore House.
Chazan, B. (1981). What is informal education? In *Philosophy of education, 1981*. Carbondale, IL: Philosophy of Education Society.
Chazan, B. (1991). What is informal Jewish education? *Journal of Jewish Communal Service, 67*(4), 300–308.
Chazan, B. (2002). *A philosophy of informal Jewish education*. Jerusalem: Jewish Agency.
Chazan, B. (2005). Toward a critical theory of Jewish education. *Journal of Jewish Education, 71*(1), 95–105.
Chazan, R. (2005). The historiography of premodern Jewish education. *Journal of Jewish Education, 74*(1), 23–32.
Chazan, B. (2007). The greening of informal Jewish education talk. *Journal of Jewish Education, 73*(2), 115–118.
Chazan, B., & London, P. (1990). *Psychology and Jewish identity education*. New York: American Jewish Committee.
Cohen, S., & Eisen, A. (2000). *The Jew within: Self, family and community in America*. Indianapolis, IN: Indiana University Press.
Feinman-Nemser, S. (2008). Learning to teach. In *What we now know about Jewish education*. New York: Tora Aura Publications.
Fox, S., Scheffler, I., & Marom, D. (2003). *Visions of Jewish education*. Cambridge, UK: Cambridge University Press.
Freud, S. (1925). Preface to Aichorn's "Wayward youth". *In* S. Freud (Ed.) (1968), *The standard edition of the complete psychological works of sigmund freud* (24 Vol.). London: Hogarth Press and Institute of Psychoanalysis.
Freud, S. (1926). Address to the society of Bnai brith. In S. Freud (Ed.) (1968), *The standard edition of the complete psychological works of sigmund freud* (24 Vol.). London: Hogarth Press and Institute of Psychoanalysis.
Gay, P. (1988). *Freud: A life for our time*. New York: Anchor Books.
Gergen, K. (1991). *The saturated self*. New York: Basic Books.
Glock, H. -J. (2008). *What is analytic philosophy?* Cambridge: Cambridge University Press.
Gregory, I. M. M. & Woods, R. G. (1970). Indoctrination in *Proceedings of the Annual Conference of the Philosophy of Education Society of Great Britain*.
Grenz, S. (1996). *A primer on postmodernism*. Cambridge, UK: Stanley Eerdsmans Publishing Company.
Hare, R. M. (1964). *The language of morals*. London: Oxford University Press.
Herman, S. (1989). *Jewish identity: A social psychological perspective*. New Brunswick, NJ: Transaction Books.

Kraemer, J. (2008). *Maimonides*. New York: Doubleday.
M. Nisan, O. Schremer (Eds.) (2005). *Educational deliberations: Studies in education dedicated to Shlomo (Seymour) Fox*. Jerusalem: Keter Publishing.
Pekarsky, D. (2008). Vision-guided Jewish education. In R. Goodman, P. Flexner, & L. Bloomberg (Eds.), *What we now know about Jewish education*. Los Angeles: Tora Aura Productions.
Phillips, D. C. (2008). Philosophy of Education in Stanford *Encyclopedia of Philosophy*. http://plato.stanford.edu/entries/education-philosophy/.
Reimer, J. (2007). Beyond more Jews doing Jewish: Clarifying the goals of informal Jewish education. *Journal of Jewish Education*, *73*(1), 5–23.
Reimer J., & Bryfman, D. (2008). Experiential Jewish education. In R. Goodman, P. Flexner, & L. Bloomberg (Eds.), *What we now know about Jewish education*. Los Angeles: Tora Aura Publications.
Rosenak, M. (1987). *Commandments and concerns: Jewish religious education in secular society*. Philadelphia: Magnes Press.
Rosenak, M. (1989). Indoctrination. In A. Shkedi (Ed.), *Studies in Jewish education*, Vol. IX. Jerusalem: Magnes Press.
Rosenak, M. (1995). *Roads to the palace: Jewish texts and teaching*. Oxford: Bergham Books.
Ryle, G. (1949). *The concept of mind*. London: Hutchinson's University Library.
Scheffler, I. (1957). *Philosophy and education*. Boston: Allyn and Bacon.
Scheffler, I. (1960). *The language of education*. Springfield, IL: Frank Thomas Publishers.
Snook, I. (1972). *Concepts of indoctrination*. London: Routledge and Kegan Paul.
Soltis, J. (1968). *An introduction to the analysis of educational concepts*. Reading, MA: Addison-Wesley (1978). 2nd ed.
Stevenson, C. L. (1944). *Ethics and language*. New Haven, CT: Yale University Press.
Stevenson, C. L. (1963). *Facts and values*. New Haven, CT: Yale University Press.
Stroll, A. (2000). *Twentieth century analytic philosophy*. Columbia University Press: New York.
Twersky, I. (1972). *A maimonides reader*. New York: Behrman House.
I. Westbury, N. Wilkof (Eds.) (1978). *J. Schwab: Science, curriculum, and education*. Chicago: University of Chicago Press.
Wiseltier, L. (1996). *Against identity*. New York: William Drentel.

Community Engagement: The Challenge of Connecting Jewish Schools to the Wider Community

Helena Miller

Introduction

British Jews are facing new and complicated challenges as they grapple with the issues of relating to the world around them in the politically turbulent years of the early twenty-first century. This challenge is not a phenomenon restricted to the Jewish schools of Britain; but the concept of schools and their relationships with the wider community is one which is especially preoccupying the British government and its Department for Children, Schools and Families (DCSF). The effect of this challenge will impact all State-funded schools in Britain. Beyond Britain, government legislation also tries to improve cohesion in societies made ever more diverse by immigration. These efforts are rarely without controversy. For example, the law passed in France in 2004 which prevents French school children in State schools from wearing visible expressions of religious identity, including the Muslim *hijab* (head scarf worn by women) and the Jewish *kippah* (head covering for males), provoked a widespread outcry (CBC News 7 September 2004). Supporters of the ban argued that in a secular state such laws help to prevent division in society. Others felt that the legislation eroded their individual rights as citizens.

Unlike in America, and indeed many other parts of the world, Jewish schooling in Britain has a long history of financial support by the State. In 1851, 12 years after the government accepted that schools of a Christian religious nature were eligible for State funding, the government agreed that Jewish schools were permitted to receive grants in the same way that other denominational schools were, provided they agreed to read the scriptures of the Old Testament every day and provided they were also prepared to submit to government inspection (Miller, 2001). Sixty years earlier, in America, in 1791, the First Amendment mandated a legal separation of Church and State and the law established religious pluralism as public policy. As a consequence, religious-affiliated schools were effectively barred from receiving

H. Miller (✉)
United Jewish Israel Appeal (UJIA), London, UK
e-mail: helena.miller@ujia.org

State funding, a situation that has remained broadly in force until the present day in the USA (Jorgenson, 1987).

Around one third of the total number of State-maintained schools in Britain are schools with a religious character (approximately 6,850 schools) out of a total of around 21,000 maintained schools. This dual system of maintained schools supported by faith organisations that exist alongside schools without a religious character is therefore at the heart of the school system in Britain. The government continues to support the benefits to society that this system brings both for parental choice and for diversity.

Within this system, approximately 26,000 Jewish children in the UK (60% of all Jewish children) are educated in Jewish faith schools. Within that number, there are 39 State-funded Jewish schools serving approximately 15,000 pupils. A further 1,000 Jewish pupils are educated in mainstream Jewish Independent schools. The remaining 10,000 are educated in 43 strictly Orthodox Independent schools that operate within the *Charedi* (ultra-orthodox) community in Britain, the majority of which are in and around greater London and Manchester.

In Britain and many other parts of the world, debate about the nature of a cohesive society and what it means to be a fully integrated and engaged citizen has led to government legislation, which has changed the nature of how Jewish schools relate to and integrate with their local and wider communities. This legislation, introduced by the Education and Inspections Act (2006), requires all State-funded schools, including all faith schools, to "promote community cohesion", and is intended to build on existing good practice in schools.

This chapter contextualises and explains what is meant by "community cohesion" in British law, and describes how well British Jewish schools already comply with the legislation. It explores to what extent and how schools need to develop in order to comply with the law, by using literature and examples from government and DCSF sources as well as from recent case studies, such as those found in the DCSF publications "Faith in the System" (2007) and the Commission of Integration and Cohesion's "Our Shared Future" (2007). The chapter looks at the extent of implementation of citizenship education in Jewish schools (NFER, 2004) through the inter-related foci of the curriculum, the school as community, and the schools' partnership with the community. It explores whether it is possible to determine if legislating for increased interaction with the community at large does indeed promote community cohesion and a greater tolerance and understanding of the world around us. It looks at successes and challenges, as well as current research (of which there is as yet very little). Whilst the focus will be on Jewish education in Britain, illustrated by examples seen by the author in British schools, this chapter will also incorporate examples of community engagement in other parts of the Diaspora and in Israel, particularly where these examples inform or challenge emerging practice in Britain. The chapter will conclude with concerns related to the development of future policy and a suggested agenda for future exploration and research.

Contextualising Community Cohesion

As early as 1897, Dewey wrote that schools "must represent life, life as real and vital to the child as that which he carries on in his home, in the neighbourhood, or in the playground". Thus, Dewey gives an educationalist's rationale for making available real-world contexts through which certain kinds of concepts and knowledge are transferred to the student.

The rationale for the British government to focus on community cohesion is a sociological and political one, namely the aftermath of the terror attacks of 9/11/2001, 7/7/2005 and the riots in Northern towns of England in 2001 (Cantle report, 2001). Government interest in faith-based communities and schools is reflected in the development of public policy since the mid-1980s (recorded by, and reflected on, amongst others by Weller, 2005; Worley, 2005; Gilroy, 1993; Bourdieu, 1985).

Goldring (2009) brings a wider, and Jewish, perspective to the context for community cohesion within schools. In addition to community collaboration for the purpose of developing social capital, paralleling the government agenda stated above, she also claims two further strands. First, that linking schools to communities is important because it will enhance learning, specifically learning that will be linked to Jewish identity development, and second that school–community cohesion has the purpose of building and developing the wider Jewish community.

Community cohesion has been defined in terms of "promoting greater knowledge, respect and contact between various sections of the community, and establishing a greater sense of citizenship" (Pearce and Howell, 2004). The emphasis here is on understanding about, as well as having contact with, the community. In addition, the British government has further defined community cohesion as "...what must happen in all communities to enable different groups of people to get on well together. A key contributor to community cohesion is integration which is what must happen to enable new residents and existing residents to adjust to one another" (Migniuolo, 2008).

This last definition explicitly recognises the role of social integration within an overall cohesion strategy, placing a distinct emphasis on society's responsibilities towards new residents. This concept of integration encompasses all existing communities within a general approach to cohesion, oriented around the relationship between citizens and local organisations, against a background of improving quality of life. Key ways of relating to the world around us are further identified by the British government. These include having a shared vision and sense of belonging, focusing on what new and existing communities have in common, and also recognising diversity, and forming strong and positive relationships between people of different backgrounds.

Community cohesion is not a widely used term within schools in Europe and the USA. Community relations, and the notion of "social capital", on the other hand, are concepts to which many schools refer. Putnam (2000) defines social capital as follows:

> whereas physical capital refers to physical objects and human capital refers to connections amongst individuals, social capital refers to social networks and the norms of trustworthiness that arise from them. (Putnam, 2000, p. 19)

Jewish school and Federation websites in the USA highlight an awareness of the importance of developing good social networks. To take one example, from information provided by the UJA Federation of Eastern Fairfield County,[1] this emphasis on community relations appears to be mostly focused internally on fostering relationships and connections within each Jewish day and supplementary school – between parents, students and staff – and not specifically on engagement with the wider community. Where there is connection with the wider community this most often seems to take place through *tzedakah* – collections of money, and working with charitable causes both inside and outside of the Jewish community.

Different stakeholders in education do not always have shared perspectives in terms of their vision of community. The move towards the increasingly secular state in France, described earlier, illustrates how the government and religious groups clearly differ in their ideas of what such a shared vision would involve. Within the Jewish education community in the UK, it is generally accepted that the meaning attributed to "belonging" is a multi-faceted issue. Many Jewish educators today would argue that, in order to feel able to "belong" to the local and wider community, children first must be securely rooted within their own, Jewish, community. Proponents of Jewish day schools argue that Jewish schooling should develop graduates who are "secure and knowledgeable in their own Jewish identity" (Miller & Shire, 2002). In addition, it is generally accepted by mainstream Jewish day schools that Jewish day schools "should encourage their pupils to engage with, and contribute to, the wider society" (JLC, 2008), although this is interpreted in different ways in different schools.

Jewish schools in Britain, have not, until the twenty-first century, had to address issues such as teaching about other religions, working with non-Jewish children from other local schools, or engaging with the local and wider non-Jewish, as well as Jewish, community. Previously, and in fact going back to the earliest days of compulsory schooling in Britain in the 1870s, Jewish schools were frequently regarded as impeding the process of social integration (Alderman, 1999). Finestein (1986) observes that these schools were regarded as appropriate only where "the foreign poor" lived. They were places where pupils were taught to assimilate, not to preserve cultural and religious knowledge and difference.

An illustration of this strategy can be taken from the Conference of Anglo-Jewish Ministers in 1911 when the Reverend S Levy was recorded as stating that education was enabling Jews to "acquire English habits of thought and character" (Lipman, 1954). The challenge to Jewish schools in the twenty-first century will be to meet

---

[1] http://www.jccs.org/uja.htm

the government criteria of cohesion without compromising the strongly Jewish ethos and curriculum of schools.

Complying with a Requirement to Connect with the Wider Community

In Britain, since 2002, citizenship education has been compulsory for all Secondary school (11–18 years) pupils and recommended for inclusion in Primary schools (DfES, 2002). The Citizenship Framework (QCA, 2002) has provided a number of key areas to explore through the formal and informal curriculum in schools. These include human rights, social justice and inclusion, sustainability, interdependence and conflict resolution, values and diversity. This framework offers faith-based schools the opportunity to explore wider issues and to encourage students to see themselves not just as members of their own religious community but also as citizens of the world, aware of the wider issues and challenges of global interdependence and responsibility. Since the launch of the Citizenship Framework in 2002, the Qualifications and Curriculum Authority (QCA, 2000) has provided information and resources to help teachers and their students learn about themselves, society and their impact on, and role within, the wider world.

The provision of citizenship education, within the National Curriculum, did not, however, go far enough in reflecting the reality of living in a multi-faith and multi-cultural society. Placing citizenship education within the National Curriculum for England and Wales led instead to an emphasis on the acquisition of theory and knowledge, and of testing and assessment, rather than of exploration and engagement. In addition, because the school day was already crowded, many schools interpreted this duty to teach citizenship in a laissez-faire way, relegating lessons to 20 minutes or less during weekly personal, social and health education sessions. The government response to this reality was to increase its commitment to the practices and principles of this challenge by promoting formal and informal relationships both within school communities and between schools and the wider community in which they are situated. The government view, echoed by Goldring (2009), has been that by promoting these relationships, learning will be enhanced through a shared understanding of each other.

Smith (2007) observes that the successes of communities with a good stock of social capital and exhibiting examples of community engagement are more likely to benefit from lower crime figures, better health, higher educational achievement and better economic growth. He states, however, that there can be significant challenges because communities and schools with high social capital also have the means and sometimes the motive to exclude and subordinate others, because they choose who to engage with, and how and when to engage with others.

In 2006, the leaders of faith communities in the UK published a joint statement which gave an assurance to the government and parents that faith schools will promote community cohesion, "welcoming the duty imposed on the governing bodies of all maintained schools in the Education and Inspections Act 2006" (DCSF, 2006).

The Jewish community in Britain has interpreted this duty in a variety of ways. Examples further on in this chapter show how schools engage with both their own community and the wider community and how they see opportunities for cohesion as a very positive aspect of school life. There are, however, many areas where sectors of the Jewish community do not feel able to comply, and feel negative about, or threatened by, the need to engage with others beyond the Jewish community. The origins of this resistance could be traced back to the *Torah*. In Deuteronomy 12:30, the Israelites are told not to enquire about pagan religions or ask "How did these nations worship their gods?" It was feared that such idolatry might lead to imitative idolatrous practices. If Israel was to be cleansed from paganism, it was best to prohibit the very knowledge of these dangerous ways. Plaut observes that the purpose of this charge was quite clear: in order to establish God as the supreme ruler of all Israel, all other religious practices and ideologies were ruled out of bounds and the very knowledge of them considered inadmissible (Plaut, 1981). Whilst Jewish religious practice is not always determined by literal and direct reference to biblical verses, these concerns have resonated down the years.

Different sectors of the Jewish community have chosen to interpret the duty towards community cohesion, and in particular the duty to teach about world faiths, very differently. In October 2004, the British government published a National Framework for Religious Education to act as a guideline for Education Authorities and other syllabus providers. It encourages the teaching of the tenets of Christianity and the five major religions represented in the UK: Judaism, Islam, Hinduism, Sikhism and Buddhism. It sets out guidelines and national standards for religious education for pupils from 4 to 16. At present, the framework is non-statutory and whilst many faith-based schools do teach some aspects of other religions, there is not yet a legal requirement for them to do so. Recent educational reform in the UK has promoted a choice model where faith-based schools are an accepted part of a wider drive to raise educational standards by expanding parental choice. Given the educational policies towards inclusion (DfES, 2006a, 2006b), faith-based schools must reconcile this legitimate parental choice of an education for their children which responds to community, religious and cultural distinctiveness, and balance this with the need for inter-community understanding, tolerance and respect.

The small number of pluralist[2] Jewish schools in Britain do teach world religions within the school curriculum. Teachers, pupils and their parents visit schools and the places of worship of other faiths, to learn from, as well as to learn about their neighbours (Miller, 2009). Orthodox Jewish schools in Britain learn about other faiths in varying degrees of depth, and may exchange visits with those from schools of other faiths, but refuse to visit the places of worship of other faiths. The United (Orthodox) Synagogue sends out guidelines to their schools explaining what may and may not be permissible. One example which caused some sectors of the

---

[2] "Pluralist" schools do not affiliate solely to one stream of Judaism, accept that there is more than one way of expressing Jewish faith and practice, and this is reflected in the Jewish education and ethos in these schools.

British Jewish community to question their level of contact with the non-Jewish community was where a Jewish school would not take part in an inter-faith initiative which included a visit to a holocaust exhibition because the exhibition was being temporarily housed in a church.

In faith schools, compliance with the duty towards community cohesion is inspected by the denominational inspectorate. In the case of the Jewish schools, this falls to Pikuach, set up in 1996 in response to the government requirement that schools have their denominational religious education inspected using a uniform framework that parallels Ofsted, the national framework for inspecting all State schools. Compliance is a grey area however. Inspectors have to judge to what extent the school exhibits community cohesion, within a context of self-evaluation against their own agreed criteria. There is much room for interpretation and so an orthodox school which learns about Hinduism through a project on "light" during which half an hour (or less) is spent learning about Diwali may still receive a top grade for inspection, depending on the school's own aims and ethos.

Community Cohesion and Engagement Within UK Jewish Schools

In 2006, the British government and the providers of State-funded schools with a religious character came together to "share understanding of the contribution of faith schools to school-based education and to society in England" (DfES, 2006). The initiative, which resulted in a document and various seminars and meetings throughout the country, highlighted "the very positive contribution" which schools with a religious character make as valuable, engaged partners in the school system and in their local communities and beyond.

Parker Jenkins (2009) researched five Muslim and four Jewish schools in the UK to explore the experiences of community cohesion and estrangement/alienation with the wider community. Her findings show the diverse approaches used in maintaining a religious focus in the curriculum and how these overlap with efforts to engage with the wider community at local, regional, national and international levels. Whilst she found that some parents expressed interest in having more inter-faith engagement, the senior management teams in schools expressed concerns over trying to increase levels of community engagement, since they felt that some parents had deliberately chosen the school so that their children did not have to mix with others.

Parker-Jenkins suggests that community "engagement" is a more likely goal for faith schools than "cohesion". She suggests that it is unclear what to cohere around, and whose values should underpin cohesion. Her research has resulted in a "typology of engagement" which may aid and guide schools as they grapple with the issues of relating to the world around them. Based on Gaine (2005) and Booth and Ainscow (2002), her typology is stated as follows:

1. Meaningful engagement: significant interaction through on-going and sustained projects.

2. Sustained engagement: strong evidence of different forms such as knowledge of and interaction with other faiths and/or the wider community.
3. Temporary engagement: perhaps due to one teacher or member of the community but which is not sustained once they have left the school.
4. Tokenistic engagement: a one off event or trip.
5. Superficial engagement: a veneer; weak and of no consequence or significance.
6. No engagement: in terms of curriculum, ethos, contact with others within and beyond the school community.

Each of these categories is, of course, open to interpretation and nuance. For example, is a permanent focus on collecting charity for distribution to non-Jewish charities either in the UK or overseas, qualitatively as engaging as regular meetings and joint projects with children in a neighbouring non-Jewish school? Both are sustained, but the first requires no personal contact, whilst the second leads to relationship building through personal contact. In each instance, knowledge of the wider world can be developed through education, but it is doubtful whether sustained engagement is possible without face-to-face commitment.

Jewish schools in the UK engage the wider community at various levels of intensity between categories two to five. In the current political climate, there is no possibility for State schools of any kind in Britain to be at level six, that is, having no contact with others within and beyond the school community. Even those Jewish schools who feel strongly that they want to have as little as possible to do with the wider community show some weak engagement with people beyond the school gates. Conversely, very few Jewish schools exhibit "significant interaction", although this may be more about having insufficient time and resources than a lack of interest or desire. Community engagement is only one of a multitude of aspects of school life to integrate into the values and practice of a school.

There are many opportunities for community cohesion and engagement within a Jewish school, especially when the "community" is the local Jewish one. Family and community are, of course, key concepts within Judaism. The importance of family and community is stressed within the fabric of the Jewish year. The regular festivals provide opportunities for family-based activities, and learning, preparation and celebration of *Shabbat* brings together the whole school community – parents, teaching and non-teaching staff and governors. One group of Jewish schools in the UK runs "Family Day" on the Sunday preceding Jewish festivals, where parents and students come together to learn as a community.

The Jewish ethos of schools provides ample opportunities for community engagement. A central value running through Jewish teaching is that of giving charity and of helping others. All Jewish schools epitomise this value with their regular collections for charities. Many schools raise money for non-Jewish, local and international causes as well as for Jewish charities. In 2006 teachers from three London Jewish schools participated in a 10-day seminar, one of the outcomes of which was to incorporate values from the Hebrew Bible into their schools. One such value, "you shall rise before the aged – *mipnay sayvah takoom*" (Leviticus 19:32) is now on display in the foyer of the school in Hebrew and English and is interpreted in practice in various ways, which include helping a teacher carry a heavy load of books to the staffroom, and letting an older passenger have your seat on the bus. These may be considered old-fashioned and outmoded concepts, but they embody the concept of *derech ertez* – behaving in the right way.

The predominant challenges for schools in relation to engaging with the wider community around them are currently located in the areas of curriculum and admissions policy. The content of the National Curriculum poses potential challenges to some Jewish schools, and curriculum selection in some Jewish schools demonstrates differing interpretations of community cohesion in practice (Osler & Starkey, 2005). For instance, in science and English literature, some of the more religiously right-wing Orthodox Jewish schools will not teach what they regard as unacceptable material. Shakespeare's "Romeo and Juliet", for example, a classic text for public examination for 16-year olds in British schools, is not acceptable to some Jewish schools. Within UK examination syllabi there is currently flexibility to accommodate such restrictions and the Board of Deputies of British Jews acts in the capacity of mediator, liaising with the government and the curriculum bodies to ensure that schools who wish to may continue to choose texts which they feel are suitable.

The structure of the National Curriculum poses further challenges to Jewish schools which look with some envy at their American colleagues who are free to teach a Jewish studies curriculum for half the school day if they choose. In the UK, all State schools, including the faith schools, are bound by a curriculum that legislates the number of hours per week to be spent on National Curriculum subjects. For example, 11–14-year olds in the UK must spend 24 hours per week studying National Curriculum subjects. School leaders have to balance the maximum number of additional hours they feel they can add to the school day with the breadth and depth of Jewish education they wish to offer their pupils. In reality this means that in Jewish schools, the working day is longer than in non-Jewish schools and that additionally strictly Orthodox secondary schools operate a 6-day school week, instead of the national 5-day school week.

Recently, the area of admissions has been a particular challenge to all-faith schools in Britain, not only the Jewish ones. In October 2006 the British government backed an amendment to the Education and Inspections Bill that would have forced faith schools to give 25% of their places to pupils of other or no faith. This measure was intended to promote community cohesion (DCSF, 2006). Whilst it would initially have affected only new schools, there was justifiable anxiety amongst all faith schools that this measure would soon after be applied to already existing schools. The Board of Deputies of British Jews, in conjunction with other faith groups, coordinated a united Jewish community voice, to oppose this sudden call for quotas. The proposal was withdrawn later the same month and the 2006 Education and Inspections Act continued to allow faith schools to give priority to applications from pupils within their own faith. Although the faith schools won this particular battle, it is likely that the relationship between faith schools and the State will continue to be a prominent political issue in the coming years. Ironically, in order to challenge a proposal which would not add to community cohesion, all sectors of the Jewish community for once came together with one another, and also united with wider faith communities to challenge this bill.

Additional challenges have been recently faced by all mainstream Jewish schools who have had to change their admissions criteria to comply with the UK Supreme Court ruling, made in 2009, which now makes it unlawful for Jewish schools to give priority to children who are born Jewish. In practice, admission to Jewish schools is now seen as a matter of faith and not one of ethnicity. To gain entry to a Jewish school, families have to show evidence of adherence to the faith (Synagogue attendance for example) and not merely birth. This brings Jewish schools' entry requirements in line with other faiths and is problematic for a religion where attending synagogue is not our test of "Jewishness".

The issue of admissions is further complicated by the changing demography of the Jewish population in the UK. State faith schools are required to enrol up to 30 pupils per class, the government recommended number. Schools in parts of the UK where there are declining Jewish populations are unable to maintain their pupil numbers without accepting non-Jewish children. Even in areas such as Greater London, with its large Jewish population (of approximately 200,000 people), there is concern about school enrolment numbers, particularly as projected over the next 10 years. The Jewish Leadership Council Report (2008) suggests that the pool of primary and secondary age children will decline by between 15 and 20% in the next 10 years. In order to address that decline and keep Jewish schools fully enrolled with Jewish students, the report recommends that between 70 and 80% of Jewish children will need to enrol in Jewish schools, a figure much higher than the current rate of between 50 and 60%.

Jewish Schools Engaging with the Wider Community

There is an emerging and possibly new story for the education service in the UK to tell about the way that its engagement with communities has the potential to improve a wide range of outcomes for young people. The concept of "public value" coined by Mark Moore (1995) has gained increasing currency amongst policy-makers and educators as a way of talking about important social products of community aspects of education. Moore argues that public value is developed when educational settings work to improve the wide range of outcomes for young people by engaging with families and communities in educational settings. Examples from Leadbetter and Mongon (2008) show the wider impact on community cohesion of individual initiatives that begin in the school and affect both the school and its local community. Ofsted reports, described in Leadbetter and Mongon (2008), praise the positive effect on students' attitudes, personal development and achievement as well as on their appreciation of and increased confidence in the school by the local community.

Jewish schools in the UK are increasingly aware of the roles they must play if they are to take full part in their local communities, and many examples of successful initiatives can be seen. Visitors from other faith groups, as well as from the local community, are welcomed into many Jewish schools on a regular basis.

For example, the students from one Jewish school in London have regular contact and programmes with the students of the neighbouring Catholic school. The local police, fire officers and shop keepers are welcomed regularly into Jewish schools to develop good community relations and to teach the pupils safe street practice. Jewish schools are well represented in local education authorities' sports leagues, music activities and extra-curricular initiatives.

A further success of cohesion is when partnerships extend beyond the students to initiatives that focus on teachers. For example, through a joint Muslim/Jewish initiative under the auspices of the British Board of Deputies of British Jews, a Jewish nursery school in South London and a Muslim nursery school begin their school year with joint professional development seminars for the teachers of both schools on topics of mutual concern and designed to foster understanding and on-going collaboration.

Jewish school buildings are available for wider community use outside of school hours with activities ranging from sports fixtures, to evening functions, to school holiday play schemes. The design of new Jewish schools specifically has to take heed of the potential for partnering with the community. Architectural drawings submitted to the DCSF on behalf of JCoSS, the new Jewish Secondary school which opened in London in 2010, have had to show clearly which areas of the school will be available for use by the local and wider community both during and after school hours. The Statutory proposals submitted to the local government offices on behalf of the same project in August 2008 were required, by law, to explain how the school will promote and contribute to community cohesion, in other words, they had to show in what ways they will invite the local and wider community into their school and how they will make real connections with the community beyond the school gates.

In the UK, the Jewish community beyond individual schools contributes to the wider society in various ways. For example, an outreach project run by one of the two Jewish teacher-training agencies in London supports non-Jewish teachers who are teaching Judaism in non-Jewish schools as part of their Religious education syllabus. Teachers who may feel insecure about teaching a faith of which they have little knowledge and even less experience are provided with resources and training. The Jewish community also hosts many non-Jewish school groups in its synagogues for programmes which demonstrate and explain Jewish religion and practice.

The Jewish community also provides a focus for one curriculum area that links it to the wider community. The National Curriculum in Britain stipulates Holocaust Education as part of the History syllabus for both 11-year olds and 14-year olds. By 1945, the Jews in Britain constituted the only intact surviving Jewish community in Europe. Many Jewish people in Britain were, however, scarred by the death of European relatives. In addition, many thousands were refugees from European persecution, often as members of the *kindertransport* – unaccompanied children sent from Germany to Britain before the start of the Second World War. The Holocaust Education Trust, the London and Manchester Jewish Museums and the Imperial War Museum are just a few of the institutions in Britain that provide education for the wider community in Britain about this dark period in European history. Outreach work, as well as the publication of a wide range of resources for teachers, ensures that powerful issues are presented appropriately to young people in Britain. This is as much a challenge as a success, however. The success is that every school child in Britain learns about the Shoah, and the challenge is that this is often the *only* aspect of Jewish life and history that the wider community learns about.

A further challenge is one of balance – of integrating without assimilating. But integration, and playing a full part in society, is a challenge in a wider society. Many local sports and music events for school students take place on Saturdays, and so are, by implication, not only barred to the Jewish schools, but to any religiously observant Jewish family in a non-Jewish school, as it would mean that they would have to break their observance of *Shabbat* in order to participate. The swimming team of one local Jewish primary school was unable to participate in the local authority gala with neighbouring schools because it took place on a Friday evening, after Shabbat had begun.

The above examples illustrate the extent of the challenge for pupils in Jewish schools to become full members of the UK community. Holden and Billings (2007) speak of "parallel lives" (p. 1) to describe the way people in local communities live separately from one another. They identify faith communities as making an important contribution towards building and sustaining cohesive communities across local communities principally by developing local leadership, providing meeting places, and encouraging values and attitudes conducive to cohesion. The mainstream adult Jewish community in Britain has always wanted to play a full role as part of British civil society. Indeed, in every synagogue in Britain, every Sabbath, a prayer is read which acknowledges and blesses the Queen and all the Royal Family. British Jews have always appreciated those occasions when they were welcomed into Britain whilst other countries at best refused them entry and at worst persecuted and massacred them. Many sectors of the UK Jewish community do, however, lead "parallel lives", as indeed do most UK citizens. This is because of where they live, their economic and social status, and their intellectual and cultural backgrounds. The contribution that faith schools can make to cohesion is significant, precisely because they are constructed as communities, and are driven by the values that underpin cohesive communities.

A challenge for those seeking to connect Jewish youth with the wider world is that the Jewish community itself provides an extensive enough infrastructure to meet so many of the needs of Jewish children and their families that their members may never have to venture beyond the community. There are religious, social and welfare institutions, informal youth provision, kosher shops and restaurants. The structure of the Jewish week, life cycle, feast and fast days are time-consuming and secure as well as being potentially restrictive in terms of engagement with the wider world. This resonates with Smith's (2007) observation discussed earlier in this chapter that groups and organisations with high social capital can have a significant downside because the experience of living in close knit-communities can lead to the exclusion of others (2007, p. 2). The challenge for Jewish schools is to develop young people who want to remain within a strong Jewish framework and who feel confident and comfortable in the wider world. Some schools perceive the challenge as unnecessary or even frightening. Once again, this reflects the difficulty of appreciating the possibilities of integration without assimilation. This challenge though is driven by a government agenda. The State is committed to confirming the ideological stance stated above, which is for schools to develop graduates who are strongly rooted in their own identity whilst playing their full part in the wider world. This is a problem for strictly orthodox schools that seek to develop graduates who are deeply knowledgeable about Jewish text, values and practice, and who principally lead their lives within a strictly orthodox community.

Jewish Schools Engaging with the Community Beyond the UK

Many successful initiatives have linked Jewish schools with the community in Europe and beyond. One such project is a European wide initiative within the Jewish community that aims to link Holocaust education with community engagement. In 2005, the European Council for Jewish Communities launched an initiative to develop a European wide citizenship curriculum which integrates Jewish values and texts into a citizenship curriculum, with particular reference to the Holocaust. This project is still in its initial stage, but with secure funding, it could be an exciting initiative in schools across Europe.

The use of technology could be extensively developed to encourage projects that enable pupils to meet each other across the globe. Rafi.ki (www.rafi.ki.co) is a large on-line community of schools, encouraging pupils to "meet" at on-line conferences, chat to each other on-line, participate in shared projects and build relationships. This virtual community aims to break down religious and cultural stereotypes and build good links between diverse groups of pupils around the world.

Jewish schools in the UK have the potential for links across Europe through biennial education conferences for policy-makers and educators, as well as occasional projects linking schools. A video link during *Hanukkah*, for example, has, in past years, enabled Jewish schools from across Europe to celebrate the kindling of the Hanukkah candles simultaneously. Individual schools make links with one another across Europe and exchanges of pupils and teachers take place. Informal education, through Jewish youth movements, teaches Jewish teenagers about Europe, through the opportunity to participate in study trips and sports competitions, as well as by inviting participants from European countries to join activities based in the UK. Each year, these initiatives and possibilities increase.

The Institute for Community Cohesion in the UK encourages pupils to engage in dialogue with schools in Europe and beyond. Jewish young adults are encouraged to engage in wider and global issues, for example, through Tzedek, a UK Jewish charity dedicated to relieving poverty in Africa and Asia. Jewish volunteers in their 20s spend 2 months at a time helping to build schools, nurse sick people and plant crops. As well as raising money for Jewish charities, Jewish schools raise money for local and global non-Jewish charities.

A particular project sponsored jointly by the "Minorities of Europe" (UK) organisation and Reut-Sadaka in Israel has linked adults from within Europe with a volunteering project in Israel that works with Arab and Jewish young people in schools, youth programmes, art and sports classes, and community projects. The purposes of the project – peace building and community cohesion – are intended to contribute to the "swapping Cultures" initiative in Europe, aimed at teaching young people to trust those of other cultures and religions through contact and joint initiatives. The project in Israel helped directly in the formation of training courses and conferences on community cohesion developed in Eastern Europe in 2007 and beyond (Minorities of Europe, 2006).

Unfortunately, ignorance and mistrust of our neighbours are two of the biggest challenges to building cohesion. Schools need help in learning how to play a role in building a mutual civility amongst different groups as well as ensuring respect for diversity. These are phrases with which no school will disagree but putting such values into practice is not so simple.

An Agenda for the Future

The heading for this section should perhaps be stated as "Whose Agenda?" In the UK, at present, there are competing agendas in relation to community cohesion and engagement. On the one hand, many individuals and groups within the wider British society view faith schools as obstacles to community cohesion or engagement. On the other hand, there are plenty of individuals and groups who view faith schools as a positive force for community cohesion and engagement. In autumn 2008, a new initiative, "Accord", was launched, chaired by a British Reform rabbi, with members from the Christian, Hindu and Humanist communities. The aims of this group were to lobby the British government to end State funding for faith schools and to "operate admissions policies that take no account of pupils' or their parents' religion or belief" (Accord, 2008). According to Accord, it is only then that a society will be able to develop which is tolerant, recognising different values and beliefs. One could argue that a useful and positive model for such an arrangement can be found in the USA where there is a strong and growing Jewish schools network, despite the fact that neither federal nor state government contribute significant funding to Jewish schools. And yet, the difficulties that the Jewish community has in maintaining and developing those schools and the elitism engendered by what is effectively a private school system is not necessarily desirable for the British community to emulate.

The position taken by Accord continues to be robustly challenged by proponents of faith schools. Apart from the educational and social benefits of faith schools, experience suggests that faith schools are no less likely to sustain a strong engagement with those of other and no faith than non-faith schools.

An additional and serious concern is that by ceasing the funding of faith schools, the government also loses hold of any power to ensure their compliance in any respect. Currently, all State faith schools in Britain are subject to the same rigorous system of accountability through both the Office of Standards in Education (Ofsted) and their denominational inspection authority, as are all State schools in Britain. If faith schools lose funding, some will close and some will comply with an open admissions policy and effectively lose their distinct faith character. It is possible that the majority of faith school providers, including the Jewish community, will move their schools into the private sector.

If this happens, there will be three key issues to face. First, there will no longer be any monitoring of curriculum and teaching standards. At present, all State schools are subject to the National State curriculum for its secular studies and able to access support and training from its local education authority. Without such controls, the more religious schools will be able to pick and choose both the content and the structure of secular studies. At present, the government is developing its agenda of collaboration between schools. The 14–19 curriculum provides a particular impetus for increased collaboration between schools. By 2013, it is estimated that all pupils will have an entitlement to this curriculum, which is planned to be delivered within consortia of schools. At present, the government is not making any provision for faith schools to opt out of this plan.

The second issue is financial. The UK is not unique in its financial support of faith schools, but at present, State-funded Jewish schools can expect to receive 90% of all development and running costs, which is considerable. The remaining 10% is raised by parental contributions and support from the Jewish community. If this level of support is withdrawn, then Jewish schooling becomes the choice only of the rich. Many Jewish schools in the USA, for example, do offer financial aid to those of lower income, but for many families there is a stigma in asking for financial help. In Jewish schools in Britain some families with low incomes refuse to ask to be put on the register to enable their children to receive free school meals, due to an embarrassment and dislike of exposing their difficulties.

The third and possibly most worrying issue to face is that by taking faith schools out of the State sector with its constraints and controls, there is little to prevent the establishment of fundamentalist schools. At the very least, the State will no longer have any authority to insist on a community cohesion or engagement policy or action from any faith school, all of which will be in the private sector and outside State influence.

These three issues all highlight the potential dangers in a withdrawal of State funding. On the other hand of course, in most parts of the world, vibrant and creative Jewish school systems do exist outside of the State sector. Yet, in Britain we are used to being within the State system of schooling, not outside of it. Surely cohesion and engagement can happen most effectively from within a system, rather than from outside it.

Visionary and committed leadership is required to drive forward the agenda on community engagement, and this is required of all schools. Jewish schools do demonstrate examples of good practice, but the debate should not be about religion and ethnicity but about education and what all schools should be doing to promote community engagement. Schools should be encouraged to map the different levels of awareness and commitment to community engagement from the different members of the school community.

There are continuing debates about the impact of faith-based schools on community engagement, including from those who promote a secular model similar to that in France (British Humanist Association, 2002). Recent controversies mentioned in this chapter, like the wearing of religious dress, reaffirm the tensions between secular and religious identities and the balance between diversity and uniformity. A future research agenda could go beyond the issues of policy raised in this chapter's final section. The outcomes and impact of community engagement should be investigated. How do we know whether, and to what extent, engagement with people and institutions beyond the school make a qualitative difference to developing young people's attitudes, knowledge and skills? Can the school, on its own, provide the locus of that development? Can change happen without the full partnership of the families of the young people, and of the media, for example?

Current conceptualisation of community cohesion is narrowly focused on a quest for greater uniformity and common values, rather than rising to the challenge of accommodating a diversity of ethnic and religious identities and institutions. There are many examples of successful initiatives and opportunities for engagement. There are also significant challenges. Whilst a small research agenda is underway, as, for example, in the work of Parker Jenkins (2009), the focus for that research has been on *how* we engage, not on the impact of engagement on the individual or on the community. This is an emerging field, which needs far greater exploration in order for us to fully understand its potential.

References

Accord. (2008). Media release. September 1, 2008.
Alderman, G. (1999). British Jews or Britons of the Jewish persuasion. In S. Cohen & G. Horencyzk (Eds.), *National variations of Jewish identity*. New York: State University Press.
Booth, T., & Ainscow, M. (2002). *Index for inclusion: Developing learning and participation in schools*. Bristol: Centre for Studies on Inclusive Education.
Bourdieu, P. (1985). The social space and genesis of groups. *Theory and Society, 14*, 723–744.
British Humanist Association. (2002). *A Better way forward: BHA policy on religion and schools*. London: British Humanist Association.
Cantle, T. (2001). *Cantle report: Community cohesion: A report of the independent review team*. London: HMSO.
DCSF. (2006). *Faith in the system*. London: DCSF.
DCSF. (2007). *Guidance on the duty to promote community cohesion*. London: DCSF.
Dewey, J. (1897). My pedagogic creed. *School Journal, 54*(3), 77–80.
DfES. (2002). *Education act*. London: DfES.
DfES. (2006). *Education and inspections act*. London: DfES.
DfES. (2006a). *Religious education in faith school*. London: DfES.
DfES. (2006b). *Making places in faith schools available to other faiths*. London: DfES.
Finestein, I. (1986). *Post emancipation Jewry: The Anglo-Jewish experience*. Oxford: Oxford Centre for Post Graduate Hebrew and Jewish Studies.
Gaine, C. (2005). *We're all white thanks*. Stoke-on-Trent: Trentham Books.
Gilroy, P. (1993). *The black Atlantic: Modernity and double consciousness*. London: Verso.
Goldring, E. (2009). Building communities within and around schools. In A. Pomson & H. Deitcher (Eds.), *Jewish schools, Jewish communities*. London: Littman Press.

Holden, A., & Billings, A. (2007). *Interfaith interventions and cohesive communities.* Lancaster, CA: University press.

Jewish Leadership Council. (2008). *The future of Jewish schools.* London: Jewish Leadership Council.

Jorgenson, L. P. (1987). *The state and the non-public school 1825–1925.* Columbia, MO: University of Missouri Press.

Leadbetter, C., & Mongon, D. (2008). *Leadership for public value.* Nottingham: National College for School Leadership.

Lipman, V. (1954). *Social history of the Jews in England 1850–1950.* London: Watts and Co.

Migniuolo, F. (2008). *Duty to promote community cohesion final guidance for schools.* London: CSN.

Miller, H. (2001). Meeting the challenge: The Jewish school phenomenon in the UK. *Oxford Review of Education, 27*(4), 501–513.

Miller, H. (2009). Beyond the community: Jewish day school education in Britain. In A. Pomson & H. Deitcher (Eds.), *Jewish schools, Jewish communities.* Oxford: Littman Press.

Miller, H., & Shire, M. (2002). *Jewish schools – A value added contribution to faith education.* London: Leo Baeck College.

Minorities of Europe. (2006). *Community cohesion and peace building Tel Aviv Jaffo, Israel.* Coventry: Minorities of Europe.

Moore, M. H. (1995). *Creating public value: Strategic management in government.* New York: Harvard University Press.

NFER. (2004). *Citizenship education longitudinal study.* London: National Foundation for Educational Research (NFER).

Osler, A., & Starkey, H. (2005). *Changing citizenship: Democracy and inclusion in education.* Berkshire, NY: Open University Press.

Parker Jenkins, M. (2009). *Terms of engagement: Muslim and Jewish school communities, cultural sustainability and maintenance of religious identity.* Derby: University of Derby unpublished paper.

Pearce, J., & Howell, J. (2004). Civil society: A critical interrogation. In B. Pratt (Ed.), *Changing expectations? The concept and practice of civil society in international development* (pp. 11–30). Oxford: INTRAC.

Plaut, G. (Ed.). (1981). *The torah, a modern commentary.* New York: Union of American Hebrew Congregations.

Putnam, R. D. (2000). *Bowling alone: The collapse and revival of American community.* New York: Simon and Schuster.

QCA (2000). *The national curriculum: Revised 2000.* London: QCA.

QCA (2002). *Citizenship at key stages 1–4.* London: Qualifications and Curriculum Authority.

Smith, M. K. (2007) Social capital, *The encyclopedia of informal education,* www.infed.org/biblio/social_capital.htm

Weller, P. (2005). Religions and social capital: Theses on religion (s), state(s) and society(ies): With particular reference to the UK and the European union. *Journal of International Migration and Integration, 6*(2), 483–496.

Worley, C. (2005). It's not about race, it's about the community: New labour and community cohesion. *Critical Social Policy, 25*(4), 483–496.

Culture: Restoring Culture to Jewish Cultural Education

Zvi Bekerman and Sue Rosenfeld

Introduction

> Given that it explicitly raises the question of its own legitimacy ... every educational system must produce and reproduce, by the means proper to the institution, the institutional conditions for misrecognition of the symbolic violence which it exerts, i.e., recognition of its legitimacy as a pedagogic institution. (Bourdieu & Passeron, 1990, p. 61)

Studies that address issues in broad strokes sometimes slip into debatable generalizations. While we are aware of this danger, we believe the issues raised in this chapter need to be accounted for even by those who might not fully agree with the analysis and suggestions we propose. The field of Jewish education is new and research in it scant; our arguments are raised not only from a formal knowledge of the field but also from the many informal venues through which we have learned about what educators, laymen, parents, and students say on this subject. We hope that the concerns and suggestions raised might be useful in any future critical reappraisal of Jewish education.

In the Diaspora, liberal Jewish education—by which we mean the wide variety of day schools and supplementary schools operated by religious and non-religious groups that profess to openness regarding the integration of tradition and modernity—is charged with preventing attrition from Jewish communities, ensuring Jewish continuity, and strengthening Jewish identity (Bloomberg, 2007; Cohen & Kelner, 2007). With such lofty goals, it is perhaps not surprising that liberal Jewish education is thought by some to be failing (Buchwald, 1999; Kress, 2007). These critics see Jewish students, the products of the liberal Jewish education system, as Jewishly illiterate, alienated from Jewish culture, and at risk of losing their Jewish identity. Many parents, too, "blame the schools for failing to really teach their children" (Prell, 2007, p. 26).

In this chapter, we wish to suggest that dissatisfaction with the liberal Jewish education system results more from a misconception of "culture" in general and Jewish culture in particular than from any failure of Jewish educators—and Jewish

Z. Bekerman (✉)
Hebrew University, Jerusalem, Israel
e-mail: mszviman@mscc.huji.ac.il

students—to meet their goals. We hope to augment the contributions of the philosophers and textual literates who have traditionally dominated the field of liberal Jewish education with an enhanced perception of culture in the hope that this might offer a better awareness of the activities of Jewish education and contribute to their improvement. We will start with a narrative of Jewish education, after which we will approach schooling and its paradigmatic foundation critically and attempt to restore the concept of culture to its historical sources. We will then develop this restored concept into a methodology—cultural analysis—and demonstrate how it allows us to shift the focus of the educational investigation from the individual (succeeding or failing according to a deficit model) to a more promising objective: the production of vital cultural contexts.

The effort might help educators and leaders to understand that culture is neither a monolithic condition nor a de-contextualized set of discrete skills transferable across all contexts. It is not static but dynamic, an ongoing dialectic rather than an externalized-to-be-internalized transmission. Culture is continuously revealed and constructed; it is not a feeding field for students, teachers, and parents to search for cues so that they may "pass" as recognizable members of their community. Jewish leaders and educators might discover, ironically, that their current understanding of culture is not good for Jewish continuity.

Restoring culture in Jewish education implies that we should halt the present attempts to identify individual failures (whether of students, teachers, schools, or curricula) and subsequently treat these failures as successful adaptations to the present socio-political contexts Jews inhabit. We will use cultural analysis to answer such questions as: Why do Jewish educators and leaders work so hard to create worthwhile educational settings and yet emerge so disappointed? When proceeding in this direction, Jewish educators will be empowered to radically (from *radix-icis*, Latin for roots, an appropriate concept for Jewish education) reconstruct their perceptions of what needs to be done and toward what goals they need to work. We posit that what liberal Jewish educators should strive for is culture as in a biology laboratory. That is, they should attempt to create working environments (cultures) that enable (cultural) growth.

The Narrative: Reflecting on Successful Failure

Researchers have noted a fundamental conflict in the way many Jews regard their place in democratic societies (e.g., Cohen & Kelner, 2007; Pomson, 2008; Sarna, 1998). On the one hand, they want to partake of the benefits of wider society; on the other, they want to preserve and transmit Jewish culture. Thus, we suggest that what is perceived as failure is actually a reflection of these contradictory goals and a successful adaptive achievement to local systemic circumstances. The most compelling account of this phenomenon is Sarna's (1998) paper on the history of Jewish education in America where he depicts it as being concerned with "the most fundamental question of Jewish life: how to live in two worlds at once, how to be both American and Jewish, part of the larger society and apart from it" (p. 9). Specifically, success at Jewish schools involves acquiring knowledge and activity that if displayed in certain wider social contexts would be considered inappropriate or dangerous. Indeed, Cohen and Kelner note that if they are to attract more Jewish parents, "schools may need to undertake symbolically important activities and practices that display their ability and interest in helping their students function in the larger society" (p. 99). Consider, for example, the potential repercussions—financial loss, social ostracism, accusations of particularity or elitism or racism—when someone adopts a dress code that differs from the dominant culture's—wearing a yarmulke, for instance—or observing the Sabbath in a capitalist economy, or asking for kosher food in a public place, or expressing Jewish communal ethics in an individualistic society.

Less threatening but just as conducive to creating failure is Jewish education's emphasis on texts that are—as currently taught—neither accessible nor relevant to the students' lives. At schools and in in-service training sessions we see youngsters and adults alike struggling with texts—Talmud, Bible, and other historical, ideological, and philosophical works. Students are asked to allow these texts—"classical and contemporary texts that are central to transmission of Jewish civilization" (Geffen, 2005, p. 28)—to become part of their associative worlds, of their cultural resources, when confronting similar situations; in short, they are asked to think about the potential relevance of these texts to their own realities. They are told that achieving Jewish textual literacy will allow them to become proud representatives of their community and partners in securing its continuity, though they are not told how this will happen, nor do they see models of it being done.

While trying to achieve this literacy, students receive continuous explanations by the "experts" (i.e., teachers) as if something prevents them from understanding these texts as they are presented. Because their reading is continuously mediated by the experts, the students' understanding is not of the text but of the experts' interpretation. This interpretation is also a text, but not the one the students have been asked to read. Of course, students are never told this. Thus, the message imparted is that understanding is a complex achievement, that students are not equal to the task of attaining this level themselves, and that the constitutive texts of the tradition that is supposed to be theirs are never accessible to them. We should ask first how texts that are not made accessible can ever become useful or relevant, and second, if we do not believe students to be capable of reaching their own understanding, why make them confront the texts at all?

But this method of textual study imparts a more dangerous message. Many students, so restricted and inept in school, act resourcefully when confronting situations similar to the ones presented in the text they had studied, without needing to refer to the text at all. What the students had been taught in Jewish education was dispensable: Life outside did not require the texts that the Jewish education system felt were necessary. If indeed the world outside the school system had no use for the knowledge being taught, why should anyone learn it? Of course, many times we learn and teach things which, though not of immediate use in our current extra-curricular experience, can become useful in the future for ourselves or our communities. This being true, we still need a better explanation for the fact that students achieve non-learning in spite of the efforts invested by their teachers. The reason may be that not only does our present environment not require this knowledge, but that the texts and rituals presented in our schools are taught as though they, and by implication, Jews themselves, are a-historical, de-contextualized, and detached from the world. Jewish education often includes a message that Jews and Judaism can—indeed, ought to—exist in isolation, without recognition of and dialogue with the Other, as though the development of the Jewish people is free from contextual influences. Fishman (2007), for example, writes that "Formal Jewish education ... is especially important for Jews living in open American societies, *in which Jewish identity is not reinforced by separation from other ethno-religious groups*" (p. 183, emphasis added). Fishman's assumption, shared by many who write about Jewish education in democratic societies, is that Jewish culture would be best preserved and maintained in isolation. (Indeed, it is difficult otherwise to explain the investment in building segregated Jewish schools.)

Such a message opposes our common (and empirical) knowledge that communities evolve and "become" through contact and dialogue with other communities (Short, 2005; Valins, 2003); they resist and react and respond to each other. Not only do cultures not spring forth, fully formed, from a vacuum, but they exist in our minds most clearly when they are differentiated from each other. This is true not only for Jews, of course, but for all world categories: They become most fully identified when there exists the possibility of being contrasted to others which can, in turn, be differentiated from them. As Bateson (1979) has stated, it takes at least two things to create a difference: Each alone is—for the mind and perception—a non-entity, a non-being, the sound of one hand clapping. Thus, Judaism does not exist by and in itself; nor is Judaism a quality of individual minds. As our students seem to realize instinctively, Judaism becomes a difference so long as it exists in concerted human activity and thus, in real world like life situations, teaching Jewishness in isolation makes little sense.

Our schools have perhaps forgotten that Judaism, to be relevant, has to be relevant not only to Jews themselves but to the rest of the world. Most importantly, Judaism has to be relevant to the Jews' world, which does not exist in isolation. A further difficulty with the vision of an isolated Judaism, devoid of actions in context and dialogue, is that Jews' claim to identity is based only on their blood ties and lineage, essentialist explanations implying arrogance and racism. If we are interested in change, we should shift the focus of our inquiry from the minds of individual students or teachers to social systems and their politics, to determine why so many Jewish leaders work hard to organize educational systems that make failure worthwhile. A first step in understanding these systems is trying to understand the historical roots of schooling, that technology most preferred by liberal Jewish educators (and other minority group leaders) to strengthen their communities and ensure their continuity.

Schools, Knowledge, Individuals, and Culture

The current educational structure, mass education through schooling, did not appear by chance but rather is closely related to the industrial revolution and the development of the nation state (Gellner, 1983). Both industry and state needed to recruit masses to their service, masses with basic cognitive and behavioral skills that could serve the needs of the nation state and its economic structure (Goody, 1987). In addition, schools have served in the modern era as an important means by which sovereigns have unified the different local groups inhabiting the areas they had subordinated to their power under one flag, one language, and one narrative. Thus schools are in no way disinterested arenas within which neutral knowledge or skills are transmitted from the minds of specialists to those of passive individuals. In the work of Lave and Wenger (1991), social knowledge and learning are settled in the social, in "communities of practice" that are powerfully differentiated by complex asymmetries. With this in mind, it is surprising that liberal Jews have chosen the school structure as the means by which to secure their future and continuity—a goal seemingly at odds with schools' historical purposes.

Furthermore, Jews already had their own strong, flourishing educational structures. Heilman (1987) describes the centuries' old tradition of study circles in which the learners try to acquire "... the ethos and world view of those who in previous generations likewise intoned or studied those words" (p. 62). Tedmon (1991) points out that "*Chavrusa* learning [a traditional format for Jewish textual study] ... has been in existence for generations" (p. 97). Copeland (1978) maintains that the traditional education system in Jewish communities, *heders* and *yeshivot*, integrated the intellectual with the emotional, in stark contrast to the West's emphasis on the intellectual, which latter emphasis, he says, "burdens, constrains, and impoverishes" (p. 24). With such a long-standing and successful tradition of educational practices, why should Jews look elsewhere?

Of course, it could be argued that their looking elsewhere should surprise no one. Jews, like most minorities in the West, have sought to adopt a preexisting structure—that of the dominant majority—in an effort to achieve success according to the measures of their new social setting (Sacks, 1994). In fact, adopting the ruling powers' educational structures is part and parcel of Jews' (like many minorities') efforts to become Western. Rather than taking pride in the success they achieved by their own communities' standards—the path chosen by many non-liberal, that is, Orthodox, Jewish communities—many liberal Jews have preferred to avoid the risks that non-conformity entails in Western societies, keeping their Jewishness under wraps, fitting in, or "passing" as part of the majority, including embracing the non-Jewish majority's values and narratives. Bourdieu and Passeron (1990) well knew the "arbitrariness" of schooling as a method for moving the young into adult positions within the hegemonic spheres. They also recognized the violence that accompanies this imposition of the hegemonic culture on a new/strange human group. They also knew that many (teachers, parents, students, system) are involved in making school a successful controlling system and that they achieve this through the use of varied methodologies and pedagogies.

The keystones of formal schooling's success are its structure and its functionality, both of which are based on and expressive of a particular paradigmatic perspective, one that cannot benefit Jews or any other minority. In other words, schools allow entrance into the reigning hegemony at the price of homogeneity. In fact, schools are a central conduit for the transmission of two interrelated beliefs of the modern Western world: belief in the autonomous self and belief in the objective existence of knowledge to which this self has access, if only properly guided (Holzman, 1997).

For centuries, these above-mentioned elements have underpinned the functioning of schools. When the first schools were created in order to produce a cast of scribes able to sustain the bureaucratic needs of growing, powerful, centralized, urban, economic human enterprises, they developed the three central characteristics which hold to this day (Cole, 2001):

1. The student was trained by strangers, separated from his kin and family.
2. The knowledge slated for transmission was differentiated and compartmentalized into fields of specialization.
3. Learning took place outside of the contexts of its intended implementation, i.e., students rehearsed knowledge "out of context."

Liberal Jewish education, which is interested in finding ways to strengthen and invigorate ethnic/religious identity, community structures, and the individuals' affiliation to them, cannot be served by a system structured around these premises. Neither can such structures lead to an understanding of Judaism as a living tradition that is able to offer answers to real socio-cultural issues.

These three characteristics are among those that reformers have periodically tried to change. However, in spite of the multiple efforts invested in this enterprise, most schools today are still structured like those of antiquity. How can a framework that is premised on distancing the individual from family and community serve to engender Jewish identity and communal integration? How can a structure that conceives of and imparts knowledge in differentiated and compartmentalized chunks serve in the cultivation of Jews who are able to view Judaism and its potential role in the world as a comprehensive whole? And, last, is it feasible to expect that schoolchildren would find what they learn relevant if they are educated in environments in which the acquisition of knowledge is segregated from the places in which this knowledge can be functional and in which the knowledge transmitted does not reflect the knowledge implemented by the community itself in the world outside?

Some Jewish educators agree that those are exactly the central issues which need to be addressed if liberal Jewish education is to succeed in the modern West. They readily point to the efforts being invested today to extend education into the surrounding school community so as to include parents and adults in general, and to the efforts to involve schools in community work so as to achieve a better fit between school and the outside world (Woocher, 1995). While such statements are encouraging, they may not be sufficiently helpful in the long run. This is because these schools and their operation are premised on two paradigmatic features which will not allow the system to be reformed, and reform is necessary if minorities (and Jews are one of these) wish to sustain a level of cultural independence and compete in the interpretative work that shapes the world they inhabit. These paradigmatic features, to which we have hinted above, are what modernity calls "universal cultural values" and those on whom these values are bestowed, "autonomous individuals" (Bekerman & Silverman, 2000; Bekerman, 2001).

Both culture, as a reified identifiable cast of behaviors and beliefs, and the individual, as an autonomous and universal entity, have been the focus of a long theoretical controversy within high and post-modernity that has successfully demonstrated the link between these features and many of the world's current maladies (Giddens, 1991; Sampson, 1993a; Taylor, 1994). These theoretical developments have pointed inter alia at two educational claims we make regarding our current understanding of culture and individual identity. The first is that culture must be understood as a verb and not a noun—as something which grows and evolves when performed, and then promptly dissolved again into the array of human activity in which it might or might not be reproduced (Bauman, 1999). Second, individual identity must also be conceived as a dialectical process of becoming and shaping through speech and action and dependent on context (Harre & Gillett, 1994; Holland, Lachicotte, Skinner, & Cain, 1998). Thus culture and individual identity are here conceptualized as evolving processes that depend on language and activity to take on form and existence (Wittgenstein, 1953).

Leaving in place these ruling paradigms of a reified culture and individual identity, together with the practices through which these perspectives are framed within school structures, can hardly be helpful to the education of Jews. The separate and isolated individual might be a good tool for domination, but not for community survival. Similarly, reified and segregated culture might be a good means of offering recognition to the politically correct multiculturalist, but, at the same time, serves to justify and perpetuate the ongoing suffering of minorities, now acknowledged but with their structural subordination left fully intact (Bekerman, 2003). In other words, the multicultural movement has opened spaces for minority cultures but has left them as before, configured in and constrained by a given space and time. Jews, for example, are allotted their space in the UK's Jewish Book Week or New York's Israel Day Parade. Instead of seeing culture as something that belongs to a person and can be internalized, or as a powerful force that shapes the individual from the outside in, the multicultural movement posits a view of culture that is constricted and discrete.

Traditional education research, working within this paradigm, explains much of the problematic encounter of students with education on the basis of families being held captive to a culture (McDermott & Verenne, 1995). That is, a person is "tied" to preconceived notions of what one culture signifies in the minds of outsiders. Culture thus internalized becomes similar to the old and unfriendly concept of race, as when within Jewish circles we hear that so-and-so does not "look like a Jew." Such an understanding of culture removes it from the realm of things we—and our students—can control; it encourages them to be passive objects of their "cultural heritage" rather than actively shaping and controlling it. Such a message—that disempowers students with relation to their own community—can hardly contribute to the creation of sustaining practices, nor can it be termed educational. These paradigms, on which current Jewish educational efforts are based, will, if left unchallenged, hinder efforts to help Jews achieve their declared goal of strengthening a vital and active Jewish identification and of making Jewish civilization a life option.

Reestablishing the concept of culture as a relevant force for strengthening Jewish identity means we must revert to its etymological roots and anthropological origins. Culture (from the Latin *cultura-ae*) means "work." Biology has maintained this sense when offering cultures as environments for growth and development. Anthropologist Margaret Mead (1942) emphasized the importance of the enculturation processes and was careful to point out that the young, whatever their biological heritage, could become members of any group, despite the dissimilarity between the adopted group and their group of origin. Claude Levi-Strauss (1955) went even further when he posited that any personality type could come into being in any culture because every human can reject the commands of the culture into which he or she was born.

According to these researchers, culture was not something to be known or learned but was an activity conducted in environments with others, coming into existence in ongoing social dialogue and within historical trajectories (Wolf, 1994). Belonging to a culture is not a predetermined, static state of being but one of active identification. Our students' cultural identification is built through their activities, molded and interpreted as classes of cultural work (Jewish or otherwise). Students are not only empowered by such a reconceptualization of culture, but also supported in it by their actual experience with the world.

Cultural Analysis: Culture as Methodology

If we see culture not as a static condition nor as a solitary cause, but the cooperative activity of many, the products of culture are unpredictable and intermittent, making this new conceptualization risky to educators who are more familiar with a stable entity whose consequences are foreseeable. But the shift in this understanding of culture should help educators focus on *process*, not *products*—on the tools, associates, and contexts in which the work is done, rather than on outcomes. So framed, our field of inquiry changes from the traditionally accepted fields of psychology and sociology to a more inclusive and complex pattern of cultural analysis.

Education has relied on both psychology and sociology to locate its shortcomings in the individual. In the former, autonomous minds in isolation are the objects of study (Holzman, 1997; Wenger, 1998). Usually, it is the student who is the target of educational reform, but it could equally be the teacher or the parent. What is central, from a psychological perspective, is that the problems that Jewish education confronts are problems of individual minds. For the most part, Jewish education—unlike mainstream education—has not proceeded along the psychological trail, thanks in large part to parents who would not easily agree to have psychologists ascribe the malfunctions of Jewish education to their otherwise successful children. Paradoxically, their willingness to do so might raise Jewish education to an unparalleled status, since the involvement of psychologists and counselors are accoutrements of "serious," i.e., public education.

Sociology, in contrast, posits that it is not the individual students, teachers, and parents who are the objects of inquiry but rather the conditions in which they were raised: Families and their trajectories are the basis of the problem. Pronouncements like "What can you expect from kids raised in families that don't care?" or "What can be expected from a school without a vision?" or "This is simply a reflection of the community's values" rest on the assumption that social structures lie at the heart of our educational frustrations, and that each of these structures contains its own cause-and-effect procedure that accounts for the failure of the educational system. Within this framework, the dream is to find a way to organize the Jewish educational system well enough to be able to identify and address the historical and social factors that cause the problems.

Just as sociology widens the scope of inquiry to include all the institutional structures (educational, charitable, political) that are organized for the purpose of benefiting the many, sociology also proposes settings to measure the success or failure of these institutions, such as the percentage of Jews who intermarry, performance of rituals, membership in Jewish social or religious organizations (Cohen & Kotler-Berkowitz, 2004; Cohen, 2007). Still other structures interpret the measurements, offer solutions, or shape policy, and in the process assuage the Jewish soul with the tacit message that the Jewish community is the product of incommensurable forces—for example, emancipation, industry, and assimilation—that are impossible to challenge or change. In fact, a look back at almost 30–40 years of this process confirms the adage that the more things change, the more they stay the same.

Given that the foundations of modern Western Jewish education are imbued with this positivist paradigmatic perspective, fundamental change is a daunting task indeed. The gatekeepers prefer linear, causal explanations with accompanying finite, predictable solutions, whether or not such solutions are successful in the long run. In their view, reform is certainly needed, but we need not worry too much if the reform fails to transform and, after 5 or 10 years, all must be reformed again.

Instead of positing causality and tracing clear historical paths, cultural analysis pays attention to work done in concert and to "the immediate and local meanings of actions as defined from the actors' point of view" (Erickson, 1986, p. 119). When applied to Jewish education, cultural analysis is not about failure or success, nor about who is responsible for these. It does not ask "What's wrong with this picture, and how do we fix it?" but rather "What's really going on in this picture; for and by whom was it drawn?" Cultural analysis asks how we have accomplished our current situations in concert with others. It examines the developing contexts in action, acknowledging in advance that neither a particular agent nor a particular cause can be identified as the driving force.

Rather than relying on the "cause-and-effect" model suggested by the current positivistic paradigm as though this was the only option, cultural analysis asks instead how the arguments of this paradigm were shaped and how they serve the same current situation the experts want (or claim to want) to change. It examines—and challenges—the options, tools, and co-participants available to produce change, not only in the Jewish liberal educational context but within the wider institutional, historical, political, and economic one, not in isolation but in unison.

Clearly, such tactics are daunting, involving as they do the possibility, if not necessity, of social change. They render the scenario of liberal Jewish education infinitely more complex and perhaps unbearably difficult. This approach is not likely to produce such facile (and appealing) "solutions" about the need to revise curricula, train better teachers, and invest in more schools—solutions which are premised on the understanding of culture we challenged in the previous section of this chapter. Moreover, simply stating that cultural analysis should propel Jewish education in different directions does not guarantee that such an analysis would fare any better, because cultural analysis is also deeply embedded in the cultural conditions it seeks to overcome. But cultural analysis is a deep and lengthy process, the first step of which is to uncover the conditions that promote the current situation, paying careful attention to the roles, goals, and interests of the participants in that setting, and revealing the connections between current solutions and their service in the roots of the problems they purport to solve. Only then can cultural analysis produce more inclusive questions that deepen our present understandings, crossing borders and producing new experimental associations—all necessary preconditions for lasting and meaningful change.

Cultural analysis could pave the way to knowing how to reconstruct, to perceive multiple problematic issues both in the strategies and in the sustaining paradigms within liberal Jewish education. Since the work remains to be done, we can only summarize here some preliminary arguments, beginning with educational strategies.

A Partial Cultural Analysis

Because culture is intimately bound to context, each and every change rearranges all the pieces in a complex puzzle. Regarding Jewish education, we must acknowledge that all the phenomena that worry liberal Jews about their education system have been shaped through history with the active participation of Jews and others. Thus, as it has been constructed, it can be reconstructed. The simple dichotomies of Jew/Non-Jew, Us/Them will not do. We work hard to make the borders between ourselves and others solid and defined, but our experience tells us that borders are both invisible and porous. Does liberal Jewish continuity require measurements on scales of identity? Does it necessitate identifying affiliations? If Jews, like every other cultural category, only exist in difference, then Jews *must* engage in dialogue with others in order to achieve true recognition (Sampson, 1993b), and dialogue with others means risking finding the others more attractive. If continuity is what Jewish education seeks to achieve, it had better find ways to make Judaism no less attractive.

When Judaism is presented as a body of knowledge and a quality of mind rather than a process of creativity and a function of action, there is little chance for any student to become engaged. Students know that in order to become lawyers, doctors, teachers, or parents, they are dependent on reciprocal work built around languages, fashion, performance—in short, a whole set of practices recognizable in context. If they fail to enact this work at the right time, with the right people, in the right interpretative moment, they will risk forfeiting their chosen identities. Most students already realize that they are primarily Americans or Israelis in their speech and behavior but Jews only in their feelings. As we explained above, this is a good bargain for students who want to succeed in the West—and it is another good reason for succeeding to fail. By failing to learn "Jewish," students are being fully adaptive to a system that has little room for cultural variance in those (typically homogeneous) domains that Western culture deems successful.

Hence Jewish educators must move from focusing on children's failure to achieve sufficient Jewish culture/literacy to studying the cultural settings in which that failure makes sense. By so doing, Jewish educators will find themselves dealing with politics, an arena that sits uncomfortably with one of the bases of liberal Jewish functioning in the Western world: the idea that particularistic cultures should be secluded to the privacy of the individual sphere, far from the public eye (Bekerman & Silberman, 2003; Maoz & Bekerman, 2009). If these cultures must exist in public, they should at least be confined to ritual events. But in spite of the current multiculturalist trends, liberal Jews do not want to become Lubavitchers, playing in the marketplace and making the fact of their Judaism a public act, any more now than they did in the past, and rightfully so. The conspicuous diversity offered by multiculturalism is risky; it offers easy recognition but not necessarily equality, and liberal Jews would prefer that things work in the opposite direction.

A cultural analysis should also question the perception of the learning processes in the Jewish educational system. Learning, we are told by recent theorists (Harper, 1987; Lave & Wenger, 1991; McDermott & Verenne, 1995; Wenger, 1998), is embedded in a myriad of activities that hold a child's attention long enough for something to change so that the next day's activities look different. It is a cumulative process involving the participation of people who have put to use the things learned over time and in multiple settings. Learning thus becomes about the contexts that allow knowledge to be seen as relevant and useful; it cannot be maintained merely as ineffectual memories. But in liberal Jewish education, learning as defined above is not available. What we have instead are students focused (or not) on texts and teachers, and interacting (or not) with each other. Jewish educators should ask whether the rehearsal of assorted rituals or the continuous pounding on texts—potentially valid activities—induces students to become sagacious in the world contexts that surround them; in short, whether or not this and the other activities that take place are conducive to the aims of Jewish education. We need to search either for ways to make the world contexts in which students live amenable to the knowledge teachers teach or, alternatively, for ways to adapt the knowledge Jews value to make it relevant in present contexts.

Again, the Western world is not helpful here in that it seems not to allow for much of Jewish knowledge to become relevant. Perhaps it is the Western world itself that Jews might need to fight rather than their own students and/or teachers! Perhaps we should be asking why dominant cultures are unwilling to accept cultural differences. Rather than ask this question, Jewish liberal schools teach the same type of intolerance, thereby reproducing within Jewish culture the same sense produced by the dominant culture, not realizing that because Jews are not dominant, the results might not benefit them. Paradoxically, while caring about their own within their educational systems, Jewish educators serve the very outside world that denies them. Intermarriage in this case could be seen not as a threat but as an adaptive response, the dissatisfaction with Jewish education as another adaptive step toward the conquest of present hierarchical positions without passing as defector, and the ghettoization of Jewish education as a secure path toward a successful assimilation.

We will conclude this section by summarizing, in brief, the main points we have raised that run contrary to received theory and practice in liberal Jewish education:

1. The perceived failure of Jewish education has little to do with the quality of individual teachers or students and much to do with the quality of the systems we cooperatively construct.
2. What appears to us as "failure" are actually adaptive moves to local and global systemic circumstances.
3. The adoption of Western positivist paradigmatic perspectives is responsible for the present educational views that guide liberal Jewish educational theory and practice.
4. In order to effect positive change in the liberal Jewish education system, we must revise our basic conceptions of the individual, the culture, and the learning process. We must realize that they are all interactional, contextualized, and dynamic processes rather than isolated, static, and impermeable states.
5. Jews should look for educational solutions in the reorganization of current Western world politics rather than in the limited parameters of their school settings or the solitude of their teachers' or students' minds.

In short, liberal Jewish education has been focused on individual learning, group membership, and school failure. We need to change these views, to acknowledge that learning is not individual, membership does not convey literacy, and schools are not the only settings in which to achieve productive, adaptive, relevant learning.

What, then, can liberal Jews do? They can start by trying to create educational settings that do not achieve success for others (the West and its expectations for the proper functioning of its minorities) and failure for their own, but that address their preferred cultural products in action, in dialogue, and in context. How to achieve this is a more difficult question on which we would like to reflect in the following section.

Cultural Education and the Liberal Jewish Educator

The moment that identity, culture, and education recover their contextual dimensions and dialectical characters, they can no longer be presented in their glorified historical remoteness, nor as static traits or as cognitive properties. Educators who have envisioned traditional cultural literacy, i.e., "mastering a body of knowledge," according to Short (2005, p. 263), as the heart of Jewish continuity can no longer content themselves with presenting texts and rituals in a de-contextualized setting; they must engage learners in interpretive activities that will make these practices relevant to their present environments. If we relocate our educational foci to the social interactional sphere, with its attendant recognition of complex socio-cultural relations, we must promote not only new educational aims and strategies, but also new models of leaders, teachers, and students who are responsive to the diverse challenges encountered in today's world.

Cultural education, in short, has little to do with the habits we train people to adopt, and everything to do with the environments we build for people to inhabit (Varenne & McDermott, 1998). But the environments we as Jews inhabit must be understood in order to be changed—if change is deemed necessary. Therefore, the first activity we need to inculcate among our leaders and educators is a reflexive process that will lead to a better and more honest understanding of their own social situation and of the powers and processes that were involved in its achievement. Educators and leaders might then stop thinking of Jewish life as a given, a natural event, but as a social construction, the result of human social activity. We might then be able to cease the self-deception we perpetuate by refusing to ask—or having our students ask—the questions about context that should be asked. For example, what is our part in the creation and preservation of the social context for Jews and other minorities? Which of our needs is being served by the present system? To what extent does this system encourage or require that Jews absorb the judgments of the non-Jewish world? What messages do students receive that make them not want to be recognized as Jews? For Jewish educators, exploring these questions will lead to the realization that their failures and successes are not so much theirs but are rather the products of complex webs of relationships taking place within cultural patterns and historical events.

Furthermore, an awareness of the connections between their cultural assumptions and the effects these have on their educational planning will raise Jewish educators' consciousness about the unequal power relationships that are endemic to educational and state institutions, i.e., hegemony at large. Indeed, cultural education attempts to cultivate in minority groups a critical consciousness of their situation as the foundation of a liberating praxis. The greatest enemy of all such groups is the belief that existing beliefs and structures are inevitable, uncontrollable, and necessary.

Imagine a child approaching a teacher and asking, "What is a Jew?" Given present realities, the teacher may be inclined to offer as a response some culturally descriptive and benevolent characteristics of the group. This response might seem appropriate given present reigning epistemologies. However, we believe that in the long run, such a response reinforces—rather than challenges—present perspectives. A better answer to the question would be a correction of the epistemological basis that, though potentially unknown to the child, substantiates his or her question. Thus, we might answer that Jews are not a "what" but a "when" and a "how" (Bekerman, 2009).

Part of becoming active in the world that surrounds us is acquiring discourses with which we can describe, uncover, and cope with the complexity of social phenomena. Language, after all, is what helps us organize experience, and although language is never fixed, social groups develop their own relatively coherent styles that help them "become-in-dialogue." We need to enrich our leaders, teachers, and students alike with descriptive powers, analytical points of view, and critical perspectives. If we currently "do" Western language but cannot successfully "do" Jewish language, we will not be able to author the world. To understand and become active agents in the world, therefore, liberal Jewish educators need familiarity with a variety of discourses:

- an economic discourse to discuss commodities, supplies, and management;
- an aesthetic discourse to discuss architecture, advertising, and display;
- a political discourse to discuss policies, planning, and discipline;
- a historical discourse to discuss change in organization, consumption, and community;
- interpretive discourses to articulate understandings of those texts that, in concert, constitute vital components of Jewish history and culture.

Language is socially and historically situated: By creating, controlling, and manipulating language, educators can contribute in large part overcoming their present educational circumstances.

One of the consequences of an increased understanding of their current situation in the world is that Jewish teachers and students alike can begin to seek out potential "cracks" in the hegemonic system, to find and create arenas in which their activities as Jews will serve the needs of their community, to work in thoughtful proactive engagement, not in acquiescence to the demands of the outside world. Indeed, if educators see that neither they nor their institutions are predestined to fall into the hegemonic trap, they can participate in proposing and producing alternative symbolic systems rather than passively accepting what is currently on offer.

Adopting and implementing a critical stance will not be easy but has, in other contexts, proven worthwhile. Teitelbaum (1991) described the Socialist movement's resistance as it was expressed in the Sunday schools in early twentieth-century America, in which the texts studied offered competing perspectives to those that were accepted as natural in the dominant society, and through which the participants were able to weigh up their arguments and examine their situation in a new light. Mirza (1999) showed how Black supplementary schools in England facilitated the creation of oppositional meanings that derailed the assumptions of mainstream schooling and, through their very existence, provided evidence of thriving Black communities.

What is not fully clear is whether the liberal Jewish educators involved are, in fact, willing to adopt critical and emancipatory strategies, thereby risking their comfortable position in Western society. (In fact, this might be the most insidious accusation of Western hegemony: that comfortably belonging to its mainstream implies relinquishing the group's sense of authenticity and risks its sense of cultural sustainability). But our existing situation, like any ideology, is not a given nor is it eternal. It is not an abstraction but is the product of socio-cultural practice expressed in speech and action. Working in the way we suggest offers the possibility of challenging the current authorial/hegemonic voice—a modest step in the right direction.

References

Bateson, G. (1979). *Mind and nature a necessary unity*. New York: Bantam Books.
Bauman, Z. (1999). *Culture as praxis*. London: Sage.
Bekerman, Z. (2001). Constructivist perspectives on language, identity and culture: Implications for Jewish identity and the education of Jews. *Religious Education, 96*(4), 462–473.
Bekerman, Z. (2003). Hidden dangers in multicultural discourse. *Race Equality and Teaching (formerly MCT-Multicultural Teaching), 21*(3), 36–42.
Bekerman, Z. (2009). Identity vs. peace: Identity wins. *Harvard Educational Review, 79*(1), 74–83.
Bekerman, Z. & Silberman, M. (2003). The corruption of culture and education by the nation state. *Journal of Modern Jewish Studies, 2*(1), 19–34.
Bekerman, Z., & Silverman, M. (2000). Education towards human dignity. In A. Hareven & C. Bram (Eds.), *Human dignity or humiliation? The tension of human dignity in Israel* (pp. 127–147). Tel Aviv: Van Leer and Hakibbutz Hameuchad Publishing House.
Bloomberg, L. (2007). An emergent research agenda for the field of Jewish education. *Journal of Jewish Education, 73*(3), 279–288.
Bourdieu, P., & Passeron, J. C. (1990). *Reproduction in education, society, and culture* (R. Nice, Trans. 2nd ed.). London: Sage.
Buchwald, E. (1999). Conversion and the American Jewish agenda. *Judaism, 48*(3), 275–277.
Cohen, S. (2007). The differential impact of Jewish education on adult Jewish identity. In J. Wertheimer (Ed.), *Family matters: Jewish education in an age of choice* (pp. 34–56). Waltham, MA: Brandeis University Press.
Cohen, S. & Kelner, S. (2007). Why Jewish parents send their children to day schools. In J. Wertheimer (Ed.), *Family matters: Jewish education in an age of choice* (pp. 80–100). Waltham, MA: Brandeis University Press.
Cohen, S. & Kotler-Berkowitz, L. (2004). *The impact of childhood Jewish education on adults' Jewish identity: Schooling, Israel travel, camping, and youth groups*: United Jewish Communities Report Series on the National Jewish Population Survey 2000–2001.
Cole, M. (2001). Remembering history in sociocultural research. *Human Development, 44*(2/3), 166–169.
Copeland, S. (1978). Values and experiences of reading aloud in traditional Jewish text learning: A study in the coordination of form and meaning. Unpublished doctoral dissertation. Harvard Graduate School of Education.
Erickson, F. (1986). Qualitative methods in research on teaching. In M. Wittrock (Ed.), *Handbook of research on teaching* (3rd ed., pp. 119–161). New York: MacMillan.
Fishman, S. (2007). Generating Jewish connections. In J. Wertheimer (Ed.), *Family matters: Jewish education in an age of choice* (pp. 181–210). Waltham, MA: Brandeis University Press.
Geffen, R. (2005). Breaking through the self-fulfilling prophecy about Jewish education. *Journal of Jewish Education, 71*(2), 227–228.
Gellner, E. (1983). *Nations and nationality*. Oxford: Basic Blackwell.
Giddens, A. (1991). *Modernity and self identity*. Stanford, CA: Stanford University Press.
Goody, J. (1987). *The interface between the written and the oral*. Cambridge: Cambridge University Press.
Harper, D. (1987). *Working knowledge: Skill and community in a small shop*. Berkeley, CA: University of California Press.
Harre, R. & Gillett, G. (1994). *The discursive mind*. London: Sage.
Heilman, S. (1987). *The people of the book: Drama, fellowship, and religion*. Chicago: University of Chicago Press.
Holland, D., Lachicotte, W., Skinner, D., & Cain, C. (1998). *Identity and agency in cultural worlds*. Cambridge: Harvard University Press.
Holzman, L. (1997). *Schools for growth: Radical alternatives to current educational models*. Mahwah, NJ: Lawrence Erlbaum Associates, Publishers.

Kress, J. (2007). Expectations, perceptions, and pre-conceptions. In J. Wertheimer (Ed.), *Family matters: Jewish education in an age of choice* (pp. 143–180). Waltham, MA: Brandeis University Press.

Lave, J., & Wenger, E. (1991). *Situated learning: Legitimate peripheral participation*. New York: Cambridge University Press.

Levi-Strauss, C. (1955). *Tristes tropiques* (J. Russell, Trans.). New York: Atheneum.

Maoz, D., & Bekerman, Z. (2009). Chabad tracks the trekkers: Jewish education in India. *Journal of Jewish Education, 75*, 173–193.

McDermott, R., & Verenne, H. (1995). Culture as disability. *Anthropology and Education, 26*(3), 324–348.

Mead, M. (1942). *And keep your powder dry: An anthropologist looks at America*. New York: W. Morrow.

Mirza, H. S. (1999). Black masculinities and schooling: A black feminist response. *British Journal of Sociology of Education, 20*(1), 137–149.

Pomson, A. (2008). Dorks with Yarmulkes": An ethnographic inquiry into the surprised embrace of parochial day schools by Liberal American Jews. In Z. Bekerman & E. Kopelowitz (Eds.), *Cultural education-cultural sustainability: Minority, diaspora, indigenous and ethno-religious groups in multicultural societies* (pp. 305–323). New York: Routledge.

Prell, R. (2007). Family formation, educational choice, and American Jewish identity. In J. Wertheimer (Ed.), *Family matters: Jewish education in an age of choice* (pp. 3–33). Waltham, MA: Brandeis University Press.

Sacks, K. B. (1994). How did Jews become White folks? In S. Gregory & R. Sanjek (Eds.), *Race* (pp. 78–102). New Brunswick, NJ: Rutgers University Press.

Sampson, E. E. (1993a). *Celebrating the other: A dialogic account of human nature*. Hertfordshire: Harvester Wheatsheaf.

Sampson, E. E. (1993b). Identity politics: Challenges to psychology's understanding. *American Psychologist, 48*, 1219–1230.

Sarna, J. (1998, Winter/Spring). American Jewish education in historical perspective. *Journal of Jewish Education, 64*(1&2), 8–21.

Short, G. (2005). The role of education in Jewish continuity: A response to Jonathan Sacks. *British Journal of Religious Education, 37*(3), 253–264.

Taylor, C. (1994). The politics of recognition. In D. T. Goldberg (Ed.), *Multiculturalism: A critical reader* (pp. 75–106). Oxford: Blackwell.

Tedmon, S. (1991). Collaborative acts of literacy in a traditional Jewish community. Unpublished doctoral dissertation. Graduate School of Education, University of Pennsylvania.

Teitelbaum, K. (1991). Critical lessons from our past: Curricula of socialist Sunday schools in the US. In M. Y. Apple & L. K. Christian-Smith (Eds.), *The politics of the text book*. New York: Routledge.

Valins, O. (2003). Defending identities or segregating communities? Faith-based schooling and the UK Jewish community. *Geoforum, 34*, 235–247.

Varenne, H. & McDermott, R. (1998). *Successful failure: The schools America builds*. Boulder, CO: Westview Press.

Wenger, E. (1998). *Communities of practice: Learning, meaning, and identity*. Cambridge: Cambridge University Press.

Wittgenstein, L. (1953). *Philosophical investigations* (G. E. M. Anscombe, Trans.). Oxford: Blackwell.

Wolf, E. R. (1994). Perilous ideas: Race, culture, people. *Current Anthropology, 35*(1), 5–12.

Woocher, J. (1995). Towards a "unified field theory" of Jewish education. In I. Aron, S. Lee, & S. Rossel (Eds.), *A congregation of learners* (pp. 33–51). New York: UAHC Press.

Curriculum Development: What We Can Learn from International Curricula

Roberta Louis Goodman and Jan Katzew

> *He used to say: "At five [one begins the study of] the Bible. At ten the* mishnah. *At thirteen [one takes on] the [responsibility for] the* mitzvot. *At fifteen [one begins the study of] the Talmud. At eighteen [one is ready for] marriage. At twenty to pursue [a livelihood]. At thirty [one attains full] strength. At forty [one gains] understanding. At fifty [one gives] counsel. ... Pirke Avot 5:21*

(Kravitz & Olitzky, 1993)

This *mishnah* from Pirke Avot demonstrates that a curriculum for lifelong Jewish learning has been a topic that is as timeless as it is timely.[1] Curriculum, with a Latin etymology that refers to a race course, is the aggregate of education and experience that enables a person to participate in and contribute to a particular community as well as to human society in general. Curriculum articulates desirable learning aims and tries to balance what is real and what is ideal, what is possible and what is desirable to learn, to do, and to be. The topics, texts, and experiences in Pirke Avot 5:21[2] articulate a lifetime curriculum for a Jew. The *mishnah* is foundational and sacred, aspirational and inspirational. Parents were obligated to teach their children about Jewish life. Jewish communities were also mandated to establish schools early in the first millennium of the Common Era. Questions focusing on who, what, how, where, and why to teach have perennially occupied Jewish educators' minds. Responses to these questions are not only educational; they have also been essential and existential to the Jewish people. Curriculum development has helped to enable the Jewish people to adapt and thrive in a variety of cultures from hostile to hospitable.

As it is a dynamic, organic process, curriculum development remains a central focus in Jewish education. It addresses conceptions of the individual, family, group, and society together with the values, purpose, and roles that each hold. Curriculum

---

R.L. Goodman (✉)
Jewish Early Childhood Education Initiative (JECEI), New York, NY, USA
e-mail: goodrl6060@aol.com

[1] For elaboration, see Maimonides Mishneh Torah, Hilchot Talmud Torah, inter alia.
[2] Note that after the age of 15, the subject matter changes to life experience.

develops as an iterative process, continually scanning the cultural environment and responding to it—sometimes with affirmation, sometimes with adaptation, sometimes with admonition, but always with translation and commentary.

Curriculum is the core expression of what an educational enterprise believes is significant and worthy. In Jewish education, as in general education, there is a wide variety of curricula: for individual programs and for entire institutions (e.g., school or camp), as well as for a system of learning institutions—internally produced by the institution itself or externally produced by a publisher. Curriculum is a fundamental part of all educational settings—formal and informal. In order to assess the impact of current curricula in Jewish education as well as to consider the communal investment of resources in them, we will consider four questions, a number chosen not at random, but because the four questions operate as a trope in Jewish education, echoing the Passover Haggadah.

1. What are the criteria for excellence in curriculum development?
2. Why is curriculum development so important to Jewish education today?
3. What are the current trends and issues in curriculum development?
4. What curricular challenges loom over the Jewish educational horizon?

What Are the Criteria for Excellence in Curriculum Development?

Tyler, a classical theorist on the topic of curriculum development, writing 60 years ago, identified four fundamental questions that need to be answered in designing any curriculum or plan of instruction (Tyler, 1949):

1. What educational purposes should the school seek to attain?
2. What educational experiences are likely to attain these purposes?
3. How can these educational experiences be effectively organized?
4. How can we determine whether these purposes are being attained?

A coherent, thoughtful, well-planned curriculum needs to reflect an institution's vision, incorporate educational experiences likely to achieve this vision, be presented in a clear and compelling way, and identify measures of educational success. These criteria make it possible for any curriculum to be analyzed and evaluated.

"When there is no vision, the people become unruly" (Proverbs 29:18). Vision is not a luxury in social organization. Vision is the foundation upon which identity is constructed and educational vision in particular constitutes the prerequisite for curricular design. Pekarsky (2008) identifies two types of vision that educational institutions should have: an existential vision of what Jewish life looks like and an institutional vision of the educational approach of how to reach that vision. While these concepts may seem lofty, they play themselves out in curricular choices that teachers make about the learning experience. For example, why have apples—how they grow, their colors, texture, and more—become the focus of so much teaching in early childhood about Rosh Hashanah? In the end, what does an apple really have to do with Rosh Hashanah? What concept or ideas do they convey? What is the purpose of this curricular focus, its connection to the holiday? What else could a teacher and children investigate that would convey a deeper understanding about the holiday? (Wiggins & McTighe, 1998; Moskowitz, 2003) Activities and experiences are not always intrinsically educational. They only become so when they are planned to achieve a desired outcome that is meaningful to the learner and the teacher at least as much outside the classroom as in one. It is fair to ask of any educational activity—so what? This question challenges the curriculum to have a purpose that transcends the time and place of the activity itself. In the absence of a vision, a curriculum may include creative and engaging activities that lack a sense of coherent meaning. Vision provides a context for educational texts and the experiences they engender. Educators can make better decisions about what to teach and how to teach if it is clear why the subject matter is being taught.

A factor that has made assessment increasingly significant in Jewish education is the influence of funders' concern for measuring the impact of a particular educational experience on its learners. The focus is increasingly on what, if anything, the learner is learning from a particular curriculum or educational experience. In response, many educators have moved away from Tyler's approach of first articulating goals (what the teacher aims to accomplish) and behavioral objectives (what the learners will be able to know, feel, or do), leaving assessment to the end to using a backward design method that identifies upfront not just what the learners will learn but also how that learning will be measured. A curriculum development approach that incorporates backward design used by many Jewish educators is Understanding by Design (UBD), as evidenced by its use in settings as diverse as some of the Reform movement's camps and the Jewish Education Center of Cleveland's Project Curriculum Renewal for congregational schools and day schools of all movements. Other methods are used to put learner outcomes in the forefront of the curriculum designing process as exemplified by the "Standards and Benchmark Project," initiated by the Melton Research Center for Jewish Education of the Jewish Theological Seminary of America that helps liberal and community day schools develop *TaNaKh* (Torah, Prophets, and Writings) curricula. The incorporation of learner assessment into the curricular process in these ways brings an increased level of accountability to Jewish education.

Why Is Curriculum Development so Important to Jewish Education Today?

Studies of formal and informal Jewish educational personnel identify two issues that connect to curriculum development:

> Issue #1—*There is a lack of qualified, credentialed teachers in Jewish learning settings in education and Jewish studies* (Kelner, Rabkin, Saxe, & Sheingold, 2005, Goodman et al. on Project Kavod 2006, Sales & Saxe, 2002; Goodman,

Bloomberg, Schaap, & David, 2009); Only 19% of teachers in day school, supplementary school, and early childhood hold credentials in both education and Jewish studies (CIJE, 1994). Although most educators participate in some type of professional development, it is questionable if these haphazard efforts adequately prepare them to implement curriculum in their settings (Wertheimer, 2009). The downsizing of central agencies of Jewish education in many communities throughout North America makes one wonder how much funding is going to be available for professional development in the near future and who will be delivering those opportunities that will exist. Our communal investment in teachers belies and defies the widespread acknowledgment that teachers arguably constitute the most important role in translating curricular theory to practice. A history of according teachers high status in the Jewish community is in jeopardy.

Issue #2—*Curricular resources could help compensate for under-qualified teachers if there were opportunities to train the teachers in the use of those resources.* What data exist suggest that curriculum is not consistently provided to formal educators in day schools, congregational schools, and early childhood schools (CIJE, 1994; Tammivaara & Goodman, 1996a, 1996b; Goodman & Schaap, 2006) nor to informal educators (Goodman et al., 2009). Educators report that one of the things that would improve their work conditions is more assistance with lesson planning and curriculum development (CIJE, 1994; Goodman & Schaap, 2006; Goodman et al., 2009; Tammivaara & Goodman, 1996a). Exemplifying this situation is a study of supplementary school educators. When asked what would most improve their job, 30% of the teachers indicated curricular or lesson planning assistance. This was second only to salary, rated at 33% (Goodman & Schaap, 2006). These data suggest that the individual teacher has a major role in devising curriculum rather than implementing it. While any good teacher would be adapting curriculum for his/her students, it appears that too often the teachers are generating and not just adapting curriculum. There is nothing inherently wrong with teachers acting as curriculum developers. However, doing so in isolation can result in one teacher repeating or contradicting what another teacher has taught in a prior class at the same school. Teaching then becomes a game of chance rather than a conscious, intentional choice, and consequently, learning suffers as well.

What Are the Current Trends and Issues in Curriculum Development?

Since few teachers receive fully developed curricula from which to plan their lessons, much curriculum development takes place within the educational setting. The curriculum specialist is arguably the least well-documented human resource in the curriculum development process. Curriculum specialists can also serve as education directors, curriculum coordinators, Judaic studies principals, head teachers, technology experts, or even volunteer education directors and clergy. For some specialists, working on curriculum is their primary focus and for others it constitutes but a minor responsibility. To a diminishing degree, curriculum specialists exist in central agencies for Jewish education or national organizations. They may be responsible for writing curriculum, working with other educators on designing curriculum, or providing support to teachers as they prepare to implement curriculum. We do not know how many Jewish educational settings have a dedicated curriculum developer, how much time they devote to curriculum development, or their preparation for this role. Furthermore, the overall process of curriculum development is generally opaque, a veritable black box. We can and should strengthen curriculum development throughout the loosely coupled Jewish learning system by building a cadre of educational professionals with curricular training and appropriate status.

Highly developed curricular resources designed for Jewish education do exist. Organizations as diverse as Hadassah, Torah U'Mesorah, JCCAssociation, American Jewish University, Institute of Southern Jewish Life, and many more have published curricula for a wide range of ages and settings. In addition, several of the publishers provide workshops on teaching methodology and consultation on how to use their materials, translating curricular theory to educational practice.

The Internet is having an increasingly profound impact on curriculum development. Whereas specialized personnel or institutional libraries or teacher centers were needed in the past for educators to do research, the Internet provides easy access to contemporary Hebrew and Israeli resources, classical Jewish texts in original languages as well as in translation, and nearly encyclopedic knowledge about Jewish life. The Internet provides the capability for creating curricular resources in synchronous or asynchronous ways around the corner and/or around the world.

The significant advantage of published curricular resources is that they can provide a framework and materials for teachers to use to stimulate learners' thinking and engagement. However, they are not a panacea. Teachers can misuse the textbook as a curriculum rather than a tool to further the educational mission of the learning institution. While many textbooks have teacher guides and some even lay out goals, objectives, and activities or experiences, it is possible that the class is achieving the publisher's goals and not the school's goals. Dorph (2003) has observed two common problems that teachers face when teaching from a textbook or curricular materials. One has to do with confusing the curricular materials or textbook with the subject matter and the other is using the materials as if they were recipes. What Dorph (2003) suggests to remedy these problems is to study the curricular materials by identifying what the material is about, the material's stated purpose, and what teachers and learners must do to reach those goals. Teachers need to adapt curriculum to particular settings, and ideally to individual students.

We selected four examples of curricular initiatives that strive to address the ramified challenges facing Jewish education as we prepare to take stock of the opening decade of the twenty-first century. Each of these initiatives is in some way exemplary and innovative, wide-ranging in its targeted age group, available to a large or Jewishly diverse audience, presented a thoughtful and coherent approach, and is international in appeal (most of the international examples were originally targeted at US/Canadian audiences):

1. JECEI's (Jewish Early Childhood Education Initiative) work with transformation school change that focuses on creating a Constructivist, Reggio-inspired approach to learning and curriculum development
2. The URJ's (Union of Reform Judaism) development of the CHAI Curriculum for elementary- and middle-school-aged children based on the Understanding by Design approach to designing curriculum
3. The work of Tal Am, NETA, and the Proficiency Approach in the teaching of Hebrew to elementary-, middle-, and high-school students based on a variety of theories, research, and standards about foreign language acquisition
4. The work of the Florence Melton Adult Mini-School (FMAMS) in creating a unique approach to curriculum development for adults

We obtained information about the various curricular efforts through a combination of reviewing the materials themselves, researching online applications, reviewing impact studies and other assessments, and consulting with people who designed the curricula.

The presentation of the curricula follows in this order: (1) a synthesis of the key findings of the trends that the curriculum development efforts share in common, (2) a brief description of the curricula, and (3) the unique element(s) that contribute to the conversation about curriculum development.

Synthesis of Key Findings

From analyzing themes in all the curricular initiatives, we identified four significant trends:

1. An emphasis on the interdependency between curricular initiatives and professional development,
2. The dedication of resources to create large-scale curricular efforts,
3. A shift from focusing on teaching to focusing on learning, and
4. A commitment to ongoing assessment of quality in search of excellence.

(1) Interdependency Between Curriculum Initiative and Professional Development

As sophisticated as some of these curricular initiatives are in terms of the materials developed, their success depends on the support to implement the resources optimally in diverse settings. All four of the initiatives strive to integrate the ongoing professional development into their curriculum design, but their effectiveness is notably inconsistent.

The CHAI Curriculum developers provide extensive support materials and a network of educational specialists. They promote the use of webinars and provide workshops on a wide range of educational and Judaic topics that can be adapted for congregational implementation. Professional development for teachers who use the URJ CHAI curriculum is recommended rather than required. This stance is reflective of an ideological commitment to congregational autonomy in Reform Judaism as well as in recognition of limited human and financial resources in attempting to reach in excess of 400 congregational schools. As its research findings indicate (Shevitz, 2009), the already widely used CHAI curriculum would derive additional benefit from more professional development workshops that could be adapted for congregational use.

The Florence Melton Adult Mini-School (FMAMS) uses a combination of professional development and ongoing monitoring and mentoring by the site director to support the curricular materials. The selection of faculty for FMAMS is rather rigorous, a conscious attempt to engage teachers, which begins with a high degree of competence and confidence. This process makes professional development especially challenging since veteran faculty may not be receptive to training.

The Hebrew curricular initiatives depend upon workshops and seminars combined with ongoing mentoring. In some cases, they mandate centralized professional development, which means that the learning environment for the teachers is artificial. Rather than learning in their familiar surroundings, they must adapt the learning and translate it to their "home" setting. In all cases, the curriculum developers recognize the need for professional development. They all make compromises – financial, organizational, and ideological – in order to come to terms with their perceived realities. They each negotiate between the real and the ideal, the possible and the desirable, in an effort to improve the status quo of Jewish learning. They are all works in process and in progress.

(2) Dedication of Extensive Resources

These curricular initiatives are ambitious, extensive, and expensive. The curriculum developers invest thousands of hours and millions of dollars in the hope that their investment will bear dividends in creating loyal institutional clients. These projects were selected for study because they were complex, sophisticated, and far-reaching in terms of educational setting and geography. The costs of the initiatives represented are high in two senses: (1) in developing the curricular resources and ancillary materials and (2) in planning for ongoing professional development for educational leaders and teachers who use the curriculum, thereby translating educational theory into practice. Most of these initiatives rely on foundations, philanthropists, or other sources of funding to support some, if not all of their work. Some have fees for their services (e.g., workshops) or materials. These fees are paid by the educational institution or sometimes through communal institutions like federations or central agencies for Jewish education. The educational institutions in the field share the cost for their paid staff members' time as well as coverage of expenses for attending professional development.

These curricular development efforts place demands on all the partners, and like any chain, each one is only as strong as its weakest link. This process has raised the stakes and expectations of all those institutions involved in serious curriculum development. They are setting a norm for the scale of what teachers and students can expect to be accomplished in Jewish education today. The investment in curriculum development by family foundations, federations, movements, universities, central agencies, congregations, schools, and camps testifies to the growing awareness that Jewish literacy and competency cannot be taken for granted. At stake is nothing less than the future of Judaism and the Jewish people. While past returns do not constitute a guarantee of future dividends, the investment in Jewish learning through curriculum development bodes well for the near term. As curricular efforts need to be constantly updated or new ones initiated to respond to changes in the Jewish community, technology, and society, curricular development costs are likely to redouble.

(3) Shift from Focus on Teaching to Focus on Learning

The shift from focusing on teaching to learning is evident in each of the curricular initiatives. For example, the Proficiency Approach for Hebrew language acquisition begins with trying to identify and then assess what the learner can do. The approach revolves around identifying student outcomes based on adapting established guidelines for Hebrew language acquisition (ACTFL), designing curriculum to achieve these outcomes, responding to learners' needs and learning styles, and monitoring and assessing students' success.

The CHAI Curriculum also brings students' outcomes to the forefront of its curriculum design, most explicitly in the lesson component entitled "evidence of understanding" when the teacher seeks to determine not what s/he taught, but rather what students learned. The CHAI Curriculum's use of backward mapping in an attempt to identify the big questions and ideas related to Jewish life that the learners should acquire is another strong example. This approach is counter-cultural for congregational schools in two respects: (1) its insistence on focusing on learner outcomes and (2) its demand to touch on one's understanding of and commitment to Jewish life rather than just information transmission and retention. Learning experiences to assess students' acquisition of concepts and questions are included in the curricular materials in an effort to focus on enabling the students to make meaning of what they are learning.

The whole concept of emergent or negotiated curriculum in the Reggio-inspired Jewish early childhood schools where the learner is a partner in providing direction to the curriculum is a learner-centric approach. Curricular choices are informed if not made based on these young children's interests and ideas. Teachers need to hone techniques like active listening and observation of children, documenting their learning in order to effectively carry out this curricular approach. Furthermore, central to constructivism is the meaning and significance that the learner associates with an educational experience, what s/he learns from it, rather than some objective or fixed meaning from an outside source.

While the Florence Melton Adult Mini-School does not explicitly state desired outcomes for its learners, graduation is based on "outputs," i.e., attendance at 2 years of sessions. The curriculum is an interactive process among learner, text, and instructor where learners interpret text, share their experiences, and raise questions all in their exploration of Jewish life. This addresses an all too prevalent pattern in adult Jewish learning where lecturing peppered by a question or two, but not real dialogue, is the dominant instructional approach, an approach that emphasizes teaching over learning.

The current focus on the learner among these curricular examples may be a corrective to prior teacher-centered curricular approaches. The distance between teacher and learner has been diminished, if not entirely eliminated. The teacher is "*ahad ha'am,*" one of the people. The teacher is a learner as well as a facilitator, researcher, listener, and guide; perhaps more so than an instructor or knower of all answers. This curricular attitude involves an attempt to humanize and personalize education. It is predicated on the non-trivial reality that in an age of choice, there must be learners in order for there to be learning.

(4) A Commitment to Ongoing Assessment in the Pursuit of Excellence

Finally, all of these curricular efforts are attempts to raise quality, expectations, and standards in the pursuit of excellence in Jewish education. They all share some measure of ongoing internal and external evaluation of their effectiveness. These curricular efforts involve field-testing in educational settings with the assistance of teachers and directors. They have advisory committees that provide input in a variety of ways. Some undergo evaluation including by hired outside evaluators. These organizations use evaluation, whether it is feedback from teachers piloting portions of the curriculum or evaluators sharing their recommendations. All these sources of information are intentional parts of the curriculum development process and have the benefit of helping improve the design and delivery of the curricular effort.

Excellence in education is an elusive pursuit, a moving target that requires continuous monitoring – challenging operative assumptions, testing hypotheses, interpreting findings, and assessing experiences. Each of the curricular initiatives has champions and detractors, successes and failures. Each of them can claim justifiably to be of quality. They represent serious, longitudinal efforts to improve the status quo in Jewish learning.

JECEI's School Transformation Process and Constructivism

JECEI (Jewish Early Childhood Education Initiative) is a national organization committed to developing schools of excellence for children and their parents through a school-wide 3–4-year intensive holistic transformation process. Consultants, retreats, readings, and accreditation standards all play an important role in fostering these Constructivist schools of excellence. While not solely a process of curriculum development, JECEI's work brings three important concepts to the forefront: (a) the entire school as part of the curriculum of the learning experience, (b) emergent or negotiated curriculum, and (c) project learning and documentation. At the end of this section, the key challenges of this curricular approach are shared.

JECEI, like other Jewish early childhood schools, has adopted a constructivist approach to learning informed by the work of theorists like Piaget (1967), Vygotsky (1978), and Dewey (1938). Constructivism is "the process by which a [person] constructs a mental explanation for her experience or perception" (Mooney, 2000, p. 97). Knowledge is socially constructed in the ongoing interaction between child and teacher. Constructivism is associated with active learning approaches emphasizing the importance of experience in generating knowledge, children learning from one another, the role of play, learning through inquiry, scaffolding learning, and much more. JECEI has focused on combining the constructivist philosophy of the schools of Reggio Emilia, Italy, with big Jewish ideas and values and change theory.

The Entire School as Part of the Learning Experience

Among Jewish early childhood educators who have become "Reggio inspired," a key idea is that the entire school experience and environment are all parts of the curriculum designed to model ideas and values and to facilitate learning and community building among children, parents, teachers, and others. The environment is often referred to as the "third teacher" as children learn through what surrounds them in terms of the social, psychological, and physical environment. Many JECEI schools have redesigned a physical space so that parents and children can spend time with one another, reflecting on the importance of creating a learning community among families, not just children. In one JECEI school, this led to moving walls, adding a fish tank and benches, so that parents could spend time talking to one another, with their children reading books or transitioning to the next part of their day, and preparing for Shabbat through story, song, and blessings. The entire school environment is carefully, intentionally, and aesthetically organized, inviting interaction and bringing the school's vision to the learning experience for all.

Emergent or Negotiated Curriculum

The approach to curriculum used in Reggio-inspired schools is often called "emergent curriculum," suggestive of the unfolding way in which the curriculum develops, twists, and turns, based on the children's inquiry. The word "emergent" does not capture the thoughtful planning that the teachers engage in to create an environment and experiences that foster this type of active learning. Carlina Rinaldi, an important educator and philosopher of the Reggio approach, contrasts *progettazione* with *programmazione*, characterized as predefined curriculum and isolated programs. For Rinaldi, *progettazione* implies a "more global and flexible approach in which initial hypotheses are made [by educators] about classroom work (as well as about staff development and relationships with parents), but are subject to modifications and changes of direction as the actual work progresses (Rinaldi, 2006, p. xi)."

Teachers plan carefully and make curricular choices, but those choices remain open, fluid, and responsive to the children, parents, and community interests and issues, as well as the teacher's own observations and assessment of the learning experience. Children's exploration, interests, and ideas contribute to the direction that the curriculum takes. Teachers are researchers hypothesizing about children's development, observing and documenting children's learning as part of the curricular process that contributes to determining the direction in which to go. The Reggio approach to curriculum development balances being reactive and responsive with being proactive, thoughtful, and structured.

How does *progettazione* occur? Building on an example from a JECEI school, in a class of 4-year-olds, the children did different blessings for different types of food – those that come from trees, the ground, or vines. The children became interested in how new plants grow from the seeds of these different fruits and vegetables. They brought in different foods with seeds or pits like apples, peaches, avocados, and grapes to see how they grow. An important part of this exploration is through dialogue; the thinking, questioning, and responding. What makes these foods so different that we have different blessings? What is needed to create an environment for the seeds or pits to grow? Why do some thrive while the others do not? How do God and human beings partner in creation together? What does the experience of trying to grow these fruits and vegetables make us realize about why we thank and praise God?

Project Learning and Documentation

Two tools for curriculum development and implementation characterize Reggio schools and their inspired Jewish versions in North America: project learning and documentation. Projects are educational investigations often done in small groups that occur over an extended period of time, even as long as the entire school year. These investigations can start with hypothesizing about children's learning, identifying a key theme or phenomenon, responding to children's interests, or reacting to some incident. The centrality of exploration and inquiry is evidenced in the project work that occurs throughout all JECEI schools. In one school, a provocation of teachers putting out film in canisters led to the children taking pictures of the outdoors, to a trip to the library to explore books of artists' expressions of flowers in the outdoors, and to the children carefully selecting water colors to paint their own exquisite flowers. The teachers shared not just the product of the flowers, but more significantly the representation of how the learning emerged and what they learned capturing the children's ideas and reactions in words and photographs.

JECEI schools commonly have documentation of the many examples of the *progettazione* process, such as daily or weekly journals for each classroom, journals of each child's experience – some that "travel" with the child for the length of their time in the school, and panels of a project's evolution. Documentation incorporates the children's voices and perspectives. These various forms of documentation are vehicles for not just sharing the learning process with parents, but more significantly as a tool for the children and teachers to use to reflect on their ideas and feelings to help set the direction for where they might extend the learning.

Challenges

Being Reggio-inspired has produced several challenges for curriculum development in JECEI schools. Curriculum needs to be developed to a large extent by each school, in each classroom, and each year in response to the cultural, social, collective, and individual values, hopes, ideals, and interests of the children, parents, and educators. How curricular ideas can be shared from school to school to stimulate thinking and collaborating on this approach in a Jewish setting remains a challenge. Teachers need to be knowledgeable about both the educational strategy and Judaism. To achieve this level of quality requires a serious commitment to professional development; this often translates into time and money, which are often both at a premium. JECEI schools must dedicate extensive time for educators to learn and plan. The holistic nature of the Reggio philosophy and approach, viewing the entire school culture as part of the learning experience, and other factors make this a complex form of curriculum development.

Adopting a Curriculum Approach

The URJ CHAI Curriculum and Understanding by Design (UBD)

The CHAI Curriculum was created to strengthen congregational education. Rabbi Eric Yoffie, President of the Union of Reform Judaism (URJ), formally launched the CHAI Curriculum at his Biennial address in December 2001. Lamenting that the congregational school is perceived by so many as failing, he explained why the URJ should invest resources in a curriculum:

> When the synagogue nurtures its school and embraces its children, the children will learn and the school will thrive. . . . religious school serves, by far, the largest number of children for the longest period of time. It is the key that opens the door to the grand adventure of Jewish learning and Jewish life. And we will not rest until our schools are a place where our children hear God's voice and see Torah as a tree of life.

In its 10th year (2009–2010), the CHAI Curriculum has an extensive reach. Approximately 65,000 students in grades 1–7 in the nearly 800 URJ-affiliated congregations with supplementary religious/Hebrew schools learn from CHAI lessons.

The CHAI Curriculum focuses on increasing the knowledge and skills of Reform Jews in the areas of torah, *avodah* (worship), and *gemilut chasidim* (deeds of loving kindness) despite the limited time spent in congregational schooling. The curriculum is a bold move to bring serious text study to elementary- and middle-school-aged liberal Jews. Rather than focus on information, it focuses on meaning, on the big questions and ideas that Jews have pondered throughout the ages.

One challenge in developing curriculum is in finding a format, an approach that not only provides a framework for writing and sharing a curriculum plan, but also captures the purpose of what a Jewish educational institution is trying to accomplish. For this reason, the URJ adopted a curricular approach used in general education, Understanding by Design (UBD), by Wiggins and McTighe that parallels its goals. UBD aims to combine active learning, "hands on" with "minds on" learning that is meaningful, purposeful, and guided by a big idea (Wiggins & McTighe, 1998, p. 21). UBD unfolds in three stages by answering the following questions:

> Stage 1: What is worthy and requiring of understanding?
> Stage 2: What is evidence of understanding?
> Stage 3: What learning experiences and teaching promote understanding, interest, and excellence? (Wiggins & McTighe, 1998, p. 18)

UBD provides a structured format that all educators could learn and follow that is well suited to promoting questioning, meaning making, and engagement with and connection to Jewish life.

In its adaptation of UBD, the following example shows how the URJ has adapted the UBD process. This example presents the elements used in the lesson plans for each 1-hour session:

- Introduction – provides Judaic background for the session focus.
- Enduring Understanding – key ideas are the same for all the lessons within each of the three sections (Torah, *Avodah*, and *G'milut Chasidim*) – e.g., Torah is real to our daily lives: it goes with us wherever we are.
- Essential Questions – these are the big questions that the student should be able to answer to show that they have acquired the enduring understanding – e.g., What does the Torah have to say to me and my world?
- Questions to Be Answered – these are more specific to the actual session content focus, e.g., *M'gilat Rut*/Book of Ruth: Mining the Text for Meaning – What is my own assessment of the meaning of the Book of Ruth.
- Evidence of Understanding – the way in which students will be assessed to make certain that they have gained knowledge of the enduring understanding, essential questions, and questions to be answered. The two sessions on the Book of Ruth included the students creating a Ruth Movie Storyboard reflecting their viewpoint about the meaning of the story.
- Lesson Overview – parts of the lesson.
- Materials Needed – includes any books, pages from student supplement, and supplies.
- Readings: Resources for Teachers – listing of books related to the topical focus.
- Lesson Vocabulary – key terms in either Hebrew or English.
- Lesson Plan – with times designated, includes set induction, learning activities, and conclusion; this section incorporates the way(s) in which the students' understanding will be assessed.

The CHAI Curriculum uses a full range of Jewish texts as a key component of the educational experience that engages the student in exploring Jewish life. It places the student in dialogue with Jewish tradition and Reform Judaism in a deep and dynamic way.

Teaching Hebrew

Hebrew is one subject that is the focus of manifold curricular efforts for all types of Jewish learning environments. That so many curriculum efforts exist probably has to do with the fact that there is a certain sequential, skill-based nature to learning a language that transcends ideological setting. Rather than develop their own Hebrew curriculum from scratch, most teachers seek outside expertise. That Hebrew is a shared interest among such a large number of Jewish educational settings contributes to an economic reality that encourages publishers or organizations to capitalize on the financial potential and foundations to invest resources in this area.

Of special interest are the curricula that have emerged for day schools to teach Hebrew as a communicative language. These include Tal Am/Tal Sela, NETA, the Proficiency Approach, and Haverim B'Ivrit as well as others. These Hebrew programs parallel the growth in day schools including the upsurge in Jewish day high schools.

A significant distinctive characteristic of these Hebrew programs is that the curricula are designed based on research and theories about second language acquisition and learning. Most of them are designed with the assistance of scholars who are associated with a university. Applying research and theories and tapping into this expertise have led to comprehensive and sophisticated approaches to curriculum development.

Tal Sela/Tal Am, for grades 1–6, is used in approximately 355 schools on six continents reaching out to an estimated 27,000 students. Its many materials for teachers and students balance communicative language and Jewish living by focusing on religious and cultural content like the Jewish year, prayer, Torah, and Israel. This program reflects the work done in second language acquisition and heritage language. In particular, Tal Am is influenced by findings from brain research that led to the Total Physical Response (TPR) approach reflected in the songs, movement, and other learning strategies that use the five senses.

NETA, designed for grades 7–12, is used in approximately 90 day schools on four continents reaching out to approximately 13,000 students. NETA has thematic-based materials for teachers and students presented from three perspectives: Jewish tradition, modern Israeli culture, and general world knowledge, e.g., science, math, and literature. The curricular themes are selected based on their interest to teenagers ranging from computers, sports, friendship, and freedom. The NETA curriculum was created by Hebrew language curriculum specialists from the Hebrew University of Jerusalem and administered by Hebrew College in Boston (Schachter & Ofek, 2008). One of the curriculum specialists from Hebrew University spent 5 years in Boston, USA, working with teachers, Hebrew or Judaic curriculum specialists, mentors, and professors connecting theory with practice as it unfolds in the field. Credit-bearing courses to prepare educators to use the NETA curriculum are offered for which participants, many of whom are working toward a bachelor's or master's degree in Judaic studies or Jewish education.

The Proficiency Approach is based on the American Council in Teaching Foreign Language (ACTFL) standards for modern language acquisition defining content standards, what students should know and be able to do (Schachter & Ofek, 2008, p. 279). The development of international standards for Hebrew language acquisition as measured against native speakers was central to launching the Proficiency Approach in Jewish day schools. A Brandeis University professor associated with the Middlebury Summer Language Schools spearheaded this effort. While initially focused on high school and college students, the ACTFL standards and Proficiency Approach are being adapted to classrooms of varying ages around the world. Schools receive assistance so that teachers within 3 years create a curriculum and materials for the school. The curriculum focuses on students gaining active knowledge of Hebrew through the four parts of communicative language – speaking, listening, reading, and writing – with content adapted to the school's vision and learners' interests.

Curriculum in Adult Jewish Education: The Florence Melton Adult Mini-School

Does curriculum development look the same for adult learners as for children? A paucity of information about curriculum is found in the field of adult education. Part of this situation is explicable by noting that adult education is a field of interest to educators from a wide variety of "content areas," e.g., science, the humanities, medicine, law, and education. In addition, teachers or facilitators of adult learning are often viewed as content experts at a high level; leading to a problematic inference that because the content is the primary focus, adult educators do not need help designing learning experiences. Curriculum development is a topic that needs to be considered in adult Jewish education as part of the conversation of engaging Jewish adults in lifelong Jewish learning.

The Florence Melton Adult Mini-Schools (FMAMS) present a unique approach to curriculum development in two respects: first, by their focus on creating a school culture and second, in the approach taken in designing the actual materials for the instructors. The FMAMS school culture is carefully crafted to shape and augment the learning experience wherever it is located throughout the world. The FMAMS operates as a franchise, setting standards or expectations for elements that are part of the school culture while incorporating the local communities' and participants' needs and interests. Whether or not the school culture is considered the content of the curriculum, it does send messages that affect the learning. The entire set-up of the school, from serving refreshments to the role of the site director, is organized to convey that adult Jewish learning is sophisticated, social, valuable, and most importantly, about Jewish learning and living. The core elements that are part of this culture are articulated to some degree in the contract with its partners and described fully in a handbook given to FMAMS site directors. Directors participate in seminars and receive ongoing support from FMAMS staff in implementing this culture.

The FMAMS is located in numerous countries throughout the world with a large concentration of learners spread throughout the United States. The curriculum is the same for all sites in the Diaspora. Staff members at Hebrew University's Melton Centre write the curriculum with input from directors and learners from around the world. It has undergone several major revisions. The purpose of the FMAMS school is to foster the acquisition of Jewish literacy in an open, trans-denominational, intellectually stimulating learning environment. The curriculum is divided into four courses, each consisting of 30 one-hour sessions. Participants take the full complement of four courses over a 2-year period. The four courses are Rhythms of Jewish Living, Purposes of Jewish Living, Ethics of Jewish Living, and Dramas of Jewish Living Throughout the Ages. Each session has a focus related to the overall theme; e.g., Purposes of Jewish Living has sessions on God, creation, mitzvot, sin, and miracles.

The FMAMS curriculum is designed to "guarantee" a consistent level of quality for the adult learner. The curricular materials are intended to make it possible to use a range of local instructors, such as clergy, Jewish educators, Judaic study academics, professionals in other fields with expertise in a Jewish-related topic, like lawyers or medical personnel, and "learned" individuals.

The instructor receives a thick curriculum guide and the learners receive the texts, including both primary and secondary sources. The curriculum guide contains the following sections for each session:

- Introduction – an overview of the big ideas presented
- Summary of Texts – listing of the texts, both primary and secondary sources included
- Texts and Analyses – the curriculum writer provides analysis of the texts often quoting other commentators or experts, elaborating on a proof text, or providing insight into a word
- Summary of Key Ideas – pulls together the analysis back in terms of the big ideas
- Suggestions for Conducting the Lesson – this provides a step-by-step outline from "set induction" through "closure"; it includes educational experiences led by the faculty member as well as *hevruta* (study in dyads); questions
- Key Terms – definitions of the main terms from a session
- Biographies – when attributed or authored texts are listed, a brief biography of the person is often included, e.g., Maimonides, Heschel
- Suggested Readings – these are additional references that are helpful for preparing a session

This curriculum guide is particularly well suited for the instructor to adapt the materials. The idea is that the curriculum guide provides a common set of texts that the instructors study to prepare for the session. The texts in the curriculum guide are referred to as "the *hevruta* partner" of the instructor, suggestive of the dialogue between the text and the teacher that occurs prior to that with the learners. These texts provide an opportunity for professional learning and a framework for the session, but this system allows the instructor to make choices about which texts to concentrate on and bring in their knowledge and interests, as well as those of the adult learners, into the conversation. The instructor's adaptation of the curriculum is shared with the learners in the form of a 1–2-page "road map" that identifies key terms, the texts the instructor is focusing on, and key questions both for the entire class to concentrate on and to inform small group *hevruta* style interaction.

This format for curricular materials provided to the instructor has many advantages. The focus on texts leads much more to discussion and active engagement of the learners rather than a lecture. It provides a methodology that is appropriate and enticing to adult learners. As the curriculum guide states, the hope is to "discover ideas and messages that are relevant and meaningful to them [the learners]" (Melton, p. xv). It presents a curriculum with scope and sequence. It addresses a pattern in some adult education offerings where instructors seem ill prepared and offerings seem to wander rather than have a progression and purpose. Furthermore, the preparation of the road map – whether it is copied from the curriculum guide, borrowed from another example on the website, or in most cases, prepared by the instructor – contributes to assuring a high-level session.

What Curricular Challenges Loom over the Jewish Educational Horizon?

Curriculum development is a dynamic, organic, and perpetual process. A curriculum is more than a document. Curriculum grows and adapts to address the needs of learners and teachers, or else it becomes irrelevant and obsolete. A thoughtful plan, even when it is emergent or negotiated, is part of a quality learning experience; curriculum development is fundamentally about this interaction among learner, instructor, and text. As the world changes socially and technologically, and as the vision and purpose of institutions change, so too must new curricula be developed and new teaching and learning processes initiated.

The landscape of Jewish organizations offering Jewish education is growing increasingly diverse, and therefore, the definition of a Jewish educator is expanding too. All of these educators, those working in schools and camps, JCCs, congregations, and central agencies for Jewish education, as well as those working in the alternative or "independent" organizations and programmatic initiatives that are becoming more and more typical of Jewish life, must engage in curriculum development whether they start from scratch or adapt a "prepared" curriculum for their learning experience. Therefore, educational leaders need expertise in curriculum development or at least curriculum adaptation. Even when a teacher is given a comprehensive curriculum with teacher's guide and student resources, the teacher is a translator – adapting the generic materials to a specific case, i.e., to fit the educational institution's vision, the learners' needs – differentiated learning, and the teacher's knowledge and skills.

Despite the number of curricular efforts that exist, an institution or organization devoted to raising the quality of curriculum development by working with educators on the curricular process remains a desideratum. Jewish education would benefit from an organization that is devoted to supporting curriculum development in its many ways, helping to set the trends for thinking and implementation about curriculum design in a technologically informed environment. Wertheimer (2009) makes a similar recommendation about the need for a resource to aid schools in the curricular process.

The Jewish Education Center of Cleveland (JECC) provides comprehensive support for curriculum development by offering local educational settings the opportunity to undertake a 3-year curriculum planning and implementation process, seminars on curriculum development – most noticeably Understanding by Design, and curriculum lesson and unit planning assistance for local educators. Complementing this is the JECC's Retreat Institute which assists schools in designing retreats including the planned learning experiences. These resources are limited for the most part to the Cleveland, OH area, but they may be worthy of further diffusion. Some programs, such as the Mandel Teacher Educator Institute (MTEI), address curricular issues as part of their methodology. While academic programs in Jewish education include courses in curriculum, these offerings are generally targeted for their degree students and provide a foundation in curriculum development, rather than a concentration in the field. Curriculum development is always a work in process; at its best, curriculum development is also a work in progress.

Final Note: A Research Agenda for Curriculum Development

Additional research could identify models or strategies for curriculum development and implementation in Jewish educational settings. How is curriculum developed or adapted? Who is doing the curriculum development? How do educators go about adapting curricular materials for use in their classrooms? What is the role of professional development in the curriculum development process? The field would benefit from cross-curricular studies and a meta-analysis that leads to theory or model building. Part of this could include looking at the personnel who support the curricular process – Who are they? What training do they have? What roles do they serve?

It may be that curricular development efforts are being evaluated more rigorously, often at the behest of a funding partner. However, often these assessments are proprietary. Research should make these evaluations part of the public domain so that their impact can be magnified. Knowledge is more powerful when it is shared, and we have yet to harness the potential of Jewish educational assessment – of individuals, institutions, and curricular resources. The ultimate beneficiaries of such collaborative evaluation would be the learners themselves and perhaps this awareness will provide the impetus for changing the status quo. Nearly 2,000 years have elapsed since Judah ben Tema established an ambitious array of goals for a lifetime of Jewish learning experiences in the *mishnah*. We are still striving to develop the curricular resources that will help to nurture and support the Jews who are committed to a lifetime of Jewish learning.

References

Council for Initiatives in Jewish Education. (1994). *Policy brief: Background and professional training of teachers in Jewish schools*. New York: Council for Initiatives in Jewish Education.
Dewey, J. (1938). *Experience and education*. New York: Collier Macmillan.
Dorph, G. Z. (2003). Studying curriculum materials: A strategy for improving teaching. In N. S. Moskowitz (Ed.), *The ultimate Jewish teacher's handbook* (pp. 311–322). Denver, CO: A.R.E. Publishing, Inc.
Goodman, R., Bidol-Padva, P., & Schaap, E. (2006). Community Report on Early Childhood Jewish Educators: Culture of Employment 2004–2005 Miami-Dade and Broward Counties, Florida. New York: CAJE (Coalition for the Advancement of Jewish Education).
Goodman, R., Bloomberg, L., Schaap, E., & David, L. (2009). Sustaining Jewish Educational Excellence in the URJ Camps.
Goodman, R, & Schaap, E. (2006, October). Jewish Heroes Wanted: Inquire Within An Advocacy Campaign for the Recruitment and Retention of Congregational Teachers, report submitted to CAJE St. Louis.
Kelner, S., Rabkin, M., Saxe, L., & Sheingold, C. (2005). The Jewish Sector's Workforce: Report of a Six Community Study, Professional Leaders Project, Report No. 2. Waltham, MA: Cohen Center for Modern Jewish Studies, Brandeis University.
Kravitz, L., Olitzky, & K. M. (Eds.) (1993). *Pirke Avot: A modern commentary on Jewish ethics*. New York: UAHC Press.
Mooney, C. G. (2000). *Theories of childhood*. St. Paul, MN: Redleaf Press.
Moskowitz, N. S. (2003). *The ultimate Jewish teacher's handbook*. Denver, CO: A.R.E. Publishing, Co.
Pekarsky, D. (2008). Vision-guided Jewish education. In R. Goodman, P. Flexner, & L. Bloomberg (Eds.), *What we now know about Jewish education* (pp. 21–30). Los Angeles: Torah Aura Productions, Inc.
Piaget, J. (1967). *Six psychological studies*. New York: Vintage Books.
Rinaldi, C. (2006). *In dialogue with Reggio Emilia: Listening, researching, and learning*. New York: Routledge.
Sales, A., & Saxe, L. (2002). *Limmud by the lake: Fulfilling the educational potential of Jewish summer camps*. Waltham, MA: Center for Modern Jewish Studies, Brandeis University.
Schachter, L., & Ofek, A. (2008). Hebrew language instruction. In R. Goodman, P. Flexner, & L. Bloomberg (Eds.), *What we now know about Jewish education* (pp. 271–282). Los Angeles: Torah Aura Productions, Inc.
Shevitz, S. L. (2009). *Report to the URJ: CHAI curriculum evaluation, phase two*. New York: Union of Reform Judaism.
Tammivaara, J., & Goodman, R. (1996a). Professional lives of Jewish educators in Washington State. In *Planning for Jewish education in Washington State* prepared for the Samis Foundation. Seattle, WA: The Jewish Education Council of The Jewish Federation of Greater Seattle.
Tammivaara, J., & Goodman, R. (1996b). Professional Lives of Jewish Educators in Cleveland 1995–1996." Prepared for the Jewish Education Center of Cleveland, OH.
Tyler, R. W. (1949). *Basic principles of curriculum and instruction*. Chicago: University of Chicago Press.
Vygotsky, L. (1978). *Mind in society*. Cambridge, MA: Harvard University Press.
Wertheimer, J. (2009). *Schools that work: What we can learn from good Jewish supplementary schools*. New York: AVICHAI Foundation.
Wiggins, G., & McTighe, J. (1998). *Understanding by design*. Upper Saddle River, NJ: Merrill Prentice Hall.

Curriculum Integration in Jewish Day Schools: The Search for Coherence

Mitchel Malkus

Introduction

Since the French Revolution, when Jews gained rights through individual citizenship rather than by communal affiliation, both elite and common Jews began to rethink their relationship to the secular world. The philosophical discourse concerning the role of the Jew in general society fostered an intellectual climate open to an integrated curricular response in the teaching of Jewish and general studies in Jewish schools. Weisel (1782), an advocate for Jewish cultural and ideological change during the Enlightenment, was the first modern Jewish thinker to address the role of secular studies and their relationship to Jewish learning in the curriculum of a Jewish school. While he does not call for "curriculum integration," in his *Divrei Shalom V'emet* (see Mendes-Flohr & Reinharz, 1980, p. 63), Weisel writes that Jewish schools should teach both *Torat Ha-adam* (general wisdom) and *Torat Ha-shem* (Jewish wisdom). He argues that *Torat Ha-adam*, which existed before the Torah was given, represents knowledge, morals, and behaviors needed for participation in the greater society. In this sense, it is a prerequisite for life and must be included in the Jewish school curriculum.

Writing almost three centuries later, Sarna (1998), suggests that Jewish day schools serve as the "primary setting where American Jews confront the most fundamental question of Jewish life: how to live in two worlds at once, how to be both American and Jewish, part of the larger society and apart from it" (p. 9). While Weisel writes with a clear ideological agenda and Sarna offers a historian's viewpoint, their shared perspective on similar concerns attests both to the significance of the topic and the still unresolved nature of how Jews may live within and embrace democratic, open societies while maintaining their distinct identity. Wertheimer (1999), among others, views the recent growth of liberal Jewish day schools in North America as a sign that Jews are reassessing what it means to be Jewish at the start of the twenty-first century.

M. Malkus (✉)
The Rabbi Jacob Pressman Academy of Temple Beth Am, Los Angeles, CA, USA
e-mail: mmalkus@tbala.org

Jewish schools in the United Kingdom have a long history of addressing both religious and secular studies. Pre-dating even Weisel, the first Jewish schools established in the mid-1600s taught mathematics, and English reading and writing, in addition to Jewish religious studies (Black, 1998). This dual curriculum was due to the need for Jewish immigrants to integrate socially into British society after being readmitted to England in 1656.

Today, most non-Orthodox and many modern Orthodox day schools subscribe to a curricular approach that attempts to integrate Jewish and general studies. This approach is rooted in a distinct worldview. Day school conferences and institutes, workshops, and symposia devote significant time to exploring the theoretical groundings of and practical strategies for implementing integrated curriculum. Schools that engage in this curricular approach are concerned equally with their students' Jewish identity development and their relationship to the larger world in which they live. The literature on curriculum integration reveals that there have always been diverse understandings of how the integration of Jewish and general studies is defined (see Malkus, 2002; Solomon, 1978; Zeldin, 1992).

This chapter begins with a review of the theoretical basis for curriculum integration and a presentation of the different definitions of the term within Jewish schools. It then explores how curriculum integration is viewed within a broader context, since the term integration was borrowed from the early-twentieth century progressive education movement. Finally, the chapter concludes with a discussion of the scholastic factors that enable integration to occur and those that mitigate against its implementation. That section of the chapter will present examples from both Jewish and general education literature.

A Theoretical Review of Curriculum Integration

While the ultra-Orthodox have always chosen separate education for their children, most of American Jewry in the twentieth century opted for public school as the vehicle for rapid enculturation. This was the case even with some of the leaders and most influential personalities within the field of Jewish education. Samson Benderly and his followers placed Jewish education within the *talmud torah*, those community schools that met in the afternoons and on Sundays. Benderly was a passionate advocate of public education and ascribed to the "Protestant model" of education. He believed that

> morality, universal values, patriotism, civics, and critical skills should all be taught in state-funded public schools to a mixed body of religiously diverse students, leaving only the fine points of religious doctrine and practice to be mastered by members of each faith in separate denominationally sponsored supplementary schools. (Sarna, 1998, p. 11)

However, a large number of Jews became convinced that Jewish identity in contemporary society was not automatic and realized that students needed a certain type of education to nurture their Jewish identity. The *talmud torah*, or supplementary schools, as they came be to be known, did not adequately embrace the complexity of Jewish life in open, democratic societies and, therefore, new all-day Jewish schools were established. Within this socio-historical context, Jewish day schools negotiated the relationship of American Jewish education to American Jewish life. In the mid-1950s, Greenberg (1957) wrote that an integrated education was essential to the future vitality of Judaism within a modern society:

> America not only permits but encourages its citizens to integrate their personal lives and their lives as distinguishable groups in American society around a religion... to fulfill this historically unprecedented task (the development of a Jewish version of American civilization) we need the help of the day school. (pp. 7 and 10).

While he writes within an American context, and it may be said that the challenges in other countries have been different, Greenberg grapples with the same issue that confronted Weisel, Sarna, and all Jewish educators who take modernity seriously.

A different historical development is evident in the growth, decline, and current revival of Jewish day schools in the United Kingdom. Jewish schools were initially established when Jews were readmitted to England after expulsion and when, later, Jews and other minority groups found themselves excluded from the Church of England schools because of the religious education that these schools required of their students. In these cases, the curriculum in Jewish schools was developed to either assist students with integrating into the social fabric of the United Kingdom or maintain students' Jewish heritage because of the compulsory study of Christianity and the New Testament in state schools (Miller, 2001). Today, Jewish day schools in the United Kingdom have experienced a resurgence, due in strong part to the creation of a multi-cultural society that supports ethnic distinction (Alderman, 1999). As Miller (2001) suggests, this changing historical context has also shaped the integrated nature of curricula in Jewish day schools.

Solomon (1978, 1979) was the first to conduct research into the definitional issues that surround curriculum integration within the context of a Jewish day school. Solomon reviews much of the literature on integration and through the use of literary and linguistic analysis identifies the sacred/secular dilemma, the structure of religious and general knowledge, and the objectives of the day school as the three major "educational and philosophical issues which must be confronted within the process of building an integrated program" (p. 13). At the same time, Lukinsky (1978) developed a typology to identify some of the existing practices within Jewish schools. He began with the "rejectionist" approach that views Western culture as at best a necessary evil and as something that must remain separate from Judaic studies and classes. He labeled a second type as the "*Torah im derekh eretz*" (Torah with the way of the land)[1] approach. In schools that ascribe to this philosophy, Lukinsky observed that the Jew's entry into the secular world is affirmed but always viewed through a Jewish lens. Another point in his classification was the "correlation" model where the Jewish curriculum is offered as an answer to the challenges of the outside world. Lukinsky concluded by suggesting a "mutual affirmation model,"

---

[1] A philosophy of Orthodox Judaism articulates by Rabbi Samson Raphael Hirsch (1808–1888), which formalizes a relationship between traditionally observant Judaism and the modern world.

where Jewish and general studies share a mutual relationship and have the ability to transform one another.

Similarly, Zeldin (1992) articulates an understanding of curriculum integration that is based on the relationship between Judaism and what he titles the "curriculum of modernity." He writes,

> [T]o clarify our understanding, we can look at the question to which integration is a response: How can the day school prepare children to live as Jews in a modern, liberal, democratic society? Living as Jews would require that children come to understand Judaism as a system of beliefs and practices that reflects a common Jewish experience. This broad understanding of Judaism would then need to be integrated into what children learn to prepare them for life in a modern, democratic society, what we might call the "curriculum of modernity": science, technology, social studies, language arts, and so on. (p. 13)

Zeldin presents four curricular approaches to meet the challenge of integration in Jewish day schools: *parallel* (where students study related topics in different classes with different teachers at the same time), *contextualizing* (where what students study in one discipline is placed within the context of knowledge, skills, or values from another area), *integrated* (where the instructor makes explicit connections between Judaism and the general studies curriculum), and *integrating* (where the instructor aims to assist students in discovering for themselves the relationships between Judaism and the curriculum of modernity). Drawing upon this work, Zeldin (1994) proposes that educators use the concept of "interaction" as opposed to "integration." The very idea of integration, Zeldin argues, carries with it the danger that as we strive to make Judaism warm and comfortable, we "will also make Judaism irrelevant" (p. 5). The concept of interaction holds the promise of presenting Judaism as a unique and distinct way of viewing the world that may be harmonious with the modern world, but which also often challenges the assumptions of modern society. Understood this way, curriculum based on the idea of interaction is "educationally potent because ... [it] create[s] the disequilibrium that is the catalyst for learning" (Zeldin, 1994, p. 9).

Building on Zeldin's writings, Ellenson (2008) explores the historical context of the shift from integration to interaction through a study of "the contemporary sociological and intellectual currents that have caused a philosophical notion of 'interaction' between minority and majority cultures to emerge" in the post-modern world (p. 246). Ellenson suggests that this interaction model might be applied to classroom situations in liberal Jewish day schools that confront the challenge of educating students to address the complex diversity of the North American world.

Pomson (2001) suggests that curriculum integration may exist on a spectrum of different models. He believes that schools committed to an integrative ideal might benefit from a re-conceptualization of integration, grounded in constructivist notions of teaching and learning. He argues that most Jewish day schools sit somewhere between complete integration and a rejection of the approach. As our contemporary knowledge of teaching and learning focuses on how students create meaning, educators in Jewish schools have an opportunity to re-evaluate an integrated approach to curriculum based on fostering an environment where students have opportunities to actively make individual meaning out of the dual curriculum.

While the term integration is widely used in day school promotional materials, its definitions have often been ambiguous and diverse. In previous research (Malkus, 2001), I identified no fewer than ten different uses of the term as it is presented in schools. Schools that emphasize this approach in their curriculum might be referring, for example, to the relationship between general and Judaic content, the integration of academic skills across the curriculum, the development of dual identities in their students, the way values are taught throughout the school, and how technology and the arts are represented across the different subject areas. One or more of these expressions of "integration" is commonly used in schools, often within the same institution. Scheindlin (2008) has added to this list in arguing for the integration of cognition and emotion within the student as an aspect of moral and spiritual education.

Curriculum integration in Jewish education is not without its critics. Reflecting on his experience at the Rabbi Jacob Joseph School of the 1930s, Scheffler (1995) discusses how the school ignored the potential integration between the general and the Jewish:

> The school said nothing about these oppositions, offered no reconciliations or philosophical rationalizations. It simply incorporated these two worlds within itself and, by offering them both to us as our daily fare, it built them both into our consciousness, bequeathing to us at the same time the ragged boundaries and the gnawing conflicts between them.
>
> Neither the school nor its faculties had any philosophy to offer capable of resolving the two-world tensions they inculcated. They had only the conviction that both worlds were vital. To choose one over the other would be worse than holding on, however uncomfortably, to both. So they left to us the task of working out in the future how to manage what they themselves could not control or foresee. They educated us by juxtaposing the incongruous realms rather than smoothing out the incongruities or offering phony reconciliations. (pp. 85–86)

The bifurcated nature of his early education did not, however, prevent Scheffler from seeking a synthesis between the two cultures he valued equally. He explains that while his teachers, transplanted from the religious culture of the old world, were charged with the task of "transporting the precious plant to new shores," his and future generations were left to synthesize the two worlds they had inherited (p. 172).

More recently, Lehmann (2008) suggests that different subject areas within the school curriculum may be predicated on different models of teaching and learning. Lehmann's study of a modern Orthodox high school reveals that in that context, English instruction was grounded in a discourse of autonomy, while *Humash* was situated within a discourse of authority. Although similar studies of non-Orthodox settings have not been conducted, this critique does call into question many of the assumptions upon which curriculum integration has been predicated in Jewish schools.

Curriculum Integration Within General Education

In general education, the concept of "integration" has its roots in the educational reform efforts of the early-twentieth century that questioned a subject-centered approach to curriculum. In his works, *The School and Society* (1915/1990b) and *The Child and the Curriculum* (1902/1990a), Dewey argues for creating curricula that unify students' life experiences with wider social issues. He claims that education "is a process of living and not a preparation for future living" (Dewey, 1992, p. 364). Dewey was primarily concerned with fostering the school's role in promoting democracy in a society of disparate immigrant groups. Drawing on the work of Dewey and the progressive movement in education, Smith (1921), at the time a student at Columbia University's Teachers College, became the first educator to use the word "integration" as she referred to an instructional approach that would facilitate learning on both the theoretical and practical levels using Kilpatrick's "Project Method."

Hopkins (1935, 1941) writings helped to shape the concept of integration in education. He defines integration as a curriculum "organized around immediate, abiding interests and assured future needs of the learner, utilizing materials selected from all areas of the social heritage regardless of subject division" (quoted in Beane, 1997, p. 27). He goes on to emphasize problem-based learning and collaboration between students and teachers as fundamental to the idea of integration. In all of his writing, Hopkins points out that what distinguishes integration from multidisciplinary approaches is the organizing philosophy of each. Multidisciplinary and cross-disciplinary curriculum are both rooted in the mastery of subject matter, while integrated approaches emphasize the personal and social as the primary organizing principles.

The Russian launch of the *Sputnik* satellite in 1957 was an unprecedented event that triggered, by way of reaction, an emphasis in American schools on technical subjects and the structure of disciplines. Bruner's work, *The Process of Education* (1963), emphasized the importance of the "disciplines of knowledge"; he endorsed subject-specific study. As a result of his work, the field of general education shifted away from curricular integration. During the 1980s, most education thinkers and curriculum scholars focused on the analysis of cultural and economic politics in making decisions about content and approach.

Since the 1990s, however, integrated curriculum has returned as a focal point of analysis and explanation. Jacobs (1989) suggests that the exponential growth of knowledge in the last half of the twentieth century, the fragmented nature of school schedules, and the search for relevance in educational programs have all contributed to the emergence of "interdisciplinary" curricula and programs as a primary concern in schools. She defines interdisciplinary as "a knowledge view and curriculum approach that consciously applies methodology and language from more than one discipline to examine a central theme, issue, problem, topic, or experience" (Jacobs, 1989, p. 8). Likewise, Beane (1997) advocates that schools move toward a "curriculum design theory that is concerned with enhancing the possibilities for personal and social integration through the organization of curriculum around significant problems and issues, collaboratively identified by educators and young people, without regard for subject-area lines" (p. 19).

The renewed movement to develop curriculum integration in general education has been criticized by supporters of the disciplines of knowledge. Critics of integrated curriculum argue that the disciplines of knowledge are weakened when schools move away from a subject-separate approach (see Bloom, 1987). Advocates of curriculum integration have responded by pointing out that the subject-separate approach in schools represents a hardening of categories that does not exist naturally in the disciplines of knowledge (Klein, 1990). Disciplines, they argue, are fluid at the edges and often combine with other disciplines. Instead of being opposed to the disciplines of knowledge, Beane (1995) suggests that curriculum integration maintains the integrity of individual subjects while shifting their function from "ends" to "means" within education.

Implementing Curriculum Integration in Jewish Day Schools

The extensive work on curriculum integration in general education provides a background for understanding how this approach is used within the context of Jewish day schools. While Jewish educators often find the philosophical and theoretical arguments for integration compelling, and many day schools articulate curriculum integration as part of their mission statements, the actual implementation of this approach within schools has been a significant challenge. In the remaining sections of this chapter I outline a number of factors that contribute to or mitigate against the implementation of an integrated curriculum in Jewish day schools. For organizational purposes, I have categorized these factors into the following three areas: instructional strategies, curricular factors, and school culture. Instructional strategies represent educational applications through which teachers put integrated curriculum into practice in their classrooms. Curricular factors are specific approaches to curriculum that are essential for implementation and that, in part, re-conceptualize the role of teachers from curriculum implementers to curriculum developers, a central concern for schools that pursue integrated curriculum. Lastly, there are a series of school-wide cultural factors that may either establish a fertile environment for integrated curriculum or, in their absence, serve as impediments to its implementation. Throughout this section, I cite examples from previous field research[2] and share reflections based on my work as a practitioner.

Theme-Based Learning

Integrated curriculum often revolves around a theme, topic, or issue that serves as the center from which inquiry and learning evolves. Theme-based learning breaks down the boundaries of disciplines and allows subject domains to serve as a means for investigating areas of interest to students (Fogarty, 1991). Theme-based learning also has the ability to promote thinking across and between subject areas. A theme may be identified from the subject areas that a teacher wants to cover as a means of connecting different disciplines.

---

[2]For a fuller treatment of this area see Malkus (2001).

In investigating one school, I saw how the kindergarten used the theme of "The Human Body" to create a context for the study of human anatomy, math, science, language arts, *Tanakh*, art, and questions about God (Malkus, 2001, p. 166). I have also seen this approach utilized at my current school at various grade levels. One first-grade teacher begins the school year with a unit on bees. Through this theme, students study science, language arts, the customs and ideas of the holiday of *Rosh Hashanah*, and Hebrew language. My middle school also employs a theme to organize a yearly one day event titled "Total Teen Expo." A recent theme was "Citizenship = Action" and teachers used the topic to explore being a global citizen, an American citizen, and a Jewish citizen. Teachers used American literature, history, sociology, and classical Jewish texts to explore the theme.

How subject areas are viewed, as ends in and of themselves that may be connected, or as means to understanding larger complex issues, is a matter of much debate among curriculum theorists and has implications for what is taught and understood as knowledge in schools. As Apple (1990) has demonstrated, curricular knowledge and what is seen as "official knowledge" in schools is not neutral, but rather represents conscious and unconscious social and ideological choices. He writes,

> One major reason that subject-centered curricula dominate most schools, [and] that integrated curricula are found in relatively few schools, is at least partly the result of the place of the school in maximizing the production of high status knowledge. This is closely interrelated with the school's role in the selection of agents to fill economic and social positions in a relatively stratified society. (p. 38)

Apple's work clarifies the highly ideological, or as he understands it, "hegemonic" role that knowledge and its uses play in the curriculum. He understands high-status knowledge and how it is used and manipulated to have a macro-effect in maintaining economic and social systems. Apple's view offers a perspective on the acceptance and rejection of integrated curriculum in day schools. While Orthodox Jewish thinkers have called for the development of an integrated worldview (Berkovits, 1962; Soloveitchik, 1983), there have been practically no educational institutions that have consistently epitomized the ethos and principles of these thinkers.

The control of and dominant position of Torah studies within Orthodox schools maintains the high status and preeminence of those subjects and the compartmentalization of religious commitment and secular society (cf. Bieler, 1986). The rejection of an integrated approach to Jewish and general studies might, therefore, be an important tool in maintaining the Orthodox social and communal apparatus. On the other hand, the (theoretical) embrace of integrated curriculum in liberal Jewish day schools could be understood as part of a larger ideological approach whereby Jewish belief and practice may be altered as it comes into contact with secular society. How integrated curriculum is conceptualized is intimately tied to a larger ideological perspective on education in Jewish day schools.

Pomson (2001) and Drake (1998), however, both argue that curriculum integration in schools may be placed along a continuum where progressively greater connections are made between subject areas. While some Orthodox schools may reject outright the ideological value of an integrated curriculum, many other schools, both Orthodox and non-Orthodox, fall somewhere between rejection and complete integration. This more pragmatic approach to understanding the appearance of integrated studies in schools offers a useful measure when observing curriculum in Jewish day schools.

Core Concepts and Essential Questions

Core concepts and essential questions are what Sizer (1985) calls lines of inquiry that are broad and rich enough for several lessons or a unit. They are few in number, a step toward learning outcomes, and often posted for all students to see. Teachers who teach with an eye toward integration often use questions and concepts in organizing student learning. In this way, core concepts and essential questions serve as important structures in enabling integration.

In one fifth-grade classroom that I visited (Malkus, 2001, p. 169), the teachers created and posted a list of four "Big Idea" questions on one of the classroom walls. All of those questions were related to the "The Role of Humans in Nature" and served as a connective thread for students and their teachers to link each of the units they studied throughout the year. At the conclusion of every unit, both the Judaic and general studies teachers would ask students to reflect on those original questions and the topic that had been covered. While the teachers may not have integrated their lessons and units, they used big idea questions to link what was studied to previous material. When teachers aim to assist students to discover for themselves the relationships between subjects, such an approach is often called integrative curriculum (see Zeldin, 1992).

In research conducted at a Jewish high school (Ingall & Malkus, 2001), Ingall and I observed a discreet unit based on the theme of "Maxims" that sought to integrate literature, history, and the study of the *Book of Proverbs*. We discovered that despite the intention of their teachers, students resisted building connections between subject areas. We found that asking high-school students to integrate was fraught with obstacles, but realized that such resistance may be appropriate to adolescent development. Using the work of Egan (1998), we suggested that high-schools students may "not [be] ready to dismantle the borders, to live with ambiguity and complexity, until they enter the age of 'ironic understanding' which comes at about the age of twenty; if it comes at all" (p. 42).

Team Teaching

The relationship between teachers is another factor at the center of developing and implementing integrated curriculum (Schlechty, 1990). Team teaching is fundamental to schools' integrated programs both in planning and in classroom instruction. When teachers work together, not only can they mindfully plan integrated curriculum together, but they often see relationships between different disciplines that they had not noticed previously. Some schools have teachers meet together both within grades and across age levels to cultivate an integrated approach both horizontally and vertically within a program (Malkus, 2001, p. 170).

While planning together may be one structure that supports integration, how teachers interact within the classroom is also an important factor to address. When general and Judaic studies teachers work simultaneously in the same classroom, they can seize on opportunities for integration spontaneously. Some schools have made this type of team teaching a hallmark of their educational culture and program. Such an approach raises questions of financial sustainability for schools but offers unique opportunities for integration.

Curricular Flexibility

When curriculum is set and static, it loses the ability to grow and expand organically around themes, core concepts, and essential questions. By contrast, curriculum without direction and boundaries is unfocused, lacks continuity, and has the potential to miss the essential skills that a school expects its students to master. In understanding the balance between flexibility and structure in integrated curriculum, it is instructive to look at the written curriculum of schools. Schools that are interested in integration need to consider how to maintain a balance between written curriculum and flexibility in organizing learning. Ben-Peretz (1990) offers a wonderful distinction between curriculum writers and curriculum developers. She writes that curriculum is often written in a general context for specific age groups of students, therefore, viewing teachers as curriculum *developers* is an essential component for some models of curriculum integration.

One of the trends in post-modern curriculum theory has been to understand curriculum as an open rather than a closed system. It is useful to take note of this movement in curriculum studies as it applies to the notion of flexibility. Doll (1993) uses the conceptual framework of chaos theory and the science of complexity in theorizing what curriculum might look like. In describing post-modern curriculum as "generated not predefined, indeterminate yet bounded ... and made up of an ever-increasing network," he touches on many of the characteristics that emerge from the schools that use integrated curriculum. It is this kind of response to the complexity of curriculum integration that has the potential to affect how schools view this approach.

Time, Scheduling, and Planning

Sizer (1985) has written about the need to rethink how time is scheduled in schools. Finding time within the school day is one of the primary challenges to implementing integrated curriculum. Educators interested in this approach view traditional forty minute block periods as obstacles to implementing integration in Jewish schools. Cushman (1995) suggests that schools need to "make time a factor supporting education, not a boundary marking its limits" (p. 1). Flexibility in scheduling coupled with broader teacher autonomy over how the day is structured are two fundamental factors in successfully implementing integrated curriculum.

Shortt and Thayer (1999) explore the use of time and its relationship to student achievement in their work on block scheduling. They conclude that block scheduling "not only improves school climate, but it also increases opportunities for learning and levels of achievement" (p. 76). This research confirms a study on flexible scheduling conducted at the Akiba Hebrew Academy (Schaffzin, 1997) by making a connection between the use of block scheduling and the establishment of an environment open to integrated curriculum. This work, together with research on curriculum integration in Jewish schools, shows the significant role that flexible scheduling plays as one of the factors that may support integration.

Teachers and administrators at Jewish day schools often identify the necessity for teachers to plan together in developing integrated curricula. The lack of time is a major factor mitigating the use of integrated approaches. The primary obstacle to joint planning in Jewish day schools is the availability of both the general and Judaic studies teachers in elementary settings and teams of teachers in middle and high schools. The issue of planning time has been identified as a major hurdle in building integrated curricula in a number of settings (Ingall & Malkus, 2001; Malkus, 2002; Beane, 1997; Drake, 1998; Jacobs, 1989).

Finally, Fogarty and Stoehr (1995) address the challenge of finding time for teams of teachers to plan together. They write that "there must be time to plan, time that is carved out of an already overloaded schedule" (p. 76). Fogarty and Stoehr suggest ten intervals of time when teachers can meet during the school day, such as borrowed time (adding fifteen minutes for four days gains one hour on the fifth day), common time (scheduling block time for teacher teams), and freed-up time (with parent volunteers, senior citizens, or visiting artists creating time). While not all of the ideas they propose may be appropriate for all schools, it is clear that making planning time a priority is an essential element for schools that implement integrated curriculum, because the need for teachers to work together requires them to find time not ordinarily allotted in their daily schedules.

School Culture

In her casebook, *Leadership skills for Jewish educators*, Rosenblum (1993) identifies "the ability to define the vision of an organization and to set goals for it" as one of the primary characteristics of leadership (p. 5). If creating a powerful vision is a central aspect of educational leadership, how that vision is developed and implemented is equally important. Addressing the issue of educational reform, Barth (1990) articulates that the relationships among adults within schools is both the most neglected and crucial area in promoting an atmosphere of learning in schools. When educators share a sense of mission and vision they begin to work together in ways that might not have been thought possible. This sense of dedication to the vision of integration is a hallmark of schools that use this approach. However, beyond vision, schools have deep organizational cultures that enable them to function in specific ways. The work of Schein (1997) has been instrumental in helping researchers and leaders understand the significance of culture in organizations. Schein views culture as "the accumulated shared learning of a given institution covering behavioral, emotional, and cognitive elements of the group members' total psychological functioning" (p. 10). Schein's framework of "shared basic assumptions," common language, and shared conceptual understanding offers a model for analyzing school culture.

Jewish schools that make curriculum integration a major goal need to explore how their school culture either supports or impedes its implementation. Based on Schein's research, the nurturing of a culture of integration with a clear mission, goals, and a concrete understanding of what is meant by integration are the key factors in developing and implementing curricular integration. At my current school, teachers have suggested that having a clear vision of what the school considers to be integrated curriculum and what practical steps the administration takes to foster an environment where faculty are supported are essential and key ingredients in developing integrated curriculum.

When teachers serve as role models for their students, the process of integration is supported in the school. For Jewish day schools that are committed to an integrated approach for their general and Jewish studies, the relationship between teacher and student is a significant factor in the success of this vision. Often, teachers can significantly influence their students through the implicit lessons they teach and through role modeling. Pomson (2000) outlines the important role that general studies teachers can play in shaping the Jewish context of day schools. When students see that their general studies teachers have knowledge, yet they also witness these same teachers speaking Hebrew together, or discussing Jewish topics, that has a profound impact on them. School cultures that stress the personal roles that teachers play in shaping their students' conceptions of life, culture, and religion have an advantage in making integration successful in their schools.

Staffing and Hiring

Finally, staffing is a perennial issue in day schools and one that bears a relationship to integrated curriculum. Schools that integrate curriculum in a deliberate way need to consider what function this approach plays in their hiring practices. In two schools I studied that were identified as being both serious and accomplished in integrated curriculum (Malkus, 2001, pp. 60 and 102–103), the principals look for specific qualities – flexibility, the ability to work with partners, and desire to integrate – as primary characteristics in the hiring choices they make. In addition to the characteristics of openness, flexibility, and being a team player, my research suggested that with respect to the integration of Jewish and general studies, the attitude of the general studies teacher to religion is an important consideration in hiring faculty that work in schools that support integrated curriculum.

Conclusion

In understanding how curricular integration is implemented in day schools, it becomes clear that virtually every facet of a school is affected by this approach. While curriculum integration is a goal of many schools, its recent re-conceptualization is an area that needs to be addressed further. In her extensive investigations toward defining how contemporary Jews express their Jewish identity, Horowitz (2000) suggests that the traditional markers of Jewish involvement and commitment may no longer apply in the twenty-first century. Similarly, Cohen and Eisen (2000) argue that the contemporary construction of Jewish meaning is personal and private and that communal loyalties and norms no longer shape Jewish identity as they did several decades ago. This redefinition of Jewish identity necessarily impacts how Jewish schools view their curricula and how they articulate the philosophical underpinning for engaging in curriculum integration. While Ellenson (2008) and Levisohn (2008) have begun to respond to these sociological developments, many unanswered questions remain. Is curricular integration an effective means of achieving such goals? How does this approach compare with traditional models of curriculum in fostering students who can integrate their dual Jewish and American heritage in meaningful ways? Are certain approaches to integration more effective than others? Ample research is needed specifically on teachers and classrooms in schools that advocate curriculum integration. In addition, while some studies have focused on Jewish schools as the primary units of analysis, further research which highlights the complexities of planning and implementing integration in classrooms is required to clarify the challenges that teachers face.

It is also apparent that curricular integration is not limited to a Jewish context. Beyond the use of integrated curriculum in public and non-sectarian private schools, other private religious and ethnic/cultural schools utilize this approach. Although studies have been conducted in these settings, comparative studies between Jewish day schools and other schools that employ an integrated curriculum would be particularly relevant with respect to dual identity integration. How do other religious groups harmonize and highlight the differences between their cultural and religious heritages and the societies in which they live? Is there a generational difference in how a community understands, implements, advocates, or rejects integration as an educational approach? What are the different rationales marshaled by ethnic groups for engaging in integration? Much work, both theoretical and practical, remains in this important area if Jewish day schools are to utilize integrated curriculum in a serious manner.

References

Alderman, G. (1999). British Jews or Britons of the Jewish pesuasian. In S. Cohen & S. Horenczyk (Eds.), *National variations in Jewish identity*. New York: SUNY Press.

Apple, M. (1990). *Ideology and curriculum*. New York: Routledge.

Barth, R. (1990). *Improving schools from within*. San Francisco: Jossey-Bass.
Beane, J. (1995). Curriculum integration and the disciplines of knowledge. *Phi Delta Kappan*, 76(8), 616–622.
Beane, J. (1997). *Curriculum integration: Designing the core of democratic education*. New York: Teachers College Press.
Ben-Peretz, M. (1990). *The teacher curriculum encounter: Freeing teachers from the tyranny of texts*. Binghamton, NY: SUNY Press.
Berkovits, E. (1962). An integrated world view. *Tradition*, 5, 1.
Bieler, J. (1986). Integration of the Judaic and general studies program. *Jewish Education*, 54(4), 15–26.
Black, J. (1998). *The history of Jews' free school, London since 1732*. London: Tymsder Publishing.
Bloom, A. (1987). *The closing of the American mind*. New York: Simon & Schuster.
Bruner, J. (1963). *The process of education*. New York: Vintage Books.
Cohen, S., & Eisen, A. (2000). *The Jew within*. Bloomington, IN: Indiana University Press.
Cushman, K. (1995). Using time well: Schedules in essential schools. *Horace*, 12(2), 1–7.
Dewey, J. (1990a). *The child and the curriculum*. Chicago: University of Chicago Press (Original work published in 1915).
Dewey, J. (1990b). *The school and society*. Chicago: University of Chicago Press (Original work published in 1902).
Dewey, J. (1992). My pedagogic creed. In K. Ryan & J. Cooper (Eds.), *Kaleidoscope: Readings in education* (pp. 363–369). Boston: Houghton Mifflin (Originally published in 1897).
Doll, W. (1993). *A postmodern perspective on curriculum*. New York: Teachers College Press.
Drake, S. (1998). *Creating integrated curriculum*. Thousand Oaks, CA: Corwin Press.
Egan, K. (1998). *The educated mind: How cognitive tools shape our understanding*. Chicago: University of Chicago Press.
Ellenson, D. (2008). An ideology for the liberal Jewish day school: A philosophical-sociological investigation. *Journal of Jewish Education*, 74(3), 245–263.
Fogarty, R. (1991). *How to integrate the curriculum*. Arlington Heights, IL: IRI/SkyLight Training and Publishing.
Fogarty, R., & Stoehr, J. (1995). *Integrating curricula with multiple intelligences: Teams, themes, and threads*. Arlington Heights, IL: IRI/SkyLight Training and Publishing.
Greenberg, S. (1957). The philosophy of the Conservative day school. *Synagogue School*, XVI(1), 7;10.
Herz Wessely, N. (1980). Words of peace and truth. In P. Mendes-Flohr & J. Reinharz (Eds.), *The Jew in the modern world: A documentary history* (pp. 62–67). New York: Oxford Press.
Hopkins, L. (1935). Arguments favoring integration. *Teachers College Record*, 36, 604–612.
Hopkins, L. (1941). *Interaction: The democratic process*. New York: Heath.
Horowitz, B. (2000). *Connections and journeys: Assessing critical opportunities for enhancing Jewish identity*. New York: UJA.
Ingall, C., & Malkus, M. (2001). Negotiating the borderlands: Implementing an integrated curricular unit in a Jewish day high school. *Journal of Jewish Education*, 67(1/2), 36–45.
Jacobs, H. H. (1989). *Interdisciplinary curriculum: Design and implementation*. Alexandria, VA: Association for Supervision and Curriculum Development.
Klein, J. (1990). *Interdisciplinarity: History, theory, and practice*. Detroit, MI: Wayne State University Press.
Lehmann, D. (2008). Calling integration into question: A discourse analysis of English and *humash* classes at a modern Orthodox yeshiva high school. *Journal of Jewish Education*, 74(3), 295–316.
Levisohn, J. (2008). From integration of curricula to the pedagogy of integrity. *Journal of Jewish Education*, 74(3), 264–294.

Lukinsky, J. (1978). Integrating Jewish and general studies in the day school. In M. Nadel (Ed.), *Integrative learning: The search for unity in Jewish day school programs*. New York: American Association for Jewish Education.

Malkus, M. (2001). *Portraits of curriculum integration in Jewish day schools*. Unpublished doctoral dissertation, Jewish Theological Seminary, New York.

Malkus, M. (2002). The curricular symphony: How one Jewish day schools integrates its curriculum. *Journal of Jewish Education, 68*(1), 47–57.

Miller, H. (2001). Meeting the challenge: The Jewish schooling phenomenon in the UK. *Oxford Review of Education, 27*(4), 501–513.

Pomson, A. (2000). Who is a Jewish teacher? A narrative inquiry into general studies teaching in Jewish day schools. *Journal of Jewish Communal Service, 77*(1), 56–63.

Pomson, A. (2001). Knowledge that doesn't just sit there: Considering a reconceptualization of the curriculum integration of Jewish and general studies. *Religious Education, 96*(4), 528–545.

Rosenblum, S. (1993). *Leadership skills for Jewish education*. West Orange, NJ: Behrman House.

Sarna, J. (1998). American Jewish education in historical perspective. *Journal of Jewish Education, 64*(1/2), 8–21.

Schaffzin, L. (1997). *Flexible scheduling project*. Philadelphia: Schaffzin and Schaffzin.

Scheffler, I. (1995). *Teachers of my youth*. Boston: Kluwer Academic Publishers.

Schein, E. (1997). *Organizational culture and leadership*. San Francisco: Jossey-Bass.

Scheindlin, L. (2008). Integrating cognition and emotion: Yirat shamayim and the taxonomies. *Journal of Jewish Education, 74*(3), 343–363.

Schlechty, P. (1990). *Schools for the twenty-first century: Leadership imperatives for educational reform*. San Francisco: Jossey-Bass.

Shortt, T., & Thayer, Y. (1999). Block-scheduling can enhance school climate. *Educational Leadership, 56*(4), 76–81.

Sizer, T. (1985). *Horace's compromise: The dilemma of the American high school*. Boston: Houghton Mifflin.

Smith, M. (1921). An educational experiment: The community project. *Survey, 46*, 301–304.

Solomon, B. (1978). A critical review of the term integration in the literature of the Jewish day school in America. *Jewish Education, 46*(4), 24–48.

Solomon, B. (1979). *Curricular integration in the Jewish all day school in the United States*. Unpublished doctoral dissertation, Harvard University, Cambridge, MA.

Soloveitchik, J. (1983). *Halachic man*. Philadelphia: JPS.

Wertheimer, J. (1999). Jewish education in the United States: Recent trends and issues. In D. Singer (Ed.), *American Jewish yearbook 1999* (Vol. 99, pp. 3–115). New York: The American Jewish Committee.

Zeldin, M. (1992). To see the world as whole: The promise of the integrated curriculum. *Jewish Education News, 13*(3), 13.

Zeldin, M. (1994). *Jewish day schools at the end of the modern era: A curricular approach*. Paper presented at the Conference of the Network for Research in Jewish Education.

Gender and Jewish Education: "Why Doesn't This Feel So Good?"

Tova Hartman and Tamar Miller

The burgeoning field of gender and Jewish education stands at the intersection of two disciplines: gender and religion, and gender and education. Paying attention to gender in education highlights the importance of education as "gender equitable... in which every voice is heard and each girl and boy has an equally wide range of educational opportunities and life choices" (Bailey, 2002). Feminism, as one of the mothers of gender studies, has made a significant impact on Jewish practice and Jewish studies by critiquing texts, traditions, and values. We are now at the stage where many women who previously felt marginalized are able to "Stand Again at Sinai" (see Plaskow, 1990).

Because there has been little systematic research on the intersection between the fields of gender and Judaism, and gender and Jewish education, this chapter highlights what a feminist lens might contribute to this new combination of disciplines. To give color and depth to our discussion, we focus on five narratives concerning Miriam, Rabbi Akiva and his wife (traditionally known as Rachel) Bruria, Hannah, Esther, and Vashti. We have chosen these stories because they are part of the Jewish curriculum in all the denominations and therefore offer an opportunity to explore educational applications of a gendered critical analysis.

Although we appreciate the important strides in gender equity in many Jewish educational institutions, we look beyond, to see what else needs attention. Inspired by the richness of gender studies, we ask in what way the inclusion of girls and women influences both the substance and methodologies of Jewish education. What does it mean today for girls and boys to study texts that are so foreign and offensive to modern sensibilities? For instance, at the beginning of the Bible, the Garden of Eden story (Genesis Ch 3:16) recounts: "your urge shall be for your husband and he shall rule over you." At a later period, Maimonides includes women in the same legal category as slaves, children, the blind and deaf regarding the prohibitions of bearing legal witness (Hilchot Edut 9:1).

If we take gender studies seriously, we are compelled to ask should these traditional texts be taught as anything but the antiquated history of ideas? How does a

---

T. Hartman (✉)
Bar-Ilan University, Tel Aviv, Israel
e-mail: TovaHartman@gmail.com

girl feel about herself, her mother, sisters, grandmother, aunts, and the Matriarchs when she studies these texts? Adrienne Rich (1986), in "Blood, Bread and Poetry," conveys the experience:

> When someone with the authority of a teacher describes the world and you are not in it, there is a moment of psychic disequilibrium, as if you looked into a mirror and saw nothing. It takes some strength of soul – and not just individual strength, but collective understanding – to resist this void, this non-being, into which you are thrust, and to stand up, demanding to be seen and heard. (p. 199)

And, let us not forget to ask what are boys' responses to these authoritative texts? Who are the boys' heroes and heroines? From the perspective of the teacher, the prime agent of socialization, into what kind of religious culture is she socializing her students?

Women and Jewish Textual Literacy

Given the novelty of gender and Jewish education, we phrase our analysis in the form of questions and recommended directions for further research. We will ask about the nature and substance of the traditional texts we choose in our Jewish educational institutions and what they might teach us about ourselves, relationships, continuity, values, and observance.

Our working hypothesis is that all Jewish education may be enhanced by reworking traditional texts through a gendered perspective. These challenges are present in the Orthodox world not only where texts are heavily weighted toward traditional hermeneutics but also where women and men do not have equal textual access. Many other Jewish denominations tend to pick and choose, and sometimes completely ignore those texts that might offend modern sensibilities regarding gender equality. By applying a gendered perspective, we suggest that Jewish educators can still use traditional texts that feel and look disturbing in the curriculum.

A significant development in Jewish education begins with the change of the status of women as learners of texts in formal settings. For centuries, only a privileged minority of rabbis' daughters and girls from affluent families enjoyed private tutoring or cautiously received a decent Jewish education "under the table" (see Stampfer, 2007). Historians of Jewish education cite the century-old, revolutionary *p'sak* of Rabbi Yisrael Meir Kagan (better known as the *Hafetz Chaim*) as one of the most important milestones for girls' Jewish education. In his commentary *Hafetz Hayim Likutei Halakhot to Masechet Sotah (1903)*, he wrote,

> ...nowadays when the tradition of our fathers has become very weakened and we find people who do not live close to the parental environment and especially that there are those who have been given a secular education, certainly it is required to teach them the Bible, the ethical writings of our sages, ... so that the principles of our holy faith will be strong for them. Otherwise, Heaven forbid they may deviate entirely from the path of God, and violate all the precepts of the Torah (trans. Menachem Lorberbaum). (unnumbered)

With this, the original Talmudic prohibition of R. Eliezer regarding women learning Torah and Talmud – "Whoever teaches his daughter Torah is as if he teaches her *tiflut*"[1] (*Masechet Sotah* 21b) – became null and void. The Hafetz Chaim, as the major Jewish legislator of his time, had the authority to respond to changing social conditions with a new enactment regarding women's learning (see Baskin, 1991, 2002; Grossman, 2004; Kehat, 2008). However, even if practice has dramatically shifted, Jewish educators have to contend with the original exclusionary and degrading Talmudic text. What is our relationship to this text? Do we read it just to see how it has evolved? Do we neutralize it? Teach it in parts or as a live text that can still compel our students? Or, should it be deleted from the curriculum completely?

The feminist lens allows us to see inequality and power imbalances regarding women's access to the treasured texts of our tradition; but more importantly, it offers the opportunity to contextualize the prohibition of women's learning and to go beyond the problems that appear to be inherent in the texts. That is, feminist studies remind those of us in Jewish education that women's restricted access to the secrets of patriarchal cultures was rather widespread, if not universal. Jewish texts could be likened to "the magic flutes" in Papua New Guinea (see Herdt, 1994, 2002) from which women were barred. Jewish education can benefit as well from the feminist project that highlights the missing voice of women, the restricted access of women to aspects of the sacred and its implications for the entire culture.

A closer look at the original text of the prohibition of women studying Torah shows that it is striking that the Talmudic discussion takes place in the context of the "bitter waters" (*mei hamarim*), described in Numbers 5 verse 11–23. The "bitter waters" were a test administered to the *Sotah*, the woman suspected by her husband of committing adultery. The intellectual, spiritual, and psychological hoops that a modern reader of this text has to go through are challenging, and so there has been and continues to be a good deal of discussion about the nature of the bitter waters (see Bach, 1997). The ritual is discussed in the *Mishnah*:

> (*Mishnah Sotah 3:4* = b.Sotah 20a) "...When a man brings a wife to the gates and they give her water... She had scarcely finished drinking (the water of bitterness) when her face turns green, her eyes protrude and her veins swell and it is exclaimed, remove her that the temple court be not defiled. If she possessed a merit (a good deed), it causes the water to suspend its effect upon her. Some merit suspends the effect (*zechut tolah lah*) for one year, another for two years, and another for three years. Hence declared Ben Azai, a man is under the obligation to teach his daughter torah so that if she has to drink she may know that the merit suspends its effect. R. Eliezer says: whoever teaches his daughter torah teaches her *tiflut*. (see footnote 1)

R. Eliezer's prohibition is cited in a variety of places in *Halakhic* literature and became predominant practice. His position is that if a wife knows traditional texts, she will be able to know how to get around the law; she will betray her husband and at the same time do a good deed, so that the bitter waters will not take effect by making her "face turn green, eyes protrude, and veins swell." R. Eliezer's claims then, that knowing the law is power and if women knew the law, they would use their

---

[1] This is typically understood to mean "frivolousness" or "licentiousness."

power in a dishonest, distorted way. In other words, this Talmudic passage reflects both an exclusionary and distrustful attitude toward women.

And so, with his influential *pesak* (binding legal decision), the Hafetz Chaim opened the gateway to radical shifts in *Jewish* literacy. This went beyond offering women access to texts and had important implications to the traditional attitudes toward women in general and to gender relations in particular. The practical changes began in the establishment of the first Beis Ya'acov School for Girls in Kraków, Poland, in 1917, by Sarah Schneirer who trained women teachers and set up similar schools in other cities throughout Europe.[2] Although only biblical texts and non-legal portions of Talmud (*Aggadah*) were permissible to girls, many more texts, such as legal portions of the Talmud and codes of Jewish law were now accessible on a more widespread basis than ever before (Weissman, 1993, 1986–1987; Wolowelsky, 2001). This radical shift changed and continues to change the balance of power and the perception of women as dangerous.

Over the last 35 years, the revolution in girls' learning has included Talmud study available in virtually *all* Jewish schools outside of the ultra-Orthodox world. We recall sitting in the first *Gemara shiur* in the Bet Midrash of Stern College for Women at Yeshiva University in the mid-1970s when Rav Solovetchik, the most influential figure of modern orthodoxy of the twentieth century, came to teach, inaugurate, and authorize young women to learn Talmud. Most of us were intellectually and spiritually elated. We felt that something special had happened and that we were part of a transformation in Jewish history. It felt like issues of gender in Jewish education were laid to rest that day in Manhattan with a quiet but radical revolution.[3]

After the endorsements of girls' Talmud study by Solovetchik and the inclusion of women in Jewish education and public life in all other Jewish denominations, is there anything more to discuss regarding gender and Jewish education? A leading theorist in the field of gender and education, Elizabeth Ellsworth, asks if we have come so far, if a revolution has taken place, "why doesn't this feel empowering" (1994, p. 300). This question resonates with many feminists who are now critically analyzing whether equal access to what was formally prohibited is sufficient for a solution to problems of inequity or invisibility.

Gender Studies and Feminist Theory

Both *liberal* and *radical* feminist theory and practice offer important lenses to understand the challenge inherent in Jewish education and suggest possible avenues of re-engagement. These are no longer purely separate categories, of course, but they

---

[2]This movement continued after WWII. Elementary, high schools, and 1–3-year seminaries were established in the United States and Israel. The schools' primary purpose was, and to a large extent still is, to prepare students to be good Jews, mothers, and wives. Secular studies are secondary, though still important, particularly in cities where Jewish girls are expected to work outside the home as the primary bread-winners while their husbands learn Torah, especially Talmud, full time.

[3]Although passages of Talmud were taught earlier to girls at the Maimonides School in Boston, which R. Solovetchik headed, this shift at Stern and the beginning of the women's Beit Midrash offered full access to Talmudic learning.

are helpful in developing our research agendas. *Liberal feminism* focuses on gender equity and sameness. Historically, much of the justification for the discrimination against women was based upon the differences between men and women – and such differences were seen hierarchically, where women were inferior, thus justifying their exclusion. In response, liberal feminism advocated equal rights for women. This was based on the premise that men and women have the same capacities for rationality, and therefore deserve equal education and political rights (see Mill (1989/1859); Stanton [1895] 2003). This conversation began over 150 years ago and focused on sameness and not difference to prove that women deserved equal rights.

Liberal feminists worked on many educational fronts in the last 30 years. For example, they initiated major textbook reforms in an attempt to alter "the highly unequal representation of the sexes in text and illustrations, blatant sex stereotyping and generic use of male pronouns..." (Tyack & Hansot, 2002, p. 36). Few women were represented in history textbooks, because women were seen as irrelevant to traditional historical foci on politics, wars, and diplomacy. Even as textbooks began to include women, the numbers were comparatively small.

Radical feminism, a later development in feminist theory and practice that bloomed in the early 1970s, addresses matters beyond sameness and equality and asks are there actual differences between boys and girls, how so, what do these differences mean, and do they matter? Is there something essential about the differences between men and women or are differences primarily a consequence of cultural conditioning? By extension, radical feminists ask about the nature of culture, religion, society, and politics; in other words, is what we assume to be natural really so or is it the imposition of patriarchy? Radical feminists ask, if women join the public sphere, what if anything shifts and changes? Do women need to join at all or should they live and create in a "room of their own?" When women write their own stories, and when history becomes herstory, what is the nature of that story? Will they write as others before them or as Helene Cixous in her classic 1976 article puts it, "there is always within [woman] at least a little of that good mother's milk, she writes in white ink" (p. 312).

Radical feminism applied to Jewish education asks, then, how has Jewish education changed in the last 100 years because girls and women have been present? A radical perspective not only asserts that woman should have an equal place in the *Beit Midrash* and equal access to texts, but also asks about the *nature and substance* of Jewish education and teacher training, and which texts we choose to teach both boys and girls (El-Or, 2002; Ross, 2004). It asks whether or how Jewish education can be or has been *transformed* as it takes gender studies and feminist theory and sensibilities seriously.

In the case of Jewish education, radical feminist approaches can only be applied after aspects of liberal feminism, such as equal access, are already achieved. Radical feminism does not align itself with traditional views of difference which insist on a hierarchical placement of men and women where their differences are used to justify the non-equal status of women. Radical feminism celebrates a "Different Voice" that is neither superior nor inferior (Gilligan, 1982).

Canonical stories from Jewish tradition take on an interesting hue as we look through the lenses of radical and liberal feminism. Although most of these narrative texts appear descriptive, over many years, the stories have become prescriptive. Women, for example, according to the Bible, sewed for the tabernacle as nomads in the desert (Exodus 35:25). In Talmudic literature, this biblical description turns into what women *must* do; in fact, it is who they are and must not transgress beyond. They sew and produce cloth in the desert which then becomes a definitive prescription: *ein chochmat nashim elah b'pelech* (Women's wisdom is only in the spindle-whirl). This is their role and this is where they must stay – within limited opportunities and constricted space. Shalom Rosenblit (d. 2000), an Orthodox rabbi in Jerusalem, brought an interesting twist to this story when he founded a girls' school in the 1970s and cleverly called the school Pelech (spindle-whirl). It was the first school in the Orthodox sector in Jerusalem to teach girls Talmud.

The Importance of Unimportant People

Masechet Ketubot (62b–63a) offers a famous story of Akiva who at age 40 goes off to study Torah leaving his wife for a total of 24 years (Miller, 1976). During that time, he gathers thousands of disciples and he remains famous until this very day. On the face of it, this is a story of hope, about starting again – that one is never too old or too late for education. However, might this narrative also be prescriptive and foundational in terms of the hierarchy of Jewish values and the ideal ways in which men and women are to relate to each other? The Talmudic narrative states,

> R. Akiva was a shepherd for Kalba Savua whose daughter saw that he was modest and of fine character. She asked him: "if I became betrothed to you will you go to the academy and study Torah?" He ... went off to learn as his wife facilitated and enabled him. R. Akiva ... sat twelve years in the academy. When he returned he brought 12,000 students... As he approached his home he heard a certain old man saying to his wife "Until when will you lead the life of living widowhood alone and impoverished?" She answered him, "if he would listen to me he would sit in the academy another twelve years." He went away for another 12 years and when he returned again, he brought ... 24,000 students this time. His wife heard of his return ... her neighbors said to her: "borrow some suitable articles of clothing and dress yourself." She said to them: a righteous one knows his animal's soul." When she reached him, she fell on her face as she was kissing his foot his attendants pushed her away, R. Akiva said to them, "Leave her alone! The portion of torah that is mine and the portion that is yours belong to her."

While this text is used to teach that it is never too late to get an education, for the modern reader, it is embedded in a painful narrative because overt abandonment and impoverishment of a wife is not part of contemporary Jewish lesson plans, her encouragement, notwithstanding (see, for comparison, Erikson's critique of Ghandi's celibacy and its effect on his young wife). R. Akiva's wife's life is nearly invisible, while her long and significant sacrifice is prominent as an emblematic badge of the good wife. Is this kind of relationship a legacy we want to pass on to our students?

Rereading this story, we notice that it is part of a series with five other Talmudic stories about men who leave their wives and families to study Torah. In those narratives, however, tragedies befall one or another of the protagonists – the man dies, the wife dies, the scholar does not recognize his children, or his wife ends up barren. A classic feminist perspective asks, why has Akiva's story become privileged throughout Jewish history over all other narratives in this Talmudic unit? When we speak about Godly relationships between men and women, why are the other stories almost totally ignored (Rapoport, Penso, & Hartman Halbertal, 1996; Valler, 2000)?

Feminist studies contextualize these stories in the larger patriarchal society where women are taught to be self-sacrificial and that the highest place for them is in the role as enabler, even when it means loneliness and impoverishment for them. The point is that this is not necessarily a Jewish problem, it is a gender problem, generally about why we privilege the "self sacrificial voice" (Gilligan, 1982). Miller (1976) notes:

> Women are encouraged to transform their own needs. This often means that they fail, automatically and without perceiving it, to recognize their own needs as such. They come to see their needs as if they were identical to those of others, – usually men or children. (p. 19)

Prevailing Jewish hierarchies and family values are part of a larger patriarchal culture. A gendered reading of the Akiva story compels us to note the patriarchal system and to question the wisdom of valorizing individual learning at the expense of relationships. Feminist theory also helps us take a look at how women are educated to be the enablers. The social system generally and Jewish tradition in particular, privileged Akiva while the text in fact had many more stories about the grave costs of leaving the family to learn Torah. This story has not merely been passed down to us as one story among many, as one description of one of the great rabbis of our time, but it alone has become a prescription for the ideal man and his ideal relationship.

If this text is to continue to be taught in Jewish educational institutions, it is a good jumping-off point to discuss matters of relationship, mutual caring, domestic responsibilities, and gendered Jewish roles. We would be doing our children a favor if we taught this text not only as an inspirational story for life-long Jewish textual learning but also as a way to engage in a discussion of Jewish family values. It is especially important that it be taught in the broader context in which it is embedded.

Boys Reading Akiva and His Wife, Named "Rachel"

This pattern is common in world-cultures: For Siddhartha, the day his wife gives birth is the very moment he commits to leaving his family's bourgeois life to become an ascetic seeker. Similarly, the ideal western man, according to the psychologist Erikson's notion of the heroic autonomous man without peer, rides off into the sunset leaving family and other relationships behind.

Is the dichotomy of learning versus family necessary? If it is not, might teaching Akiva and Rachel in the usual way actually harm men and boys and not just pain girls and women? The ideal man who goes away to learn and the ideal self-sacrificial woman are dichotomous definitions and prescriptions that go far beyond the traditional feminist concerns that women's voices have virtually been ignored for centuries (Thorne, 1990).

When boys in school study the story of Akiva and Rachel, do they recognize themselves? Do they want to comply with this grand vision? When the ideal is to leave home, wife, and children, what does it do to them psychologically and spiritually? What parts of their *neshamot* (souls) do they have to cut off and leave behind? Even if the ideal is an aspiration and not a prescription in our tradition, it does guide gender roles and mediates conflict of values. This is one of the challenges of Jewish education; this particular Jewish "alpha man" is not only unattainable for most boys, it is also undesirable for most men and women (Kimmel, 2008; Gilmore, 1990).

To take gender and Jewish education seriously, we need to consider deconstructing its texts, and study the complexity of dichotomous characteristics. In many of the new multi-denominational and even in some modern orthodox schools in the United States, and in Jewish culture generally, we are seeing different kinds of acceptable and broader expressions of gender. While this Akiva story is well known and commonly taught, gender studies underscore the need to reconsider how to teach the variety of ways of being a Jewish man and a Jewish woman.

The Exceptional Woman in Biblical and Talmudic Legacy

Several stories from our tradition that include women are discussed at length by many feminist scholars of religion. We revisit these canonical narratives with an eye toward the educational challenges embedded in them. Liberal and radical feminist lenses shed light upon Jewish educational agendas and research questions. Miriam, Bruria, Hannah, Vashti, and Esther are well-known characters among educated Jews and each story highlights particular educational challenges.

Miriam

Miriam is one of the few named central female figures in the Bible, equated in Micah 6:4 with her more famous brothers: "And I sent before you Moses, Aaron, and Miriam." In Exodus 15:20, she is explicitly called a prophetess, and she is highlighted, albeit negatively, in the story in Numbers 12, where along with Aaron she speaks critically of Moses, and she (alone) is punished with "leprosy."[4] The nation refuses to de-camp until she recovers. Quite exceptionally for a female figure, even her death and burial are recorded (Numbers 20:1).

Given her prominence in the Bible, it is not surprising that Miriam was one of the first female biblical figures claimed by Jewish feminists. In modern Jewish education and holiday celebration, she has become the focal point of a new ritual.

---

[4] Trible comments poetically on Miriam's leprosy: "a searing emotion gets a scarred body," punished by God: "Red hot anger becomes a cold white disease."

Many add a Miriam's cup of wine to the *Seder* table at Passover, paralleling the more traditional cup of Elijah.

The recovery of Miriam as an important biblical figure represents the influence of liberal feminism on Judaism, including Jewish education, as it highlights her as a prophetess, equal to her brother Aaron. The radical feminist approach goes further, most dramatically represented by Phyllis Trible, one of the founders of modern feminist biblical hermeneutics. For Trible, Miriam is much more than a central biblical figure. Trible adduces important evidence that the Song of the Sea (Exodus 15:1) attributed to "Moses and the Israelites" was originally Miriam's song. Over time, Miriam's words were put into the mouth of Moses, relegating Miriam to a "footnote" at the end of the chapter. From the perspective of gendered biblical hermeneutics, this may be an example of how a patriarchal culture rewrites its stories, marginalizes its women, and gives men credit for important activities of women.

Trible's analysis is compatible with the more traditional liberal feminist analysis, which emphasizes that women too were prophets and leaders in antiquity. But as a radical feminist, she ventures beyond this observation. Trible claims that Miriam, in her maternal role, was *different* from male leaders.

Beyond Miriam's status as prophetess and poetess, Trible celebrates Miriam's maternal contribution to the very foundation of Judaism. After all, Moses' sister plays a central role in saving him from death (Exodus 2:7). From her Christian perspective, Trible connects the birthing of the Jewish people to the central role that the two later Miriams, namely the two Marys, play in the birth of Christianity (the one who gave birth to Jesus and Mary Magdalena who saw him rise). Thus, Miriam is a progenitor of religions, a legacy that Trible insists must be reclaimed (Trible, 1994).

When we strip Miriam of likely ownership of the composition of the Song of the Sea, we give the singing and recitation of poetry rights to someone who stutters, her brother Moses. If we give away her gifts to someone else, then in fact, we lose them. What happens to Jewish tradition when we lose women's song and generativity as part of its spirit? What happens when the tradition attributes to men what originally belonged to a woman?

Bruria

In the Talmud, Bruria is admired as a scholar. The rabbis admire her for her competence, and she becomes an example of superior knowledge and ability (See Pesachim 62b). This recognition challenges Talmudic norms regarding a woman's place.

In the next two Talmudic anecdotes, Bruria meets up with a rabbi and student in the Beit Midrash and chides them, perhaps even with a bit of humor, cleverness, and irony (*Erubin* 53b–54a):

> R. Jose the Galilean was once on a journey when he met Beruriah. "By what road," he asked her, "do we go to Lydda?"

> "Foolish Galilean", she replied did not the Sages say this: "Engage not much in talk with women? You should have asked: 'By which to Lydda?!'
> Bruria once discovered a student learning and mumbling "in an undertone." (54a) Rebuking him (literally *Batsha bei:* kicked him), she exclaimed: "Is it not written, *Ordered in all things, and sure*: If it is *ordered* in your two hundred and forty eight limbs it will be *sure*, otherwise it will not be sure?"

Bruria is rebuking the student for studying in the disembodied way of the talking heads. She wants him to learn with his whole body and whole being.

In *Berachot* 9b-10, another story:

> ... Some highwaymen ... caused him a great deal of trouble. R. Meir ... prayed that they should die. His wife Bruria said to him: 'How do you make out (that such a prayer should be permitted)? Because it is written Let *khata'im* (sins) cease? Is it written *khotím* (sinners)? It is written *khata'im*! Further look at the verse: and let the wicked men be no more, since the sins will cease, there will be no more wicked men! Rather pray for them that they should repent, and there will be no wickedness.' He did pray for them and they repented."

In these Talmudic stories, we do not hear any echoes of the self-sacrificing archetypal woman, but rather of a woman (with a name!) who is famous for her erudition and scholarship. Does this text come to teach us that there is more than one perspective in Jewish tradition? With this, can our students connect to a multi-layered tradition and find themselves within the vast sea of tradition, even while some voices have been louder than others over the centuries?

Historically, women are absent as Torah scholars; however, there were few exceptions. How do we teach the exceptions to the rule? Is Bruria the exception to the rule, to reinforce the rule, or is her legacy to teach the possibility of equality? Or, was the tradition actually less monolithic than later generations presume (see Boyarin, 1993)? To seek subtle undercurrents and shifts in the tradition, feminist scholars often find marginal stories and hushed voices and give them a place of honor or in Bell Hooks (2000) terms, bring these stories and their teachings "From Margin to Center."

From a radical feminist perspective, we listen to Bruria's unique voice as cultural critic not only as an exceptional example of erudition. She admonishes the rabbi, the student, and her husband. She critiques disembodied learning and her husband's desire for others' demise rather than praying for them to repent. Bruria teaches us another way to act in the world.

The educational possibilities in Bruria stories are of course about women's equal participation in Jewish life with equal voice and power; but perhaps more to the transformative point, Bruria offers a model that is a radical critique of traditional ways of studying and behaving. It is significant that it is the Talmud itself that brings a woman – an outsider – to make this possible.

Who are Esther and Vashti?

Megillat Esther [The Scroll of Esther] is one of two biblical books named after a woman and depicts two exceptional women, Esther and Vashti. Although a great deal has been written about this story, there has been no serious treatment of the curricular implications for how the story might be taught through a gendered lens.

There are two sharply contrasting responses to the Purim story. It is still common to see young girls, year after year, dressed up as their heroine, Queen Esther, the winner of the Persian beauty contest, in their Barbie-like costumes. It is also now common for Vashti to be the new feminist heroine – the first of the "Just say no" Jewish leaders. In that frame, Esther is typically deprecated as the "true" hero is elevated. Vashti, in this new scenario, is the good woman concerned about her dignity and able to make independent strong decisions, while Esther is a pawn in the hands of kings and their men.

Depicting Esther and Vashti as dichotomous characters is simplistic and ultimately not educationally helpful. Truly, there is a great deal of ambiguity in both of these figures, and *Megillat Esther* can be taught by highlighting the complexity of the story in a way that is surprisingly relevant to modern life.

Megillat Esther is very concise concerning Vashti; it simply notes the royal degree, her refusal, and the king's anger (1:11–12):

> To bring Queen Vashti before the king wearing a royal diadem, to display her beauty to the peoples and the officials; for she was a beautiful woman. But Queen Vashti refused to come at the king's command conveyed by the eunuchs. The king was greatly incensed, and his fury burned within him.

Perhaps Vashti personifies the ultimate feminist who in the face of the humiliation of unjust requests chooses to maintain her dignity and refuses to succumb to the objectifying, offensive whims of the king. In the face of tyranny and humiliation to her body, she stands up and faces the consequences. She knows that conversation is not possible and so just says NO. Fully aware of the repercussions of being exiled or whatever else is in store for female insubordination, she exits (see Gilligan et al., 1988).

As is their hermeneutical practice, the rabbis filled in this terse account in a variety of ways. Typically they assumed that the text meant that Vashti should appear wearing a "royal diadem" and nothing else. But their elaboration of the text goes even further as they explore why Vashti might not want to appear naked. For example, in the Babylonian Talmud, Megillah 12b, we read:

> And Queen Vashti refused.... What is the reason she did not appear when Achashverosh ordered her to appear naked? R. Yose bar Chanina said this teaches that she broke out in leprosy, so she did not want to appear naked, In a *baraisa*, a different reason why she did not want to appear naked was taught – the angel Gavriel came and made her grow a tail....

This is quite a remarkable elaboration on the text. While *Megillat Esther* depicts Vashti as simply refusing, the rabbis suggest that she refused because she was embarrassed about her body; something happened to her that day, otherwise of course she would have been happy to come naked. In this rabbinic reading, there is no dignity in Vashti. She does not embody a heroic stance against objectification, but is a narcissistic woman having a bad hair day.

Stripping Vashti of her dignity, the rabbis misread the original text itself, which continues with a royal decree (1:20) that explains her banishment so that "all wives will treat their husbands with respect." In other words, the text itself understands that Vashti's punishment for her disobedience by her husband, the King, is in order to prevent other women from refusing their husbands' commands.

Esther, on the other hand, is depicted in the Megillah as doing what women are thought of as doing – getting what she wants by using her body, her beauty, her sexuality. She uses all the "sneaky" ways women employ. It appears *as if* Esther succumbs to what is thought of as women's ways, but we would like to suggest otherwise. It may seem like a stretch in a book that is populated with caricatures of women and men who seem to do everything that goes bad between the sexes, but Esther models how a heroine acts when those dependent upon her are in dire circumstances.

Esther carries the fate of the Jewish people on her shoulders – no, in her entire body. She did not have the choice that Vashti had to exit and suffer individual consequences, because Esther had a sense of responsibility for others. She acted in the *only* ways that were available to her as many women before her – through her body, through the "woman's way." It helps to enlist feminist psychology's critique of traditional psychology regarding the latter's inability to distinguish between the way women acted in context and the essence of womanhood; that is, confusing behavior produced by the limited range of possibilities in a patriarchy, with essential character traits.

Are women by nature dependent or are they dependent because punishment for independence is severe?[5] Are women devious by nature? If they have no straightforward power, they must do things in crooked ways. The Purim story, educationally, opens up rich opportunities in the classroom to discuss stereotypes of many disempowered groups who must use non-traditional methods – the only methods available to them – to survive, and are then accused of being "devious."

In other words, it is possible to teach Esther in her context. Imagining that she should have said "no" (like Vashti) to Mordecai's request because she did not want to be humiliated is noble on the one hand, but does not recognize that she would then have abdicated her responsibility to the community. This suggests that though we may celebrate Vashti, she cannot be our only model. She reflects one positive way of being, but we must not celebrate her at the expense of Esther, who did what all traditional women do when the stakes are so high.

The nature of women is not to be prostitutes; but, heroic women, when faced with the suffering of family and community, will do almost anything, even *play* the prostitute. In this way, we do not see Esther through the male gaze; we do not view her as the idealized woman whom we should aspire to emulate; nor do we look down upon her from our place of privilege. When she cannot speak directly, she must act in the ways that are available to her, like all acts of subversion under ethnic or religious persecution (see Strauss, 1988). The challenge for Esther was how to

---

[5]Likewise, Freud says women overvalue love, but as feminist scholar Karen Horney answers that it is not love they overvalue; it is the prizes from love they need. If women were not able to work, have access to sexual satisfaction or protection *except* in the framework of marriage, then they would put a lot of emphasis on marriage.

save her people. The means by which she achieved this goal – through prostitution of her body – is the classroom conversation we should have with modern Jewish students, even though the story has been sanitized and therefore a woman's heroism made invisible, over time.

Beginning with the *Septuagint*, the Greek translation of the Bible, and in much of rabbinic commentary, the image of Esther is cleaned up. In the Greek Esther, Addition C puts the following into Esther's mouth:

> (16) You know my necessity–that I abhor the sign of my proud position, which is upon my head on days when I appear in public. I abhor it like a filthy rag, and I do not wear it on the days when I am at leisure (17). And your servant has not eaten at Haman's table, and I have not honored the king's feast or drunk the wine of libations.

We do not need to whitewash Esther and to make believe that she is the perfect beauty queen. We must not foster what traditional psychologists or the rabbis did, and claim that what women did was a reflection of their deepest essence. Instead, we must simultaneously look, name, and shudder as we see what behavior they had to choose and we also must be in awe and in gratitude to Esther and to all the brave women who came before us, to our grandmothers, and great-grandmothers who did not have the luxury to "exit," but stayed in horrific situations to nourish and protect others. These are deeply important modern lesson plans.

The didactic strength of *Megillat Esther* comes from the manner in which it depicts gender stereotypes gone amok, since its men too are depicted stereotypically: the caricatured King acts upon his sexual desires; Haman needs all to admire and exalt him; and Mordechai sends the woman to do his work. This story is a particularly good source for exploring issues of gender and relationship, leadership and gender stereotypes, and challenges educators to grapple with powerful covert teachings and dynamics.

Hannah

In the Talmud, Hannah's prayer serves as the very basis for the traditional prayers that we pray today. Tractate Berachot 31a states:

> How many important laws can be learned from these verses relating to Hannah? Hannah, she was speaking in her heart, from here we learn that one who prays must direct his heart towards God; only her lips moved, from here we derive that that one who prays must pronounce the words with his lips . . . . . .

The rabbis study and endorse Hannah's prayer for inspiration, guidance, and substance. They analyze every word of her prayer, developing over time multiple laws concerning prayer. Many people pray in the Bible and the rabbis mention them elsewhere in the Talmud as well, but it is very striking that Hannah's prayer is emblematic. Yet, the rabbis of this same sacred text, the Talmud, do not allow women to be included in a quorum, in the community of prayer. If Hannah showed up today, she would not be permitted to be part of a minyan in Orthodox synagogues or schools. This absurdity is historically important and still exists today. An

Orthodox rabbi, in a famous article forbidding women's prayer groups used Hannah as the symbol of the ultimate praying individual (Twersky, 1998). How can Hannah's prayer be the archetype we hold up and honor in traditional Judaism, and yet as a woman she cannot be part of the religious ritual community?

Hannah brings to mind Daphne Hampson (1990), a former Christian theologian who taught theology to men training for the priesthood at an Anglican seminary for 10 years. When she asked to be ordained, she was constantly rebuffed and she left Christianity because of this glaring inequity. Of course, some Jewish denominations fully include Hannah's legacy in their synagogues and would cherish her role as a prayer leader.

The issue in Jewish education from a liberal feminist perspective, however, is broader than who is included in a *minyan* (prayer quorum) and who is not. This matter is not only related to the Orthodox community, but also to the liberal Jewish community that does include "Hannah" in prayer. This is so because Jewish educators have to make sense of a religious mindset that can simultaneously celebrate and marginalize women. In underscoring this tension, we are assuming that Jewish education is not merely studying our past as a history of ideas, namely as how rabbinic patriarchy thought then, but also, as how it informs the present. Our texts speak to us about whether there are values to glean from our tradition and not only whether we corrected the past.

After the Talmudic rabbis analyze every word and action relating to Hannah's prayer, they continue adding words to her biblical prayer:

> "From all the legions upon legions of creatures that You have created in Your universe, is it difficult in Your eyes to grant me one son?".... She goes on and pleads: "Master of the Universe Of all that You created in a woman, You did not create a single thing for naught you created eyes to see.... and breasts with which to nurse – These breasts that you have placed upon my heart what are they for? Are they not to nurse with? Grant me a child that I may nurse with them..." (Berachot 31b)

The rabbis understand Hannah's prayer, directly connected to her inability to give birth, as an expression of her womanhood. Hannah appeals to God's powers in creation, in divine wisdom, and feels that her very being is not fully expressed. Why would God create her as a woman and not enable her to be a mother? Moreover, the two men in Hannah's life did not understand her. Her husband thinks he is as good as 10 children (1 Samuel 1:8), and believes that his presence is a comfort to her; he does not understand the despair and betrayal she feels in a body that God gave her. Eli, the priest, in the face of her mumbling cannot see the intense religious passion of a woman, and relegates it to madness; he is sure she is a drunkard. What is it that the men in her life were not getting? What is the story telling us?

Liberal feminists have helped recover the story of Hannah and have raised the important issue of the place of woman in prayer. Radical feminists ask in addition: What is the significance of being in a particular body? Can men understand women's way of being? By enhancing Hannah's position, making her the prototype for Jewish prayer, the Talmudic rabbis who celebrate and honor her by adding to her *tefillah* seem to be beginning to heal the misunderstanding between the genders that appears glaring in the biblical story (see Adler, 1998; Plaskow, 1990). This can be a powerfully didactic story for Jewish educators to discuss inclusion and exclusion, compassionate listening to another in pain, non-standard ways of divine worship, and betrayal of one's deepest desires in the context of a religious embrace.

Conclusion

We hope it is clear that the challenges of gender and Jewish education go beyond the following famous poem that provides an epigram for many chapters on gender and education.

> And they shall beat their pots and pans into printing presses,
> And weave their cloth into protest banners,
> Nations of women shall lift up their voices with other women,
> Neither shall they accept discrimination anymore.
> Mary Chagnon, quoted in Sandler (2002, p. 11)

The lenses of liberal and radical feminism are helpful methodological tools for mapping research agendas in gender and Jewish education. They are not, of course, the only possible theoretical frameworks. In her "Introduction" to *The Education Feminism Reader,* Linda Stone (1994) also uses educational, intellectual, and political contexts to look at gender and education. These categories could enhance a study of gender and Jewish education, raising provocative questions for further inquiry.

The *educational context* focuses on "instruction and curriculum, classroom and schooling organization, the relationships of teachers, students, parents and the larger community." (p. 3) For Jewish educators, some questions are related to the multiple goals of Jewish education. Who *is* the educated Jewish man or woman? What should they know? Do boys and girls have an equal range of educational opportunities that feed into Jewish life choices and careers? Is one of the goals of Jewish education to explore hidden voices or to create a gender-neutral education, as much as possible? Furthermore, education is a gendered field and teachers are gendered. How do teachers, as agents of Jewish socialization mediate some of the harsh texts and male-centered stories, and into what sort of family and community are they socializing our children?

In the *political context,* Stone focuses primarily on the agenda of school reform and the leadership that authorizes it. For our purposes here, the dimension of religious leadership and authority is important; that is, who makes the decisions and how? The research questions Jewish educators can ask in this context are: what is the *nature* of citizenship in the Jewish community? Who may lead and how? Who defines who is in and who is out and does the community change with different membership? Are men and women authorized equally to facilitate reform?

Today's *intellectual milieu* includes the effect of post-modernism on Jewish life and academic research. Stone claims that:

> Whatever its label, all agree that the modern search for certainty is over. This change is recognized in the spate of "postisms" often under the broad umbrella called post-modernism. Intellectually, postmodern theorization exhibits the tentativeness and ambiguity of the age,

> the giving up of certainty that is central to the period changes the ways that science and knowledge and their discourse practices are undertaken and considered... Knowledge to most is becoming knowledges. (Stone, 1994, p. 4)

For Jewish education, in the context of diversity, we do not have an agreed upon singular truth theologically, historically, or *halakhically*, and we do not even have a definitive answer to the "who is a Jew" question. Post-modern perspectives engage the meaning of Jewish education to individual, communal, and national identities in flux.

These permeable boundaries of identity have enabled the establishment of "alternative *yeshivot*" that emphasizes the arts or nature with expanding notions of gender, as well as Jewish identity. How does this square up with traditional texts and prescribed roles? How are altered power relationships in the variety of Jewish educational settings reflected in the curriculum explicitly? Even the definitions of who is a boy and who is a girl are now part of public inquiry.

If in the past, a definition of manhood was one who had access to special knowledge, what happens when everyone has access to all forms of study and ways of being? What happens to Jewish boys when text study is no longer the defining claim to power and prestige for the 'alpha Jewish man'? How can a boy or man be involved in Jewish life when he does not come close to identifying with this particular type of man? Moreover, where are the rest of the boys who are not in the *Beit Midrash* (or the soccer field)? Do we have questions to ask of the other boys' interests and achievements, both actual and perceived? Who is this new Jewish man?

The field of gender and Jewish education is much larger and more complex than developing gender-sensitive hermeneutics. The educational challenges of gender and Jewish education are more than an intellectual challenge in how to teach text with gender neutrality or as in some schools, in not teaching problematic texts at all. Others say, we should teach them with subversion and resistance but how *do* we teach resistance of sacred texts?

Orthodoxy is often criticized because of the inequality of what boys and girls learn. This chapter attempted to go beyond inequality and underscore the challenge of why "this (*education*) still doesn't feel so good" in all of the Jewish denominations. The issue is much larger than equal access when we take a good look and ask equal access to *what*?

The discussion of gender and Jewish education takes place within the context of a post-modern world still steeped in tradition. The field of gender and education generally sensitizes us to the fact that issues of gender are still very much alive. Even though there is greater equality – such as new interpretation of texts, women's Midrash, women rabbis, and heads of schools – our work continues to uncover the covert messages and covert imbalances of power.

Feminism humanizes and makes it possible to stay in our tradition because we know that the problems of inequality and gender-stereotyping can follow us around in many places, having nothing whatever to do with Rabbinic Judaism. The study of gender and Jewish education helps us re-engage and re-negotiate without an illusion that the rest of the liberal world has given us definitive answers to these issues. This contextualization, however, does not absolve us from continuing to re-visit and re-mediate the current challenges within the Jewish educational world. As Tractate Avot 2:21 famously notes: "It is not your responsibility to complete the work, nor are you exempt from engaging in it."

> Biblical quotations generally follow Jewish Publication Society, Tanakh. Talmudic translations (including Mishnah) generally follow *The Schottenstein Talmud Bavli*.
> Apocrypha is quoted from the New Revised Standard Version.

References

Adler, R. (1998). *Engendering Judaism: An inclusive theology and ethics*. Philadelphia: Jewish Publication Society.
Bach, A. (1997). *Women in the Hebrew Bible: A reader*. New York: Routledge.
Bailey, S. (2002). Forward. In S. Bailey (Ed.), *Gender in education (*pp. xxi–xxiv). San Francisco: Jossey-Bass.
Baskin, J. (Ed.) (1991). *Jewish women in historical perspective*. Detroit, MI: Wayne State.
Baskin, J. (2002). *Midrashic women: Formations of the feminine in rabbinic literature*. Hanover, MD: Brandeis University Press.
Boyarin, D. (1993). *Carnal Israel: Reading sex in talmudic culture*. Berkeley, CA: University of California Press.
Cixous, H. (1976). The laugh of the Medusa. *Signs, 1*(4), 875–893.
El-Or, T. (2002). *Next year I will know more: literacy and identity among young Orthodox women in Israel*. Trans. by Haim Watzman. Detroit, MI: Wayne State University Press.
Ellsworth, E. (1994). Why doesn't this feel empowering? Working through the repressive myths of critical pedagogy. In L. Stone (Ed.), *The education feminism reader*. New York: Routledge.
Gilligan, C. (1982). *In a different voice: Psychological theory and women's development*. Cambridge: Harvard University Press.
Gilligan, C. (1988). Exit-voice dilemmas in adolescent development. In C. Gilligan, et al. (Eds.), *Mapping the moral domain*. Cambridge: Harvard University Press.
Gilmore, D. (1990). *Manhood in the making: Cultural conceptions of masculinity*. New Haven, CT: Yale University Press.
Grossman, A. (2004). *Pious and rebellious: Jewish women in medieval Europe*. Lebanon, NH: Brandeis University Press.
Hampson, D. (1990). *Theology and feminism*. Cambridge: Blackwell.
Herdt, G. (1994). *Guardians of the Flutes, Vol. 1, Idioms of Masculinity*, Chicago, IL: The University of Chicago Press.
Herdt, G. (2002). *The Sambia: Ritual and gender in New Guinea*. New York: Holt, Rinehart and Winston.
Hooks, B. (2000). *Feminist theory: From margin to center*. Cambridge, MA: South End Press.
Kehat, H. (2008). *Jewish education of women: The idea and its meaning*. Ramat Gan: Bar-Ilan (Hebrew).
Mill, J. S. (1989/1859). In S. Colini (Ed.), *On liberty and other essays*. Cambridge: Cambridge University Press.
Miller, J. B. (1976). *Toward a new psychology of women* (2nd ed.). Boston: Beacon.
Plaskow, J. (1990). *Standing again at Sinai: Judaism from a feminist perspective*. San Francisco: Harper & Row.
Rapoport, T., Penso, A., & Hartman Halbertal, T. (1996). The artistic selfhood of adolescent girls: Two improvisations of cultural scripts. *Journal of Contemporary Ethnography, 24*, 438–461.
Rich, A. (1986). *Blood, bread, and poetry: Selected prose 1979–1985*. New York: Norton.
Ross, T. (2004). *Expanding the palace of Torah*. Waltham, Ma: Brandeis University Press.

Sandler, R. R. (2002). "Too strong for a woman" – The five words that created Title IX. In *The Jossey-Bass reader on gender in education* (pp. 2–11). San Francisco: Jossey-Bass.

Stampfer, S. (2007). How Jewish society adapted to change in male/female relationships in 19th/early 20th century Eastern Europe. In R. Blau (Ed.), *Gender relationships in marriage and out* (pp. 64–83). New York: Yeshiva University.

Stanton, E. C. (1993/1895). *The woman's Bible: A classic feminist perspective*. Boston: Northeastern University Press.

Stone, L. (1994). Introducing education feminism. In L. Stone (Ed.), *The education feminism reader*. New York: Routledge.

Strauss, L. (1988). *Persecution and the art of writing*. Chicago: University of Chicago.

Thorne, B. (1990). Children and gender constructions of difference. In D. L. Rhode (Ed.), *Theoretical perspectives on sexual difference*. New Haven, CT: Yale university press.

Trible, P. (1994). Bringing miriam out of the shadows. In A. Brenner (Ed.), *A feminist companion to Exodus to Deuteronomy* (pp. 166–186). Sheffield: Sheffield Academic Press.

Twersky, M. (1998). Halakchic values and halakchic decisions: Rav Soloveitchik's pesak regarding women's prayer groups. *Tradition, 32*(3), 5–17.

Tyack, D., & Hansot, E. (2002). Feminists discover the hidden injuries of coeducation. In *The Jossey-Bass reader on gender in education* (pp. 12–28). San Francisco: Jossey-Bass.

Valler, S. (2000). *Women in Jewish society: In the Talmudic period*. Tel Aviv: Hakibbutz Hameuchad (Hebrew).

Weissman, D. (1986–1987). Education of Jewish Women. In *Encyclopedia Judaica Yearbook*, pp. 186–187, Jerusalem: Keter, pp. 29–36.

Weissman, D. (1993). Education of religious girls in Jerusalem during the period of British rule: The crystallization and institutionalization of five educational ideologies. Hebrew Univ. Ph.D. dissertation (Hebrew).

Wolowelsky, J. B. (2001). *Women and the study of Torah: Essays from the pages of tradition*. Hoboken, NJ: Ktav.

Historiography of American Jewish Education: A Case for Guarded Optimism

Jonathan Krasner

In his 1998 article, "American Jewish Education in Historical Perspective," historian Jonathan Sarna lamented the dearth of high-caliber scholarship on the history of American Jewish education. He characterized the bulk of existing works as "parochial and narrowly conceived studies, long on facts and short on analysis" (1998, p. 8). Sarna was hardly alone in his assessment (see, for example, Jacobs, B.M., 2005). Nor was his negative appraisal the result of a contemporary academic sensibility. Thirty years earlier, Lloyd Gartner categorically concluded, in his landmark *Jewish Education in the United States: A Documentary History*, that "What has been written on the history of American Jewish education is largely inadequate." Gartner included a seven-page bibliography at the end of the book's introduction, but observed that "less than half the historical works listed here are good." He included a plea for "serious research, within the double framework of American and Jewish educational history" (1969, pp. 33–40).

That the state of the field has arguably changed so little since Gartner wrote in the late 1960s calls into question the value of another survey barely a decade after Sarna's appraisal. Indeed, if my purpose here was primarily to add my voice to the chorus, there would be little value added. To be sure, I share my colleagues' dim assessment. And yet, a survey of recent scholarship provides reason for cautious optimism. While more than a few studies continue to be penned by educational researchers with little training in historical methodology and suffer from what B. M. Jacobs referred to as a "dilettantish" quality (2005, p. 42), a growing number of articles and monographs defy this categorization. They are being written by a small but growing coterie of younger specialists in Jewish educational history as well as an increasing number of generalist American Jewish historians and social scientists, who are studying the development of Jewish education as one of many facets of American Jewish culture and society. Equally noteworthy is the widening focus of these studies to include heretofore neglected or underemployed interpretive lenses and lines of inquiry. The most significant of these engage in educational

J. Krasner (✉)
Hebrew Union College, New York, NY, USA
e-mail: jkrasner@huc.edu

history as a means of exploring the evolution of American Jewish identity and the American Jewish condition.

Historiography as a Tool in the Professionalization of Jewish Education: The Early Pattern of American Jewish Educational History

As Gartner recognized, the deficient quality of American Jewish educational historiography should be understood as a function of a dynamic that similarly diminished the general field of American educational history. According to critics like Bernard Bailyn (1960), American educational historiography suffered from a host of abuses. Most could be traced to the tendency to write educational history from a position of defense, motivated by a desire to gain professional legitimacy.

Tasked with an essentially apologetic errand, the narrative that these writers of educational history fashioned became essential in investing educators with a nobility of purpose. With the stakes so high, educationalists were loath to leave this project in the hands of professional historians. Bailyn mercilessly lampooned these "educational missionaries," who "with great virtuosity... drew up what became the patristic literature of a powerful academic ecclesia" (1960, p. 8). In his view they were guilty of a multiplicity of sins. In particular, they could not resist the urge to read present interests and meanings into the past. As a result, their work was laced with anachronisms.

Taking the writing of history largely out of the hands of historians also served to isolate the historiography of American education from the wider field of American history. Moreover, the overriding concern with locating antecedents to contemporary systems and institutions caused the writers to define their subject narrowly. In particular, they made little distinction between schooling and education, devoting their attention almost exclusively to formal settings. The overriding subject of these histories was the triumph of the public school system. Education, as defined by Bailyn, involved "the entire process by which a culture transmits itself across generations," and was not merely within the purview of schools (1960, p. 14).

The transition from antiquarian musings to bona fide educational history in Jewish education may be traced to the 1918 publication of Alexander Dushkin's Columbia University Teachers College doctoral dissertation *Jewish Education in New York City*, by the New York Bureau of Jewish Education. Primarily devoted to a survey of the contemporary educational scene, the volume also included an almost 150-page historical study based almost exclusively on primary sources. Even today, Dushkin's work stands out for its thoroughness. Both sections remain invaluable sources of data for contemporary historians. Yet perusing the historical chapters brings to mind Bailyn's criticism of the educational history of his day: "The facts, or at least a great quantity of them are there, but they lie inert, they form no significant pattern" (1960, p. 4).

In one respect, this criticism is unjust, as the narrative is propelled by an unambiguous teleology, namely, the celebration of the Bureau and its indefatigable director, Samson Benderly. Jewish education prior to 1881 is treated as mere prelude to the proliferation of educational institutions of varying configurations and ideological loyalties during the period of great Eastern European Jewish migration. To the extent that Dushkin's narrative exhibits a modicum of drama, it comes with the Bureau's effort to professionalize the educational field and to organize out of the prevailing chaos a modernized supplementary school system. "The year 1910 marks the beginning of a new era in Jewish education in New York City," Dushkin declared. "The 8 years which followed were more productive in the creation of new schools, and in the improvement and coordination of old ones, than any previous period in the Jewish educational history of New York" (1918, p. 90).

Dushkin's narrative followed an outline suggested by Mordecai Kaplan and Bernard Cronson's 1909 report on the state of Jewish education in New York City, which originally recommended the Bureau's establishment as an arm of the New York *Kehillah*, a communal self-governing body that operated from 1909 until shortly after World War I. Kaplan and Cronson surveyed the range of Jewish educational agencies, highlighting the poor conditions and low quality of education that prevailed in most schools. They noted the lack of a standardized curriculum, a mechanism for teacher quality control or a coordinated system of organization and financing, and successfully urged the *Kehillah* to step into the vacuum (Kaplan and Cronson, 1949, pp. 113–116). Dushkin's history reads as a vindication of *Kehillah*'s efforts.

As a member of the Bureau's staff and a protégé of its director, Dushkin was hardly a disinterested party to the events about which he was writing. Just as contemporaneous general educators made the ascendancy of public education their central theme, so, too, did the writers of American Jewish educational history craft a narrative that climaxed with the triumph of the principle of community responsibility for Jewish education as epitomized by the proliferation of a federation-supported network of central educational agencies and the growth of the communal Talmud Torahs.

Like their counterparts in general education, Dushkin and his colleagues were also heavily invested in endowing their traditionally disparaged field with an air of legitimacy. Their strategy involved creating as much distance as possible between themselves and the teachers and institutions outside of the Bureau's orbit. The traditional *khayder*, the private one-room school, was the subject of especial disparagement, in part because it exemplified the immigrant educational mindset and defied efforts at standardization, but also because it provided the most serious competition to the communal Talmud Torah schools that the Bureau co-opted. The itinerant teachers who operated these establishments were a favorite object of ridicule by progressive and Hebraist teachers alike.

Dushkin's gaze was fixed almost exclusively on formal institutional settings, thereby reducing education to schooling. Interestingly, a theoretical chapter at the beginning of the book hinted at a more expansive view. He offered an operating definition of American Jewish education as "the process of enriching the personality of American Jewish children, by transmitting to them the cultural heritage of the Jews, and by training them to share in the experiences of the Jewish people, both past and present," and characterized it as a process of "mental and social adjustment" (p. 26). Yet even in this chapter he was quick to equate social attitudes with systems. To his credit, however, Dushkin cast a wide net in his volume. He considered a broad range of educational institutions, venturing into the fields of pre-school and higher education, and even flirting with informal education in his discussion of the Bureau's extension activities. He provided relatively judicious if comparatively perfunctory treatment of the Yiddish folk schools and mostly Reform Sunday schools, although he personally had little use for either institution as safeguards of Jewish continuity.

Along with Emanuel Gamoran's erudite 1924 two-volume history of Jewish education in Eastern Europe and North America, *Changing Conceptions in Jewish Education*, Dushkin's study set the pattern for a generation of Jewish educational historiography. As Gartner intimated, much of it was "pedestrian," expedient, and rarely rose to the level of these two classic works. Weaknesses became magnified, including the lack of a comparative frame of reference and the relative inattention to schools that did not share a cultural Zionist orientation. Over time, the master narrative was sharpened, reaching its apogee in the later historical essays of Leo Honor, an early disciple of pioneering Jewish educator Samson Benderly, and Judah Pilch's 1969 edited volume *A History of Jewish Education in the United States*.

Although both men were generally careful, they were not beyond the occasional resort to hyperbole in the interests of heightening the drama of their narratives. In one memorable example, from a 1952 article on elementary education, Honor asserted that "the negative and harmful influences" of the watered-down Sunday schools and the backward-looking *khaydarim* provoked "a hue and cry… in one community after another during the first decade of the twentieth century, and a growing realization developed that something must be done to put an end to this intolerable condition" (Gannes, 1965, pp. 60–61). In fact, documentary evidence suggests that to the extent that immigrant dissatisfaction with the state of Jewish education existed, few were sufficiently exercised by prevailing conditions to take any action. In New York, the impetus for reform came largely from the professionals, who had a difficult time winning support from the masses, and was financed by the wealthy as a means of social control and amelioration (Goren, 1970). As for the Sunday schools, while their lamentable state became a recurring subject of discussion at the annual conventions of the Central Conference of American Rabbis, efforts at intensification and standardization were generally unsuccessful (Marcus, 1993, pp. 594–611).

In the 1940s and 1950s the outlines of a counter-narrative began to congeal, as reflected in the writings of Teachers Institute professor and textbook author Zevi Scharfstein, who portrayed Benderly and his followers as unnecessarily quick to make concessions to the dominant culture. As a result of a willingness to compromise their standards and dilute their educational program they became inadvertent agents of a rarefied American Jewish culture, he argued (1960–1965; Scharfstein, 1955). Early proponents of the revisionist view, including Boston Bureau of Jewish Education superintendent Louis Hurwich, tended to be ardent Jewish nationalists who despaired at the apparent failure of a small but dedicated immigrant-dominated Hebraist movement to make deep and enduring inroads on American soil. Their perspective was shared and elaborated by a younger generation that came to prominence in the 1960s and 1970s when the communal agenda was shifting from facilitating integration to concern about assimilation. The standout voice in the group belonged to Walter Ackerman, a Harvard-trained educator who wrote historical and other educational studies over the course of a half-century, while serving in a variety of positions, including camp director, day school principal, and university professor and administrator. Not coincidentally, Ackerman was a product of the Boston Talmud Torah system and Boston Hebrew College, where he internalized the maximalist educational philosophy of Hurwich and his successor Benjamin Shevach (Band, 1998; Reimer, 1995, pp. 279–301; Ackerman, Alexander, et al., 2008).

Despite its dissenting ideological perspective, the revisionist history resembled its older counterpart in important ways. It was written primarily by educational practitioners rather than professional historians and functioned as a rationalization for their work in the field. The focus continued to be on schools, although other educational institutions, particularly camps and community centers, garnered some attention. Finally, it was uneven in quality, and of negligible quantity.

The Turning Point in Jewish Educational Historiography

By the time Gartner was writing in the late 1960s, a reformation was well underway in the field of general educational historiography. Spurred by a scathing report issued by the Committee on the Role of Education in American History of the Ford Foundation's Fund for the Advancement of Education, it was spearheaded by Bailyn's study of education in the colonial period and exemplified by Lawrence Cremin's masterful three-volume *American Education* (1970, 1980, 1988). A similar transformation in the writing of American Jewish educational history was slower in coming. With the possible exception of Gartner himself, whose scholarship includes a seminal essay on Jews and public school education (1976, pp. 157–189), prior to the 1970s there were no American Jewish historians eager to take up Bailyn's cause. Jacobs pointed out that with a few notable exceptions, like Jacob R. Marcus, American Jewish historians took little interest in educational history. He postulated that the lack of attention was a function of their disconnection from Jewish schools. Unlike American historians who were intimately involved in the so-called "history wars"—the public school curricular debates relating to teaching of history and social studies—American Jewish historians had little to say about Jewish history instruction in supplementary and day schools (Jacobs, B.M., 2005, p. 38). This disparity can be attributed to two factors: the focus of formal Jewish education on the elementary and middle school grades, when students are developmentally ill-equipped to engage in critical historical study, and the relative youth of American Jewish history as a recognized sub-field of Jewish history. American Jewish historians harbored a lingering sense of disciplinary inferiority, which probably discouraged them from tackling perceived "soft" topics, like the history of the professions.

Gartner's (1969) documentary history, which included an introductory essay outlining major themes in American Jewish educational history, encouraged scholarly activity. So, too, did Pilch's edited history, published the same year, which provided a useful if conventional narrative framework and included extensive footnotes. Pilch assembled an eclectic group of writers, including the historian Hyman Grinstein, a scholar of the colonial and nineteenth-century New York Jewish community; educator and sociologist Uriah Z. Engelman, whose knowledge of the contemporary educational scene was enhanced by his involvement in the 1959 national Jewish education survey; and education professor and scholar of modern Jewish thought Meir Ben-Horin (Pilch, 1969).

The choice of Ben-Horin to write on the decisive period between 1900 and 1940 was inspired. The European-born and European-educated Ben-Horin was able to maintain critical distance from his subject. Ben-Horin accurately portrayed the Jewish educational establishment's embrace of a supplementary educational system as an attempt to balance the dual imperatives of American integration and Jewish survival, rather than an abdication to unfettered Americanization. He reminded readers that the organization in the early twentieth century of an extensive day school system modeled upon the Catholic parochial schools was an economic and political impossibility. At the same time, however, he faulted the establishment's inability "to go beyond the recognition of opportunity and to envisage 'trans-fusion' " (Pilch, 1969, p. 55).

Ironically, Ben-Horin's personal biography—his coming of age in Nazi Danzig, his avid Zionism and eventual departure for Palestine in 1937—also contributed to the chapter's weaknesses. His analysis fell short in its comparative lack of attention to the devastating impact of the Depression on the Jewish educational system and its impulse to read the era retrospectively in the light of the Holocaust and the creation of the State of Israel. If most Jewish educators turned a blind eye to "the speed and the fury of nazidom's 'gathering storm'" (p. 55), as Ben-Horin charged, they were certainly not alone. As for his contention that they failed to grasp, "the passion and the muscle of European Jewry's efforts on behalf of Jewish statehood in Palestine ever since the issuance of the Balfour Declaration in 1917" (p. 55), it implied a unanimity of purpose and action on both sides of the Atlantic that simply did not exist. The upbuilding of Palestine before the 1930s was viewed by most observers as a fledgling and quixotic enterprise and the prospects for Jewish statehood seemed doubtful to all but the most enthusiastic Zionist partisans. In fact, cultural-survivalist Jewish educators in the United States were often far ahead of the majority of their constituents, in their dogged commitment to a cultural Zionist curriculum that prioritized Modern Hebrew instruction.

Jewish Education and the Creation of an Americanized Judaism

It was Arthur's (Goren, 1970) *New York Jews and the Quest for Community: The Kehillah Experiment, 1908–1922* that broke considerable ground and set the pattern for more recent works incorporating educational history into treatments of wider topics. Goren devoted two chapters to a study of the Bureau of Jewish Education, which comprised a centerpiece of the *Kehillah*'s program. Goren contextualized the Bureau's philosophy and activities within the political, social, and cultural currents of the 1910s. His research not only demonstrated how the *Kehillah*'s educational work provided its leaders with an opportunity to elaborate and propagate their cultural-survivalist theories of Jewish communal life, it also revealed how the *Kehillah*'s activities were blunted by various rejectionist elements within the Jewish community (1970, pp. 86–133). [On the New York Bureau of Jewish Education see also, Winter (1966).]

Goren was trained at Columbia University by social historian Robert D. Cross, whose scholarship on the history of American Catholicism accorded considerable attention to religious education. Cross's research interests and his sympathetic attitude toward Bailyn's plea to transform educational history no doubt influenced Goren's approach. His influence, in turn, is clearly visible in the work of Deborah Dash Moore. Her studies of second generation New York Jews (1981) and the growth of the Jewish sun-belt communities in Los Angeles and Miami (1994) both incorporate educational history into their broader narrative. The former volume, in particular, made education a central focus of inquiry, and pointed to the formative role that both secular and religious education played in shaping the collective consciousness of interwar Jewry.

If Moore used the sociological category of generation as a lens through which to explore the shaping of urban American Jewish identity, her graduate school colleague at Columbia, Jeffrey Gurock, chose to explore similar themes through the case study of a single neighborhood, Harlem. Both Moore and Gurock agreed that the Jewish "love affair" with the city gestated first in the ethnic neighborhood. Unlike earlier Jewish neighborhood studies which focused primarily on institutions, like Alter Landesman's volume on Brownsville (1969), Gurock's work emphasized group social dynamics, in particular, the tensions between the working-class immigrants, who attempted to recreate the spirit of the Lower East Side ghetto, and the upwardly mobile, acculturated "alrightniks," who sought to distance themselves from old-world and ghetto values without relinquishing their Jewishness. As Gurock demonstrated, a primary arena for this inter-group squabbling was the Jewish school. Institutions like the Uptown Talmud Torah and Rabbi Salanter Talmud Torah became incubators for an Americanized modern Orthodoxy; sites where the "first efforts were made to separate the essence of traditional Judaism from its old-world shell." But the efforts of acculturated and newly affluent lay leaders to introduce a modernized educational program in cooperation with the Bureau of Jewish Education provoked fierce resistance from the traditionalists. Gurock pointed out that a similar struggle played out within the much smaller segment of the community that chose to reject public school education and the supplementary Talmud Torahs in favor of all-day Jewish schools (Gurock, 1979, pp. 86–113).

In their challenge to the prevailing sociological model of immigrant assimilation popularized by scholars like Ernest Burgess and Louis Wirth, Moore and Gurock spotlighted institutions that promoted ethnic identification, including educational settings. Their example was followed over the next two decades by historians like

Jenna Weissman Joselit (1990) and David Kaufman (1999), who amplified, refined, and gently critiqued their pioneering work. Kaufman explored the genesis and development of the synagogue center, questioning the prevailing view that it first emerged from the experiments of Jewish Center founder Rabbi Mordecai Kaplan and Institutional Synagogue leader Rabbi Herbert Goldstein. Among the institutions that he viewed as a forerunner was the Central Jewish Institute, a communal school center that was brought to life during World War I by two Benderly disciples, Isaac Berkson and Albert Schoolman. Joselit explored the solidification of New York's modern Orthodox identity in the interwar period and included a chapter on the transition from community Talmud Torahs to modern all-day schools. She too used CJI as a case study, pairing it with the Ramaz School, the modern Orthodox day school that purchased CJI's building in the mid-1940s.

More recently, the history and significance of CJI as an agent of Americanization and ethnic identity construction and perpetuation was considered by Miriam Heller Stern (2007) and Jonathan Krasner (2009, pp. 411–467). Stern, who was trained at Stanford University's School of Education, also wrote an insightful reappraisal of the Benderly era utilizing analytical templates that she borrowed from the work of leading historians of American public school education, David Tyack and Larry Cuban (2004, pp. 16–26). Krasner (2011) wrote a reconsideration of the development on American Jewish education in the first half of the twentieth century, including the rise of the bureau system, the impact of progressive education of Jewish school curricula, and the transition from a communal to a congregationally based supplementary school system. He also published a three-part series on the history of *Jewish Education*, the journal that served as the primary organ for Benderly's protégés. The journal played a central role in creating a national community of like-minded educators, providing a platform for debate on the major issues and educational trends of the day as well as a venue for the sharing of programs and pedagogies (2005, pp. 121–177, 2005, pp. 279–317, 2006, pp. 29–76).

Accommodation and Resistance as a Theme in Orthodox Educational Historiography

Gurock's magnum opus, *Orthodox Jews in America* (2009) is a model for the seamless integration of educational history into a synthetic American Jewish historical narrative. Other scholars who study the Orthodox community, including Etan Diamond (2000) and William Helmreich (1982) also have devoted considerable attention to education. This is hardly surprising given the central role that Jewish education has assumed in virtually all segments of the Orthodox world. As Haym Soloveitchik elucidated in his seminal essay "Rupture and Reconstruction," in recent times the prevailing "mimetic" style of education that centered on the Jewish home has been replaced by a text-centered formal style of education that takes place primarily in the *yeshiva* (1994). Soloveitchik demonstrated that the ascendancy of the text-centered model had far-reaching implications for Orthodox Jewish ritual practice and cultural life.

The growth of Orthodox *yeshiva* day schools is one of the most important sociological trends of the post-War era. Jack Wertheimer pronounced it "the most significant factor in the revival of Orthodoxy" (1993, p. 130). The history of the day school movement was treated by Alvin Schiff (1966) and Doniel Zvi Kramer (1984), but it was only in more recent studies, including Gurock (1989), Diamond (2000) and Seth Farber (2004) that the phenomenon was analyzed using the categories of social class, geography, and gender. Diamond explained that post-War Orthodox day schools served two crucial social functions: They "provided an arena for the expression of Orthodox Jewish religious suburbanization" and were instrumental in "transmitting the styles of religious suburbanization to the second and third generations" (2000, p. 89). As Soloveitchik observed, this new Orthodox culture was characterized by rigorous observance and conspicuous material consumption.

Two of the trailblazing modern-day schools, the Ramaz School in Manhattan and the Maimonides School in Boston, were actually established prior to World War II, in 1937. Farber's treatment of the origins and development of the latter institution, founded by the venerable modern Orthodox leader, Rabbi Joseph Soloveitchik, emphasized how American mores influenced Orthodox culture. Two of the defining features of these modern-day schools were coeducational classes and advanced Talmud instruction for girls and young women. Both innovations were controversial, and debate continues today as to whether Rabbi Soloveitchik, in particular, viewed coeducation as an expedient concession or a matter of principle. Regardless, these features served to separate Ramaz and Maimonides from more traditional day schools and *yeshivas*, highlighting how adherents to Orthodoxy would continue to define themselves based on their responses to the challenges of modernity; liberals would chart a path of accommodation, while traditionalists would insist upon resistance.

As Farber and Gurock demonstrated, the modern Orthodox day schools were recognized by their supporters as a break from the European-style *yeshiva*; their mission was to train Jewishly literate laypeople who were completely at home in American society, as opposed to the traditional *yeshivas*, which devoted themselves to shaping an intellectual elite. To this end, the schools would offer a secular education that rivaled the best private schools and a rich variety of extra-curricular sports, clubs, and cultural activities. They also refrained from holding classes on Sundays. Ramaz's founder Rabbi Joseph Lookstein readily acknowledged that the schools were intent upon removing from the students "the consciousness of being different." There was little or no compunction about emulating "the ways of the Gentiles" (Farber, 2004, p. 87; Gurock, 1989, pp. 42–44, 62).

On the opposite end of the spectrum from Ramaz and Maimonides were the educational institutions that strove to recreate the spirit of great Lithuanian and Polish *yeshivas*. In the interwar years, the standout institution was Mesivta Torah Vodaath in the Williamsburg section of Brooklyn, which was led by Rabbi Shraga Feivel Mendlowitz. The center, meanwhile, was occupied by the Mizrachi movement and the community that coalesced around the Rabbi Isaac Elchanan Theological

Seminary (RIETS) and Yeshiva College in Washington Heights. The competing cultures and the interactions between these schools were captured nicely in Gurock's portrait of interwar Brooklyn (2002, pp. 227–241, 2009, pp. 184–198) and his volume on Jews and American sports (2005). Mendlowitz also founded Torah U'Mesorah, the National Society for Hebrew Day Schools (Kramer, 1984).

Formal education for girls was relatively neglected in the *yeshiva* community until the post-War years. It was not until 1937 that an American affiliate of the European Bais Yaakov girls' schools was opened in Williamsburg. However, the system grew rapidly in the decades after the Holocaust. Historical research into this phenomenon is a significant lacuna, which promises to be filled by the work of Leslie Ginsparg, who is in the midst of completing her doctoral dissertation at New York University. Yeshiva education for girls was likewise becoming normative in more centrist segments of the community. In 1948, Yeshiva University established the Central Yeshiva High School for Girls, and in 1954 opened Stern College for women. By the 1960s, girls made up over 40% of children studying in all-day Jewish schools. In addition to the growing number of coeducational day schools, 14 girls' schools were operating across the country by 1963 (Gurock, 2009, p. 211). Newfound interest in girls' education among the centrist and rigorously Orthodox reflected growing communal fears not only about the inadequacy of home-based socialization, but also the embourgeoisement of the Orthodox community.

The *yeshiva* community was considerably strengthened and diversified by the influx of European refugees in the years immediately preceding and after World War II. Significantly, the rigorously Orthodox began to branch out geographically. Although Brooklyn and Washington Heights attracted many newcomers and continued to serve as hubs of Orthodox life, significant refugee communities and august *yeshivas* were established across the Hudson in Lakewood, New Jersey, and in more remote cities, including Cleveland, Ohio, and Baltimore, Maryland. "For all of them in their holy quests to recapture the past, yeshiva education, of the separatist variety was a *sine qua non*," Gurock concluded. "Thus in the first post-War decades, these aggressive aggregations of foreign-born Orthodox Jews began building a network of schools designed to keep America out of their children's development to the fullest extent that the law allowed" (2009, p. 216).

A New Lens of Inquiry: The Impact of Gender on Jewish Educational History

The use of gender as a lens to explore issues in Jewish educational historiography was hardly limited to studies focusing on the Orthodox community. Indeed, gender studies opened entirely new lines of inquiry as well as shedding new light on seemingly exhausted topics. Standout studies in the past two decades include Dianne Ashton's volume *Rebecca Gratz: Women and Judaism in Antebellum America* (1997) and Melissa Klapper's *Jewish Girls Coming of Age in America, 1860–1920* (2005). Both scholars presented identity formation as an ongoing process of negotiation. Moreover, their interests included both the history of Jewish girls and women and the construction of Jewish girlhood and womanhood.

It is no accident that Gratz founded the first Jewish Sunday school in Philadelphia, the same city where the Protestant American Sunday School Union emerged. An appreciation for Gratz's educational work is considerably enhanced by Ashton's use of a comparative perspective, particularly her reading of the sources in the light of Anne Boylan's scholarship on the Protestant Sunday schools. Under Ashton's microscope, Gratz's Sunday school likewise becomes an enlightening case study of the impact of gender on curricular development. Under the influence of Gratz and her all-female staff, the school's curriculum came to reflect the values of Victorian culture and feminized religion, particularly "the importance of domestic piety, the heart's longing for and devotion to God and God's loving-kindness." Even the choice of Biblical texts, which was heavily weighted toward stories with prominent female characters, suggested a womanly influence (1997, pp. 149–169).

Equally fascinating is Ashton's treatment of the role that Gratz and the Hebrew Sunday School played in shaping a "domesticated" American Judaism. Ashton located Gratz within a subculture of upper- and middle-class white women who participated in and helped to legitimate "domestic feminism," the use of "a rhetoric of domesticity" to legitimate vocations beyond homemaking and childrearing. In effect, the domestic realm was expanded to include a range of voluntary organizational work, including teaching in the Hebrew Sunday School (1997, pp. 19 and 22–23).

Klapper's book, which explores the construction of American Jewish adolescence among girls in the late nineteenth and early twentieth centuries, similarly approaches education as a social phenomenon, a process of enculturation and acculturation. To be sure, the schools—both public and Jewish—were important settings for this type of learning and Klapper dedicates considerable attention to both. But so were the myriad other places where girls and young women lived their everyday lives. Indeed, with the working-class family economy often unable to support secondary schooling, let alone university, alternative educational venues took on an exaggerated importance in working-class children's lives, particularly as they struggled to Americanize. Klapper devoted an entire chapter of her volume to "Alternative Forms of Education for Working-Class Girls," by which she meant to include the Anglo-Jewish press, recreational institutions, settlement houses, night schools, and specialized institutions like orphanages and working girls' homes (2005, pp. 105–142, esp. 107).

Like Ashton, Emily Bingham (2003), and other scholars of the American Jewish women's experience, Klapper was attuned to the intersections between gender and class. To become an American Jewish woman was synonymous with internalizing middle-class values and gender norms. Ultimately, however, whether her protagonists were bourgeois or members of the "upwardly mobile working class," their common endeavor involved finding a balance between tradition and modernization. Adding her voice to those of Moore and Gurock, Klapper averred that the pathways to acculturation and assimilation were hardly uniform and seldom linear (2005, pp. 109 and 235–239).

Education as Enculturation and Socialization: Reading the Sources

Klapper's work was also distinguished by its attention first and foremost to descriptive sources, produced by the girls themselves—diaries, memoirs, letters, scrapbooks, etc.—rather than the prescriptive sources that usually capture the attention of cultural and gender studies scholars. She was careful not to treat American Jewish "girl culture" monolithically (2005, p. 1–5). Of course, as Klapper herself acknowledged, prescriptive materials played an important role in the education process. Riv-Ellen Prell (1999), Joselit (1994) and others have been attuned to the impact of representations in books, newspapers, and magazines on socialization and the shaping of American Jewish identity in youth and adults. Children, meanwhile, were encouraged to take their cues about Jewish holiday observance from the pages of Jewish children's books, including Sadie Rose Weilerstein's 1935 *The Adventures of K'tonton*. Simultaneously, at a moment when the movement was re-embracing traditional rituals and ceremonies, Mamie Gamoran was similarly instructing a generation of Reform Jewish children (Krasner, 2003, pp. 344–361; Grant, 2010). Somewhat older children and youth were able to turn to the pages of Jewish educational magazines, which served a significant educative function. Sue Levi Elwell (1986, pp. 240–250) and Naomi Cohen (2004, pp. 1–35) have written on this subject, but the topic is ripe for further research.

Another line of inquiry has been to analyze the representations of insiders and outsiders in Jewish textbooks (Krasner, 2002). While it is difficult to accurately gauge the impact of schoolbooks on their student consumers, in part because teachers play an important mediating role when the books are used in formal classroom settings, they often govern what students learn, as teachers look to them to set curriculum and organize subject matter. Their power is only enhanced by the general public's tendency to treat them as authoritative (Apple & Christian-Smith, 1991, p. 5). Moreover, as distillations of the values, stories, and culture that a society itself considers essential to transmit to the next generation, textbooks provide an important perspective on the socialization process. In the case of American Jewish textbooks, images of archetypal others, like Christians and Arabs, as well as depictions of various Jewish sub-groups who were negatively viewed by the social and cultural elites provided a foil. They enabled the authors to frame Jewish distinctiveness contextually and discursively, in opposition to a countertype. Simultaneously, by defining the boundaries of the in-group, they played an important role in promoting a sense of *Klal Yisrael* (Jewish unity).

Another important contribution to the literature on textbooks is Penny Schine-Gold's examination of the role of children's Bible's and Bible story collections in shaping the identities of second- and third-generation Jews of Eastern European descent (2004, esp. 96 208). Schine-Gold's work emphasized how the Bible replaced the Talmud as "the binding text of Judaism and Jewish education" (p. 206). She further reflected on the books' application of moral and character education in a Jewish context. Jacobs' study of social studies curricula (2005) also contributed important insights into the motivations and objectives of early twentieth-century progressive Jewish educators.

All of these historians ultimately interpreted their sources in light of the American Jewish integrationist agenda that guided the mission of mainstream educators, reflecting upon the difficulties that authors and pedagogues experienced in applying the tenets of progressive education to Jewish education, particularly given its traditional emphasis on text learning. Rona Sheramy's history of Holocaust education in Jewish settings (2001), which focused on the past half-century, likewise stressed how educational narratives are shaped by the wider community and national discourse. Their work contributes substantially to a literature that until the 2000s was distinguished primarily by a pair of articles by Ackerman on Jewish history and Israel studies textbooks (1984, pp. 1–35, 1986, pp. 4–14). Of course, as mentioned above, the limitation of all of these studies was that they shed only limited light on what was actually taught in the classroom. Klapper's observation that, "the most rewarding history may lie in the intriguing spaces between representation and lived experience," is indubitably on target (2005, p. 4).

The New Focus on Youth

In focusing her attention on adolescent girls, Klapper was anticipating a recent upsurge in scholarly interest in Jewish youth. At an October 2008 conference entitled "Jewish Youth and Social Change," which was convened at the Center for Jewish History, participants were charged with no less as a task than the rethinking of American Jewish history through the use of youth as both a subject and an interpretive category.

Of course, youth is not an entirely new subject. For example, American Jewish historians have long been cognizant that young people made up a disproportionate number of immigrants from Eastern and Central Europe. Susan Glenn wrote compellingly of how immigrant girls and young women were socialized by the garment industry sweatshop and the trade union. Her point was reflected evocatively in a poem she quoted that was penned by one of the young factory workers:

> I would like to write a poem
> But I have no words.
> My grammar was ladies waists
> And my schooling skirts. (Glenn, 1990, p. 2)

Ruth Gay wrote of the young immigrants as "unfinished people." Many left their home towns and villages before they were old enough to intensely imbibe its traditions, folkways, and culture, yet most arrived when they were too old to become seamlessly integrated into American society. As such, they were a transitional generation (2001, pp. 4–5).

Similarly, Sarna (1989, 1995) and others (Pearlstein, 1993; Rogow, 1993; Schwartz, 1991) have taken note of the role of American-born young people in

Philadelphia and New York in spearheading a Jewish revival in the late nineteenth century. Many of the institutions that emerged from this renewal movement were broadly educational in orientation, including the *American Hebrew* (1879), the Jewish Publication Society (1888), the American Jewish Historical Society (1892), Gratz College (1893), the Jewish Chautauqua Society (1893), and the National Council for Jewish Women (1893). In its early years, the revival was associated with the burgeoning Young Men's Hebrew Associations (1870s), the forerunner of the Jewish Community Centers. The median age of the revivalists was about 25, although some like Cyrus Adler and Henrietta Szold were in their teens when they first became active. It is worth remembering that until the post-War era, the term "youth" was commonly used to refer to people under 30.

Prell's contribution to the growing discourse on youth focused predominately on camping (2006, 2007, pp. 77–106). She argued that in the aftermath of the Holocaust, rabbis, educators, and other Jewish professionals tried to shape the Jewish youth in the 1950s and early 1960s into a "redeemer generation." Jewish educational summer camps, which grew in number and popularity in the 1940s and 1950s (Sarna, 2005), and in which Jewish values and culture could be lived as well as taught, were recognized as an ideal venue in which to mold a "saving remnant."

The earliest serious scholarly work on the history of Jewish camping was Daniel Isaacman's unpublished doctoral dissertation (1970). More recently both Ackerman (1999, pp. 3–24) and Zola (2006, pp. 1–26) provided useful introductions to the history of organized Jewish camping, including its debt to the Young Men's Christian Association—Young Women's Christian Association camps, the Fresh Air movement, and American scouting. The history of the first Americanized Jewish culture camp, Cejwin (1919), is treated by Stern (2007) and Krasner (2011). Sarna's essay (2006, pp. 27–51) in the Lorge-Zola volume focuses on the "crucial decade" from 1941 to 1952, which witnessed the founding of many influential educational camps and heralded a golden age of Jewish camping. According to Sarna, the 1940s was a turning point in the history of the Jewish camping movement, as the focus shifted from philanthropic and community-based camps to privately owned camps catering to the wealthy and educational camps associated with denominational groups or cultural institutions.

A growing historical literature on Jewish educational camping has focused primarily on the non-Orthodox denominational camps. The best histories of the Conservative movement's Ramah camps are arguably a pair of articles by Shuly Rubin Schwartz (1987) and Ackerman (1999), which focus on the early years, and Michael Brown's (1997, pp. 823–854) overview of Ramah's development through the 1970s, which appeared in *Tradition Renewed*. The Lorge-Zola volume, *A Place of Our Own* (2006), which constituted the major contribution on the history of Reform camping, focused primarily on the first Reform camp, Olin Sang Ruby Union Institute, in Oconomowoc, Wisconsin. One particularly interesting essay in the volume, by Judah M. Cohen (2006, pp. 173–208), focused on the critical role that music and song-leading played in creating the culture of the Union-Institute camps, and how the camp music ultimately influenced the development of Reform synagogue liturgical music.

Outside of the histories of Cejwin, Ramah and the Union-Institute camps, the scholarship on educational camping is considerably thinner. The standouts are Moore (1999, pp. 201–221) and Bruce Powell (2003, pp. 171–184) treatments of Shlomo Bardin's founding of the Brandeis Camp Institute. Full-scale histories of the Hebrew-speaking and Yiddish-speaking camps and Orthodox camping remain to be written.

Neglected Areas of Research

Sparse as the history of Jewish camping may be, it is substantial when compared to the literature on other settings for informal Jewish education. With the exception of the Intercollegiate Menorah Association (Greene, 2011; Joselit, 1978, pp. 133–154; Korelitz, 1997, pp. 75–100; Fried, 2001, pp. 147–174), little of note has been written on the history of American Jewish youth organizations since Samuel Grand's dissertation in 1958, although, J.J. Goldberg and Elliot Kling's sourcebook on Habonim (1993) is useful. Nor has the "Israel experience" or Eastern European youth trip phenomena been treated historically, although a growing sociological and anthropological literature (see, for example, Kelner, 2010; Mittelberg, 1992, pp. 194–218; Helmreich, 1995, pp. 16–20; Heilman, 1999, pp. 231–249; Kelner, 2003, pp. 124–155; Sheramy, 2007, pp. 307–325; and Saxe & Chazan, 2008) should prove useful to future researchers. Adult education has fared only marginally better. Among the great experiments in adult education were the Jewish Chautauqua Society (Pearlstein, 1993) and the havurah movement (Prell, 1989). Sarna's recent overview of the history of adult education (2005, pp. 207–222), pointed to three periods of heightened activity prior to the present day: the 1840s, the late nineteenth century, and the late 1930s–1940s. Following Robert Peers' theory, Sarna asserted that adult education tended to flourish in periods of great social change.

Another area that has received scant attention is the history of Yiddish-speaking schools. At their height, in the 1930s, the Yiddish schools enrolled about 10% of those children receiving a Jewish education (Fishman, 2007, p. 271). But they have been the object of considerable misconception, wittingly or unwittingly perpetuated by Zionist and religious educators, which, in turn, resulted in their marginalization by scholars of education. Two recent articles by David Fishman (2007, pp. 271–285, 2009) and Tony Michels history of Yiddish socialists in New York (2005, pp. 179–216) have begun to fill the void. Our knowledge of the history of Yiddish schools in North America promises to expand with Fradle Freidenreich's new volume *Passionate Pioneers: Yiddish Secular Education in North America, 1910–1960* (2010).

Likewise, the history of non-Orthodox day schools, including community schools, has been largely neglected. While these schools account for only about 20% of day school enrollments (Schick, 2004, p. 1), until recently they comprised the fastest-growing segment of the day school pie. Valerie Thaler's history of Akiba Academy in Philadelphia (2008) and M. Schreiber's study of the origins of the Agnon school in Cleveland (1970, pp. 66–79) are among the few available case studies.

Scholarship on Higher Education

One area of educational history that has received considerable attention in recent years is higher education. Jewish Studies has undergone a veritable revolution over the past half-century, and it is only natural that its phenomenal expansion would attract the interest of historians. In 1945 there were only a dozen full-time faculty positions in Jewish studies at American universities. By the time Arnold Band published the first broad treatment of the growth of Jewish studies, in 1966, the number had grown to over 60 (1966, pp. 3–30). Despite this impressive growth, practitioners of Jewish studies still considered themselves to be pioneers (Neusner, 1985, p. 41). By the end of the 1980s Jewish studies scholars were operating in an entirely remade landscape, with over 600 academic positions in Jewish studies (Band, 1989, p. 17). The proliferation of Jewish studies courses and departments on college campuses was accompanied by rising student enrollments, translating into a growing audience for Jewish education.

The early history and mainstreaming of Jewish studies in American universities was explored in depth by Paul Ritterband and Harold Wechsler (1994). Edward Shapiro provided a concise but useful summary of post-War developments, including the founding of the Association for Jewish Studies in 1969 and the general burgeoning of Jewish studies between 1965 and 1985 (1992, pp. 71–88). Among the more focused studies, of particular note is Shuly Rubin Schwartz's account of the publication of the Jewish encyclopedia (1991), Robert Liberles' intellectual biography of Columbia University historian Salo Baron (1995) and Harriet Pass Freidenreich's focus on the mainstreaming of Jewish women academics (2007). The historical resistance of English literature departments in particular to the appointment of Jewish faculty is explored in a pair of books by Susanne Klingenstein (1991, 1998). Among the stories that have not adequately been told is the contribution of Brandeis University to the promotion of Jewish scholarship, particularly through its recruitment of refugee scholars Nahum Glatzer and Alexander Altmann.

If by the 1980s Jewish studies were firmly ensconced in the university, scholars were not entirely sanguine. To be sure, concerns that the field was growing too quickly to safeguard the quality of scholarship and instruction (Cohen, 1970, p. 144; Fox, 1986, p. 143) were eventually put to rest. But these gave way to new anxieties, including the apparent marginalization of Jewish studies in the new multicultural academy (Horowitz et al., 1998, pp. 116–130). A perennial concern was the conflict that many Jewish studies scholars felt between their commitment to academic rigor and their concern for Jewish survival. This problem was only magnified and complicated by the influx of huge contributions into Jewish studies programs by funders who were primarily concerned with shoring up Jewish students' religious and ethnic identities (Shapiro, 1992, pp. 83–84).

Until the second half of the twentieth century, the loci of the Jewish scholarship in North America were the non-Orthodox seminaries. As Wechsler and Ritterband explained, "seminaries provided an alternative to intellectual exclusion from universities," and by the 1910s were widely viewed as the most promising venue for

Judaic scholarship. But even before they were eclipsed by the universities in the post-War era, they were hobbled by withering criticism from respected quarters in intellectual circles and the academy. Among the complaints against the seminaries were middling academic standards, narrow scholarship, curricular superficiality, and petty faculty politicking. Members of the Jewish Theological Seminary faculty contributed to their own marginalization within the American academic world (as well as the Conservative movement) by publishing much of their scholarship in Hebrew (Ritterband & Wechsler, 1994, pp. 139–147; Meyer, 1992, pp. 63–67; Sarna, 1997, pp. 67–68).

Significant anniversaries were judged to be opportune occasions for thorough studies of the largest rabbinical seminaries. The first of these surveys appeared in 1976 to mark the centennial of Hebrew Union College-Jewish Institute of Religion. Historian Michael Meyer set the standard for his and the subsequent volumes with his commitment "to tell the story of the HUC-JIR with utmost honesty, including the failures and the unpleasant wrangles no less than the accomplishments and expressions of unity, the struggles for power no less than the lofty idealism" (Meyer, 1992, p. 3). Gurock's history of Yeshiva University, with its meditation on that school's ongoing efforts to negotiate the tensions inherent in its *Torah U'Mada* philosophy, followed in 1988. The latest and most ambitious effort, dedicated to the history of the Jewish Theological Seminary, was the two-volume collection of essays *Tradition Renewed* (1997), edited by Jack Wertheimer, which appeared in that institution's 110th year. Comprised of 40 essays by an array of scholars, some of whom have no direct connection to the institution, the collection was almost universally hailed for its breadth, depth, and level of candor. Historians of Jewish education and religion will find much of interest in the chapters devoted to the institution's history and relationship with the movement and the wider Jewish, religious, and academic communities. Of particular interest will be Kaufman (1997, pp. 565–629), Alan Mintz (1997, pp. 81–112) and Virginia Lieson Brereton's (1997, pp. 737–765) studies of the history, culture, and influence of Teachers Institute, Schwartz (1997, pp. 293–325), Robert Liberles (1997, pp. 329–351), Harvey Goldberg (1997, pp. 355–437) and Sarna (1997, pp. 53–80) articles on the Seminary's faculty, Rela Mintz Geffen's study of Teachers Institute alumni (1997, pp. 633–653), and David Ellenson and Lee Bycel's (1997, pp. 525–591) analysis of the evolution of the rabbinical school curriculum.

The association of Teachers Institute with the Seminary and the crucial role its longtime dean Mordecai Kaplan played both in the areas of training and articulating a vision and a rationale for American Jewish education accounts for the disproportionate attention to this institution in the historical literature (Kaufman, 1997, pp. 611–612). In formulating his vision, Kaplan derived inspiration from both Schechter and Benderly. He liked to think of TI as born of two parents, the Seminary and the *Kehillah*. "If Kaplan was ideologically located midway between Schechter and Benderly, then the Teachers Institute would similarly be situated as the connecting link between the greater Jewish community and the insular Seminary, between the downtown masses and the uptown (rabbinical) classes," Kaufman observed

(582). Considerable light is shed on the early years of TI in biographies of Kaplan (Scult, 1993) and Seminary professor Israel Friedlaender (Shargel, 1985), as well as Kaplan's diaries, which were edited and published by Mel Scult (2001).

Of course, TI was not the only Hebrew teacher-training school. By the 1930s there were ten Hebrew teaching colleges, including four in New York City and one each in Baltimore, Boston, Chicago, Cleveland, Philadelphia, and Pittsburgh. The earliest of these schools was Gratz College, in Philadelphia, which opened in 1887. Its history was recounted by Diane King (1979) and Jerome Kutnick (1998, pp. 321–348). The impact of Boston's Hebrew College was explored by Ackerman (1983, pp. 16–26) and Reimer (1995, pp. 285–307), while the general phenomenon of Hebrew teaching colleges was surveyed by Ackerman (1993, pp. 105–128).

The Jewish experience in the United States also intersects in significant ways with the history of American education more generally. Of especial concern has been the impact of social anti-Semitism on admissions at elite universities during the interwar years, and the eventual easing of restrictions as anti-Semitism declined in the decades after World War II. Books by Marcia Graham Synnott (1979) and Wechsler (1977), explored the legacy of discrimination at Harvard, Yale, Princeton, and Columbia. The most recent contribution to this literature, Jerome Karabel's *The Chosen*, covered similar ground but was considerably enhanced by the availability of new documentary sources (2005).

Conclusion

At the beginning of the twenty-first century, there is reason for guarded optimism about the future outlook for American Jewish historiography. Historians of the American Jewish experience increasingly appear to recognize education not only as a process of cultural transmission, but also as an expression of culture and an engine of cultural production. Some of the most prominent voices in the field have devoted considerable attention to education in their personal research and have encouraged their graduate students to explore topics with an educational history component or focus. Other scholars, in related humanities and social science fields like literature, anthropology, sociology have enriched the discourse with interdisciplinary studies that sometimes introduce novel categories of inquiry. At the same time, the slim ranks of Jewish educational historians have lately grown to include a few promising scholars who trained in history of education programs at schools of education. Conference programs at annual conferences of Jewish studies and Jewish education reflect the growth of scholarship in the modest but steady inclusion of panels devoted to the history of education, even if the conveners sometimes prefer to frame the scholarship in other terms, like childhood, youth, and gender. Journals like *American Jewish History* and the *American Jewish Archives Journal* occasionally publish in educational history, while a revitalized *Journal of Jewish Education* promises to enhance the stature of the field.

No doubt the increased consideration from these various quarters has been reinforced by the growing level of attention and financial support that education has lately enjoyed from federations and prominent philanthropic foundations. At least one of the latter has also had a direct impact on scholarship. As one young scholar observed at a recent conference of the Network for Research in Jewish Education, the lion's share of responsibility for the small but discernable increase in the number of Jewish educational historians and sociologists must be credited to the Wexner Foundation Graduate Education Program, which almost single-handedly subsidized their education.

Another encouraging sign was the inclusion of an essay devoted to the history of American Jewish education in the recently published *Columbia History of Jews & Judaism in America*, edited by Marc Lee Raphael (Klapper, 2008, pp. 189–216). This thoughtful thematic essay, along with Wertheimer's wide-ranging, sociologically focused overview of the past half-century of Jewish education in the 1999 edition of the *American Jewish Year Book* (1999, pp. 3–115), and a brief overview of recent scholarship by Gil Graff (2008) constitute the first serious attempts at historical syntheses since Pilch, 1969 volume. While it is overly optimistic to interpret these publications as a sign of increased commitment to the field of Jewish educational history, they seem to indicate that the rising profile of education on the Jewish communal agenda can produce a modest trickle-down effect.

Despite these encouraging developments, the field has hardly found secure footing. With fears of contracting resources and fewer faculty positions in the years ahead any tentative gains may well be transitory. Even the current state of affairs is hardly satisfactory. Only a single faculty position in the history of Jewish education currently exists at the various schools and programs of Jewish education. Few if any courses in the history of Jewish education are included in university Jewish studies programs, and education rarely even commands a single session in most American Jewish history survey courses. Meanwhile, educational foundations have thus far expressed little interest in supporting historical studies, preferring instead to funnel their money into applied research that promises to have a direct impact on student outcomes. Perhaps they can be enticed with more articles like Sarna's exploration of the late nineteenth-century Jewish "great awakening" (1995) and Zeldin's consideration of nineteenth-century day schools (1988, pp. 438–452), both of which mined the history for contemporary policy implications. More established sources of funding for Jewish historical research have meanwhile declined to consider proposals focusing on education. In short, the traditional disregard for educational history as trivial and lightweight continues to hold considerable sway.

And so, historians of Jewish education find themselves in a Catch-22 situation: Only unremitting advocacy, perseverance, and the sustained dissemination of first-rate scholarship will ensure the consolidation of the tentative gains of the past few years. Yet, until the history of American Jewish education achieves widespread recognition within the communities of scholars and benefactors, and faculty positions are secured, the quality of the research will continue to be uneven.

References

Ackerman, W. (1983). From past to present: Notes from the history of Jewish education in Boston. *Jewish Education, 51,* 16–26.
Ackerman, W. (1984). "Let us now praise famous men and our fathers in their generation": History books for Jewish schools in America. *Dor le Dor, 2,* 1–35.
Ackerman, W. (1986). The "Land of our fathers" in the "Land of the free": Textbooks on Israel in American Jewish schools. *Jewish Education, 54,* 4–14.
Ackerman, W. (1993). A world apart: Hebrew teachers colleges and Hebrew-speaking camps. In A. Mintz (Ed.), *Hebrew in America: Perspectives and prospects.* Detroit, MI: Wayne State University Press.
Ackerman, W. (1999). Becoming Ramah. In S. Dorph (Ed.), *Ramah: Reflections at 50: Visions for a new century.* New York: National Ramah Commission.
Ackerman, A. (2008). From historical reconstruction to social criticism: Walter Ackerman on American Jewish education. In A. Ackerman, et al. (Eds.), *Jewish education: For what? And other essays by Walter Ackerman* (pp. vii–xxiii). Jerusalem: Schechter Institute for Jewish Studies.
Apple, M., & Christian-Smith, L. (Eds.). (1991). *The politics of the textbook.* New York: Routledge.
Ashton, D. (1997). *Rebecca Gratz: Women and Judaism in Antebellum America.* Detroit, MI: Wayne State University Press.
Bailyn, B. (1960). *Education in the forming of American society: Needs and opportunities for study.* Chapel Hill, NC: University of North Carolina Press.
Band, A. (1966). Jewish studies in American liberal arts colleges and universities. *American Jewish Year Book, 67,* 3–30.
Band, A. (1989, December, 8). Jewish studies: A generation later. *Sh'ma, 20,* 17–20.
Band, A. (1998). Confluent myths: Two lives. In H. Morantz (Ed.), *Judaism and education: Essays in honor of Walter I. Ackerman.* Beer Sheba: Ben Gurion University.
Bingham, E. (2003). *Mordecai: An early American family.* New York: Hill and Wang.
Brereton, V. L. (1997). Religious educators at JTS and the wider educational world. In J. Wertheimer (Ed.), *Tradition renewed* (pp. 737–765). New York: Jewish Theological Seminary.
Brown, M. (1997). It's off to camp we go: RamahLTF and the seminary in the Finkelstein era. In J. Wertheimer (Ed.), *Tradition renewed.* New York: Jewish Theological Seminary.
Cohen, G. (1970). An embarrassment of riches: On the condition of American Jewish scholarship in 1969. In L. Jick (Ed.), *Teaching of Judaica in American universities: The proceedings of a colloquium* (pp. 135–150). New York: Ktav.
Cohen, N. W. (2004). The Ark: An early twentieth century periodical. *American Jewish Archives Journal, 56,* 1–35.
Cohen, J. (2006). Singing out for Judaism: A history of song leaders and song leading at Olin-Sang-Ruby union institute. In M. Lorge & G. Zola (Eds.), *A place of their own: The rise of reform Jewish camping* (pp. 173–208). Tuscaloosa, AL: University of Alabama Press.
Cremin, L. (1970). *American education: The colonial experience, 1607–1783.* New York: Harper & Row.
Cremin, L. (1980). *American education: The national experience, 1783–1876.* New York: Harper & Row.
Cremin, L. (1988). *American education: The metropolitan experience, 1876–1980.* New York: Harper & Row.
Diamond, E. (2000). *And I Will Dwell in their Midst: Orthodox Jews in Suburbia.* Chapel Hill, NC: University of North Carolina Press.
Dushkin, A. (1918). *Jewish education in New York City.* New York: Bureau of Jewish Education.
Ellenson, D., & Bycel, L. (1997). A seminary of sacred learning: The JTS rabbinical curriculum in historical perspective. In J. Wertheimer (Ed.), *Tradition renewed* (pp. 525–591). New York: Jewish Theological Seminary.
Elwell, S. L. (1986). Educating Jews and Americans: The influence of the first American Jewish juvenile monthly magazine. *Religious Education, 81,* 240–250.

Farber, S. (2004). *An orthodox dreamer: Rabbi Joseph B. Soloveitchik and Boston's maimonides school*. Hanover, NH: University Press of New England.

Fishman, D. (2007). From Yiddishism to American Judaism: The impact of American Yiddish schools on their students. In J. Wertheimer (Ed.), *Imagining the American Jewish community* (pp. 271–285). Hanover, NH: University Press of New England.

Fishman, D. (2009). Yiddish schools in America and the problem of secular Jewish identity. In Z. Gitelman (Ed.), *Religion of Ethnicity?* New Brunswick, NJ: Rutgers University Press.

Fox, M. (1986). Some reflections on Jewish studies in American universities. *Judaism, 35*.

Freidenreich, H. P. (2007). Joining the faculty club: Jewish women academics in the United States. *Nashim, 13*, 68–101.

Freidenreich, F. P. (2010). *Passionate pioneers: The story of Yiddish secular education in North America, 1910–1960*. New York: Holmes & Meier Publishing.

Fried, L. (2001). Creating Hebraism, confronting Hellenism: The *menorah journal* and its struggle for the Jewish imagination. *American Jewish Archives Journal, 43*, 147–174.

Gamoran, E. (1924). *Changing conceptions of Jewish education*. New York: MacMillan Company.

A. Gannes (Ed.). (1965). *Selected writings of Leo L. Honor*. New York: Reconstructionist Press.

Gartner, L. (1969). *Jewish education in the United States*. New York: Teachers College Press.

Gartner, L. (1976). Temples of liberty unpolluted: American Jews and public schools, 1840–1875. In B. W. Korn (Ed.), *A bicentennial festschrift for Jacob Rader Marcus*. New York: Ktav.

Gay, R. (2001). *Unfinished people: Eastern European Jews encounter America*. New York: W.W. Notton & Company.

Geffen, R. M. (1997). The shaping of a cultural and religious elite: Alumni of the teachers institute, seminary college, and graduate schools, 1930–1995. In J. Wertheimer (Ed.), *Tradition renewed* (pp. 631–653). New York: Jewish Theological Seminary.

Glenn, S. (1990). *Daughters of the Shtetl: Jewish immigrant women in America's garment industry, 1880–1920*. Ithaca, NY: Cornell University Press.

Gold, P. S. (2004). *Making the Bible modern: Children's Bibles and Jewish education in twentieth century America*. Ithaca, NY: Cornell University Press.

Goldberg, H. (1997). Becoming history: Perspectives on the seminary faculty at mid-century. In J. Wertheimer (Ed.), *Tradition renewed* (pp. 353–437). New York: Jewish Theological Seminary.

Goldberg, J. J., & King, E. (1993). *Builders and dreamers: Habonim Labor Zionist youth in North America*. New York: Herzl Press.

Goren, A. (1970). *New York Jews and the quest for community*. New York: Columbia University Press.

Graff, G. (2008). *"And You Shall teach them diligently": A concise history of Jewish education in the United States, 1776–2000*. New York: JTS Press.

Grand, S. (1958). *A history of Zionist youth organizations in the United States from their inception to 1940*. Ph.D. diss., Columbia University.

Grant, L. (2010). Mamie Gamoran: Modeling her Jewish life through Jewish textbooks. In C. Ingall (Ed.), *The women who reconstructed American Jewish Education, (1910–1965)*. Waltham, MA: Brandeis University Press.

Greene, D. (2011). *The Jewish origins of cultureal Pluralism: The Menorah association and American diversity*. Bloomington: Indiana University Press.

Gurock, J. (1979). *When harlem was Jewish, 1870–1930*. New York: Columbia University Press.

Gurock, J. (1988). *The Men and Women of Yeshiva: Higher education, orthodoxy, and American Judaism*. New York: Columbia University Press.

J. Gurock (Ed.). (1989). *Ramaz: School, community, scholarship and orthodoxy*. Hoboken, NJ: Ktav.

Gurock, J. (2002). Jewish commitment and continuity in interwar Brooklyn. In I. Abramovitch & S. Galvin (Eds.), *The Jews of Brooklyn*. Hanover, NH: University Press of New England.

Gurock, J. (2005). *Judaism's encounter with American sports*. Bloomington, IN: Indiana University Press.

Gurock, J. (2009). *Orthodox Jews in America*. Bloomington, IN: Indiana University Press.

Heilman, S. (1999). From t-shirts to peak experiences: Teens, the Israel trip and Jewish identity. In Y. Rich, M. Rosenak (Eds.), *Abiding challenges: Research perspectives on Jewish education, studies in memory of Mordechai Bar-Lev*. Ramat Gan: Bar-Ilan University.

Helmreich, W. (1982). *The world of the Yeshiva: An intimate portrait of orthodox Jewry*. New York: Free Press.

Helmreich, W. (1995). Visits to Europe, Zionist education and Jewish identity: The case of the march of the living. *Journal of Jewish Education, 61*, 16–20.

Horowitz, S. (1998). The paradox of Jewish studies in the new academy. In D. Biale, et al (Eds.), *Insider/Outsider: American Jews and multiculturalism*. Berkeley, CA: University of California Press.

Isaacman, D. (1970). *Jewish Summer Camps in the US and Canada*. Ph.D. diss., Dropsie College.

Jacobs, B. (2005). *The (Trans)formation of American Jews: Jewish Social Studies in Progressive American Jewish Schools, 1910–1940*. Ph.D diss., Columbia University.

Jacobs, B. M. (2005). What's wrong with the history of American Jewish education? *Journal of Jewish Education, 71*, 33–51.

Joselit, J. W. (1978). Without Ghettoism: A history of the Intercollegiate Menorah Association, 1906–1930. *American Jewish Archives Journal, 30*, 133–154.

Joselit, J. W. (1990). *New York's Jewish Jews: The orthodox community in the interwar years*. Bloomington, IN: Indiana University Press.

Joselit, J. W. (1994). *The wonders of America: Reinventing Jewish culture, 1880–1950*. New York: Hill & Wang.

Kaplan, M., & Cronson, B. (1949). First community survey of Jewish education in New York city. *Jewish Education, 20*, 113–116.

Karabel, J. (2005). *The Chosen: The hidden history of admission and exclusion at Harvard, Yale and Princeton*. Boston: Houghton Mifflin Company.

Kaufman, D. (1997). Jewish education as a civilization: A history of the Teachers Institute. In J. Wertheimer (Ed.), *Tradition renewed: A history of the Jewish theological seminary of America* (pp. 565–629). New York: Jewish Theological Seminary.

Kaufman, D. (1999). *Shul with a pool: The "Synagogue-center" in American Jewish history*. Hanover, NH: Brandeis University Press.

Kelner, S. (2003–2004). The impact of Israel experience programs on Israel's symbolic meaning. *Contemporary Jewry, 24*, 124–155.

Kelner, S. (2010). *Tours that bind: Diaspora, Pilgrimage and Israeli Birthright tourism*. New York: New York University Press.

King, D. (1979). *A History of Gratz College, 1893–1928*. Ph.D. diss., Dropsie College.

Klapper, M. (2005). *Jewish Girls coming of age in America, 1860–1920*. New York: New York University Press.

Klapper, M. (2008). A history of Jewish education in America, 1700–2000. In M. L. Raphael (Ed.), *The Columbia history of Jews and Judaism in America* (pp. 189–216). New York: Columbia University Press.

Klingenstein, S. (1991). *Jews in the American academy, 1900–1940: The dynamics of intellectual assimilation*. New Haven, CT: Yale University Press.

Klingenstein, S. (1998). *Enlarging America: The cultural work of Jewish literary scholars, 1930–1990*. Syracuse, NY: Syracuse University Press.

Korelitz, S. (1997). The Menorah idea: From religion to culture, from race to ethnicity. *American Jewish History, 85*, 75–100.

Kramer, D. Z. (1984). *The Day schools and Torah Umesorah: The seeding of traditional Judaism in America*. New York: Yeshiva University Press.

Krasner, J. (2002). *Representations of Self and Other in American Jewish History and Social Studies School Books: An Exploration of the Changing Shape of American Jewish Identity*. Ph.D. diss., Brandeis University.

Krasner, J. (2003). A recipe for American Jewish integration: The Adventures of K'tonton and Hillel's Happy Holidays. *The Lion and the Unicorn, 27*, 344–361.

Krasner, J. (2005–2006). *Jewish education* and American Jewish education. *Journal of Jewish Education, 71*, 121–177; 71, 279–317; 72, 29–76.

Krasner, J. (2009). The rise and fall of the progressive Talmud Torah: The Central Jewish Institute and interwar American Jewish identity. In R. Medoff (Ed.), *Rav chesed: Essays in honor of Rabbi Dr. Haskel Lookstein*. Hoboken, NJ: Ktav.

Krasner, J. (2011). *The Benderly boys and American Jewish education*. Hanover, NH: Brandeis University Press.

Kutnick, J. (1998). Serving the Jewish community, pursuing higher Jewish learning: Gratz College in historical perspective. In R. M. Geffen & M. B. Edelman (Eds.), *Freedom and responsibility: Exploring the challenges of Jewish continuity* (pp. 321–348). Hoboken, NJ: Ktav.

Landesman, A. (1969). *Brownsville: The birth, development and passing of a Jewish community in New York*. New York: Bloch Publishing Company.

Liberles, R. (1995). *Salo Wittmayer Baron: Architect of Jewish history*. New York: New York University Press.

Liberles, R. (1997). Wissenschaft des Judentums comes to America. In J. Wertheimer (Ed.), *Tradition renewed* (pp. 327–351). New York: Jewish Theological Seminary.

Lorge, M., & Zola, G. (2006). *A place of our own: The rise of reform Jewish camping*. Tuscaloosa, AL: University of Alabama Press.

Marcus, J. R. (1993). *United States Jewry, 1776–1985: The Germanic period (Part II)*. Detroit, MI: Wayne State University Press.

Meyer, M. (1992). *Hebrew Union College-Jewish Institute of religion: A centennial history, 1875–1975*. Cincinnati, OH: Hebrew Union College Press.

Michels, T. (2005). *A fire in their hearts: Yiddish socialists in New York*. Cambridge, MA: Harvard University Press.

Mintz, A. (1997). The divided fate of Hebrew and Hebrew culture at the Seminary. In J. Wertheimer (Ed.), *Tradition renewed* (pp. 81–112). New York: Jewish Theological Seminary.

Mittelberg, D. (1992). The impact of Jewish education and an "Israel experience" on the Jewish identity of American Jewish youth. *Studies in Contemporary Jewry, 8*, 194–218.

Moore, D. D. (1981). *At home in America: Second generation New York Jews*. New York: Columbia University Press.

Moore, D. D. (1994). *To the golden cities: Pursuing the American Jewish dream Miami and L.A.* New York: Free Press.

Moore, D. D. (1999). Inventing Jewish identity in California: Shlomo Bardin, Zionism and the Brandeis Camp Institute. In S. M. Cohen & G. Horenczyk (Eds.), *National variations in Jewish identity* (pp. 201–221). Albany, NY: State University of New York Press.

Neusner, J. (1985). *The public side of learning: The political consequences of scholarship in the context of Judaism*. Chico, CA: Scholars Press.

Pearlstein, P. (1993). *Understanding through Education: One Hundred Years of the Jewish Chautauqua Society, 1893–1993*. Ph.D. diss., George Washington University.

J. Pilch (Ed.). (1969). *A history of Jewish education in America*. New York: National Curriculum Research Institute of the American Association of Jewish Education.

Powell, B. (2003). Shlomo Bardin's Eretz Brandeis. In A. Kahn & M. Dollinger (Eds.), *California Jews* (pp. 171–184). Hanover, NH: University Press of New England.

Prell, R.-E. (1989). *Prayer and community: The Havurah in American Judaism*. Detroit, MI: Wayne State University Press.

Prell, R.-E. (1999). *Fighting to become American: Jews, gender and the anxiety of assimilation*. Boston: Beacon Press.

Prell, R.-E. (2006). *Jewish summer camping and civil rights*. Ann Arbor, MI: Frankel Center for Judaic Studies, University of Michigan.

Prell, R.-E. (2007). Summer camp, postwar American Jewish youth and the redemption of Judaism. *The Jewish Role in American Life: An Annual Review, 5*, 77–108.

Reimer, J. (1995). Passionate visions in contest: On the history of Jewish education in Boston. In J. Sarna & E. Smith (Eds.), *The Jews of Boston* (pp. 279–301). Boston, MA: Combined Jewish Philanthropies of Greater Boston.

Ritterband, P., & Wechsler, H. (1994). *Jewish learning in American Universities: The first century.* Bloomington, IN: Indiana University Press.

Rogow, F. (1993). *Gone to another meeting: The national council of Jewish women, 1893–1993.* Tuscaloosa, AL: University of Alabama Press.

Sarna, J. (1989). *JPS: The Americanization of Jewish culture.* Philadelphia, PA: Jewish Publication Society.

Sarna, J. (1995). *A great awakening: The transformation that shaped twentieth century American Judaism and its implications for today.* New York: Council for Initiatives on Jewish Education.

Sarna, J. (1997). Two traditions of seminary scholarship. In J. Wertheimer (Ed.), *Tradition renewed* (pp. 53–80). New York: Jewish Theological Seminary.

Sarna, J. (1998). American Jewish education in historical perspective. *Journal of Jewish Education, 64,* 8–21.

Sarna, J. (2005). The cyclical history of adult Jewish learning in the United States: Peers law and its implications. In M. Nisan & O. Schremer (Eds.), *Educational deliberations: Studies in education dedicated to Shlomo (Seymour) Fox.* Jerusalem: Keter Publishing.

Sarna, J. (2006). A crucial decade in Jewish camping. In M. Lorge & G. Zola (Eds.), *A place of our own: The Rise of reform Jewish camping.* Tuscaloosa, AL: University of Alabama Press.

Saxe, L., & Chazan, B. (2008). *Ten days of birthright Israel: A journey in young adult identity.* Hanover, NH: University Press of New England.

Scharfstein, Z. (1955). *Arba'im Shanah Be-Amerikah.* Tel Aviv: Masada.

Scharfstein, Z. (1960–1965). *Toldot ha-hinukh be-Yiśrael ba-dorot ha-aharonim.* Jerusalem: Reuben Mass.

Schick, M. (2004). *A census of Jewish day schools in the United States, 2003–2004.* New York: Avi Chai Foundation.

Schiff, A. (1966). *The Jewish day school in America.* New York: Jewish Education Committee Press.

Schreiber, M. (1970, April). The Agnon school of Cleveland: An unlikely birth of a day school. *CCAR Journal, 17,* 66–79.

Schwartz, S. R. (1987). Camp Ramah: The early years, 1947–1952. *Conservative Judaism, 40,* 12–42.

Schwartz, S. R. (1991). *The emergence of Jewish scholarship in America: The publication of the Jewish Encyclopedia.* Cincinnati, OH: Hebrew Union College Press.

Schwartz, S. R. (1997). The Schechter faculty: The Seminary and Wissenschaft des Judentums. *In* J. Wertheimer (Ed.), *Tradition renewed* (pp. 293–325). New York: Jewish Theological Seminary.

Scult, M. (1990). *The American Judaism of Mordecai Kaplan.* New York: New York University Press.

Scult, M. (1993). *Judaism faces the Twentieth century: A biography of Mordecai M. Kaplan.* Detroit: Wayne State University Press.

Scult, M. (Ed.). (2001). *Communings of the spirit: The journals of Mordecai M. Kaplan.* Detroit, MI: Wayne State University Press.

Shapiro, E. (1992). *A time for healing: American Jewry Since World War II.* Baltimore: Johns Hopkins University Press.

Shargel, B. R. (1985). *Practical dreamer: Israel Friedlaender and the shaping of American Judaism.* New York: Jewish Theological Seminary of America.

Sheramy, R. (2001). *Defining lessons: The Holocaust in American Jewish education.* Ph.D. diss., Brandeis University.

Sheramy, R. (2007). From Auschwitz to Jerusalem: Re-enacting Jewish history on the march of the living. *Polin, 19,* 307–325.

Soloveitchik, H. (1994). Rupture and reconstruction: The transformation of contemporary Orthodoxy. *Tradition, 28,* 64–130.

Stern, M. H. (2004). "A dream not quite come true": Reassessing the Benderly era in Jewish education. *Journal of Jewish Education, 70,* 16–26.

Stern, M. H. (2007). *"Your Children, Will they be Yours?"—Educational Strategies for Jewish Survival: The Central Jewish Institute, 1916–1944*. Ph.D. diss., Stanford University.
Synnott, M. (1979). *The half-opened door: Discrimination and admissions at Harvard, Yale and Princeton, 1900–1970*. Westport, CT: Greenwood Press.
Thaler, V. S. (2008), *The reshaping of American Jewish identity, 1945–1960*. Ph.D. diss., Yale University.
Wechsler, H. (1977). *The qualified student: A history of selective college admission in America*. New York: Wiley.
Wertheimer, J. (1993). *A people divided: Judaism in contemporary America*. New York: Basic Books.
Wertheimer, J. (1997). *Tradition renewed: A history of the Jewish theological seminary*. New York: Jewish Theological Seminary of America.
Wertheimer, J. (1999). Jewish education in the United States: Recent trends and issues. *American Jewish Year Book, 99*, 3–115.
Winter, N. (1966). *Jewish education in a pluralist society*. New York: New York University Press.
Zeldin, M. (1988). The promise of historical inquiry: Nineteenth century Jewish day schools and twentieth century policy. *Religious Education, 83*, 438–452.
Zola, G. (2006). Jewish camping and its relationship to the organized camping movement in America. In M. Lorge & G. Zola (Eds.), *A place of their own: The rise of reform Jewish camping* (pp. 1–26). Tuscaloosa, AL: University of Alabama Press.

Janush Korczak's Life and Legacy for Jewish Education

Marc Silverman

Introduction

Janush Korczak (1878–1942) is renowned worldwide for his heroic stand of non-violent opposition to the Nazis' decision to liquidate the Jewish ghetto of Warsaw (July–August 1942) and deport all the Jews in it, including the children, to the death camp of Treblinka. Korczak refused to accept the offers made by close friends or admirers that would have afforded him escape from the ghetto and from the fate awaiting his fellow Jews. His decision to stay with his charges, the hundred and more orphans and the staff of the Jewish orphanage he had headed since 1912, and to accompany them through all the travails, including death, that deportation would hold for them was as unequivocal as was his refusal to consider escaping from the ghetto (Bernheim, 1989, pp. 137–146; Lifton, 1988, pp. 325–346; Perlis, 1986, pp. 208–217; Regev, 1996, pp. 195–208).

The ethos of accepting radical responsibility for the welfare of others, of lending support to the weakest sectors of the Warsaw ghetto population out of profound compassion for all that lives, breathes, creates, and suffers, and the uncompromising search for justice and truth as essential components of humanity are expressed powerfully in the final chapters of Korczak's life. However, this rather exclusive focus on his Warsaw ghetto years (1940–1942) and his heroic and tragic end in Treblinka do not give him, his work and works the attention they so richly deserve.

In fact, Korczak was one of the outstanding humanist educators of the twentieth century in the Western world; indeed, some would say he was the most outstanding (see Kohlberg, 1981). In the Polish-Jewish orphanage he headed for 30 years (1912–1942) and in the Polish one in which he served as its head educational supervisor (1919–1936), he developed and implemented a rich array of educational practices, methods, and frameworks later dubbed the Korczakian system. This "system" enabled deprived and abused children, who came from dysfunctional families and suffered from considerable social pathologies, to undergo significant self-reformation during their residence in the orphanage over a period of 6–8 years.

M. Silverman (✉)
Hebrew University, Jerusalem, Israel
e-mail: msmrs@mscc.huji.ac.il

In this chapter I propose that the following four major features of Korczak's educational works are strongly relevant to, and can be incorporated into, Jewish education worldwide today:

1. *God-wrestling* (Waskow, 1978)—"Implicit religion" plays a central role in Korczak's own personal search for the meaning of life and toward leading a meaningful life. His religiosity is articulated in many of his literary, reflective, and pedagogical works, and it underlies and significantly influences his educational approach and practices;
2. *The "humanization" of the world*—Lending true "weight" to human, animate, and inanimate others is the hallmark of Korczak's "brand" of humanism. Paraphrasing Dostoyevsky, Korczak traveled on the lending respect to real persons in their respective concrete, physical, and mental particularities including "the–person-coughing–next-to-you-on-a-bus" road of humanism. He never traveled on its "easy to love humanity" road. His humanism expressed itself in a highly egalitarian ethos. Democracy, reciprocity, mutuality, cooperation, partnership, sharing, and gracious dialogue were the cornerstones of the human social and interpersonal relationships he constructed, implemented, and sustained. Ever striving toward self-improvement and improvement of the world—increasing care, concern, fairness, and justice in human beings' interrelationship and relationship to the world—was the ultimate cultural–educational goal and project of his life-work.
3. *Character and moral education*—Korczak was an outstanding, indeed exceptional social pedagogue, a character educator and an educator toward ethical fairness and justice. Analysis of the network of interrelated educational practices, methods, and frameworks he devised and implemented in the two orphanages referred to above demonstrates the realization of a moral education embedded in and realizing an integration between justice-seeking and care-lending types of ethic.
4. *Types of modern Jewish identity and identification*—As a person of Jewish origins, strongly educated in and highly acculturated to Polish culture and patriotism, Korczak's struggle with his Jewish identity is an engaging story in itself. In many ways it emblematizes strongly acculturated European and Western Jews'—including Anglo-American ones'—struggles with this existential issue in the nineteenth, twentieth, and twenty-first centuries. Of no less significance, Korczak's "non-Jewish Jewish identity" was composed of integration between his Jewish solidarity and his uncompromising concern regarding decisive perennial existential—personal, social, and political—issues facing humanity. This concern was a highly proactive one which expressed itself in his untiring attempts to contribute to their resolution.

Singling out these four features from Korczak's life and legacy as the ones most significant to Jewish education worldwide today is based on my understanding of Jewish education and of the major challenges it faces. This understanding comprises the following main assumptions:

Religious education—Irrespective of their specific approaches to the Jewish historical religious tradition, most if not all Jewish educational frameworks include in their curriculum learning about, and/or experiencing Jewish religious ideas and rituals. Talking about, relating to, and "wrestling" with God is one of the constitutive features of Jewish culture and civilization throughout the ages. Affording opportunities and offering tools to Jewish learners to address these religious existential issues plays an important role in formal and informal Jewish educational frameworks and settings.

Political–civic education—Jews understand themselves and other peoples understand them as a particular people holding at once their own particular religion and contending, at the same time, that their religion–ethnicity ultimately holds universal meaning for all of humankind. Confronting the internal tension between religious–ethnic centricity and a world-embracing humanism has played a central role in Jewish life throughout the ages. Consequently, Jewish education needs to and does include important features of political–civic education. Specifically, in the context of the Jewish democratic state of Israel, the nature of the relationship between its Jewish and its democratic dimensions is the main political–civic question Jewish education needs to address; in the context of Jews living in diverse nation-States throughout the world as citizens and as a distinct ethnic or cultural–religious group in these polities, Jewish education needs to address the latter's nature and the extent its political structure and policies are congruent with Jewish perspectives on them.

Moral education—"We will do and then we'll hear/understand" (*Na'aseh ve'nishma*); and "our hearts—habits and tendencies—follow in the footsteps of our deeds" (*ha'levavot nimshachim achar ha'ma'asim*) are at the core of Jewish conceptions of ethics. Consequently, as in the case of God-relating, irrespective of their specific approach to them, Jewish educational streams and frameworks include moral education as an important component in their educational program.

Cultural-identity education—The interface between the Jews' and other peoples' cultures has been and remains a perennial theme throughout world history. Today, as in previous historical periods, Jewish education is called upon to develop ways to realize a satisfactory integration between Jewish culture and general cultures.

I now turn to presenting in detail Korczak's approach to these four cultural and educational issues. Following this presentation, I will explore possible direct connections between his approaches and the concerns of Jewish education today.

Korczak's Religious Humanist Social–Pedagogical Legacy

Implicit Religion

Opening

An examination of Korczak's writings and life experiences, from his youthful through his mature and older adult years, discloses the consistent presence of an interrelated number of basic religious existential senses and sensibilities in his experience and understanding of the world. A considerable number of these sensibilities are expressed in the two passages from Korczak's semi-autobiographical work *Confessions of a Butterfly* published in 1914:

January 20
This morning I really prayed the way a human being should pray... I was completely aware of what I was saying, not so much in the words, but in my thought and spirit. Only this type of praying can strengthen a person; only this type of praying becomes a reflective being. The other type of praying can be likened to the ramblings of a beggar on the church's steps (As I now experience infinite harmony in God I'm no longer surprised this Being has no beginning and no end. The cosmos and the stars, not the priest, lend testimony to me of the "Creator of worlds" existence). I've created for myself a new type of faith. Its direction is not yet entirely clear to me; but I know it is based on the purity of the human spirit. It claims God exists. What's God's nature? Human reason does not have an answer to this question. Behave fairly and do good deeds, pray not to petition God but in order to never forget Him because we can see God in everything. (Korczak, 1999, pp. 146–147)

April 10
... I'm afraid of the dark, afraid of hallucinations, I'm more afraid of the emotional than of the visual ones: If a cold, bony twisted hand suddenly reached out to catch me I would not be able to stand it. Books seem to make me nervous but they protect me from something even worse. I have come to deny and reject ritual practices. But I still believe in God and prayer. I preserve them because it's not possible to live without them. It's not possible that human beings are a mere accident. (ibid., pp. 156–157)

The following religious sensibilities, assumptions, or contentions can be derived from these two passages:

1. God, a Supreme Being, exists.
2. The strong sense of this Being's existence is derived from human encounters with nature.
3. This Supreme Being is infinite and is experienced and conceived of in terms of re-presenting an infinite harmony.
4. Human reason cannot comprehend the nature of this Infinite Being.
5. This Supreme Being's presence can be experienced by human beings in everything.
6. The presence of God is experienced mainly in ethical behavior and in prayer.
7. The praying experience befitting humans as rational–reflective beings should be a purely spiritual personal one; it should not resemble a business-like transaction where the attempt is made to trade off the spiritual wares of faith for the sake of receiving material goods.

Creation

With the help of passages from works he penned in other periods of his life, I develop and explore these sensibilities further. Korczak's conception of God and of this Supreme Being's relationship to the world is articulated most clearly and powerfully in his essay on the first year of the human infant "Bobo" (Polish term meaning baby). This essay also published in 1914 combines rich insightful empirical comments on an infant's mental and motor development in its first year of life with rich poetic metaphors and philosophical reflections on the process and meaning of life. Bobo, the human infant, is at once a real human infant and a metaphor of human life and human life forces in general (Korczak, 1999, pp. 68–70).

Korczak places Bobo within the context of the creation of the world. In its primordial stage, Korczak envisages the world as having been in a state of chaos; atom-like particles exist separately and unrelated to each other in this chaos. The actual creation of life and Bobo within it takes place when God calls out to these atoms and commands them to relinquish their separate estranged existence from each other and to join themselves together in cooperative interdependent relationships (ibid.).

Creation and not the particular-historical revelation of any specific explicit religion, such as Christianity, Judaism, Islam, etc., is the centerpiece of Korczak's implicit religiosity. Korczak experiences and perceives divine revelation through "Creation" and human phenomena emerging out of it. In Korczak's eyes these human phenomena intimate God's presence in the world:

- Human longings, aspirations, and need to pray for a better life and world;
- Human strivings to realize goodness in the world;
- The respect, love, and support human beings can and often do lend to human others (as well as to animate and inanimate ones).

These human signals of the divine presence are articulated most powerfully in the prayer book Korczak composed after his mother's death in 1920 and in the parable "How God took to His feet and ran away from the sanctuary the townspeople built for Him" which appears in the play, *The Asylum of the Insane*, he penned in 1931.

Korczak's Book of 18 Prayers

Korczak entitled the prayer book composed of 18 prayers he penned and collected together *A Person with Her/His God: Prayers of People Who Do Not Pray* (1921/1922; Korczak, 1996a). The title as well as the subtitle of this collection provides some insights regarding Korczak's sense of God's presence and of his response to it. *A Person with Her/His God*—It is not humanity with its God or human beings with their God but an individual singular human being with her/his God. Implicit here is the supposition that God's presence in the world is experienced and conceived within the concrete, particular, subjective context of each and every human individual's life. *Prayers of People Who Do Not Pray*—The paradox in this subtitle intimates that the prayers in this prayer book are prayed by people who pray and the people to whom this prayer book is addressed are also people who pray. However, these praying people do not pray in conventional traditional religious places, and their prayers are not and cannot be found in particular, historical, institutionalized fixed canonized liturgy.

In these prayers, Korczak takes great liberty employing ironic, playful, and at times radical and shocking anthropomorphic imagery in his prayers' God-talk and in his images of God in general (see below). This tendency apparently stems from the uncompromising anthropocentric nature of his implicit religiosity or religious humanism. Since rational–critical reflective human beings cannot possibly gain access into the essence of the infinite Supreme Being as the young girl states in her prayer to God "I know man's mind is too tiny to comprehend God, it's like a drop in the ocean" (Korczak, 1996a, pp. 23–24), the best they can do is to "imaginare" this Being in terms of the human at its best—of humanity in its finest actual achievements and highest aspirations. Many of Korczak's prayers are shot through with such imaginerings—like this one of the young woman who prays the prayer of "Playfulness":

> But after all, You are not only present in a human being's tears but also in the lilac flowers' scent. You are not only in the heavens but also in a kiss. Sadness and longings arise after every festivity. Embedded in these longings like in the mist are mom's face, whispers from the homeland, a human other's plight, and the fate of Your secret, God. (ibid., p. 26)

Summarizing these points, we can say Korczak's God is human beings' Wise and Closest Friend of Friends who ever lends them support and encouragement to grow, flourish, and create, and to accompany and do good to the world and to all others in it, to human ones especially, and to human children most especially.

Korczak's Parable About God

In the seventh scene of Korczak's play, *The Senate of the Insane* (Korczak, 1996a, pp. 59–100), the "old man," one of the more sane patients in this fictional insane asylum, shares a legend about God with a young boy named Yazik (nicknamed Yank). This parable is rich, intricate, and full of daring and delightful images, humor, and irony. Tying together the many threads and themes in it and interpreting these offers the following major insights regarding Korczak's conception of God and his response to this Being's presence:

- *God's wisdom and human beings' recalcitrance*—Images characterizing God as very old, lonely, tired-out, sad, and disappointed abound in this parable as they do in Korczak's prayer book. God speaks directly to the multitude of people gathered around him only once. God issues the following command consisting of seven words to them: *My children—love each one their neighbor!* (ibid., p. 78). Both the command and the Commander are very ancient and in great age lay great wisdom—the wisdom of many generations. However, despite this wisdom and its ancient pedigree, human beings all-too-often neither accept nor practice it! They do not let God's real and true Presence "in"—into themselves. It is precisely here, in the in-between between the "presence" of this eternal command of loving one's neighbor issued to human beings throughout the ages and their unwillingness to follow and fulfill it that God's profound "feelings" of exhaustion, sadness, disappointment, and despair emerge.
- *Acts of loving-kindness and justice*—God's travels, encounters with people, temporary dwelling places, and self-transformations intimate Korczak's understanding of what this singular command entails. It can be formulated through mirroring the Rabbinic hermeneutic model of *Imatatio Dei* (*Sifre'-Devarim*, 49) while introducing specific ideas of Korczak into it:

Just as God lends respect and deep affection to inanimate and animate non-rational beings in the natural word—forests, forest berries, lilacs, the Sun, stars, the Vistula river, lightening bugs, sparrows, larks, etc. —so too humans should lend such respect and love to them. And just as God cares deeply about, lends compassion and assistance to common and simple folk (workers, soldiers, church-goers), to poor, weak, oppressed, and outcast members of society in general and to children in particular, so too humans should lend such care, accompaniment, and assistance to them.

Ever striving to develop interpersonal and social sensitivity to the "trials and tribulations" of human others and an active orientation to lending assistance to them, to the weak and oppressed among them in particular, and most particularly to children whom Korczak considered as the outstanding members among these latter types of people, is the true way to imitate God's Presence in Creation and to realize this Being's single and singular command.

Jewish Education: Implications and Applications

As stated in the opening section above, most Jewish educational frameworks include learning about and experiencing Jewish religious ideas and ritual in their curriculum; "God-talk" and "God-relating" are part and parcel of their educational programs. Consequently, lending Jewish learners concepts and tools to address religious existential issues is an important objective of most formal and informal Jewish educational frameworks and settings.

Korczak's life story, his educational work and his final march with the children of the Jewish orphanage are deeply embedded in his implicit religious sense of the world. Both the prayer book and the parable on God can be considered true gems of implicit religiosity. The prayers in this prayer book could be studied toward and within student prayer services. These prayers could encourage students to compose their own "personal" prayers. A careful considered reading of Korczak's parable could increase the religious sensitivity of the students and generate serious discussion among them on the nature of God and this Infinite Being's presence in the world.

Korczak's implicit religion can serve Jewish education in two main ways: (1) as a vehicle to inspire Jewish learners to deepening the inwardness of their existent observance of the historical–traditional precepts and practices of Judaism as a historical–particular explicit religion and/or (2) as a vehicle toward the development of these learners' growth as free, critical–rational, and ethical human beings who care deeply about the world and actively engage in trying to improve it.

Religious Humanism and the "Humanization" of the World

Opening

Korczak derived the basic components of his political and pedagogical orientation from "Warsaw positivism" (Frost, 1983). This positivism was held by a group of Polish intellectuals, academics, social activists, and educators in Warsaw who saw themselves and were seen by others as positivist, progressive liberals, or socialists. Korczak met the members of this circle during his student years in Warsaw University's medical school (1896–1904). He came to admire many of them. Their personalities, ideas, and actions exercised considerable influence on him, and he took part in many of their social, cultural, and educational activities (Cohen, 1988; Eden, 2000; Perlis, 1986).

Their ideas and deeds are clearly discernible in Korczak's version of humanism. The main features of this circle's humanism and Korczak's intensification of them are:

- The improvement of the lives of the oppressed, impoverished, and weakest sectors of Polish society is conceived as the ultimate end of social, cultural, and educational work. The target population of this circle's work was Polish common folk, mainly members of the working class; in distinction from them, Korczak's target audience was children. He considered them as a greatly and unfairly ignored underprivileged and oppressed social class in general; and he considered the homeless or abused among these children as the most oppressed sub-sector among them.
- "Organic work"—work from the "bottom-up." This circle contended that social reform and improvement can be best realized through specific and concrete forms of social–economic and cultural–educational work and legislation. This path of social–positivist reconstruction of Polish society organically entailed daily, patient, hard, getting-ones'-hands-dirty practical work.
- This circle's members' political orientation was liberal or socialist. They identified with social–progressive political trends and parties, and were opposed to revolutionary Marxist ones.

Korczak's political orientation was social–democratic. However, he refused to become a member of the "Social–democratic party of Lithuanian and Polish workers" with which he identified. Strong echoes of this circle's members' distrust of ideologies, theories, and programs, and their insistence on people's actual doings as the litmus test of their ethical stature can be heard in Korczak's familiar quip about political parties and their platforms: *Rain water is pure but becomes filthy upon its passage through the street-drains* (Perlis, 1986, p. 17).

Were we asked to devise a caption that would encapsulate the ethos of this circle of activists, the following possibilities come to mind: *We are what we give (to others); To live is to give and to give is to live; Not our theories but our practices— doings and deeds—constitute and define us.* The litmus test of a persons' humanity is the way they actively relate to human others in real-life conditions. Another decisive criterion for the assessment of a persons' humanity is their authenticity, honesty, and integrity as these are articulated in their efforts to practice what they preach.

The correlation between Korczak's words and his deeds is truly exceptional. Few would contest the claim that honesty, sincerity, authenticity, and integrity were among the most decisive characteristics expressed in and constituting his personality and character. Underlying and lending form and shape to this ethos is the principle of respect to human beings as persons—lending genuine respect to all human beings in their respective real, concrete, physical as well as historical–cultural particularity. This humanism expressed itself in a highly egalitarian ethos. A firm commitment to democratic, egalitarian, and dialogical human relationships and interrelationships, uncompromising advocacy of equal rights for the downtrodden, and a strong opposition to relationships based on forms of hierarchies are among the decisive political–cultural ramifications of this ethos.

Korczak's educational work was based on this radical egalitarian ethos. In one of the last entries in his Warsaw ghetto diary entitled "Why I collect dirty dishes," he insists on lending equal respect to menial and intellectual tasks, and to the persons who do either or both of them. In his own words:

> I carry on a struggle to make sure that in the orphanage there shall be no work called delicate or ordinary, smart or stupid, clean or dirty—work fit for dainty young ladies and for the plain crowd. The orphanage should not have members doing exclusively physical or mental work... I respect honest working people. Their hands are always clean for me and their opinions I weigh at the price of gold. (Korczak, 1972, p. 166)

Korczak struggled against dichotomous conceptions of human beings that maintained antagonistic divisions between the physical, the affective, the intellectual, and the behavioral dimensions of human personality and tasks of life.

Jewish Education: Implications and Applications

There are two major ways Korczak's humanism and his tireless efforts to humanize the world can be meaningfully applied to Jewish education today:

1. Engendering Jewish learners' political awareness and encouraging them to become reflective and critical of the sources of social–economic inequality, to consider the ethical implications of different and oft-opposing political theories, parties, and movements, and to take proactive stands toward realizing ethical policies and opposing unethical ones is one of these ways. Korczak's firm commitment to democracy and to democratic-socialism always out-weighed his strong Polish patriotism and nationalism. His affirmation of the latter as a decisively important framework of human belonging was predicated on the assumption that it would serve as an instrument through which to realize humanistic–social–democratic values. Korczak's attitudes and deeds can assist toward facilitating the development of Jewish learners who will actively lend priority to realizing the humanistic–democratic over Jewish national or ethnic or religious ethnic aspirations and values when they are clearly in conflict with each other. In Israel this would mean civic education that insists on democracy as the qualifier of Israel's Jewishness; and among Diaspora Jewish communities this would mean placing social–economic justice as a sine qua non-component of a Jewish education worthy of its name.
2. As Kohlberg (1981) suggests, Korczak refrained from imposing his exceptionally high ethical–humanist standards on the children and educational staff in his

charge. However, this admirable self-limitation does not prevent us from viewing his life and work as a model of humanity at its highest expression and level. Korczak's life is a powerful expression of the contention that our humanity is constituted by what we give to others and not by what we get from them. Korczak's life can inspire all those who learn about it and for Jewish learners, in particular, to develop and adopt altruistic attitudes and deeds to others. Indeed, there is an interesting ideational correlation between Korczak's view of lending help to others as a self-understood human duty or obligation and the Jewish view of *tzadaka* (the Hebrew term for lending assistance to an oppressed human other), not as a special allowance, not as charity, but as *tzedek* (Hebrew for justice).

Character and Moral Education

> To cultivate the goodness that does exist, despite peoples' weaknesses and inborn negative instincts, such goodness indeed does exist. Are not Trust and the Belief in people precisely the goodness that we can cultivate and foster as an antidote to the badness we sometimes cannot eliminate, and whose growth we are barely able to curtail through very hard and concentrated effort. (Korczak, 1978, pp. 255–256)

> When I consider the facts in an unbiased fashion without any illusions, I believe educators primarily need to know: To lend full forbearance to every child in every case. The meaning of "to understand every thing" is to lend it forgiveness [...] Educators [...] are called upon to adopt in their hearts and for their own sake a compassionate stand in their judgment of children's misdeeds, failings and culpability [...] children act wrongly—sin—out of ignorance [...] because they succumbed to temptation, to an other's manipulation [...], because they could not find a way to act differently [...]. Those who are angered and agitated by children for being what they are, for being as they were born or as their experiences have taught them to be, are not educators. (ibid., pp. 253–254)

Opening

Korczak developed and implemented a rich array of educational practices, methods, and frameworks in the orphanages he led that were later dubbed the Korczakian system. This system achieved considerable success in engaging deprived and abused children (ages 8–14) from dysfunctional families, who suffered from considerable social pathologies, in processes of ethical growth, that led to significant improvement in their relationships to themselves and others over the usual 6 year period of their residence in the orphanage. The extensive success Korczak realized in the reformation of these children from potentially anti-social and criminal to fair-minded, fair-playing young adults, justifiably earns him distinction as an exceptionally gifted moral and character educator.

What were the most salient features of Korczak's social pedagogy? The two quotes above from Korczak's short and seminal essay "Principles and Action—Theory and Practice" (1924–1925) articulate in a nutshell his understanding of the overarching aim of education and his basic educational approach toward its realization. As the first intimates, educating children's character in the wholeness of their personalities in the present and encouraging their will toward goodness are the quintessential aims of education. In Korczak's eyes true education worthy of this name is moral education.

In the light of this aim and these tasks, the basic question educators are called upon to address is: Through what processes can the will toward goodness be advanced and the will to badness reduced and re-channeled to more constructive life-building directions? Korczak himself was keenly aware that it is much easier to pose this question than it is to locate adequately compelling responses to it. The main difficulty in finding such responses stemmed from what he perceived to be the in-built limitations and frailties of humankind. The educational approach he developed to address the latter can be called "Compassionate reformation." Its fundamental meaning is well conveyed in the following lines taken from the well-known Tranquility prayer, penned by the Protestant existentialist theologian, Reinhold Neibhur:

> Dear Lord—Please grant me the fortitude to accept those things not in my power to change; the courage to change those things in my power; and the intelligence to be able to discern between these two. (Ring, 1985, p. 184)

Response-ability, the ability to respond in compassionate reformation to the difficulties and aspirations of their charges, is the hallmark of good educators. Korczak constructed and implemented an interrelated web of educational practices, methods, and frameworks that fostered an ethos of "compassionate re-formation" among all the members of the orphanages' community—its children, educational and administrative staff. The most outstanding among these practices and frameworks were *the children's parliament and law court*; this court's *constitution*; the *apprenticeship* system; *gradated citizenship status; ethical-improvement wagers and growth charts; work assignments, units, and points*, and others. Each of these frameworks independently and through their interrelationship engendered educational processes that assisted members of the orphanage community to learn to relate to each other through the prism of an ethical ethos that integrates between a relational–caring ethic and a rational–cognitive justice-seeking one.

These educational processes work themselves out through three interrelated sequential steps that will be presented and discussed in terms of the nature of the children's law court, its constitution, and its proceedings. Similar steps unfold in most of Korczak's educational methods, practices, and frameworks. However, an explication of these is beyond the scope of this chapter.

Step 1: Educational Forgiveness

Korczak insisted that the education of children must be achieved *with* them and *through* genuine dialogical cooperation between them and their educators. He translated this principle by establishing self-governing frameworks with "real teeth" in which children were called upon to undertake responsible roles and to perform genuine tasks. Among these frameworks, the children's law court he established and the constitution he penned for its proceedings were his favorite. Through it he hoped to find a "constitutional system" of education and to become a "constitutional educator" (Korczak, 1996, pp. 224 and 264). Staff members and not only children were subject to the proceedings and rulings of the law court according to its constitution. Such an equality-for-all constitutional framework strongly militated against the possibility of educators projecting their own needs, wants, and whims onto their educatees and of their adopting dominating-despotic relational modes toward them.

The constitution Korczak composed has no laws defining right or wrong, and good or bad deeds. The deeds' rightness or wrongness is first defined by the plaintiff, the child who accuses another child of committing a misdeed against her. Then, the court judges—four children who had not been accused of an offence over the previous week, and one educator in an advisory but no-vote capacity—are called upon to determine the extent to which this misdeed is indeed wrong and the extent to which its perpetrator is responsible and deserves blame for its commission. Consequently, the ethical nature of a deed is defined in relational, inter-subjective terms by the plaintiff and the children and staff member who serve as judges in the court.

Taking a considered look at this constitution's preamble will shed light on this first step as well as on the next two that follow it. Here is the full text of the preamble:

> *If a person does something bad, the best thing to do is to forgive her.* If she did something bad because she did not know better, she now already knows this. If she did something bad unintentionally, she will be more careful in the future. If she does something bad because she finds it difficult to adjust to norms unfamiliar to her, she'll try harder to adjust to them in the future. If she did something bad because she was tempted by others, from now on she will not pay attention to them.
>
> *If a person does something bad, the best thing to do is to forgive her, and to wait for her to mend her way in the future.*
>
> However, at the same time, the law court has an obligation to protect the quiet from being treated unfairly by the pestering and pushing ones; it has an obligation to protect the weak ones so that the strong ones will not be able to rise up to bother them; it has to protect the conscientious and industrious ones so that the neglectful and lazy ones won't disturb them; the law court has to make sure that order will be maintained, because disorder mainly hurts the good, quiet persons with a conscience.
>
> The law court is not justice but it is called upon to aspire towards realizing it; the law court is not truth but it is devoted to seeking it. (Korczak, 1996, pp. 224–225; translation from Hebrew, M.S., emphasis added)

Taking a look at the first two of the four passages comprising the full text of this preamble, it is important to note that the phrase "If a person does something bad, the best thing to do is to forgive him" appears twice. This repetition suggests that Korczak considered such forgiveness as a constitutive postulate of the very possibility of engaging in moral educational work with children. Indeed the substance of the second passage quoted from Korczak's essay "Principles and Action—Theory and Practice" heading this section (see Section "Character and Moral Education" p. X) is very similar to that of these two passages from the preamble.

A deep respect for children as persons combines together to create forbearance for their misdeeds. This forbearance is based on an attitude of compassionate understanding regarding the diverse conditions and circumstances that diminish children's capacity to do good things or increase their capacity to do bad ones. Korczak views this forbearance as an imperative, commanding ethical respect for the pupil's "given" presence, and not as a special favor. Furthermore, blaming a child for the way he genuinely "is" not only demonstrates a lack of respect toward his personhood but also strongly militates against any possibility of the child reconsidering specific pernicious aspects of his behavior. Angry accusation locks the "gates of mending one's bad ways" through which educatees could enter; while educational forgivingness unlocks and opens them widely.

To sum up, the first step on this compassionate reformation path entails lending genuine respect to children as persons and adopting an attitude of educational forgivingness toward them in their present "presence." Proceeding now from this first step and taking note of another crucial passage in this preamble, we arrive at its second step.

Step 2: Offering Mending-One's-Way(s) Opportunities

The last clause of the key sentence discussed above in its second appearance warrants attention: "If a person does something bad, the best thing to do is to forgive him, and to wait for her to mend her way in the future."

The forbearance Korczak proposes is not meant in any way to grant a do-wrong free pass to the child. Instead, the understanding acceptance of the bad deed is predicated upon the hopeful notion that in the future when an opportunity for the child to repeat this bad deed presents itself again, she will "mend her way" and refrain from committing it again. The Korczakian system abounds with "offerings" of second, third, fourth, and more improving-behavior opportunities, such as, children entering into a wager with Korczak regarding a negative behavior they wanted to overcome (ethical-improvement wagers); raising one's citizen's status in the orphanage by virtue of having become more socially cooperative (upgrading citizen status); and many more.

Suffice to say, the abundance of opportunities to mend one's way in Korczak's network of frameworks clearly demonstrates that his hope of his charges accepting response-ability for mending their ways was neither pious nor empty. On the contrary, it was based on his conscious, creative, wise design of a relatively inexhaustible array of *mending-ones-way* opportunities: individual and social tasks and frameworks that became practice fields for improving oneself and one's relationship with others.

Step 3: Not Just Caring but Just-Caring

Interpreting the last passages of this preamble will lead us to the third and final step in Korczak's approach to and practice of moral education. In the very last sentence of this preamble, Korczak states explicitly that the pursuit of justice and truthfulness is the motivating force underlying the children's court. These sentences and those preceding it suggest that in Korczak's conception of moral education, interpersonal, and social relationships should not be based just on relational caring but also on a caring and concern for just relationships. In light of this, the third step entails encouraging children not just to care for each other but also to care about conducting relationships between themselves and others that are just.

Consequently, educational forgivingness is not only predicated on the hope of children mending their ways in the future but also limited by considerations of justice. There are borders which the respect of children-as-persons and educational forgiveness should not traverse: Respect and forgiveness cannot permit the development of an unjust social climate in which the aggressive, mischievous, and irresponsible children become stronger while the cooperative, industrious, and responsible ones become weaker.

The pursuit of justice provides the grounds on which the diverse "self-improvement practice fields" are built and it underlies and shapes the children law court's constitution and proceedings. Constructing these practice fields on these grounds and this paradigm assisted children to learn and internalize rational ethical principles of give-and-take, effort and outcome, input and output.

The many interactive social frameworks, in which the children engaged, encouraged them to pursue knowledge and understanding of themselves and of others, and to exercise moral reasoning based on rational, critical reflection, and judgment, on the one hand, and compassion for and beneficence to others and themselves, on the other hand. It is therefore responsible to argue that Korczak's theory and practice(s) of the moral education of children can be identified and located in the "in-between" between a care-lending and justice-seeking ethical ethos. There are two subject matters, "subjects" that matter deeply to Korczak, in the context of his educational project: lending respect to children as persons, and the pursuit and establishment of justice in their interpersonal and broader social relationships. Constructing a holistic educational environment anchored in an integration between a relational ethic and a critical–reflective one is at the very core of Korczak's system of moral education.

Jewish Education: Implications and Applications

The cultivation of *Midot* (the Hebrew term for qualities of character), *Derech Eretz* (the Hebrew term for etiquette, good habits, and manners), personal, and social–ethical behavior in Jewish learners usually plays an important role in Jewish educational frameworks. Polish and Israeli schools whose leadership is strongly committed to assisting their learners to internalize the two ethical "r's" of respect and response-ability (Lickona, 1996) in conjunction with their realization of the three traditional cognitive "r's" of schooling ("righting, reading, and rithmatic") have employed key components of Korczak's system in their schools' climate and culture. There is strong anecdotal evidence that these components are among those that have indeed facilitated the ethical growth of these schools' teachers and learners (Bernholtz, 1988; Hecht, 2005).

In light of this evidence, a strong case can be made to call upon Jewish educational leadership today who genuinely seek to practice moral education to study Korczak's system in depth, and to consider which components in this system could prove to be significant in different Jewish educational settings.

Types of Modern Jewish Identity and Identification

As Yitzhak Perlis, one of the important Israeli-Jewish biographers of Korczak's life and legacy, contends, Janush Korczak was born assimilated: he was broadly and deeply acculturated into Polish culture (1986, p. 224). Korczak's Polish national–cultural identity was quite natural to him. In contrast to the naturalness of his Polish identity, Korczak's Jewish identity was a matter of constant existential struggle and choice. These dynamic–existential–volitional dimensions of Korczak's "Jewishness" are perhaps at the inner-most core of the relative abundance of competing and often opposing interpretations of the nature and place of Korczak's Jewish origins in his national–cultural as well as religious identity (Arnon, 1962; Eden, 2000; Bernheim, 1985; Cohen, 1988; Lifton, 1988; Mortakovich-Oltzakova, 1961; Perlis, 1986; Regev, 1996; Zaks & Cahana, 1989).

The salient differences between Korczak's biographers' understandings of Korczak's Jewishness can be located in their respective interpretations of the ever-increasing extent of solidarity Korczak demonstrated toward his Jewish sisters and brothers in Warsaw from the 1930s onward up to his deportation to the Treblinka death camps in August, 1942. In the way of one example, Perlis, who openly acknowledges the depth and strength of Korczak's Polish acculturation and the existential, dynamic, and volitional nature of his identification with Jews and of his own Jewishness, argues that Korczak advanced from a position of assimilation to one of Jewish solidarity, and then to one of complete Jewish identification and ultimately to one of a total return to the Jewish people as the true constitutive source and force of his national identity (Perlis, 1986, pp. 23 and 224).

There, indeed, is strong historical–empirical evidence for the existential volitional nature of Korczak's Jewishness and that his connection with and active participation in the lives of Warsaw's Jews from the early 1930s up to his death in 1942 intensified and thickened significantly. At the same time, there is barely any evidence to support the latter two interrelated claims that Perlis registers:

- The Jewish people were the true source of Korczak's national identity.
- In the unceasing support he lent to his fellow Jews in the ghetto period in general (1940–1942) and especially in his accompaniment of the Jewish children under his charge into the train cars bound to Treblinka, Korczak returned completely to the true Jewish foundation of his national identity.

Coming from the opposite direction, there is considerable evidence to support the claim that Korczak's national identity remained Polish and that his increased solidarity with his Jewish sisters and brothers stemmed from a web of interrelated sources other than an awakening of his Jewish origins and a reclaiming of his "primordial" Jewish national origins. Foremost and first among these was the escalation of anti-Semitic forces in Polish society and in government policies in the 1930s. Korczak was ever being turned back onto and into his Jewish origins by these forces. Due to his ultra-humanistic world-embracing ethos and outlook, he chose to actively demonstrate loyalty to the group undergoing severe persecution. It can be said that more than Korczak returned, he was turned back into the Polish-Jewish community in Warsaw and into the fledgling pioneering communities in Palestine in particular; in short, being turned, Korczak re-turned.

It was the following features of Korczak's version of humanism that made the fortification of his solidarity with Jews, including his adoption of certain selected

Jewish religious and national practices, the only possible path he could take: authenticity, sincerity, straightforwardness, honesty, and integrity; lending respect, love, and real-life accompaniment to all of the world's creations; a powerful faith in the ever-possible ethical corrigibility of human beings—evil in the world is real but it can be overcome. Recognizing and accepting his Jewish origins as a distinct part of himself and his identity as he always did, how could he possibly be insensitive and uncaring to the weak and oppressed among the children, sisters, and brothers of the religion into which he himself was born, and in a web of events and circumstances of unheard oppression and suffering?

Indeed, a strong case can be made that it was Korczak's Jewishness, his situation as a Jew living among a Polish-Catholic majority society hostile toward all the national minorities living within it and especially the Jews among the latter that inspired his ultra-humanism. In his article on the prominence of European intellectuals of Jewish origins in modern European society (1991), Paul Flohr argues that it is not mere coincidence that a disproportionate number of persons of Jewish origins are found among European intellectuals who developed innovative ways of understanding human beings and human society. On the one hand, these European intellectuals' situatedness as persons of Jewish origins engenders in them an especially powerful drive to master the high culture of the European nation-State in which they reside. Many of them indeed often succeeded in achieving this mastery and thereby became a part of the cultural elite. Korczak's knowledge and understanding of Polish culture was outstanding, and the mastery, richness, and creativity of his Polish language are renowned.

On the other hand, at the same time, their Jewish origins also inspire in them a relatively invisible floating sense of alienation between themselves and their more naturally rooted national colleagues. The existential awareness of being at once a part of and apart from the respective societies they inhabit affords them a less accommodating and more innovative, often radical perspective on these societies and their respective cultures.

As we learned, Korczakian humanism was directly influenced by the humanism prevalent among the Polish circle of intellectuals with whom he identified. In the discussion of his humanism, I suggested that what makes it unique is the radical nature of its inclusiveness on the one hand and its boundlessness on the other. In the context of the conceptual framework Flohr offers, it makes sense to postulate that it was likely Korczak's own situation as a Polish intellectual of Jewish origin that underlies the radical nature of his humanist ethos.

The foci of Korczak's concerns were securing the rights of children as human persons and their well-being, irrespective of the color of their skin, ethnicity, race, and religion. Korczak's exceptional humanism, expressed in all his work and works, centered on "repairing the world by repairing education, most importantly the education of children." He combined his endless engagement in trying to realize this repair with loyalty to his Jewish brothers and sisters and proactive solidarity with their plight, oppression, and suffering during the period before and during World War II. In a manner that may at first glance appear contradictory, the historical distortion that is embedded in attributing undeserved importance to the Jewish components of

Korczak's national identity leads to a devaluation of his radical inclusive and boundless humanism. This humanism comprised the very praiseworthy courageous and unbending solidarity with Jews, especially Jewish children, that Korczak, indeed, did demonstrate.

Jewish Jews who view themselves as full-time twenty-four-hours–seven-days-a-week Jews can derive significant religious or cultural national pride out of the fact that Janush Korczak, this truly exceptional humanist and social pedagogue, is a human being of Jewish origins.

Jewish Education: Implications and Applications

Affording Jewish learners the possibility of conducting a relatively in-depth study of the vicissitudes that Korczak underwent in the process of his working out for himself and others, the place and role of his Jewish origins in his identity will lend them insights regarding their own personal confrontation of the place of Jewishness and Judaism in their own identities. Such a study, if properly designed, will also provide critical–reflective conceptual tools to explore the tensions, challenges, dilemmas, and limitations contemporary Jews ever face between their loyalty and commitment to Judaism, the Jewish people and Jewish life and between their loyalty and commitment to the culture and life of their fellow citizens in the respective nation-States they inhabit as well as to transnational, world-global culture and life.

In one of the entries in the diary he kept between May/June and August, 1942, in the Warsaw ghetto, Korczak writes:

> My life has been full of difficulties but also quite interesting. Indeed the life I've led is precisely the life I prayed to God and asked Him to lend me when I was a young boy: Grant me Lord a difficult but beautiful, rich and majestic life. (1972, p. 151)

As this chapter hopefully provides strong evidence, Korczak's life was indeed a rich, meaningful, and majestic one. Hopefully, too, it demonstrates that educators in general and Jewish educators in particular can learn a great deal from Korczak's humanist, social–pedagogic legacy; and that furthermore they can implement these learnings into the curriculum, culture, and climate of Jewish schools and educational institutions worldwide today.

Bibliography

Arnon, Y. (1962). *Janush Korczak's educational system Merhavia*: Sifriat Ha'Poalim (in Hebrew) (*Shitato ha'chinuchit shel Janush Korczak*).
Bernheim, M. (1989). *Father of the orphans – The story of Janush Korczak*. New York: Lodestar Books/E.P. Dutton.
Bernholtz, Y. (1988) An educational intervention plan towards schools as just communities (*Tochnit hitarvut chinuchit likrat chevra hogenet be'beit ha'sefer*), Summations from a conference on Janush Korczak's legacy and on children's society held at Beit Berl (in Hebrew).
Bruner, J. (1985). Narrative and paradigmatic modes of thought. In E. Eisner (Ed.), *Learning and teaching the ways of knowing* (pp. 79–115). Chicago: National society for study of education.

Buber, M. M. (1963). *In the secret space of dialogue – On human beings and their standing before Being (Be'sod siach: Al ha'adam ve'amidato nochach ha'havaya)*. Jerusalem: Bialik institute publications (in Hebrew).

Calderhead, J. (1992). The role of reflection in learning to teach. In L. Vali (Ed.), *Reflective teacher education: Cases and critiques* (pp. 79–115). Albany, NY: State university of New York press.

Cohen, A. (1988). *To be the sun, to be a light: Education as love (Lihyot shemesh, lihyot or: Ha'chinuch ke'ahava)*. Haifa: University of Haifa (in Hebrew).

Dewey, J. (1933). *How we think*. Boston: Heath and Co.

Dewey, J. (1960). *Experience and education (Nisayon ve'chinuch* – Kleinberger, trans.). Jerusalem: Hebrew University School of Education (in Hebrew).

Eden, S. (2000). *Henrik Goldsmith – Janush Korczack*. Jerusalem: Israeli Korczak association (in Hebrew).

Erikson, E. H. (1950). *Childhood and Society*. New York: W. W. Norton.

Flohr, P. M. (1991). *Divided passions – The Jewish intellectual in European society*. Detroit, MI: Wayne state university press.

Frost, S. (1983) Humanism: A Leitmotif in Korczak's world outlook (an unpublished essay)

Hagar-Poznanski, E. (1989). *The stubborn person Janush Korczak up-close (Ha'ish ha'akshan Janush Korczak me'karov)*. Tel Aviv: *Ha'Kibbutz Ha'meuchad* (in Hebrew).

Hecht, Y. (2005). *Democratic education (Chinuch democrati)*. Jerusalem: *Keter* and the Israeli institute of democracy (in Hebrew).

Joseph, S. (1999). *A voice for the Child*. London: Thorsons.

Kirchner, M. (2002). Janush Korczak: Child as text of hieroglyphs, paper presented at international conference on Janush Korczak in Warsaw, September 19–21.

Kohlberg, L. (1981). Education for justice: The vocation of Janush Korczak. In *Essays in moral development* (Vol. 1). San Francisco: Harper and Row.

Korczak, J. (1972). *Writings-Volume 4 – From the Ghetto (Ketavim 4 – Min Ha'getto)* (Z. Adar, Trans.). Tel-Aviv: *Beit Lochamei Ha'getaot* and *Ha'Kibbutz Ha'meuchad* (in Hebrew).

Korczak, J. (1974). *Writings-Volume 1 – With a child (Ketavim 1 – Im Ha'Yeled)* (Z. Adar, Trans.). Tel-Aviv: *Beit Lochamei Ha'getaot* and *Ha'Kibbutz Ha'meuchad* (in Hebrew).

Korczak, J. (1976). *Writings-Volume 2 – A childhood of respect (Ketavim 2 – Yaldut shel Kavod)* (D. Sadan & S. Meltzer, Trans.). Tel-Aviv: *Beit Lochamei Ha'getaot* and *Ha'Kibbutz Ha'meuchad* (in Hebrew).

Korczak, J. (1978). *Writings-Volume 3 – The religion of childhood (Ketavim 5-Dat Ha'Yeled)*, (Z. Adar & D. Sadan, Trans.). Tel-Aviv: *Beit Lochamei Ha'getaot* and *Ha'Kibbutz Ha'meuchad* (in Hebrew).

Korczak, J. (1989). The asylum of the insane *(Senat ha'meturafim)*. S. Eden, A. Y. Cohen, & R. Yatziv (Eds.), *Studies in Janush Korczak's legacy – 2 (Iyunim be'morashto shel Janush Korczak-2)*. Haifa: Haifa University, Israeli Korczak Association and *Beit Lochamei Ha'getaot* (in Hebrew).

Korczak, J. (1995). The school of life *(Beit sefer shel ha'chaim)*. S. Eden, A. Cohen, Y. Guttman, & Y. Rotem (Eds.), *Studies in Janush Korczak's legacy – 5 (Iyunim be'morashto shel Janush Korczak-5)*. Haifa: Haifa university, Israeli Korczak association and *Beit Lochamei Ha'getaot* (in Hebrew).

Korczak, J. (1996). *Collected works (Vol. 1) (Ketavim 1*, Y. & A. Sand, Trans.). Tel-Aviv: *Yad Va'Shem, Beit Lochamei Ha'getaot* and *Ha'Kibbutz Ha'meuchad* (in Hebrew).

Korczak, J. (1996a). *Collected works (Vol. 2) (Ketavim 2*, U. Orlev, Trans.). Tel-Aviv: *Yad Va'Shem, Beit Lochamei Ha'getaot* and *Ha'Kibbutz Ha'meuchad* (in Hebrew).

Korczak, J. (1999). *Collected works (Vol. 5) (Ketavim 5*, U. Orlev, Trans.). Tel-Aviv: *Yad Va'Shem, Beit Lochamei Ha'getaot* and *Ha'Kibbutz Ha'meuchad* (in Hebrew).

Kurzweil, Z. (1969). *Dr. Yanush Korczak's educational thought (Mishnato Ha'chinuchit shel Doktor Janush Korczak)*. Tel-Aviv: Israeli ministry of culture and education (in Hebrew).

Langhanky, M. (2002) The ethnography of childhood: Korczak's contribution to modern childhood research, paper presented at international conference on Janush Korczak in Warsaw, September 19–21.

Lickona, T. (1996). Eleven principles of effective character education. *Journal of Moral Education*, 25(1), 93–100.
Lifton, B. J. (1988). *The king of children – A biography of Janush Korczak*. New York: Farrar, Straus and Giroux.
Martel, Y. (2001) *Life of Pi*.
Mckernan, J. (1988). The countenance of curriculum action research: Traditional, collaborative, and emancipatory-critical conceptions. *Journal of curriculum and supervision*, *3*, 173–200.
Mortakovich-Oltzakova, H. (1961). *Janush Korczak's life* (*Chayei Janush Korczak*). Tel-Aviv: Ha'Kibbutz Ha'meuchad (in Hebrew).
Perlis, Y. (1986). *A Jewish man from Poland* (*Ish Yehudi me'Polin*). Tel-Aviv: Beit Lochamei Ha'getaot and Ha'Kibbutz Ha'meuchad (in Hebrew).
Power, C. (1988). The just community approach to moral education. *Journal of Moral Education*, *17*(3), 195–208.
Regev, M. (1996). *To touch a person: Korczak's personhood and thought* (Laga'at Be'adam: Demuto ve'haguto shel Janush Korczak). Jerusalem: Akademon (in Hebrew).
Ring, Y. (1985). *The taste of life (Ta'am ha'chaim)*. Tel-aviv: Sifriat Ha'poalim (in Hebrew).
Sartre, J. P. (1988). *Existentialism is humanism* (Existentialism hu Humanism, Y. Golomb, Trans.). Jerusalem: Carmel press (in Hebrew).
Schon, D. A. (1987). *Educating the reflective practitioner*. San Francisco: Josey-Bass.
Schwab, J. (1970). *The practical: A language for curriculum*. Washington, DC: National Education Association.
Sharshevsky, M. (1990). *Two homelands: Janush Korczak's national identity (Shtei molodot: Al zehuto ha'leumit shel Janush Korczak)*. Tel Aviv: Tel-Aviv university.
Silverman, M. (1999) How to lend respect to human others? Janush Korczak's humanist pedagogy, *Be'shvilei Ha'zikaron* (Down the paths of memory) – No. 32, April–May/*Nissan-Iyaar*, pp. 23–28 (in Hebrew).
Silverman, M. (2004). Korczaks Weltanschauung und Gottesbild. In *Janush Korczak in Theorie und Praxis* (pp. 45–67). Gutersloh: Gutersloher Verlagshaus (in German).
Silverman, M. (2005). Korczak's anti-theory of education (*Ha'anti teoria chinuchit shel janush korczak*). In *Educational deliberations – A collection of research papers in honor of Shlomo Fox* (Ma'aseh be'chinuch: kovetz mechkarim le'chvod Shlomo Fox) (pp. 210–229). Jerusalem: Bialik institute and Mandel institute for leadership.
Silverman, M. (2006). Janush Korczak's implicit religiosity: Its place in his educational approach and its relevance to education today. In *Studies in Jewish Education* (*Vol. XI*, pp. 289–324). Jerusalem: Magnes Press.
Simon, E. (1949). *Pestalotzi and Korczak: Pioneers of social-pedagogy* (*Pestalotzi ve'Korczak: Halutzim shel ha'chinuch ha'chevrati*). Tel-Aviv: Urim. Tractate *Nezikim* (Damages), *Ethics of the fathers 5–21*.
Van Manen, M. (1977). Linking ways of knowing with ways of being practical. *Curriculum Inquiry*, *6*, 205–228.
Van Manen, M. (1995). On epistemology of reflective practice. *Teachers and Teaching: Theory and Practice*, *1*, 33–49.
Waskow, A. (1978). *God wrestling*. New York: Schoken.
Zaks, S., & Cahana, Y. (1989). *Korczak: memories and reflections* (*Korczak: Zichronot ve'hagigim*). Tel-Aviv: *Papirus* (in Hebrew).

Jewish Identities: Educating for Multiple and Moving Targets

Stuart Charmé and Tali Zelkowicz

"I am in love with being Jewish," declared Diane Troderman, a former board chair of JESNA (Jewish Education Service of North America) recently.[1] Judaism, she explained, gives meaning to everything in her life, influences her everyday decisions and actions, and inspires her to do work that will strengthen and enhance the Jewish identities of other people. Many Jewish educators have chosen the work they do precisely because they share this deep emotional attachment to the fact of being Jewish and an appreciation of its centrality in their lives. So it is natural for them to wonder what went "wrong" in the cases of people whose relationship to being Jewish is a less central or less intensive part of their identities. Was there something flawed or inadequate in their Jewish education? Did their families lack a strong commitment to Judaism? Why didn't a strong Jewish identity take root?

The Survivalist Frame

For many years, the language of crisis and loss has pervaded discussion of Jewish identity. The tone has often been one of lamentation over what is seen as the weakened, eroded condition of Jewish identity in America, laced with nostalgia for a purportedly more authentic and vital form of Jewish life in the past. According to one common narrative, Jewish immigrants arrived in the USA with strong Jewish identities and no American identities, and within several generations many of their grandchildren sported strong American identities and weak Jewish identities, lacking in Jewish literacy, values, or commitment. In a narrative focused on waning Jewishness, Jewish identity formation is urgent and crucial, since, hopefully, it will offer a protective shield against the threat of the non-Jewish world, particularly the dangers of assimilation and intermarriage.

Yet, such an approach can be unrealistic in its search for an antidote for the impact of modernity on Jews and Judaism. The weakening in traditional religious

---

S. Charmé (✉)
Rutgers University, Camden, NJ, USA
e-mail: scharme@camden.rutgers.edu

[1] JESNA newsletter, Summer 2008

beliefs and communal insularity are not recent "problems." They reflect a process that dates back at least several centuries, when the impact of the enlightenment and emancipation transformed the relationship of Jews to both their own traditions and culture and also to the wider secular world and culture. The weakening of the power of tradition and the new element of individual choice in constructing religious and ethnic identities is a fact of modern civilization (Berger, 1979).

For many educators and communal leaders, interest in Jewish identity formation has been driven by deep and abiding concerns about Jewish survival and by visions of the strong Jewish identities that will somehow safeguard this survival. When survivalist aims and anxieties about collective Jewish life are ascendant, educational leaders and teachers often turn to Jewish identity formation in a frantic effort to discover what "works" for making and keeping Jews Jewish, not just throughout childhood and adolescence, but into adulthood. In the process, educators can easily become distracted from the ongoing, unfolding educational processes of Jewish identity formation in the present and be more focused on a larger mission of saving Jews and ultimately Judaism.

Hoping to build Jewish identities that will endure throughout the lives of their students also puts Jewish educators in a significantly different situation from teachers of secular subjects such as mathematics. For math teachers, there is no investment in creating lifelong mathematicians out of each and every student, nor in expecting them to socialize with and marry other mathematicians, nor in raising the next generation of young mathematicians. In contrast, students are well aware of the special expectation of Jewish education to influence their life choices now and into the future, and this can be a tension in the teacher–student relationship that teachers of other subjects do not face. Jewish education seeks to instill a long list of values and behavioral attitudes. To offer just a few examples, Jewish teachers generally want and need their students to learn Hebrew, give *tzedakah,* light Shabbat candles, love Israel and go there, celebrate all the holidays, learn about their history, interpret ancient Jewish texts to make them relevant today, say prayers, give *divrei Torah,* date Jews, marry Jews, join Jewish organizations and institutions, attend synagogue and life cycle events, observe or at least grapple with *kashrut,* etc.

Inevitably, researchers have tried to measure the level of Jewish identity by calculating the amount of traditional religious practices like fasting on Yom Kippur, lighting Shabbat or Hanukkah candles, or keeping kosher. In doing so, it became easy to assume that those who do more have "stronger" Jewish identities, and those who do less have "weaker" Jewish identities. But such measurements generally tell us only who is more *traditionally* religious in their practice. It is risky and misleading to assume that a person who observes more Jewish ritual is "more Jewish" than one who observes less, or that such a person can be described as having a *stronger* Jewish identity. Too often, the chosen criteria for measuring Jewish identity produce a range of scores in which the "strongest" Jewish identities are found among Orthodox Jews and "weakest" among reform, reconstructionist, and unaffiliated Jews. Yet, such evaluations will always be relative to one set of prescriptive criteria or another. Whose blueprints for normative Jewish identity should be accepted and on what is their authority based?

Changing Paradigms for the Study of Jewish Identities

Not surprisingly, despite vast amounts of research on American-Jewish identity in the last 40 years, individual researchers have not been able to agree on just what Jewish identity is, much less how it is formed (Cohen, 1988; Goldscheider, 1986; Herman, 1977; Himmelfarb, 1974; Horowitz, 1999; Liebman, 2001; Perry and Chazan, 1990; Prell, 2000; Sklare & Greenblum, 1967; Tennenbaum, 2000). For many of them, the utopian dream has been first to devise a precise and systematic yardstick of Jewishness against which Jews' identities could be diagnosed, and eventually to concoct a Jewish educational elixir capable of recreating these identities for future generations, thereby guaranteeing the survival of the Jewish people. Social psychologist Bethamie Horowitz, a researcher of adult Jewish identity formation has described this research paradigm of Jewish identity in America as preoccupied with the question "How *Jewish* are American Jews?" in contrast to what we could be asking, which is "*How* are American Jews Jewish?" (Horowitz, 2002, p. 14, emphasis in original).

It is important for both scholars and educators alike to be aware of the criteria they employ to determine what counts as legitimate expressions of Jewish survival and how those criteria inform their work. After all, what does it look like to have a "strong Jewish identity," when Jewish identity, like other aspects of personal and collective identities, occupies differing amounts of space, time, and emotional commitment in the lives of different people? If every Jew "packages" his or her Jewish identity in a slightly different way, Jewish educators and Jewish identity researchers alike must wrestle with the question of how to determine what counts as authentically, legitimately, and ultimately generatively Jewish.

Some have talked about the relocation of the boundary between Jewish and non-Jewish and a reconfiguration of what counts as "authentic Jewishness." Sylvia Barack Fishman (1995) calls this process "coalescence" or an "incorporation of American liberal values such as free choice, universalism, and pluralism into the perceived boundaries of Jewish meaning and identity." In addition, increases in numbers of conversion, intermarriage, and international adoptions mean that the "non-Jewish" world is not just "out there"; it is now an element found within Jewish communities, families, and within the identities of individual Jews. The result may represent not necessarily the dilution or erasure of Jewish identity but rather a complementarity and synergy between Jewish identity and the wider cultural context in which Jews live. American-Jewish historian Jonathan Sarna described the most fundamental question of American-Jewish life as "how to live in two worlds at once, how to be both American and Jewish, *part* of the larger American society *and apart from it*" (1998, pp. 9–10, emphasis added). Yet, these two worlds are increasingly hard to differentiate in many people's identities.

Jews today are constantly juggling a variety of social identities which may be triggered by different contexts. People will constantly modify their identities, consciously and often unconsciously, with different elements becoming strengthened, weakened, revised, abandoned, and reconstituted, in response to a mix of innate qualities and a range of social influences, such as ethnic and cultural background influences. For some Jews, old recipes are being abandoned and new ones discovered.

After studying differences among college students from different college settings, Sales and Saxe (2006) observe, "... students will speak of their 'identities' as opposed to a singular identity. They are vegans, ecologists, artists, Zionists, conservative Jews, lesbians, and so on ... any efforts to stimulate Jewish life on college campuses must be flexible, adaptable to vastly different college settings and different types of Jewish students." Thus, as Jewish history unfolds over time, the manifestations of Jewish identity have likewise evolved, mutated, fragmented, and been deconstructed and transformed in a kaleidoscope of possible Jewish identities that are negotiated in relationship with a person's other identities and in relation to one's socio-historical realities. To the extent that all the categories of religion, culture, and peoplehood are defined and constructed in a variety of ways, the result is that those who try to find out what Jewish identity is or who try to measure it, are more likely to come face to face with the multiple forms of Jewish identities, cultures, and spiritualities.

Since the late 1990s, a shift has taken place from pre-ordained inventories quantifying *how Jewish* the American-Jewish community is to a more fluid investigation into the diverse constructions of Jewishness that have emerged among American Jews. The shift has major implications for how Jewish educators might approach their highly complex task of helping learners of all ages to develop their Jewish identities. In the remainder of this chapter, we aim to describe how the paradigm shift represents an alternative to solely survivalist orientations for Jewish identity formation and offers new ways of conceiving the relationship between Jewish education and Jewish identity building.

The Problem of Authenticity: What's a Real Jew?

Every period of Jewish history has involved struggles over who controls expressions of Jewish identity. As power and authority shift, or rather flow, between the elite (educators, rabbis) and the folk (students, congregants) in new and unprecedented ways, culturally accepted norms of what constitutes standard content and canon become contested arenas. In short, what counts as tradition, who gets to decide, and why?

Today, the leaders of liberal Jewish day schools of all denominations seek to live in both Jewish and American cultural worlds simultaneously and to search for new ways of negotiating their multiple and competing loyalties and allegiances to American and Jewish values and worldviews. By combining both Jewish and secular general studies curriculum in one education, they face identity dissonances daily. Often, the integrationist goal of bringing together general, American values with Jewish teachings comes to a screeching halt when it comes to American holidays like Valentine's Day or Halloween. Despite the fact that few Jewish students or parents find participation in these common American customs and holidays worthy of concern, formal and informal administrative policies that discourage open discussion and observance of Halloween and Valentine's Day exist at many Jewish day and supplemental schools. Some educational leaders express their concern about possible pagan and Christian roots and want to create Jewish schools as "a space where students and parents will not have to feel the pressure to engage in secular or non-Jewish traditions" (Hyman, 2008, p. 128).

Such policies attempt to *protect* Jews from dissonance and reduce or eliminate a sense of conflict with the "outside" culture that American Jews, especially liberal ones, regularly face. But an educational culture that aims primarily at reducing tensions and conflicts becomes irrelevant, in time, to the real needs, concerns, and identities of Jews in the contemporary world. Issues related to Israel and Zionism, for example, have become increasingly complicated for American Jews who are trying to balance multiple and often competing values of peoplehood, history, and language, along with social justice for all nations and freedom for all peoples. The moment that educators become apologists for a single perspective on secular/religious tensions in Israel or on the Israeli/Palestinian conflict, they have abandoned the necessary engagement with tensions and complexity of these issues and they make the error of identifying Jewish identity with only a limited range of ideological options.

The same can be said about the necessary educational approach to vast numbers of Jews for whom belief in God and/or Jewish ritual observance may be the locus of tension and ambivalence within their Jewish identities. The paradox of Jewish identity is that it can thrive in the presence *or absence* of particular beliefs or practices that may be considered indispensable to some Jews. Neither atheism nor lack of interest in traditional Jewish observances should ever be treated as disqualifications for Jewish identity or evidence of educational failure. There will always be tensions and dilemmas in Jewish identities as individuals navigate dissonances that surface at the interface between local and global, particularist and universalist, rationalist and spiritual, and secular and religious dimensions of Jewishness.

New educational approaches might explore the educational value of these tensions and contradictions as a central and creative task of being a Jew in the midst of a broader cultural world. For Jewish educators in twenty-first century America, in particular, curricular experiences will be most powerful when they are designed to (a) acknowledge the friction created by multiple and competing categories of Jewish and American, (b) normalize the tensions as potentially creative and productive, (c) engage with colleagues and students in ongoing, open, and collaborative dialogue about their various experiences of those tensions, and (d) articulate existing and possible new strategies for coping with, and even using, the tensions.

The study of Jewish identity has gradually begun to track the empirical experience of being Jewish rather than any one researcher's prescribed or hoped-for ideals of Jewish identity formation. Jewish identity research has had to catch up with newer theoretical and methodological innovations that have radically revised ideas about religion, culture, and identity (see cultural studies theorists from as early as the 1990s, such as Stuart Hall et al., 1992, 1996; Ulf Hannerz, 1991; bell Hooks, 1992; Cornel West, 1990). Like all cultural identities, Jewish identity is something that is constantly in motion. As Stuart Hall notes, "Cultural identity ... belongs to the future as much as to the past. It is not something which already exists, transcending place, time, history, and culture. Cultural identities come from somewhere, have histories. But, like everything which is historical, they undergo constant transformation" (Stuart Hall et al., 1992 cited by Hooks, p. 5). Identity formation is a process of becoming, a journey without a clear itinerary or destination.

As individual Jews and individual Jewish communities have begun choosing and constructing their own Jewish religious practices, Jewish traditions, and ultimately Jewish identities, it makes little sense to develop and defer to standard inventories against which Jewish identity can be measured. To understand that different people make sense of their own Jewish identities in different ways is to make the shift from asking "How Jewish are American Jews?" to asking "*How* are American Jews Jewish?" (Horowitz, 2002, p. 22).

Tradition and Spirituality

If teachers acknowledge that contemporary Jewish identity formation processes are contingent, provisional, variable, tentative, shifting, and changing, then what could possibly be the appropriate *content* to teach, and how should one teach it? What exactly constitutes an adequate understanding and experience of Jewish tradition? Jewish educators must still make selections among endless possibilities of classical texts, modern literature, ethics, laws, practices, histories, holidays, and values from which to teach. Teachers must still determine specific teaching goals and observable, measurable learning objectives. Indeed, educational integrity is marked, in part, by the very content choices teachers make and by the thoughtful rationales in which those choices are grounded. This important educational task must not be abandoned even as "tradition" itself is destabilized through ongoing redefinition.

How should educators now approach the issue of tradition? Certainly, tradition provides a degree of emotional comfort and belonging, even in the absence of intellectual commitment to the religious basis for individual ideas or practices. It offers a set of sacred guidelines that religious leaders use to sustain community, build identity, and make meaning of human life. However, to raise the question of *how* people are Jewish, rather than how Jewish they are, requires a reevaluation of our understanding of tradition. To be sure, most people think of tradition as that which is passed down, intact from the past. As such, it provides a window into the world of one's ancestors. For many people, this connection to the past provided by tradition is an important anchor to their identities. From this point of view, one might consider the enemy of tradition to be innovation and change, since any alteration of tradition from the way things were done in the past is tantamount to a loss of who one is or was. Tradition has often been construed in a conservative way that identifies real, authentic Judaism with immutable and authoritative texts and practices from the past.

Scholars who write about tradition, however, go to great pains to challenge the static view of tradition as fixed and unchanging. For example, Judith Plaskow (1991) began her feminist reinterpretation of Judaism, *Standing Again at Sinai,* by trying to reclaim tradition as a feminist value and by challenging the view that feminism and Jewish tradition are inevitable adversaries. She rejected the idea that Jewish tradition is monolithic and static, something that can be accepted or rejected, but which remains relatively constant over time. Rather, she proposed a view of Judaism as a "complex and pluralistic tradition involved in a continual process of adaptation and change – a process to which I and other feminist Jews could contribute" (1991, pp. ix–x). Tradition is anything but stable or static. Rather Jewish identity rests upon an endless reappropriation of tradition by each generation of Jews.

When new or revised ritual practices are introduced, they are often resisted and criticized by so-called traditionalists as illegitimate innovations that violate tradition. The concept of tradition is thus intimately intertwined with that of authenticity. It is precisely during periods of dramatic change that those who oppose such change will raise the banner of tradition and challenge changes as inauthentic and dangerous. Over time, nevertheless, ways of being Jewish that at first were seen as inauthentic or too innovative can take root and become part of the lived experience of new generations who know nothing but them. Women rabbis, for example, might still disturb some Jews who consider themselves "traditional," but they are probably far outnumbered by those who accept this development as a legitimate element in Jewish tradition. Today's more fluid forms of Jewish identity are better supported by an appreciation of the intrinsic flexibility of our cultural traditions.

The search for personal meaning through Jewish identity also means that it is now necessary to consider Jewish identity not only as a potential ethnic identity and religious identity, but also as a spiritual identity. While religious identity is a collective, social identity, reflected in a sense of belonging to a specific group of people and history, spiritual identity may or may not involve this sense of belonging. Many people now report a weak sense of religious identity but a strong sense of spiritual identity (Templeton and Eccles, 2005, pp. 254–55). Indeed, it is often when traditional religious beliefs and practices seem inadequate that people turn away from the collective for personal meaning making. "This mature spiritual identity usually develops in private as individuals give new personal meanings to traditional religious beliefs or seek out what is personally sacred in other ways" (Templeton and Eccles, 2005, p. 255). How these relatively new concerns with Jewish spirituality will affect methods of Jewish education has yet to be determined.

Beyond Survival: Toward New Understandings of Jewish Identity Formation

When Jewish identity formation is analyzed apart from anxieties about survival, what emerges is a multi-dimensional phenomenon that requires interdisciplinary analysis. For example, psychologists need to consider the developmental connections between Jewish identity and the developmental tasks and challenges that occur in identity over the life cycle from childhood through adolescence and into adulthood. Regrettably, Jewish education has not seen a serious attempt at this since Perry London and Barry Chazan's 1990 article, *Psychology and Jewish Identity*

Education. Social psychologists must look into the dynamics of inter-group and intra-group relations (such as beginning with the now classic work *Jewish Identity: A Social Psychological Perspective* (1970), by Simon Herman; and the more recent 1998 study by Bethamie Horowitz titled, "Connections and Journeys: Shifting Identities Among American Jews"). Quantitative sociologists have had perhaps the loudest voices, and have plotted connections between aspects of Jewish identity and long-term demographic trends,[2] but recent work in the sociology of Jewish education employs qualitative methodologies (such as studies of Jewish identity formation through adult education by Lisa Grant and Diane Tickton-Schuster, 2005, for example). Anthropologists must continue to explore the lived texture of the processes of Jewish identity formation through ethnographic explorations (see, for example, Heilman, 1998; Prell, 1989; Schoem, 1989; and Meyerhoff's classic and exquisite work in 1978).

In addition to the social scientists, scholars in the humanities also provide valuable knowledge about Jewish identity formation. Philosophers will ponder what Jewish identity may tell us about the characteristics of identity in a post-modern world (Charmé, 2000; Goldberg & Krausz, 1993) and educational philosophers such as Fox, Seymour, Scheffler, and Marom (2003) deal with content, curricular ideals, what could and should be at the core of what is taught, and why. Finally, historians of Jewish education such as Jonathan Krasner are increasingly filling in gaping

---

[2] At least since 1976, a long sociological tradition of "impact studies" exists that has attempted to relate the effect of Jewish education in childhood to levels of Jewish identification in adulthood. Some of the earliest of these include, for example, Geoffrey Bock's *The Jewish Schooling of American Jews: A Study of Non-Cognitive Educational Effect*, 1976; Harold Himmelfarb's *Impact of Religious Schooling: Effects of Jewish Education*, 1974; and Steven M. Cohen's "The Impact of Jewish Education on Religious Identification and Practice" (Jewish Social Studies) 1974. Cohen and others have continued this quest throughout the decades with articles such as Steven M. Cohen's "Jewish Education and Its Differential Impact on Adult Jewish Identity," in Jack Wertheimer (ed.), *Family Matters: Jewish Education in an Age of Choice* (University Press of New England), 2008; Steven M. Cohen's highly charged and controversial work "A Tale of Two Jewries: The 'Inconvenient Truth' for American Jews'" which warned of dire decline in American Jewish identity as a direct result of intermarriage (Jewish Life Network/Steinhardt Foundation) 2006; and Steven M. Cohen and Ari Y. Kelman's less survivalist-driven study called *Cultural Events and Jewish Identities: Young Adult Jews in New York* (UJA NY) 2005. Also, in 2005, Jack Wertheimer introduced an important policy paper, a metaphor which entered into the field of Jewish education, called *Linking the Silos: How to Accelerate the Momentum in Jewish Education Today* (Avi Chai Foundation). Calling for the linking of silos of Jewish educational settings and initiatives, Wertheimer's research team consisted of Steven M. Cohen, Sylvia Barack Fishman, Shaul Kelner, Jeffrey Kress, Alex Pompson, and Riv-Ellen Prell. They explored the relationship between pre-school attendance and later Jewish educational experiences and the impact of parents' Jewish schooling on children's Jewish education, of parents' Jewish youth group experience and children's Jewish education, of parents' Israel travel as students on their children's education, and grandparents' observance upon their grandchildren's education. Focusing on Jewish camp and Israel travel experiences, Amy Sales and Leonard Saxe published the report *Limud* [learning] *by the Lake: Fulfilling the Educational Potential of Jewish Summer Camps* (Cohen Center for Modern Jewish Studies, Brandeis University), 2002; and Leonard Saxe et al.'s produced a study called "A Mega-Experiment in Jewish Education: The Impact of birthright Israel" (Cohen Center for Modern Jewish Studies, Brandeis University), 2001.

holes in our knowledge of the field's development, major influential factors upon Jewish identity formation, and radical transitions and recurring trajectories. In order to approach the complexities of Jewish identity formation in the twenty-first century, Jewish educators must turn to scholarship from multiple disciplines and scholarship that is not framed by survivalist motivations alone.

Psychological Approaches

In the field of psychology of religion, a long-standing research practice has explored different *ways of being religious*. If religiosity were merely a switch that is either in the "on" or "off" position, it might be measured by simple checklists of beliefs or activities that a person may or may not believe or do. But religiosity manifests itself in a variety of ways, and psychologists have tried to identify some of the different ways it may function in a person's life. Although most of this research was designed with Christians in mind, the basic principles apply to Jews as well.

Gordon Allport, one of the most important figures in this area, developed ways of measuring what he described as "extrinsic" and "intrinsic" forms of religion (Allport, 1950). By "extrinsic" religion, he wanted to highlight the ways in which some people approach religion in instrumental and utilitarian ways. They participate in religion for the sake of various secondary benefits, such as the social status provided by religion, a sense of belonging to a particular group, a sense of security, etc. By intrinsic religion, Allport intended to describe people whose commitment is to the religion itself, people who genuinely live it in their daily lives. These are not mutually exclusive categories but dimensions of religion that may be more or less salient in different people. When religion is approached in this way, the list of one's beliefs and religious behaviors is less important than the attitudes motivating a person (consciously or unconsciously). Accordingly, Jews who join synagogues and/or observe traditional Jewish rituals mainly because they think it is "good for the Jews" to do so have a different relationship to Judaism than those whose main concern is the personal meaning they derive from their involvement in Judaism.

Subsequent researchers noticed limitations to Allport's categories, which tend, like much research on Jewish identity, to use more conservative, traditional forms of religion and morality as the primary yardsticks for religion and are thereby apt to miss other forms of religion that may be present today. In response, Daniel Batson developed measures for identifying a different way of being religious, which he called the "quest" orientation (Batson & Ventis, 1982). What is important about people who engage their religion in the quest mode is that they tend to be dissatisfied with traditional answers, values, or practices. Instead, the quest orientation highlights the process of searching, as opposed to the mechanical repetition of childhood religious doctrines or practices, or conformity to the consensus of the religious community. For people in a religious quest mode, there is a heightened awareness of the tentativeness and incompleteness of religious answers, of the importance of doubt as a part of the quest process, and of the urgent need to deal with existential questions (Batson and Ventis, 166). In Batson's research, interviewees who agree with statements like "Doubting is an important part of being religious," "As I grow and change, I expect my religion to grow and change," and "Questions are far more important to my religious experience than answers" are not regarded as weaker in their religious identities than those whose religious identities are not rooted in such questions.

By focusing only on traditional belief and practice, research on Jewish identity has often missed this and other equally important dimensions of Jewish religiosity. One can imagine, for example, Jews who disagree with statements about the importance of adhering to Jewish law, keeping kosher, or accepting traditional beliefs about God, and who agree with the idea that doubting and questioning are important elements of their Jewish identities, and that their Jewish identities will continually change as they change throughout their lives. They may be asking questions about how Jewishness is related to their overall sense of identity or who they really are.

Jewish Identity Formation and the Human Life Cycle

Jewish identity also needs to be examined in light of the different ways it may manifest itself at different points in a person's life. Some researchers describe Jewish identity less as a fixed thing than as a journey (Horowitz, 1998) or an unfolding spiral (Charmé, Horowitz, Hyman, & Kress, 2008). The work of developmental psychologists raises two additional issues: first, how does cognitive development affect a person's understanding of religion, particularly in childhood and adolescence, and second, how does Jewish identity interface with other kinds of developmental challenges throughout the course of life?

In one of the earliest studies of Jewish identity, developmental psychologist David Elkind (1961) confirmed the stages of cognitive evolution in Jewish children's understanding of aspects of being Jewish. Using a series of questions including "What makes you Jewish?" "Can a dog or cat be Jewish?" "Can you be Jewish and American at the same time?" "How do you become a Jew?" Elkind showed that children's understanding of Jewish identity goes through predictable Piagetian stages. For younger children, the understanding of Jewishness as a quality is fairly concrete and rigid, externally determined by one's family. Somewhat older children learn to define Jewishness in terms of different behaviors. Finally, as children approach adolescence and mature in their ability to reason more abstractly and symbolically, their understanding of the meaning of being Jewish becomes more complex and abstract.

Work by cognitive psychologists of religion have repeatedly shown the ways in which children's understanding of their religious identities are quite different from that of their parents, even though both may be saying and doing similar things. Ronald Goldman, another researcher who uses a Piagetian model of cognitive development has raised the question of just what children understand about religious ideas they are taught during childhood. In most cases, magical and literal views of religion persist until about age 13 (Goldman, 1964). Educationally speaking, this is problematic if not tragic, since age 13, or the age of becoming a Bar or Bat Mitzvah, is often the end of formal Jewish education for many Jewish children.

How does this situation affect the Jewish identity of older adolescents and young adults? For those whose Jewish education continues and provides transition to a more abstract, complex, symbolic view of Jewish texts and rituals, a more mature form of Jewish identity is possible. On the other hand, for those whose view of Judaism remains at the magical and literal level, there are two common possibilities: they may continue to accept this form of Judaism as true and suppress doubts or questions about it, or they may feel alienated from ideas which become increasingly dissonant with their evolving views of the world and reject them outright (Goldman, 1965).

Adolescence is probably the period of life when there is not only a huge physiological growth spurt, but a psychological one, as well, in relationship to personal identity. Erik Erikson considered identity to be the main developmental task of adolescence. Cognitive development allows children a more mature understanding of their identities, and their growing independence enables them to evaluate and internalize various social roles and identities. It is a time when a person begins to commit to particular elements of his or her identity, which includes religious, ethnic, and other group identities. This commitment requires a period of searching and experimentation (Erikson, 1980). For this reason, a genuine commitment to one's religious and ethnic identity (or identities) involves more than merely reproducing the identities of one's parents.

Jewish identity consists of more than personal religious beliefs and family traditions. It also includes the formation of a Jewish ethnic identity, which defines one's relationship to a larger group, the Jewish people. Like other parts of identity, Jewish ethnic identity emerges in stages and includes both cognitive and affective dimensions. At first it may be unexamined or taken for granted, but further personal explorations of the meaning of group membership produce various forms of commitment and/or resistance to that identity, positive feelings of belonging, identification with Jewish history, particularly recent parts involving the Holocaust and the modern state of Israel, and participation in group traditions (cf. Phinney, 1990).

Feminist Approaches

One of the important insights of feminism as it developed its analysis of women's issues and identities has been the realization that there is no "generic" woman's identity, that women's identities are inflected by factors of race, class, culture, ethnicity, religion, etc. Jewish identities are no different. In his classic study of Jewish identity, Simon Herman wrote: "Nowhere in the world does Jewish sub-identity exist in isolation as an individual's exclusive ethnic identity. It is everywhere linked with another ethnic sub-identity with which it interacts and by which it is influenced" (Herman, 1970, p. 43).

In the last generation, feminism has not only changed the roles for women in Judaism, it has explored the unspoken world of women's Jewish identities. Until recently, most research on Jewish identity in general and children's Jewish identity in particular has seemed blind to possible gender differences in the emergence, development, and maintenance of Jewishness. The failure to find gender differences in Jewish identity, however, may be a result of neglecting to investigate all aspects of the issue. Cohen and Halbertal note that even similar Jewish identity outcomes may conceal different underlying processes. Men and women may arrive in equal numbers at certain Jewish identity destinations, but they get there by different routes (Cohen & Halbertal, 2001, pp. 39–40). Anthropologist of American-Jewish life, Riv-Ellen Prell, questions whether Jewishness can truly be measured by conventional lists of beliefs and activities. She argues that if Jewishness is a gendered and relational concept, then Jewish men and women have not experienced their lives in identical ways.[3] More recently, too, sociologist Debra Kaufman discovered significant gender differences among groups of young Jews. Kaufman found that young Jewish women tended to describe their identities in more gendered and relational terms than Jewish men their age, who saw themselves in more individualistic terms (1999, pp. 11–12, 1998, pp. 54–55). Jewishness for women is more deeply embedded in social relationships, particularly those with parents, children, friends, and community.

When the question of gender was explicitly posed to Jewish children, girls were found to be more sensitive to issues of equal rights and sexism, more ambivalent about their proper roles, and more aware of the contributions of Jewish women, while boys were more likely to defend more traditional gender roles in Judaism and to be less familiar with important Jewish women (Charmé, 2006). Neither educators nor researchers should assume that gender differences are a non-issue in understanding the Jewish identities of children.

Faced with the reality of Jewish identity formation as an unfolding, unpredictable process and activity that is inextricably connected to the array of one's other multiple and competing identities, Jewish teachers educate multiple moving targets. There are at least three realms in which new understandings of contemporary Jewish identity formation could represent a major paradigm shift for Jewish education. These three include Jewish education's pedagogical methods, educational cultures, and its overall capacity for trust.

Pedagogical Methods

Jewish teaching that focuses more on processes than outcomes would create classroom and learning settings well-positioned to preserve critical rigor in the intellectual and emotional "play" of concepts and ideas. Students would be given the same opportunities to dismiss a *midrash* as bearing the weakest proof-texts, challenge a course or institution's particular ideological orientation to Israel attachment

---

[3]See, for example, Prell (1988) ethnography, "Laughter that Hurts: Ritual Humor and Ritual Change in an American Jewish Community," where Purim becomes a keen window into painful gender inequalities and unnamed taboos within a learning community. Prell demonstrated how that community's ritual celebration of Purim revealed tensions regarding gender roles and religious authority in a group that consciously described themselves as officially and proudly egalitarian.

as historically problematic, or interrogate the various theologies represented by Jewish liturgies, as they are to denounce the Shakespearean play *Romeo and Juliet* for its flat plot and undeveloped characters. Students and teachers would be willing and able to determine excellence in their topics of Jewish content through a rigorous assailing of the subject matter, asking genuine questions and providing genuine answers. Sometimes these indictments could be contained within Jewish tradition, but sometimes they would not. Moreover, the task and responsibility for defending and redeeming Jewish tradition and applying it to contemporary life, would belong increasingly to the students, and not primarily, or at least not solely, to the teacher. Identifying excellence in a subject matter also involves the capacity for identifying mediocrity and the ability to support those evaluations with compelling and informed analytical explanations. In order to foster rigorous processes of Jewish identity formation in their students, Jewish teachers will need to strengthen their self-awareness about their own Jewish identity tensions to avoid being either apologetic or defensive as they model and facilitate thorough explorations and examinations of their content.

Educational Culture

The problems facing Jewish identity formation do not lie simply in how it is being taught, however. Profound educational change will come when institutions move beyond the important work of teachers in developing new methods and curriculum. It will also require a culture change at the institutional level in which the qualities of resilience and rigor, strength and "durability" are nurtured.

While it may at first appear counterintuitive, teachers' willingness and ability to poke intellectually critical and analytical holes at their subject matter does not weaken their authority. Similarly, the judicious use of humor and jokes which can permit expression of both hostility and love that teachers and students alike may experience toward the subject matter, also need not compromise the learning. Such acts do not need to become tantamount to self-deprecation or disrespect of the learning process. In fact, they often achieve precisely the opposite effect (Hyman, 2008, p. 151). The rough and rigorous treatment of a course's content demonstrates the resilience, strength, and permanence, both of the subject matter and the teacher. It can also communicate to the students that they, themselves, are worthy and trustworthy investigators of that content. The capacity for critical distance from one's subject matter area creates a classroom culture well cushioned to absorb, survive, and *use* productively the many normal hostilities and anxieties that are a part of identity-building work. When teachers feel confident enough that their course content can not only survive, but thrive from rigorous and ongoing critique from within their fields, they are transforming learning environments into "durable educational cultures."

Often, the best examples of durable Jewish educational cultures are found at summer camps and youth groups. This is because in those settings, the leaders are most willing to consciously and purposefully encourage participants—campers, CITs, counselors, and advisors alike—to create, appropriate, and perpetuate their cultures. Members of those communities often learn that they are enfranchised voices who can create the norms and rituals of camp and youth group life. As a result, they tend to have forums for open and critical discussion about what matters and what counts in constructing their Jewish identities, even if they do not label it as such. These durable Jewish cultures are most able to withstand and absorb the hostility, frustration, and disillusion that children as well as adults can experience with regard to being Jewish. Camp cultures allow for play, humor, and even a modicum of mockery, which all contribute to the necessary cushion of experimentation and risk-taking that a culture that is not obsessed with its own survival can sustain.

Without needing to tip-toe around loaded and formally unaddressed dissonances, teachers of general studies are free and obligated to create classrooms where one need not tread softly at all. In fact, general studies teachers and students jump and stomp around in their subject matter knowing that it has survived many previous teachers and students poking at it, and that it will continue to survive many more teachers and students engaging with it, long after them. The central, orienting difference is that general studies classroom cultures tend to exhibit the features of educational durability, so important for the dynamic activity of identity building, while Jewish studies classroom cultures are often fraught with fragility. Although more formal Jewish educational cultures, such as schools, are probably better at imparting specific Jewish knowledge and skills, they tend to lack capacities or productive strategies for responding to students who say "I hate this, this means nothing to me, I resent being here," not only with their words, but also with their actions.

However, the ongoing activity of identity formation thrives in rigorous, risk-taking, and safe learning cultures. Thus, consciously working toward creating learning cultures of durability rather than fragility could become powerful messages to students that they, their teachers, and the subject matter can and will survive rigorous engagement. Indeed, creating cultures where it is not only acceptable and normalized to name and examine one's Jewish identity tensions, but where there are also strategies developed collaboratively for coping with these tensions, could produce a new kind of Jewish educational culture that is based more on creativity than anxiety.

Trusting and Entrusting the Students

Jewish educators must let go of the urge to control the *outcomes* of their students' Jewish futures. Instead, they can hold on closely and carefully to their students' collective *processes* of grappling with Jewish subject matter, trusting and entrusting students with their own future outcomes. This may be the most difficult and profound shift necessary for making it safe and inviting enough for students—children and adults alike—to take personal risks and participate willingly and genuinely in the meaning-making conversations that ultimately contribute to productive, durable, identity building.

It is not likely that avoiding or distrusting formal, public exploration of loaded and complex topics will make them disappear. Avoidance may even intensify the counter-productive aspect of the dissonances, making them seem more dangerous and threatening. Simply admitting that there are multiple and competing visions for what constitutes Jewish literacy and serious Jewish learning need not compromise Jewish identity building, and may even be necessary for it. Official and unofficial cultures that could make it easier and possible for students and teachers alike to find the language to talk about any and all dissonances openly may allow the dissonances to be used, rather than magnified and dreaded.

Lingering in the Conflicts

As educators and academics continue to analyze the multi-dimensional character of Jewish identity formation, they must take care to linger in the *conflicts* and *contradictions* of identity formation, and not rush into homogeneous harmonies. Jewish educational approaches that focus on reducing or eliminating the dissonances that are generated by multiple and competing cultures, values, and worldviews have left us with little understanding about the conscious and unconscious strategies that Jews develop to negotiate these tensions. Whether these tensions have an impact on the apparent quantitative and qualitative decline of American-Jewish life that many sociological studies have reported will require further analysis. However, as researchers broaden their conceptions of Jewish identity formation in the design of new research, we can begin to learn about a much wider set of issues than those focused on in much of the current research on Jewish identity.

First and foremost, the field of Jewish identity research is starving for methodological approaches that can appreciate and document identity formation as a series of multiple and moving targets. We need tools capable of studying processes in flux, and over time. In other words, the field needs more ethnographic research and more systematic, longitudinal studies. With greater attention to both of these approaches, separately and together, and through an embrace of the reality of identity conflicts and dissonance which this chapter has addressed, a number of intriguing specific directions for future research emerge:

1. Cultural differences and tensions related to Jewish identity appear, of course, in interfaith families. How each member in such families affects the Jewish identity formation of the others is an important area to investigate. Yet, we bear precious few qualitative studies that could teach us how families and institutions navigate these multiple and competing constructions of theology, ritual, history, heritage, and authenticity.
2. The relatively new definitions of, and interest in, "Jewish spirituality" and "faith development" have yet to be thoroughly studied, but they undoubtedly are important considerations for methods of Jewish education.
3. Research literature on heritage tourism has already begun to explore the meaning of travel to Israel for Jewish identity, particularly the impact of Birthright trips

(Kelner, 2001). However, we still need much more knowledge about what it can mean to make pilgrimages to a "homeland" during this time when all nostalgic and mythic assumptions about Israel are contested and under revision. At the same time, we also need to consider how and why Jews choose to take vacations to other places like Thailand or Italy and what it can mean to people to be in those places, as Jews.
4. Jewish identity formation must be considered in the context of the full range of young people's various identities, Jewish and non-Jewish. As children weave in and out of explicitly Jewish settings like supplemental or day schools, their involvement in Jewish education needs to be examined in the context of the full range of children's supplemental activities, from soccer to ballet to fencing. How does each of these activities fit into a Jewish child's overall identity and how is limited time apportioned and prioritized among the variety of activities they participate in?
5. Those children who do attend religious school or Jewish day school will likely find themselves receiving Hebrew instruction from native Israeli women whose cultural backgrounds, values, and approaches to Jewish education may be quite different from what Jewish-American students are accustomed to in other classes. We do not know how students' associations with Israel and Hebrew are influenced by the differing backgrounds, cultures, and teaching styles of their teachers.

If we are to better understand the Jewish identities that both influence and are influenced by formal Jewish educational efforts, we will need to ask about the tensions, gaps, and contradictions; in short, the dissonances, inherent in Jewish identity formation. As more research of these sorts emerge, Jewish educators will have richer qualitative data that could inspire curricular and pedagogical experimentation that is attuned to the range of sociological and psychological tensions that contemporary Jews face. Jewish educators will have access to new conceptual models, language, and specific vocabulary with which to think about the complex craft of teaching for Jewish identity formation.

Bibliography

Allport, G. (1950). *The individual and his religion*. New York: Macmillan.
Ammerman, N. (2006). Religious identities in contemporary American life: Lessons from the NJPS. *Sociology of Religion, 67*(4), 359–364.
Batson, C. D. & Ventis, W. L. (1982). *The religious experience: A social-psychological perspective*. New York: Oxford.
Berger, P. L. (1979). *The heretical imperative*. New York: Anchor Press/Doubleday.
Bock, G. E. (1976). *The Jewish schooling of American Jews: A study of non-cognitive educational effects*. Doctoral Dissertation, Harvard University.
Charmé, S. (2000, March). Varieties of authenticity in contemporary Jewish identity. *Jewish Social Studies, 6*(2)
Charmé, S. (2006, Winter). The gender question and the study of Jewish children. *Religious Education, 101*(1), 21–39.

Charmé, S., Horowitz, B., Hyman, T., & Kress, J. S. (2008). Jewish identities in action: An exploration of models, metaphors, and methods. *Journal of Jewish Education, 74*, 115–143.

Cohen, S. M. (1974). The impact of Jewish education on religious identification and practice. *Jewish Social Studies, 36*, 316–326.

Cohen, S. M. (1988). *American assimilation or Jewish revival?* Bloomington, IN: University of Indiana Press.

Cohen, S. M. (1991). *Content or continuity? Alternative bases for commitment.* New York: American Jewish Committee.

Cohen, S. M. (2006). *A tale of two Jewries: The 'inconvenient truth' for American Jews.* New York: Jewish Life Network/Steinhardt Foundation.

Cohen, S. M. (2008). "Jewish education and its differential impact on adult Jewish identity. In J. Wertheimer (Ed.), *Family matters: Jewish education in an age of choice* (pp. 19–38). Lebanon, NH: University Press of New England.

Cohen, S. M. & Halbertal, T. H. (2001). Gender variations in Jewish identity: Practices and attitudes in conservative congregations. *Contemporary Jewry, 22*, 37–64.

Cohen, S. M. & Kelman, A. Y. (2005). *Cultural events and Jewish identities: Young adult Jews in New York.* New York: The National Foundation for Jewish Culture and the UJA Federation of New York.

Cohen, S. M. & Kotler-Berkowitz, L. (2000–2001) The impact of Jewish education on adults; Jewish identity: Schooling, Israel travel, camping, and youth groups, Report #, July 2004, United Jewish Communities Report Series on the National Jewish Population Survey. 20 pp.

Elkind, D. (1961). The child's conception of his religious denomination: The Jewish child. *Journal of Genetic Psychology, 99*, 209–225.

Erikson, E. (1980). *Identity and the life cycle.* New York: W.W. Norton.

Fishman, S. B. (1995). *Negotiating both sides of the hyphen: Coalescence, compartmentalization, and American–Jewish values*, Judaic studies program. Cincinnati: University of Cincinnati.

Fox, S., Scheffler, I., & Marom, D. (Eds.) (2003). *Visions of Jewish education.* Cambridge and New York: Cambridge University Press.

Gitelman, Z. (1998). The decline of the diaspora Jewish nation: Boundaries, content, and Jewish identity. *Jewish Social Studies, 4*, 112–133.

Goldberg, D. T. & Krausz, M. (1993). *Jewish identity.* Philadelphia: Temple University Press.

Goldman, R. (1964). *Religious thinking from childhood to adolescence.* London: Routledge.

Goldman, R. (1965). *Readiness for religion: A basis for developmental religious education.* New York: Seabury.

Goldscheider, C. (1986). *Jewish continuity and change: Emerging patterns in America.* Bloomington, IN: Indiana University Press.

Grant, L. D. (2007, Summer). Israel education in reform congregational schools. *CCAR Journal*

Grant, L. D. & Marmur, M. (2007). The place of Israel in the identity of reform Jews. In D. B. Moshe (Ed.), *Israel, world Jewry, and identity.* London: Sussex Academic Press.

Hall, S. (1992). Cultural studies and its theoretical legacies. In L. Grossberg, et al. (Eds.), *Cultural studies* (pp. 277–294). New York: Routledge.

Hall, S. (1996). Introduction: Who needs identity? In S. Hall & P. du Gay (Eds.), *Questions of cultural identity.* London: Sage.

Hannerz, U. (1991). Scenarios for peripheral cultures. In A. King (Ed.), *Culture, globalization and the world system: Contemporary conditions for the representation of identity.* Binghamton, NY: MacMillan.

Hartman, H. & Kaufman, D. (2006). Decentering the study of Jewish identity: Opening the dialogue with other religious groups. *Sociology of Religion, 67*(4), 365–385.

Heilman, S. C. (1998). *Synagogue life: A study in symbolic interaction.* New Brunswick, NJ: Transaction Publishers.

Herman, S. (1970). *Israelis and Jews: The continuity of an identity*. Philadelphia: Jewish Publication Society.
Herman, S. N. (1977). *Jewish identity: A social psychological perspective*. Beverly Hills, CA and London: Sage Publications.
Himmelfarb, H. (1974) *Impact of religious schooling: Effects of Jewish education upon adult religious involvement*. Doctoral Dissertation, University of Chicago.
Himmelfarb, H. (1980). The American Jewish day school: A case study. In *Consultation of the anthropology of the Jewish classroom*. New York: American Jewish Committee.
Hooks, B. (1992). *Black looks: Race and representation*. Boston: South End Press.
Horowitz, B. (1998). Connections and journeys: Shifting identities among American Jews. *Contemporary Jewry, 19*, 63–94.
Horowitz, B. (1999). *Indicators of Jewish identity: Developing a conceptual framework for understanding American Jewry*. New York: Mandel Foundation.
Horowitz, B. (2002). Reframing the study of contemporary American Jewish identity. *Contemporary Jewry, 23*, 14–34.
Hyman Tali, E. (2008) The liberal Jewish day school as laboratory for dissonance in American Jewish identity-formation. Unpublished doctoral dissertation. New York University, New York.
Kaufman, D. R. (1998). Gender and Jewish identity among twenty-somethings in the United States. In M. Cousineau (Ed.), *Religion in a changing world* (pp. 49–56). Westport, CT: Praeger.
Kaufman, D. R. (1999). Embedded categories: Identity among Jewish young adults in the U.S. *Race, Gender, and Class, 6*(4), 86. New Orleans, LA.
Kelman, H. (1976). The place of Jewish identity in the development of personal identity. In *Issues in Jewish identity*. New York: American Jewish Committee.
Kelner, S. (2001) "Authentic sights and authentic narratives on Taglit." Maurice and Marilyn cohen center for modern Jewish studies, Steinhardt Social Research Institute, Presented at 2001 Association for Jewish Studies conference, http://dcoll.brandeis.edu/bitstream/handle/10192/23022/AJS2001.pdf?sequence=1
Krasner, J. (2005). *Jewish education* and American Jewish education, Part I. *Journal of Jewish Education, 71*, 121–177.
Liebman, C. S. (1973). *The ambivalent American Jew*. Philadelphia: Jewish Publication Society.
Liebman, C. S. (2001). Some research proposals for the study of American Jews. *Contemporary Jewry, 22*, 99–114.
Liebman, C. S. (2003). Jewish identity in the U.S. and Israel. In Z. Gitelman, B. Kosmin, & A. Kovacs (Eds.), *New Jewish identities*. (pp. 291–316). New York: Central European University Press.
London, P. & Chazan, B. (1990). *Psychology and Jewish identity education*. New York: American Jewish Committee.
Miedema, S. & Wardekker, W. L. (1999). Emergent identity versus consistent identity: Possibilities for a postmodern repoliticization of critical pedagogy (67–83). In T. S. Popkewitz & L. Fendler (Eds.), *Critical theories in education changing terrains of knowledge and politics*. New York and London: Routledge.
Myerhoff, B. (1978). *Number our days*. New York: Simon and Schuster.
Phinney, J. S. (1990). Ethnic identity in adolescents and adults: Review of research. *Psychological Bulletin, 108*(3), 499–514.
Plaskow, J. (1991). *Standing again at Sinai*. San Francisco: Harper.
Prell, R. -E. (1988). Laughter that hurts: Ritual humor and ritual change in an American Jewish community. In J. Kugelmass (Ed.), *Between two worlds: Ethnographic essays on American Jewry*. Ithaca, NY: Cornell University Press.
Prell, R. -E. (1989). *Prayer and community: The havurah in American Judaism*. Detroit, MI: Wayne State University Press.
Prell, R. -E. (2000). Developmental Judaism: Challenging the study of American Jewish identity in the social sciences. *Contemporary Jewry, 21*, 33–53.

Rosen, S. (1995). *Jewish identity and identity development* (pp. 1–25). New York: American Jewish Committee.

Sales, A. L. & Saxe, L. (2002). *Limud [learning] by the lake: Fulfilling the educational potential of Jewish summer camps*. Boston: Cohen Center for Modern Jewish Studies, Brandeis University.

Sales, A. L. & Saxe, L. (2006). *Particularism in the University: Realities and opportunities For Jewish life on campus*. New York: Avi Chai Foundation.

Sarna, J. D. (1998, Winter/Spring). American Jewish education in historical perspective. *Journal of Jewish Education, 64*(1 and 2), 8–21.

Sarna, J. D. (1998, Fall/1999, Winter). The cult of synthesis in American Jewish culture. *Jewish Social Studies, 5*(1–2), 52–79.

Saxe, L., Kadushin, C., Kelner, S., Rosen, M. I., & Yereslove, E. (2001). *A mega-experiment in Jewish education: The impact of birthright Israel* (Birthright Israel Report 1). Cohen Center for Modern Jewish Studies, Brandeis University

Schoem, D. (1989). *Ethnic survival in America: An ethnography of a Jewish afternoon school*. Atlanta, GA: Scholars Press.

Schuster, D. T. & Grant, L. D. (2005, Fall). Adult Jewish learning: What do we know? What do we need to know? *Journal of Jewish Education, 71*(2), 79–200.

Sklare, M. & Greenblum, J. (1967). *Jewish identity on the Suburban frontier: A study of group survival in the open society*. New York and London: Basic Books, Inc.

Templeton, J. L. & Eccles, J. S. (2005). The relation between spiritual development and identity processes. In E. Roehkepartian, P. E. King, L. Wagener, & P. Benson (Eds.), *The handbook of spiritual development in childhood and adolescence (*pp. 252–265). Thousand Oaks, CA: Sage.

Tennenbaum, S. (2000). Good or bad for the Jews? Moving beyond the continuity debate. *Contemporary Jewry, 21*, 91–97.

Wertheimer, J. (2005). *Linking the silos: How to accelerate the momentum in Jewish education today*. New York: Avi Chai Foundation.

West, C. (1990). The new cultural politics of difference. In R. Ferguson, M. Gever, T. T. Minh-ha, & C. West (Eds.), *Out there: Marginalization and contemporary cultures* (pp. 19–38). Cambridge, MA: MIT Press.

Jewish Identity and Jewish Education: The Jewish Identity Space and Its Contribution to Research and Practice

Gabriel Horenczyk and Hagit Hacohen Wolf

"Ethnic identity could be maintained through education"—this statement seems self-evident, even trivial, to Kwon Young Gun, director of the "Overseas Korean Foundation." More and more diaspora groups are turning to ethnic education in order to foster a sense of ethnic belonging and to bring their members closer to their heritage and to their homeland. Many of them are turning to Jewish educators for advice and guidance, assuming that the Jewish people have succeeded in strengthening their Jewish identity through Jewish education.

This chapter examines this basic assumption and proposes a conceptualization and mapping of the Jewish Identity Space as a tool for better understanding, exploring, and applying aspects related to the relationship between Jewish education and identity. The Jewish Identity Space defines the various aspects and manifestations of identity and behavior in terms of five levels of inclusiveness (personal, family, community, local, and global) and of three components of identity and its expressions (affective, cognitive, and behavioral).

The area to be surveyed is large, with a varied landscape, and no clear boundaries. Theories, conceptualizations, and research reviewed and proposed in this chapter will draw primarily from the discipline of psychology—primarily social and developmental. It should be noted that the areas of Jewish education and identity (and the connection between them) have been informed primarily by sociological and educational theory and research. We believe that our psychological perspective will contribute to the expansion and refinement of the conceptualizations and methodologies by developing and importing new constructs, distinctions, and measures.

We will start with a brief review of the research, focusing on the two causal directions of the relationship between education and collective identity—one that examines the impact of ethnic identity on educational outcomes and the other, less explored, that investigates the effects of education on ethnic identity. This will provide the basis for our summary of the research in the area of Jewish education and identity, and a discussion of the diverse conceptualizations of the variables included

---

G. Horenczyk (✉)
Hebrew University, Jerusalem, Israel
e-mail: Gabriel@vms.huji.ac.il

in the different studies. We will then propose an overarching framework—the Jewish Identity Space—for the mapping and design of research in the area.

Collective Identity and Educational Outcomes

As indicated recently by Feliciano (2009), the influence of ethnic identity on educational achievement has been the subject of much research, but little attention has been paid to the effects of education on ethnic-identity formation. In one of the few studies in this direction, Ng (1999) compared Chinese-American children who attended a heritage school program to Chinese-American children who did not receive education in their heritage language and culture. Her findings showed complex patterns of relationship between Chinese language fluency and ethnic identification.

The vast majority of research, however, focuses on the effects of ethnic/minority identity on educational achievement. Fuligni, Witkow and Garcia (2005) summarized research conducted among African-American students, documenting positive relationships between ethnic identity and a variety of educational outcomes: academic performance, academic efficacy, educational motivation, higher levels of college enrollment, and general academic adjustment. They report findings of their own study showing that, regardless of their chosen ethnic labels, adolescents from diverse cultural backgrounds who considered their ethnicity to be a central aspect of their selves and felt positively regarding their ethnic identity were more positive about education, tended to like school, found their studies more interesting, and believed in their value for their future. Another study (Huynh & Fuligni, 2008) found that adolescents with higher levels of cultural socialization reported higher levels of intrinsic and utility values of school. Along similar lines, Altschul, Oyserman, and Bybee (2006) report that racial-ethnic identity—in its various aspects—is associated with better academic achievement. Ethnic identity was also found to moderate the negative effects of low-socioeconomic status on academic achievement (Ong, Phinney, & Dennis, 2006). Research evidence also suggests that American-Latino students with strong ethnic identity are more likely to capitalize on parental support to excel academically (Cabrera & Padilla, 2004). More recently, Supple and his colleagues (2006) found that adolescents reporting higher levels of ethnic affirmation are rated higher by their teachers in terms of grades, cooperation, and schoolwork. On the other hand, ethnic-identity exploration and resolution were unrelated to school performance and behavior. This finding calls for a careful examination of the differential effects of the various dimensions of ethnic identity, a suggestion that will be discussed later in this chapter.

Thus, most research evidence provides strong support for the view that group affiliation is protective, facilitating minority youths' development of positive achievement beliefs and subsequent academic adjustment. They are largely inconsistent with the "disidentification" perspective on African-American youth, according to which adolescents who recognize societal inequity in economic and social mobility for their group tend to conclude that education has little value for their future personal and professional lives. Strong group identification, then, results in the development of oppositional identities around education and academic values (Chavous et al., 2003).

In the acculturation psychology literature, various studies have examined the relationship between acculturation attitudes and school adaptation among members of immigrant and minority groups. The prevalent finding is the one showing the adaptational advantage of the "assimilative" orientation—one that favors the new society and culture while rejecting ties with the former/minority heritage (van de Vijver, 2005). Horenczyk and Ben-Shalom (2001) provided support for their "cultural identity accumulation hypothesis," showing that among immigrants to Israel from the former Soviet Union, the more positive cultural identities ("Russian," Israeli, and/or Jewish) held by the adolescent the better his or her psychological and school adaptation, regardless of the specific combinations of cultural identities.

Jewish Education and Identity

Research regarding Jewish education and identity has focused almost exclusively on the effect of various types of Jewish education on Jewish identity—conceptualized and measured in a variety of ways.

The components of the studies in this field can be classified into three categories—predictor (or independent) variables, predicted (or dependent) variables, and intervening variables. It is important to note that, notwithstanding the fact that the various studies refer repeatedly to the same measures, quite often researchers use the same labels for indices with different conceptual or operational meaning.

The predictors or independent variables are generally the educational experiences, divided into formal and informal education. The variables used in studies of formal Jewish education include the extent of exposure to Jewish education, i.e., number of hours, number of years of study in Jewish education (Bock, 1977; Himmelfarb, 1974); the "intensity" of education, i.e., none at all, minimal, moderate, substantial (e.g., Goldstein & Fishman, 1993); the type of education, i.e., day schools, private tutor, partial, and Sunday school (Cohen, 1995; Rimor & Katz, 1993); timing of education, i.e., participation in Jewish education in the early/later years of schooling, Jewish education during the high school years (Schiff, 1988; Schiff & Schneider, 1994b). Variables in informal education include participation in trips to Israel, youth movements, summer camps of religious institutions, and Zionist youth movements (e.g., Cohen, 1995).

The predicted or dependent variables are usually those related to Jewish identification, measured in the studies through a variety of indices that may be broadly classified into a number of categories: (1) *General Jewish practices* (observance of customs and rituals), such as lighting Shabbat candles, Chanukah candles, participation in a Passover seder, observing kosher laws and fasting on Yom Kippur, not having a Christmas tree at home (Goldstein & Fishman, 1993), carefully adhering to private religious practices such as buying kosher meat, using separate dishes, not carrying money on Shabbat (Rimor & Katz, 1993), Sabbath observance—Kiddush on Friday night, going to synagogue on Shabbat, and refraining from traveling (Schiff & Schneider, 1994b). (2) *The intellectual and artistic area*—reading, studying and accumulating Jewish books, listening to Jewish music and purchasing Jewish art (Himmelfarb, 1977), and Jewish knowledge (Schiff, 1988). (3) *Social and community Jewish involvement*—involvement in informal social networks with other Jews (Bock, 1977), membership in Jewish organizations, synagogue membership, volunteering for and donations to Jewish causes, subscription to Jewish periodicals, living in a Jewish neighborhood or the desire to live in a Jewish neighborhood, and participation in JCC activities (Rimor & Katz, 1993; Goldstein & Fishman, 1993; Lipset, 1994). Horowitz (2000) suggested measuring "Jewish engagement" by means of seven modes of behavior, including language, memberships/interactions with other Jews, participation in social organizations (e.g., synagogue or Jewish Federation membership), preserving cultural traditions, and political activity. In addition to these indices there may also be included, under the heading of "Jewish involvement," attitudes toward social issues such as mixed marriages (Lipset, 1994), as well as visits to Israel and participation in JCC activities (Lipset, 1994; Rimor & Katz, 1993).

An overview of the indices used for measuring Jewish identity in studies of the relation between identification and Jewish education points to the use of indices based primarily upon intellectual aspects of identity (knowledge of Jewish culture and history), social aspects (involvement with Jewish people and Jewish causes), and on rituals (maintaining customs). Glock & Stark (1965) classic classification of religiosity includes aspects missing from the list of indices, like those that focus on beliefs, feelings, and spirituality. We shall deal with these aspects further on in the chapter. In addition, most of the indices used to measure Jewish identification are indices with "traditional" content (i.e., connected to the Jewish religious tradition, such as Jewish holidays, Shabbat, mezuzah, kashruth, Yom Kippur, etc.), and only a few of them are indices of the "national" content of Jewish identity (i.e., indices that do not stem from the Jewish religion, such as—"ingathering of the exiles," "Holocaust," "self-defense," etc.).

Chapter "Jewish Identities: Educating for Multiple and Moving Targets" by Charmé and Zelkowicz, in this volume, sees these types of indices as reflecting a "survivalist" perspective of Jewish identity that has tended to narrow the field's theoretical conceptions and resulting in largely static and monolithic formulations. They argue for an approach that conceives identities as being multiple and shifting processes that people practice and rehearse, and propose to take into account new or revised ritual practices, spiritual aspects of Jewish identity, and developmental processes and changes throughout the lifecycle.

Intervening Factors

With the increase of research on the effect of Jewish education on Jewish identity, a number of researchers argued that these studies failed to take into account variables that may influence the very decision to send children to the various frameworks of Jewish education, first and foremost among them—the family environment and parental Jewish identity. It was suggested that, in effect, the studies did not measure the influence of Jewish education but rather the influence of the family and its lifestyle (Cohen, 1995; Philips, 2000; Schoenfeld, 1998). Additional variables likely to affect the relationship between Jewish education and identity that were examined in some of the studies are gender, Jewish lifestyle and observance of mitzvoth in the home, birth in another country, and the stream of Judaism in which the respondents grew up (Goldstein & Fishman, 1993). Philips (2000) focused on mixed marriages, and argued that analyses of Jewish education must take into account, in addition to Jewish parentage, variables such as generation (third, fourth), connection to the synagogue, and family income.

A methodological clarification is needed here. Some of these intervening factors can be seen as confounding variables – variables extraneous to the study that are likely to influence the outcome variable, and become a source of "corruption" (Black, 1999). We would like to suggest that some of these additional variables affecting identification outcomes (such as Jewish family variables) should be looked at in terms of their intervening role in the Jewish education – Jewish identity relationship. These variables can play two major types of roles—moderating and mediating. According to Baron and Kenny (1986), a variable may be said to function as a *mediator* to the extent that *it accounts for* the relation between two variables, while a *moderator* is a qualitative or quantitative variable that *affects the direction and/or strength* of the relationship between two variables. Let's take, for instance, the variable of the number of Jewish friends. This variable can play a mediating role: Jewish education impacts Jewish identity via its effect on the Jewish social network. Very likely, mediation will be partial rather than full, with other internal and external factors also accounting for the relationship between Jewish education and identity. As to moderation effects, we could examine the moderating role of Jewish observance at home on the Jewish education – identity relationship. It could be the case that education affects identity more (or perhaps only) when the level of home Jewish observance is low as compared to a high level of home Jewish observance.

Selected Findings from Studies on Jewish Education and Jewish Identification

Most studies report positive correlations between the length and quantity of exposure to Jewish education and various indices of Jewish identification, but also point to differences between various types of Jewish schools in terms of their influence on Jewish identification: Day schools have been consistently shown to strengthen Jewish identity, including connections with other Jews and Jewish behaviors (Cohen, 1995; Lipset, 1994; Rimor & Katz, 1993; Schiff & Schneider, 1994a, 1994b) and they are the most influential of all the kinds of education. According to Rimor and Katz (1993), there is a positive relationship between the number of years of Jewish education and general Jewish identification, expressed in synagogue attendance, community involvement, and religious behavior. Moreover,

Schiff & Schneider (1994b) noted that Jewish education has a greater impact when it continues beyond high school.

Chertok et al. (2007) found that graduates of Jewish day schools exhibit greater involvement in Jewish life on campus than graduates of private and public schools, as expressed in the following indices: involvement in formal Jewish studies, observance of holidays, participation in courses on Judaism, programs on the Holocaust, Israel and Jewish culture, community work under the auspices of a Jewish organization, knowledge about Israel or informal celebration of Jewish holidays with friends. Graduates of an Orthodox background are generally more involved in Jewish life on campus and in observing rituals. In addition, it was found that Jewish day schools, especially those with a non-Orthodox orientation, succeeded in influencing the sense of civic and social responsibility of their students and that the graduates of Orthodox schools expressed a greater obligation toward the Jewish community, in addition to universal values of civic responsibility and social involvement.

Only a few studies were conducted on supplementary schools. In one of these, children viewed their studies in the regular school as much more important than those in the supplementary school, and did not want to spend additional hours in a Jewish school (Schiff, 1988). Cohen (2007) summarizes the scarce evidence in the impact of supplementary Jewish education, concluding that the effect may be somewhat positive, negligible, or even somewhat negative.

According to Himmelfarb (1974), it is not the kind of education (i.e., day school or other) that is the factor influencing Jewish identification, but rather the quantity of the exposure to Jewish education and for what length of time this education continues. Bock's study (1977) supports this assertion, and suggests that the number of hours of Jewish instruction is the best predictor of Jewish identification as expressed in greater religiousness, more involvement in informal social networks with other Jews, a feeling of more knowledge of Jewish culture, and greater support of Israel. Himmelfarb (1974) claimed that at least 3,000 hours of religious education is necessary in order for Jewish schools to have a lasting impact. Since this condition is practically non-existent, Himmelfarb argued that the Jewish education of approximately 80% of the Jews in the United States is not effective. However, later on, Himmelfarb (1977) noted that Jewish schools have a non-negligible influence on the observance of customs or on the intellectual-artistic area of reading, study, and accumulation of Jewish books, music, and art. However, as indicated earlier, some research did reveal impact, albeit limited, of part-time supplementary Jewish education (see Cohen & Kotler-Berkowitz, 2004; Cohen, 1988, 1995).

The studies reported so far were conducted almost solely in North America. Quantitative data on Jewish education and its relationship to Jewish identity from outside North America is scarce. Chapter "Latin America: Jewish Education in Latin America—Challenges, Trends, and Processes" by Goldstein and Ganiel, in this volume, attributes the lack of studies on these topics in Latin America to the absence of community or academic research institutions working on Jewish studies in general, and on Jewish education in particular due to the low awareness on the part of the community leadreship about the value of research. Among the few investigations of Jewish education in the Spanish-speaking world is a comprehensive study currently underway of Jewish schools in Argentina—the Mifné project—coordinated by Yaacov Rubel. Jmelnizky and Erdei (2005) report findings from a survey showing that the major consideration of parents in Latin America for sending their children to a Jewish school is academic excellence. But the study also reveals a high level of consensus among Jewish parents regarding the positive effect of Jewish schools on the Jewish identity of the children. Interestingly, this belief is also shared by the Jewish parents who do not send their children to Jewish schools. Goldstein concludes his analysis by arguing that nowadays the Jewish school is not merely an agent of socialization for Jewish values and identification with Israel, but also plays a significant role in the preparation of the student for professional success and upward social mobility, as well as acculturation to the local-national environment—echoes of a new era characterized by values of diversity, pluralism, and social integration (Chapter "Latin America: Jewish Education in Latin America—Challenges, Trends, and Processes" by Goldstein and Ganiel, this volume).

Research on Jewish education and identity in Europe is also very limited. Cohen (2009) examined the connection between the kind of school (Jewish, general, and non-Jewish private) and family values among Jewish families in France. He found that traditionally religious families at times choose to send their children to public schools and non-religious families at times choose to send their children to Jewish day schools. However, beyond everything else, families that send their children to private Jewish schools are more religious and more connected to Israel, put more emphasis on the family, the community, and religious belief, while families with children in non-Jewish education place an emphasis upon universal values of autonomy and hedonism.

Criticism of the Studies

The expansion of studies on Jewish education and identity is accompanied by various types of criticism that challenge the conceptualizations underlying the studies or their conclusions. As we mentioned above, some of the criticism is methodological and relates to confounding variables (such as Jewish lifestyle at home) that may exert stronger effects on Jewish identification than does Jewish education (see also Chapter "Jewish Identity: Who You Knew Affects How You Jew: The Impact of Jewish Networks in Childhood upon Adult Jewish Identity" by Cohen and Veinstein, this volume). In order to overcome this criticism, a number of studies were carried out that controlled for various possible intervening variables, such as family background and gender, and a high level of correlation was still obtained between Jewish education and aspects of Jewish identification such as community ties (Cohen, 2007), Jewish involvement, knowledge of Jewish culture, and connection to Israel (Dashefsky, 1992). As to the type of education, it was found that day schools have a relatively high influence, whereas no differences were found between those learning in supplementary Sunday schools and those who did not receive any Jewish education at all (Cohen, 1995). In addition, it was found that Jewish identification is enhanced by informal educational activities—youth movements, summer camps, visits to Israel, and especially the combination of all of these. Indeed, such informal education was found to be more effective for youth than any form of formal education (with the exception of day schools). In other words, even partial education provided in the high-school years and combined with informal education provides a rather significant influence from the perspective of Jewish identity (Cohen, 1995; Dashefsky, 1992).

Notwithstanding these studies, researchers point to additional variables that were not examined as intervening variables and that are likely to significantly affect Jewish identification, such as—previous experience at home, the subjects' perception of their parents' Jewish commitment, the emotional climate at home, etc. (Charmé, Horowitz, Hyman, & Kress, 2008). In addition, Chertok et al. (2007) note that in all of the studies that were surveyed there is no solid evidence of a direct causal relationship between a formal Jewish school and various indices of adult Jewish identity. According to them, in order to prove such a connection there would be a need for random experimental conditions, which is of course impractical, or a longitudinal study, for which funding is largely unavailable.

Schoenfeld (1998) raised additional methodological problems, that were not addressed up to now, in the examination of the relationship between Jewish education and identity: the vast internal differences between various types of Jewish education (e.g., Orthodox day schools are totally different from non-Orthodox schools), the use of different variables in order to measure a particular aspect of Jewish identity, whereas, in effect, various components of Jewish identity should be measured since Jewish identity is multidimensional; biases caused by the evaluation of modern-educational projects ("experimental effect"); the absence of attention to the dynamic of identity and to the fact that Jewish identity can change over the course of a lifetime; and the absence of sufficient attention to the changing environmental contexts and the inter-generational differences that render the traditional indices that were used in the past to measure Jewish identity less relevant at present (see also chapter "Jewish Identities: Educating for Multiple and Moving Targets" by Charmé and Zelkowicz, this volume).

From a different angle, Wertheimer (2005) challenge a number of assumptions underlying Jewish education, such as that an institution of a particular type can address various educational needs; that schools are the sole educators of children; that outside of the Orthodox world identification with a particular stream in Judaism has little importance; that efficiency is the best way to strengthen Jewish education and that duplication is a wasteful and incorrect use of expensive resources; and that it is only the family that determines whether Jewish education will succeed. They contend that the success of Jewish education in bringing about Jewish identification depends upon a variety of factors, including the social and community contexts in which the child or adolescent grew up; simultaneous and/or accumulative participation in a variety of Jewish educational frameworks; the availability to the parents of educational choices and their belonging to a particular denomination, which itself influences their educational decisions; the parents' perception of themselves as agents of Jewish education and the mutual influence of parents and children on one another from the perspective of Jewish involvement. According to their assertion, in view of the multitude of internal factors and connections between them, Jewish educational leaders must find ways to connect between formal and informal educational programs, between families and schools, between educators of different kinds, and between central community organizations supporting Jewish education.

The primary current criticism of the conceptualization of Jewish identity and identification is grounded in post-modern conceptualizations arguing against the modern conception of Jewish identity as a relatively clear and stable entity, with clear boundaries based upon known demarcations between "Jew" and "non-Jew," and positing clear criteria for "strong" or "weak" Jewish identities (Charmé et al., 2008). According to Kress (Charmé et al., 2008) most studies ignore the fluid, dynamic, and changing nature of post-modern Jewish identity, characterized by interplay with many other identities which a person has (Charmé et al., 2008), and new dimensions that have lately penetrated the experience of Jewish identity, i.e., synchronic and diachronic diversity.[1]

According to this perspective, these changes in the conceptualization of identity in general, and Jewish identity in particular, mandate adjustments in the underlying assumptions of the studies. Instead of relying on normative linear models of Jewish identity according to which there is a need for accumulation of Jewish experiences throughout childhood and adolescence in order to achieve a strong Jewish identity, Charmé et al. (2008) argue for a spiral model that relates to the post-modern era in which other cultures and identities in a person's environment may influence his or her personal identity more than his or her Jewishness does. The new Jewish identity may find expressions in various ways, unique to each person, notwithstanding characteristics shared with others, and develops with time in a non-linear manner, by returning over and over to the fundamental Jewish questions, albeit in different contexts, throughout a lifetime. The spiral image also challenges the essentialist view of identity. According to Yair (2006), the linear model also includes the assumption of accumulative experiences and is largely appropriate to formal education, whereas those who support the decisive influences of informal Jewish education rely, explicitly or implicitly, on the assumption of transformative experiences.

These claims are consistent with the assertion of Cohen and Wertheimer (2006) that increases in indices of Jewish identification (such as membership in a synagogue or Jewish community center, observance of customs such as Passover seder, lighting Shabbat candles, etc.) do not necessarily point to an increase in the feeling of ethnic solidarity of Jews or their feeling of peoplehood, but rather are consistent at times with the disappearance of such feelings of identification. The researchers interpret this as a result of the changes that occurred in recent decades in the perception of Jewish identity by Jews in the United States, from the perception that it

---

[1] "Synchronic diversity" refers to the multiple forms of Jewish identities that comprise the "Jewish community" at any particular moment. "Diachronic diversity" looks at the phenomenon of Jewish identity as a journey over time (Charmé et al., 2008).

expresses identity of a collective with a shared culture to the perception of an identity with personal, individual, private significance (Cohen & Eisen, 2000). Along these lines, Horowitz (2000) suggested a relatively new variable in research on Jewish identity—namely, the degree of integration between the Jewish part of the individual's identity and the whole person, i.e., an examination of the relative weight of Jewishness (being Jewish) as compared with other significant areas in the person's life (leisure, work, family).

In addition, the post-modern approaches challenge the "natural" and self-evident basis of belonging—a basis that was perceived as unassailable. In other words, a primordial discourse is being replaced by a constructivist one (Burr, 1995; Nagel, 1994), and identities that in the past were conceptualized as ascribed are currently perceived as being a matter of choice. Just as discourse about sexual identity became a conversation about gender, so the constructivist revolution has also not passed over ethnic identity in general, and Jewish identity in particular (Horenczyk & Bekerman, 1999). Therefore, research must relate to the fact that identity, which in the past was perceived as congenital and "ascribed," becomes an "achieved" identity.

It seems that this critique mandates re-examination of the assumptions underlying the studies seeking to explore the connection between Jewish education and identity. For example, Charmé et al. (2008) detail the implications of such wide-ranging changes in the concept of identity. First, a more dynamic research perspective regarding identity is necessary, in order to recognize changes in identity over a lifetime. Second, conclusions regarding Jewish identity cannot be drawn from behaviors or activities reported but rather the self-understanding of a person regarding the place of Judaism in his life/experience must be examined independently of the normative Jewish image—"good" or "bad"/"strong" or "weak." In addition, research methods are needed to enable expression of multiple Jewish "selves" in different contexts.

In order to capture the rich and multifaceted nature of contemporary ethnic identity in general, and Jewish identity in particular, we wish to propose a broad conceptualization informed by theoretical development in the social psychology of collective identity. This framework, we suggest, will allow for better mapping and research on the relationship between Jewish education and identity.

A Social Psychological Perspective on Jewish Identity: The Jewish Identity Space

As a theoretical construct, identity has a rich tradition that offers a wide variety of possible meanings. These are grounded in different disciplines, such as philosophy, sociology, and anthropology (Baumeister, 1987, 1995). In most of the literature in the field, such as that described above, concepts of "identity" and "identification" are used synonymously, with no clear distinction between them. Identification with a group appears in some of the studies as "social identity," "group identification," "group identity," "in-group identity," "intra-group identity," or "group commitment" (see, e.g., Brewer & Kramer, 1986). Ashmore, Deaux, and McLaughlin-Volpe (2004) propose an overarching term—collective identity or identification shared with a group of others who have (or are believed to have) some characteristic(s) in common ... This shared position does not require direct contact or interchange with all others who share category membership; rather, the positioning is psychological in nature. (p. 81)

Some researchers have conceived Jewish identity as an ethnic identity (see, e.g., Dor-Shav, 1990; Elias & Blanton, 1987; Elizur, 1984; Herman, 1970, 1977). Phinney (2003) defined ethnic identity as:

a dynamic, multidimensional construct that refers to one's identity or sense of self as a member of an ethnic group. Ethnic groups are subgroups within a larger context that claim a common ancestry and share one or more of the following elements: culture, phenotype, religion, language, kinship, or place of origin. Ethnic identity is not a fixed categorization but rather is a fluid and dynamic understanding of self and ethnic background. (p. 63)

Different researchers emphasize distinct components of ethnic identity. Some focus upon attitudes and emotions: Ethnic identity as the ethnic component of social identity; self-identification as a member of a group; a sense of belonging and a sense of commitment; a feeling of shared values; the attitude of a person toward his or her group and his or her membership in the group; and ethnic involvement (social participation, observing cultural customs, and holding cultural positions). Some conceptualizations place the emphasis on the cultural aspects of ethnic identity, such as language, behavior, values, and knowledge of the history of the ethnic group (Deaux, 1993; Phinney, 1990).

Along similar lines, Tur-Caspa, Pereg, and Mikulincer (2004) proposed an integrative model of Jewish identity dividing between three types of components: (1) factors that influence formation of Jewish identity, such as values and beliefs, inter-family relationships and relations with Jews and non-Jews, characteristics of the Jewish community, etc.; (2) components of Jewish identity, such as religion, community, Israel, "the Jews," "the goyim," history, etc.; and (3) expressions of Jewish identity, such as the performance of mitzvoth and rituals, marriage patterns, connection with the State of Israel, etc.

We would like to put forward, as a starting point, a rather "pared-down" and inclusive definition of Jewish identity. Jewish identity, we suggest, *is the attitude of the individual towards Jewishness, towards Jews, and towards his or her own Jewishness*. This definition makes no reference to specific contents or to the normative implications of the person's Jewishness. Jewish identity profiles are likely to differ in terms of contents as well as in the extent to which the person feels a duty to express his or her Jewish identity. It is up to researchers to examine these variations in contents, and the relationship between Jewish identity (which is conceived here as an attitude or a conglomerate of attitudes) and Jewish behavior.

The three major components of Jewish identity within our definition (attitudes toward Jewishness, Jews, and one's own Jewishness) are likely to be interrelated— as is the case with other facets of Jewish identity and identification mentioned in this chapter. But for our purposes, as social psychologists and educators, it is the discrepancies among the various aspects of Jewish identity that require theoretical, empirical, and educational attention, such as to students with positive attitudes toward Jews, but less favorable attitudes toward Judaism, or students with a positive attitude toward Judaism but without feeling a personal connection to their

Jewishness. These increasingly common patterns call for educational approaches rich and multifaceted enough in order to confront complex identity dilemmas.

For the purpose of mapping components of Jewish identification, we can then adopt the well-known distinction between three components of the attitude – affective, cognitive, and behavioral (or behavioral intentions) (Ajzen, 1982). Ashmore et al. (2004) also make use of this distinction, classifying the various dimensions of collective identity into cognitive elements (e.g., self-categorization, explicit and implicit importance), affective elements (e.g., attachment and sense of interdependence), and behavioral elements (e.g., behavioral involvement and social embeddedness).

In the wake of this, we can define three *components of Jewish identity* according to three principal groups of questions: (1) *The affective/emotional dimension*—what does the person feel about his Jewishness—is he happy that he is Jewish? Is he proud of his Jewishness? What does the person feel about other Jews and about the Jewish people? Does he feel that there is an internal connection between himself and other Jews? What closeness does he feel toward them? (2) *The cognitive dimension*— does the person place herself within the Jewish people? Does she view herself as a typical member of the category? What is the degree of importance that she attributes to her belonging to the Jewish people? Does she have a positive or negative position regarding her belonging to the Jewish people? Does she carry within herself the narrative of the Jewish people? What are the beliefs and opinions that the person has regarding her Jewishness, Jews, and the Jewish people? Does she hold beliefs and opinions regarding the ways in which Jews need to act? (3) *The behavioral dimension*—what are the behavioral inclinations in the private sphere and in the public sphere, which express his cognitive and emotional relationship to other Jews? Toward the Jewish people? Toward belonging to the Jewish people? What are the explanations that he supplies for such behavioral tendencies?

In addition to the components of identity, Brewer and Gardner (1996) distinguished between three *levels of identity*, according to the level of inclusiveness of the identity: (1) *Personal identity*—relating to the person as a unique individual, her attributes, her personality, her inclinations, without reference to other people; (2) *interpersonal identity*—relating to the person's belonging to small groups with whose members of she/he has daily interactions (such as family, work team, etc.); and (3) *collective identity*—relating to the person's belonging to large groups or abstract categories (such as political tendencies, interest groups, etc.).

Each of these levels of identity can be related to each of the components of collective identity: affective, cognitive, and behavioral. In the context of Jewish identity, in our opinion it is possible to derive four levels of identity from the model of Brewer and Gardner: personal Jewish, two levels of interpersonal Jewish (family and community levels), and collective-global Jewish.

In addition, a comprehensive analysis of contemporary Jewish identity would benefit from the inclusion of a fifth level, namely the local level. This level has not been accorded appropriate attention in the theoretical and research literature until now, but is becoming increasingly prominent in current global Jewish discourse.

The "diaspora" discourse emphasizes the local connection as one of the components that not only describe, but also fashion, the place and experience of the ethnic group. This primarily involves not only the group that is scattered, but it can also be applied to a group residing in its homeland. Jewish identity in the United States has unique characteristics and this is true as well with respect to Jewish identity in France or in Argentina. Each of these identities is the result of historical, demographic, and intra-Jewish cultural processes, but its fashioning was and is also significantly influenced by social and cultural forces in the non-Jewish context in various places. In this vein Aviv and Shneer (2005) argue against the widespread viewpoint according to which Jews throughout the world have "legs" and not "roots," and they advocate researching the ways in which Jews of today fashion identities, not as people in the diaspora—lacking a home—but rather as people rooted in unique places and connected to them.

In this manner, the inclusion of the local level in the mapping of the identity space will enable an examination of the differences between various geographic and cultural contexts in the nature and extent of various expressions of identity. It will also direct us to a measuring of local intra-diaspora connections in the broad framework of Jewish identity and identification. The local level also enables a separate location, in the theoretical analysis and the empirical studies, of the Jewish-Israeli identity that with time becomes more distinct than the identity fashioned in other places in the world (Ben-Rafael & Ben-Chaim, 2006; Cohen & Liebman, 1990).

From the integration of both dimensions, the components of identity (affective, cognitive, behavioral) and the levels of identity (personal, family, community, local, global) we can sketch the identity space (as presented in Table 1) which allows for a multidimensional and multilevel mapping of Jewish identity and its possible behavioral manifestations.

The multidimensional model enables an examination of various issues in the discourse of Jewish identity, as theoretical questions as well in an empirical manner. For example, through use of the model, variables used in the social-psychological studies of Jewish identity from the 1960s and onward in Israel and in the diaspora may be mapped, as is demonstrated in Table 2. The placement of the variables in the table is tentative at this point and may offer a basis for further discussion and refinement. It should be noted that our proposal for a multidimensional mapping of Jewish identity is supported by studies showing how different facets of ethnic identity have differential relationships with psychological and educational outcomes (e.g., Chavous et al., 2003).

Table 1 The identity space

Level	Affective	Cognitive	Behavioral
Personal			
Family			
Community			
Local			
Global			

Table 2 Examples of Jewish identity variables in the identity space

Component level	Affective	Cognitive	Behavioral
Personal	• Motivation for Jewish continuity • Feeling of ownership of Jewish sources	• Perception of Judaism as relevant to everyday life • Knowledge of concepts in Jewish sources	• Observance of customs (fasting on Yom Kippur, Passover seder, celebrating Jewish holidays) • Visiting Israel • Integrating content from Jewish culture in creative works • Volunteering for Jewish causes
Family	• Feeling of connection to roots • Feeling of pride in family tradition	• Self-perception as a link in the generational chain • Familiarity with values of the family culture	• Preserving customs in the home (lighting candles, Kiddush, kashruth) • Holding family ceremonies connected to the life cycle and the cycle of the year
Community	• Feeling of belonging to the community	• Involvement or initiating of social projects in the community	• Synagogue/JCC membership • Initiation and participation in activities connected to Jewish culture
Local	• Pride in local Jewish institutions	• Familiarity with local Jewish institutions • Knowledge of local Jewish history	• Contribution to local Jewish causes • Membership in local Jewish organizations • Membership in Jewish clubs
Global	• Feeling of connection and brotherhood with Jews throughout the world • Feeling of belonging to the Jewish people • Emotional involvement with Israel	• Familiarity with Jewish traditions in the world • Positive and negative positions regarding Jews/the Jewish people • Learning about Israel in the past and in the present	• Making contact with Jews throughout the world • Donation to non-local Jewish causes • Visiting Israel • Contributing to Israeli causes

The suggested conceptualization can generate basic and applied research on various aspects and issues related to Jewish identity and Jewish education. A study conducted by Wolf (2004) examined aspects of Jewish identity using a complex and rich conceptualization based on a number of important distinctions: (1) a distinction between classic measures of social identity derived from group membership (ascribed identity) common to all kinds of identities, and cultural measures unique to Jewish identity (cultural identity); (2) a distinction among cognitive, affective, and behavioral measures; (3) a distinction between measures of national content, measures of traditional content, and those based upon a variety of facets of Jewish identity (cultural, religious, anti-Semitic, political, etc.); (4) a distinction between identification with the category (the Jewish people) and identification with the members of the category—contemporary Jews; and (5) a distinction between identification with the Jews in Israel and identification with the Jews outside of Israel. The study's findings supported the multidimensional perception of Jewish identification and statistically identified a number of factors underlying the complex construct of Jewish identity, such as (1) "feelings towards the Jewish people and the importance of its continuity," (2) "centrality of Judaism in life," (3) "ideology regarding the essence of Judaism," and (4) "connection to Judaism and Jews outside of Israel."

Conclusions and Implications

Jewish education is considered to be one of the major vehicles for fostering a sense of belonging and commitment to Jewishness and to the Jewish people. Most evidence suggests that continuous and extended participation in Jewish educational programs (formal and non-formal) tends to contribute to the strengthening and maintenance of positive Jewish identity.

In this chapter, we referred to some of the conceptual and methodological criticisms raised regarding studies in this area and the conclusions derived from them. It is widely claimed that the measurement of Jewish identity in many of these studies fails to capture the diversity, richness, complexity, and fluidity of Jewish identity in these times throughout the Jewish world (see also Chapter "Jewish Identities: Educating for Multiple and Moving Targets" by Charmé and Zelkowicz, this volume).

It is possible to see the "fluidity" of identity in general, and of Jewish identity in particular, that researchers refer to as stemming, among other things, from only a partial look that focuses each time on another aspect of identity, and as a result, of this resulting in the conclusion that identity is changing, fragmented, and inconsistent in our times. In our opinion, an inclusive approach that accounts for the various aspects and dimensions comprising identity would permit a more complex and appropriate view of identity. Those concepts common to the post-modern discussion of identity, such as "fluidity," "instability," "fragmentation," and "inconsistency" will be replaced by the notion of gaps between various dimensions and aspects of identity or transition from one particular identity profile to another.

Informed mainly by theory and research in social and cultural psychology, we proposed an overarching framework for mapping Jewish identity concepts and variables, and for exploring and describing Jewish identity patterns. The suggested Jewish Identity Space makes room for complexity and richness by enabling the examination of profiles and the analysis of possible discrepancies.

Thus, the multidimensional model of the Jewish Identity Space enables the examination of various issues in the discussion of Jewish identity as theoretical questions, as well as empirically. For example, the model can help to examine and describe the prevailing and developing patterns of connections between the various components of identity, and to provide empirical answers to questions such as: To what extent is the behavioral expression of Jewish identity related to other internal aspects? What characterizes those who have an internal expression (emotional and/or cognitive) but not behavioral, as opposed to others whose Jewish identity is reflected in their behavior? The model will also enable a more differentiated examination of the differences between different groups in Jewish identity—there can be differences on certain levels but not on others, in certain components but not in others, or even in unique combinations of components and levels. The conceptualization of Jewish identity through the proposed model allows, and even calls for, the sharpening of theoretical questions and to the integration of empirical findings from various studies in the Jewish world. This will enable comparison between these studies, and the identification of missing information calling for additional research.

Beyond this, the distinction between the various components of identity enables, e.g., an examination of the differential effects of various educational variables. For example, it may be that supplementary education is more directed—and/or more effective—for strengthening identification at the community and local level, whereas day school education is likely to have more significance on the personal and family level. It may be that accumulated experiences may lead to more significant outcomes in the aspects connected to the cognitive and behavioral components while experiences that constitute turning points are more directed to the emotional component, etc. These distinctions have particular importance in these times, when financial dictates compel restrictions on the educational scope of programs. Policy makers in this area have to be more modest—and especially more aware—of the goals they set for themselves, according to a well-thought out order of priorities, which can be assisted by the distinctions enabled by a model like this. Obviously, there is no expectation that all of the factors will be simultaneously examined in one study, however, if we aspire to multidimensional and comprehensive understanding, our aggregate knowledge must relate to most of these aspects.

In summary, our suggested conceptual model can enrich the toolbox available for the study of Jewish identity and the ways in which Jewish identity is—or is not—influenced by various types of Jewish education. Those who assert that current conceptualizations are inadequate for an understanding of "post-modern" Jewish identity usually do not expect systematic socio-psychological models to provide new tools and measures that are appropriate. We suggest that a multifaceted and context-sensitive approach to the mapping of Jewish attitudes and behavior can provide research—and also other domains of Jewish-identity discourse—with these necessary tools. We also believe that such a conceptually diverse and pluralistic approach can help to better define the goals of Jewish education—not uniform goals for all kinds of Jewish educational interventions or programs, but rather specific, focused, and achievable objectives.

References

Ajzen, I. (1982). On behaving in accordance with one's attitudes. In M. Zanna, E. Higgins, & C. Herman (Eds.), *Consistency in social behavior: The Ontario symposium (Vol. 2)*. Hillsdale, NJ: Erlbaum.

Altschul, I., Oyserman, D., & Bybee, D. (2006). Racial-ethnic identity in mid-adolescence: Content and change as predictors of academic achievement. *Child Development, 77*(5), 1155–1169.

Ashmore, R. D., Deaux, K., & McLaughlin-Volpe, T. (2004). An organizing framework for collective identity: Articulation and significance of multidimensionality. *Psychological Bulletin, 130*(1), 80–114.

Aviv, C. & Shneer, D. (2005). *New Jews: The end of the Jewish diaspora*. New York: New York University Press.

Baron, R. M. & Kenny, D. A. (1986). The moderator-mediator variable distinction in social psychological research: Conceptual, strategic, and statistical considerations. *Journal of Personality and Social Psychology, 51*, 1173–1182.

Baumeister, R. F. (1987). How the self became a problem: A psychological review of historical research. *Journal of Personality and Social Psychology, 52*, 163–176.

Baumeister, R. F. (1995). Self and identity: An introduction (ch.3). In A. Tesser (Ed.), *Advanced social psychology*. New York: McGraw-Hill, Inc

Ben-Rafael, E. & Ben-Chaim, L. (2006). *Jewish identities in an era of multiple modernities*. Tel-Aviv: The Open University of Israel.

Black, T. R. (1999). *Doing quantitative research in the social sciences*. London: Sage.

Bock, G. (1977). *Does Jewish schooling matter?* New York: American Jewish committee. Cohen, S.M. (1974). The impact of Jewish education on religious identification and practice. *Jewish Social Studies, 36*, 316–326.

Brewer, M. B. & Gardner, W. (1996). Who is this "we"? Levels of collective identity and self representations. *Journal of Personality and Social Psychology, 71*, 83–93.

Brewer, M. B. & Kramer, R. M. (1986). Choice behavior in social dilemmas: Effects of social identity, group size, and decision framing. *Journal of Personality and Social Psychology, 50*, 543–549.

Burr, V. (1995). *Introduction to social constructionsim*. London: Routledge.

Cabrera, N. L. & Padilla, A. M. (2004). Entering and succeeding in the "culture of college": The story of two Mexican heritage students. *Hispanic Journal of Behavioral Sciences, 26*, 152–170.

Charmé, S., Horowitz, B., Hyman, T., & Kress, J. (2008). Jewish identities in action: An exploration of models, metaphors, and methods. *Journal of Jewish Education, 74*(2), 115–143.

Chavous, T. M., Bernat, D. H., Schmeelk-Cone, K., Caldwell, C. H., Kohn-Wood, L., & Zimmerman, M. A. (2003). Racial identity and academic attainment among African American adolescents. *Child Development, 74*(4), 1076–1090.

Chertok, F., Saxe, L., Kadushin, C., Wright, G., Klein, A., & Koren, A. (2007). *What difference does day school make? The impact of day school: A comparative analysis of Jewish college students*. Maurice and Marilyn Cohen Center for Modern Jewish Studies. Boston: Brandeis University.

Cohen, S. M. (1988). *American assimilation or Jewish revival?* Bloomington, IN: Indiana University Press.

Cohen, S. M. (1995). The impact of varieties of Jewish education upon Jewish identity: An intergenerational perspective. *Contemporary Jewry, 16*, 68–96.

Cohen, S. M. (2007). The differential impact of Jewish education on adult Jewish identity. In J. Wertheimer (Ed.), *Family matters: Jewish education in an age of choice*. Boston: University Press of New England.

Cohen, E. H. (2009). Attitudes, behaviors, values and school choice: A comparison of French Jewish families. In A. Pomson & H. Deitcher (Eds.), *Jewish day schools Jewish communities*. Portland, OR: Oxford.

Cohen, S. M. & Eisen, A. M. (2000). *The Jew within: Self, family and community in America*. Bloomington, IN: Indiana University Press.

Cohen, S. M. & Kotler-Berkowitz, L. (2004). The Impact of Childhood Jewish Education upon Adults' Jewish Identity: Schooling, Israel Travel, Camping and Youth Groups, United Jewish Communities Report Series on the National Jewish Population Survey 2000–01, Report 3, www.ujc.org/njps.

Cohen, S. M. & Liebman, C. S. (1990). *Two worlds of Judaism: The Israeli and American experiences*. New Haven, CT: Yale University Press.

Cohen, S. M. & Wertheimer, J. (2006, June). Whatever happened to the Jewish people. *Commentary, 121*, 33–37.

Dashefsky, A. (1992). The effects of Jewish education on Jewish identification. In S. L. Kelman (Ed.), *What we know about Jewish education* (pp. 103–114). Los Angeles: Torah Aura Publications.

Deaux, K. (1993). Reconstructing social identity. *Personality and Social Psychology Bulletin, 19*(1), 4–12.

Dor-Shav, Z. (1990). Development of an ethnic self-definition: The ethnic self-concept "Jew" among Israeli children. *International Journal of Behavioral Development, 13*(3), 317–332.

Elias, N. & Blanton, J. (1987). Dimensions of ethnic identity in Israeli Jewish families living in the United States. *Psychological Reports, 60*, 367–375.

Elizur, D. (1984). Facet analysis of ethnic identity: The case of Israelis residing in the U.S. *Journal of General Psychology, 111*(2), 259–269.

Feliciano, C. (2009). Education and ethnic identity formation among children of Latin American and Caribbean immigrants. *Sociological Perspectives, 52*, 135–158.

Fuligni, A. J., Witkow, M., & Garcia, C. (2005). Ethnic identity and the academic adjustment of adolescents from Mexican, Chinese, and European backgrounds. *Developmental Psychology, 41*(5), 799–811.

Glock, C. & Stark, R. (1965). *Religion and society in tension*. Chicago: Rand McNally.

Goldstein, A. & Fishman, S. B. (1993). *When they are grown they will not depart: Jewish education and the Jewish behavior of American adults*. Research Report 8. Waltham, MA: Brandeis University, Cohen Center for Modern Jewish Studies.

Herman, S. (1970). *Israelis and Jews: The continuity of an identity*. Philadelphia: Jewish Publication Society.

Herman, S. N. (1977). *Jewish identity: A social psychological perspective*. Beverly Hills, CA: Sage.

Himmelfarb, H. (1974). The Impact of Religious Schooling: The Effects of Jewish Education Upon Adult Religious Involvement. Ph. D. dissertation, University of Chicago: Chicago.

Himmelfarb, H. (1977). The interaction effects of parents, spouse, and schooling: Comparing the impact of Jewish and Catholic schools. *The Sociological Quarterly, 18*(Autumn), 477–494.

Horenczyk, G. & Bekerman, Z. (1999). A social conatructivist approach to Jewish identity. In M. S. Cohen & G. Horenczyk (Eds.), *National variations in Jewish identity: Implications for Jewish identity*. Albany, NY: State University of New York Press.

Horenczyk, G. & Ben-Shalom, U. (2001). Multicultural identities and adaptation of young immigrants in Israel. In N. K. Shimahara, I. Holowinsky, & S. Tomlinson-Clarke (Eds.), *Ethnicity, race, and nationality in education: A global perspective* (pp. 57–80). Mahwa, NJ: Lawrence Erlbaum.

Horowitz, B. (2000). *Connections and journeys: Assessing critical oppurtunities for enhancing Jewish identity*. A Report to the Commission on Jewish Identity & Renewal. New York: UJA Federation of New York.

Huynh, V. W. & Fuligni, A. J. (2008). Ethnic socialization and the academic adjustment of adolescents from Mexican, Chinese, and European backgrounds. *Developmental Psychology, 44*(4), 1202–1208.

Jmelnizky, A. & Erdei, E. (2005). *The Jewish population in Buenos Aires – Sociodemographic survey*. Buenos Aires: Joint DC & AMIA.

Lipset, S. M. (1994). *The power of Jewish education*. Los Angeles and Boston: The Susan and David Wilstein Institute of Jewish Policy Studies.

Nagel, J. (1994). Constructing ethnicity: Creating and recreating ethnic identity and culture. *Social Problems, 41*, 152–176.

Ng, E. (1999). The impact of heritage education on self-esteem and ethnic identity *ETD Collection for Pace University*. Paper AAI9925491.

Ong, A. D., Phinney, J. S., & Dennis, J. (2006). Competence under challenge: Exploring the protective influence of parental support and ethnic identity in Latino college students. *Journal of Adolescence, 29*(6), 961–979.

Philips, B. A. (2000). Intermarriage and Jewish education: Is there a connection? *Journal of Jewish Education, 66*(1), 54–66.

Phinney, J. S. (1990). Ethnic identity in adolescents and adults: Review of research. *Psychological Bulletin, 108*(3), 499–514.

Phinney, J. S. (2003). Ethnic identity and acculturation. In K. M. Chun, P. B. Organista, & G. Marín (Eds.), *Acculturation: Advances in theory, measurement, and applied research* (pp. 63–81). Washington, DC: APA.

Rimor, M. & Katz, E. (1993). *Jewish involvement of the baby boom generation: Interrogating the 1990 national Jewish population survey*. Jerusalem: The Louis Guttman Israel Institute of Applied Social Research.

Schiff, A. I. (1988). *Jewish supplementary schooling: An educational system in need of change*. New York: Board of Jewish Education of Greater New York.

Schiff, A. I. & Schneider, M. (1994a). *The Jewishness quotient of Jewish day school graduates: Studying the effect of Jewish education on adult Jewish behavior*. New York: David J. Azrieli Graduate Institute of Jewish Education and Administration, Yeshiva University, Research Report 1.

Schiff, A. I. & Schneider, M. (1994b). *Far reaching effects of extensive Jewish day school attendance: The impact of Jewish education on Jewish behavior and attitudes*. New York: David J. Azrieli Graduate Institute of Jewish Education and Administration, Yeshiva University, Research Report 2.

Schoenfeld, S. (1998). Six methodological problems in forecasting the impact of Jewish education on Jewish identity. *Journal of Jewish Education, 64*(1–2), 87–101.

Supple, A. J., Ghazarian, S. R., Frabutt, J. M., Plunkett, S. W., & Sands, T. (2006). Contextual influences on Latino adolescent ethnic identity and academic outcomes. *Child Development, 77*(5), 1427–1433.

Tur-Caspa, M., Pereg, D., & Mikulincer, M. (2004). *Psychological aspects of identity formation and their implications for understanding the concept of Jewish identity: A review of the scientific literature*. Ramat Gan: The Rapaport Center for Assimilation Research and Strengthening Jewish Vitality, Bar-Ilan University.

Van de Vijver, F. J. R. (2005). Theory and research in acculturation and school adjustment. In C. L. Frisby & C. R. Reynolds (Eds.), *Comprehensive handbook of multicultural school psychology* (pp. 651–673). Hoboken, NJ: Wiley.

Wertheimer, J. (2005). *Linking the silos: How to accelerate the momentum in Jewish education today*. New York: The Avi Chai Foundation.

Wolf, H. (2004). *Perceptions of the ingroup and group identification: The case of Jewish identity*. Ph. D. dissertation, Bar-Ilan University, Ramat Gan.

Yair, G. (2006). *From key experiences to transformative points – On the intensity of educational impact*. Tel Aviv: Poalim Library Publishers.

Jewish Identity: Who You Knew Affects How You Jew—The Impact of Jewish Networks in Childhood upon Adult Jewish Identity

Steven M. Cohen and Judith Veinstein

The Well-Established Impact of Jewish Education

The long-term impact of Jewish education upon adult Jewish identity in the United States is well established. Studies that date back until the early 1970s (e.g., Bock, 1976; Cohen, 1974, 1995a; Dashefsky & Lebson, 2002; Dashefsky, 1992; Himmelfarb, 1974, 1979; Fishman, 1987; Goldstein & Fishman, 1993; Grant, Schuster, Woocher & Cohen, 2004) have validated, in broad terms, the effectiveness of Jewish education upon adult Jewish identity. In one form or another, the studies find that several instruments of Jewish education (e.g., schools, camps, youth groups) exert a positive influence upon the levels of several indicators of adult Jewish identity (e.g., ritual observance, communal affiliation), and that this relationship holds up even after taking into account several parents' Jewish engagement and other background factors. In other words, to take an illustration, day school alumni are more likely to attend Shabbat services, even after we recognize that those who went to day schools as children also were more likely to be raised by parents who themselves went to Shabbat services. The link between Jewish education, in its many varieties, and Jewish identity outcomes, and their many varieties, holds up even after we recognize that those with more and better Jewish educational experiences were raised by parents and in communities that also contribute to their chances of higher levels of Jewish involvement in adulthood.

Not all instruments of Jewish education (supplementary schools, day schools, Israel trips, etc.) exert equal influence upon all adult identity outcomes. Day schools in particular stand out as exerting the most profound influence on adult Jewish identity outcomes (Cohen, 1988, 1995a, 2007; Cohen & Kotler-Berkowitz, 2004). Supplementary schools before Bar/Bat Mitzvah exert little impact and one-day-a-week schools seem to even promote intermarriage later in life, probably by reinforcing the weak Jewish commitment of the youngsters whose parents provide them only with a one-day-a-week education. At the same time, positive effects (not

---

S.M. Cohen (✉)
Hebrew Union College & Berman Policy Archive, NYU Wagner, New York, NY, USA
e-mail: steve34nyc@aol.com

quite in the range of day schools) are associated with other forms of Jewish education: supplementary school in the teen years and youth group participation (Cohen, 1988, 1995, 2007; Cohen & Kotler-Berkowitz, 2004), trips to Israel (Mittelberg, 2007; Sasson, Saxe, Rosen, Selinger-Abutbul, & Hecht, 2007; Saxe & Chazan, 2008; Saxe, Sasson, & Hecht, 2006; Saxe, Sasson, Phillips, Hecht, & Wright, 2007) and attending Jewish overnight camps in the summer (Cohen, 2000; Keysar & Kosmin, 2002, 2005; Sales & Saxe, 2002, 2003). Still other studies point to the long-range impact of Jewish pre-schools, as well as to the lasting effects of taking Jewish Studies classes and participation in Hillel or other such campus-based activities.

The effects not only vary by educational instrument, they also vary by the outcomes measured. An early paper in this tradition, for example, pointed to the greater impact of school on knowledge of Hebrew as contrasted with positive feelings about being Jewish (Cohen, 1972), emblematic of what may be schools' greater impact upon Jewish knowledge as compared with Jewish commitment. A study of applicants for Wexner fellowships demonstrated a link between type of Jewish education and type of Jewish professional career aspiration. Day schools seem to be more associated with Jewish Studies professors-in-the-making; Jewish camps from the denominational movements may be especially effective at producing future rabbis; and youth group participation seems to produce a large number of Jewish communal professionals (Cohen, 1995b).

In short, we may still have questions about which sort of Jewish education produces what sorts of outcomes for which types of Jews. But we ought to regard the question as to whether Jewish education matters in terms of fostering strong Jewish identity in the long run as a settled issue, albeit one demanding ongoing investigation and further elaboration.

In contrast, we have little direct investigation of another major aspect of Jewish socialization: Jewish social networks in childhood. Above and beyond everything else we may know about people's childhood lives, do their levels of Jewish engagement measures as adults depend in part upon their parents and friends, even after we statistically account for the impact of their Jewish education?

We do know that children of two Jewish parents score far higher than those with just one Jewish parent on almost all measures of Jewish identity (Beck, 2005; Cohen, 1998, 2006; Fishman, 2004), be they related to belief (attitudes), behavior, or belonging, be it formal or informal. (Throughout this chapter, we regard "Jewish identity" as embracing not merely what one feels; but it is also about behavior, knowledge, formal ties with communal institutions, and informal ties with family, friends, and neighbors. For some, Christian identity may be primarily about faith; for us, Jewish identity is about so much more.) We also know that current levels of Jewish friendship are related to current levels of other forms of Jewish engagement. And we know that a mounting body of evidence points to the impact of social networks in powerful and unexpected ways. For example, a recent study that examined the spread of obesity during a 30-year period among friends, siblings, and spouses concluded:

> A person's chances of becoming obese increased by 57%... if he or she had a friend who became obese in a given interval. Among pairs of adult siblings, if one sibling became obese, the chance that the other would become obese increased by 40%.... If one spouse

became obese, the likelihood that the other spouse would become obese increased by 37%. (Christakis & Flower, 2007, p. 370)

More directly related to this topic, a recent study of longitudinal data on the shaping of religiosity among American adolescents reported: "We found that parents and friends strongly influenced the religious service attendance habits of adolescents and that these, as well as school context, shaped how important religion is in adolescents' lives" (Regnerus, Smith, & Smith, 2004, p. 27; see also Uecker, Regnerus, & Vaaler, 2007). Research on the Jewish engagement of Birthright Israel alumni in North America points to the power of friendship in numerous ways, including influencing the chances and nature of participation in programming for Jewish young adults:

> The alumni we interviewed repeatedly told us that social network factors play a prominent role in decision-making about what programs they will and will not attend. Moreover, analysis of the alumni survey underscores the significance of having friends who also attend activities. In the survey data, participation in specific activities is highly correlated with having friends who participated in those activities. Indeed, between one-fifth and one half of the variance in attendance can be traced to the friendship circle phenomenon. Although this does not prove causation, since alumni may go to a program because their friends go, or the friends may go because the respondent went, it does indicate that participation is strongly tied to network factors. (Chertok, Sasson, & Saxe, 2009, p. 24)

If family and friends influence the chances of growing obese, to say nothing of adolescent religiosity, they also figure to influence the chances of growing up Jewish. Judaism and Jewishness are socially determined, socially constructed, and socially supported. Hence, social networks should be especially valuable in shaping and sustaining Jewish engagement. For good reason the Rabbis placed a premium upon family, community, and institutions, to say nothing of the group character of Jewish prayers, rituals, and ceremonies.

What About Jewish Social Networks?

In light of the proven power of education to influence adult Jewish identity outcomes, one wonders whether social networks exert the same sort of impact upon adult Jewish identity. Analytically, the issue is complicated by the empirical overlap of three major components that undoubtedly come into play in shaping Jewish commitment: parental engagement, Jewish education, and Jewish social networks. Thus, people whose parents were religiously observant and communally active are also likely to report more intensive Jewish educational experiences. The more engaged parents are also more likely to be in-married and to bestow more extensive Jewish friendships on their children. Likewise, Jewish education and Jewish networks are related: people with more extensive and intensive Jewish educational experiences are more likely to derive from in-married homes and to develop Jewish friendships in their childhood and adolescent years.

The overlap in parents' engagement, Jewish education, and Jewish networks in adolescent years raises questions about which factor is genuinely producing positive

Jewish identity outcomes in adulthood. Does education appear to "work" because education is linked to stronger Jewish social networks? Do people who have experienced strong Jewish networks exhibit higher levels of Jewish engagement later in life simply because their parents were unusually engaged or because they experienced more extensive and intensive Jewish educational experiences? In short, what really makes the difference later in life: Is it parents, Jewish education, or Jewish networks? Or, is it all three? (The answer: It is all three.)

Moreover, "Jewish identity" is far from a unitary concept. While no clear consensus defines its boundaries or its content, researchers, policymakers, practitioners, and observers readily agree that it is multifaceted, consisting of several dimensions and expressions. The choice as to which dimensions to emphasize is not simply a scientific exercise, but one influenced by time, place, and ideology. The features of Jewish identity that may be considered more important or most relevant can (and should) differ for younger Jews and older Jews, for Jews in the early twenty-first century versus those in the mid-twentieth century, Jews in the US as opposed to those in other countries, and for Jews who see themselves as religious or secular, Orthodox, Conservative, Reform or post-denominational. As an example, whether one belongs to a national Jewish organization may be a useful sign of engagement for older Jews today or most adult Jews 50 years ago; but it is a less compelling indicator for today's Jews in their twenties and thirties. For them, whether they read Jewish-oriented blogs and websites may be a statistically and substantively indicator of underlying Jewish engagement—and was, of course, simply unavailable to almost anyone during much of the twentieth century.

Fully recognizing these conceptual, problematic, and operational difficulties, we believe that common to members of the contemporary American Jewish population are certain shared dimensions or expressions of Jewish engagement. Among them are:

- Jewish social networks—in-group friends and in-marriage,
- ritual observance—be it the most popular rituals that are observed by vast majorities of American Jews, or some of the more traditional practices observed by minorities of American Jews,
- communal affiliation—of which synagogue membership is the most widespread and the affiliation measure that is, empirically, the most efficient predictor of other measures of Jewish engagement, and
- self-ascribed importance of being Jewish

These measures bear different relationships with different characteristics of the Jewish population. That is, major axes of social differentiation, such as age, gender, social class, family status, socioeconomic status, region, and Jewish ideology, vary in the extent to which and the manner in which they matter for different dimensions of Jewish engagement. The unmarried, for example, score especially low on measures of communal affiliation, but they resemble their married counterparts with respect to several important Jewish feelings (Cohen & Kelman, 2008). To take another example, younger Jews score especially low on measures of Israel attachment (Cohen & Kelman, 2007), but they score not much lower than their elders with respect to celebrating the most widely observed Jewish holidays.

Similarly, the studies of Jewish education have found quite understandable and meaningful variations in the impact of Jewish educational experiences. Not surprisingly, Israel trips produce a much bigger bounce in attitudes with respect to Israel attachment than they do for other measures of Jewish engagement.

Given the variety of Jewish identity measures, the variation in their relationship with external variables, and the differential impact of Jewish education upon different measures of Jewish identity, we would not be surprised to find the same patterns with respect to Jewish social networks. That is, the presence of Jewish friends in childhood and having two Jewish parents rather than one should affect Jewish engagement in adulthood in varying ways, depending upon the measure of Jewish identity.

Is this supposition true? Do childhood Jewish social networks exert an effect upon Jewish identity that can be observed decades later, even when taking into account parental characteristics and the Jewish educational experiences they underwent as children? That is the core question this analysis seeks to answer.

The Data, the Measures, and the Analytic Strategy

To systematically examine, perhaps for the first time, the impact of childhood Jewish social networks upon adult Jewish identity, we turned to the (American) 2000–2001 National Jewish Population Study (Kotler-Berkowitz et al., 2003). For conceptual clarity, we limited our analysis to those who:

- were age 25–64, and who
- were unquestionably Jewish (dropping those regarded as simply "Jewish connected"), and to those who
- were raised at least partially Jewish or had at least one born-Jewish parent (i.e., we dropped the converts to Judaism and those who switched to Jewish identity without undertaking formal conversion under rabbinic auspices).

These criteria limited our respondent pool to 2,064 potential respondents, reduced even further by random non-response to the survey questions we drew upon for the analysis.

The Measures

To measure *Jewish identity outcomes in adulthood*, we focused upon seven particular measures:

- proportion of close friends who are Jewish (32% report that most are Jewish);
- in-marriage, that is, the proportion of those married who are married to a born-Jew or convert to Judaism (67% in this sample);
- observance of more popular rituals, consisting of attending a seder, observing Chanukah, fasting on Yom Kippur, and High Holiday service attendance (47% perform three or four of these);

- observance of more traditional rituals that is, at least monthly service attendance and, regularly lighting Sabbath candles (32% do at least one);
- synagogue membership (46% affiliated);
- communal affiliations, consisting of membership in synagogues, JCCs, and other Jewish organizations (47% with no affiliations, 28% with one, and 25% with two or more);
- subjective feelings about the importance of being Jewish, as measured by the answers to the question, "To what extent is being Jewish important in your life?" (47% answer, "very").

We examined both Jewish education in childhood and Jewish social networks in childhood, separately and together. We defined *childhood Jewish educational experiences* as a combination of Jewish schooling and informal Jewish educational experiences, consisting of participating in Jewish camping, Jewish youth group, and a teen trip to Israel. We experimented with different configurations so as to maximize the impact of the Jewish education measure on the outcome variable and derived the following categories:

- Day school attendees (13% of the weighted sample)
- Attended "Hebrew school" of any frequency 7 or more years (15%) [other terminological equivalents: "religious school," "Talmud Torah," "supplemental school."]
- Had some informal Jewish experiences, but did not attend day school or Hebrew school for 7 or more years (34%)
- Had no informal Jewish experiences but some formal Jewish education (18%)
- No formal Jewish education and no informal Jewish experiences (21%)

For *childhood Jewish social networks* we experimented with various combinations of parents' in-marriage and the number of friends in high school who were Jews, leading us to create the following four categories:

- Parents were in-married and the adult respondent had all or mostly Jewish friends in high school (36%)
- Parents were in-married and half of the respondents' friends were Jewish in high school (16%)
- Parents were in-married but the respondent had just some or no Jewish friends in high school (33%)
- Parents were intermarried (15%)

Throughout our analysis, we controlled for *socio-demographic* and other variables in order to ensure that differences in the adult Jewish identity measures were, in fact, attributable to childhood social networks and/or Jewish educational experiences, and not to the demographic variables with which they may be correlated. We experimented with a variety of possibilities, settling upon a parsimonious list that could adequately represent the impact of the Jewish education that took place in the parental home (we take the view that parents, by their very nature, function as Jewish educators and that the home provides children with motivation, knowledge, connections, and all elements of Jewish education), and current circumstances that are known to influence the expression of Jewish identity. The three factors relating to the *parents' Jewish engagement* for which we controlled were comprised of the following:

- Denomination raised
- No Christmas tree in the home when the respondent was about 10 years old
- The frequency with which Shabbat candles were lit when the respondent was about 10 years old

The socio-demographic characteristics for which we controlled consisted of the following:

- Gender
- Age (25–64)
- Education
- Income
- Family type: unmarried with no children, married with no children, single parents, parents of young children, parents of school-aged children, empty nesters, and widow(er)s.

The Findings

Childhood Friends Linked to Most Adult Outcomes

First, we present the extent to which childhood social networks are linked with expressions of adult Jewish identity, without dealing with the matter of causality or other related factors. As can be seen in Table 1, those raised by two Jewish parents and who had mostly Jewish friends in high school received the highest adult Jewish identity scores on every measure. That is, they had the highest rates of Jewish friendships as adults, were more likely to be in-married, more likely to observe popular and traditional rituals, more likely to be synagogue members and members of other Jewish institutions, and were more likely to feel that being Jewish was an important part of their life. Those respondents with two Jewish parents and about half of their friends were Jewish in high school outscored respondents with two Jewish parents and no Jewish high school friends, who, in turn, outscored respondents whose parents were intermarried.

Of note is that childhood friends matter considerably. With respect to their adult Jewish outcome measures, those with one Jewish parent closely approximate the scores of those whose parents were in-married but reported mostly non-Jewish friends. The only large gap is with respect to in-marriage, with children of the in-married with few Jewish friends reporting more in-marriage than their counterparts who were raised by intermarried parents (58 vs. 44%). But on all other measures, the gaps are small.

Table 1 Childhood social network means, unadjusted

	Jewish friends now	Jewish spouse	Popular ritual observance	Traditional ritual observance	Synagogue member	Jewish affiliations	Importance of being Jewish
2 Jewish parents, most/all J HS friends	63	80	83	34	60	50	84
2 Jewish parents, ½ Jewish HS Friends	47	68	80	22	48	42	79
2 Jewish parents, none, some Jewish HS friends	35	58	69	16	39	33	73
1 Jewish parent	32	44	64	15	36	30	74

At the same time, for today's adults whose parents were in-married, the friendships they had decades ago, in childhood, influence Jewish identity measures today. For these grown children of the in-married, we may compare those who had mostly non-Jewish high school friends with those who reported having mostly Jewish friends in high school. For the two groups, synagogue membership moves from 39 to 60%—friendship patterns years are linked with synagogue affiliation today. The results are even more dramatic in terms of the proportion reporting that most of their current friends are Jewish: 35 versus 63%—again, friendships then are associated with friendships today. The link with in-marriage is telling as well: 58% for those with mostly non-Jewish friends in their high school year to 80% who had mostly Jewish friends. More Jewish friends then (in high school) mean more in-marriage today.

Another way to look at these findings is as follows. Among the children of in-married parents, the chances that one's child will intermarry was only 20% for those with mostly Jewish friends in high school; but it more than doubles (to 42%) for their counterparts with mostly non-Jewish friends.

As noted above, assessing the impact of childhood Jewish social networks requires removing the effects of parents' Jewish engagement, and current socio-demographic variables. Using Multiple Classification Analysis, we examined whether the effects of childhood social networks on adult Jewish identity would remain substantial after controlling for all of the covariates: denomination raised, no Christmas tree in home at age 10, the frequency of lighting Shabbat candles at age 10, gender, age, education, income, and family type (note that at this stage, we do not take into account Jewish education).

As can be seen in Table 2, the differences between each of the childhood social networks groups became narrower on the measures of adult Jewish identity, but

Table 2 Childhood social network means, adjusted for covariates

	Jewish friends now	Jewish spouse	Popular ritual observance	Traditional ritual observance	Synagogue member	Jewish affiliations	Importance of being Jewish
2 Jewish parents, most/all J HS friends	61	77	79	27	53	44	82
2 Jewish parents, ½ Jewish HS Friends	48	70	81	26	50	44	80
2 Jewish parents, none, some Jewish HS friends	37	60	71	20	43	37	74
1 Jewish parent	33	47	69	20	43	36	76
Eta	.467	.264	.236	.215	.198	.201	.198

in every case, they remained substantial. The patterns demonstrated that higher childhood socialization scores are associated with higher levels of Jewish identity in adulthood, even after controlling for the covariates. This pattern was again consistent across every measure of adult Jewish identity—friendship and marriage patterns, ritual observance, affiliation, and subjective feelings—demonstrating that childhood social networks are, in fact, a significant predictor of Jewish identity in adulthood.

Next, to place the results with respect to childhood Jewish social networks in context, we performed the same analysis for Jewish educational experiences. We examined the link of the respondents' childhood Jewish educational experiences with the same adult Jewish identity measures. We present the mean scores for each of the outcomes by level of Jewish education (Table 3), and we control for other variables in Table 4.

These findings reveal some both expected and some curious patterns, as follows:

1. Day school alumni generally outscore all the others. The effects of having attended a day school are most pronounced for in-marriage; less pronounced for Jewish friends, traditional ritual observance, and synagogue membership; and negligible for popular rituals, communal affiliation, and the subjective importance of being Jewish.
2. For most intents and purposes, we find similar outcomes for two groups: those who went to Hebrew school in their adolescent years, and those who stopped Hebrew school, but had some informal Jewish education in adolescence.
3. On many measures, in particular in-marriage, those with no Jewish schooling outscore those with minimal Jewish schooling. This non-intuitive finding occurs

Table 3 Jewish education means, unadjusted

	Jewish friends now	Jewish spouse	Popular ritual observance	Traditional ritual observance	Synagogue member	Jewish affiliations	Importance of being Jewish
Day school	67	91	91	58	75	60	92
Hebrew school, 7+ yrs	48	63	86	23	53	46	81
Some informal exp, did not attend Day or Heb 7+	47	66	76	22	48	42	79
No informal, some formal J ed	36	51	64	10	37	31	69
No informal or formal J education	42	66	62	15	30	24	74

several times in the research literature for these two groups at the lower end of the education scale. Perhaps minimal Jewish education that does not continue or "take" serves to bring together those with weaker parental backgrounds and weaker commitment and actually reinforces their diminished interest in things Jewish.

Table 4 Jewish education means, adjusted for covariates

	Jewish friends now	Jewish spouse	Popular ritual observance	Traditional ritual observance	Synagogue member	Jewish affiliations	Importance of being Jewish
Day school	59	85	81	42	59	48	85
Hebrew school, 7+ yrs	48	61	82	24	50	45	80
Some informal exp, did not attend Day or Heb 7+	48	66	76	24	49	42	80
No informal, some formal J ed	39	54	67	13	41	35	71
No informal or formal J education	44	72	70	19	41	32	77
Eta	.319	.262	.333	.398	.267	.267	.267

Table 5 Social network means, adjusted for covariates, including childhood Jewish education

	Jewish friends now	Jewish spouse	Popular ritual observance	Traditional ritual observance	Synagogue member	Jewish affiliations	Importance of being Jewish
2 Jewish parents, most/all J HS friends	60	75	78	25	52	43	81
2 Jewish parents, ½ Jewish HS Friends	48	71	80	26	50	43	80
2 Jewish parents, none, some Jewish HS friends	38	62	72	22	45	38	75
1 Jewish parent	33	46	70	20	43	37	77
Eta	.467	.264	.236	.215	.198	.201	.198

The findings so far clearly indicate that both childhood social networks and Jewish educational experiences affect how respondents manifest their Jewish identities as adults. We tested whether childhood social networks would remain a powerful predictor of adult Jewish identity if we also controlled for the respondents' childhood Jewish education.

As can be seen in Table 5, even after controlling for childhood Jewish educational experiences, childhood social networks remained a significant predictor of adult Jewish identity. In fact, the same patterns seen earlier again emerged across all categories of adult identity measures. Those respondents with higher levels of childhood social networks also had higher levels of adult Jewish identification even after controlling for a host of socio-demographic variables, denomination raised, and childhood Jewish education.

We also examined whether the effects of childhood Jewish education would be diminished if we introduced childhood social networks as a covariate into those regression equations. That is, would childhood social networks reduce the impact of Jewish education on adult Jewish identity? The answer, illustrated in Table 6, is clearly, no.

Even after introducing childhood social networks into the equation, the earlier patterns remained. Childhood Jewish education remained a significant predictor of adult Jewish identity across all of the identity measures.

These analyses demonstrate that both childhood social networks and Jewish educational experiences influence several measures of adult Jewish identification, even when taking into account parental Jewish engagement and current socio-demographic characteristics. But which factor is more important? Is it social

Table 6 Jewish education means, adjusted for covariates, including childhood social networks

	Jewish friends now	Jewish spouse	Popular ritual observance	Traditional ritual observance	Synagogue member	Jewish affiliations	Importance of being Jewish
Day school	53	83	80	41	57	47	84
Hebrew school, 7+ yrs	48	60	82	23	50	45	80
Some informal exp, did not attend Day or Heb 7+	48	67	76	24	49	42	80
No informal, some formal J ed	42	57	68	14	42	36	71
No informal or formal J education	47	73	72	19	41	32	77
Eta	.315	.259	.329	.404	.268	.267	.270

networks or Jewish education? And when, for what measure of adult Jewish identity, is one more important than the other?

Figure 1 illustrates each variable's overall measure of impact (measured by the Eta coefficient—a measure of impact that ranges from 0 to 1.00, much like a correlation or standardized regression coefficient) on each of the measures of adult

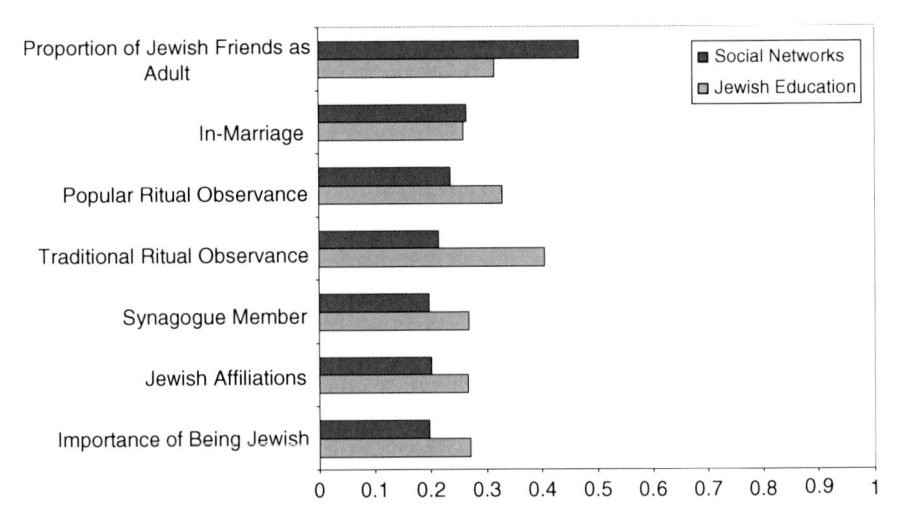

Fig. 1 Overall measures of impact (Eta) for childhood social networks and Jewish education on measures of adult Jewish identity

Jewish identity. By comparing the coefficients for social networks and education, we learn that childhood social networks exert a greater impact upon adult Jewish friendship. For predicting in-marriage, the two childhood experiences are about equally important. In contrast, the impact of childhood Jewish educational experiences is more pronounced upon ritual observance, communal affiliation, and subjective Jewish identity in adults. Nevertheless, the differences in impact are small, with social networks coming close to Jewish education on all adult outcomes with the exception of traditional ritual observances where the education lead is substantial.

Conclusion: Networks Work

In summary, both of these childhood indicators—social networks and education—play an important role in adult Jewish identity, independently of each other. Above and beyond Jewish education, having Jewish friends (and parents) in the childhood years matters especially for having Jewish friends later in life, and to a lesser extent, for in-marriage, and for all other measures of Jewish identity. While Jewish education generally matters more than networks, in all instances except for the more traditional rituals, childhood Jewish friendships and having two Jewish parents are almost as important, if not sometimes more important.

We can reasonably infer that Jewish education, like all forms of education that take place in a social context, exerts its impact in part by creating, sustaining, and reinforcing Jewish friendships. And we need to recognize that Jewish friendships, apart from Jewish education, exert an independent effect upon adult Jewish identity outcomes. In fact, these results echo the position one of us took a few years ago with respect to in-marriage, but which can be extended to other expressions of adult Jewish engagement:

> The role of Jewish education in promoting in-marriage is fairly well-recognized in Jewish communal circles. In contrast, the equally powerful (if not more powerful) influence upon intermarriage of proximity to other Jews, Jewish residential density, and association (informal ties among Jews—friends, neighbors, co-workers, and the like) has received far less recognition than this domain deserves.
>
> Who one happens to meet or know has as much to do with the chances of marrying a Jew as does one's Jewish commitment and education. Jews living in areas of high density (with lots of Jews relative to the surrounding population) are more likely to marry Jews. Thus, Jews in Nassau County (for example) report lower intermarriage rates than those in Suffolk, while Jews in Philadelphia report lower rates than those in, say, Denver. Also linked to more in-marriage is having had more Jewish friends in high school and college, which is a corollary of living in areas with high Jewish residential density. Zip code may in fact be more predictive of in-marriage than Jewish education in that people still date and marry those they live near. (Cohen, 2006, p. 17)

Moving beyond intermarriage to adult Jewish identity more generally, the implications for educators and other practitioners are quite clear: The impact of Jewish education can be augmented by the creation and sustenance of strong Jewish social networks. If so, then mere Jewish association, such as that which may be brought about by Jewish neighborhoods, organizations, or Jewish Community Centers, can play a valuable role in building Jewish social networks, Jewish community, and lifelong Jewish engagement.

Over time, the boundaries and content of "Jewish education" have shifted in line with the changing understandings and changing needs of the Jewish people. This analysis has demonstrated the influence of Jewish social networks in childhood upon Jewish identity in adulthood. But, of course, the lesson is broader: Jewish social relationships (marriage, friendships, neighbors, co-works) operate to nurture, sustain, and encourage Jewish engagement of all sorts. This scientific realization (well known to the Rabbis or old) comes at a time when Jewish social relationships (again: marriage, friendships, neighbors, and co-workers) have been in sharp decline over the last several decades. These circumstances, then, argue for a broadening of the very concept of "Jewish education" to embrace the formation and bestowal of Jewish social networks. If part of what a Jewish education and Jewish educator are expected to do is to teach commitment to Israel, or the importance of *Tikkun olam* (repairing the world) or the virtues of text study, so too should their explicit mission now incorporate the bestowal of Jewish friendship networks upon youngsters (and adults) who are decreasingly likely to find them on their own. For Jewish marriage, friendship, and community are not only instrumentally valuable (they promote and buttress other forms of Jewish engagement), they are also intrinsically valuable to the Jewish life, tradition, and culture Jewish educators seek to perpetuate and enrich.

The research agenda pertaining to Jewish social networks is rich, and parallels the agenda pertaining to social networks in general. A very fundamental question concerns where, and when, and how are networks and identity indicators causes and effects—or chickens and eggs. What leads to what and when and how? A related question concerns how are networks formed and how can Jewish educators help form them at various stages of life—childhood, adolescence, undergraduate years, young adulthood, and beyond? Finally, just as social scientific research repeatedly has demonstrated that well-connected individuals exert more influence on others than social isolates, the question for researchers is to determine the extent to which and the manner in which centrally located and engaged (or unengaged) Jews influences their circles of relationships. And the challenge to educators is to locate such influential youngsters (and others) and mobilize them, in particular, on behalf of Jewish interests and Jewish engagement—both for their own benefit and for that of their surrounding circles of contacts and intimates.

References

Beck, P. (2005). *A flame still burns: The dimensions and determinants of Jewish identity among young adult children of the intermarried—Findings and policy implications*. New York: Jewish Outreach Institute.

Bock, G. (1976). *The Jewish schooling of American Jews: A study of non-cognitive educational effects*. Doctoral dissertation, Harvard University, 1976.

Chertok, F., Sasson, T., & Saxe, L. (2009). *Tourists, travelers, and citizens: Jewish engagement of young adults in four centers of North American Jewish life*. Waltham, MA: Maurice and Marilyn Cohen Center for Modern Jewish Studies.

Christakis, N. A., & Fowler, J. H. (2007). The spread of obesity in a large social network over 32 years. *New England Journal of Medicine, 357*, 370–379.

Cohen, S. M. (1974). The impact of Jewish education on religious identification and practice. *Jewish Social Studies, 36*, 316–326.

Cohen, S. M. (1988). *American assimilation or Jewish revival?* Bloomington, IN: Indiana University Press.

Cohen, S. M. (1995a). The impact of varieties of Jewish education upon Jewish identity: An inter-generational perspective. *Contemporary Jewry, 16*, 68–96.

Cohen, S. M. (1995b). "The coming generation of Jewish communal professionals, Cohen Center for Modern Jewish Studies, Brandeis University. In S. M. Cohen, S. B. Fishman, J. D. Sarna, & C. S. Liebman (Eds.), *Expectations, education and experience of Jewish professional leaders: Report of the Wexner Foundation research project on contemporary Jewish professional leadership* (pp. 1–30). Waltham, MA: Cohen Center for Modern Jewish Studies, Brandeis University, and Argov Center for the Study of Israel and the Jewish People, Bar Ilan University.

Cohen, S. M. (1998). *Religious stability and ethnic decline: Emerging patterns of Jewish identity in the United States.* New York: Jewish Community Centers Association.

Cohen, S. M. (2000). Camp Ramah and adult Jewish identity. In S. A. Dorph (Ed.), *RAMAH: reflections at 50: Visions for a new century* (pp. 95–129). New York: National Ramah Commission.

Cohen, S. M. (2006). *A tale of two Jewries: The "inconvenient truth" for American Jews.* New York: Jewish Life Network/Steinhardt Foundation.

Cohen, S. M. (2007). The differential impact of Jewish education on adult Jewish identity. In J. Wertheimer (Ed.), *Family matters: Jewish education in an age of choice* (pp. 34–58). Lebanon, NH: University Press of New England.

Cohen, S. M., & Kelman, A. Y. (2007). *Beyond distancing: Young adult American Jews and their alienation from Israel.* New York Andrea and Charles Bronfman Philanthropies.

Cohen, S. M., & Kelman, A. Y. (2008). *Uncoupled: How our singles are reshaping Jewish engagement.* New York: Andrea and Charles Bronfman Philanthropies. http://www.acbp.net/About/PDF/uncoupled.pdf

Cohen, S. M., & Kotler-Berkowitz, L. (2004). The Impact of Childhood Jewish Education upon Adults' Jewish Identity: Schooling, Israel Travel, Camping and Youth Groups, United Jewish Communities Report Series on the National Jewish Population Survey 2000–01, Report 3, www.ujc.org/njps.

Dashefsky, A. (1992). The effects of Jewish education on Jewish identification. In S. L. Kelman (Ed.), *What we know about Jewish education.* Los Angeles: Torah Aura Publications.

Dashefsky, A., & Lebson, C. (2002). Does Jewish schooling matter? A review of the empirical literature on the relationship between formal Jewish education and dimensions of Jewish identity. *Contemporary Jewry, 23*, 96–131.

Fishman, S. B. (1987). *Learning about learning: Insights on contemporary Jewish education from Jewish population studies.* Waltham, MA: Brandeis University, Cohen Center for Modern Jewish Studies.

Fishman, S. B. (2004). *Double or nothing? Jewish families and mixed marriage.* Waltham, MA: Brandeis University Press.

Goldstein, A., & Fishman, S. B. (1993). *When they are grown they will not depart: Jewish education and the Jewish behavior of American adults. Research Report 8.* Waltham, MA: Brandeis University, Cohen Center for Modern Jewish Studies.

Grant, L. D., Schuster, D. T., Woocher, M., & Cohen, S. M. (2004). *A journey of heart and mind: Transformative Jewish learning in adulthood.* New York: Jewish Theological Seminary of America.

Himmelfarb, H. (1974). *The impact of religious schooling: The effects of Jewish education upon adult religious involvement.* Doctoral dissertation, University of Chicago.

Himmelfarb, H. (1979). Agents of religious socialization. *The Sociological Quarterly, 20*(Autumn), 477–494.

Keysar, A., & Kosmin, B. A. (2002). *The camping experience—The impact of Jewish summer camping on the conservative high school seniors of the "four up" study.* New York: National Ramah Commission.

Keysar, A., & Kosmin, B. A. (2005). *Research findings on the impact of Camp Ramah: A companion study to the 2004 "eight up" Report on the attitudes and practices of conservative Jewish college students.* New York: National Ramah Commission.

Kotler-Berkowitz, L., Cohen, S. M., Ament, J., Klaff, V., Mott, F., & Pekerman-Newman, D. (2003). National Jewish population survey 2000–01: Strength, challenge and diversity in the American Jewish population. *United Jewish Communities*, http://www.ujc.org/page.aspx?id=33650

Mittelberg, D. (2007). Israel visits and Jewish identity. In D. Ben-Moshe & Z. Segev (Eds.), *Israel, the Diaspora and Jewish identity.* Eastbourne: Sussex Academic Press.

Regnerus, M. D., Smith, C. S., & Smith, P. B. (2004). Social context in the development of adolescent religiosity. *Applied Developmental Science, 8*, 27–38.

Sales, A. L., & Saxe, L. (2002). *Limud by the lake: Fulfilling the educational potential of Jewish summer camps.* New York: Avi Chai Foundation.

Sales, A. L., & Saxe, L. (2003). *How goodly are thy tents: Summer camps as Jewish socializing experiences.* Waltham, MA: Brandeis University Press/University Press of New England.

Sasson, T., Saxe, S., Rosen, M., Selinger-Abutbul, D., & Hecht, S. (2007). *After birthright Israel: Finding and seeking young adult Jewish community.* Waltham, MA: Maurice and Marilyn Cohen Center for Modern Jewish Studies.

Saxe, L., & Chazan, B. (2008). *Ten days of birthright Israel: A journey in young adult identity.* Lebanon, NH: University Press of New England.

Saxe, L., Sasson, T., & Hecht, S. (2006). *Taglit-birthright Israel: Impact on Jewish identity, peoplehood and connection to Israel.* Waltham, MA: Maurice and Marilyn Cohen Center for Modern Jewish Studies.

Saxe, L., Sasson, T., Phillips, B., Hecht, S., & Wright, G. (2007). *Taglit-birthright Israel evaluation: 2007 North American cohorts.* Waltham, MA: Steinhardt Social Research Institute.

Uecker, J. E., Regnerus, M. D., & Vaaler, M. (2007). Losing my religion: The social sources of religious decline in early adulthood. *Social Forces, 85*, 1667–1692.

Jewish Thought for Jewish Education: Sources and Resources

Jonathan A. Cohen

Introduction

In recent years, a noteworthy proliferation of descriptive, empirical research has shed a great deal of light on the way Jewish education is actually conducted in various settings: denominational and non-denominational, day school and supplementary, formal and informal. The growth of academic research in Jewish education has also generated a felt need for a more rigorous consideration of the *ends* of Jewish education – the "oughts" that might orient educators with regard to the purpose of their practice, as they become more knowledgeable about the situation as it "is." It is this need that has informed both the composition and the reception of the well-known anthology and commentary: *Visions of Jewish Education* (Fox, Scheffler, & Marom, 2003) – a rich compendium of plural conceptions of the educated Jew conceived and coordinated by my esteemed teacher Seymour Fox, of blessed memory. The mentor to whom I owe my personal initiation into the field of the philosophy of Jewish education, Michael Rosenak, has made the ends of Jewish education his primary academic focus in foundational books such as *Commandments and Concerns* (Rosenak, 1987) and *Roads to the Palace* (Rosenak, 1995).

Fox, together with Israel Scheffler and Daniel Marom, asked premier Jewish scholars and thinkers such as Isadore Twersky, Moshe Greenberg, Michael Meyer, and Menachem Brinker – to explicitly set forth their conceptions of the educated Jew. Rosenak drew upon modern Jewish thinkers such as Buber, Heschel, Liebowitz, and Soloveitchik as resources for the articulation and justification of his own vision of "Jewish Religious Education in a Secular Society." Both of these projects have yielded rich fruit and I strongly recommend these works for Jewish educational leaders who perforce cannot avoid being concerned with the clarification and formulation of ends. Another approach to Jewish educational thought (one that I have been concerned with in my own work) involves "thinking through" issues of principle occupying Jewish educators today through the eyes of Jewish thinkers who represent different worldviews, even if those thinkers did not necessarily address

J.A. Cohen (✉)
Hebrew University, Jerusalem, Israel
e-mail: jonny@mscc.huji.ac.il

those issues directly. The aim of this pursuit is to present Jewish educational leaders and policymakers with plural perspectives on fundamental issues, perspectives derived from the work of recognized philosophers, theologians, and scholars. It is my hope that this kind of inquiry can enrich contemporary discourse on the overall aims of Jewish education.

The kind of question that will posed in this chapter, then, goes something like this: If I were Mordechai Kaplan, or Martin Buber, or some other outstanding modern Jewish thinker, and I saw things the way they see things, and a certain issue of principle that has been perplexing Jewish educators today were placed at my doorstep – how might I conceivably think through that issue? How might I thereby offer a measure of guidance to educators who are searching for orientation in their work?

For example, if we were to focus on some of Schwab's famous educational "commonplaces" (Schwab, 1964, pp. 5–6), with regard to the *learner*, should the ideal student or the ideal graduate of a Jewish educational institution possess a disposition for "spirituality?" Is "spirituality" a good thing? What do we mean by this term, one that has become something of a Jewish-educational buzzword? Should we judge our success or failure in Jewish education by the degree to which we foster "spirituality" in our students? What might thinkers like Julius Guttmann or Emmanuel Levinas have to say about this issue, if we were to confront them with it?

Concerning the commonplace *subject matter*, is the Jewish traditional literature that many of us are laboring to impart and illuminate actually "translatable" to young people whose consciousness has been shaped by modernity and post-modernity? Can ancient texts, permeated with values, mores, and conceptions so different from our own be "translated" for us without being distorted out of all recognition? If such "translation" is at all possible, what is "lost" and "gained" in such translation? Can we translate Jewish traditional texts in a way that preserves their "authenticity" while still being "relevant" (Rosenak, 1986, pp. 35–45, 1995, pp. 98–100)? What might scholars and thinkers such as J.B. Soloveitchik and Martin Buber have to say about this issue?

Schwab always emphasized that a full educational deliberation should include discussion of all four commonplaces. Toward the end of his career, he even came to feel that the commonplace *teacher* was perhaps the most neglected of the four (Schwab, 1983). He therefore thought it particularly important not to pass over the commonplace *teacher* in any deliberation meant to issue in practical decisions. The limited scope of this brief chapter, however, will allow us to treat only two commonplaces (the "learner" and the "subject matter"). For an extended treatment of Schwab's fourth commonplace – the *teacher* – I refer the reader to my article "Subterranean Didactic: Theology, Aesthetics and Pedagogy in the Thought of Franz Rosenzweig" (Cohen, 1999a). As far as the commonplace *milieu* is concerned, I am planning a paper comparing the views of Yeshayahu Liebowitz and Menachem Brinker on the issue of Jewish "peoplehood."

In the framework of a handbook, I am also not able to give an account of how I arrived at my interpretations of the thought systems under discussion. I can only provide a brief summary of the relevant views of the thinkers I have chosen to "mine" for insights into Jewish educational issues. Interested readers are directed to the bibliographical items presented at the end of this chapter, wherein both the methodology and the canons of interpretation used to reach the conclusions offered here are extensively discussed.

Julius Guttmann and Emmanuel Levinas on "Spirituality"

Jewish thinkers and sociologists advise us of the recent decline of ethnic solidarity and "visceral Judaism" as primary characteristics of Jewish identity among contemporary Jews (Cohen & Eisen, 2000). In this generation, individual Jews are often said to be seeking out experiences of "spirituality," joining groups that offer the promise of "spiritual experience," rather than groups that place a premium on collective action for "national" causes. Talk about "spirituality," however, tends to be vague and unfocused. It is often difficult for people who are enthusiastic about it to give a coherent account of it. What exactly do we mean by "spirituality" and how is it different from other kinds of consciousness or feeling? Does "spirituality" entail certain beliefs or commitments, or is it a catch phrase for pleasant experiences with religious overtones? What might education for spirituality require from the learner or can any and all "get the spirit" if only the right mood is set?

Searching for guidance on some of these questions, let us turn to two towering Jewish thinkers of the twentieth century – Julius Guttmann and Emmanuel Levinas. Julius Guttmann is perhaps the less known of the two, since Levinas' fame as a world-class philosopher and as an original Jewish thinker has been growing in recent years. Guttmann, however, can and should be regarded as one of the premier scholars of Jewish philosophy in the twentieth century. After heading the Academy for the Science of Judaism in Berlin in the 1920s and early 1930s, he made his home in Jerusalem in 1934, where he was professor of Jewish philosophy at the Hebrew University until his death in 1950. His famous book, *Philosophies of Judaism* (Guttmann, 1964) published in German, Hebrew, and English, remains a foundational text for anyone who wishes to gain entry into the field. Guttmann, however, was not only a scholar of Jewish philosophy. His writings, though written in a scholarly vein, reveal a thinker with a definite philosophical position of his own. I believe his insights into what is today called "Jewish spirituality" can serve as a paradigm and a resource for Jewish educators who are seeking to understand what "spirituality" is and how to educate toward it.

First of all, Guttmann would probably prefer the term "religiosity" to "spirituality." Guttmann was of the opinion that religiosity is a universal human potential. All people, so he thought, have an innate disposition to connect with some supreme "Other" regarded as the ultimate source of Being and Value. Just as human beings have a natural capacity for rationality and the making of intellectual distinctions (true and false); just as they are endowed with an innate moral sense (that allows them to distinguish right from wrong) and with a native aesthetic sense (by way of which they separate the beautiful from the ugly) – so too are they endowed with the capacity to experience a religious dimension within which they sense the difference between the holy and the profane. Religiosity, then, for Guttmann, is not a psychological crutch (as the Freudians might have it) or an avenue of escape from the material causes of the human condition (as the Marxists might claim). It is rather a natural, healthy state – reflecting the best and the highest in human consciousness (Guttmann, 1976, pp. 11–38, 61–80).

For Guttmann, there are two basic modes by way of which human beings have been, and can be, "religious." One mode he called "mystic-pantheistic" and the other he called "personalist." Religiosity in the first mode involves some kind of desire for unity with the Absolute. The Ultimate Reality is thought or felt to be inside one, or one senses oneself to be a part or an aspect of it. This mode is mystical because it posits an ultimate unity to all Being, with all separation and distinction regarded as temporary or illusionary. It is pantheistic because it ultimately regards the world and the human as part of the oneness of God. The world and the human may have temporarily separated from Him, but they are destined to reunite with Him. Such reunification can be accomplished in different ways. Some variations of this mode see the reunification as taking place within the realm of the intellect. For Maimonides, for example, the human mind, gradually gaining knowledge of the rational essences and principles underlying nature, unites with the mind of the author of nature – God. Others see this reunification as taking place by way of some kind of extra-rational experience.

It is the "personalistic" mode of religiosity that Guttmann regarded as most typical of Judaism, although many Jewish thinkers, as well as whole Jewish communities, may have deviated from it in varying degrees in the course of Jewish history. Personalistic religiosity implies that God and the human remain distinct from each other always, confronting each other as integral, separate beings. God is conceived after the model of a willing person, one who makes moral demands on humans. He may confront us as a powerful king or an exacting judge, or He may meet us as a merciful father. Humans are charged not to seek unity with God, but rather to actively respond to His moral call. Only the realization of His moral will in the world can bring human beings closer to Him. Such an experience of intimacy, however, is discretely "religious," and represents a dimension beyond the ethical sense of having fulfilled a moral duty for its own sake. It is a blissful experience of communion with a supreme person, an experience that has a similar structure to, and yet transcends, the inter-human realm (Guttmann, 1964, pp. 3–10, 1976, pp. 93–101).

Religious "readiness," then, is not something that has to be manufactured in the learner. All people have an innate "readiness" for the religious relation. What, then, could be considered as religious maturity from a point of view derived from the thought of Julius Guttmann? Mature religiosity, from Guttmann's perspective, involves the coexistence and interaction of two dimensions: one "subjective" and "personal" (sometimes expressed by way of strong emotions) and another "objective" and "critical" (expressed by way of cognitive analysis and reflection). The religious relation can beget a sense of trust and faith in the goodness of God and the world. This can issue in strong feelings of love for the God who has given us our being as well as the wherewithal to enact His moral will. Such a relation, however, can also beget fear of the awesome and demanding side of the Divine. Such feelings can erupt suddenly, and it is of their essence that they are not calculable or controllable.

Although no religiosity could be authentically "personal" and "subjective" without such a spontaneous, emotional dimension – so, too, no mature religiosity would be complete without a rational-critical dimension. For Guttmann, the rational and moral aspects of human consciousness play an active part in the constitution of the religious domain itself. For God's word to be appropriated by human beings who retain their integrity, it must pass through those prisms and categories by way of which humans autonomously judge things as true or false, good or bad. Indeed, these capacities have been bestowed upon us as a gift from God himself. They have been bestowed, however, in order that we might use them autonomously. The rational-critical capacity helps us to distinguish between the various "objects" toward which we might be tempted to direct our penchant for worship. It also helps us to realize when we are experiencing truth, goodness, beauty, or holiness – and when we are not. These "filters" protect us against idolatry, "false prophecy," and self-delusion. Mature religiosity, then, for Guttmann, involves both emotional spontaneity and rational reflection. In fact, it could be said, perhaps paradoxically, that the mature religious person is possessed of a kind of "reflective spontaneity" (Guttmann, 1955, pp. 299–301; Cohen, 1991, pp. 135–138, 336).

To be a Jew in the quintessential sense, then, for Guttmann, means not to be an adherent of the law, or to be a believer in a certain doctrine or to be the proud member of an ethnic group. It actually has to do with what is today called "spirituality," but in a very specific sense. It means partaking in a certain quality of subjective, personalistic religious intimacy with God, yet one that is dependent for its realization on the enactment of God's moral will. While awarded in response to ethical action, religious intimacy itself takes place in a realm distinct from the ethical.

From an educational point of view, the potential to draw near to God and to experience oneself in a relation with Him resides in every person. Religion does not subsist *outside* the learner, with the task of education being to somehow place it *inside* the learner. Religion preexists *inside* the learner, though perhaps in a latent or dormant state. Educationally, then, we can say that religion is not "instilled" in a person, as perhaps obedience to the law or the assent to a doctrine can be "instilled." Religiosity – as Guttmann understands it – is "drawn out" of a person. Education would not involve inculcation from the outside, but rather the creation of an environment that would be congenial to the growth and expression of an inner capacity (Cohen, 1991, p. 344).

Much more could be said, of course, regarding Guttmann's understanding of religious experience and the educational implications that could be extrapolated from it. We nonetheless turn, at this point, to another thinker whose views on "religiosity" and all that goes with it were very different from those of Guttmann – Emmanuel Levinas. Levinas' conception of religious maturity was quite different from that of Guttmann, and unique in the world of modern Jewish thought. In one of his more incisive articles on Jewish themes, Levinas calls Judaism a "religion for adults." In that article, as well in other essays that appear in the collection called *Difficult Freedom* (Levinas, 1990), Levinas offers insight into what he considered a mature religiosity, as distinct from modes of religiosity that he regarded as either "childish" or "adolescent."

Levinas, in contradistinction to Guttmann, expressed a marked aversion to all attempts to stake out and characterize a discrete area of experience known as "religiosity" or "spirituality" (whether "awe" in the presence of the "numinous" or "ecstasy" in the presence of the "sacred"). For Levinas, this tendency represented a "childish" need to be gathered up and comforted by an all-encompassing presence – a "womblike" experience that has the effect of turning one's attention away from the immediacy of human need and the difficult trials of moral decision making. Levinas did not believe that the universal yearning for the Beyond represents humanity at its best – as Guttmann did. For Levinas, it represents an escape from the arduous task of active service directed toward vulnerable, suffering human beings. Absolute responsibility to the other human being – expressed in actions that penetrate the most "petty" details of life – is the only posture wherein even a trace of the transcendent may be intimated (Levinas, 1990, pp. 14–16; Cohen, 2002, pp. 353–354).

In mid-twentieth-century France Levinas already observed Jews flocking to forums where they can "savor metaphysical anxiety and the presence of the Sacred in social quietude" (Levinas, 1990, p. 248). This kind of "spirituality" seemed to him to be taking the place of what had traditionally been regarded as Jewish activity par excellence: arduous training in the details of the Talmudic law (for Levinas, the quintessence and ramification of ethics) with a view to applying them to the most prosaic areas of life. He believed that the current trend is rooted in an immature mode of religiosity, one that derives from an inability to postpone gratification. People want instant and unmediated "spirituality" – issuing perhaps in intense feeling but without a great deal of cognitive or ethical rigor. One of the virtues of the mature, educated Jew, then is "the virtue of patience," the "ability to wait and suffer" (Levinas, 1990, p. 155) through the inevitable frustrations of the life of ethical service. "Religious" education, then, would not involve the "drawing out" of a universal propensity for the "spiritual," but rather rigorous training and exercise in those intellectual and ethical disciplines that might prepare (and fortify) the individual for the enactment of his/her primordial and incalculable ethical responsibility.

The above description of Levinas' educational ideal might be read as a critique of certain tendencies within what is sometimes referred to as "liberal" Judaism. Other characteristics of his worldview, however, could be read as a critique of tendencies more commonly observed in "traditional" circles. For example, another expression of religious immaturity for Levinas can be found in certain Jews' sense of "chosenness," wherein they feel that they are somehow "better" than other people. Many people, it would appear, need, like children, to feel that their group is better than other groups. This provides them with the motivation to continue to belong to the group, and to make the sacrifices necessary to keep the group going. Levinas, however, interprets the experience of chosenness in an entirely different way. For Levinas, to sense oneself as "chosen" means that within a specific ethical situation, *I know that there is no one else who can enact responsibility for the other in the precise way that I am called upon to do.* I am irreplaceable in my responsibility. Only I can carry the burden of the other, actually "substituting" for him, as if it were my own. Though I must substitute for him, as far as this particular situation of encounter is concerned, no one can substitute for me (Levinas, 1997, pp. 88–125). To sense oneself as chosen, then, is not to consider oneself essentially superior. Nor is it to feel (as Freud did, for example) that one's Jewish side is one's best side. It is to be aware of oneself as "singled out" to come to the aid of this particular person at this particular time in this particular way.

The mature, educated Jew, then, is also one who sees himself/herself as both personally "chosen" and as a member of the "chosen people," namely that people that have responded to the call to embody the posture of ethical irreplaceability in the world. The fully mature ethical person understands himself/herself as bound to the service of the other whether or not the other feels and acts in the same way. The ethos of service is asymmetrical and not dependent on reciprocity. So, too, to be a Jew is to join those who collectively represent the orientation of disinterested service as a living possibility. This individual and collective "being-for-the-other" is the only way that "mere being," dedicated only to self-preservation, can be transcended. It is therefore the only legitimate locus for anything that might be termed "spirituality."

In *Difficult Freedom* and elsewhere, Levinas also confronts "religious" dispositions that appear to him as characteristic of adolescence. What Barry Holtz has called a "hunger for wonders" (Holtz & Rauch, 1988, pp. 74–76) would probably be seen by him as originating from an adolescent fascination with the bizarre and the mysterious. Levinas would likely diagnose this hankering for the holy as resulting from the kind of alienation and ennui that often propels young people to search out exciting new stimuli (Levinas, 1990, pp. 100–101). In his view, it would probably be better to foster a different kind of "heightened awareness" in young people: namely a hyper-attentiveness to the needs of the other, and a willingness to do unconventional things in order to aid the vulnerable and the downtrodden.

As is well known, adolescents can fall prey to an excess of either individualism or conformism. In religious communities, over-individualism can sometimes take the form of a penchant for religious virtuosity or idiosyncrasy. People who believe that they are "special" or "different" seek out what Levinas has called a personal "tete-a-tete" with God, far from the madding crowd of community and tradition (Levinas, 1990, p. 248). On the other hand, compulsive conformism to the details of communal practice can often dull the individual conscience. Such obsessive observance has the effect of diverting a person from his/her individual "calling" to serve the other in ways that only he or she can.

The romantic virtues of "spontaneity" and "naturalness" have also been associated with the ethos of adolescence. Praise is reserved for those who have the "courage" for uninhibited self-expression, while those who structure their lives around routines are considered dull and uninteresting. The ethos of mediation cultivated by the Torah, on the other hand, encourages one to pause between one's wants and one's deeds (Levinas, 1990, p. 288). The rituals of Halacha inject a measure of formality and distance into human discourse – restraining the desire for immediate experience and fulfillment. Such is a "religion for adults."

In sum, for Levinas, Judaism, as a "religion for adults," does not thematize "religion" as such. In contradistinction to Guttmann, Levinas did not see a discrete kind of "religious experience" as the effect or reward of ethics. For him, only *within* the very fabric of the ethical gesture itself (the orientation of "being there" for the other) can any trace of the transcendent be intimated. Only human acts of succor testify to the possibility of the moral transcendence of reality as it is. God does not "appear." He does not "make things right" in history. He does not "dish out prizes, inflict punishment and pardon sin" (Levinas, 1990, p. 143). The only revelation we can experience comes to us in and through the needy countenance of the other person, whose vulnerable face commands us to protect him/her from violence.

Educators who have been exposed to Levinas' "adult" version of Judaism sometimes complain that it is too demanding, and that the posture of infinite responsibility can lead to feelings of unremitting guilt and inadequacy. Such feelings, they say, paralyze the will rather than motivate it. Remarks such as these must be taken with the utmost seriousness, since those of us who are dedicated to education must confront not only the "essence" of a philosophical worldview, but also its psychological and developmental implications. In responding to remarks such as these, I have often found it useful to distinguish between psychological guilt and existential guilt. It could very well be that in preparing young people to bear the kind of existential guilt that is one of the hallmarks of the human condition for Levinas, it might, at least initially, be necessary to cultivate a sense of adequacy rather than inadequacy. Readiness to take on the burdens of maturity, including the consciousness that one is never done with one's moral responsibility, must be preceded by feelings of security and capability (Cohen, 2002, pp. 359–360). Whatever the case, this is an example of the kind of educational discourse that might issue from a serious consideration of the views of a thinker like Levinas in the context of Jewish education.

Soloveitchik and Martin Buber on "Translation"

Turning now to the commonplace "subject matter," I propose a further consultation with modern Jewish thought as a resource for thinking about another important educational issue. Above, I asked what are some of the typical dispositions of the mature Jew as we see him/her. What difficulties might we encounter in trying to cultivate these dispositions? At this point I ask what is the nature of this traditional corpus we feel committed to transmit. Is this tradition given to "translation" to the "language" (the cultural ethos or the underlying worldview) of the contemporary Jew?

With regard to these questions, two extreme positions are possible. One is that the Jewish tradition is ultimately "untranslatable." Therefore, any attempt to "translate" the tradition into terms more understandable, palatable, or congenial to modern consciousness necessarily entails violating it. To do this, one would have to distort the tradition to such a degree that it would no longer be continuous with itself. Educationally, the only "solution" to this problem would be to represent the tradition in its "original" dimensions as authentically as possible, hoping that it might inspire those who are fortunate enough to "see the light." Modern Jews who wish to link up with tradition would have to undergo, whether overtly or covertly, some kind of "conversion," thereby leaving their modern assumptions behind.

The other extreme position would be that the "translation" of tradition is eminently possible and presents no fundamental problem. Judaism and, say, contemporary humanism, are ultimately identical and no great changes in form or content need be made in order to demonstrate this identity. When we consider these two alternatives, however, many of us working in Jewish education have an intuition that the situation is, to say the least, somewhat more complex than either of these two extreme positions would allow.

Two important modern Jewish thinkers, J. B. Soloveitchik and Martin Buber, also sensed that the issue of translation cannot be approached with an either/or attitude. They believed (each is his own way) that the tradition could be *partially*, if not entirely, translated such that moderns could genuinely appropriate at least some aspects of it (Rosenak, 1995, pp. 132–133). Neither the tradition nor the contemporary Jew need sacrifice their authenticity in order for this to come about.

Soloveitchik maintained that certain aspects of the tradition are legitimately and even eminently translatable. Others, however, are not. Buber, on the other hand, believed that the tradition is not really divisible into a "translatable" and a "non-translatable" part. His view was that any aspect of tradition considered by moderns would have to be "translated" in order for it to be appropriated without intellectual or personal dishonesty. On the other hand, he also believed that moderns, if they genuinely wish to reconnect with the tradition, would also have to "translate," or reinterpret, *themselves*. On the one hand, traditional texts would have to be re-understood so that they could speak to contemporary Jews and still retain their integrity. On the other hand, however, modern Jews would also have to expand their worldview and open themselves to new insights that tradition makes available without relinquishing their modernity (Cohen, 1996, pp. 173–181).

Soloveitchik's position on this issue is based on the famous distinction he makes between "Adam 1" and "Adam 2" in his well-known essay "The Lonely Man of Faith" (Soloveitchik, 1992) – a distinction that derives from a close reading of the first three chapters of Genesis. "Adam 1" represents the rational-technological side of human beings – that aspect that strives to improve the status of the human race vis-à-vis nature. Through civilization and culture, human beings aspire, in the words of Leo Strauss (1997, p. 154), to become the "masters and owners of nature." To this end, human beings commute immediate empirical experience into scientific concepts and networks of interaction – like "waves," "particles," "causes," and "correlations." These concepts and networks help human beings understand the world as a set of intelligible regularities. Constructing the world in this way enables us to predict the course of natural processes, to intervene in them if possible, and thereby bring nature under a measure of control. Mathematics, physics, chemistry, biology – all these matrices – assume the kind of predictability that makes technology possible. Technology, whether in the form of new medicines or new engineering techniques, helps to change the status of human beings from victims to masters of nature. According to Soloveitchik, the mandate to do this is given by God Himself, who, by way of those famous passages from Genesis, commands us to "rule" the world and to "conquer" it.

Adam 1, however, is typified not only by scientific-technological rationality, but also likes to take stock of his achievements and place them in a larger, philosophical perspective. He wants to be convinced that his pursuits have absolute sanction, not only by passively accepting the Biblical mandate, but through the use of his own reason. To this end, he has recourse to philosophy and theology, by way of which he tries to understand his divinely instilled motivation in rational, systematic terms. In order to do this, he has to "translate" the givens of religious experience (which he is not willing to accept blindly) and the givens of Scripture (which he is not willing to accept on mere authority) into terms and concepts that make sense in his rationalized world. After much reflection, he finds that he *needs* religious concepts, like God and the Transcendent, in order to lend dignity and legitimacy to his own pursuits. For example, he finds that there is an amazing correlation between the concepts and causal links that he constructs in his mind and the way that nature actually "behaves." This is not self-understood, since there is no concept, either immanent to the human mind or immanent to the world that could explain why reality seems to respond to our rational construction of it – so much so that we can even create technologies that domesticate it to a certain extent. If the correlation between human thought and the patterns of nature is to be rationally and systematically understood, a third, "transcendent" concept is needed – the concept of God. For Descartes, for example, the concept of God underwrites the connection between human thought and the workings of the world. The living God of religion, then, "translates out," for Adam 1, into the guarantor of the possibility of science and technology.

Another important example of "translation" mentioned at length by Soloveitchik is one that he learned from the great German philosopher Immanuel Kant. The "conquest of nature" for the "relief of man's estate" (Strauss, 1989, p. 88) cannot take place under conditions of anarchy and moral disintegration. Society must be ordered; moral and political norms must be given absolute sanction. But, just as it is not self-understood that there is a real correlation between thought and nature, so it is not self-understood that there is a real correlation between moral norms and nature. It is not at all clear that this world, and human society within it, is amenable to ethical reconstruction. A third, transcendent concept is needed here as well, in order to guarantee the possibility of moral progress.

Both of the above concepts of God – as guarantor of the parallel between thought and reality and as guarantor of the possibility of the application of moral norms to an indifferent world – are examples of "translation" at its best. When Adam 1 engages in "translating" the immediacy of faith into God-concepts that give absolute sanction to the projects of science and ethics, he is doing no less than performing the will of God. God Himself enjoins that human beings "translate" primordial religious experience and language into concepts that enhance his projects. This is true, however, only if "Adam 1" doesn't get carried away with these projects, and doesn't forget that there is another side to his humanity – equal to if not more important than his quest for a civilized, dignified life.

"Adam 2" does not "advance" and "conquer" in order to become the "theoretical and practical lord of his life" (Strauss, 1987, p. 13). His mode is rather one of "retreat," wherein he tries to experience reality in its "original" dimensions. He is concerned more with the unique moment of meaning – something like the poet or artist, and not so much with recurring patterns. Looking, say, at a waterfall, he would not immediately think of its contribution to the water supply, or of its potential as a source of electrical energy. He would rather perceive it precisely as it appears in the moment – in its unique configuration and in its own right. His gesture is, as the Bible says, one of "service and protection."

He is also very different from Adam 1 in everything that has to do with human relations. Adam 1 relates to other human beings first and foremost as work partners. He can be neighborly, collegial, civil, and even convivial – but he is not concerned with the other in his/her own right, in his/her individual uniqueness. He might be capable of cooperation for common, pragmatic ends, but not of genuine empathy for the unique suffering of the other, or of a willingness to sacrifice himself for the other's sake.

Ultimately, the hallmark of Adam 2 is his primordial faith commitment, an orientation that grows out of his sensitivity to the ultimately problematic character of the human condition. Adam 2 has come to understand that the grand achievements of civilization do not relieve his sense of existential loneliness, meaninglessness, and inadequacy. He senses that he has been "thrown" into existence without his consent and that his death will be similarly arbitrary. He is not sure if he can really make any "mark" on the world before he must leave it. While all people experience thoughts and feelings like these, each of us undergoes them in a radically individual way, one that cannot really be appreciated by others. Such experiences often lead us to "close up" and distance ourselves from others, as we become preoccupied with our own anxieties and uncertainties.

The living God, however, so testifies Soloveitchik, approaches the human being in her solitude, and offers her the gift of love and existential confirmation. After the experience of God's turning, the individual gains the strength to come out of herself and offer the very same gift of love and existential confirmation to others. God has whispered to her: "I am here for you. Your life and its course are of concern to me." By dint of this experience, she is now empowered to approach other human beings with the same message. The miracle of human self-revelation to others comes as the result of the miracle of God's self-revelation to us.

Such experiences, so believed Soloveitchik, are "untranslatable" into the common discourse of contemporary Westerners. True, all humans are possessed of the potential to act, feel, and think as both Adam 1 and Adam 2. In modernity, however, the ethos of Adam 1 has become dominant and the orientation of receptivity, retreat, and sacrifice characteristic of Adam 2 has become dormant. "Men of faith" cannot really "translate" their faith experience into the pragmatic, utilitarian language of moderns, and so they end up being rejected, ridiculed, and misunderstood. This situation, for Soloveitchik, is ultimately irremediable and tragic – although people of faith are enjoined not to waver in their testimony.

As far as education is concerned, then, the Adam 2 aspect of the Jewish tradition cannot really be "translated" to moderns, as long as moderns cling to their compulsive preoccupation with rational control. Moderns can only "get" that aspect of tradition that speaks to their need to domesticate nature. Tradition, then, is only *partially* translatable to contemporary consciousness. Yes, the living God can also be understood as a concept – one that can support the modern project of civilization. Yes, the idea of God can be shown to be rationally plausible and serviceable. This gesture, of translation, however, most certainly does not exhaust what the tradition is trying to get across. To open oneself to the mysterious God who comes out of hiding in order to bestow His infinite love on human beings, thereby enabling them to genuinely empathize with others – one would have to set aside crucial aspects of one's modern identity and mind-set. At this point, an educator would seem compelled to ask: If this aspect of the Jewish tradition is "untranslatable," how could it conceivably be communicated to others? A possible answer to this question might be: Perhaps education by example, whereby singular individuals and groups simply live out their faith unself-consciously, might have a chance of inspiring others to dedicate themselves to the service of God and other human beings – more than any attempts at "explanation."

Martin Buber can also serve as an important resource when considering the issue of the "translatability" of the tradition. As mentioned above, Buber did not believe that some aspects of the tradition are in principle translatable while others are not. He wrote for those of his contemporaries who could not authentically relinquish the modern categories by way of which they make sense of the world. He hoped, however, to influence his readers such that they would not dogmatically discount ancient Jewish texts as a resource for insight into the human condition. For people like this, Buber believed, the encounter with tradition would have to have a different structure. He was convinced that *any and all aspects* of the tradition had the potential to "speak" to even the most culturally assimilated Jew, if he/she did not close himself/herself off to them in principle. Yet, in order for this to happen, a process of mutual reinterpretation would have to take place. As sometimes happens in situations of true dialogue between human beings, mutual openness to the other's point of view can bring about a basic transformation in the perspective of both speakers. In genuine dialogue this happens, perhaps paradoxically, without either of the parties losing their basic identity and self-understanding.

Buber applied this dialogical model to the encounter between modern Jews and ancient Jewish texts (Cohen, 1999b; Kepnes, 1992). The Bible, for example would have to be reinterpreted such that it could enter the thought world and value structure of the modern person without losing its "Biblical" character and identity. The modern person would have to reinterpret the his/her own possibilities of thought and feeling in order to open himself/herself to the Biblical horizon. Yet he/she would have to do this without losing his/her sense of self as a modern person.

We can watch Buber applying this dialogical approach in practice if we examine the manner in which he interprets the Biblical notion of miracles – a notion that remains distant and remote for many moderns (Buber, 1998, pp. 74–79). When one reads the Bible, one is struck by the manner in which God intervenes in the workings of the world in accordance with His purposes. While the Bible may not have a concept of "nature," like the Greeks, it certainly does have a notion of the cycle of the seasons and the typical "ways" of the different creatures. This regularity and stability is enjoined by God Himself when He promises, after the Flood, that the cycles of "planting and reaping, cold and heat, summer and winter, day and night will not cease" (Genesis 8:22). Yet we find that in the Biblical narrative, God overturns these regularities when He so wills. Many moderns, who have been reared on an all-pervasive naturalism and empiricism, find these narratives downright incredible. Those of us who have been taught, whether explicitly or implicitly, to always seek a "natural" or a "historical" cause for events – however strange or unusual those events might be – find it very difficult to trust Biblical miracle stories. Many of us tend to see this issue in a dichotomous fashion. Either the Biblical account is "right" and "accurate," and then we must sacrifice everything we know about nature and history, or our modern naturalism and historicism is "right" and "accurate," and then we must relegate the Bible to the doubtful category of myth and fable. Such a situation leaves the Bible in an ultimately "untranslatable" state (Buber, 1998, pp. 13–19).

Buber, however, believed that there is a genuine way out of this quandary. For this to happen, however, the Bible has to be "translated" such that its message is made available to moderns while its core testimony remains intact. Similarly, moderns have to "expand their consciousness" so that new insights can be admitted while remaining true to their modern orientation. As far as Biblical wonder narratives are concerned, a new conception of the miraculous – one that is neither supernaturalistic nor naturalistic – must arise out of the dialogue between the Bible and its modern readers. In his famous book *Moses*, in the chapter called "The Wonder on the Sea," Buber claims that the receding of the sea at the time of the Egyptians' pursuit of the people of Israel was a thoroughly natural and historical event, one that scientists or historians could give an account of by all the methods at their disposal. This, however, does not exhaust the significance of the event. For Buber, the meaning of an event, for those who experience it, is part of its character as an event. The salvation on the sea was an event of cardinal and foundational significance for those to whom it occurred, and for their descendants. For this reason, the event was experienced as pointing beyond itself. It was not the *physical* dimensions of the event that were of ultimate importance, but its *ultimate value* for those who bore witness to it. The "Wonder on the Sea" finally guaranteed the salvation of the Israelites from the "House of Bondage" and gave them the wherewithal to build a society that could become, metaphorically, a "Home for God."

For Buber, the "Wonder on the Sea" is not only a "historical" event that represents a record of "what once happened," it is also paradigmatic. It exemplifies "what always happens" when so-called natural events become "transparent," such that individuals or whole peoples experience a transcendent guiding hand in and through the intelligible causality that is perceived to inform them. Biblical miracle stories, then, when addressed to us as moderns and genuinely heard by us as moderns, are not "extraterritorial" events, immune to the matrices and networks of causal relations that make the world understandable to us. They are simultaneously "immanent" and "transcendent" – immanent in that they are intelligible by rational means and "transcendent" in that we can likewise experience them as pointing to a beneficent will.

"Partial translation," then, for Buber, would not involve distinguishing between aspects of the tradition that are congenial to modern consciousness and aspects that are not – as it would for Soloveitchik. For Soloveitchik, moderns legitimately get some dimensions of tradition in "translated" form, while others are closed to them unless they "demodernize" themselves. For Buber, all dimensions of tradition must undergo "translation" if they are to be "heard" by moderns, and this is as it should be. Moderns qua moderns do not suffer from a congenital theological disease, making it impossible for them to "hear" the address of the divine in its "original" dimensions. Any dialogue partner, even God speaking through the Bible, must meet his interlocutors on their own ground, and not expect them to divest themselves of the scientific and historical "lenses" that structure their world.

From a certain traditional perspective, it might be said that Buber, by "filtering out" the supernatural dimension of miracles, has given moderns "only" a "partial translation" that "loses" an important part of the "original." Buber would answer, however, that this seeming "partiality" actually contributes to greater "wholeness" on two fronts. First, with regard to contemporary readers, by rejecting the naturalist-supernaturalist dichotomy, one allows a "core" insight of the Biblical sensibility to "speak" in a manner that can be "heard" and understood by moderns as whole persons. Second, it could well be that the very same move actually lets the "original," pristine Biblical teaching shine through, namely that the events of individual and collective life, as we know them, are carriers of transcendence – speaking to us in our here and now. "Partial translation," then, in the Buberian sense, should not be understood as a "negative," quantitative subtraction but rather as a "positive," qualitative shift – enhancing the meaning-making capacity of the Bible rather than restricting it.

Educators working under the aegis of Soloveitchik's conception of partial translation (division of tradition into translatable and non-translatable components) would necessarily have to conceive of their charge and go about their business in a different way from those who follow Buber's conception of partial translation (modified understanding of all for all) (Cohen, 1996). A student of Soloveitchik would first set about determining whether a certain piece of "subject matter" (a text, an attitude, a value, a skill) – is "translatable" to moderns. He would then know whether he can leave his students' modern mind-set intact when trying to transmit it or not. If he is working with an "untranslatable" aspect of tradition, he will not really be able to ultimately "explicate" or "justify" it. At best, he will be able to authentically live out his faith position against all odds, and hope that his students might react positively to his own courageous self-consistency.

For a "Buberian" educator, on the other hand, nothing Jewish should in principle be considered strange to the modern qua modern. Conditions for dialogue would have to be created, however – so that the text is in a position to "open itself" to modern students (through reinterpretation) and students are in a position to "open themselves" to the text (by allowing for a possible shift in their own self-understanding). These conditions do not arise of themselves. In order that they arise, teachers might have to invest a great deal of time and energy in dispelling stereotypes, demystifying reigning theories, and questioning ideologies that prevent students from seeing the textual "other" in a charitable or sympathetic light. They will also have to foster an atmosphere of "creative reading," such that traditional texts are seen to address the modern sensibility without selling themselves short. While the above points represent only some very general educational guidelines, they most definitely do valorize certain kinds of educational practices, while calling others into question.

Conclusion

Within the framework of this chapter, I hope to have allowed the reader an initial acquaintance with certain normative perspectives drawn from the works of modern Jewish thinkers. These perspectives were treated with a view to highlighting their possible import for educational issues relating to two of Schwab's four commonplaces. My main questions were as follows: (1) Should a disposition for "spirituality" be regarded as an essential characteristic of the educated Jew (learner)? (2) Can ancient, religiously oriented texts be "translated" so they resonate with the sensibility of this-worldly moderns (subject matter)?

As I hope to have shown, the contribution of Jewish thought to these discussions can be twofold. From the perspective of what Michael Rosenak (1987, pp. 15–47) has called "normative" philosophy of Jewish education, it is obvious that different thinkers have different and often conflicting worldviews on the issues of "spirituality" and "translation." The same word or buzzword can be the carrier of very different norms, visions, and values. It is important to distinguish between these plural visions on given issues so that educators might clarify where they stand on them. From the perspective of "analytic" philosophy of Jewish education (as exemplified in Chazan, 1978, pp. 58–76) the question that has been the focus of my attention has been what do we mean when we say "spirituality," or "translation." The two perspectives overlap, in that thinkers with different normative worldviews often give the same terms very different meanings. The making of clear distinctions between the rival meanings of terms avoids those "dialogues of the deaf" that so often plague educational discourse.

As mentioned above, I have been able to touch on only two out of four of Schwab's commonplaces. In partial compensation for this limitation, I hope also to have shown that insights relevant to a particular commonplace (i.e., translatability of subject matter) can have repercussions for other commonplaces (i.e., teaching as creating conditions for dialogue). At this concluding point, I remind the reader that plural normative insights regarding questions such as the dispositions of the educated Jew and the translatability of Jewish subject matter, however they might enlarge our awareness of Jewish educational possibilities and desiderata, are not sufficient to inform a genuine educational deliberation. Educational ends deriving from normative worldviews must be brought into contact with empirical readings of the very same commonplaces. In any deliberation that is to issue in responsible decision making, plural formulations of the ends of Jewish education, as derived from the works of our best Jewish thinkers, should and must be brought into contact with the growing empirical knowledge that Jewish educational research has been providing us with in the course of the last generation. How do young people today actually experience what they call "spirituality?" How do teachers "translate" texts in practice, and what is their hidden philosophy of translation? Only if research into possible Jewish "oughts," of the kind briefly illustrated here, interacts with the growing reservoir of research on the condition of the Jewish "is," do we have a chance of moving that "is" in the direction of some "ought," however conceived.

References

Buber, M. (1946, reprint 1998). *Moses: The revelation and the covenant*. Amherst, NY: Humanity Books.
Chazan, B. (1978). *The language of Jewish education*. New York: Hartmore House.
Cohen, J. (1991). Selected trends in contemporary scholarship in Jewish philosophy: Implications for curriculum, Unpublished doctoral dissertation, Hebrew University of Jerusalem.
Cohen, J. (1996). Machshevet Yisrael LeShem Chinuch: Ha'Im HaMasoret HaYehudit Nitenet Le'Tirgum? In T. Lamm (Ed.), *ItzuvVeShikum: A collection of articles in memory of Akiva Ernst Simon and Carl Frankenstein* (pp. 164–182). Jerusalem: Magnes Press.
Cohen, J. (1999a, Winter). Subterranean didactics: Theology, aesthetics and pedagogy in the thought of Franz Rosenzweig. *Religious Education, 94*, 24–38.
Cohen, J. (1999b). Hermeneutic options for the teaching of canonical texts: Freud, Fromm, Strauss and Buber Read the Bible. In *Courtyard* (pp. 33–65). New York: Jewish Theological Seminary Press.
Cohen, J. (2002). Postponing spiritual gratification: Levinas' perception of religious maturity as an orienting notion for Jewish education. In B. Cohen & A. Ofek (Eds.), *Essays in education and Judaism in honor of Joseph S. Lukinsky* (pp. 347–365). New York: Jewish Theological Seminary Press.
Cohen, S. & Eisen, A. (2000). *The Jew within: Self, family and community in America*. Bloomington, IN: Indiana University Press.
Fox, S., Scheffler, I., & Marom, D. (2003). *Visions of Jewish education*. Cambridge, UK and New York: Cambridge University Press.
Guttmann, J. (1955). *Dat U'Madda*. Jerusalem: Magnes Press.
Guttmann, J. (1964). *Philosophies of Judaism*. New York: Holt, Rinehart, & Winston.
Guttmann, J. (1976). *On the philosophy of religion*. Jerusalem: Magnes Press.
Holtz, B. & Rauch, E. (1988). Education for change. In *Studies in Jewish education* (Vol. 3, pp. 62–90). Jerusalem: Magnes Press.
Kepnes, S. (1992). *The text as thou: Martin Buber's dialogical hermeneutics and narrative theology*. Bloomington, IN: Indiana University Press.
Levinas, E. (1990). *Difficult freedom: Essays on Judaism*. Baltimore: Johns Hopkins University Press.
Levinas, E. (1997). *The Levinas reader*. Oxford, UK & Cambridge: Blackwell Publishers.
Rosenak, M. (1986). *Teaching Jewish values: A conceptual guide*. Jerusalem: Nachala Press.
Rosenak, M. (1987). *Commandments and concerns: Jewish religious education in a secular society*. Philadelphia: Jewish Publication Society.
Rosenak, M. (1995). *Roads to the palace: Jewish texts and teaching*. Providence, RI, and Oxford, UK: Berghahn Books.
Schwab, J. (1964). Problems, topics and issues. In S. Elam (Ed.), *Education and the structure of knowledge* (pp. 4–47). Chicago: Rand McNally.

Schwab, J. (1983). The practical 4: Something for curriculum professors to do. *Curriculum Inquiry, 13*(3), 239–265.
Soloveitchik, J. B. (1992). *The lonely man of faith.* New York: Doubleday.
Strauss, L. (1987). *Philosophy and law.* Philadelphia: Jewish Publication Society.
Strauss, L. (1989). *An introduction to political philosophy: Ten essays.* Detroit, MI: Wayne State University Press.
Strauss, L. (1997). *Jewish philosophy and the crisis of modernity.* Albany, NY: SUNY Press.

Philosophy of Jewish Education: Some Thoughts

Michael Rosenak

Introduction

A close friend and professor of Jewish education, the late and lamented Professor Joseph Lukinsky, liked to tell the story of a boy in prep school who is being taught there to play baseball. In his daily e-letters home he describes how he and his friends are learning all about the game. They are given lessons on how to hold the bat, the modes of throwing a ball, the appropriate foot movements, and even a brief history of the game. On the fifth day of studies, the boy happily reports to his family: "Everybody here is very excited. Tomorrow they are going to let us actually play baseball."

In beginning with this story I take a risk: many of my readers may turn the page to the next subject, for this witticism may convince them that philosophy of education, and all the more so, philosophy of Jewish education, is not a serious affair, that it is worthy of sustained interest mainly for doctoral students in "Education."

There are a number of reasons for this disdain:

(a) We may note that education, Jewish or otherwise, is known as a practical enterprise. Educational philosophy may be useful to a certain type of scholar who has been habituated to explore such spurious matters as the relationship between education and the world of theory and who thinks that there is some profound value in acquiring ever clearer conceptions of the "field" while spurning all interest in the practical wisdom associated with it. "Real" teachers tend to be scornful of such "theorists" who seem to keep their distance from actually *doing* something, that is, from *educating*! So why would practitioners of such down-to-earth enterprises like law, medicine, *and education* wish to theorize about them? It would seem that the very idea of theoretical reflection upon such practical pursuits undermines the desire and ability of educators (for example) to hone their expertise and to make their practice more useful in dealing with the issues at hand. In other words, it can plausibly be argued that "the field" in

M. Rosenak (✉)
Hebrew University, Jerusalem, Israel
e-mail: msros@mscc.huji.ac.il

which educators work is distinguished by non-theoretical habits of practice. In line with the habits of practice, the task at hand is to learn vital facts, to set goals, to identify problems that impede reaching these goals, and, hopefully, to solve them. Hence as a good physician treats disease, and as a good attorney faithfully defends a client, so too does a skillful and wise teacher educate! We all know, at least so it is said, what that means.

(b) Furthermore, even if we admit that it is legitimate to cultivate a reflective and philosophical element in education, so that there may be "well educated persons," why specifically a Jewish one? After all, the very term "philosophy," in the classic-educational context, points to what is universal in education and comes into play wherever there is an engagement with thought and reason. Certainly one can argue for discourse on Jewish education on religious grounds or on the basis of historical memory or social consciousness and identification. Yet, many scholars will insist that such frameworks, though they deal with ideas, are not "really" philosophical. They maintain that only if Jewish educators relinquish the authority of memory and turn wholeheartedly to reason, as exemplified by such thinkers as Aristotle and Plato and Dewey, they may legitimately be called philosophers or the disciples of philosophers. These savants think that religious, ideological, and other ways of thinking that smack of indoctrination cannot be called philosophical in the normative and classic senses of that term. Yet for most teachers to give up these ideologies would be tantamount to relinquishing that which is most essentially Jewish about Jewish education!

Should, or can, teachers do this? Or would it, perhaps, be legitimate for them to say that Jewish education plays by different rules and that the vocabulary in which it speaks is unique unto itself?

Normative and Analytic Philosophy of Education

To deal with such questions we need to distinguish between two types of activity in which educators are engaged and about what they argue. At the risk of oversimplifying and "over-theorizing" we may say that some educators speak in the language of normative philosophy of education while others have an analytic philosophy of education. Though there is controversy about what these terms connote exactly, we may differentiate between them as representing two schools of thought and practice, two ways of doing education and thinking about it.

The normative-philosophical scholar, the classic Jewish one no less than others, considers the great minds of philosophy, like Plato and Maimonides and Kant, to have taught us, by their far-ranging discourse on the nature of human life, of knowledge, and of reality as a whole, what, why, and how to transmit the "goods" of culture to the young generation. Hence because they are philosophers, these sages may be expected to deal extensively with the issues of how to transmit wisdom to the young. Indeed they may claim that they, more than more-practical educators, cultivate a vision of the educated person. They are necessarily philosophers of education; they set norms for noteworthy and worthwhile human existence, norms that should be made accessible to coming generations; they discuss in depth the nature of human beings and ways to cultivate exemplary men and women on the basis of some ideal, some vision. Normative philosophers of education are considered by their followers to be mentors of humankind with regard to the issues they consider most central in human existence. For those who accept their leadership, their philosophies are philosophies of education; education itself thus corresponds to inquiry into human existence. Having written extensively on wisdom, the philosophers give prescriptions for becoming and being; having delved into knowledge, they can be expected to teach us of what knowledge consists; and having thought extensively on education and its principles, their thought is said to lay foundations of educational vision. Vision, they say, is truly the rock on which philosophy of education is built.

But why should there be a philosophical Jewish vision? Is philosophy not, ideally, the same for everyone? And if it is not, is it still philosophy?

To illustrate this problem: When we speak of Greek philosophy do we mean that certain ideas that arose in Greece could only have originated there, for Greek philosophy is Greek by its very character and in a broad cultural sense. Or, do we mean that much great philosophy was (historically) Greek by chance? In this case, a great thinker need not feel deprived if he does not carry a Greek passport. In this case, the Greek origins of this philosophy are irrelevant to its teachings.

Speaking of Jewish philosophy: Can we say, with the medieval Jewish thinker Rabbi Yehuda Halevi and his followers, that there is a sense in which outsiders cannot fathom Jewish philosophy completely for it is founded upon the prophetic character of the people of Israel? Or should we say that just as there is no German or French physics so there is no specific Jewish philosophy. So, what, in the latter case, can be understood by philosophy of Jewish education?

Normative Philosophy of Education

Let me attempt to clarify these terms—analytic and normative philosophy of education—that we have now brought into our discussion. We must remember that discussion of such terms as "Jewish philosophy of education" reflects not only various definitions, but also diverse purposes ascribed to education. Such terms are not as self-understood as the reader was given to understand in the previous passages. In fact, especially in modern times, many educators find themselves irritated by what sounds like "high falutin" verbiage that, they claim, serves the cultural and even the social needs of the "ruling class" who "sell" ideological notions designed to serve their interests. For them, what we have said here is "ideology;" a flawed and subtly dishonest intellectual pursuit. So, we find, philosophers of education who make normative statements, as philosophers, as to "who is the educated person" and how such persons should be instructed in wisdom; how to be taught to live by the moral and cultural and educational ideas and ideals of her society and culture. Thus, it is claimed, the Jewish products of normative education are to *know* the norms of their civilization, to have *mastered* them, and to endeavor *to live* by them.

Is this a bombastic slogan or a profound truth? Normative philosophers can be expected to defend such a statement, for it is part and parcel of teaching us to distinguish between good and evil, as between worthy knowledge and trivia, and to expect from the agents of education that they transmit their knowledge and their insights to the learners. To carry out their mission, normative teachers can be expected to turn to thinkers who they find congenial to their own worldviews and from whom they wish to learn the uses of philosophy in educational practice. For example, an educator may discover in the dialogical writings of Martin Buber (1963), on the one hand, or in the sociological approaches of Mordecai Kaplan (1967), on the other hand, two differing philosophical views of (human and Jewish) life and differing views of worthwhile knowledge. In studying these diverse sources and their prescriptions for education, we come across philosophies of education; different conceptions of worthwhile activity, and different views of the educated person and of God.

Analytic Philosophy of Education

By way of contrast to those philosophers of education who make normative statements, there are those who dismiss such normative concerns and practices as no more than ideological beliefs and commitments disguised as "self-understood" and sublime truths. Such "truths," they say, are, in fact, grounds for indoctrination and thus they are instruments for robbing children of the autonomy that is their right and, ultimately, their duty. (Here, of course, the normative educator may ask: But isn't this a normative statement in itself?)

Now, analytic philosophers of education will agree that educators should cultivate autonomy, without which independence and clarity of thought are precluded. They might agree among themselves, normatively, that our children will benefit from an education that fosters autonomy. But, as analytic philosophers, they will ask what exactly *is* autonomy? How do diverse thinkers understand the concept? What allegedly makes one statement more or less "ideological" than another? What is an "ideological" statement? What is the difference between "philosophy" and "ideology?"

The normative thinker will frequently claim that she too is describing, clarifying, distinguishing, and analyzing. But philosophers who "do" analytic work maintain that their way of doing philosophy of education is uncomfortable with "large" questions and metaphysical discourse. They do not look to any oracle that answers ultimate questions and tells us how to educate children in the light of ultimate verities. The analytical philosopher of education presents his field of study as one that analyzes the terms and practices of education, not shying away from such fundamental yet complex questions as: What is the difference between educating and teaching? When does the teaching of values become brain washing? What is indoctrination? Who accords it a negative connotation, and for what professed reasons? And yet, the chief concern of the analytical philosopher is not to answer the question of "what is the good and how might it be transmitted," but the question: "what does X mean when he uses Y?"

All these questions are raised in the course of engaging in a practical pursuit in which the distinctions between success and failure seem self-evident. Either the goals, say of reading and writing, or assembling the parts of a motor have been achieved or they have not. What is the need here for detached theory? These are questions that might trouble the analytic philosopher.

In response to this, a normatively oriented teacher will maintain that one is called upon to determine what is the philosophical basis of one's practice, and to consider what good it serves? To this, the analytically oriented educator could conceivably answer that lack of clarity here can lead to confused thought that endangers the spirit and threatens free society. When leaders cannot distinguish between dictatorship and lawful society, or between freedom and anarchy, demagogues will have ample opportunities to replace freedom with tyranny. How to educate toward understanding such matters is the central question of philosophy and of education. The analytic thinker is also uncomfortable with the idea that all Jewish education is by definition normative and impervious to the analytic thought which asks, in the Jewish classroom as elsewhere: "What is really going on here – and why?"

The normative philosopher wishes to cultivate a moral person and he is much concerned with what constitutes such a person and decent society. But in the course of trying to locate the essence and the value of philosophy of Jewish education, we have also discovered problems such as, what are the meanings ascribed to a particular word or phrase (as used by educators), and, what is involved in deciding when education is really something else (for example, indoctrination or "training")? These are analytic questions, questions that have to do with the clarification of terms and the making of distinctions.

An Immoral Society?

A pithy example of the tension between normative and analytical inquiry and educational thought concerns fictitious research findings made in a particular city. It appears that despite normatively inspired efforts in the schools there to teach values, achievements have been sparse indeed, practically non-existent. It appears that 90% of the pupils in that city's school system have cheated on examinations in the past, and would do so again wherever feasible; in fact most pupils do not see it as a moral issue!

The city's leaders and educators express deep shock at these findings. From a normative point of view, they deduce that the children in this city's schools have not had enough formal and informal education on moral issues; apparently the time and effort devoted to values education, as well as the allocation for moral education, is totally inadequate. More concentrated efforts to educate the children seem called for. Moral education is apparently a more difficult task than previously held to be.

An analytically oriented educator who has been invited to this conversation listens not only with some exasperation, but also with amusement. She asks herself: what assumptions are these leaders making about the relationship between classroom hours on moral education and the actual behavior of children and between what children perceive as the real issues and problems in their own lives? How do teachers in this city claim to be identifying the real problems and what do they think could count as solutions to these problems? On what basis should pupils think that the "answers" given by the adults oblige them? What do these teachers think makes pupils act "immorally?" What, indeed, do they consider immoral and why? Can we assume on the basis of their "shock" that they never cheated and would counsel their children never to do so?

Clearly our two educators, the normative and the analytic, are hardly speaking the same language here!

Now I return to the first paragraph of our reflections. "Today we are going to actually play baseball!" Meaning: Having talked at length about some basic categories of philosophical-educational thinking and even some of philosophy of education, we can now move our discussion to where the action is. Finally, we arrive at Jewish education and the philosophy of it. Our previous discussion should have made it clear that it is not an easy task. Can there be Jewish education without norms? What makes education Jewish? Can there be Jewish education without religious instruction?

In attempting to clarify these and related queries we must keep in mind that philosophy of education is in the category of "philosophies of ..." It is like, for example, philosophy of law, or philosophy of aesthetics or philosophy of religion. That is, it consists of systematic reflection on a specific field or phenomenon or aspect of human activity and experience though it is itself not an integral part of that being reflected on. Hence, one need not be a jurist to be a philosopher of law or an artist to unravel problems of aesthetics or a moral person to teach moral philosophy. The discussion on these topics may present itself as analytic, for example, the philosopher being studied is likely to claim that there are various ways to interpret and understand what is going on in the field; what scholars who are dealing with these topics think, and of course, what teachers think they are doing.

These topics all bring into view areas of research, for they provide rich sources for possible answers to the manifold questions that educators must confront: For example: By which "picture(s)" of the world do most people today conduct their lives? What knowledge is most important and useful to persons educated to a given worldview? What do they see as happiness, what as truth? What made them think how they do? What made them what they are "essentially" and true to what they are? What do people in today's world mean by educating to virtue? Can one educate to virtue? Is the observance of mitzvoth and its teaching an example of virtue? When people speak of values are they referring to some substance "out there" or of discovering what they value? In the Jewish community, a community that traditionally has valued texts, what is the authority of text in diverse views? What is the role of textual commentary in an educational system that values text? What, if anything at all, should be learned from others and where should lines be drawn between "us" and "them?" When are the others within ourselves as well as beyond our selves in a state of confrontation with "us?" How are various views of Jewish education explained and justified? Should lines be drawn between modern culture and Judaism? Do they speak the same language, and if so, what strains are placed on "loyalty" (if modern culture is normatively accepted and even demanded)? How much openness is desirable, for given publics, and how much commitment? What do we mean by commitment? What are distinct yet diverse normative answers to such questions in various Jewish settings?

Judaism, Education, and Philosophy

These questions and many others that we might legitimately present for discussion and analysis are all, in our context, aspects of reflection on Judaism. This makes sense for before there is philosophy of Jewish education specifically, there is a specific subject "that invites reflection," that is, both Judaism and Jewish experience themselves. But what do we understand by the term "Judaism?" Is using this term already an indicator of a position? (That is, is a school that teaches "Judaism" more or less inclined to teaching Bible with medieval commentary than one which teaches "the Jews" and their civilization?) What ideological justifications for their diverse positions may diverse thinkers present to curriculum writers?

All the above questions are intended to show that while what we may call the language of Judaism is likely to contain accepted "terms" and (seemingly) common "assumptions" that are identical or extremely alike, non-philosophers, be they ever such excellent teachers, are seldom clear as to what may be meant by the basic terms being used until we grasp what various thinkers and educators understand by them and do with them. Different thinkers organize the material being studied differently. Thereby they enrich our grasp of a particular model, or a particular "story" of Judaism and its transmissions, and its discrete visions.

In all cases the curricular task placed before philosophers of Jewish education is to present a picture of Jewish life or of Judaism that tells a story that can be understood within "the community" and that delineates the community by the story/stories it tells. This story must be portrayed for education in a manner that hangs together by virtue of the educational, cultural, or theological prism through which a "picture" is being presented. Through study of the picture and using the tools it provides, it expands and enriches what education can do. On the normative level there will be more vision, and on the analytic level, where the practitioner learns to become a more thoughtful educational practitioner, there can be more understanding of what is being taught.

Let me be specific. The heritage of Judaism is multifaceted and it tells various stories that interlock: historical, religious, cultural, and existential.

The great complexity of Judaism, as both an historical and "national" phenomenon, on the one hand, and a "religious," one on the other hand, invites diverse approaches to Jewish education. For example, concepts such as "nation" and "religious" suggest examining varying relationships that are plausible between them. The analytic thinker is likely to ask questions that arise from modern Jewish identity while the normative one will ask how to maintain the vision in light of the variety of challenges and paradoxes that arise from Jewish modernity, challenges that (may) undermine the normative bases of Jewish education or, conversely "reconstruct" Jewish life and education as believed to be needed.

These questions may be presented as three short queries: *What? How? Why?*

First, *what* should we transmit to the young? What do we want them to know and experience? What constitute priorities in our times? Is the acquisition of languages more important in our view of the good life than scientific expertise? Are the skills, aptitudes, and actions cherished by one's (Jewish) particular culture more central and pressing than the skills of a universal technology and its diverse "fields?" Is Talmud more important than modern Hebrew literature, or vice versa? While the shelves of culture are always stock full, they demand constant replenishment as a result of ever changing realities that demand attention and present new challenges. What, then, should be removed or taught in a cursory manner?

To complicate this matter: we often find ourselves changing our perceptions of what is most important. Which skills do we want students to master and how do we defend our choices of what is to be taught and learned? What is to be deleted from our syllabus and what do we find worthwhile or essential?

Our first question, then, asks us to carefully consider what we need on already (and always) crowded shelves; it tells us what we cannot do without.

The second question, "How?" directs us to pedagogic concerns. How are the valued materials to be acquired or mastered, and what are the difficulties in this transmission that are affected by who we and our pupils are, and what they and we have previously experienced. Here we also must consider the diversities around and within us, and the different problems they pose: for identification and identity. How is this transmission of values, goods, and abilities to be achieved? What must teachers know, what kinds of people should they be? When does the teacher constitute a role model, and when does she threaten children's autonomy by the perhaps unavoidable transference of her presence that demands, sometimes silently and even stealthily, that they become like her? If it is agreed that Talmud study is important, how may the impediments to understanding its (mostly Aramaic) language be overcome?

If the second question raises the pedagogical question, *how* are the aims of the education, the desired outcomes, to be achieved, the third question (which the normative philosopher of education considers to be the main one, and the only pristinely philosophical one for it requires radical decisions on the nature of human beings and their being brought into the human family) focuses on the word, "why." Here we are called upon to justify our choices and priorities on philosophical grounds. The key concern of educational philosophy is with the questions, "Why should I teach this set of texts or values and not others? What are the plausible justifications for my chosen educational policy?" I venture the thought that here considerations, assumptions, and discourse, for Jewish educators, will be essentially Jewish. Here the word "Jewish" refers the learner back to Jewish study and reflection. After all, the Jewish philosopher of education wishes to examine how Judaism and Jewish experience can "make a difference" in the individual who is being educated, in the communities that we wish to have reflect Jewish civilization and in the world to which Judaism and the Jews have something to say.

Clearly we may expect large disagreements here and on various levels: Why study "sources:" because they are interesting, or because they are Torah? What makes education Jewish? Why be Jewish? This question of "why" troubles Jews of our generation far more than the other two. The entire educational structure rests on an answer or answers given to them, for in a free society there is no self-evident social reality that makes it possible to dismiss this question as simply theoretical or as pristine philosophy, or for that matter, sociology or psychology.

This situation is the converse of the pre-modern social reality. Our ancestors were not much troubled by the question, "why?" They had a clear picture of what the normative world was, which of course was important for within it alone there was true meaning; they knew that God had given the Torah to His people. Present troubles and suffering were certain to end when the Messiah came and vindicated Jewish stubbornness in waiting for the redemption of Israel and of the world. They all knew that Israel was a people living alongside others, whether in friendship, or in a state of unease or fear; they knew that Jews were a distinct and distinctive people, not a part of the civilization of others, though there could, at times, be a meeting of minds. But as Jews, they naturally did different things and they did them because they were Jews, and had been educated as Jews. As an American-Jewish educator of the twentieth century, Maurice Pekarski, once said: "Our parents did not keep kosher. They were Jews and so they ate only kosher food." For most people, being educated, before Enlightenment and the (sometimes illusionary) Emancipation, education meant socialization. Eating only kosher food came naturally: everyone did it. Those who didn't because they were not Jews, or sinners, didn't count.

Today it is different. To keep kosher is to have made a decision—to eat only kosher food, or at least to maintain a kosher home. But clearly there is disagreement about the act of doing it and what it means and why one should or should not do it. Moreover, not only don't Jews agree but they are not of one mind as to what they are agreeing about! Are they carrying out religious obligations, as members of a "kosher keeping" community; do they see themselves as directly commanded by God to observe His commandments; or are they pledging allegiance to an ancient history? The possibilities and their educational manifestations are innumerable and they all require, finally, turning to the first two questions and what is behind them, such as the question, what are some ways to solve the paradoxes of human life?

I have begun a conversation in philosophy of Jewish education. We have found that, at times, it is normative and at times analytical. Which is the right way? It seems to me that a philosopher of Jewish education might answer this question with other ones: Does your study include deliberation on hopes and visions? Does it build on a conception of the human being? Is it grounded in a view of a Jewish life that is worthy of continuation and transmission? Does the discussion and study point in a direction that suggests how to proceed toward the resolution of real problems? And as a religious philosopher of education I would add: Is this Jewish life, which is at the core of both the practice and the theory, conducted for the sake of Heaven? Or as some might prefer to state it: Does it all really make a difference?

References

Buber, M. (1963). *Israel and the world: Essays in a time of crisis*. New York: Schocken Books.
Kaplan, M. M. (1967). *Judaism as a civilization*. New York: Schocken Books.

Planning for Jewish Education in the Twenty-First Century: Toward a New Praxis

Jonathan S. Woocher

The following scenario is all too familiar. A major challenge or opportunity has been identified. Perhaps it is a school seeking to increase enrollment, improve its educational program, and/or strengthen its financial condition. Perhaps it's a community that wants to engage unaffiliated populations or redesign supplementary education. Or, perhaps it's a national commission or a consortium of organizations that seeks to recruit and retain more highly qualified Jewish educators.

If these actors follow a traditional pathway, a planning process will be launched. There will be meetings, probably some data gathering, perhaps interviews with stakeholders. Options will be identified, strategies articulated, and specific action steps laid out. The planning group will issue a report with objectives, recommendations, timetables, perhaps a multi-year budget.

And then .... Well, usually something happens (though not always). But, what unfolds is rarely what is in the plan. The first few steps may proceed smoothly, but then, more often than not, things get off course. Unexpected developments overtake the plan—the departure of a key actor, urgent exigencies, resistance and inertia, a new leader with different ideas. Recommendations prove unworkable or bring results other than those anticipated. New problems demand attention. Eventually, often sooner, rather than later, the plan is off the table and on to a shelf, its objectives at best partially realized, the entire process a disappointment.

This has been the story of Jewish educational planning in North America over the past few decades: much effort, modest results. The question is: how can we do better? This chapter is an attempt to answer this question, to lay out a conceptual and practical framework for Jewish educational planning in the twenty-first century.

J.S. Woocher (✉)
Jewish Educational Services of North America, New York, NY, USA
e-mail: jwoocher@jesna.org

Planning and Change

Planning is about making orderly change.[1] Planning attempts to guide the flow of what might otherwise be chaotic events, laying out a course for getting from here to there, from the current situation to a desired destination or goal. Planning seeks to make that journey a smooth, orderly, and predictable one, to make change a relatively benign process. Planning is not only an exercise of reason, but also an act of faith—of faith in rationality's ability to shape the course of unfolding events. Planning affirms that by using our rationality, by following an orderly set of steps—amassing information, applying insight and analysis, and organizing activities in a logical sequence—we can increase the likelihood that we will arrive at our intended destination and get there in one piece.[2]

The problem, though, is that things often do *not* work out as they should. Although almost no one expects planning to unfold perfectly, the gap between what rational planning promises and what occurs is frequently substantial.[3] Part of this gap may be attributable to poorly implemented planning processes. But, we would suggest that there is a deeper problem: the rational model of planning is itself flawed. This is certainly the case, we would argue, for planning in Jewish education, for a number of reasons that we will outline below. The ultimate question then becomes: is there a better model, a way of planning that holds greater promise of leading to desirable change? We believe there is. But first, a look at why rational planning does not work for Jewish education is in order.

---

[1] In his book, *The Rise and Fall of Strategic Planning*, Henry Mintzberg cites a number of different definitions of planning: "Planning is action laid out in advance" (G. C. Sawyer); "Planning is the design of a desired future and of effective ways of bringing it about" (R. L. Ackoff); Planning is "those activities which are concerned specifically with determining in advance what actions and/or human and physical resources are required to reach a goal" (N. Snyder and W.F. Glueck). All of these definitions emphasize the idea of planning as projective, as attempting to set and control the direction of change (Mintzberg, 1994, pp. 5–13).

[2] For an example of this kind of orderly and sequenced planning process applied to the domain of Jewish education/identity, see JESNA's *Handbook on Planning for Jewish Continuity* (Shluker & Isaacs, 1995). The Handbook outlines eleven steps in the planning process: initiating the process, organizing the planning effort, understanding community needs, visioning, choosing a planning strategy, identifying goals and objectives, designing/adopting programs to meet goals and objectives, planning for program evaluation, implementing programs, evaluating programs, continuing continuity planning.

[3] Mintzberg devotes a lengthy chapter in his book to the considerable evidence that conventional rational planning simply does not produce the results that its proponents expect from it (Mintzberg, 1994, pp. 91–158). Douglas Reeves, writing about educational change, offers an equally blunt critique: "Perhaps the most pervasive myth in change leadership is that planning – particularly complex, large-scale, and supposedly 'strategic' planning – leads to effective change …. [T]he evidence for that proposition is absent not only in education but in the business world as well" (Reeves, 2009, p. 42).

The Planning Context in Jewish Education

Planning is as much a part of North American Jewish education as it is in other aspects of our lives.[4] Teachers plan lessons; schools plan curricula; institutions plan new initiatives; communities plan how to allocate resources among diverse programs and settings. As a field, Jewish education is growing increasingly sophisticated in its use of planning and of a host of techniques that may be part of the planning process. It is no longer uncommon to read and hear about planning processes in Jewish education that employ quantitative data gathering and analysis, focus group interviews, values clarification activities, logic modeling, scenario building, benchmarking, and other "state of the art" methodologies. Schools and other educational organizations now create and update strategic plans on a regular basis, and growing numbers of institutions engage in market and business planning. Local communities, through their federations and central agencies, undertake planning around "macro"-issues like how better to engage broad populations in Jewish learning or how to deliver educational services to front-line institutions more effectively. Nationally, major foundations, organizations like PEJE and the Foundation for Jewish Camp that serve particular sectors of the educational system, religious movements, academic institutions, and trans-denominational umbrella agencies like the JCC Association and JESNA are all involved—singly and together with others—in planning to address issues of educational quality, access and affordability, personnel recruitment and development, capacity-building, and the like (Cousens, 2008).

There is no reliable data on how much is spent each year on Jewish education—for North America, estimates range between $2 and $4 billion (Sales, 2006, p. 2)—but it is clearly substantial. Worldwide, Jewish education engages millions of individuals as learners, teachers, administrators, and funders. The Jewish community and Jewish people place great hope in Jewish education. There is ample evidence that the more Jewish education an individual receives, the more likely it is that she or he will be engaged in a wide range of Jewish activities and will be motivated in turn to educate her/his children.[5] Thus, it is no wonder that Jewish education is almost universally regarded as critical to the continuing vitality of Jewish life.

However, the environment in which North American Jewish education is operating is both challenging and changing. Social changes over the past 30 years

---

[4]The discussion that follows deals only with Jewish education in North America. Readers who are knowledgeable about Jewish education in other communities are invited to consider the extent to which the description and analysis offered here apply to those communities as well.

[5]Many studies have documented the effects of Jewish education on adult Jewish identity, including the most recent large-scale study of the American-Jewish population, the National Jewish Population Survey 2000–2001. The summary statement in the NJPS report on The Impact of Childhood Jewish Education on Adults' Jewish Identity reflects the findings generally: "Many, but not all, forms of Jewish education exert measurable, positive impacts upon almost every form of Jewish identity examined here" (Cohen & Kotler-Berkowitz, 2004, p. 17).

have reshaped Jewish identity, making it more fluid, more diverse, less insular. Technological changes are transforming how we work, play, communicate, and learn. A large majority of Jews continue to take Jewish education seriously, and they want a greater voice in the kind of Jewish education they and their children will receive. Recent decades have seen many positive developments in North American Jewish education—long-term trends like the steady growth of day schools, intensive efforts to strengthen and transform supplementary schooling and summer camping, and the emergence of new phenomena like Birthright Israel and Jewish learning tied to social and environmental activism. At the same time, a group of seemingly intractable problems—a chronic shortage of top-flight personnel, inconsistent and often mediocre quality, steep declines in participation during the teen years, lack of coordination across modes and settings, inefficient and inadequate funding—persist and have clearly limited Jewish education's potential reach and impact.

Not surprisingly, therefore, Jewish education is seen today as a domain in need of change. And this belief, in turn, has given new urgency to the question of how we can use planning to help identify and effect the changes that are required. Unfortunately, Jewish education is also a domain that resists efforts to plan effectively. Perhaps no area in Jewish life is as highly fragmented and localized. Thousands of institutions and programs provide Jewish learning—schools, synagogues, camps, centers, and a myriad of organizations that embody virtually every Jewish interest and ideology imaginable. The vast majority of these are entirely autonomous, free to educate whom and how they see fit—and to compete with one another for the right and resources to do so. Because they often disagree on the ends of Jewish education—the goals toward which we should strive—it is difficult to get them to cooperate on the means—the steps to be taken to reach these goals. Even internally, many educational organizations operate less on the basis of well-thought out plans than some mix of good intentions, personal beliefs and preferences, and instinct.

Further, efforts to plan effectively in Jewish education are often thwarted, or at least complicated, by factors in the environment, both Jewish and general. Alongside the hopes invested in Jewish education is a persistent skepticism about its ability to realize these hopes and an accompanying devaluation of those who actually do the work in the field. This ambivalence (which affects education in general) expresses itself in both a casualness about planning (how valuable is it, really?) and a tendency toward what might be termed "hit and run" planning—quick forays that are not rooted in deep knowledge of the field nor followed by consistent attention to what comes afterward. Above all, planning in Jewish education is often held hostage to the overall economic condition of the field that is consistently undercapitalized. As a result, ambitious plans are often doomed by the lack of resources to implement them, further weakening the impact of traditional planning efforts.

The Search for a Planning Paradigm

The key question we wish to explore is, therefore: Given the environment in which Jewish educational planning takes place, what models of planning make sense and are likely to help us reach the ambitious goals we have set for Jewish education?

To answer this question, we need to consider a little more deeply the nature of the Jewish-educational system itself. In a seminal article published in 1991, Susan Shevitz introduced the concept of Jewish organizations and organizational systems as "organized anarchies." This concept was developed to describe organizations characterized by multiple, problematic, and/or unclear goals; under-developed technologies for reaching those goals (operating mostly on the basis of trial and error, past precedent, and ad hoc preferences and inventions); and highly fluid participation (Cohen & March, 1986). An organized anarchy might be imagined as a game in which a myriad of players coming in and out almost at random kick multiple balls toward different goals on a shifting field using different rulebooks (Shevitz, 1991).

This is an apt description of how the game of Jewish education is played, both within and among institutions. Take a typical supplementary school. Although it may have a set of nominal goals, it is likely that parents, teachers, administrators, synagogue leaders, clergy, and students all bring very different values and personal objectives to the table that influence their conduct far more than the articulated goals. Parents want their children to have an enjoyable experience while they come to appreciate their Jewishness and pick up the skills necessary for a Bar or Bat Mitzvah. Teachers want to cover the material they've been assigned to teach, keep order, and feel that they're helping to transmit the Jewish tradition as they understand it. Administrators want the school to run smoothly and be well-regarded by parents, the Board, and the Rabbi. The Rabbi in turn wants to be known as having a "good school" and to have a personal relationship with students, but may not be able to invest the time and energy required to have a consistent and positive influence on what goes on.

At the same time, it is frequently unclear how to translate any of these objectives effectively into an educational program that can actually produce the outcomes it seeks. What curriculum, what schedule, which types of teachers, what activities for children and parents, will work best? Schools lack the rigorous empirical data to make these kinds of decisions, so they fall back on opinions that may or may not be well-informed. And, for all the participants (with the possible exception of the educational director), involvement in the school is likely to be a sometime thing—intense for brief periods when something personally important is at stake, but otherwise minimal and intermittent. At the end of the day, decisions in such a setting are not likely to be the result of rational planning, but rather of circumstance and serendipity.

On the communal level, the situation is likely to be even more anarchic. Ideological divisions compound normal institutional differences. Participation in collaborative decision-making is even more inconsistent and self-interested. Solutions to system-wide problems are even less obvious, and the knowledge and abilities needed to identify and implement them less likely to be available. These characteristics combine to make conventional models of planning highly problematic. As Shevitz concludes: "The uneven participation, unclear technology, and multiple goals that characterize an organized anarchy suggest that a linear, rationally-based planning model will prove frustrating to even an able practitioner" (Shevitz, 1991, p. 197).

Another useful lens through which to view planning in the Jewish-educational system is provided by Lee G. Bolman and Terrence E. Deal in their work on leadership, organizational development, and change (Bolman & Deal, 2008). Bolman and Deal argue that every organization and every change situation needs to be viewed through four "frames:" the structural, the human resource, the political, and the symbolic. The structural frame is the domain of conventional rational planning in which one seeks to manage the environment, set organizational goals, and put in place the structures and procedures necessary to pursue these successfully. A structural view assumes that organizations have the information, technology, and control systems needed to move steadily toward their objectives.

What Bolman and Deal demonstrate, however, is that this way of understanding and managing organizations is at best partial, and unlikely to be effective in the real world except in rare cases. The other dimensions of organizational life operate on the basis of different "logics"—the need to deal with the individuals who comprise the system and their personal aspirations, abilities, and anxieties; the reality of power relationships and conflicting interests that need to be negotiated; the human desire for rituals and symbols that inspire, provide confidence or comfort, and build community. These logics determine what happens in an organization as much (or more) than formal structural arrangements, official goals, and codified procedures.

What this means is that planning and effecting change cannot be a strictly rational process, at least if by that we mean a process that focuses almost exclusively on the structural frame. The other frames must be given their due, and these introduce all sorts of "non-rational" forces and considerations into the mix, ranging from what people involved are actually capable of doing (think, under-trained, part-time teachers in a supplementary school) to the deeply felt, almost ritualized attachments that institutions develop to specific arrangements or practices (think, the idea that every synagogue must operate its own school).

Jewish education is clearly an arena where all four dimensions of organizational life are powerfully at work and color the way in which planned change endeavors must be approached. We might look, for example, at an issue prominent on today's American communal educational-planning agenda: the effort to "link silos" more effectively. Essentially, this effort seeks to make it easier for Jewish education's "consumers" to move along a pathway of connected educational experiences, with the aim of both extending educational participation (as one experience leads to another) and intensifying its impact (taking advantage of a documented "multiplier" effect as educational experiences accumulate). In order for this to happen, it is clear that institutions need to become both more "customer-centric" in their approach, facilitating awareness of and access to a range of educational options, and more willing to and adept at "handing off" participants to other providers for reinforcement and continuation of their educational journeys.

Looking at this issue through a structural frame, we can envision arrangements that would need to be made for better data gathering about consumers and their preferences, expanded marketing, sharing of information, and perhaps a new coordinating position in the community. But, if the "plan" stopped here, it would be unlikely to succeed. Digging deeper we would see the following:

- Educators are neither trained nor rewarded for guiding individuals toward other educational experiences.
- Institutions worry about holding on to their constituents and about the ideological differences that color their educational offerings.
- "Consumers" may feel disoriented when confronted with too many choices, and seek settings where they can feel "at home" and well-supported.

Viewed through all four frames, "linking silos" turns out to be more difficult than it initially appears and to require a "plan" that is attuned to a multitude of non-rational and even cross-cutting factors (does building a strong familial identification with one setting, say a summer camp, increase or decrease the likelihood that they will seek out other settings?). Bolman and Deal's "four frames" perspective allows rational planning a place in our efforts to make change in Jewish education; but, it warns us that planning in practice must be broad and flexible enough to deal with non-rational factors not as annoying intrusions, but as essential elements of the organizational context.

Looked at in another way, the example of "linking silos" helps us to see yet another reason why conventional planning is poorly suited to the Jewish educational environment. In their work on leadership, Ron Heifetz and Marty Linsky differentiate between "technical" and "adaptive" challenges (Heifetz & Linsky, 2002). Technical problems have known solutions (albeit sometimes difficult to implement), but adaptive challenges are complex and often fuzzy. Meeting them requires not the exercise of expertise or authority, but the engagement of individuals with diverse views and values in a process that involves learning new ways of doing things. Adaptive challenges, Heifetz and Linsky suggest, have a number of characteristics in common:

1. There is a gap between aspirations and reality.
2. Progress requires responses outside the organization's standard repertoire.
3. Narrowing that gap will require difficult learning.
4. Part of the learning will require distinguishing, among all that is valued, what is essential to be carried forward and what is expendable, which will involve loss.
5. The losses often involve learning to refashion loyalties and develop new competencies.
6. Painful choices must be made between competing loyalties and values.
7. The people with the problem are both the problem and the solution. Problem-solving responsibility must shift from authoritative experts to the stakeholders.
8. Adaptive work requires a longer time frame than technical work.
9. Adaptive work involves experimentation.
10. Adaptive challenges generate disequilibrium, resistance, and work avoidance (Cambridge Leadership Associates, 2005).

This fairly describes, I would argue, the context for doing effective planning in Jewish education. While some challenges may be purely technical, even apparently simple ones—like coming up with a schedule for religious schooling that maximizes participation, satisfaction, and learning—frequently turn out to be far more complex than they first appear to be. Consider the choice of whether to hold supplementary school classes on Sunday morning or on Shabbat (leaving aside for the moment the many other options, like flexible scheduling with "on line" schooling, that might be imagined). The factors that come into play here are manifold: how Jewish schooling is seen in relation to other dimensions of Jewish religious and synagogue life; parental preferences and expectations; the potential impact on the curriculum and on what may or may not be done in the class; what is being asked of teachers; the use of physical facilities and space; the symbolism of seeing a large community of learner – worshippers in the synagogue on Shabbat; and a host of others. The decision of when the religious school should meet *is* an adaptive challenge that will undoubtedly awaken strong emotions, require difficult choices, and—if handled well—both incorporate and result in a great deal of individual and institutional learning.

When we shift the focus from the individual institution to the communal stage, the prominence of adaptive challenges becomes even clearer. We simply do not know today how to do most of the things that we earnestly wish to do, whether it be to keep a majority of young people involved in Jewish learning past Bar or Bat Mitzvah, to strengthen their attachment to Israel and the Jewish people, to make effective use of new communications technologies, to recruit and retain an adequate supply of quality educators, or (as above) to get institutions to cooperate and share information. The real challenge in confronting these "big" issues lies, as Heifetz and Linsky would have it, in the need for individuals and institutions to go beyond their customary repertoires of behavior, to be both patient and flexible, to learn lessons as we go and apply these, and for those affected to "own" the problems and the solutions. Conventional planning is not irrelevant to meeting adaptive challenges, but neither is it sufficient nor especially well-suited to this work.

We might ask at this point: If the Jewish educational "system" is something other than the rational system that traditional planning imagines and is designed for, what kind of system is it, and can we derive any additional guidance from theory in the attempt to identify a framework for planning that is likely to be successful?

There is a theory that enables us to better understand Jewish education as a system amenable to planning—as long as the planning model itself grows out of that theory: complex adaptive systems theory.

Complex adaptive systems theory—also called simply "complexity theory" and sometimes (less accurately) "chaos theory"—originated in the scientific community to describe and study a variety of phenomena ranging from weather patterns to cellular biology to artificial intelligence. Social scientists as well began to use complexity theory to better understand the operation of everything from single businesses to entire societies (Baltram, 1998; Coveney & Highfield, 1995; Lissack & Roos, 1999; Waldrop, 1992). The core of complexity theory is its recognition that systems are made up of multiple actors who in their interactions continuously affect one another, thereby changing the behavior of the system as a whole, and that these changes, while following certain patterns, are not predictable or controllable in advance. That is, the system adapts and evolves, but not in a simple linear way. It is this element of "patterned indeterminacy," straddling the border between order and chaos that gives complex systems their vitality.

Drawing on a synthesis of literature in the field, we can identify a number of characteristics of complex adaptive systems that are relevant to understanding the Jewish-educational system and the behaviors that typically characterize it:

1. *Unpredictable lines of development.* Elements of the system and the system as a whole often display unexpected behavior. The future cannot be simply extrapolated from the past (examples might include: individuals who dramatically change their beliefs and behavioral systems (e.g., *ba'alei teshuvah*), the rapid growth of day schools in the late-twentieth century; the disruptive effects of unexpected events—the death of a key professional, an economic downturn).
2. *Sensitive dependence on initial conditions.* This is the famous "butterfly" effect, where the movement of a butterfly's wings in Japan eventually leads to a tornado in Kansas. In more general terms, micro-interactions often determine macro-effects. Feedback loops may lead to larger and larger changes, rather than to equilibrium (examples: the impact of a chance meeting with a rabbi on an individual's trajectory of Jewish development; the multiplier effects of a chain of educational experiences).
3. *Emergence.* Complex behavior and new phenomena emerge from the interaction of agents, even when the individual agents are following relatively simple rules of action. Parts get recombined to make new wholes that cannot be reduced to those parts (example: how the typical patterns of post-war suburban synagogue life, the 1960s political and cultural environment (including the draft), and experiences at Jewish summer camps, combined to give birth to the *Havurah* movement in the late 1960s and early 1970s).
4. *Holarchy.* Systems are nested within other systems. Wholes at one level are parts at another, and vice versa (example: the ecology of almost any synagogue, where, e.g., the school is nested within the larger institution, which is itself nested within a community and a movement, and where each system affects the others in complex ways).
5. *Self-organization.* Order emerges from within the system, rather than being imposed upon it. Order is achieved as a dynamic "coherence" or "alignment," rooted in shared purpose and identity, rather than as a uniformity among the elements of the system. Coherence is often achieved in the form of the following:

    1. *Attractors*—"basins" toward which many elements of a system appear to gravitate as a "natural" consequence of their individual trajectories (examples: the drawing power of a charismatic leader who may draw together individuals with diverse backgrounds and sensibilities; an idea "whose time has come" [Zionism, feminism]).
    2. *Networks*—frameworks for the exchange of energy and information which help to achieve/maintain coherence in the absence of hierarchical structures (example: the early success of the Coalition for Alternatives in Jewish

Education in the 1970s and 1980s in drawing together disparate and otherwise unconnected individuals and institutions who shared a commitment to creating "alternatives" in Jewish education).

6. *Bifurcations.* Systems may "split" at certain key points in their evolution, with two (or more) dynamic, but relatively stable, "sub-systems" emerging that continue to develop along separate pathways while remaining in communication and (frequently) dynamic tension with one another (example: the domains of day school and congregational education).
7. *Co-evolution.* The system and its elements change in continuous interaction with one another and with their environment. Complexity theory posits that systems continually face new challenges and opportunities thrown up by the environment as "peaks" that can either be scaled or ignored (e.g., the situation of teen trips to Israel after the success of Birthright Israel). To maximize their survivability and robustness, the system and its elements typically need both to "exploit" nearby opportunities (e.g., synagogues that incorporate healing services in order to engage those seeking spiritual support in times of difficulty) and to "explore" more distant possibilities (e.g., creating entirely new organizations to give expression to young Jews' concern for the environment).
8. *Learning as the process that allows for successful adaptation.* In natural systems, variability and natural selection determine outcomes. In human systems, the ability to learn from experience and to communicate the results of this learning across system boundaries is frequently the key to maintaining robustness and survivability (example: the success of some synagogues in remaking their educational programs as a result of participating in projects like the Experiment in Congregational Education, NESS [Nurturing Excellence in Synagogue Schools], or La'atid: Synagogues for the Future) (Woocher, 2001).

The idea of Jewish education as a complex adaptive system and the use of complexity theory as a framework for approaching issues of change and planning for change are not nearly as radical as they may initially appear. A rich literature has developed in recent years applying complexity theory to change in the business and social sectors. And, perhaps the leading academic figure in the world of educational reform, Michael Fullan, has grounded his recent work on change in the public education sector in complexity theory. As Fullan writes:

> The jury must surely be in by now that rationally constructed reform strategies do not work. The reason is that such strategies can never work in the face of rapidly changing environments. Further, rapid change is endemic and inevitable in postmodern society – a system which self-generates complex dynamics over and over and over again. (Fullan, 1999, p. 3)

Whether we approach the Jewish-educational system through the lens of organized anarchy, Bolman and Deal's four frames, Heifetz and Linsky's adaptive challenges, or complexity theory, we end up with essentially the same conclusion: Those who aspire to bring positive change to Jewish education will not be able to do so via conventional rational planning. The system, and the challenges it faces, simply do not lend themselves to this approach. The planning processes in Jewish education that often attract the greatest attention—national commissions, local strategic plans—are probably least likely to have a significant impact, because they misconstrue how change takes place and the way in which "planning," i.e., the activities that planners typically undertake, can actually shape such change. It is not the activities per se or the skills and techniques used in carrying them out that have rendered much Jewish-educational planning problematic, but the *framework*, one drawn from conventional rational planning models, in which these have often been employed.

Yet, change clearly is needed, and some measure of planning must guide that change if it is to achieve the results we seek. So, we need a different model of planning, one attuned to the nature of Jewish education as a complex adaptive system and to the adaptive challenges it faces in the twenty-first century.

A Planning Praxis for Twenty-First Century Jewish Education

The alternative model of planning that we propose is one that is firmly embedded in the "doing" of Jewish education, what might be called "praxis planning." "Praxis" refers to the practical application of a science, art, or skill—doing that is guided by a body of learning. We call the type of planning being advocated here "praxis planning" because the emphasis is not on theoretical constructs or even on the outcome of the planning process (i.e., the "plan"), but on the process itself—on "planful doing," if you will. In such planning, the key elements are going on continuously and simultaneously: value-determination, observation, reflection, direction-setting, testing, recalibration, theorizing, and exploring, all at the same time.[6] Classical planning certainly also involves seeking and using feedback as one moves through the plan. But, praxis planning goes a step further: Rather than creating a plan of action, implementing it, and modifying it (if need be—which it almost always is) along the way, praxis planning is the process of actively addressing an issue with an objective in mind, but no certain sense in advance of how to get there, and using a broad range of analytic, imaginative, and relational skills to gradually steer the process ever closer toward that objective.

A variety of metaphors have been proposed for this type of endeavor. In an early article on the topic of school change (which can serve in many ways as an exemplar of a wide set of planned change endeavors in Jewish education), Shevitz, borrowing from Thomas Sergiovanni, used the metaphor of "surfing," as opposed to "pitching," to describe the process whereby one must "ride the waves" in order to make change (Shevitz, 1992). In a later article revisiting the topic, she adopted a musical metaphor from Orlikowski: Like a jazz ensemble, we need to learn to "improvise,

---

[6]This is similar on an organizational level to what Schon urges as the appropriate model for professional practice on an individual level. Schon's concept of the "reflective practitioner" calls for the same type of continuous thoughtful but open monitoring of the situation at hand in order to achieve one's purposes (e.g., teaching or healing). Reflection-in-action becomes the primary driving force for forward movement, and it allows for surprise and improvisation. But, it is also a discipline that must be learned and refined (Schon, 1983).

not conduct" (Shevitz, 2008). We might employ a third metaphor, as well, that of sailing: The sailor works with the elements of the situation—wind, currents, sails, rudder, crewmates—to steer toward a destination, constantly monitoring the variables, tacking when necessary, occasionally getting wet, using both intellect and instinct, and hoping to avoid capsizing along the way. The good sailor is planning constantly as she or he goes, but knows that in the end, what matters is the sailing, not the plan.

This type of planning is both empirically grounded and improvisational. It is empirically grounded in that it demands faithful attention to what is actually going on in real time as new actions are introduced. It is improvisational in offering actors the freedom to change what they do as needed in order to keep the process moving toward its goal.

Regardless of which metaphor we prefer, the point in all of these comparisons is the same: effective planning in Jewish education is not about moving ahead in a straight line or seeking to control the unfolding of events. It is about artfully steering events as they unfold, being hyper-aware of the environment in which these events are unfolding, and being agile enough to keep things on course by changing direction when necessary. This approach to planning is firmly grounded in what we know today about social and educational change. The literature about change and how to make it—in schools, organizations, communities, even countries—is vast and constantly growing. Increasingly, however, a consensus is emerging that sees change, even in systems that are more "tightly coupled" and less anarchic than is Jewish education, as an organic process with emergent properties that rarely proceeds in a linear or pre-determined fashion.

Fullan, in his trilogy of volumes on *Change Forces*, articulates a number of "rules" to guide educational change-makers.[7] These emphasize the need to treat change "as a journey, not a blueprint" and as a guided collective endeavor, not one that can be imposed from without (or simply left to "happen" from within). In the third book of his trilogy, Fullan suggests the following as "common sense" principles for educational reformers:

- Start with the notion of moral purpose, key problems, desirable directions, but don't lock in.
- Create communities of interaction around these ideas.
- Ensure that quality information infuses the interaction and related deliberations.
- Look for and extract promising patterns, i.e., consolidate gains and build on them (Fullan, 2003, p. 23).

These ideas provide planners with useful guidance as to the particular and unique contributions they can make to a change process. The classical tasks of defining problems, identifying potential directions for solutions, mobilizing stakeholders,

---

[7]The lists, each consisting of eight "lessons," can be found in Fullan (1993, pp. 21–22, 1999, p. 18, 2003, p. 24).

providing good information to guide deliberations, and monitoring results to ascertain the effects of action all remain relevant. What is different is the context in which they are employed—one in which planning does not take place prior to and above the action, but as an integral part of it.

In their book, *Getting to Maybe: How the World is Changed*, the authors Frances Westley, Brenda Zimmerman, and Michael Quinn Patton, focus on social innovation through the lens of complexity theory. They argue that successful social innovators do so not like "generals on their horses" and are rarely guided at the outset by some grand strategy. Rather, they see a situation calling for change, take some tentative steps, and, if they have correctly intuited the patterns that are causing the problematic situation, find that the steps they take become "attractors" around which new patterns of interaction grow. Westley, Zimmerman, and Patton describe the key elements in this process of social change as

- "standing still"—observing, thinking, analyzing, pondering, and acting in order to understand deeply the system and the situation one is trying to change
- engaging potential allies, including those who may represent oppositional power, and building networks
- getting in the flow—letting the power of emergence and the networks that have been created carry the work forward and generate strategies
- accepting the inevitability of failures and using them as opportunities for new questions and new learning
- finding the moment when a small success is ready to become a system-wide transformation, the moment when "hope and history rhyme" (Westley, Zimmerman, & Patton, 2006, p. 188).

This process cannot be expected to unfold smoothly or in predictable ways (we are talking about complexity, after all). But, it is a process that is amenable to human guidance, if not control. There is a critical need for thoughtful "steering" at many points along the way—from the initial vision of what must be changed (and the passion to pursue it), to the deep analysis of the patterns that prevent change, to the forging of relationships, to the design of structures and processes (like "developmental evaluation") that enable learning and the emergence of refined strategies, to the effort to sustain and expand successes even while being open to still more change. As described by Westley, Zimmerman, and Patton, social innovators are assuredly not conventional "planners," but the skills they employ are ones that Jewish educational planners needs to embrace if they are to be effective in guiding the changes they seeks to make.

Experience with change initiatives in the Jewish educational world lends support to this understanding of change and of the role that "planning" and planners can play in it. Recent research conducted by JESNA's Lippman Kanfer Institute looked at lessons learned from a dozen major congregational-educational change initiatives. The research identified eight lessons about the change process that held with great consistency across the initiatives and that can likely be extrapolated to Jewish educational change processes in general:

1. Substantial change takes time and does not proceed smoothly.
2. It is important to take action and be ambitious.
3. In a systemic approach to change, vision, action, reflection, and conversation feed off one another to drive the process forward.
4. Getting the (right) people engaged and empowering them is critical.
5. The change process is powered by and largely about learning.
6. Quality outside assistance can help the process tremendously.
7. Because change is complex, a multi-pronged support system is necessary.
8. Financial resources can help "lubricate" change (JESNA, 2008b).

As in Fullan's understanding and that of the authors of *Getting to Maybe*, this research emphasizes change as an organic, emergent process, but not one that simply unfolds haphazardly. There is a bias for action and experimentalism in this approach (Fullan early on advocated for a motto of "ready, fire, aim" [Fullan, 1993, p. 31]), and certainly a strong belief that those in the best position to design change are those who will implement it and be affected by it. But, there is also a clear role for expertise, for good information, for brainstorming options, for building consensus, for close monitoring—i.e., for the things that "planners" do. Fullan warns against believing that change can happen from the bottom up alone (Fullan, 1993, p. 37), and the clear record in congregational-educational change initiatives is that outside guidance and support is generally critical to the success of the change process.

But, the other side of the story is equally important: To be effective, planning must be part of the change process, not apart from it. To try another metaphor: Effective planning is more like operating a GPS system in a car, where the route is recalculated as needed to take account of decisions made and eventualities encountered along the way, than it is like drawing a route line on a map in advance of the journey. The latter may be needed to get started. It is even useful to have available as a reference point. But, unless the trip is a very simple one—which most journeys in Jewish education are not—the line on the map is as likely to impede the journey as to advance it if one tries to stick to it regardless of intervening events and emerging preferences.

What does this type of planning look like in practice? Unfortunately, serious case studies of Jewish-educational planning in general, much less of this type of adaptive "praxis" planning, are few and far between. However, the type of planning that we have been advocating is not entirely new. It is already being practiced in at least one important arena, that of congregational-educational change. The literature on synagogue change offers a number of examples of how individual congregations have pursued change in ways that honor the complexity of the change process and of the environment in which it unfolds. These accounts and many of the key lessons from these change efforts, for example, that change requires a vision of potentiality, but must unfold organically, that learning is the key driving force of change, and that participants must be empowered and equipped to take ownership of the changes being prescribed, lend support to the model for planned change proposed here (Aron, 2000, 2002; Reimer, 1997; Shevitz, 1991, 1992, 2008; Aron, Cohen,

Hoffman, & Kelman, 2010; Aron, Lee, & Rossel, 1995; Hoffman, 2006; JESNA, 2008a, 2008b; Wolfson, 2006).

When it comes to descriptions and analyses of educational planning and change efforts at the community and national levels, we face an even greater dearth of examples to cite. As noted earlier, large-scale planning efforts like the Commission on Jewish Education in North America, whose report, *A Time to Act*, was issued in 1990, and local commissions on Jewish Continuity that operated in many communities often attracted considerable attention at the time. However, little follow-up has been done on the actual effects of these planning efforts, nearly all of which followed a traditional model.[8] A recent review of Jewish educational activity in seven communities across the United States done by Jack Wertheimer (2007) mentions only a handful of educational-planning initiatives in these communities (even though each has undertaken initiatives of varying scope in recent years), thereby providing perhaps inadvertent evidence of the overall lack of impact of such planning on educational activity (with a few notable exceptions, such as Boston, Massachusetts). Thus, we are left to imagine what a praxis planning process of the type we are advocating *might* look like at the community level.

Here, for example, is how a Jewish federation and/or central agency for Jewish education seeking to increase the number of teens who are involved in Jewish formal and informal learning and other activities through their high-school years (a not uncommon goal today) might mount such a planning process: The agency (or agencies) driving the planning process might begin by articulating the vision (initially for itself) in clear terms: every Jewish teen involved in some personally meaningful Jewish activity. Then begins the fun: The agency would undertake a wide ranging set of conversations—with teens themselves, with organizations already offering programming for Jewish teens (synagogues, youth movements, JCC, Chabad, Jewish Student Union, Community Hebrew High School, etc.), with youth workers, with parents, with public and private school personnel, with organizations working successfully with youth in the wider community—listening and learning. What engages teens? What turns them off? What are the characteristics of successful engagement opportunities? What roles does social networking play? What are the constraints and concerns that need to be dealt with?

An inventory of existing opportunities would be created and data about current patterns of participation gathered. Current providers might be brought together for a candid discussion about their successes and failures, their dreams, the gaps they see, what would be needed to engage more teens. At this point, a leadership group for the effort would emerge—a "coalition of the willing," individuals from a variety of

---

[8]My own sense, based on a fairly extensive, but non-systematic, monitoring of these planning processes and as the chief staff person for one national commission (the Commission on Jewish Identity and Continuity, convened by the Council of Jewish Federations in the mid-1990s), is that these commissions produced a number of new initiatives in the short-term, and perhaps contributed to, even as they reflected, an overall cultural shift in the Jewish community over the longer term, but rarely were successful in catalyzing and guiding substantial change. That is, few if any came close to meeting their ambitious goals.

settings who clearly evidence a passion for this challenge, a readiness to experiment with new approaches, and a willingness to work collaboratively.

Experimentation would then begin. An initial set of ideas would be implemented—not a "master plan," but a few new initiatives that seem most promising. These might be new programs and engagement opportunities, imagined by the leadership group or brought to the table by entrepreneurs (some of whom may not even wait for "permission" to do their thing), or additional investments in existing activities. Some might come from teens themselves. The initiatives might involve new partnerships or ways of leveraging and connecting programs and resources.

The progress of these initiatives would be intensively monitored, at the outset not to judge their success or failure, but to see what patterns begin to emerge: Is anything changing? If so, what and for whom? What new issues are coming to the surface (perhaps a need for different kinds of personnel; perhaps a need to "track" teens as they participate in different activities and effect smoother "hand-offs" from program to program; perhaps the need to reach out more aggressively to teens who are unresponsive to what is currently available, but have their own ideas for things that would work for them)? It may take some time for these patterns to become clear, so patience and urgency need to be held in tension. Once patterns do appear, they provide cues for where to go next. Initiatives that seem to offer little promise are dropped. Promising ones are tweaked. New ones get added to the mix. Assessment is continuous, as are conversations with all of the stakeholders. A shared commitment to learning and a mix of patience and persistence drive and guide the process.

It is unlikely that the initial vision of "every teen meaningfully engaged" will be fully realized (truly big visions rarely are). But, hopefully, out of this type of process real change will take place. The change is likely to be messy, with a number of things going on simultaneously and not always in perfect harmony. A key role of the leadership group, however, is to keep everyone focused on the vision and to interpret the unfolding events in a way that makes them coherent to those involved—to identify where progress is being made, to suggest how the pieces fit together (and in so suggesting, probably help them to in fact fit better). In this model there may never be a "plan," i.e., a consolidated blueprint of everything that is to happen, but there will be constant planning, judgments made in the course of events concerning what has happened, what it means, and where to go next. This is planning that can work in the real world of Jewish education, with its multitude of actors, ideas, and interests.

Over the next few years we hope to see major initiatives in various domains of Jewish education and try this type of "praxis planning" to see if it can indeed help in solving some of the field's most persistent problems and in meeting the high aspirations we hold for Jewish education. Several of the large agenda items we have mentioned—the quality personnel shortage in the field, the need to create a more accessible and seamless system—would seem to lend themselves well to being addressed through the kind of experimental—analytic—collaborative—open-ended process that we have described.

Regardless of how Jewish educational planning proceeds over the coming years, it is incumbent on us to initiate serious research on planning and change efforts in arenas beyond the synagogue. This research agenda should include the following:

1. Case studies of planning efforts at a number of different levels (institutional, communal, national)—What approaches were employed? How did the process unfold? What happened as a result?
2. Attempts to understand the factors that make for successful planning—How important are such elements as the planning model employed, the scope of participation, the use (or non-use) of "hard" data, process facilitation by experts, time allocated, leadership, etc.?
3. Action research—using new approaches, like that advocated in this chapter, and monitoring the process for lessons learned. The model of praxis planning that we have proposed is well grounded in the literature on change and in what we know about the characteristics of Jewish educational and communal life. But, we have no evidence of its feasibility or efficacy as an alternative to conventional planning.

We return at the end to the roles of reason and faith in planning. Both, we would argue, remain at the core of what planning is and what it must be. Even in a complex and unpredictable world, reason, properly understood and applied, is critical to our efforts to bring a measure of order out of potential chaos. The reason we employ is not one that limits itself to the logic of cause and effect or seeks to impose order at the expense of stifling the unexpected. It is a measured and mature reason that understands that disorder can also be good, that out of it emerges novelty and new patterns of organization. Our faith too is different. It is not faith in the power of reason per se, but in the possibilities that are inherent in any situation if we are both committed to change and trusting of ourselves, our fellows, and nature's thrust toward self-organization.

The sensibility we need today in our planning is in the end, we would suggest, a very Jewish one. It recognizes both our power (we are created in the image of God) and its limitations (but we are not God). It affirms that as we do (*na'aseh*), we will come to understand more deeply (*v'nishma*). And, it trusts that Jewish education—and the world—can be made better, one deed (*mitzvah*) at a time.

References

Aron, I. (2000). *Becoming a congregation of learners*. Woodstock, VT: Jewish Lights Publishing.
Aron, I. (2002). *The self-renewing congregation*. Woodstock, VT: Jewish Lights Publishing.
Aron, I., Cohen, S. M., Hoffman, L. A., & Kelman, A. Y. (2010). *Sacred strategies: Transforming synagogues from functional to visionary*. Herndon, VA: The Alban Institute.
Aron, I., Lee, S., & Rossel, S. (1995). *A congregation of learners: Transforming the synagogue into a learning community*. New York: UAHC Press.
Baltram, A. (1998). *Navigating complexity: The essential guide to complexity theory in business and management*. London: The Industrial Society.

Bolman, L. G. & Deal, T. E. (2008). *Reframing organizations: Artistry, choice, and leadership* (4th ed.). San Francisco: Jossey-Bass.

Cambridge Leadership Associates (2005). *Adaptive leadership: What is adaptive leadership?* Cambridge, MA: CLA (http://www.cambridge-leadership.com/adaptive/index.php4)

Cohen, S. M. & Kotler-Berkowitz, L. (2004). *The impact of childhood Jewish education on adults' Jewish identity: Schooling, Israel travel, camping and youth groups.* New York: United Jewish Communities.

Cohen, M. & March, J. (1986). *Leadership and ambiguity: The American college president.* Carnegie commission on higher education. Boston: Harvard Business Press.

Commission on Jewish Education in North America (1990). *A time to act: The report of the commission on Jewish education in North America.* Lanham, MD, New York and London: University Press of America.

Cousens, B. (2008). Community planning – Continuity efforts. In P. A. Flexner, R. L. Goodman, & L. D. Bloomberg (Eds.), *What we now know about Jewish education.* Los Angeles: Torah Aura Productions.

Coveney, P. & Highfield, R. (1995). *Frontiers of complexity: The search for order in a chaotic world.* New York: Fawcett Columbine.

Fullan, M. (1993). *Change forces: Probing the depths of educational reform.* Philadelphia: The Falmer Press.

Fullan, M. (1999). *Change forces: The sequel.* Philadelphia: The Falmer Press.

Fullan, M. (2003). *Change forces with a vengeance.* New York: RoutledgeFalmer.

Heifetz, R. & Linsky, M. (2002). *Leadership on the line: Staying alive through the dangers of leading.* Boston: Harvard Business School Press.

Hoffman, L. A. (2006). *ReThinking synagogues: A new vocabulary for congregational life.* Woodstock, VT: Jewish Lights Publishing.

JESNA (2008a). *Compendium of complementary school change initiatives.* New York: JESNA (http://www.jesna.org/sosland/resources/Complementary-Education/Compendium-of-Complementary-School-Change-Initiatives/details)

JESNA (2008b). *Transforming congregational education: Lessons learned and questions for the future.* New York: JESNA (http://www.jesna.org/sosland/resources/Complementary-Education/Transforming-Congregational-Education-3A-Lessons-Learned-and-Questions-for-the-Future/details)

Lissack, M. & Roos, J. (1999). *The next common sense: Mastering corporate complexity through coherence.* London: Nicholas Brealey Publishing.

Mintzberg, H. (1994). *The rise and fall of strategic planning.* New York: The Free Press.

Reeves, D. B. (2009). *Leading change in your school: Hoe to conquer myths, build commitment, and get results.* Alexandria, VA: Association for Supervision and Curriculum Development.

Reimer, J. (1997). *Succeeding at Jewish education: How one synagogue made it work.* Philadelphia: The Jewish Publication Society.

Sales, A. L. (2006). *Philanthropic lessons from mapping Jewish education.* Waltham, MA: Fisher-Bernstein Institute for Jewish Philanthropy and Leadership.

Schon, D. (1983). *The reflective practitioner: How professionals think in action.* London: Temple Smith.

Shevitz, S. L. (1991). Communal planning in a nonrational world: A shift in paradigm and practice. In L. I. Sternberg, G. A. Tobin, & S. B. Fishman (Eds.), *Changing Jewish life: Service delivery and planning in the 1990s* (pp. 187–210). New York: Greenwood Press.

Shevitz, S. L. (1992). Changing Jewish schools. In S. Kelman (Ed.), *What we know about Jewish education.* Los Angeles: Torah Aura Productions.

Shevitz, S. L. (2008). "Don't conduct, improvise!" New approaches to changing congregational schools. In P. A. Flexner, R. L. Goodman, & L. D. Bloomberg (Eds.), *What we now know about Jewish education.* Los Angeles: Torah Aura Productions.

Shluker, D. & Isaacs, L. (1995). *Planning for Jewish continuity: A handbook.* New York: JESNA.

Waldrop, M. M. (1992). *Complexity: The emerging science at the edge of order and chaos.* New York: Simon and Schuster.

Wertheimer, J. (2007). Cultures of Jewish education: How communities address local educational needs. In J. Wetheimer (Ed.), *Family matters: Jewish education in an age of choice*. Waltham, MA: Brandeis University Press.

Westley, F., Zimmerman, B., & Patton, M. Q. (2006). *Getting to maybe: How the world is changed*. Toronto, ON: Random House of Canada.

Wolfson, R. (2006). *The spirituality of welcoming: How to transform your congregation into a sacred community*. Woodstock, VT: Jewish Lights Publishing.

Woocher, J. S. (2001, Fall). A Jewish education strategy for the 21st century. *Torah At the Center*, 5, 26–35.

Pluralism in Jewish Education

Bryan Conyer

Introduction

Pluralism is a deceptive term – on the one hand, it is easily and often applied to nearly any field of study from astrophysics to zoology. On the other hand, it is a complex term with some obvious and subtle significance for each of the areas to which it is applied. Over the last two decades, many Jewish educational institutions including rabbinical seminaries, adult education programmes and Jewish Day Schools have adopted pluralism as one of their core values. These institutions are located primarily in the USA, but also can be found in Australia, Canada, England, Israel and Mexico, amongst others. Parallel to and preceding this development of pluralistic Jewish educational institutions is an abundant scholarship primarily debating the theoretical relationship between pluralism and Judaism and its implications for contemporary Jewry. Furthermore, a Google search of "Jewish + pluralism" reveals a plethora of newspaper and magazine articles, Jewish organisations, speeches and blogs that dedicate time, space and resources to promoting and exploring pluralism within Judaism, indicating that it has become part of the vernacular. Despite this increased usage of the term within the Jewish world, the practical consequences of adopting pluralism as a central organisational value remains virtually unexplored. Despite growing interest, the first empirical research appeared only as recently as 2006, and continues to be published in small numbers.

By drawing upon general academic literature regarding pluralism, as well as research specifically on Jewish education and pluralism, this chapter will attempt to bring some clarity to the term primarily from the perspective of theory, while focusing upon its implications for praxis, with Jewish education remaining the focus. This overview is intended to support the visioning process for any pluralistic Jewish education organisation, as well as to stimulate thought amongst the teaching faculty and policy-makers who ultimately retain responsibility for bridging the gap between vision and practice.

B. Conyer (✉)
Emanuel School, University of Sydney, Sydney, Australia
e-mail: b.conyer@edfac.usyd.ed.au

Three Broad Applications of Pluralism

As the term pluralism is a concept with a multiplicity of meanings, scholars have called it "ambiguous" (Shamai, 1987, p. 97) and even "maddening" (McLennan, 1995, p. 7). Consequently, within the many conversations about pluralism in a Jewish context, different parties unknowingly emphasise one meaning of the term over another, thereby creating confusion, frustration and even conflict, all the while neglecting other meanings. In his brief overview of pluralism, McLennan (1995) identifies three broad and interrelated categories which help to articulate how the term is generally applied: the methodological, political and socio-cultural. A brief description of each of these categories will provide some clarity and insight into the hidden complexity that underlies the concept. It will also highlight some of the implications that pluralism has for Judaism and Jewish education and allow individuals to purposefully distinguish between all three areas. Each of the examples provided throughout this chapter is drawn from actual challenges faced by Jewish pluralistic educational institutions.

At a methodological or philosophical level, pluralism is often the antonym for monism, a philosophically grounded and absolutist belief that there is only one unifying entity, value or substance such as God or Truth, or that there is only one valid methodology for accessing that single Truth. Several examples can help to illustrate this. For instance, in Jewish terms, it asks the questions whether and how Judaism can be validly represented through the prism of each of the major denominations, or whether there is only a singular Judaism. In Jewish educational terms, when teaching *Tanakh* (the Bible), should a pluralist school be teaching biblical criticism or only traditional rabbinic commentators? Finally, in practical terms, should an educational institution allow a student who is Jewish by patrilineal decent to read the blessings over the Torah that affirm the particularistic identity of Jews, when there are other students in that same *minyan* (prayer quorum) who reject patrilineal descent and therefore that person's Jewish status?

At the political level, pluralism is often used as an ideology that strives to recognise and protect the rights of individuals and groups. In this context, pluralism is often discussed through the labels of multiculturalism and interculturalism, and refers to the prism through which a corporate body considers its responsibility to its constituents, including whether power is distributed primarily along a horizontal or vertical axis. In this regard, pluralism encapsulates liberal notions of individualism, including the right to choose, associate, dissent and self-growth, each deemed to be a critical quality for the maintenance of democracy (Dewey, 1968; Feinberg, 1996; Mill, 1991). In Jewish terms, political pluralism considers when one individual's conception of Judaism is being privileged over another person's conception of Judaism. In Jewish educational terms, when does the organisation change its Jewish practices and standards to reflect or accommodate the desires of its student and parent body, and when is the student expected to change his or her practices to fit with that of the school? In practical terms, if the family of a student supports their child playing competitive sports on Shabbat as being consistent with their Jewish identity, should a Jewish pluralist school provide the opportunity for that student to do so or does the pluralist school have a right or responsibility to say 'no'?

At a socio-cultural level, Horace Kallen, a German-born, American Jewish sociologist popularised the concept of pluralism when he coined the term Cultural Pluralism (Kallen, 1915). This was a theory designed to counter the Melting Pot ideology that then prevailed in the USA. The notion of Melting Pot argued that the cultural heritage of America's migrants needed to be amalgamated into and replaced by a newly emerging and homogenous American identity (Zangwill, 1909). In other words, diverse identities are valued only to the degree that they are willing to contribute to the creation of a new, common and uniform identity, all the while relinquishing themselves. Cultural Pluralism opposed this idea and linked the right to maintain one's particularistic identity with the protection of personal autonomy, and by extension, democracy. Cultural Pluralism argued, therefore, that an individual could simultaneously maintain multiple identities, and hence maintain his or her particularistic ethno-cultural micro identity while being loyal to the macro culture. The Melting Pot and Cultural Pluralism provide two distinct models for responding to socio-cultural plural populations.[1] In Jewish terms, are there specific Jewish behaviours, beliefs and values to which all Jews must subscribe? In Jewish educational terms, is the pluralist institution responsible for maintaining the self-defined Jewish identity of the family or transforming the Jewish identity of the student to something different? At a practical level, when a pluralist institution offers *tefillah* (prayers), is it preferable for it to always offer choices that reflect the existing practices of the surrounding synagogue communities or should it offer only one common prayer option? If only one prayer option, which customs and traditions should it follow?

Hence, these three categories provide a cursory overview of how pluralism is applied, influencing the domains of ritual, values, beliefs, cultural norms, policy creation and more, each an area of significance for Jewish education. At the lowest common denominator, each of these applications of pluralism shares an acknowledgement of diversity at many and varied levels. Any institution committed to pluralism needs to determine in which of these three categories it intends to be pluralistic – the methodological, political and/or socio-cultural.

Common Considerations of Pluralism

When considering the broader scholarly discourse surrounding the meaning and purpose of pluralism, certain central and interconnected considerations become apparent. For pluralistic Jewish educational institutions to fully consider and articulate the implications of adopting pluralism as a defining value, they first need to determine whether they intend to be pluralistic in the methodological, political or

---

[1] Many other models also exist. See Walzer (1997) for examples of political arrangements that facilitate cultural pluralism, Appleton (1983) for socio-cultural models and Sleeter and Grant (2003) for socio-cultural models within an educational context.

socio-cultural domains, and then they need to address each of these other common considerations as well.

1. Internal or external pluralism: Pluralism can be external, referring to the relationship between independent phenomena, as well as internal, referring to diversity within the same phenomenon. In the first context, questions relating to Judaism and its ability to recognise, coexist, critique and even validate another religious tradition are considered (Rosenak, 1984; Sacks, 2002; Stone, 2003). In the second, an intra-Jewish context is created, whereby the diverse groups that comprise Judaism consider their ability and the desirability to coexist (Borowitz, 1987; Greenberg, 1985; Rosethal, 2004). These relationships can occur at only a methodological level, whereby theological and value differences are emphasised; a socio-cultural level, where their co-existence as social groups are explored; or at a political level, whereby they protect, support or diminish the rights and social standing of the other.
2. Category formation: Category formation refers to identifying the parts that are to comprise the whole. If pluralism refers to the recognition of diversity, it is imperative that there is clarity regarding the composition and characteristics of the diversity. Category formation is a subjective process whereby a distinctive marker or a set of markers is utilised to identify a common attribute around which a category can be formed (Turner, 1987). This selection of the marker has significant implications for how a pluralist system understands its inner-diversity and which of its internal components are recognised, prioritised or ignored. For example, a pluralistic institution that emphasises denominations to represent Judaism's inner-pluralism uses denominations as its primary marker. Consequently, in a curriculum on Jewish bioethics, it may choose to include material that articulates each denomination's theological perspective on the issue at hand. By selecting such a marker, the school may unintentionally emphasise this methodological expression of pluralism, while underemphasising the socio-cultural expression and its considerations of factors such as national heritage (American-Jew, Russian-Jew or Ethiopian-Jew) and its influence upon a student's self-understanding of Judaism and his/her community's attitudes to such socially contentious matters. Research repeatedly identifies national heritage as exercising a significant influence upon Jewish identity, in a manner that is not necessarily consistent with denominational divisions (Ament, 2004; Rutland & Gariano, 2005; Waxman et al., 2007). Category composition, therefore, significantly impacts the way in which an organisation is able to articulate, recognise and represent its pluralism, including which categories of pluralism are ignored or prioritised.
3. Qualitative definition: On the one hand, pluralism is used as a descriptive, phenomenological term whose purpose is to acknowledge that methodological or socio-cultural diversity is present. Within the Jewish community, this may include the recognition of the presence of diverse denominations as well as the distinct racial, linguistic, national, gender and socio-economic groups that comprise the community. Susan Shevitz (2006) labels this as demographic

pluralism. At times, being acknowledged is sufficient and very important. On the other hand, others argue that for pluralism, merely being acknowledged is inadequate. For them, pluralism also requires an embrace of a concurrent values dimension that evaluates the diversity as being an inherent good that is worthy of cultivating (Dewey, 1968; Feinberg, 1996; Skeie, 1995). Additionally, many maintain that for a plurality to become pluralism certain attitudinal prerequisites must be present, including tolerance (Mittleman, 2001) and a reciprocal willingness to dialogically engage with others (Ingram, 2004), amongst others. When this values and attitudinal approach relates to the existent demographic plurality, Shevitz (2006) labels it as coexistence pluralism. When this approach relates to an intellectual process that generates new thoughts and understandings about Judaism, through an encounter with diverse viewpoints and social arrangements maintained by Jews throughout history, Shevitz (2006) labels it as generative pluralism. It is only through the embrace of this values and attitudinal dimensions, which permits an active engagement with pluralism at a political level, that existing power structures are then open for discussion and evaluation.

4. Pluralism and goodness: Pluralism is usually presumed to be a positive liberal value that is inherently good. However, is pluralism a guarantee of goodness? At a political level, pluralism has been used as an ideology to protect a dominant social group's own interests, often when it feels threatened by the presence of diversity (Bullivant, 1984; Gollnick & Chinn, 2002). When used in this way, certain social groups and their corresponding values and beliefs are consistently privileged over others by giving its members easier access to socially valued goods, including positional power, education or financial assets (Walzer, 1983). The decision to privilege these groups is usually justified by a values-based ideology or theology and is reflected during category formation, when an individual or organisation chooses the constituent components of their pluralism. It is inevitable that this choice will often accord with the worldview of the dominant group, thereby inadvertently or intentionally excluding or partly delegitimizing other potential groups. For example, when a visiting dignitary visits the *Knesset* (Israeli government), arguably a representative of Israel's plurality, it is customary for only the males who comprise the official choir to lead the singing of *HaTikvah* (Israel's national anthem), thereby excluding the other two-thirds of the choir's membership who are women (Alfon, 2008). This arrangement is designed to be inclusive and respectful of the needs of Israel's Ultra-Orthodox community whose understanding of Judaism prohibits a woman's voice from singing in public. If the Knesset chose gender as its primary marker for its pluralism, rather than "religious", the outcome of this same decision would be different. Most probably, the women would have sung, while the Ultra-orthodox would have been excluded. A pluralistic Jewish organisation needs to consider when their pursuit of pluralism is, inadvertently or intentionally, alienating a segment of the Jewish community, and whether that alienation is consistent with its value structure. When reviewing the standards of Jewish practice within the organisation, are certain groups more frequently privileged over

others? Furthermore, which Jewish identities and values does the Jewish Studies curriculum emphasise, leave out or understate when representing Judaism?

5. Relativism: Relativism is often perceived by critics as the unavoidable methodological consequence of pluralism. Relativism maintains that the perceived integrity of any one phenomenon is diminished when it is deemed to be as good as any other. Peter Berger, the influential sociologist of religion and modernity, explains that relativism is an inevitable problem of the post-modern condition where each person is confronted with an endless array of choices around which they construct their own personally meaningful narrative (Berger, 2006). This value-neutral position of post-modernity establishes relativism as a fact. Norman Lamm, while President of Yeshiva University, made this concern explicit within a Jewish context. When considering the ramifications of the traditional notion that there are "seventy faces of Judaism", Lamm maintains that:

> a pluralism that accepts everything as co-legitimate is not pluralism, but the kind of relativism that leads to spiritual nihilism. If everything is kosher, nothing is kosher. If "Torah" has an infinite number of faces, then it is faceless and without value or significance. (Lamm, 1986)

While the proponents of pluralism reject the notion that relativism is a necessary and inevitable problem of pluralism, they do recognise that it is an ongoing challenge. They argue that the capacity to maintain a personal identity or to hold a particular set of values or beliefs does not preclude others from doing the same. Dissent is compatible with pluralism and even a necessary prerequisite (Sartori, 1997). Hence, at a methodological level, Isaiah Berlin, the eminent philosopher of values pluralism, argues that in a plural society competing values will always be present and human beings, in order to be free, need to be able to make personally meaningful choices by rejecting possible choices (Hardy, 2002). These choices may be made in accordance with one's moral conviction, and even though these choices may change over time, "principles are no less sacred because their duration cannot be guaranteed (ibid, p. 217)." Rabbi Irving Greenberg, the scholar and Orthodox rabbi whose lifework is a commitment to Jewish pluralism, reinforces this sentiment:

> Pluralism requires a higher level of internal conviction so that one's convictions are not undermined by allowing for the existence of other valid but alternative truths or systems. This enables believers to function at a higher level of choice. (Greenberg, 2006, p. 44)

David Hartman, the Jerusalem-based scholar, an Orthodox rabbi and an advocate of Jewish pluralism, makes this clear within the Jewish context:

> it is important that we learn that respect for others' points of view does not imply relativism. One can simultaneously maintain that the way one lives reflects the truest interpretations of Judaism and yet respectfully recognise that this position is not held by all Jews. (Hartman, 2001, p. 199)

Hence, the counter-arguments to relativism as a problem demands a conception of a methodological pluralism whereby individuals and ideas must be willing to permit the coexistence of differences without necessarily agreeing with them.

6. Parameters of pluralism: Flowing directly from the above concerns is a question regarding how a pluralist system, which strives to be inclusive, establishes limits. While few scholars maintain that pluralistic systems are ideally able to be inclusive of everything (Watson, 1990), the majority recognise that no one pluralist system can be entirely universal. McLennan notes that there is "a point at which healthy diversity turns into unhealthy dissonance" (1995, p. 8). As has been previously discussed, limits are inevitable and consciously and unconsciously imposed by the selection of the marker used to identify the parts that comprise the pluralistic whole. The challenge remains, how to consciously and purposefully determine where to establish those limits.

   At a practical level, Greenberg maintains that "pluralism means more than allowing others to do and believe things which one cannot accept. Pluralism implies that people must accept limits for the sake of living together" (1988, p. 25). This would include what Berlin calls negative liberties, those pragmatic constraints that prevent an individual doing whatever he or she wishes, so that individuals are able to live within a group (Hardy, 2002). This includes the rejection of the right to harm others even though one may have the means and opportunity to do so. It also includes the right to compel our children to receive an (Jewish) education, sometimes against their will. Connolly, a professor of political science, argues that "the limit point is reached when pluralism itself is threatened by powerful Unitarian forces that demand the end of pluralism" (2005, p. 67). Accordingly, when considering conceptions of political pluralism, any attempts to diminish the right to dissent, associate, choose or self-growth cannot be tolerated or included within the pluralism. Kekes (1993, 2000), a philosopher of moral pluralism, argues that the adoption of absolutist standards lies outside of the parameters of any pluralistic system. For him, pluralistic systems need to constantly reassess what they regard as acceptable, by binding themselves to external measures that can be used for determining their validity. These external measures could include deeply held moral convictions, such as the prohibition against murder or support of egalitarianism. It is imperative, however, that these external measures are also constantly re-evaluated, as their meaning changes over time and within shifting contexts.

   Hence, pluralistic Jewish educational institutions must be able to establish and identify parameters for their pluralism – at a methodological, socio-cultural and political level. This includes determining which ideas, standards and values cannot be compromised, and which groups and individuals can and cannot be included so that the essential character and integrity of its Jewish community and pluralism will not be undermined. In addition, the process used to determine the integral qualities of the institution must itself be open to revision.

7. The maintenance of unity: Another key concern relates to the question of whether it is possible to maintain a sense of unity within a system that focuses upon diversity. Group identity traditionally focuses upon a cohesive, overarching and unifying quality such as Jewish, Secular or Israeli. Pluralism reassigns the focus from this one unifying quality to one that focuses upon divisions within a group. The concern is that this change of focus leads to a fragmentation and

weakening of the whole.[2] How do the Jewish people remain a people when the focus is on the multitude of differences within them – denominational, racial, linguistic, gender, religious observance level, socio-economic and more? Advocates of political and socio-cultural pluralism maintain that those individuals who persist in this argument are usually from the dominant social group and are attempting to protect a status quo that continues to privilege them (Banks, 2005; Bullivant, 1984; Howard, 1999).

Many scholars are unperturbed by this accusation as they maintain that individuals work together in groups in order to achieve a greater good that requires their interdependence (Levey, 2007). Yet this existential challenge of group coherence is very challenging for Judaism, Jewish education and pluralism. What greater good is achieved when pluralism within Judaism is both encouraged and embraced? What greater good is served by actively nurturing greater homogeneity within Judaism? If pluralism is the preferred greater good, then how does a school allow its constituents to share in its understanding of what is the greater good?

8. Process of pluralism: The continuation and maintenance of a values-based pluralism requires a purposeful and deliberate process to do so. For example, at a socio-cultural level, individuals, students and teachers need to be given opportunities to consciously explore and identify their own heritages and values constructs (Howard, 1999) while schools also need to cultivate purposeful spaces that permit meaningful social engagement between distinct groups (Eck, 1993). Racial, linguistic, denominational, national, economic and other differences must be explicitly acknowledged within a classroom, in a non-prejudicial way, so that their influence upon these students can be fully acknowledged, rather than unwittingly ignored (Schofield, 2005). At a methodological level, students should be exposed to diverse biblical interpretive traditions (Tanchel, 2008) and learn to recognise their own biases and the biases of others (Banks, 2005). At a political level, students need to be taught how knowledge and societal arrangements are subjectively constructed, and learn to critically evaluate and then reconstruct them in a more equitable manner (Banks, 2005). If Jewish pluralist institutions do not want to leave their pluralistic convictions to chance, they need to determine their preferred process for nurturing and maintaining them.

As can be seen, pluralism is a fluid concept that easily weaves a multilayered and multi-textured quality through methodological constructs, political considerations and socio-cultural identities. While pluralism can function as both a process and a product, its visible expression will ultimately reflect the conscious and unconscious specificities of each organisation's unique context. Consequently, while these eight theoretical concerns described above are shared by all pluralistic systems, the way that each pluralistic system chooses to respond to each will provide it with its unique quality and character. This spectrum of differences becomes clearly apparent

---

[2] For example, at the political level, see Schlesinger (1992).

when considering the many voices within Judaism that contemplate the relationship between Judaism and pluralism, and ultimately, how the concept of pluralism shapes the educative process of an institution of Jewish learning.

The Jewish Discourse

There are a myriad of voices within Judaism that consider the theoretical relationship between Judaism and pluralism. While most scholars who write on the subject are self-described supporters of pluralism, they hold conflicting definitions of pluralism and insist upon very different limits for it. There is also a general consensus that the inner-plurality of Judaism is categorised primarily, if not exclusively, according to the denominations and that Jewish pluralism is deemed to serve the greater good of preserving and strengthening *klal Yisrael* (Community of Jews). These arguments tend to fit into two broad categories – the theological–philosophical and the sociological. Each of these arguments describes the preferred visions for the three pluralism categories – the methodological, the political and the socio-cultural.

The majority of scholars who speak from a theological–philosophical perspective present themselves as a spokesperson from within a particular denomination. At the heart of their discourse is a challenging methodological question deliberating upon whether pluralism is an authentically Jewish construct and whether pluralism can be congruent with Judaism. Predictably, Orthodox Judaism finds pluralism to be the most challenging as it views itself first and foremost as representing an understanding of Judaism that is bound by *halacha* (Jewish legal and ethical system) with an authority structure that determines appropriate ways to interpret the *halacha*. Hence, the political construct of Orthodox Judaism maintains that any aspect of Judaism that works outside of this *halachik* framework stands accused of being outside of authentic Judaism (Eisen, 2005; Lamm, 1986; Wurzburger, 2001). Following this logic, the current Chief Orthodox Rabbi of the Commonwealth, Jonathan Sacks (1993), maintains in his important study on intra-Jewish pluralism, that there is no *halachik* sanction for the existence of denominations within Judaism, and they are, therefore, incompatible with Judaism. Hence, Orthodox Judaism is regarded as being synonymous with the only authentic expression of Judaism.

While normative Orthodox Judaism rejects denominational pluralism, its socio-cultural responses acknowledge their presence, and they fall upon a spectrum. On one end is the eminent *halachist*, Rabbi Moshe Feinstein, who in his *Igrot Moshe* (*Halachik* rulings), prohibits any meaningful interaction with non-Orthodox Judaism.[3] On the other end are Orthodox Rabbis David Hartman (2000, 2001) and Irving Greenberg (1981, 1988) who find halachically sanctioned ways for the various denominations to co-exist. In between are a plethora of rabbinic authorities who see the need for meaningful interactions with non-Orthodox Jews as Jews, sanctioned by the axiological imperative *klal Yisrael* – the unity of the Jewish people,

---

[3] See Kellner (2008), chapter "Curriculum Integration" for further exposition on this.

without sanctioning their understanding of Judaism (Eisen, 2005; Lamm, 1986; Wurzburger, 2001).

While denominational pluralism is theologically problematic, normative Orthodox Judaism does not dismiss pluralism from Judaism per se, but does limit its influence. For example, Sacks (1993, 2002) maintains that pluralism is compatible with Judaism's interpretive tradition, the established methodology for determining valid answers and Judaism's willingness and ability to engage in inter-religious dialogue, all conditioned upon them being consistent with valid *halachik* precedent. Any Jewish educational pluralistic institution that intends to include Orthodox Judaism within its pluralism needs to be cognisant of these perspectives.

Reform Judaism has always had an easier time with pluralism. As a non-*halachik* system built between the poles of autonomous choice and communitarian considerations (Ellenson, 1999), methodological and socio-cultural pluralisms are assumed. For example, the most recently adopted platform of the Central Conference of American Rabbis (Principles for Reform Judaism, 1999) includes the term pluralism to broadly reject monist conceptions of Truth and to affirm cultural and religious diversity within Judaism. Reform Judaism's relationship to political pluralism is usually expressed in relation to combating Israel's Orthodox majority's monopoly upon Jewish public decision-making (Regev, 2005), which excludes both them and the Conservative movement from receiving public funds, access to decision-making and other social goods.

The Conservative movement regards Judaism as being bound by *halachah*, yet affirms the simultaneous co-existence of multiple halachik systems (Dorff, 1991; Gordis, 1990; Rosethal, 2004). Like the Reform movement, it strongly supports methodological and socio-cultural pluralisms, made clear by the inclusion and repetition of the word "pluralism" in its statement of principles, *Emet v'Emunah*[4] (Gordis, 1990). In this context, pluralism is used to refer to the affirmation of divergent viewpoints within Judaism, the array of individuals who are consulted prior to an official Rabbinic law and standard being rendered, and the prerogative of congregational rabbis to determine which of the endorsed laws and standards are to apply to his/her community. Again, consistent with the Reform movement, political pluralism is also used to decry the monopoly upon Jewish public decision-making within Israel by Orthodox Judaism. In other words, the Conservative movement wants to see a changed power structure to enable it to be more equitably represented.

Methodologically, Conservative Judaism, like Orthodox Judaism, struggles with non-adherence to *halachah*. Hence, while Orthodox Judaism is critiqued for being too rigid in its application of *halachah*, *Emet v'Emunah* critiques Reform Judaism for giving too much latitude to the individual. Yet, two influential scholars and rabbis, Elliot Dorff (1996) and Neil Gillman (1983), both on the committee that wrote *Emet v'Emunah*, provide a theological basis for authenticating these other relationships to Judaism.

---

[4]Literally translated at "truth and belief" though the statement is never translated in Conservative Movement publications.

The sociological voice within Judaism is usually descriptive of the growing socio-cultural and demographic plurality within Judaism, without attempting to prescribe an ultimate methodological form for it. Sociologists often demonstrate how theological considerations remain a concern for the elite of each denomination, but not for the broader membership of their communities (e.g. Ament, 2005). The sociological voice usually focuses on the growing influence of individuation upon Jewish identity (Cohen & Eisen, 2000), the fluid and changing nature of those individuated identities (Horowitz, 2003) or the growing racial and cultural diversity within Judaism (Tobin, Tobin, & Rubin, 2005). While Tobin et al. (2005) draw upon this to promote a political ideology that encourages a broad tent approach for recognising Jewish status, other sociological thinkers emphasise the changing assumptions underpinning Jewish identification to which Jewish education must adapt if it is to effectively engage such pluriforms of contemporary Jewry.

Hence, Jewish theological–philosophical and sociological scholarship provides a plurality of responses to Jewish pluralism at a methodological, socio-cultural and political level, while also negotiating each of the eight common considerations of pluralism in its own unique way. In turn, each offers a theoretical paradigm for at least one conception of Jewish pluralism.

Visions for a Pluralistic Jewish Education

The advantage and need for clearly articulated visions for Jewish education is not new (Fox, Scheffler, & Marom, 2003; Pekarsky, 2006). When pluralism becomes a foundational value for a Jewish educational institution, it unavoidably becomes at least one component of the guiding vision for that institution. Emanating directly from the concerns of pluralism and Judaism are voices that strive to articulate diverse visions for pluralistic Jewish education. Feuerman (2000) represents a view that is consistent with normative Orthodox methodological and political pluralism. In response to the acclaim of the growth of Pluralistic Jewish Day Schools, he encourages these schools to establish a tripartite model for their Jewish education. The first track would be available for all Jews who are recognised by Orthodox Judaism as being Jewish. The second is a conversion track for those who desire that their Jewish status, currently not sanctioned by Orthodox Judaism, be recognised as such. The third track is for those students whose Jewish status is not sanctioned by Orthodox Judaism and having no interest in being recognised as such. In other words, Feuerman uses Orthodox conceptions of *halachah* as the primary marker by which Jewish pluralism would be organised. In this model, Orthodox Judaism serves as the dominant group and retains the authority to establish, nurture and maintain the value structures by which the phenomenological pluralism can be managed.

David Hartman offers an educational vision that begins with an acknowledgement of Jewish socio-cultural pluralism. He maintains that if Judaism is unable to build bridges between its inner-plurality, it is "in danger of splitting Israeli society and of creating sectarian forms of Judaism in the diaspora (Hartman, 2001, p. xiv)". His central educational concern is the alienation that many facets of the community experience towards Jewish tradition. His solution is to transmit a Judaism that retains its own integrity, and speaks to a broad spectrum of contemporary Jews. Hartman encourages, therefore, an education system that uses as role models the rabbinic sages who struggled with their understanding of Judaism such that they were forced to reconsider pre-existing beliefs. In other words, reiterating the notion that both – one's Jewish commitment and understanding of Judaism – constitute a dynamic process built upon deliberate choices. In order to bridge the gap between halachically observant and non-observant Jews, they must be taught to share the same spiritual language. Hence, he encourages the curriculum to develop a common language that can simultaneously convey particularistic Jewish understandings of concepts while also conveying meaning to those who subscribe to more universal values. In other words, a *mitzvah* would be spoken about in regard to its inherent ability to advance justice, as well as exposing students to normative *halachik* practices and their diverse inner spiritual workings. This approach would allow Jews from different backgrounds to participate in the same learning programme with the potential to positively shape all students' characters, and when a student is committed to a *halachik* lifestyle, inform that student's *halachik* choices. Hence, it would allow all students to share *halachik* aspirations without insisting upon *halachik* prescriptions, as well as provide students with insights into the methodological pluralism of Judaism's interpretive tradition and its commitment to the uniformity of *halachik* practice.

Michael Rosenak (1987, 2003) expands upon Hartman's socio-cultural concern for the need for a shared language of understanding between Jews with different orientations. For him, the contemporary lived experience of Jews makes pluralism an inescapable part of Jewish life. His fear, like Hartman's, is that the different groups of Jews will become alien to one another. Pluralism, therefore, is not a choice or a luxury, but a necessity for the maintenance of the Jewish people. Rosenak maintains that the challenge for Jewish education is to create a curriculum that encourages students to cultivate a relationship with both the external (outward expressions) and the internal (subjective experiences) dimensions of Judaism. In a post-modern context, each individual will ultimately determine a personally meaningful balance between the internal and the external, thereby establishing an inevitable pluralistic context. Methodological pluralism is, therefore, also unavoidable. Rosenak maintains that the best way to create a Jewish education that meets the needs of all Jews is to identify the common elements that link each expression of Judaism. He does this by identifying 10 common characteristics of an educated Jew, regardless of how that person understands and lives out his/her Jewish identity. These characteristics include being literate about Judaism, having the competencies to represent one's own understanding of Judaism, a willingness to defend *Klal Yisrael* – the whole people of Israel with its disagreements, allowing honest critique to co-exist with loyalty, and a desire to solve problems facing the Jewish people. If these educated Jews, with their pluralistic conceptions of Judaism, are to be able to communicate with one another about Jewish matters at a practical level, then a common communal agenda must be identified. Rosenak suggests that the first common element of this agenda is the study of sacred literature, with each Jew retaining the space to interpret and engage with the text in diverse ways. The second is the development of a common sacred vocabulary for Jewish life, again, permitting different conceptions of the meaning behind this vocabulary. For example, Shabbat must begin on Friday night and end on Saturday evening, but how one observes Shabbat remains the prerogative of the individual. Rosenak does not attempt to prescribe what this sacred vocabulary shall be, but encourages the educational community to jointly create it. The third challenge is to create common practices between communities, which he recognises as being the most "sticky" area. If this is to work, all participants need to be flexible and continue to negotiate what is appropriate "for everyone has to pay a price for community" (2003, p. 194). Hence, a reciprocal willingness to create the space for others to be different from oneself is an ongoing assumed value within Rosenak's work. His final common element is the goal of identifying problems and addressing them.

Empirical Research

The majority of the work cited so far is theoretical in nature, indicative of the literature currently available on Jewish Pluralism and Education. Yet, the gap between the theory and praxis of pluralism is slowly being narrowed through the emergence of a small number of case studies, many still ongoing, and seeking to better understand the lived experiences of pluralistic Jewish educational institutions. Most of these focus upon Jewish Day Schools that adopt pluralism as a guiding ethos. Some case studies provide insight into the larger issues influencing pluralistic Jewish educational organisations, while others focus primarily upon the way that pluralism shapes the pedagogical process of such an institution.

Kramer (2000), the executive Director of RAVSAK, the network of pluralistic Jewish Community Day Schools, found that most heads of Jewish Community schools, as well as their teachers, have no formal training to prepare them for working specifically in a pluralistic ethos. Pekarsky (2006) demonstrates how a school vision that includes pluralism can meaningfully inform the pedagogical choices for every facet of a school. Grant et al. demonstrates how pluralism facilitates meaning-making in adult learning (2004).

Ben-Chorin (2006) and Conyer (2006, 2011, forthcoming) observe that Jewish educational institutions that identify pluralism as a central value do not articulate a consistent or coherent meaning of the term for their organisations at a methodological, socio-cultural or political level. Conyer (2011, forthcoming) demonstrates how the social milieu of an institution influences the prevailing understandings of pluralism in that institution. Pluralism also assumes different purposes in Jewish Community Day Schools over time. In three disparate schools, while pluralism was initially an espoused value, it was usually confined to the socio-cultural fact that the student body included a diverse array of Jewish backgrounds. Pluralism, at this time, assumed a utilitarian role, principally enabling the school to market to and attract a broad range of potential fee-paying students. Consistent with this, accommodating denominational distinctions remained the primary focus of the school curriculum and policies. With the passage of time, however, each school purposefully transitioned in its relationship to pluralism from one of pragmatic acknowledgement of having a diverse student population to one where pluralism assumed a values and attitudinal dimension. This impacted upon diverse facets of the school's programme, including an expectation that attitudes such as tolerance for difference be required of all school members. This shifting relationship led to different conceptions of pluralism and competing pedagogical visions existing within the same school.

This absence of a clear definition forces the employed educators in all institutions to inductively develop an understanding of the term. These educators then use this inducted understanding to influence their curriculum construction, preferred teaching methods and other pedagogical choices. While Ben-Chorin focused upon *madrichim* (facilitators/guides) within an Israeli adult informal education programme, and Conyer is focusing upon how different stakeholders (policy-makers, faculty, students and parents) within and between Jewish Community Day Schools in California and Australia develop an understanding of pluralism, and how that understanding then influences their interpretation of pedagogical decision-making within the school, this similarity is significant. Ben-Chorin's study ultimately posits *midrash* (genre of textual interpretation) as an effective mode for pluralist pedagogy. *Midrash* permits a pluralistic discourse that enables individuals to construct personal meaning, helps to establish a language to convey pluralistic concepts and provides an inherently Jewish form for the pedagogy of pluralism.

As part of the attempt to gain further clarity regarding the way the term pluralism is being used, Kay (2009) focused on the ideological understandings of pluralism within two US Jewish Community Day Schools on the East Coast. He observes that three primary concepts of pluralism prevail. He calls these: (1) Atmospheric – where the school culture facilitates the co-existence of difference; (2) Informational – the transmission of information pertaining to diverse approaches to Judaism; and (3) Interactional – where purposeful engagement between diverse individuals is encouraged. He also proposes that the successful implementation of pluralism within these schools occurs only when context-specific limits are acknowledged and respected, whether determined by historical, external or internal factors.

Shevitz and Wasserfall (2006) and Wasserfall and Shevitz (2006) have focused on the process of pluralism in Jewish educational institutions. They observed how a Jewish Community High School socialised its students to understand its conception of pluralism and how that school constructs a cohesive sense of community amidst a culture that emphasises differences. Their focus, as with Ben-Chorin, was upon the chosen language of the teachers and the concepts they conveyed, and the way that public rituals were negotiated. This school emphasises pluralism as a process, which it calls cognitive pluralism; that is, the intellectual ability to simultaneously consider multiple perspectives, correlating with methodological pluralism. The school also references "engaged pluralism", a presumption that students must be seriously engaged in the pluralistic conversations, including offering critiques of both their and other people's ideas, correlating again with a methodological pluralism. A significant part of this process is establishing what the school's secular teachers call the creation of a "safe enough" space in which such a risky pluralistic ethic can exist.

When students and staff are open to new ideas, they call this "generative pluralism". Consistently, the research regarding each of these self-defined pluralistic Jewish educational institutions was upon methodological and socio-cultural pluralism of the student body, the learning process and how Judaism was represented. Hence, research is beginning to provide some understanding of how pluralism is being understood and utilised within Jewish education, with many areas of understanding still waiting to be investigated.

Research Agenda of the Future

Theoretical deliberations upon pluralism in Jewish education continue to dominate the available literature. Only a small amount of empirical research considers specifically how pluralism influences Jewish education, problematising the ability to generalise from any conclusions. With the proliferation of such institutions around the world, it is critical that a more comprehensive research agenda be pursued. To date, there has been a focus on only one institution in Israel, one in Australia and six in the USA. There is significant scope for additional descriptive research to identify the internal dynamics of what is happening within other Jewish pluralistic institutions, in other parts of the Jewish world, in a comparative manner as well. With the proliferation of pluralistic institutions of Jewish learning within Israel, this is of particular importance. All existing research employs qualitative methodology. Quantitative studies utilising larger sample size will help further contextualise the qualitative research and provide a broader picture. The existing research suggests that most pluralistic institutions emphasise methodological and socio-cultural understandings of pluralism. It is important to understand why the Jewish expression of pluralism within education has chosen to understate the political understanding. As there is little pedagogical training available specifically to prepare teachers for a pluralist Jewish education, it would be important to identify which pedagogical tools educators employed in pluralistic institutions believe are most impactful, while also consulting the students on the impact they believe they have. None of the existing research has yet been willing to do an efficacy study. A study observing how students, families and a school's employees change their understandings and attitudes towards pluralism within Judaism over time will provide insight into whether this new pluralism agenda is impacting the individual in the desired manner. Finally, it is important to understand how pluralistic Jewish educational institutions address each of the eight common considerations discussed above.

Conclusion

While Jewish educational programmes that self-define as pluralist still comprise a minority of Jewish educational options, they are a growing minority. Pluralism as a concept is as capable of being intellectually infuriating as it is stimulating, emotionally explosive as it is inspiring, and practically a provocateur of endless problems as it can be a utilitarian solution to other challenges. Pluralism can exist as a liberal, universalistic concept or it can be adapted to articulate a particular value, existential or historical lens through which to understand Judaism. This chapter has attempted to offer any person concerned with Jewish education and pluralism an opportunity to bring clarity to the many possible meanings of the term and sensitivity to the promise and challenge that it can offer too.

References

Alfon, D. (2008, July, 23). 'Hatikva' belongs to women, too *Haaretz.com*
Ament, J. (2004). *Jewish immigrants in the United States* (Vol. 7). New York: United Jewish Communities.
Ament, J. (2005). *American Jewish religious denominations* (Vol. 10). New York: United Jewish Communities.
Appleton, N. (1983). *Cultural pluralism in education: Theoretical foundations.* New York: Longman Inc.
Banks, J. A. (2005). Multicultural education: Characteristics and goals. In J. A. Banks & C. A. McGee-Banks (Eds.), *Multicultural education: Issues and Perspectives* (5th ed., pp. 3–30). NJ: Wiley, Jossey- Bass Education.
Ben-Chorin, G. (2006). *Educating for pluralism from a Jewish perspective in an Israeli institution of informal education.* Unpublished Ed.D., The Jewish Theological Seminary of America, United States – New York.
Berger, P. (2006, July, 21). *Religion in a globalizing world.* Paper presented at the Faith Angle Conference Key West, Florida.
Borowitz, E. B. (1987, Summer). Co-existing with orthodox Jews. *Journal of Reform Judaism*, 53–62.
Bullivant, B. M. (1984). *Pluralism: Cultural maintenance and evolution.* Clevedon: Multilingual matters.
Cohen, S. M. & Eisen, A. (2000). *The Jew within: Self, family, and community in America.* Bloomington, IN: Indiana University Press.
Connolly, W. E. (2005). *Pluralism.* Durham, NC: Duke University Press.
Conyer, B. (2006). *Teaching Jewish pluralism in a Sydney Jewish day school* Unpublished MEd (Research), University of Sydney, Sydney.
Conyer, B. (2011, forthcoming). *Considering pluralism in Community Jewish Day Schools: Three case studies in New South Wales and California.* Unpublished PhD, University of Sydney, Sydney.
Dewey, J. (1968). *Democracy and education.* New York: The Free Press.
Dorff, E. N. (1991). The Concept of god in the conservative movement. *Judaism, 40*(4), 429–441.
Dorff, E. N. (1996). *Knowing god: Jewish journeys to the unknowable.* Northvale, NJ: Jason Aronson Inc.
Eck, D. L. (1993). The challenge of pluralism. *Nieman Reports, 47*(2). Available: http://www.pluralism.org/articles/eck_1993_challenge_of_pluralism?from=articles_index
Eisen, C. (2005). A discussion of pluralism: Rx for Orthodox intolerance. *Jewish Action. The Magazine of the Orthodox Union* Spring. Retrieved August 15, 2005, from http://www.ou.org/publications/ja/5758/spring98/pluralismeisen.html
Ellenson, D. (1999, Spring). Autonomy and norms in reform Judaism. *CCAR Journal*
Feinberg, W. (1996). The goals of multicultural education: A critical re-evaluation. *Philosophy of Education.* Available: http://www.ed.uiuc.edu/EPS/PES-Yearbook/96_docs/feinberg.html
Feuerman, C. (2000). Jewish community school high school education for everyone; really? Counteracting intermarriage and assimilation. *Ten Da'at, 12.* Available: http://www.lookstein.org/resources/jewishcommunityschool.htm

Fox, S., Scheffler, I., & Marom, D. (Eds.) (2003). *Visions of Jewish education*. Cambridge: Cambridge University Press.
Gillman, N. (1983). Toward a theology for conservative Judaism. *Conservative Judaism, 37*(1)
Gollnick, D. M. & Chinn, P. C. (2002). *Multicultural education in a pluralistic society* (6th ed.). Columbus, OH: Merrill Prentice Hall.
R. Gordis (Ed.) (1990). *Emet ve-emunah: Statement of principles of conservative Judaism*. New York: Jewish Theological Seminary of America, Rabbinical Assembly, United Synagogue of America, Women's League for Conservative Judaism, and Federation of Jewish Men's Clubs.
Grant, L., Schuster, D. T., Woocher, M., & Cohen, S. M. (2004). *A journey of heart and mind: Transforming Jewish learning in adulthood*. New York: The Jewish Theological Seminary of America.
Greenberg, I. (1981). *The third great cycle of Jewish history*. New York: National Jewish resource centre.
Greenberg, I. (1985). Will there be one Jewish people by the year 2000? *Perspectives*, 1–8.
Greenberg, I. (1988). Toward a principled pluralism. In R. Kronish (Ed.), *Towards the twenty-first century: Judaism and the Jewish people in Israel and America* (pp. 183–205). NJ: KTAV Publishing.
Greenberg, I. (2006). *Judaism and modernity: Realigning the two worlds*. Paper presented at the Principal's Seminar, Bar Ilan University.
H. Hardy (Ed.) (2002). *Isaiah Berlin: Liberty*. Oxford: Oxford University Press.
Hartman, D. (2000). *Israelis and the Jewish tradition: An ancient people debating its future*. New Haven, CT: Yale University Press.
Hartman, D. (2001). *A heart of many rooms: Celebrating the many voices within Judaism*. Vermont: Jewish Lights Publishing.
Horowitz, B. (2003). *Connections and journeys:Assessing critical opportunities for enhancing Jewish identity*. New York: UJA-Federation of Jewish Philanthropies of New York.
Howard, G. (1999). *We can't teach what we don't know: White teachers, multiracial schools*. New York: Teachers College Press.
Ingram, P. O. (2004). "That we may know each other": The pluralist hypothesis as a research program. [Essay]. *Buddhist – Christian Studies, 24*, 135–157.
Kallen, H. (1915). Democracy versus the melting pot. *The Nation*. Available: http://www.expo98.msu.edu/people/Kallen.htm
Kay, M. A. (2009). *The paradox of pluralism: Leadership and community building in ideologically pluralistic Jewish high schools*. Unpublished PhD, New York University, New York.
Kekes, J. (1993). *The morality of pluralism*. Princeton, NJ: Princeton University Press.
Kekes, J. (2000). *Pluralism in philosophy: Changing the subject*. Ithaca, NY: Cornell University Press.
Kellner, M. (2008). *Must a Jew believe anything?* (2nd ed.). Oxford: Littman Library of Jewish Civilization.
Kramer, M. N. (2000). *The pathways for preparation: A study of heads of Jewish community day schools affiliated with the Jewish Community Day School Network, 1998–1999*. Unpublished Ed.D., Columbia University Teachers College, United States – New York.
Lamm, N. (1986). Seventy faces. *Moment*, 2(6).
Levey, G. B. (2007). The antidote of multiculturalism. *Griffith Review, 15*, 197–208.
McLennan, G. (1995). *Pluralism*. Minneapolis, MN: University of Minnesota Press.
Mill, J. S. (1991). *On liberty*. New York: Oxford University Press.
Mittleman, A. (2001). Pluralism: Identity, civility, and the common good. *Modern Judaism, 21*, 125–145.
Pekarsky, D. (2006). *Vision at work: The theory and practice of Beit Rabban*. New York: Jewish Theological Seminary of America.
Principles for Reform Judaism (1999, May). Retrieved March 9, 2007, from http://ccarnet.org/Articles/index.cfm?id=44&pge_prg_id=3032&pge_id=1656
Regev, U. (2005, Winter). Respecting pluralism in the Jewish state. *National Council of Jewish Women Journal*

Rosenak, M. (1984, November, 25–28). *The religious person and religious pluralism*. Paper presented at the The meaning and the limits of religious pluralism in the world today, Cambridge.

Rosenak, M. (1987). *Commandments and concerns. Jewish religious education in secular society*. New York: Jewish Publication Society.

Rosenak, M. (2003). Educated Jews: Common elements. In S. Fox, I. Schleffer, & D. Marom (Eds.), *Visions of Jewish education* (pp. 178–200). Cambridge: Cambridge University Press.

Rosethal, G. (2004). "Both these and those": Pluralism within Judaism. *Conservative Judaism*, 56(3), 3–20.

Rutland, S. D. & Gariano, A. C. (2005). *Survey of Jews in the diaspora: An Australian perspective final report*. Jerusalem: The Jewish Agency of Israel and The Zionist Federation of Australia.

Sacks, J. (1993). *One people? Tradition, modernity, and Jewish unity*. London: The Littman Library of Jewish Civilization.

Sacks, J. (2002). *A clash of civilizations. Judaic sources on co-existence in a world of difference*. London: Continuum.

Sartori, G. (1997). Understanding pluralism. *Journal of Democracy*, 8(4), 58–69.

Schlesinger, A. M. (1992). *The disuniting of America*. New York: Norton.

Schofield, J. W. (2005). The colorblind perspective in school: Causes and consequences. In J. A. Banks & C. A. McGee-Banks (Eds.), *Multicultural education: Issues and Perspectives* (5th ed., pp. 265–288). NJ: Wiley, Jossey- Bass Education.

Shamai, S. (1987). Critical theory of education and ethnicity: The case study of the Toronto Jewish community. *Journal of Education*, 169(2), 89–144.

Shevitz, S. L. (2006). Pluralist education (Vol. March): Shma.com.

Shevitz, S. L. & Wasserfall, R. (2006). *Building Community in a Pluralist Jewish High School: Balancing Risk and Safety, Group and Individual in the Life of a School (Work in progress)*. Unpublished work in progress, The Mandel Center for Studies in Jewish Education, Brandeis University, Waltham, MA.

Skeie, G. (1995). Plurality and pluralism: A challenge for religious education. *British Journal of Religious Education*, 17(2), 84–91.

Sleeter, C. E. & Grant, C. A. (2003). *Making choices for multicultural education: Five approaches to race, class, and gender* (4th ed.). New York: John Wiley and Sons.

Stone, S. L. (2003). Tolerance versus pluralism in Judaism. *Journal of Human Rights*, 2(1), 105–117.

Tanchel, S. E. (2008). "A Judaism that does not hide": Teaching the documentary hypothesis in a pluralistic Jewish high school. *Journal of Jewish Education*, 74(1), 29–52.

Tobin, D., Tobin, G. A., & Rubin, S. (2005). *In every tongue: The racial and ethnic diversity of the Jewish people*. San Francisco: Institute for Jewish & Community Research.

Turner, J. C. (1987). *Rediscovering the social group: Self-categorization theory*. Oxford, UK and New York: B. Blackwell.

Walzer, M. (1983). *Spheres of justice: A defense of pluralism and justice*. New York: Basic Books.

Walzer, M. (1997). *On Toleration*. New Haven, CT: Yale University Press.

Wasserfall, R. & Shevitz, S. L. (2006). *The Language of Pluralism in a Jewish Day School (Work in progress)*. Unpublished Work in progress, The Mandel Center for Studies in Jewish Education, Brandeis University, Waltham, MA.

Watson, W. (1990). Types of pluralism. *The Monist: An International Quarterly Journal of General Philosophical Inquiry*, 73(3), 350–367.

Waxman, C. I., Arazi, A., Bar-Yosef, A., DellaPergola, S., Dror, Y., Elimeleh, N., et al. (2007). *Jewish people policy planning institute annual assessment*. Jerusalem: Jewish People Policy Planning Institute.

Wurzburger, W. S. (2001). *Ethics of responsibility pluralistic approaches to covenantal ethics*. Skokie, IL: Varda Books.

Zangwill, I. (1909). The Melting Pot. Retrieved May 12, 2008, from http://www.gutenberg.org/files/23893/23893-8.txt

Post Modernism Paradoxes: After Enlightenment – Jewish Education and the Paradoxes of Post Modernism

Hanan Alexander

Introduction

Postmodernism in the broadest sense is concerned with how discourses of power saturate and corrupt every aspect of our lives, our pursuit of knowledge, our interpretations of the world and of human conduct, our understanding of language and law, the stories we tell ourselves and our children about who we are and how we ought to live and the religious, cultural, artistic, and other forms in which we express them, our interpersonal and gender relations, our sexual attitudes and orientations, and our institutions of personal and social governance. Those who embrace this complex array of attitudes, suspicions, questions, and analyses ask us to be aware of the myriad ways in which we dominate one another and to consider whether or to what extent we can conceive social relations that ameliorate if not all, then at least some of the most egregious effects of this domination. The term is most often associated with a strand of what Isaiah Berlin (2001) called 'Counter-Enlightenment' that includes such intellectual descendents of Friedrich Nietzsche (1989, 2005) and Karl Marx (1970, 2008) as Michel Foucault (2001); Jacques Derrida (1998), and Jean-Francois Lyotard (1984) who oppose forms of oppression embedded in Enlightenment thought. The prefix *post* in the term *post*modern, and other related terms such as *post*-structural, *post*-colonial, and *post*-Zionist, may be understood more properly as 'counter' than 'after,' since these critiques do not necessarily signal or bring about the end of the trends they criticize. Proponents of modernism, structuralism, colonialism, and Zionism continue to thrive and respond to their critics even as putative power relations hidden in their thought and practice are disclosed by what Paul Ricoeur (1977) dubbed the 'hermeneutic of suspicion.'

This sort of analysis has much to contribute to our understanding of Jewish education in Israel and the Diaspora today since Enlightenment ideas have heavily impacted the most influential ways in which the Jewish condition is currently conceived and transmitted across the generations. However, the postmodern concern for

H. Alexander (✉)
Haifa University, Haifa, Israel
e-mail: hanana@construct.haifa.ac.il

the corrupting influences of power is more useful in exposing than alleviating domination. According to this sort of analysis, for example, each of the three responses to Enlightenment that have most influenced contemporary Jewish education—liberal religion, ultra-Orthodoxy, and secular Zionism—embraces unproductive assumptions about power, one concerning autonomy, another law, and a third national sovereignty (Alexander, 2003a). Addressing these difficulties, however, requires an ethics that makes a distinction between appropriate and inappropriate power eschewed in postmodern thought but found in softer post-, in the sense of counter, Enlightenment orientations. Proponents of such alternatives, including Emmanuel Levinas (1969, 1998, 2003), Michael Oakeshott (1962), and Isaiah Berlin (1990), conceive moral agency in terms of particular histories, languages, and cultures not universal reason, and favor receiving others over asserting the self.

This chapter is divided into four sections. In the first section 'The Dynamics of Enlightenment and Jewish Education' I discuss how Enlightenment assumptions about autonomy, law, and sovereignty have influenced contemporary Jewish education. The second section, 'Postmodernism and Contemporary Jewish Education,' considers why postmodern discourse might lead one to be skeptical of these assumptions, and the third section, 'Three Paradoxes of Postmodernism' considers some paradoxes inherent in this sort of skepticism. The final section 'Post-Enlightenment Jewish Education' explores how Jewish education might address this postmodern critique.

The Dynamics of Enlightenment and Jewish Education

Contemporary Jewish life is shaped by the eighteenth-century intellectual revolution known as Enlightenment which challenged the assumptions of medieval Mediterranean society. This society was based on the idea that the laws which govern how we ought to conduct our lives were created by the same God and so have the same authority as those which govern the physical universe. Political power comes from God, so leaders anointed by those who represent Him should govern according to His will. In Europe this meant rule by Christians and in North Africa and the Middle East by Moslems. Jews were a protected minority in both Christian and Moslem societies based on laws inherited from the Romans and so lived as distinct corporate entities. However, the structure of medieval Jewish life was fundamentally the same as that of its Christian and Moslem counterparts; the power to determine what to believe and how to behave was vested in religious authorities. To be educated in each case entailed coming to confess one or another of these faith traditions, the truth of which is sustained by revelation if not also by reason (Wolfson, 1977, pp. 17–38).

Enlightenment changed this by asserting a new form of skepticism according to which we are to accept only those statements about how we ought to behave or organize society and how the world works that pass an objective test (Gellner, 1992). Moral and intellectual authority, in this view, rests in the autonomous individual not a transcendent God; and the question of whether to accept the dictates of scripture should be decided on the basis of reason built, according to the great Enlightenment philosopher Immanuel Kant (1969, 1994), into the structure of human thought. This set the stage for a new sort of liberal democratic politics sometimes called Emancipation that allocates to the citizens of a society rather than those closest to God the right to choose leaders, public policies, and personal life paths. Education according to this perspective entails the cultivation of personal autonomy, not religious faith, based on one or another account of rationality. This challenged the political power and spiritual influence of Christianity in Europe and of Islam in North Africa and the Middle East. It also undermined the corporate identity and religious faith of Jews who were now offered citizenship in secular states independent of their faith or ethnic origins and empowered them to choose whether or in what ways they would continue to adhere to the beliefs and customs of Judaism.

Three responses to Enlightenment have come to dominate contemporary Jewish education. Liberal religion essentially accepts it, while ultra-Orthodoxy and secular Zionism to one degree or another reject it (Alexander, 2003a). Liberal religion, which includes Progressive, Liberal, Reform, Reconstructionist, Conservative, and to some extent modern Orthodox Jews, accepts Enlightenment and Emancipation by authorizing individuals rather than rabbis to determine how Jewish life ought to be lived, thereby acknowledging one degree or another of personal autonomy; and by embracing citizenship in the liberal democratic state, thereby deemphasizing the corporate aspect of Jewish identity. Jewish education should assist individuals in negotiating the tension between rational autonomy and traditional heteronomy, in this view, by providing them with information about and experience of Jewish tradition so that they can choose for themselves how to participate in Jewish religious and cultural life. Those on the more liberal end of this spectrum place a greater emphasis on personal autonomy and so subject the beliefs and practices they are prepared to inculcate to one or another rational test. Nineteenth and early twentieth-century liberals (e.g., Cohen, 1995) tended to believe, with Kant (1989, 1997), that the exercise of personal autonomy involves applying a universal rationality whereas their mid to late twentieth-century counterparts (e.g., Kaplan, 1981) were influenced by the great American philosopher John Dewey (1916, 1997) who thought that intelligent choice must take into account a person's own felt needs. This emphasis on the individual in Jewish life resulted in religious innovations such as changes to the worship service, or recognition of a child as Jewish whose father, but not mother, was born a Jew, or inclusion of women or homosexuals into synagogue leadership. Those on the more traditional end (e.g., Heschel, 1967; Soloveitchik, 2000), on the other hand, tend to believe that people can only make intelligent choices when exposed to classical rabbinic Judaism, which is sufficiently attractive if properly introduced to inspire the individual to adopt most or all of a traditional Jewish lifestyle.

Modernity, however, is comprised not only of Enlightenment ideas and Emancipation politics but also of reactions against them. Isaiah Berlin (1997, 2001) referred to these trends as the Counter-Enlightenment. Many of them are rooted in G.W.F. Hegel's critique of Kant. Whereas Kant believed that all reason originates in the very structure of human thought, prior to experience with 'things-in-themselves,' Hegel (1995) held that reason is embedded in that very experience, expressed in the historical evolution of national culture and language. Through a process of dialectical criticism in which each generation critiques the ideas of its predecessors, human society slowly corrects its mistaken beliefs and comes to be liberated from error. The society that represents the ultimate end of this process embodies Absolute Freedom. These Hegelian ideas have been interpreted in many complex and conflicting ways across the political spectrum. Those who envisage this freedom as embodied in a particular national culture are sometimes called right-leaning Hegelians, even if they also embrace the sort of economic egalitarianism often associated with the left, while those who combine liberty conceived as a cosmopolitan or universal ideal with egalitarian economics are usually called left-leaning Hegelians.

One right-leaning Counter-Enlightenment trend entails a rigid account of faith, sometimes called fundamentalism, or among Jews ultra-Orthodoxy, which takes one particular interpretation of sacred scripture as the literal word of God and so also, as with Hegel, the absolute truth. All forms of Jewish Orthodoxy—neo-Orthodoxy, modern Orthodoxy, religious Zionism—tend to embrace rabbinic exegesis as the correct understanding of the Hebrew Bible and are ambivalent to one degree or another about Enlightenment ideas (Salmon, Ravitzki, & Ferziger, 2006), but ultra-Orthodox Judaism is distinguishable by its complete rejection of Enlightenment and Emancipation altogether (Sofer & Stern, 1996). Christian fundamentalists read the Hebrew Bible (what they call the Old Testament) in light of a literal interpretation of the Christian Bible (their New Testament) and Moslem fundamentalists read the Hidath (a form of Islamic midrash) as if it were the literal meaning of the Koran. Ultra-Orthodox scholars tend to embrace what is sometimes called a positive theory of law, which holds that the unequivocal meaning of a legal text is to be found within a legal tradition alone without reference to any external sources offering other moral, political, or legal perspectives (Austin, 1995). This position in legal philosophy actually emerged under the influence of scientific and historical positivism, or the view that the truth about nature, society, and history is only to be discovered within the confines of empirical rationality (Dilthey, 1989). This is an Enlightenment idea that seeks precise and definitive results to legal deliberations similar to those found in the empirical sciences. However, in the ultra-Orthodox context this view takes on a decidedly Hegelian meaning that texts can only be properly deciphered within the organic context of the cultures and traditions in which they were written. Jewish education according to this view involves inculcating adherence to an insular, rigid, and absolute account of positive Jewish law, born of a deep suspicion that Enlightenment ideas will result in the ultimate demise of the Jewish people and of God's plan for the redemption of the world.

A second Counter-Enlightenment tendency, which held particular sway over important trends within Zionist thought, involves a messianic (some would say chauvinist) form of nationalism that views a particular culture as the end of history or the embodiment of ultimate ethical ideals. This sort of thinking is often associated with right-leaning Hegelianism even when it is combined with left-leaning egalitarian economics such as that of the kibbutz movement or other embodiments of labor Zionism (Sternhell, 1998). According to this view, the establishment of the State of Israel constitutes the culmination of Jewish history in which the values of the Hebrew Bible are to be translated into a modern national culture. This is to bring about a resolution of the so-called Jewish problem—how Jews could become citizens of non-Jewish societies and yet remain Jews—and the consequent problem of anti-Semitism—the hatred of Jews because they are different—by normalizing Jews as citizens in their own state. The new secular state should also signal an impending end to human (or at least European) history. By translating the ethical ideals of the Hebrew prophets into a biblical form of humanism—Buber (1997) called it Hebrew humanism—the new secular state would serve as a 'light unto the nations.' This spirit is seen in the writings of most leading political, labor, cultural, and revisionist Zionists (Hertzberg, 1997, pp. 199–389, 556–571). It is also embraced in one form or another by both religious *Zionists* who combine strict religious Orthodoxy with commitment to Israel as a secular Jewish state as well as religious *nationalists* who interpret the Jewish return to Zion as a literal harbinger of the messianic era and envisage an Israeli Jewish society that reflects positive Jewish law much like the ultra-Orthodox (Hertzberg, 1997, pp. 390–427). Secular Zionism then does not reject Enlightenment ideas altogether, but only the view of Emancipation politics that Jewish life as a minority culture could thrive in large diverse democracies, since the public square of such a society will always favor the majority. Cultural survival on this view requires political sovereignty. Jewish education then must entail learning to embrace the State of Israel as the embodiment of ancient Jewish values translated into a modern national culture.

Postmodernism and Contemporary Jewish Education

As heir to left-leaning Hegelianism, postmodernism is critical of both Enlightenment and right-leaning Counter-Enlightenment thought. It combines the skepticism of Hegel's disciple Karl Marx (1970, 2008) concerning the unequal distribution of power embedded in economic, political, and social relations with that of Friedrich Nietzsche concerning the possibility of any grand narrative adequately explaining the meaning of human existence. Like Hegel, Marx believed that historical progress was motivated by social conflict. However, unlike is predecessor, he understood this conflict in economic rather than intellectual terms. Those who control the production of wealth also control the ideas used to justify its unequal distribution. Marx called these sorts of ideas 'ideologies.' All societies are divided between haves and have-nots, on this view, and the former use their power to force the latter, often by means of schooling, to believe that the current circumstance in which some are weak and others strong is as it should be. Marx dubbed the material or economic conditions that create power the 'basic structure' of society, and the 'false consciousness' or ideology used to justify them its 'super structure.' The task of social criticism, in this view, is to bring about liberation from these illusions by divulging how they serve the interests of those in charge in order to promote a redistribution of wealth and power.

Neo-Marxists such as Max Horkheimer, Theodor Adorno (Horkheimer & Adorno, 2002), and Antonio Gramsci (1991) also believed that liberation from false consciousness and redistribution of power is possible. However, they placed a greater emphasis than Marx on the importance of ideology in producing as well as justifying and maintaining power. The ideological super structure of society is not merely a passive by-product of its economic basic structure, they argued; the right ideas can also serve as a source of power. They called this view 'critical theory,' which discloses the ways that some cultures, languages, and political ideas dominate others, a process they called hegemony, and advocated that liberation requires the equalizing of cultural as well as economic resources. Marxist and neo-Marxist thought is sometimes called modern critical social theory because of its belief in an 'objective' ideology that could bring about a utopian end to social conflict. Postmodernism, however, was also influenced by Nietzsche (who like Hegel has been interpreted as both an advocate and an opponent of absolute power). This led many to abandon the optimistic attitude of modern critical theory that liberation from the corrupting influence of power can be achieved for the more pessimistic view that discourses of power are present in all human endeavors.

Consider how Michel Foucault (2001) might assess the role that autonomy has come to play in liberal religious Jewish education. Foucault's post-structuralism rejected as naïve the Marxist and neo-Marxist position that the adverse effects of unequal power relations can be ameliorated by properly understanding the political–economic structure of society. Acknowledging the errors of one's ideology only leads to another which is no less erroneous. In liberating the peoples of Eastern Europe from oppression by the Russian Czars, for example, the Bolsheviks did not eliminate the adverse consequences of domination but transferred them from one regime to another. All epistemological and moral claims entail power relations. These are embedded in complex networks of belief and practice that justify and maintain regimes of domination built into our very conceptions of self and society. The task of social inquiry in this view is to illumine discourses of power, not social laws or structures, which are the genuine and often hidden forces that explain human behavior.

From a post-structuralist perspective the liberal idea that Jewish education can provide knowledge relevant to making informed choices about Jewish life based on universal rational standards, as Kant would have it, or personal felt needs, as Dewey proposed, is an illusion. The 'knowledge' transmitted as well as the 'choices' made, indeed even the very idea that people are capable of free choice, cannot be separated from the power relations in which they are embedded. Liberal Jews tend to combine an appreciation for traditional rabbinic knowledge with a desire for objective historical understanding. Classical rabbinic interpretations might be combined in a Bible curriculum, for example, with various forms of historical criticism. According to Foucault's analysis, however, both entail domination. The former is tied to the power that the rabbinate exercises over Jewish life and the latter to European colonialism which imposed a belief in objective history on Jews in order to dominate their culture by means of one form or another of 'rational' discourse. Both are nothing more than false ideologies. One replaced the authority of biblical religion with that of the rabbis and the other the power of rabbinic tradition with Enlightenment knowledge.

Even the view that an individual person has the capacity to choose freely is embedded in Enlightenment power-discourses, since the idea of a self unencumbered by socio-economic class, culture, or language, is unimaginable other than in the context of Kant's and Locke's liberalism that reflects the interests of modern secular society.

Or consider how Jacques Derrida (1998) might evaluate the positive account of Jewish law associated with ultra-Orthodoxy. Derrida applied skepticism about power relations similar to that of Foucault to the meaning of language and the interpretation of texts. There is no essential relation between signifiers—linguistic symbols such as words and phrases that purport to say something about human experience—and that which they allegedly signify, he argued; rather any assertion that language means this as opposed to that is an act of domination imposed upon someone trying to understand it. The task of interpretation on this account is not to uncover the intentions of an author or speaker or meanings embedded in the linguistic or conceptual context in which something was written or said but to deconstruct the techniques used by writers and commentators to impose meanings on readers, in order to liberate them from traditional hermeneutics and open up new possibilities of understanding.

This process is not unlike *midrash*, rabbinic literary interpretation, which admits the possibility of eisegesis, or reading new meanings into a text, in addition to exegesis, the discover of meanings already present within a text, except, as mentioned above, ultra-Orthodoxy has tended to read the Hebrew Bible in a closed manner as if this ancient *midrashic* eisegesis is its correct exegetical interpretation. From a deconstructionist perspective, however, any attempt to close the meaning of a text or limit the possibility of new understandings is a morally perverse act of domination that undermines the inherent freedom of the reader to find in the text whatever meaning he or she deems appropriate. The idea that Jewish education should promote a heteronymous commitment to a limited set of religious rituals and customs tied to so narrow and authority-seeking reading of sacred texts is deeply problematic, on this account, since in an effort to secure the control of a particular brand of rabbis over Jewish life, it attributes a limited interpretation to biblical and rabbinic sources that cannot withstand criticism.

Or consider how Jean-Francois Lyotard (1984) might respond to central themes in Zionist education. Lyotard associated what he called 'the postmodern condition' with an incredulity toward meta-narratives or grand theories, that human history progresses in a linear fashion, for example, or that everything can be known by means of science or everyone liberated from domination. We have ceased to believe in all-encompassing stories of this kind, he argued, since they impose a single interpretation of reality on everyone regardless of whether it conforms to one's own experience. Hence, we have become alert to the incompatibility of rival aspirations, beliefs, and desires, to different cultures, identities, and world views, to our participation in a diversity of inconsistent ways of life. Postmodernity is characterized in this view by an abundance of micro-narratives, 'regimens of meaning,' or competing identities. We live in a multiplicity of semantic communities, according to Lyotard, distinct and often incommensurable systems in which meanings are produced and rules for their circulation created.

The difficulty with Zionist education, on this account, is that it has all too often sought to impose a single, linear, and in many instances messianic meta-narrative according to which the trajectory of Jewish history is ultimately and inevitably toward a return of the Jewish people to political sovereignty in the land of Israel (Gur-Zeev, 2003). But this homogeneous story does not allow for the many complexities of Jewish history, the variety of languages Jews have spoken, the diversity of religious and cultural lives in which they have expressed their connections to other Jews, sacred texts, and God, or the multiplicity of localities and communal structures in which Jews have lived and in many instances continue to live (Boyarin, 1997). Nor does it ring true to many Jews today, even those who among their many identities choose to affiliate as citizens of Israel. Indeed, some would argue that by eschewing the traditional Jewish ambivalence toward power and placing it at the center of collective Jewish existence, Zionism has exacerbated not ameliorated anti-Semitism, and by secularizing and nationalizing fundamentally religious forms of cultural expression Zionism has not redefined traditional Jewish values for a new age but robbed Jewish life of its most essential ideals, beliefs, and practices.

Postmodernism is sometimes associated with the term post-Zionism, which includes a variety of sociological and historical critiques of Israeli society based loosely on critical social theory (Silberstein, 1999). However, post-Zionism has also been influenced by post-colonial ideas that Foucault, Derrida, and Lyotard did not necessarily endorse. Zionism is a hegemonic ideology, according to the post-colonial critique, based on nineteenth-century European nationalism that imposed itself on the indigenous Arab people of Palestine with the assistance of the British who were granted a mandate to rule the region by League of Nations—predecessor to the United Nations—in 1917. This ideology was created for the purpose of controlling the local Arab population by inserting European power into the region. Zionism on this account is a form of colonialism, the corrupt power relations of which seep into every aspect of the Israeli state. The task of any sort of education worthy of the name ought to be liberation from the oppression imposed by this hegemonic regime not its proliferation (Gur-Zeev, 1999). The difficulty with this view from a postmodern perspective lies in the presupposition that Zionism is somehow unique in the evil domination it has perpetrated against the Palestinian Arabs and that liberation from oppression of this kind is possible. This privileges an Arab over a Jewish narrative concerning who is indigenous to the land that lies between the Jordon River and the Mediterranean Sea, which could itself be understood as an oppressive act. One does not need to adopt such a naïve faith in the possibility of liberation or one-sided reading of the meta-narratives that have sought to dominate the region to acknowledge the monistic and power-centered character of Zionism (Alexander, 2000, 2006). This is not to say, of course, that postmodern analysis has nothing to say concerning power relations among Jews and Arabs, rather acknowledging that liberation from one regime of meaning is likely to lead to subjugation under another affords a more balanced look at the myriad ways in which they have sought to dominate one another over time.

Three Paradoxes of Postmodernism

Both postmodern and modern critical social theories shine light on forms of domination that might otherwise go unnoticed. The brief illustration offered above makes plain, for example, that each of the three most influential Jewish responses to Enlightenment, which form the conceptual basis for contemporary Jewish education, imposes regimes of meaning in ways that assert power over others by restricting rather than enhancing the capacity of students to find meaning in Jewish life. But if modern critical social theory failed to acknowledge that liberation from one false consciousness leads only to another, the postmodern position suffers from at least three defects that stem from its departure from its modern predecessors. I have called these the fallacies of excessive determinism, relativism, and authority, though they might also be called paradoxes since they reveal contradictions inherent in postmodern thought (Alexander, 2003b). Each paradox raises doubts about postmodern critiques of liberal autonomy, positive law, and Jewish national sovereignty, respectively.

One paradox, which undermines the postmodern critique of liberal autonomy, is concerned with the relation between power and perspective in postmodern thought. Modern critical social theories supposes a tight connection between context and consciousness according to which beliefs and behaviors are conditioned by the forces ruling one's life at any given time. While one is under the sway of false consciousness, the dominant ideology is imposed. When one has been liberated from falsehood and comes to realize that one's true interest lies with this or that disenfranchised group, a new ideology takes its place. Although critical theories expect that one can come to recognize the ways in which a dominant ideology is oppressive, this is only from the position of a perspective in which socio-economic and cultural power is distributed equitably. At no point in this process are beliefs and behaviors chosen; they are always determined by one orientation or another. This is as true for the powerful as the powerless, since on this theory those who dominate are themselves corrupted by the evils of the oppression they perpetrate and are all too often unaware of the ways in which their own hegemonic ideologies compel them to believe and behave as they do.

It is the recognition of this fact that led postmodern theorists to abandon what they saw as the naïve optimism of modern critical social theory for the more pessimistic view that we can never escape domination. Under these circumstances, however, it is hard to know what to make of the ethical critique of oppression inherent in postmodernism or its moral preference for the disenfranchised, since neither the rulers nor the ruled are actually the agents of their own actions, which are determined by socio-economic, cultural, and other power-related interests. Yet, if false ideologies not people are responsible for oppression, why should people be held accountable for their attitudes or actions? The naïve optimism of modern critical theory at least allowed for the possibility of a better society in which power interests would be equalized and people free to choose their own life paths. However, on the postmodern view which holds that liberation from one false consciousness leads only to another, there is no escape from the determining effect of power interests and so no way to hold agents accountable for their actions. What could it possibly mean, then, to say that it is wrong to dominate or oppress another person? The postmodern critique of liberal autonomy undermines its own concern for the morally corrupting influence of power, therefore, even while it highlights that very influence.

A second paradox, which raises questions about the postmodern critique of legal positivism, concerns the postmodern assertion that knowledge claims are tainted by the impulse to dominate, since they assert that evidence *compels* one to believe this and not that. On the postmodern view beliefs cannot be reduced to raw data independent of one regime of meaning or another. Power interests are embedded in the very ways in which we formulate what we count as data, not to mention how we go about collecting it or arranging it to draw conclusions. The difficulty with this position, however, can be seen when we apply this same sort of analysis to the assertion that all knowledge claims entail power relations, by asking whether that assertion itself is not also embedded in power relations. Should we not challenge the epistemological authority of this assertion along with all the rest? But if we are to be skeptical of the very postmodern concern for the ways in which power seeps into all knowledge claims, the epistemological status of postmodern analysis in its own right is called into question, which leads, in turn, to the paradoxical conclusion that the postmodern critique of ultra-Orthodox legal positivism as arbitrary act of domination is itself such an oppressive act.

A third paradox, which relates to the postmodern critique of Jewish sovereignty, is connected to political authority. Drawing on a tradition that goes back to Plato, postmodern theorists tend to view power as absolute. Power is evil, they argue, so the weak should be privileged, and since power relations cannot be neutralized, this means enfranchising them. But this not only infects them with the corruption entailed by power, it disenfranchises those who were once in charge, placing them in the position of weakness that was held by those who have now been elevated into the dominant position. This is a recipe for never-ending conflict. Why privilege the weak if it means transforming them into a version of those who oppressed them, which is the only option available to the postmodernist since he denies the possibility that power relations can be equalized? If everything is saturated with power there is no room for justice, since privileging the weak over the strong itself entails an exercise of unjustifiable power. In order to conceive a just society, there needs to be a realm that allows for the possibility of normative right, not mere political might, which is precisely what postmodernism denies in its critique of modern critical theories. Power is not always evil. Most of us would like the police to respond with an appropriate use of force, for example, if our home has been burgled. A chief challenge of political education is to distinguish between the just and unjust exercise of force. From the fact that Zionism entails an assertion of Jewish power, therefore, it does not follow that the establishment of Israel moves Jews or Zionists from the category of the powerless and righteous to that of the powerful and evil, which has led some to reject the legitimacy of Israel as an expression of Jewish sovereignty. Rather Zionist education ought to cultivate an ability to distinguish between the just and unjust exercise of Jewish power.

Post-Enlightenment Jewish Education

How then is it possible to acknowledge the strengths of postmodern analysis in Jewish education, particularly when it comes to highlighting inappropriate uses of power, without succumbing to these paradoxes? One answer can be found in critiques of Enlightenment that do not flow from left-leaning Hegelianism but that offer alternative accounts of autonomy, law, and sovereignty (Alexander, 1995).

Consider, for example, how Emmanuel Levinas (1969, 1998, 2003) might respond to the liberal concept of autonomy. Like Hegel, Levinas was a phenomenologist. He believed that knowledge is derived from the phenomena of human experience which cannot be separated from the contexts of history, language, and culture. He did not learn this from Hegel, however, but from Edmund Husserl (1999), who was not interested in hidden power relations. The difficulty with both modern and postmodern critical theories, according to a Husserlian perspective, is that they conceive liberation or the lack thereof as objects over against experiencing subjects. Marxists and neo-Marxists believed that the equalization of power relations constitute an objective standard, independent of concrete human experience, against which all ideologies could be judged, while their postmodern critics decried this very quest for objectivity as hopelessly naïve and unattainable. However, Husserl thought that this whole subject–object discourse was incomprehensible, since all that can ever really be known is experienced within the consciousness of a perceiving subject. Knowledge begins according to Husserl with the experience of receiving another into one's self, not the assertion of a rationally autonomous self, as with Kant, or the critique of domination hidden in that assertion, as in Marx, neo-Marxism or postmodernism. It was Levinas, the student of Husserl, who recognized that 'receiving the other' is first an ethical act and only secondarily epistemological. Ethics, on this view, not epistemology, is first philosophy. Hence, though it is well known that Derrida was influenced by Levinas, the latter stopped short of some of the paradoxical conclusions reached by the former. But it was Levinas, the student of Talmud, who realized that this other rather than self-centered ethic is deeply rooted in the Hebrew Bible as read by the rabbis.

Self-determination—autonomy or agency—is to be found on this account in receiving not asserting, contracting not imposing, acknowledging the other not centering on the self. Moral independence is achieved by entering into relation with another subject in an intimate I–Thou moment experienced as a 'meeting' or 'dialogue' in which, to use Buber (1970) words, the other fills the firmament, not by confronting a subject with an object to achieve an instrumental purpose. In a subject–subject encounter we set aside interest in order to receive the other with no end in view other than the meeting itself. The result is neither 'objective' nor 'interested' knowledge, but a form of insight into oneself and others achieved by a letting go, at least in part, in order to receive another subject. Parker Palmer (1983) called this self-knowledge as one might be perceived by another, by God or a beloved friend. It is a form of what Israel Scheffler (1983) called personal as opposed to propositional or procedural knowledge. Nel Noddings (1984) called it 'engrossment' (p. 30), a process in which the one-caring receives the feelings of the one-cared-for, which confirms in each an elevated sense of self. Terence McLaughlin (1984, 1985) dubbed it 'autonomy-via-faith,' in contrast to Kant's 'autonomy-via-reason.' It is characterized by the Hebrew notion of *emunah*—belief or trust in another person, rather than the more rational Greek *pistis*—belief that something is the case on logical or empirical grounds (Buber, 1951). The appropriate response, Levinas pointed out, blurs autonomy and heteronomy in a felt sense of responsibility for or duty toward the other, not an individual right to choose for oneself. Here is an ethic that can distinguish between the just and unjust exercise of power, according to the extent to which it involves acknowledging a responsibility for the other (Alexander, 2010a).

Or consider how Michael Oakeshott (1962) might assess the sort of legal positivism that has come to characterize ultra-Orthodoxy. Like Hegel, Oakeshott was critical of the false idea that human affairs can be adequately captured by means of abstract and rigid concepts and techniques such as those taught in empirical science and by both universal liberals and critical social theorists. All of these are but convenient techniques for summarizing more complex manners, customs, symbols, and stories by means of which people live with others. The summaries he called technical and the lived complexities practical knowledge. One can be formulated in propositions, rules, principles, directions, and maxims; the other exists only in the human relations in which communal life is conducted and is shared by means of practical traditions not theoretical doctrines. Oakeshott traced the source of this fallacy to a preoccupation with certainty by the likes of Descartes and Bacon, but it, in fact, goes back to Plato's preference for theory over practice and his idea that power should be vested in those whose belief is free from error.

Ironically, the rigidity that legal positivists attribute to the interpretation of law and ultra-Orthodoxy to religious tradition belongs more properly to the rational principles born of 'arid technique' (Oakeshott, 1962, p. 31), which entered into religion in response to Greek philosophical rationalism (Kellner, 1999). A tradition of practice is not an inflexible manner of doing things. 'It is neither fixed nor finished; it has no changeless centre to which understanding can anchor itself' (Oakeshott, 1962, p. 128). Some parts may change more slowly than others, but none is immune from change. What accounts for the continuity of tradition on this account is the diffusion of authority between past, present, and future, in which nothing that ever belonged is completely lost. Change within a tradition of practice emerges gradually not abruptly, by means of undirected evolution not preplanned revolution, in part through contact with other viewpoints; and the engine of this change is found in the ways in which individuals engage culture in order to create themselves.

Selves are historical achievements, not rational or legal abstractions. Each human being is self-made, not out of nothing, but from a self-understanding acquired by learning to recognize oneself in the mirror of a cultural inheritance, that 'reaches us, as it reached generations before ours, neither as long-ago terminated specimens of human adventure nor as an accumulation of human achievements we are called upon to accept, but as a manifold of invitations to look, to listen, and to reflect' (Oakeshott, 1989, p. 29). It is in joining conversations that connect past and present to future, deciphering artifacts that have been handed down and creating new ones to pass along, speaking the languages and appreciating the literatures of a culture that a particular biological body, or locus of psychological or sociological traits, becomes a recognizably human life (Alexander, 2008). The relevant educational issue concerns a faith's openness to learning from alternative perspectives, not the uniform authenticity of its beliefs (Alexander, 2005).

Or consider how Isaiah Berlin would relate to the issue of national sovereignty. Rationalism tends toward universal political theories in which power is allocated to those who have achieved self-control by freeing themselves from error. Kant's 'autonomy-via-reason' is an example. Traditionalism of the sort embraced by Oakeshott inclines toward political pluralism in which power is vested in those who resist the impulse to impose themselves on others, which is an alternative sense of self-control born of relations to individuals, community, history, or God, similar to McLaughlin's 'autonomy-via-faith.' Berlin (1990) called one positive, the other negative liberty; the former has to do with self-definition or control of one's destiny, the latter with the absence of constraints on, or interference with a person's actions. Berlin had deep reservations about the former because of the tendency among those who advance positive accounts of freedom to distinguish between one's actual self that acts in the day-to-day world and some occult entity referred to alternatively as a 'true' or 'real' or 'higher' self of which a person might not be fully aware. Thus, it is argued that although one's empirical self may indeed feel free, one's true self may actually be enslaved. As Berlin (1990) put it so aptly, 'once I take this view, I am in a position to ignore the actual wishes of men or societies, to bully, oppress; torture them in the name, and on behalf, of their "real" selves, in the secure knowledge that whatever is the true goal of man (happiness, performance of duty, wisdom, a just society, self-fulfillment) must be identical with his freedom—the free choice of his "true", albeit often submerged and inarticulate, self' (p. 133). It should come as no surprise, then, that Berlin (1997, pp. 1–24) leveled this critique against the potential authoritarianism inherent in left-leaning Hegelianism upon which the postmodern critique of the Zionist quest for Jewish power relies.

It may be surprising, however, to learn that Berlin's reservations concerning the excesses of positive liberty were addressed no less to the monist moral and political theories of Kant and Locke than to critical social theorists. Liberalism is normally associated with pluralism, grounded in the right of citizens to choose a concept of the Good over any particular goods they may prefer. This assumes that they can pick freely based on relevant reasons (Brighouse, 2005) and engage in reasonable deliberation to adjudicate disagreements (Rawls, 2005). However, Berlin followed Hegel in holding that our choices are not always as free nor our deliberations as reasonable as they might appear, since the very idea of rational evaluation is itself historically situated; and though preferring negative freedom, he recognized it too as an historical achievement which tends toward its positive counterpart when transformed into a doctrine that strives for comprehensive influence over the lives of citizens. Thus, he counted as a fairly extreme version of positive liberty the concept of rational autonomy and the pursuit of liberal toleration as a universal ideal found in Kant and Locke.

Berlin parted company with Hegel, however, especially his left-leaning followers, when it came to the idea that choices can be genuinely free only when we strive to equalize power relations. The ultimate source of human power, Berlin argued, lies in the presumption that people can step outside of their current circumstances to choose a new path, despite all of the influences upon them or the forces stacked against them. This is so precisely because our circumstances are not given and even though our choices cannot be based on one view or another of universal reason (Gray, 1996). His views were thus closer to communitarians such as Alastair MacIntyre (1989) and Charles Taylor (1991), who held that there is no way to assess rational evaluation other than by appeal to the very rational standards in question, which without a satisfactory justification of rationality may be reduced to expressions of mere personal feeling. This confuses freedom with caprice and isolates people from one another as they center increasingly on themselves. Meaningful assessment must be based on values that emanate from beyond the self, linked to historically contingent communities, traditions, or cultures in which people live.

Like Oakeshott, Berlin was a value pluralist. He believed that there are many incommensurable cultures founded on distinct and often conflicting values and ideals. The task of political theory is to consider ways for peoples of distinct difference to live together in peace, within one society or across national boundaries, not to impose a particular conception of liberty on all as a universal ideal. John Gray (2002) called this the other face of liberalism. Berlin agreed with Oakeshott that our identities are formed in the mirror of inherited traditions, from which it follows that each person is entitled to receive or engage her own cultural tradition in the public square, without imposing it on others or having another's imposed on her. Here is the justification of national sovereignty, in acknowledging the other not asserting the self (Tamir, 1995). But we can only truly respect a culture different from our own when we have engaged our own cultural inheritance (Alexander, 2010b).

A post-Enlightenment view of Jewish education acknowledges unproductive power relations inherent in the conceptions of personal autonomy, positive law, and political authority that inform contemporary Jewish education without succumbing to the paradoxes of postmodernism. It does this by reconstituting the significance of self-determination, traditional practice, or national sovereignty, as receiving the other rather than asserting the self, by engaging a dynamic not a dogmatic tradition of practice, in the public as well as the private sphere. This entails coming to understand myself, both past and present, and being prepared to assume responsibility for my future. It also requires coming to understand others who are different from me, both past and present, and recognizing that it is they, not I, who should assume responsibility for their future. Following Jonathan Sacks (2003), and in contrast to pedagogies of the oppressed which tend to place responsibility for one's plight on social structures or power relations rather than on oneself, I have called this the pedagogy of difference. Whereas modernity tended to sever the organic links between self, tradition, and sovereignty in Jewish education, and the postmodern critique exacerbated this tendency toward disintegration, this post-Enlightenment view provides the basis for a possible reintegration of these fundamental ingredients of Jewish life.

References

Alexander, H. A. (1995). Religion and education in multicultural society. *Religious Education*, *90*(3–4), 377–387.
Alexander, H. A. (2000). Education in the Jewish state. *Studies in Philosophy of Education*, *19*(5), 489–505.
Alexander, H. A. (2003a). Jewish education in extremes: A prolegomenon to postmodern Jewish educational thought. *Religious Education*, *98*(4), 471–493.
Alexander, H. A. (2003b). The Frankfort school and post-Zionist thought. In S. Sharan (Ed.), *Israel and the post Zionists* (pp. 71–86). Brighton: Sussex Academic Press.
Alexander, H. A. (2005). Education in ideology. *Journal of Moral Education*, *34*(1), 1–18.
Alexander, H. A. (2006). Zionist education at the crossroads. In D. Breakstone & A. Feldestein (Eds.), *From Altneuland to Tel Aviv: Of dreams and deeds* (pp. 61–77). Jerusalem: The Zionist Library.
Alexander, H. A. (2008). Engaging tradition: Michael Oakeshott on liberal learning. In A. Stables & S. Gough (Eds.), *Learning to live with the future* (pp. 113–127). New York: Routledge.
Alexander, H. A. (2010a). Autonomy, faith, and reason: McLaughlin and Callan on religious initiation. In G. Haydon (Ed.), *Faith in education: A tribute to Terence McLaughlin*. London: Institute of Education.
Alexander, H. A. (2010b). Literacy and citizenship: Tradition, reason, and critique in democratic education. In Y. Raley & G. Preyer (Eds.), *Philosophy of education in the era of globalization* (pp. 30–50). New York: Routledge.
Austin, J. (1995). *The province of jurisprudence determined*. Cambridge: Cambridge University Press.
Berlin, I. (1990). *Four essays on liberty*. Oxford: Oxford University Press.
Berlin, I. (1997). *Against the current: Essays in the history of ideas*. Princeton, NJ: Princeton University Press.
Berlin, I. (2001). *Three critics of enlightenment: Vico, Hamann, and Herder*. Princeton, NJ: Princeton University Press.
Boyarin, D. (1997). *Unheroic conduct: The rise of heterosexuality and the invention of the Jewish man*. Berkeley, CA: University of California Press.
Brighouse, H. (2005). *On education*. New York: Routledge.
Buber, M. (1951). *Two types of faith*. New York: HarperCollins.
Buber, M. (1970). *I and Thou*. New York: Charles Scribner's Sons.
Buber, M. (1997). *Israel and the world*. Syracuse, NY: Syracuse University Press.
Cohen, H. (1995). *Religion of reason out of the sources of Judaism*. American Academy of Religion.
Derrida, J. (1998). *Of grammatology*, G.C. Spivak (tr.). Baltimore: The Johns Hopkins University Press.
Dewey, J. (1916). *Democracy and education*. New York: Macmillan.
Dewey, J. (1997). *Experience and education*. New York: Free Press.
Dilthey, W. (1989). *Introduction to the human sciences*. Detroit, MI: Wayne State University Press.
Foucault, M. (2001). *The order of things: An archeology of the human sciences*. New York: Routledge.
Gellner, E. (1992). *Reason and culture*. Oxford: Blackwell.
Gramsci, A. (1991). In D. Forgacs & G. Nowell-Smith (Eds.), *Selections from cultural writings*, W. Boelhower (tr.). Cambridge, MA: Harvard University Press.
Gray, J. (1996). *Isaiah Berlin*. Princeton, NJ: Princeton University Press.
Gray, J. (2002). *The two faces of liberalism*. London: New Press.
Gur-Zeev, I. (1999). *Philosophy, politics, and education in Israel*. Haifa: University of Haifa Press and Zemora-Bitan (Hebrew).
Gur-Zeev, I. (2003). *Destroying the other's collective memory*. New York: Peter Lang.
Hegel, G. W. F. (1995). *Reason in history*, R. S. Hartman (tr.). Englewood-Cliffs, NJ: Prentice-Hall.

Hertzberg, A. (1997). *The Zionist idea: A historical analysis and reader*. Philadelphia, PA: The Jewish Publication Society of America.
Heschel, A. J. (1967). *The insecurity of freedom*. New York: Noonday.
Horkheimer, M. & Adorno, T. (2002). *The dialectic of enlightenment*, E. Jephcott (tr.). Sanford, CA: Stanford University Press.
Husserl, E. (1999). *The idea of phenomenology*, L. Hardy (tr.). The Hague: Springer.
Kant, I. (1969). *Critique of pure reason*. Bedford Books.
Kant, I. (1989). *Foundations of the metaphysics of morals*. Englewood Cliffs, NJ: Prentice Hall.
Kant, I. (1994). *Prolegomena to any future metaphysics*. Englewood Cliffs, NJ: Prentice Hall.
Kant, I. (1997). *Critique of practical reason*. Cambridge: Cambridge University Press.
Kaplan, M. (1981). *Judaism as a civilization*. Philadelphia, PA: The Jewish Publication Society.
Kellner, M. (1999). *Must a Jew believe anything*. Portland, OR: Littman Library of Jewish Civilization.
Levinas, E. (1969). *Totality and infinity: An essay on exteriority*, A. Lingis (tr.). Pittsburgh, PA: Duquesne University Press.
Levinas, E. (1998). *Otherwise than being: Or beyond essence*, A. Lingis (tr.). Pittsburgh, PA: Duquesne University Press.
Levinas, E. (2003). *Humanism of the other*, N. Poller (tr.). Urbana, IL: University of Illinois Press.
Lyotard, J. -F. (1984). *The postmodern condition: A report on knowledge*, G. Bennington & B. Massumi (trs.). Minneapolis, MN: University of Minnesota Press.
MacIntyre, A. (1989). *Whose justice, which rationality?* Notre Dame, IN: University of Notre Dame Press.
Marx, K. (1970). In J. O'Malley (Ed.), *Critique of Hegel's philosophy of right*. Cambridge: Cambridge University Press.
Marx, K. (2008). In D. McLellan (Ed.), *Capital: An abridged edition*. Oxford: Oxford University Press.
McLaughlin, T. H. (1984). Parental rights and the religious upbringing of children. *Journal of Philosophy of Education, 18*(1), 75–83.
McLaughlin, T. H. (1985). Religion, upbringing and liberal values: A rejoinder to Eamonn Callan. *Journal of Philosophy of Education, 19*(1), 119–127.
Nietzsche, F. (1989). *Beyond good and evil*, W. Kaufman (tr.). New York: Vintage.
Nietzsche, F. (2005). *This spoke Zarathrustra*, G. Parks (tr.). Oxford: Oxford University Press.
Noddings, N. (1984). *Caring: A feminine approach to ethics and moral education*. Berkeley, CA: University of California Press.
Oakeshott, M. (1962). *Rationalism in politics*. London: Methuen.
Oakeshott, M. (1989). *The voice of liberal learning*. New Haven, CT: Yale University Press.
Palmer, P. (1983). *To know as we are known: Education as a spiritual journey*. San Francisco: Harper Collins.
Rawls, J. (2005). *Political liberalism*. New York: Columbia University Press.
Ricoeur, P. (1977). *Freud and philosophy: An essay on interpretation*, D. Savage (tr.). New Haven, CT: Yale University Press.
Sacks, J. (2003). *The dignity of difference* (Rev ed.). London: Continuum.
Salmon, Y., Ravitzki, A., & Ferziger, A. (Eds.) (2006). *Jewish orthodoxy*. Jerusalem: Magnes Press.
Scheffler, I. (1983). *Conditions of knowledge*. Chicago: University of Chicago Press.
Silberstein, L. J. (1999). *The post-Zionism debates: Knowledge and power in Israeli culture*. New York: Routledge.
Sofer, M. & Stern, Y. (1996). *Chasam sofer on torah*. New York: Artscroll.
Soloveitchik, J. B. (2000). *Fate and destiny: From the holocaust to the state of Israel*. Hoboken, NJ: Ktav.
Sternhell, Z. (1998). *The founding myths of Israel*, D. Maisel (tr.). Princeton, NJ: Princeton University Press.
Tamir, Y. (1995). *Liberal nationalism*. Princeton, NJ: Princeton University Press.
Taylor, C. (1991). *The ethics of authenticity*. Cambridge, MA: Harvard University Press.
Wolfson, H. (1977). *From Philo to Spinoza*. New York: Behrman House.

Spirituality: The Spiritual Child and Jewish Childhood

Michael J. Shire

Introduction

Since the early work of James Fowler (1981) in faith development there has spawned a vast array of research and studies in the area of children's spirituality, religious development, theologies of childhood and educational approaches to religious growth. For Jewish educators, however, questions and concerns abound about defining children's spirituality in a Jewish context as well as understanding the roles of the Jewish educator in enhancing it. Jewish educators have offered critiques of both the definition of spirituality and the intended outcomes of spiritual education (Bekerman, 2003; Gottlieb, 2006). However, in some settings, spiritual development has become a normative feature of children's education even resulting, for example, in its assessment of attainment in British schools by the Office of Standards in Education (National Curriculum Council, 1993).

Prompted by this newly developed field of educational development, Jewish educators need to ask questions about the nature of educating for religious growth and spirituality and the relationship of religious development to religious learning and practice. Specifically they will want to know how the faith of the child can be characterised and expressed in Jewish terms. What conceptual tools can be used to best understand the nature of the spiritual child? How can faith be formed and nurtured authentically in Judaism and how can young people be personally enriched and their faith enhanced through Jewish religious education?

Literature concerned with the religious development of children can be broadly categorised into three groupings. The developmentalists (Fowler, 1981; Goldman, 1964; Oser & Scarlett, 1991) understand faith change as a sequenced process of development that is characterised by predetermined stages of faith which are universal and invariant. Since these stages are described as structural, relating to a process of 'making meaning' relevant to all human beings, a number of Jewish educators have applied faith development theory to Jewish education (Blumberg, 1991; Goodman, 2003; Shire, 1987). Though providing new and useful ways of

M.J. Shire (✉)
Leo Baeck College, London, UK
e-mail: michael.shire@lbc.ac.uk

understanding religious development, faith development theory has been criticised extensively especially for its use of stage development and its claims to universal structural processes.

A second generation of studies arose in the 1990s (Berryman, 1991; Coles, 1990; Hay & Nye, 1998) that sought to understand religious identity and spiritual expression in childhood as expressed by children themselves. These studies focused on the spiritual awareness expressed by children and the inherent nature of the child as a naturally spiritual being. Though largely ignored by contemporary Jewish educators, these studies reflected some of the expressions of Jewish childhood described earlier in the century by Solomon Schechter (1938); Martin Buber (1979) and Janusz Korczak (Cohen, 1994). Their writings reflect an approach that values the whole child and focus on the nature of childhood in its theological and psychological dimensions.

Finally, a third strand to this investigation of the spiritual lives of children has focused on a concentration of theological works about childhood particularly in Christianity but now more and more in an inter-religious framework (Bunge, 2001; Jenson, 2005; Mercer, 2005; Miller-McLemore, 2003; Yust et al., 2006; Shier-Jones, 2007). Some Jewish educators responding to this Christian framework have attempted a description of Jewish theological understandings of childhood spirituality (Sasso, 2001; Shire et al., 2006). Drawing upon the classical Jewish sources, a theological understanding of the child as blessed is seen, as well as conceptions of childhood as a highly intimate sacred relationship. The key indicators of this perception are 'learning' and 'goodness' both of which are categorised as the 'spiritual tasks of childhood'.

This chapter will review the major findings in each of the three paradigms and describe the attempts by Jewish educators to refine and apply them to Jewish education. It will draw together the often-competing theories regarding the spiritual nature of the child and provide a comprehensive overview of the most important thinkers in this field. Due to the large majority of studies having taken place outside Judaism, it is important that the reader understands the general scope of the field but specific reference to Judaism will be made in each case. Finally the chapter will suggest further ways this area can be studied and researched in Jewish education, and will provide a summary of the educational approaches that are suggested by the theories.

Spiritual Development

What is meant by spiritual development? Is it different from spirituality, religious development or religiosity? There is little consensus about the nature and scope of this particular dimension of life. Where there is research, it has situated itself within the field of the psychology of religion. The originator of this field of study combining theological enquiry with psychological development is Professor James Fowler of Emory University in Atlanta. Fowler's theory of faith development is summarised as follows:

> Faith may be characterised as an integral, centring process underlying the formation of beliefs, values and meanings that (1) give coherence and direction to people's lives, (2) links them in shared trust and loyalties with others, (3) grounds their personal stance and loyalties in relation to a larger frame of reference and (4) enables them to face and deal with the conditions of human life. The stages of faith aim to describe patterned operations of knowing and valuing that underlie our consciousness. (Fowler, 1991, p. 56)

Fowler uses a broad definition of the word faith. Rather than limiting faith to religious belief, Fowler denotes a process of making meaning which is shared by all human beings. Faith is therefore a process of trusting and structuring meaning making that incorporates belief but goes beyond it.

Fowler conducted research interviews with hundreds of people from a variety of different backgrounds, ages, sexes and religious affiliations. From these interviews, he derived six stages of faith through which an individual passes though he contends that the higher stages are present in only certain highly developed individuals. These stages are structural; they characterise the inner operations by which a person makes meaning of the world. These stages are claimed to be common to all people. Though the content of the stage will change from individual to individual, Fowler suggests that all people at the same stage compose meaning in a structurally similar manner. The stages are sequentially ordered with each stage incorporating the processes of the one before while adding to it in a new dimension. Each stage has its own integrity so that stage four is not categorised as more faith-full than stage three, rather it has developed in a qualitatively new way. The transition from stage to stage becomes apparent when the individual is no longer able to make meaning using their familiar processes and seeks to move beyond them. These transitions are often triggered by life crises where new ways are sought to understand painful and difficult circumstances.

The faith of the young child (Stage 1: intuitive-projective faith) is one in which meaning is made intuitively and by imitation. Knowledge and feeling are fused and formed by significant people in the child's life. Here the importance of sensitive and caring teachers who foster trust in the child is important as are the images, stories, and symbols which are formative at this stage. Fact and fantasy may be undifferentiated leading to imaginative and creative images of God. Religious meaning is associated with concrete images and symbols. At the stage of schooling (Stage 2: mythic-literal faith), the child is conscious of being part of a larger group than just his/her family as the child engages with the stories, myths and values of a religious tradition. These can be particularly understood in very literal terms as God is portrayed as the ultimate powerful being or force. Stage 3 (synthetic-conventional faith) according to Fowler is conventional in that the individual is anxious to respond to the expectations of significant others. There is a strong tendency to rely upon institutional authority as the holder of religious authority. Symbols become more deeply understood allowing for symbolic meaning to become important. A personal relationship with God can be expressed and a sense of community is valued. Religious feelings are deeply felt but tacitly held before they become examined more critically later on. This is the time for confirming a religious identification and belonging to a community or religious heritage.

As the congruence of this position breaks down in the adolescent who questions authority, there comes more of a position of individual choice with regard to meaning making, authority and belief. Stage 4 (individuative-reflective) coinciding with Piaget's formal operational thinking becomes more inner dependent in which a way of making meaning is more personally chosen and self-consciously different from the religious identity of others. Prayer and spiritual feelings can take place in any location not necessarily connected to a religious institution. Ritual shared with like-minded individuals is preferred over a large community. Stage 4 faith diminishes the power of the concrete symbol in favour of the central idea it represents. The person ready for transition in young adulthood finds that their faith is excessively reliant on their individual consciousness. This leads to an awareness of the purely personal perspective of truth and meaning without regard for a historical or community-based conception.

Stage 5 (conjunctive faith) combines what one knows and trusts from within, with the perspectives of others even from outside one's own community of faith. In stage 5 there is a universal perspective to one's faith as well as a return to ritual and symbol as sacred roles and objects. At this stage the symbols of a religious tradition have deep meaning resonant in their historical and contemporary identification. Often individuals can infer new meaning in the role of these symbols and rituals.

The final and most comprehensive stage according to Fowler (Stage 6: universalising faith) is seen in someone who has the ability to perceive paradoxes in life and yet create unity in their spiritual life combining a particularistic religious tradition with a universal humanitarian outlook. Fowler suggests that this is rare in human beings and only some exceptional individuals achieve it.

Fritz Oser & Scarlett (1991), Swiss researchers in religious development and moral reasoning, drew upon similar strands in developmental psychology as Fowler particularly from the work of Piaget and Kohlberg. Oser's approach to developmental stages was to propose a hierarchy of religious behaviours dependent on the ever-developing religious judgements of individuals. For Oser, religious judgement is how people construct their own religious meaning. To understand this particular feature of religious behaviour, Oser posed a series of dilemmas to individuals based on core religious issues such as making promises to God, responding when bad things happen to good people and counting one's blessings. The response to these dilemmas produced patterns that demonstrate how people structure their solutions to religious problems and challenges. According to Oser there are five stages which are similarly hierarchical, sequenced, and universal. For Oser a higher stage is a more reasoned construction of the relationship between God and human beings. Movement from one stage to the next is not automatic as the structures of thinking within the stages are stimulated through life experience. The stages are however universal in that they occur in all peoples regardless of religious background. For Oser, each individual structures his or her reasoning in a similar manner though at different stages.

The work of faith development in the United States and Switzerland, coupled with the work of spiritual development in the United Kingdom as part of the Religious Education National Curriculum has prompted much debate about the nature of spirituality in education. This has resulted in philosophical reflections on spirituality and psychological approaches to learning for the development of spirituality. This bringing together of theology and developmental psychology marked the innovative uniqueness of the faith development school. These approaches, including those of Canadian writer Clive Beck (1989) and British writer Kevin Mott-Thornton (1998), all attempt a universalist approach to the nature of spirituality. This approach widens the definition of spirituality so as to allow those without a religious heritage or affiliation to accept the notion that one can be spiritual without being religious. However, such a universalist and syncretistic approach blurs the significant differences between religious traditions and often assumes a Western rationalist position where the cognitive predominates over the affective.

Critiques of these developmental theories take issue with the normative linear structure of a stage theory that leads to an endpoint that is highly individuative, rationalist and universalistic. The predominant feature of Jewish religious life is the increasing nature of one's obligation to community.

Where faith is defined as leading to a universal norm, it does not take into account such specifics within differing religious traditions. For Judaism, the corresponding Hebrew term for faith, *emunah*, denotes a relationship of trust between God and humankind, one in which trust is put into a transcendent reality with the expectation of a covenantal relationship in return. However, *emunah* is not merely an idea. It is expressed in Judaism through the performance of *mitzvoth*. These *mitzvoth* become the ways in which Jews act out *emunah* in the world. The relationship to God is developed by the deepening consciousness of the *mitzvoth*. However, mere performance will not necessarily engender a spiritual awareness. Medieval philosopher Bachya Ibn Pakuda (1978) in eleventh-century Spain already warned of a life based on *mitzvoth* that had no inner significance. He called for priority to be given to 'Duties of the Heart' that underpin and make meaningful the traditional practices of faith. If this inner dimension is not nurtured then the external commandments cannot be properly fulfilled. It is necessary therefore to have intention (*kavannah*) in carrying out the *mitzvoth*.

Jews have been uncomfortable with the use of the word 'spiritual' when it has been related merely to a series of inner spiritual virtues. For Jews, spiritual awareness without explicit religious expression is incomplete. Martin Buber therefore used the word 'religiosity' to describe a spiritual openness within a religious tradition. For Art Green, Jewish religiosity is described as 'striving for the presence of God and fashioning a life of holiness appropriate to such striving' (1987, p. xii). Jewish spiritual life is thus a continual task of creating holiness even in the most mundane of daily acts as Jews seek to build a life of holiness for communities and for individuals.

Educational Implications for Spiritual Development

Jewish educators place significant emphasis on the key issues described by the developmentalists. They recognise the vital role that spirituality as a form of meaning making takes in the lives of individuals and the inner structural operations that operationalise such meaning making, during childhood especially. This entails

Jewish educators being able to discern the pathways and expressions of an inner religiosity in their students and to have the capability to nurture their development. They would be sensitive to the transitions of spiritual change in their students' lives and engage with them in religious decision-making and judgment that reflects current core understandings of their own religiosity. They would be attuned to the dissonance that occurs between inner and outer expressions of spirituality, particularly as students enter adolescence. Educators would need to have the means to reintegrate a religiosity of mind, spirit and heart as a centring thread in their lives.

This inner expression however needs to be matched and integrated with external religiosity as lived through a Jewish life and language. Jewish education today is mainly concerned with the transmission of knowledge, the development of ritual skills, the formation and strengthening of Jewish identity and the affirmation of values. It deals little with the nature of religious experience, the development of religious growth or the field of spirituality in general. It has found these areas of religious education difficult to promote in a modern secular society with teachers and parents ambivalent about their own religiosity, let alone about transmitting it to others. Jewish education has primarily been concerned with the outer dimensions of religion; the historical, social and theological forms of religious expression. It has been less concerned with elements of spiritual experience such as trust, awe and love especially beyond early childhood. Where it has focused on inner dimensions, it has not considered the relationship between inner and outer dimensions. Aspirations for graduates of Jewish educational programmes often focus on evidence of knowledge, pride of association and expression of moral values. Where spirituality is included, it is often regarded as a separate entity, perhaps expressed in music or experiences removed from the home and synagogue such as camping or Jewish travel.

However, religiosity is a vital component of Jewish life and experience; as such, it needs to be integrated into the very fabric of Jewish education. Many Jewish educators are uncertain as to how it can be translated into educational objectives incorporated into the curriculum of Jewish educational settings. One of the key issues for Jewish education is how to make spiritual development an explicit objective of educational programming. Roberta Louis Goodman (2003) posits three implications for Jewish education that emerge from the developmentalist approach to spiritual development:

1. It is necessary for the Jewish educator to facilitate the learner's relationship with God. Our educational curricula need to incorporate God explicitly into the curriculum of the educational setting within which we work. It is our responsibility as educators to bring our tradition and its texts to bear on this relationship.
2. Jewish educators should recognise the potential of religious education to enable students to develop their understanding and relationship with God. We therefore need to provide learners with the experiences and subject matter that will facilitate this development.
3. We need to engage in this educational activity throughout the lifetime of our students since it is a changing and developing experience for them. It is a lifelong activity for making meaning.

When Jewish educators come to understand the nature of faith and spirituality as a core human activity expressed through inner and outer forms of meaning making, ritual, symbol, values and language, they will come to know the ongoing search and the means for human growth of all of their students.

The Child as Spiritual Being

A second generation of studies of children's spirituality focused on the expressed spirituality of children themselves, seeking to determine the particular characteristics of the phenomenon in its own natural state. David Hay and Rebecca Nye took a grounded theory approach (Hay & Nye, 1998) in using data collected from interviewing children to guide the construction of a theory that best described how children themselves described their spirituality. They started with the presupposition that the world into which children are socialised (modern Britain, in their case) is often destructive of their spirituality and that children become reluctant to use traditional religious language and symbol to express their spiritual life. Hay and Nye proposed three interrelated categories to describe this self-definition, including (1) awareness sensing as a means to understand present experience; (2) mystery sensing pertaining to wonder, awe and imagination; and (3) value sensing referring to the moral sensitivities of the child. Hay and Nye noted high levels of consciousness exhibited by the children in all of these categories. Nye coined the term 'relational consciousness' to describe a quality of children's spirituality that expresses:

> An unusual level of *consciousness* or perceptiveness, relative to other passages of conversation spoken by that child. (Authors italics) (Hay & Nye, 1998, p. 113)

She further explained this as

> Conversation expressed in a context of how the child related to things, other people, him/herself, and God. (Hay & Nye, 1998, p. 113)

Here the nature of children's spirituality is not divided by age or stage of development. In describing 'relational consciousness', Nye stresses that consciousness implies a degree of awareness in children that allows them to appreciate the wonder of their own mental ability. She goes on to define 'relational' as occurring not in a narrow awareness of those nearest but in a much broader context that allows children to consider their relationship to all sections of their life experience including their personal relationship to the world and to God.

In contrast to Fowler, Nye warns against judging spiritual development in a linear fashion that looks for stages of progress. She urges judgements to be conducted in a more feminine mould that would allow for development 'around collaboration, reciprocity and co-construction' (Hay Nye, 1998, p. 9). Carol Gilligan (1982) had previously identified a clear male gender bias in the theoretical assumptions made by Kohlberg and Fowler in positing an individuative faith as more highly developed than a relational faith.

Two particular characteristics stood out in Hay and Nye's research. The first was the individuality of each child. Relational consciousness was described as a personal signature that pertained to that child. Hay and Nye concluded that educators need to attend to each child's personal style and expression of spirituality if they are to discern their spiritual pathway. The second feature was children's ability to draw upon religious language to make meaning of their discussed experiences. This ability was present despite the fact that many of the children they studied had little or no religious knowledge of a faith tradition. The ability of children to engage in profound philosophical reflections concerning ultimate meaning and value demonstrated the powerful nature of the spiritual child. Hay and Nye pointed out the danger of suppressing this personal signature and capacity for philosophical reflection through use of religious teachings from an organised faith tradition.

Elaine McCreery (1996) entered into conversations with young people that did not involve specific 'God talk' but rather discussed their perceptions and understanding of the world, including birth, death, school, television, etc. She was interested to see the ways in which children themselves used language to express their spiritual understandings and insights. She argued that these personal narratives, constructed out of personal experience, become the framework with which children construct their own spiritual awareness.

Tobin Hart (2003) identified five spiritual capacities through which children's spirituality seems naturally to flow: wisdom, awe/wonder, the relationship between self and other, seeing the invisible and wondering in relation to ultimate questions. Hart maintained that children have a capacity greater than adults to be open to the deep perceptions and wonder in life leading to great joy and insight. Importantly, Hart also argued that young children are not self-centred in this capacity but rather capable of natural empathy and compassion which they express through care and concern for others. Hart therefore posited children as natural philosophers. Though they may not have adult logic and language, Hart considered that children have a capacity for consideration of existential questions of value and meaning.

The emphasis on the individual child and their singular inner life is reflected in the earlier work of twentieth-century Polish educator and humanitarian, Janusz Korczak. Putting himself in the position of the child, he wrote revealingly

> Our language is limited and hesitant (so it seems to you) for it is not completely grammatical. Because of this it seems to you that our thinking is confused and our feelings shallow. Our beliefs are naive for they are not based on bookish learning and the world is so wide ... we live as a nation of dwarves vanquished by giants, by priests who derive their coercive power from the occult. We are an abused class, which you would keep alive in exchange for tiny concessions and very little effort. We are very very complex creatures – taciturn, suspicious and close lipped and the scholar's glass and eye will tell you nothing if you do not believe in us and sympathise with us. (Korczak, 1988)

In his book *When I shall be little again*, Korczak described the mental life of a child in the course of a day. 'He is an Eskimo and a dog, chasing and fleeing from pursuit, a victor and an innocent victim of circumstance, a loving friend and a frustrated mate, a philosopher and a painter, a sportsman and a dreamer' (Korczak, 1988, p. 90).

Korczak dealt with each child individually, recognising his or her special talents and interests and needs. It is for this reason that he rejected any attempt to impose accepted predetermined forms of living and society on the child. He feared the kind of conformity that breeds uniformity, diminishing the individual worth of each child. He strove to discover the optimal conditions for a child's development and growth.

Korczak's view was that childhood is not a period preparatory to life but an essential and integral part of life itself which cannot be measured by its usefulness for adulthood, but is absolutely valued for itself:

> Clumsily we think of the years as of greater or lesser maturity; (yet in truth) no day is immature. There is no hierarchy of age and pain and happiness, hopes and disappointments cannot be graded. (p. 13)

Educational Implications for the Child as Spiritual Being

Placing children at the centre of their own spiritual experience is a key feature of this genre of studies. Jewish educators must get to know the child fully, and understand his or her spirit and unique understanding of the world. They are to acknowledge and respect the child's own perspective while helping the child discover the beauty and sublime values that are within him or her.

A particular methodology for the development of awareness, mystery and value sensing was established by Jerome Berryman (1991) in his work on 'Godly Play' as scriptural story telling within a liturgical framework. *Godly Play* is an innovative approach to biblical story telling that seeks not so much to tell stories in order that children will 'know' them, but as a spiritual action for finding meaning, identity and God through 'wondering'. The pedagogical ideal of this approach is that, from the earliest age, children are invited to experience and become increasingly aware of the spiritual call within sacred stories and of their own deep response as something naturally afforded by religious narrative. *Godly Play* was developed as an outcome of the work of Maria Montessori combined with a contemplative reading of sacred texts (lectio divina). In Berryman's analysis, this is a return to the nonverbal, relational communication system that is foundational to spirituality and with which children started before shifting to a reliance on language. The inner child thus experienced is full of energy, creativity, spontaneity and is deeply centred.

Godly Play uses specially created artefacts and symbolic objects to enable a trained storyteller to powerfully engage children (and adults) in the wonderment of the Hebrew Bible including stories from the Tanach, the lives of the Prophets and some Psalms. It might be considered much more than an 'Encounter' with the text. *Godly Play* is not merely an educational method, but a means also to enact the theology and liturgy of a religious tradition. The time spent together in *Godly Play* is an enactment of a liturgical experience as much as it is a telling of a story. In a similar manner, the Shabbat morning Torah service serves as both liturgical and scriptural in the experience of the worshipper.

Jewish education needs to balance opportunities for spiritual experience with expectations of children. Jewish educators should not only listen to children and their spiritual experiences, but listen for them. As educators begin to hear their students' spiritual narratives, some will be philosophically profound, others unsettling to the perception of adults. All of them will be singular probing questions about the nature of life. This searching is an expression of a child's spirituality and their identity. Educators may encourage children on a philosophical quest but words cannot fully express a spiritual experience, suggesting that play, creativity, stories and music are essential elements of a spiritual education. Rather than encouraging children to become adults, educators should value them as being children.

> The emphasis should not be on teaching children correct or orthodox doctrine about God. Rather the emphasis should be on enriching children's vocabulary and through conversation developing images and concepts which will enable children to grapple at their own level with the issues and experiences involved in God-talk. (Hull, 1990, p. 15)

Relational consciousness of self, others and God needs to include spiritual feelings, thought, attitudes, actions and even fantasies of each individual child. It is about not limiting expression about spirituality to religious vocabulary solely. Third, it is about wonder and wondering, curiosity and openness, mystery and awe such that the child's perceptive abilities in these areas may be crystalline only to be potentially diminished by exposure to closed religious instruction.

Theologies of Childhood

A third approach to understanding the religious views of children and childhood has been prevalent in Christianity through Catholic teachings on Catechesis and Christian doctrines of theological education (Groome, 1980; Moran, 1983). Questions that such theologians ask include: What is God saying to us in the existence of childhood, in the necessity that life must begin with childhood and that all peoples must enter into a time of formation and education? To whom do children belong and who should determine their future and growth?

Childhood therefore is seen not merely as a stage to pass through as the developmentalists would have it, but rather a state of being profoundly spiritual 'a part of our being before God' (Shier-Jones, 2007, p. xii). Theologians of childhood believe that there needs to be a fuller understanding of this state of being and how religion can contribute to the way childhood is shaped and formed. Here there is a distinction to be made between children and childhood. There has been very little theological speculation, especially in Judaism, on the nature of childhood, though thought has been given in the tradition to the moral and spiritual status of the child. The following exploration of a Jewish theology of childhood is compared and contrasted in part with Christian theologies.

The Blessing of Children and the Blessings Children Bestow

The blessings of childhood are reflected in Christian and Hebrew readings of the Hebrew Bible. From a Christian perspective, children are viewed as gifts from God, a sign of God's blessing and a source of joy to parents and the community (Bunge, 2001; Jenson, 2005; Shier-Jones, 2007; Watson, 2007). However, they are also depicted as capricious, ignorant and in need of strict discipline. Children are also considered a great gift in Judaism. Parents who produce children are considered to be blessed and there are many and varied customs and ceremonies to introduce a child into the Jewish community. Just as children are received as a blessing, they, in turn, bless their own parents as well as the larger community as indicated in the concept of *Zechut banim* – through the merits of the children, the parents deserve honour.

The distinct nature of the spirituality of children in Judaism is therefore expressed as a purity of nature and a potential for the highest aspiration of holiness and goodness. Treasured and cherished, Judaism values children and childhood as perhaps the most pure form of being created in God's image (*b'zelem elohim*). A classic passage from the *midrash* illuminates the incomparable status of the child in the very act of God's revelation:

> When God was about to give the Torah to Israel, he asked them, will you accept my Torah? And they answered, we will. God said, give me surety that you will fulfill its ordinances. They said let Abraham, Isaac and Jacob be our pledges. God answered, but the patriarchs themselves need sureties .... Then Israel said, our children shall be our sureties. God said such as these pledges I will indeed accept. Straight away the Israelites brought their wives with their children, even infants at the breast, even babes yet unborn. And God gave them power of speech even to those yet in the womb. He said to them, I am about to give your parents the Torah, will you pledge yourselves that they will fulfill it. They said, we pledge ourselves. Then God rehearsed command after command and to each in succession the children promised obedience. (*Tanhuma Vayiggash*)

This favours comparison with Christian attitudes to children as a blessing and childhood as a sacred and protected state. Marcia Bunge (2001) quotes Christian theologian Kahl Rahner as saying that children have value and dignity in their own right and are fully human from the beginning. They are to be respected, have reverence given to them, held in sacred trust and to be protected. Rahner sees childhood as not just one stage of existence but as a spiritually mature state which is the potential of all human beings and in which there is an attitude of infinite openness and wonder. Talmudic aggadah gives emphasis to this understanding of childhood when stating that childhood is a garland of roses. One rabbi states that the very breath of children is free of sin (Shabbat 119a) while the Jerusalem Talmud pronounces, 'Better are the late fruits we ate in our childhood than the peaches we ate in our old age' (*J.Talmud Peah* 87:4). Children are regarded as the hope for the future in that they have been entrusted to parents as a Divine gift.

What then is the theological purpose of children in the scheme of creation? A famous story from the rabbinic tradition seeks to affirm the purity of God's realm while acknowledging the task of humanity as being growing and learning creatures: Newborn children are contrasted with angels and lowly beasts of the field:

> On the second day of creation, God created the angels with their innate goodness. Then God created beasts with animal instincts not knowing right or wrong. Since God was unhappy with these extremes, God created humanity who would combine characteristics of both angel and beast in order to have free will to follow his good or evil inclination. In order for free will to be truly exercised, the child is made to forget all that he or she has learned as an unborn soul. Before it enters the world, an angel strikes it on the upper lip and all knowledge and wisdom disappear. The ridge in the upper lip is the result of this stroke. (Seder Yezirat HaValad)

From investigation of attitudes in the *Midrash* based on biblical narratives of the childhood experiences of Joseph, Samuel and David, we can see emerge a state of childhood being treasured for a special role. Childhood is seen as a condition of purity and deep spiritual connection especially through awe and wonder of God's creation and Divine purpose. Biblical stories about children demonstrate their ability to see what others cannot as in Joseph's dreams or Samuel's call in the Temple. Childhood is a state treasured in the young and one to be fostered even into adulthood. Invoking the prophet Elijah, harbinger of the Messiah at a boy's circumcision demonstrates that each newborn has the potential to change the world and bring it to completion and perfection. The sublime notion of harmony and perfection as described by the prophet Isaiah incorporates a young child playing with a wolf and lamb, leopard and goat and lion and calf at the end of days.

Ritual and Moral Obligations of the Child

However, there is no single picture of childhood in Judaism and the promotion of childhood to an elevated status in the *aggadic* (narrative) literature is balanced by the *halachic* (legal) treatment of children as minors. Minors do not have obligations or responsibility in contrast to adults. *Halachaic* restrictions are placed on what children can be obliged to do ritually; they are treated differently within Jewish law and practice from adults, particularly in regard to obligations in the public domain. However, there is a strong understanding that the purpose of childhood is to carry out the commandments and learn to enter the world of duty and religious obligation.

The thirteenth-century scholar Maimonides viewed children as unaware of the knowledge of good and evil so that parents are given a fundamental obligation to instil the values which will lead them to choose well while they are yet young. Therefore, children cannot fulfil the commandments for which they have no sense of their moral rightness. These early years are precisely to set children on the right moral path of life based on knowledge of the unique nature of children and their innate qualities and character. Tradition then holds that only at the time of Bar Mitzvah does the 'moral inclination' – *yetzer hatov* – enter the soul (Ecclesiastes Rabbah 69). Now the adolescent is able to make a positive choice in carrying out the commandments and becomes obligated to a greater or lesser extent depending on gender. The spiritual elements of the soul are now in place to carry out the Jewish task of learning and living as an adult.

Study and Learning as Quintessential Childhood Activities

The vital role of learning in fulfilling the purpose of childhood and finally entering the adult world is richly described in Jewish literature. The elaborate ceremonies developed from early rabbinic times continue to this very day with influences from all the cultures and countries in which Jews have lived. The traditional approach to learning was to start with the study of Leviticus and its sacrificial order. The rationale for this priority was that just as sacrifices are pure, so are children . . . 'therefore let the pure learn about the pure' (Leviticus Rabbah 7:3). Children are seen as pure of heart and mind and therefore regarded as potential for ultimate service to God through the priesthood. This is echoed in the story of Samuel who is indentured to the High Priest in the Temple by Hannah, his mother, in thanksgiving for his long awaited birth. His innocence as a child is emphasised in God's call to him in the Temple being the only one who can hear God's voice. Only a child's receptivity has the ability to perceive God's presence and respond to a call for duty and lifetime of service. Samuel as he grows and develops becomes the paradigm for the child's potential as Priest and Prophet teaching others through wisdom and moral conscience.

This innate insight of the boy Samuel leads to the downfall of the High Priest's dynasty and its replacement by prophecy. It is a challenging and potentially transformative state of being. The Christian writer David Jenson (2005) when commenting on Jesus' challenge to his disciples to 'become like children' in the Gospel of Mark (9:37) is not suggesting a comfortable escape into sweet romanticism, but rather it is to open eyes to the violence that surrounds them and to reconnect with God who protects and 'saves'. For Jensen, childhood is not something outgrown, not a time that has been completed but rather a time that remains and indeed comes back to the individual. To enter into childhood is to enter into a state in which the individual is open to expect the unexpected. Learning to become more like children will mean becoming more curious, frank, challenging, hopeful and eager to relate and communicate (Herzog, 2005).

Childhood as Symbolic of God's Relationship with the Children of Israel

The description of the covenanted people in Jewish literature as 'the children of Israel' places these views of childhood on a theological plane. This understanding of childhood (as distinct to the status of the child) becomes reflective of the Divine–human relationship. Even though the People of Israel are often depicted as failing in their duty to fulfil God's mission, nevertheless their status as child to a Divine parent is never questioned. This concept emphasises the unconditional love of parents to children. As children are the fulfilment of their parents' hopes, so Israel is the crowing glory of God's creation. When Rabbi Akiva living under Roman occupation in Judea describes man's belovedness by virtue of being created in the image of God, he emphasises the nature of the child–Divine relationship.

> Beloved is Man for he was created in the image of God. Beloved are the people of Israel for they are called the children of God. Beloved are the People of Israel for a precious tool was given to them with which the world was created. (Mishnah Avot 3:14)

Within humanity as a whole, the Jewish people occupy a special position as the 'children of God'. This love for children is enduring and eternal. Even when children cease to behave, they are still their parents' sons and daughters. Similarly Israel's special position is one that does not change according to Israel's behaviour.

> *You are children to the Eternal One your God* (Deut 14:1). When you conduct yourselves as children you are called children. When you do not conduct yourselves as children, you are not called children. These are the words of Rabbi Judah. Rabbi Meir says: In either case you are called children as it says *'They are foolish children'* (Jer 4:22) and it says *'Children in whom there is no faith'* (Deut 32:20) and it says *'A seed of evildoers; children acting corruptly'* (Isaiah 1:4). Instead therefore of saying 'you are not my children', it shall be said to them *'children of the living God'*. (Hos 2:1) Talmud Kiddushin 36a

The varying conceptions of childhood in Jewish literature encompass a view of children as a blessing but with ritual and moral obligations to grow in learning and in goodness. This is the quintessential task for childhood and entails 'learning to be righteous' (Shire et al., 2006). Childhood is also seen as symbolic of the human – Divine relationship particularly in the relationship of the children of Israel to a parent God. This theological construct is reflective of the way in which the rabbis viewed the exalted and pure nature of childhood.

Educational Implications for a Jewish Theology of Childhood

Judaism's view of learning is not just as a means to train children but to educate them to be engaged in a higher purpose. Thus, the Hebrew word for education is *hinukh* – dedication or commitment. Knowledge of Torah does not necessarily lead to commitment or engagement. Rather, living a life of religious sensibility with a duty to others is the determinant of the pious Jew. For Judaism, education is essentially an ethical activity. Studying, practicing and celebrating Torah is what leads to spiritual renewal and commitment to God's moral purpose for all. The Jewish notion of education is not instrumental in that it seeks to achieve something extrinsic to the learner, rather it is spiritual in that it offers God's vision of goodness for all (Alexander, 2004). Children learning and studying are therefore elevated to the highest connotation and their teachers are perceived as the very guardians of the world in which they live and a security against evil:

> Rabbi Judah Hanasi sent Rabbi Hisda, Rabbi Assi and Rabbi Ammi to traverse the cities of the land of Israel in order to appoint Bible and *Mishnah* teachers. They came to a city and they found no teacher of Bible or *Mishnah*. They said; bring us to the guardians of the city. So they brought them to the senators of the town. They said, 'are these the guardians of the town? They are the destroyers of the town'. Who then, they said, are the guardians of the town? They said the teachers of Bible and *Mishnah*, as it is said; *Unless God guards the city, its watchmen stay awake in vain.* (Psalm 127:1) Pesikta D'Rav Kahana 15:5

Understanding this role for Jewish educators is to conceive of Jewish education as a powerful and compelling task enabling learners to fulfil Judaism's highest aspirations. Childhood becomes a state of being to be cherished and nurtured on which is built a lifetime of insight and formative perception. Robert Coles in deep conversation with four Jewish children saw them being 'soulful in the ways they reveal themselves as spiritual beings' (Coles, 1990). For Coles, spiritual awareness is a universal human predisposition though he did not see this in the same terms as the developmentalists. Coles did not draw theories from the spiritual portraits of the children or generalise to all children. He did however identify a common trait in Jewish children of 'righteous humility' that he felt marks a Jewish spirituality in children:

> In years of work with Jewish children, I have encountered such moments over and over again to the point that I feel it makes up an aspect of the righteousness those children keep espousing, describing, urging upon one another. At its best this is a righteousness that avoids the fatal deterioration of self-righteousness precisely because it is not accompanied by professed certainty. I know exactly what the Lord wants and why he wants it and anyone within my sight or sound of my voice had better take heed. On the contrary, as these four children kept reminding us all "God doesn't let on all his plans but He'd like us to show we trust Him and the best way to do it, is by doing some good while we're here". (Coles, 1990, p. 266)

These Jewish conceptions of childhood encompass a powerful potential to grow in wisdom and goodness. Judaism understands childhood to be both formative and life-long and indeed a paradigm for the holiness and moral purpose of life and symbolic of the human – Divine relationship itself.

Questions for Further Study

Jewish education has drawn upon the general research about the spiritual child and childhood over the past 30 years adopting the language of religious development and spirituality. It has not only adapted some of this research to a Jewish milieu, but also remained sceptical about its place in normative Jewish education. The very definitions of spirituality and spiritual education as appropriate to Judaism continue to draw criticism from Jewish educational thinkers and practitioners.

However, the evolving critique of developmental psychology and the emerging field of childhood studies as an academic discipline demonstrate that the nature of a spiritual life in childhood is worthy of greater understanding. Jewish educators themselves are responding to the common culture of spirituality and seeking to find ways to appropriately and 'Jewishly' incorporate it into Jewish educational settings. Some of these ways may look back to former Jewish methodologies of encouraging piety or enhancing spiritual experience. Others may seek to devise new and appropriate methodologies for Jewish spirituality in education. The following areas of study would provide the field with greater clarity; they would contribute operational definitions and would increase confidence in the place of spirituality in Jewish learning environments:

1. Further study is needed on the wide variety of opportunities for spirituality in Judaism in order that these are authentic expressions of an education for religious growth. Here the question needs to be asked, 'What is the relationship between Jewish religious commitment and inner spiritual awareness?' Concern is often expressed about the evaluation of educational programmes as to their success in enhancing Jewish spirituality? What are the means to assess religious

commitment and spiritual awareness? In light of the need to educate for spiritual awareness, how are educators to be prepared and trained for the work of spiritual pedagogy?
2. Many of the studies mentioned above emphasise the need to listen to and for children's spirituality. Further studies directly with Jewish children would highlight ways in which Jewish childhood is experienced and spiritual issues addressed. What are the formative influences that promote spirituality and how is this to be fostered and nurtured through Jewish educational experiences? Anecdotal evidence suggests that informal-educational settings more readily contribute to heightened spiritual awareness but little is actually known about this. Questions also remain about the predisposition of some children more than others to spirituality and the comparative nature of their sensitivities.
3. The theological construct that suggests Jewish education is essentially 'learning for righteousness' requires further investigation, especially as to the connection between the variables of 'learning' and 'goodness'. What is the connection, if any, between spiritual development and moral development? Does Judaism have a uniquely expressed relationship between Jewish education and commitment? In what ways does Jewish education impact on a developing spiritual and moral Jewish childhood?

These further areas of study may enable Jewish educators to more fully incorporate religious development, the child as spiritual being and Jewish theologies of childhood into their practice. They may also challenge current conceptions of Jewish education as primarily seeking to achieve transmission of a heritage, the construction of identity and the acquisition of knowledge and skills. The new and rich field of inquiry of the spiritual child may transform Jewish education itself.

Bibliography

Alexander, H. (1999). A Jewish view of human learning. *International Journal of Children's Spirituality*, 4(2), 155–164.
Alexander, H. & Glick, S. (2003). The Judaic tradition. In R. Curren (Ed.), *A companion to the philosophy of education*. Oxford: Blackwells.
Alexander, H. (2004). *Spirituality and ethics in education*. Brighton: Sussex Academic Press.
Beck, C. (1989). *Better schools: A values perspective*. New York: Routledge.
Bekerman, Z. (2003). Spiritual exploration: Following my head or my heart? In J. Boyd (Ed.), *The sovereign and the situated self*. London: UJIA.
Berryman, J. (1991). *Godly play*. Minneapolis, MN: Augsburg.
Best, R. (1996). *Education, spirituality and the whole child*. London: Cassell.
Blumberg, S. H. (1991). *Educating for religious experience*. PhD dissertation, Los Angeles: Hebrew Union College.
Buber, M. (1979). *Between man and man*. London: Fontana books.
Bunge, M. (2001). *The child in Christian thought*. Grand Rapids, MI: William B. Eerdmans Publishing.
Cohen, A. (1994). *The gate of light*. London: Associated University Presses.
Coles, R. (1990). *The spiritual life of children*. Boston: Houghton Mifflin.

Cooper, J. (1996). *The child in Jewish history*. Lanham, MD: Jason Aronson.
Feldman, W. M. (1917). *The Jewish child*. London: Bailliere, Tindall and Cox.
Fowler, J. (1981). *Stages of faith*. New York: Harper and Row.
Fowler, J., et al. (1991). *Stages of faith and religious development*. New York: Crossroad Press.
Fowler, J., Nipkow, K., & Schweitzer, F. (1992). *Stages of faith and religious development*. London: SCM press.
Gilligan, C. (1982). *In a different voice: Psychological theory and women's development*. Cambridge, MA: Harvard University Press.
Goldman, R. (1964). *Religious thinking from childhood to adolescence*. New York: Seabury.
Goodman, R. (2003). In R. Goodman, S. Blumberg (Ed.), *Nurturing a relationship to god and spiritual growth: Developmental approaches in teaching about god and spirituality*. Denver, CO: ARE.
Gottlieb, E. (2006, Spring). Development of religious thinking. *Religious Education, 101*(2), 242–260.
Green, A. (Ed.) (1987). *Jewish spirituality* (Vol. 1). New York: Crossroad Publishing co.
Groome, T. (1980). *Christian religious education*. San Francisco: Harper and Row.
Hart, T. (2003). *The secret spiritual world of children*. Novato, CA: New World Library.
Hay, D., & Nye, R. (1998). *The spirit of the child*. London: Fount.
Herzog, K. (2005). *Children and our global future: Theological and social challenges*. Cleveland, OH: Pilgrim Press.
Heschel, A. J. (1966). *The insecurity of freedom*. New York: Farrar, Straus and Giroux.
Hull, J. (1990). *God-talk with young children*. Birmingham Papers in Religious Education No.2, University of Birmingham, Birmingham.
Ibn Pakuda, B. (1978). *Duties of the heart*. Jerusalem: Feldheim Publishers.
Jenson, D. (2005). *Graced vulnerability*. Cleveland, OH: The Pilgrim Press.
Korczak, J. (1988). When I shall be little again. In B. J. Lifton (Ed.), *The king of children*. Washington, DC: American Academy of Pediatrics.
Madge, V. (1965). *Children in search of meaning*. London: SCM Press.
Magnes, I. (1966). *Rituals of childhood: Jewish acculturation in medieval Europe*. New Haven, CT: Yale University Press.
Matzner-Bekerman, S. (1984). *The Jewish child-halachaic perspectives*. New York: Ktav.
McCreery, E. (1996). Talking to god about things spiritual. In R. Best (Ed.), *Education spirituality and the whole child*. Cassell: London.
Mercer, J. A. (2005). *Welcoming children: A practical theology of childhood*. St Louis, MO: Chalice Press.
Mott-Thornton, K. (1998). *Common faith: Education, spirituality and state*. Brookfield, VT: Ashgate.
Miller-McLemore, B. J. (2003). *Let the children come: Reimaging childhood from a Christian perspective*. San Francisco: Jossey-Bass.
Moran, G. (1983). *Religious education development*. Minneapolis, MN: Winston Press.
National Curriculum Council, 1993, April. Spiritual and moral development: A Discussion Paper.
Oser, F. & Scarlett, W. G. (1991, Summer). Religious development in childhood and adolescence. *New Directions for Child Development, 52*, (pp 5–13) San Francisco: Jossey-Bass Inc Publishers.
Roehlkepartain, E. (2006). *The handbook of spiritual development in childhood and adolescence*. Thousand Oaks, CA: Sage Publications.
Rosenak, M. (2001). *Tree of life, tree of knowledge*. Boulder, CO: Westview Press.
Sasso, S. (2001). When your children ask. In J. Erricker, C. Ota, & C. Erricker (Ed.), *Spiritual education: Cultural, religious and social difference: New perspectives for the 21st century*. Brighton: Sussex Academic Press.
Schechter, S. (1938). *Studies in Judaism, first series*. Philadelphia: JPSA.
Shier-Jones, A. (2007). *Children of god*. Peterborough: Epworth.
Shire, M. J. (1987). Faith development and Jewish education. In *Compass*. New York: UAHC.

Shire, M. J. (1998, Winter). Enhancing religiosity in Jewish education. *CCAR Journal: A Reform Jewish Quarterly*, 74–83.
Shire, M. J. (2003). Educating the spirit. In S. Blumberg & R. Goodman (Eds.), *Teaching about god and spirituality*. Denver, CO: ARE.
Shire, M. J. (2006). Learning to be righteous: A Jewish theology of childhood. In K. M. Yust, et al. (Eds.), *Nurturing child and adolescent spirituality*. Langham: Rowman and Littlefield.
Watson, N. (2007). Expecting or on being open to children. In A. S. -J. Angela (Ed.), *Children of god*. Peterborough: Epworth.
Yust, K. M., et al. (2006). *Nurturing child and adolescent spirituality*. Langham: Rowman and Littlefield.

Visions in Jewish Education

Daniel Pekarsky

Introduction

The basic idea, the context, and the animating concerns. Significantly influenced by earlier work on the part of the late Professor Seymour Fox (e.g., Fox, 1973), who was long a lone voice crying out in the wilderness, the last 15 years in the field of Jewish education have featured an interest, more widespread and popular than usual, in the possibility that attention to questions relating to the nature, significance, and purposes of Jewish life is profoundly relevant to the formulation of an adequate agenda for contemporary Jewish education in settings that range from schools, to adult education programs, to so-called informal education programs (e.g., those found in Jewish Community Centers, summer camps, and Israel-experiences). The intuitive idea behind this turn can be articulated both positively and negatively. Positively, the idea is that the use of educational programs and institutions as vehicles for enhancing the robustness and vitality of the Jewish people and Judaism under contemporary conditions (what is sometimes referred to as *the continuity agenda*) is unlikely to be serious and effective unless these initiatives are animated by inspiring educational purposes that speak powerfully to the nature and significance of Judaism. Negatively, the idea is that too often Jewish education has failed to do anything of the kind, being instead a mish-mash of under-developed strands (history, holidays, Bible, *Tfillot* [prayer], Israel, etc.) that are not united by any larger sense of the point of the enterprise.[1] Practiced in this way, as long as the learners are satisfied and come back, the enterprise goes along unchallenged. But even when it proves successful in this limited way, it may well be, as some thoughtful observers have come to believe, that the absence of meaningful content often undermines the long-term effectiveness of Jewish education as judged by the criterion that educators

---

D. Pekarsky (✉)
University of Wisconsin, Madison, WI, USA
e-mail: pekarsky@education.wisc.edu

[1] Similar critiques that emphasize the thoughtless incoherence of the enterprise and the negative consequences for quality-education have also been made in relation to general education. See, for example, Powell et al. (1985) for discussions on this matter.

and communal leaders often take to be bottom-line: whether Jewish life continues to engage the hearts and minds of contemporary Jews who have gone through this kind of an education. Too many of them, it is feared, end up leaving the orbit of Jewish life altogether or engaging with it in increasingly marginal ways (Commission on Jewish Education, 1990).

In the period under consideration, a number of people who identify with this critique have championed the idea that a key dimension of any effort to improve things demands acquainting contemporary Jewish learners, both children and adults, with the profoundly important ideas and practices that are at the heart of Judaism at its best and revealing to these people the potential of these ideas and practices to enrich their lives. This belief has suggested an educational agenda designed to infuse powerful Jewish ideas into the heart of Jewish education; and this agenda has, during this period, often been identified with variants of the term *vision*. As will be discussed below, reliance on this term to flag the relevant concerns and insights is problematic, the reason being that there is a vast literature in arenas that span business, politics, organizational development, and the like, as well as in general education that uses terms like "vision" and "visioning" in extremely varied ways and contexts. I will return to this matter briefly below, but it is pertinent to note at the outset that I will not attempt to discuss all or even most of this literature on this occasion, although some of it may overlap the concerns of this chapter. Rather, I will focus on the relatively narrow set of concerns already intimated, and to be further explained below, with emphasis on the way they have influenced recent debates and research in Jewish education. Moreover, I will adopt as a basis for discussion a version of the vision-lexicon that is grounded in the concepts of *educational vision* (Fox, Scheffler, & Marom, 2003) and *existential vision* (Pekarsky, 2006, 2007)—concepts that I have found particularly useful in exploring and writing about the terrain in question. Generally speaking, an *existential vision* is a *conception of Jewish life at its best* in its individual and social dimensions, one grounded in beliefs about the nature, significance, and/or purposes of Jewish life—ideally, beliefs that are the product of serious reflection that is informed by profound understandings of Jewish ideas, texts, and culture. An *educational vision* is a *thick conception of the entirety of the educational process that is organized around an existential vision*. It is an educational conception that embodies and reflects beliefs concerning the way to encourage the most important and authentic learning (as interpreted through the lens of the relevant existential vision) in the kinds of learners one is likely to encounter (along dimensions like age, background, outlook, interests, motivations, preconceptions, and knowledge-base) in the particular cultural, technological, and economic environment in which the educational process is going to take place. Related to these ideas, *a vision-guided program/institution* is one that embodies, down to its details, an educational vision in the sense just specified; or, more modestly, it is an institution or program that is engaged in a continuing but serious effort to become more fully organized around such a vision, always on the lookout for ways to reduce the gap between actuality and ideal. It is noteworthy that some organizations that are vision-guided in one of the preceding senses (and some would say the best of them!) are also characterized by a willingness to periodically reconsider the adequacy not just of their strategies but also of their most basic purposes and even of their existing guiding existential vision.

Obstacles to progress and a reformulation of the core issues. The agenda of theoretical and practical activity suggested by the challenge of establishing vision-guided education in the sense just intimated has been hard to unfold for more than one reason. For example, not only are some educators and others concerned with Jewish education sometimes intimidated by the challenge of thinking about questions of basic purpose, it is sometimes also difficult to convince them that attention to these matters has the power to advance educational practice in important ways. Historically, they have been more likely to respond positively to those who promise techniques that will keep learners excited or tools that will enhance effectiveness in teaching particular skills and bodies of subject matter. Although less likely at present than in many other periods, exploring questions relating to core Jewish ideas and how views that are responsive to these questions are pertinent to the work of educators has often been viewed as a frill—window-dressing that may adorn "mission-statements" but that is largely a distraction from the serious enterprise of making, implementing, and evaluating educational decisions. Less harshly, due to a variety of circumstances, even when not viewed as a frill, activities organized around such explorations tend to be pursued intensely but only episodically and briefly; and while the conclusions may be of interest, other circumstances and concerns typically interfere with serious efforts at translation into practice.

As already intimated, another obstacle to advancing our thinking about guiding visions in the sense specified above, and one on which I want to focus in this context, is that terms like "vision" and "mission" get used in so many different ways within different research and professional communities within and beyond the world of Jewish education that their capacity to point us toward any particular set of concerns may be dissipated. Thus, in contrast with the cluster of ideas that I have been pointing to with terms that use the word "vision," we find some people using the term to refer to an *organizational* ideal—what our institution needs to become if it is to most effectively and efficiently realize its mission. Even more commonly, we find the term "vision" used by many people as shorthand for a conception (ours or someone else's) of *anything*—be it teaching, a congregation, a school, a curriculum, etc.—*at its best.* There is, of course, nothing inherently wrong with the latter use of the term; indeed, it may do something valuable to the extent that it signals to readers or hearers that the speaker is discussing "the something" in question as it is at its best, i.e., that we have moved into a normative or evaluative context. But to the extent that "vision" gets used in this way, its ability to serve as a shorthand for any specific set of concerns (in the ways that people like the author have sought to use the term "vision" to direct us to concerns relating to the whys and wherefores of Jewish life as they figure in education) is drastically weakened.[2]

---

[2]For a rich discussion of the ways in which definitions, and more generally, language, can both illuminate and confuse educational discourse, see Scheffler (1960).

I make this point for two reasons. The first is to urge that when the reader comes across references to "vision" in conversation, in research, or in other arenas, he or she should recognize the need to seek clarity (through questions or attention to context) about the way the term is being used. The second is to suggest that those interested in focusing the field of Jewish education on the concerns I am indicating with the terms "existential vision" and "educational vision" may want to consider the possibility of dropping the term altogether. The reasoning for this view is straightforward: When language, which is supposed to be a tool that facilitates communication, has the opposite effect—that is, when a term regularly invites confusion and an inordinate amount of energy regularly needs to go into getting beyond this confusion (with no enduring effects beyond the immediate context), it may be reasonable to consider abandoning the term and finding other ways of getting at the matters one wants to address. Indeed, in the present instance, it may well be possible to address the matters that are central to my discussion without recourse to the term "vision." And as a way of re-emphasizing and more fully specifying the terrain in which I am interested in this chapter, I will, before proceeding, now suggest what the pertinent questions would look like if they were articulated without relying on the term "vision":

1. *Basic purposes and outcomes.* In the service of what important and intrinsically desirable Jewish end-states (at the level of the individual and the community) should Jewish education be designed? Related to this, what guiding dreams and aspirations will give the leaders of Jewish educating institutions the energy and the sense of direction to go forward with their various challenges in the face of obstacles and distractions, as well as reasonable criteria for judging success in its most important sense?
2. *Rationale for basic purposes and outcomes. Why* are the outcomes identified in #1 important to encourage? Based on what considerations, Jewish and other texts, ideas, values, etc., should they get singled out as the most important things for us to achieve? *For example*: Are these purposes and hoped-for outcomes more *Jewishly authentic* (in a sense that would require a defensible explanation) than alternative guiding purposes that might be proposed? In what/whose authority are they grounded? More basically, how do a person's views on these matters reflect his/her *personal stance*—what the person stands for—in relation to the indispensable heart and soul of Jewish life?
3. *The practical value of clarity of purpose.* What are the ways in which the achievement of clarity concerning #s 1 and 2 can effectively guide the formulation of aims for, as well as the practices of, Jewish educating institutions like schools and camps and in domains that encompass curriculum, pedagogy, hiring, budget allocations, and educational evaluation?
4. *Creating a change-friendly cultural and organizational infrastructure.* What organizational and cultural considerations, processes, activities, resources, obstacles, etc. need to be attended to if, in any given setting, an overall approach to education is to emerge that is animated by profound purposes and is otherwise sound? And what do educational leaders (professional and volunteer) need to be

able to understand, to be able to do, and to do—what kinds of people do they need to be—if they are to attend to these matters effectively under real-world conditions without burning out in the process?
5. *Ownership of the change-agenda and process.* What constellation of stakeholders in an educating community/congregation needs to "own" or identify with answers to some or possibly all of the matters alluded to above in order for these answers to foster the progress of the educating institution in an effective and ethically justifiable way? Through what kind of activities or processes might such shared understandings (the requisite sense of shared ownership or buy-in) emerge?
6. *The field of Jewish education's need for leadership in this domain.* [For those interested in advancing the agenda of work intimated in the preceding questions by cultivating appropriate kinds of educational leaders, the following question becomes critical:] What kinds of people should be recruited to transform Jewish education so that it is genuinely organized around clear, important, and inspiring purposes? Related to this: By means of what kinds of materials, questions, inquiries, strategies, and activities can these change-agents be helped to achieve sufficient sophistication concerning the matters identified above to proceed effectively with this work?
7. *The skeptic's question.* Is it really true that the practice of education would profit from attention to all of the foregoing questions on the part of educational leaders, programs, and organizations? Are there times and situations in which systematic attention to some or all of these matters is unnecessary or counter-productive?

It may be clear but, in case not, worth noting that the set of concerns I have tried to identify without reference to the "V"-word are equally relevant to education outside the Jewish context—a world in which comparable confusion complicates discussions of "vision." But this matter is beyond the scope of this chapter. My more modest intention in identifying these concerns in the ways that I have is not to illuminate the challenges of general education but to specify the constellation of concerns that I want to explore. And having now done so, I will be using the term "vision" as a short-hand for these concerns.

Against this background, I move on now to indicate some of the more significant streams of research that have been emerging in the terrain under consideration. I will then go on to consider some additional research-challenges that need attention if the field of Jewish education is to take full advantage of the potentialities opened up by the recent interest in encouraging practice that is more vision-guided.

Research Directions to Date

1. *The need for and the nature of guiding visions: conceptual/theoretical pieces.* Some of the research in this domain has sought to clarify the concept of vision and, more importantly, to make the case for educational visions that are grounded in profound ideas concerning the whys and wherefores of Judaism and the Jewish

people. Those writing in this stream of research (e.g., Fox, 1973; Fox et al., 2003; Levisohn, 2005; Marom, 2005; Pekarsky, 1997, 2007; Katzman & Marom, 2007) have focused on the way attention to these matters can bring educators and the communities they serve to an energizing appreciation of why the enterprise of Jewish life and education is worth investing in and the many ways in which this appreciation, if grounded in understanding, has the power to guide and give coherence to educational practice and evaluation. Attention to these matters has also given rise to a variety of related conversations concerning, for example, the sources of worthy visions, the ways in which philosophical ideas might meaningfully be translated into practice (if "translated" is really the right word), whether attention to vision is always necessary or desirable, and various ethical matters that relate to the role of leaders, ordinary people, and others in identifying core religious and/or other ideas that should guide education in a particular community.

2. *Competing visions.* A second line of research has been organized around the challenge of articulating and making available to those deliberating the future of Jewish education powerful but competing understandings of what is most important and worth preserving in Judaism and the Jewish people—understandings which differently embody (interpret, assign value/significance to, prioritize, etc.) key concepts like God, Torah, Israel, Diaspora, and the Jewish people. The concern that has given rise to recent research in this area is twofold. On the one hand, decisions of educational leaders and their communities concerning an appropriate vision to guide their educational efforts should be based on more than activities of simple values-clarification and consensus-building; for too often these activities are grounded in relatively uninformed, idiosyncratic or conventional preconceptions and platitudes concerning the nature of Judaism that the decision makers happen to bring with them by virtue of immersion in a particular community. They should, so it is alleged, have the chance to encounter and wrestle with profound ideas that may challenge and take them beyond their existing understandings.

On the other hand, those deliberating this important matter should not be limited by any single philosophical or other perspective on Judaism that someone—some authority or expert—has predetermined. Rather, this liberal perspective holds that informed choice demands an awareness of more than one serious alternative. On the way to a decision concerning the aims of Jewish education, people should have the chance to embark on a process of thoughtful deliberation that is grounded in an examination of more than one potentially powerful perspective on the nature and significance of Jewish life. The most significant project in this domain to date is embodied in *Visions of Jewish Education* (2003), in which world-class scholars like Professors Menachem Brinker (2003), Moshe Greenberg (2003), Michael Meyer (2003), Michael Rosenak (2003), and Isadore Twersky (2003) thoughtfully lay out informed visions of Jewish life and education representing very different religious and other perspectives, all of them anchored in Jewish culture. Accompanied by discussions of the ways in which commitment to any one of these visions can illuminate the challenges and the design of practice, this book has been playing an invaluable role in helping relevant constituencies that are concerned with strengthening Jewish education in the twenty-first century understand why and how attention to questions of vision can enhance the quality and outcomes of practice.[3]

3. *Examples of vision-guided institutions.* In the spirit of "one picture is worth a thousand words," a number of pieces have been written that attempt to vividly portray specific vision-guided educational programs and institutions (Fox with Novak, 1997; Pekarsky, 2006).[4] Such case studies are intended to convey, at one and the same time, what a guiding vision is, what it might mean for this vision to be embodied in every nook and cranny of institutional life, as well as the power of such a vision to offer those charged with determining the direction of education in a particular context an invaluable, non-arbitrary basis for decision making and evaluation. The animating hope is that, in combination with theoretical pieces that make the case for the practical value of investing time and energy in thinking about "the big questions," such case studies will catalyze a desire on the part of educational institutions and their leaders, as well as those shaping policy for larger communities, to consider embracing a serious "educational visions" agenda.

4. *The process of change.* Attention to the social processes through which new visions emerge and come to be shared, embodied, and institutionalized is, of course, essential if an educating institution is to move toward a vision-guided identity and reality. It is therefore not surprising that another stream of recent and continuing research focuses on the process of change in its social, psychological, and organizational dimensions, often with attention to the role of "the change-agent" in the process (e.g., Aron, 1998, 2000, 2002; Marom, 2003; Schein, 2005, 2009). This work has significantly illuminated the cultural and social realities that need to be taken into account in seeking to encourage the emergence of a focused community agenda that encourages and supports enthusiastic buy-in and its meaningful implementation in an actual organizational setting. This body of research draws from theory but also from a number of change-initiatives, from which researchers continue to learn down to the present. Like some of the work pointed to above, this work was prefigured in some of Fox's early work. In particular, following his own teacher, Joseph Schwab (1970), Fox, in his article "The Art of Translation" (2003), reiterated his view, also stressed in his other writings, that some of the best ideas of all in education, both Jewish and general, have failed to significantly influence practice because of insufficient or naïve attention

---

[3]Powerful guiding visions have also been articulated in relation to the challenges of general education in the United States. See, for example, Dewey (1901); Noddings (1984); Schrag (1995); Nussbaum (1997).

[4]Though not as plentiful as one might imagine, there are also examples of vision-guided institutions in the world of general education, some of which have been written up. The most famous is the school developed by John Dewey in Chicago at the end of the nineteenth century (Mayhew & Edwards, 2007; Dewey, 1901).

to the creation of the cultural, organizational, and intellectual infrastructure that meaningful implementation would demand.[5]

Challenges in Need of Attention

For those (like the author) who believe that the recent, relatively general, interest in matters relating to guiding educational visions is an important but fragile step forward, this is not a moment for complacency—especially since the promise implicit in this development has a long way to go before it is significantly realized, and there is a danger that the interest in vision will prove a passing fad. Below I identify a number of matters that need attention in the field, and on the part of researchers and others, if the desired progress is to be made.

From initial desire to vision-guided practice. As already suggested, in part due to publications that have emerged in the last 20 years and other efforts at conveying the need for guiding visions in Jewish education, many educators and lay leaders have come to believe that attention needs to go into developing and actualizing existential and educational visions with the power to guide practice in their communities and institutions. But because the work is hard and delicate, there is a danger that an institution (or community) that undertakes it on its own and unaided will prove unsuccessful. Among the many worrisome possibilities are the following: the effort may never move beyond a very superficial level; or the process may surface underlying tensions in the community or organization in ways that prove paralyzing or otherwise counter-productive; or it may, for various reasons, lead to a process-undermining sense of frustration or demoralization. To proceed effectively with the challenge of developing and implementing a guiding vision in a way that allows for the necessary kinds of shared ownership and that makes good educational sense may often require a thoughtfully designed, evolving process that is guided by sophisticated good sense. A major part of this challenge is practical: making available to institutions and especially to those who would lead change-efforts the intellectual and human resources that will support, enrich, and guide their efforts. But this practical challenge itself demands continuing research concerning both the best ways to navigate the change-process and the kind of scaffolding that will help those who have decided to embark on it. Marom's *Limud Halimud [Learning Learning]* (2008) offers an example (in Hebrew) of an effort to create such scaffolding in an Israeli context.

This may be the appropriate moment to emphasize the need for a particular kind of research (and practice) agenda, the core elements of which were separately discussed in the preceding section. On the one hand, there has been research

---

[5] Prominent among thinkers outside of Jewish life who have been concerned with the organizational challenges associated with meaningfully introducing powerful ideas into practice include Edgar Schein (1992) and Peter Senge (2006), although it is important to add that Schein, like many others who write on this subject, pays less attention than one might hope to the work an organization needs to do to identify a *worthy* vision (a topic to which I return below).

focused on how to navigate the change process in light of organizational and cultural realities. On the other hand, as also noted earlier, a recent research stream has focused on the identification of varied content-rich visions of Jewish life and education at their best, as well on the associated challenge of identifying a fruitful process for engaging those who are leaders at institutional and communal levels in a serious encounter with these visions, in the service of their arriving at inspiring, content-rich, and profound visions that can guide their efforts. Unfortunately, these two research streams have not sufficiently spoken to each other, and there is a need for dialogue and research that crosses this troubling divide. Specifically, there is a need to think about how to encourage organizations struggling to be more vision-guided not just to devote more, and more content-rich, attention to the challenge of thoughtfully arriving at visions that are rich in powerful Jewish ideas that are also resonant with contemporary needs and sensibilities, but also to do so in ways that are simultaneously sensitive to organizational and cultural realities and needs. Research that focuses on this challenge may play a useful role in helping organizations achieve practice that is meaningfully vision-guided.

A significant part of the needed research would seek, with careful attention to the challenges of practice, to integrate two of the research-streams referred to above: the one concerned with a community's effort to thoughtfully identify and embrace a compelling existential vision (i.e., an understanding of the aims of Jewish education that is anchored in a profound and inspiring conception of the nature and significance of Jewish life) and the one concerned with the cultural and organizational considerations that need to be attended to if an institution/community is to successfully actualize this guiding idea in its practice.

If vision-guided practice is to become more than a dream or a very occasional exception to the rule, it is important that researchers and others pay serious attention to the role of lay people (i.e., the nonprofessional volunteers—especially leaders but also the rank-and-file individuals who are the heart and soul of educating institutions, congregations, and communities) in the move toward vision-guided practice. Too often, the professionals who occupy roles of communal and educational leadership have viewed lay people with mixed feelings: on the one hand, they need their money, their enthusiastic advocacy, and their active participation; on the other hand, there has, historically, been a tendency to view them as being (with significant exceptions) unsophisticated if not ignorant, Jewishly and/or educationally. Fortunately, this situation has begun to change. For one thing, communal and educational professionals have come to realize that the lay community brings a wealth of practical and other kinds of wisdom and expertise to questions of Jewish life and education. Second, even if the older stereotypes contained a measure of truth, through important cultural changes in the Jewish community the lay leadership in contemporary Jewish life has been developing increasing sophistication concerning the nature of Judaism and the challenges of Jewish life. Third, those concerned with change have come to realize that the lay community—both leaders and others—can only become effective ambassadors for new ideas if they genuinely appreciate and have a sense of ownership in relation to these ideas—which may only come about if they play a non-perfunctory role in the institution/community's effort to identify the core ideas that will guide it.

These and other circumstances have begun to foster an important and salutary change in attitude with respect to the role of lay leaders in the process of moving toward vision-guided education. But the promise implicit in this change is unlikely to be realized unless greater clarity is achieved concerning the following basic question: What *is* the appropriate role of lay people in the process of determining the aims and design of a vision-guided educational program or institution? There are both pragmatic and ethical dimensions to this question. Pragmatically, the question is this: If the enthusiastic desire for vision-guided change is to effectively travel a journey that includes the identification of a worthy vision around which to mobilize knowledgeable and enthusiastic support, and an effective effort to actualize it in a meaningful way, what understandings, attitudes, inputs, and involvements are necessary on the part of lay leaders? Ethically, questions cluster around matters like: Who (morally speaking) *should* be deciding on behalf of whom what the guiding Jewish educational vision of an organization or community should be? Whose views should the vision reflect? To what extent, if any, should the views of rabbis and educational leaders carry more moral and intellectual weight in the process than those of others members of the community, and what is it ethical for rabbis and other professionals to do in order to encourage adoption of their favored views? These matters would benefit from the work of thoughtful researchers who are both savvy about organizations and contemporary Jews *and* sophisticated and concerned about ethical matters.

A corollary of this is the need for serious inquiry concerning the way to educate the leaders and the educators who will be called on to encourage and guide vision-guided educational change and practice. Fortunately, a number of significant Jewish educational leadership programs and educator-preparation programs have been seriously engaging with the challenge of educating professionals who will have the requisite competencies and attitudes to do meaningful work in this territory, and some have been writing about what they are learning (e.g., Nisan, 1997; Saks, 2008). Continuing practice-enriched research in this domain will be invaluable. And because, as already suggested, lay leaders must play a central role in the advancement of vision-guided practice, research that illuminates what professionals need for this work needs to be complemented by research, some of it based on past experience and on imaginative pilot projects, that helps the field think about ways in which to encourage and prepare talented *lay leaders* to engage in fruitful ways with the challenges of vision-guided change and practice in their domains of leadership.

The challenge of truth. My discussion of this matter is indebted, most immediately, to conversations with my teacher Israel Scheffler and, more generally, to what might be described as the Socratic perspective on the journey toward human well-being. As is well known, Socrates (e.g., Plato, 1969) took great pains to distinguish his educational agenda from that of the sophists, as he understood them. From his perspective, the sophists were individuals skilled in arts like rhetoric, public speaking, and advocacy who advertised themselves as capable of transmitting these skills to others so that they could more effectively convince others of whatever they wanted to convince them. "We have a powerful weapon," the sophists (as viewed by Socrates) proclaim, "and, for a price, we will pass it on to you to use for whatever purposes you want." To Socrates, this was a superficial and morally repugnant use of language and the human capacity to reason: The challenge, he urged, was not to help people learn how to convince others of their views, but to help them figure out whether their views could withstand genuinely critical scrutiny, to help them move closer to the truth, and, most importantly, to help them acquire the attitudes and intellectual tools that would encourage them to continue on a serious pursuit of true ideas. All of this flowed, of course, from Socrates' conviction that whether or not our beliefs are true (or grow closer to the truth than they have been) makes all the difference, and that it is possible, if not to arrive at final truths in any particular inquiry, to arrive at more adequate beliefs and to realize that one has continuing work to do.

Located within this Socratic tradition, Scheffler (unpublished comments, made in a Mandel-sponsored seminar at Brandeis University, 2005) has pointed to the danger that those championing the idea of vision in Jewish education will limit their efforts to helping educators to clarify their guiding educational commitments and to identify relevant implications for educational practice and evaluation. Not that these efforts are, in his view, unimportant; but they should not displace or compromise another key dimension of what might be called "vision-work." This dimension is organized around the question "Is the vision—the guiding set of intellectual and moral commitments that you champion and want to use as a basis for influencing the lives of individuals and communities—really defensible? Does it pass the test of truth?".

Scheffler and others associated with this view are not naïve about the difficulties of addressing these matters. Among other things, they realize that achieving reasonable epistemological and/or moral warrant for one's ideas cannot be accomplished via any kind of single, obvious procedure, or that it can be established in a knock-down, irrefutable, and permanent way, such that further critical deliberation is beside the point. Indeed, serious questions can and should be asked concerning the criteria that a truer, more defensible, more worthy view would need to satisfy, and the kinds of activity and inputs that are likely to give rise to views that satisfy these criteria. But this is precisely the point I want to emphasize. Serious philosophically grounded research is needed that will illuminate this question—research that can help those who seek to guide Jewish life and education to struggle with the question "How can we best assure ourselves that the key ideas we champion are worthy?"

A related research question concerns why it is that those charged with guiding Jewish communal life and education—including many of those charged with cultivating educational leaders—often shy away from serious engagement with these basic questions concerning the intellectual and moral warrant for the agendas they believe important. More than one possibility suggests itself: is it, for example, because they fear or believe that there is no way of making progress in the direction of truth and worthiness—that, in the spirit of relativism, all views are on a par and that the most anyone can reasonably hope for is that they will become clear enough to guide practice in a systematic and/or consistent way? Is it because it will be thought socially awkward, insensitive, offensive, or divisive to put serious challenges to people who have struggled to articulate their heart-felt understandings and commitments—understandings and commitments that may be inseparable from their personal identities? Or might it be because the social and/or cultural powers-that-be have settled views about the commitments to be emphasized and do not want to create situations in which these views, like others, will be submitted to genuinely critical thinking that might call the worthiness of these views into question? Perhaps none of these hypotheses is meritorious, and perhaps, to different degrees in different circumstances, some or all of them are—and, of course, there might be other hypotheses that we have not identified. Research into these matters, in this case not philosophical but perhaps sociological and social psychological, may have significant potential to illuminate some of the field's difficult, practical challenges.

The dance of theory and practice. Debates concerning the best way to organize Jewish education are often contaminated by an undercurrent of tension. At the risk of caricature, here is how the situation might be described: On the one side, a cultural/intellectual elite made up of people whose lives have been profoundly shaped by a lifetime of immersion in and inquiry concerning significant spheres of Jewish culture sense that in the typical situation, well-intentioned, but poorly educated practitioners set about the education of new generations of Jews in hackneyed, conventional ways that reflect ignorance, misunderstandings, and criteria of success that have more to do with keeping learners satisfied and coming back than with any more serious agenda. As far as this elite is concerned, Jewish life will be more vital, robust, and meaningful if Jewish education is organized around the kinds of powerful Jewish ideas to which they have access—ideas which, unfortunately, have been marginalized, if not completely lost sight of, by those usually charged with the challenges of Jewish education. Hence, their strong desire to influence the field. It is important to add that, in many cases, the hope animating these people is not that their particular beliefs concerning the nature of Judaism and its major challenges will be adopted but that those who will shape the direction of practice will decide their fundamental direction based on a serious encounter with a range of possibly competing ideas. The point—and the challenge as understood by those who have championed the need to infuse Jewish education with serious ideas—is to ensure that the work of Jewish educators is informed by profound (*relevant* and *authentic* are often code-words here) Jewish ideas that go beyond what, so these critics believe, those who typically set and enact the agenda for Jewish education can be assumed to possess under contemporary cultural circumstances.

On the other side, practitioners sometimes resent what feels like the smug and patronizing (top-down) attitude of the other group. Not only, they feel, is this elite of intellectuals out of touch with the challenges of practice in the contemporary world, they do not recognize that the practitioners and lay leaders often embody in their hearts, minds, and work profoundly important intuitions concerning the nature and direction of Jewish life and education—an idea captured in the phrase "the wisdom of practice" (and of ordinary people). Associated with this outlook is the belief that long before the intervention of the elites, practice was already (as it continues to be) saturated with profound ideas—ideas that may be as worthy if not more worthy than those that these patronizing intellectuals bring to the allegedly boorish masses.

In the spirit of John Dewey (1901, 1963), the unhealthy tension just described calls on those interested in improving Jewish education to consider the possibility that important truths lurk in both perspectives just articulated, and that serious inquiry would help us understand what these truths are and how they might be meaningfully honored in our approach to the field's development. More generally, there is a continuing need to better understand the nature and value of a fruitful *interplay* in education (both Jewish and general) between practice, on the one hand, and the world of big ideas and theory, on the other. In the effort to respond to this need, university-based researchers, in particular, would do well to take more account than we usually do of the views of thoughtful philosophical conservatives like Michael Oakeshott (1962) who believe that the world of practice is much richer with finely integrated and invaluable, if not always articulated, ideas and intuitions than intellectuals and others typically realize. In entitling this section "The dance of theory and practice" I mean to suggest as an hypothesis for this inquiry that the relationship between theory and practice in Jewish education is, at its best, a dynamically changing non-hierarchical, web-like interplay of ideas and practice, enriched by continuing evaluation that regularly introduces the need for adjustments, big and small, throughout the entire system. As those familiar with the relevant fields can attest, these ideas have long been articulated within domains like the philosophy of science and ethics, and they have also been sometimes been voiced in Jewish education by thinkers like Fox and Schwab. But precisely because these ideas are, at a cost to progress in Jewish education, often only honored in the breach, they need continuing attention on the part of researchers and others whose work may have the power to influence Jewish communal life and education. Their challenge is to help interested individuals and organizations think productively about how to overcome the generally false and counter-productive divides between theory and practice, "intellectuals" and "practitioners," and "visionaries" and "implementers."

Conclusion

This chapter has been guided by several purposes. One of them is to identify a constellation of ideas that relate to what I have referred to as existential and educational visions, and I have tried to suggest why attention to these matters has been thought important for the advancement of Jewish life and education. I have also sought to indicate some obstacles that have attended the effort to advance vision-guided Jewish education, with special emphasis on the ways in which the language of vision, as currently employed, has itself sometimes ill-served those who have sought to communicate the importance of the terrain in question. Against this background, I have sought to identify major directions of recent research, as well as to signal some directions worthy of further inquiry. Since I identify strongly with the idea that Jewish education needs to be organized around guiding visions that give pride of place to powerful ideas concerning the potentialities and significance of

Judaism and Jewish life, I also believe strongly that the challenges herein identified deserve serious attention. As many readers may know, we live at a time when many thoughtful people are proclaiming that Jewish educational practice and policy are insufficiently driven by *empirical* data concerning what Jewish education looks like "on the ground" and the effects of different variables, practices, and policies on educational outcomes, and I fully agree about the importance of these kinds of empirical research. At the same time, it is important that we not lose sight of the need for continuing research, much of it more philosophical, that focuses on questions of basic educational purpose, including the matters raised in this chapter and associated with the concept of guiding visions.

References

Aron, I. (Ed.). (1998). *A congregation of learners: Transforming a synagogue into a learning community*. New York: Union of Reform Judaism.
Aron, I. (Ed.). (2000). *Becoming a congregation of learners: Learning as a key to revitalizing Jewish life*. New York: Union of Reform Judaism.
Aron, I. (2002). *The self-renewing congregation: Organizational strategies for revitalizing congregational life*. Woodstock, VT: Jewish Lights Publishing.
Brinker, M. (2003). Jewish studies in Israel from a liberal-secular perspective [With supplement by editors]. In S. Fox, et al. (Eds.), *Visions of Jewish education* (pp. 95–121). Cambridge, England: Cambridge University Press.
Commission on Jewish Education. (1990). *A time to act*. New York: University Press of America.
Dewey, J. (1901). *The child and the curriculum/the school and society*. Chicago: The University of Chicago Press.
Dewey, J. (1963). *Experience and education*. New York: Collier Books.
Fox, S. (1973). Towards a general theory of Jewish education. D. Sidorsky (Ed.), *The future of the American Jewish community* (pp. 260–271). Philadelphia, PA: Jewish Publication Society.
Fox, S. (2003). The Art of Translation. In S. Fox, et al. (Eds.), *Visions of Jewish education* (pp. 253–294). Cambridge, England: Cambridge University Press.
Fox, S. with Novak., W. (1997). *Vision at the heart: Lessons from camp Ramah on the power of ideas in shaping educational institutions*. Jerusalem: Mandel Institute.
Fox, S., Scheffler, I., & Marom, D. (Ed.). (2003). *Visions of Jewish education*. England. Cambridge University Press: Cambridge.
Greenberg, M. (2003). We were as those who dream: An agenda for an ideal Jewish education [With supplement by editors]. In S. Fox, et al. (Eds.), *Visions of Jewish education* (pp. 122–148). Cambridge, England: Cambridge University Press.
Katzman, A. & Marom, D. (Fall 2007). Introduction to the Hebrew Edition of Visions of Jewish Education—Medabrim Chazon. *Journal of Jewish Education, 73*(2), 107–113.
Levisohn, J. A. (2005). Ideas and ideals of Jewish education: Initiating a conversation on visions of Jewish education. *Journal of Jewish Education, 71*(1), 53–66.
Marom, D. (2003). Before the gates of the school: An experiment in developing educational vision from practice. In S. Fox, et al. (Eds.), *Visions of Jewish education* (pp. 296–331). Cambridge, England: Cambridge University Press.
Marom, D. (2005). Theory in practice. In M. Nisan & O. Schremer (Eds.), *Studies in education dedicated to Shlomo (Seymour) Fox* (pp. 51–70). Jerusalem: Keter Publishing House and Mandel Leadership Institute.
Marom, D. (2008). *Limud HaLimud [Learning Learning]: A pedagogical handbook for pluralistic Beit Midrash educators in Israel [In Hebrew]*. Jerusalem: Mandel Foundation and Hamidrasha Cetner for Jewish Renewal in Israel.

Mayhew, K. K. & Edwards, A. K. (2007). *(Re-issued). The Dewey school.* New Brunswick, NJ: Aldine Transaction Publishers.
Meyer, M. (2003). Reflections on the educated Jew from the perspective of reform Judaism [with supplement by editors]. In S. Fox, et al. (Eds.), *Visions of Jewish education* (pp. 149–177). Cambridge, England: Cambridge University Press.
Nisan, M. (1997). *Educational identity as a primary factor in the development of educational leadership.* Jerusalem: The Mandel Institute.
Noddings, N. (1984). *Caring.* Berkeley: University of California Press.
Nussbaum, M. (1997). *Cultivating Humanity.* Cambridge, MA: Harvard University press.
Oakeshott, M. (1962). *Rationalism in Politics.* London, England: Metheun.
Pekarsky, D. (1997). The place of vision in Jewish educational reform. *Journal of Jewish Education, 63*(1–2), 31–40.
Pekarsky, D. (2006). *Vision at work: The theory and practice of Beit Rabban.* New York: Jewish Theological Press.
Pekarsky, D. (2007). Vision and education: Arguments, counter-arguments, Rejoinders. *American Journal of Education, 113,* 423–450.
Plato. (1969). Meno. W. K. C. Guthrie. trans. The Collected Dialogues of Plato. Princeton, NJ: Princeton University Press. 353–384.
Powell, A. G., Farrar, E., & Cohen, D. K. (1985). *The shopping mall high school.* Boston: Houghton Mifflin.
Rosenak, M. (2003). Educated Jews: Common elements [With supplement by editors]. In S. Fox, et al. (Eds.), *Visions of Jewish education* (pp. 178–218). Cambridge, England: Cambridge University Press.
Saks, J. (2008). *Spiritualizing Halakhic education: A case-study in modern orthodox teacher development.* Jerusalem: Mandel Foundation.
Scheffler, I. (1960). *The language of education.* Springfield, IL: Charles C. Thomas.
Schein, E. (1992). *Organizational culture and leadership.* San Francisco: Jossey-Bass.
Schein, J. (2005, Spring). "In Search of Bezallel: Can Educational Craftsmen and Visionaries Live in the Same Place?" Jewish Education News. CAJE.
Schein, J. (2009). "The Pedagogy of Teaching Vision." (Unpublished) To appear on the Mandel Foundation Website and currently under journal review.
Schrag, F. (1995). *Back to basics.* San Francisco: Jossey-Bass.
Schwab, J. (1970). *The practical: A language for curriculum.* Washington, DC: National Education Association.
Senge, P. (2006). *The art and practice of the learning organization.* New York: Doubleday Paperback Edition.
Twersky, I. (2003). What must a Jew study – and why [with supplement]. In S. Fox, et al. (Eds.), *Visions of Jewish education* (pp. 47–94). Cambridge, England: Cambridge University Press.

Section Two: Teaching and Learning

Introduction

Teaching and learning are the essential processes of education. The chapters in this section explore the nature of teaching and learning in Jewish education from 14 different perspectives, focusing on aspects of curriculum, instruction and learner engagement. Our authors have explored elements of curriculum as a body of knowledge to be transmitted and as an attempt to achieve certain ends in the learners. There is also a strong thread running through these chapters which shows the relevance of curriculum as process. Curriculum is not just a physical set of objectives but rather the interaction of teacher, learner and knowledge. While the emphasis throughout is on current educational models, these chapters also look at the possibilities and challenges of change and development. Throughout, the chapters explore teaching and learning through the lens of Jewish-educational research.

A recurring theme in these chapters is the impact of aspects of teaching and learning on the individual lives of the learners. Whether it is through learning a language with the intent to facilitate integration into society, as Nava Nevo explores, or through the growing interest in Jewish life-cycle education, as examined by Howard Deitcher, it is clear that the themes in these chapters play a critical role in shaping individual Jewish lives. As both Nevo and Deitcher show in their analyses of subject matter structured by shared commonplace components but conceived for widely different curricular purposes, the context of Jewish education (in Israel and the Diaspora, in orthodox and liberal religious settings) makes as sharp a difference to the content of Jewish education as do the needs of the learners in view, whether children or adults.

Our relationship to community is also explored in other chapters of this section of the *International Handbook*. Several authors touch upon the relationship between Jewish-travel education and community. Travel in general, as a Jewish-educational tool in contemporary-Jewish education, is explored by Erik Cohen. More specifically, Scott Copeland observes the centrality of Israel travel in the development of Jewish communal life. Similarly, in another chapter on travel, Jeremy Leigh draws on empirical research to address elements of community. This perspective is challenged by David Mittelberg, who argues for Jewish peoplehood education, asserting that today, Jewish youth seem to feel in little existential need to belong to the Jewish collective, whether local or national. Hence, he argues for focused attention on Jewish-peoplehood education in order to cultivate a stronger sense of belonging. Mittelberg's peoplehood paradigm has some resonance with Leigh in that both consider how travel can instil in young people a need for belonging. Both Leigh and Mittelberg also pose research questions designed to move this particular discourse forward. In turn, they respond to difficult questions posed by Erik Cohen in earlier important work in this field. Copeland and Mittelberg both also cite Michael Rosenak's works, whose philosophical explorations of both the paradigm of Jewish peoplehood and the thick cultural context around community show a variety of interpretive possibilities. For Jewish students and teachers coming to Israel, exposure to the tough issues facing Israeli society, with all of their complexities and heterogeneity, is a challenge towards engagement with the possibilities of exploring Jewish and non-Jewish literatures in debate. Jewish peoplehood fuels the continuing search for shared meaning within the current ambiguity and ambivalence that Jews face both in Israel and abroad.

Travel gives us an opportunity to recall the past and link that past to our present through experiential means. In their chapter on teaching Jewish history, Benjamin Jacobs and Yona Shem-Tov look at how recalling, reviewing and remembering the past plays a central role in most Jewish schools. They are interested in the formal curriculum and their chapter focuses on the main orientations towards Jewish history education today – identification, group citizenship, moral response, integration and adjustment, and intellectual pursuit. Again the two themes of individual Jewish identity and community identity feature in their work.

Holocaust education is frequently placed within the history curriculum, although it is considered a field of inquiry on its own. In her chapter, Simone Schweber explores the current state of Holocaust education and asks what might Holocaust education do if conceptualised not from the standpoint of building nations or concretising collective memory but as a project of global citizenship and human understanding. Again, the notion of what it means to be part of the Jewish people and where Jews situate themselves among other peoples resonates with themes explored by Mittelberg, Cohen and Leigh.

Part of the challenge of looking outwards and placing the Jewish community within the wider community in a teaching and learning framework concerns the approach taken towards religious plurality in Jewish schools. Michael Gillis acknowledges that teaching other religions as an integral part of Jewish education is an uncommon practice, both in Israel and most of the Diaspora. In many countries, the reality of plurality has prompted a re-thinking of the teaching of religion in general education. Using Israel, Britain and America as the sites through which to explore this issue, Gillis argues that not only is there no incompatibility between learning about other religions and Jewish education, but also that such learning can be viewed as a necessary part of a Jewish education.

Subject matter knowledge acquisition is a central aim of education and Barry Holtz explores the nature of Bible education in contemporary Jewish education through an examination of the history of Jewish Bible interpretation, reflecting the content of Bible teaching. He explores these distinctions by researching various curricular projects and pedagogies. His chapter concludes by looking at research which draws upon work in pedagogical content knowledge and specific orientations to subject matter, exploring the implications of this scholarship for Bible teaching.

Using a model for encouraging critical thinking in Talmud pedagogy indicates to students that such a mode is internal to Jewish tradition. The chapter by Marjorie Lehman and Jane Kanarek shows how rabbinic texts can be interrogated and put into conversation with one another, and how through Talmud study students can question their teachers. Questions provoke anxiety, and debate fosters intellectual growth. But, at the root of this inquiry is a desire to embed rabbinic tradition in the hearts and minds of its participants. When this model is followed, whereby conversations are rooted in a set of authoritative texts, students are asked to learn to speak a specific language and to think along with a particular tradition.

Whilst cognitive curricular areas traditionally focus on intellectual growth, as expounded by Holtz, Lehmann, and Gillis, the arts provide questions and concerns for both Jewish education and educational research. In this section of the *International Handbook*, two chapters explore contemporary issues relating to Jewish arts education. In the first, Robbie Gringras explores what he terms as the 'seam-line' between education and art. He explores the questions and concerns that engage educators interested in creating culturally significant meaning, encoded in an affecting and sensuous medium. Using song, literature and poetry to illustrate his argument, Gringras suggests, from his place within Israel, that art can be a significant aspect of any Jewish curriculum, particularly in the informal sector.

Ofra Backenroth takes a different, and Diaspora-oriented, perspective as she focuses on the value of the arts in the formal Jewish education system, where, in the context of a dual curriculum, they must wrestle for time and budget. She examines the goals, content and methodology of how the arts are being taught in today's Jewish day schools in North America. Both she and Gringras call for a continuum of curricular integration, where the teaching of the arts ranges from arts as discrete disciplines to multidisciplinary integration.

Finally, this section focuses on two aspects of teaching and learning that are very much twenty-first-century additions to the field, namely the environment and technology. Of course, an interest in caring for the environment has been a Jewish concern since the earliest times. In the Bible, in *Bereshit* (Genesis 2:15), humanity is called upon as stewards put on this earth to look after it, but in the twenty-first century, caring for the environment has taken on new and acute significance. For Eilon Schwartz, that there is no academic field of Jewish environmental education today, mirrors the peripheral status of environmentalism within the Jewish-educational establishment, and within society in general. Shwartz proposes that like so many shifts in educational theory and practice, change in public consciousness and political will not come from the top-down, but from the bottom-up. It will come from a growing field of educational innovators whose central challenge will be to take their intuition as to what needs to change, and transform it into a reflective educational practice. The Jewish future, he suggests, depends on the collective ability to re-imagine educational and communal institutions, and to build a Jewish community where continuity does not begin and end at the Jewish doorstep as if Jewish existence lives apart on the only planet on which humanity has been created to live.

Brian Amkraut's chapter is no less grounded in a sense of the current historical moment. Amkraut writes about the digital era and shows how perspectives on Jewish continuity in general and approaches to Jewish education in particular are now, and will continue to be, shaped by a new world in which traditional notions of authority, community and identity are challenged and redefined. As Schwartz does in his chapter with reference to environmentalism, Amkraut argues that embrace of new technologies does not only call for extending the subject matter of Jewish education, it calls for thinking anew about its purposes and practices, texts and contexts.

In summary, this section of the *International Handbook* explores both subject matter and transmission of that subject matter, formal and informal curricular opportunities, the cognitive and the affective, and traditional and new areas of teaching and learning for the Jewish education academic and practitioner. It promises to engage theorists and practitioners, scholars and students.

Helena Miller
Lisa D. Grant
Alex Pomson

Art: Educating with Art Without Ruining It

Robbie Gringras

Introduction

In education circles it has become fashionable to state that "Art is a text." This is a deceptively problematic statement. It signals, on the one hand, the educator's admirable desire to broaden horizons and to allow for non-prose and non-academia to play a role in the educative process. In this sense, the statement is to be welcomed. On the other hand, as T.S. Eliot pointed out, "Form is content, and content is form." The form of the statement, its language, reveals its hidden message. While granting art some educational "status" by naming it as text (as opposed to an irrelevant ornament!), at the same time describing art as "text" co-opts art as a form of education. According to this formulation, art is not something else entirely, it is "just" another kind of text. This is problematic, because it encourages a misunderstanding of the nature of art and its ambivalent relationship with education. We as educators need to work a little harder before we so smoothly grasp art to our bosom.

So how should we understand art? What is it about art that makes it a different "animal" from education? How may we navigate the differences between the two, in a healthy way?

We might sketch out the parameters of our work by trying to understand what it is we mean by "art." The academic and artistic worlds abound with definitions of art. All of them contain differing amounts of truth, many are obscure, several incomprehensible, a few simplistic, others deep. In the end we should draw on the definition that helps us move beyond the philosophizing, and into work. A suggested beginning is a definition of art offered by Richard Anderson:

> Art is [1] culturally significant meaning, [2] skilfully encoded in an [3] affecting and sensuous medium. [my numbering] (Anderson, 2004)

This definition, that may be split into three distinct values, offers us an accessible way to understand the unique nature of art and points to the role of the educator in developing the receptive audience. The definition does not offer a sealed

R. Gringras (✉)
Makom, Jerusalem, Israel
e-mail: robbieg@jafi.org

contradiction-free litmus test of what is art. It calls for judgment and exploration of how these values may be interpreted in our work in Jewish education.

Culturally Significant Meaning

The educator's first choice when working with art in an educational context is to decide what song, or book, image, or film, contributes to the overall educational aim. In Jewish education, what guidelines do we have for ourselves when searching for something of culturally significant meaning? We might perhaps set a baseline for a piece of art that contributes something significant to Jewish culture. In so doing, we begin the process of narrowing down our options, while, at the same time, opening up a can of worms. For when was the last time anyone succeeded in defining Jewish culture in any inclusive and persuasive way?

While not presenting an overarching cultural theory, Asaf Inbari wrote an article several years ago (Inbari, 2004) critiquing the way in which Israeli culture detaches itself from what he would define as Jewish culture. He takes a swipe at two "camps," and in so doing reveals our goal. He suggests that Jewish culture should address the experience and understanding of Jewish life in the present, while taking into account the traditions and approaches of the past. Those cultural "cultivators" who are unable or unwilling to make this connection should be understood as being outside Jewish culture:

> The cultivators [of Jewish culture] understand the present as the continuation of a living flow. Time, for them, is a river, not a puddle... The neglecters, on the other hand, stagnate in the puddle of mono-dimensional identity, secular and religious... The former live in a present with no past, and the latter in a past with no present. Both of them spend their lives throwing mud at each other from the bottom of the puddle. (Inbari 2004)

An ultra-orthodox approach to Jewish culture, that would prefer automatic reverence for past expressions of culture without addressing the present day context, is, in Inbari's understanding, living "in a past with no present." The more secular Jew who creates with no reference to past Jewish expressions is "living in a present with no past."

That which has culturally significant meaning addresses the connection between the Jewish past and present. The music of Jeremiah Lockwood's New York-based Sway Machinery (Machinery) is a fascinating example of art that splashes noisily in the river of Jewish culture. Lockwood's style combines the craziness of a David Byrne, his grandfather's chazanut (cantorial singing), and the challenging doom-laden tone of a Maggid on drugs. Lockwood's contribution to Sway Machinery draws on detailed and loving research into Jewish cantorial traditions, and a post-punk klezmer-like fusion.

Some would easily classify Sway Machinery's music as firmly in the "river" of Jewish culture. An extremely talented and internationally acclaimed Israeli pop star, Asaf Avidan (Avidan), creates Janis Joplin-like rock laments. Yet, he sings in English and makes little reference in content or style to anything Jewish or for that matter, Israeli. Far from being in the puddle or the river, we might say that

Asaf Avidan does not feel the need to even get his feet wet... But a song by Mook E (a well-known Israeli performer) asks more questions of us. *The Earth Weeps* (Mook E) laments immoral behavior, and, in particular, man's detrimental impact on the environment. Musically, the song is a mixture of folk protest and rap. The language is Hebrew, peppered with occasional phrases that refer to a shared Jewish past ("We were once slaves/Apparently so we will remain"). According to a simplistic expectation of a Jewish song that it either sound like synagogue or klezmer, then Mook E's song is not "culturally significant" for us. But if we were to ask to what extent the song swims in the flow of the Jewish river of culture, we might emerge with alternative and more fruitful answers.

Important here are not clear-cut differentiations, but the dimensions of the argument. "When a tradition is in good order it is always partially constituted by an argument about the goods the pursuit of which gives to that tradition its particular point and purpose... A living tradition ... is a historically extended, socially embodied argument" (MacIntyre, 1981). When we begin to argue about the location of a piece of art in the river or the puddle of Jewish culture, one can be confident our tradition is alive!

Extending the Canon

Inbari also frees us from the assumption that a Jewish text or artifact must be so defined according to the extent to which it draws on *Torat Yisrael*. *Torat Yisrael* is a phrase that refers to Jewish traditional practice, learning, and text. A Jewish piece of art in this sense would be one that draws on or makes specific reference to *Torat Yisrael*. The more mature among us may cite Leonard Cohen's adaptation of the *piyut* (hymn) *Unetane Tokef* (Cohen), while the under 30-year-olds would draw our attention to Matisyahu's song Jerusalem (Matisyahu) ("If I forget you, let me right hand forget what it suppose' to do ...").

Inbari suggests that there is another source of inspiration for Jewish creativity: that which emerges not necessarily from *Torat Yisrael*, but from Jewish *experience*. When Primo Levi wrote about the Holocaust, he did not necessarily make reference to the Torah. And yet a creation that speaks to the experience of Jews in the world, this is a text of *Am Yisrael*—the People of Israel—and as such, Inbari would suggest, has its place in the river of Jewish culture.

Limmud Jewish Education Conference in the UK once famously hosted the Israeli funk/rap band HaDag Nachash. Though the performance was a great popular success, the leadership of Limmud was ambivalent about the band's place at the conference. They felt the music was "not Jewish enough"—that it spoke to the Israeli experience, and not to the Jewish world. Limmud's leadership at the time saw *Torat Yisrael* as the key identifier for Jewish music. Inbari would push them to check themselves. Bearing in mind that Israel is the Jewish State, populated by a significant majority of Jews, might not art created from and about this context be seen as emerging from *Am Yisrael*?

Choosing According to Priorities

Having developed a broad definition of what we mean by art that is culturally significant, and expanded our horizons beyond *Torat Yisrael*, we can feel confident we will choose the "right" pieces of art to present to our students. We shall work with art that has "culturally significant meaning."

The next question is to what extent does this cultural significance present itself in the experience of the art itself, and how much should the educator impart?

If the educator is mainly interested in encouraging the student to interpret the piece of art individually and freely, with little necessity to refer to the cultural significance of the art, then one need not necessarily impose any criteria. But if we are suggesting that there is learning to be done from an encounter with a piece of art, then we need to enter into the *discourse of meaning* that is constructed through a partnership between the artistry and the audience. Some art, such as popular film, ventures deep into the discourse of meaning, in that it will add narration, emotional soundtracks, full scenery, and make-up. Other art is performed live, with the possibility of a mutual dialog over the event developing with the audience as it unfolds. Other arts, such as the plastic arts, will often leave far more room for the interpretation of the audience.

Teachers, who wish their students to understand the cultural significance of the art with as little mediation from the educator as possible, should choose art forms that are most active in the discourse of cultural meaning about the work itself. For example, the opening scene of *Fiddler on the Roof* (Tradition) provides the viewer with an historical, sociological, economic, and religious context to the trials of Tevye, the central character in the story. The narrative form and clear use of camera work indicate to us that Tevye is our central character, through whose tribulations we are expected to experience the film, and the music—both sung and background—works to influence our emotional preferences. Exposition and contextualization is built into the art form itself. As a result, ignorance of Eastern European Jewish life is no barrier to an audience picking up the cultural significance of the film.

By contrast, a Chagall painting offers hints, but does not enter into the contextual conversation in anything like such a proactive way. An outsider or newcomer to Jewish culture would gain little of substance from certain Chagall paintings, without some form of explanation or information external to the painting itself. For example, a well-visited site celebrating Chagall's work refers to The Blue Violinist (Chagall). The interpretation of this ethereal and celebratory *Fiddler on the Roof* that is offered by the site's creator makes absolutely no reference to Jewish culture, other than the acknowledgment that the background features a Jewish village (Paintings). Without an educator or Jewish art critic pointing out the almost direct visual reference to Shalom Aleichem, the uninitiated would have no reason to assume a Jewish aspect to the painting. By contrast, the same art lover would not be able to leave a screening of *Fiddler on the Roof* without knowing a great deal about Jewish shtetl life—for the genre is far more active in the discourse of meaning.

Culturally Significant Meaning—Summary So Far

Our choices of art can thus be guided by Inbari's river/puddle "rule of thumb," so that we may choose art that is culturally significant to our Jewish educational aims. Our choices also may be guided by the extent to which we search for art forms that are more or less involved in the discourse of their own meaning.

Once these choices have been made, we are then faced with the key challenge for the educator: when, in what fashion, and to what extent do we wish to explicate for our students the cultural significance we judge the piece of art embodies? How much do we feel we need to "feed" our students with context, or information? How much information or processing is enough? When should this work be done—before, during, or after experiencing the art? What pedagogy should we use?

We shall address all these questions later, after having tackled the other two key phrases in Anderson's definition: "skilful encoding," and "moving and affecting." Appreciation of these two phrases will aid us in our decisions.

Skillfully Encoded

When an observant Jew enters a house, she does not make a speech about her connection to the history of the Jewish people. She does not quote from Deuteronomy, nor does she attempt to explain her emotional connection to her Jewish roots. She most certainly does not express her fear of demons, her belief in the divine, or talk about the feeling of security she has on entering a house that may not be her own. She probably would not tell us all about the tenth plague in Egypt. She will simply reach out her hand, touch it gently to the decorative mezuzah on the doorpost, and then kiss her hand.

This evocative combination of movement and the visual arts that says so much with such concision and beauty is an excellent example of "skilful encoding." Beyond the physical skills involved in the calligraphy of the rolled-up text, the design of the mezuzah casing, and the development of Jews' touching the mezuzah and then kissing their hand—the gesture itself skillfully refers to deep expressions without spelling them out in harsh prose. Touching a mezuzah and kissing one's hand has symbolism and depth: It leaves room for interpretation, for individual intention, for the echoes of history. As such, an educator attempting to explain this gesture to a non-Jew, or to a student from a non-observant household, would need to do a significant amount of *de-coding* in order for the full cultural significance of the gesture to be made clear. The gesture

> ... has meaning and interest only for someone who possesses the cultural competence, that is, the code, into which it is encoded... A beholder who lacks the specific code feels lost in a chaos of sounds and rhythms, colors and lines, without rhyme or reason ... The "eye" is a product of history reproduced by education. (Bourdieu, 1984)

The work of the educator when dealing with art is to "reproduce" this "eye" with our students. It is not our work to choose to present our students with art that needs no "eye." Too often we are tempted to work with art that is literal, explanatory, mono-dimensional—in short, that which Anderson would tell us is not art at all! We must first take care to choose a piece of art that has skillfully encoded its meaning, displaying talent, craftsmanship, and concision.

Next, we must begin to assess what "code" is lacking on the part of our students, and establish strategies to impart these "codes." Clearly one form of code might be language. A rhythmic poem by Yehuda HaLevi, the dense overwhelming language of the book of Job, or the expansive prose of Amos Oz, are encoded in the first instance by their being in the "code" of Hebrew. But, of course, beyond such easily identifiable codes we must uncover those concise evocations that are such only to those who are familiar with the cultural settings in which they are presented.

In Yehuda Amichai's poem, *An Arab shepherd is searching for his goat on Mount Zion* (Amichai) there is more encoding than just the Hebrew. For example, to the educated Jewish ear, Amichai's brief yet telling reference to the Passover song *Had Gadya* (One Goat) is rich with echoes of mortality, violence, family, and Jewish tradition. A simple "translation" of the meaning of the two Aramaic words does not unlock their code. Art is often more a celebration of "that which is not said" (Berger, 1995) than of what is expounded fully.

Great art is enriched and fired with such "skilful encoding." A stroke of a brush that references a past master, the use of a particular idiom that conjures an era, a wordless glance that speaks beyond words. These are what make art so evocative since they open doors to shared human and cultural experiences, without forcing one to enter. It is this gentle invitation to interpretation that makes good art so inviting and powerful. As educators choosing to work with art, we must value our sense of such "skilful encoding." Not all that is immediately explained and unequivocally defined is inviting. Rather than searching to present only the most "accessible" art (read: "poorly or barely encoded"), we must explore pedagogical techniques for giving our students their own access to the appropriate code.

John Berger, when exploring the idea of narrative, points out what Walter Benjamin had noted several years earlier: The value of a story is measured by its distance from "information." Berger writes about story, but as Jewish educators concerned with the connection between that which is taught and the Jewish identity of the learner, we might read "story" as "art in education":

> No story is like a wheeled vehicle whose contact with the road is continuous. Stories walk, like animals or men... Every step is a stride over something not said... All stories are discontinuous and are based on a tacit agreement about what is not said... when a story makes sense of its discontinuities, it acquires authority as a story. (Berger, ibid.)

As educators, our concern will always be to make sure that our students are able to "fill in the space between the strides." At the same time, we must never forget that the engaging power of the art lies precisely in the fact that it does "leave space." This space between expression and meaning frees us to make assumptions, to draw contradictory conclusions, and to insert ourselves into the interpretation. This invitation to create meaning from a piece of art is what allows the student to feel "ownership"—another way of saying that the story emerging from the piece of art has become part of the student's own story.

Here the tension comes clear. On the one hand, we wish the art experience to leave room for the student to "fill in the space" from his or her own experiences and understandings for the experience to be personal. On the other hand, we wish for the student to appreciate the codes that the artist is using, so as to share interpretations of the art with all the Jewish world, and not just themselves. How do we de-code the art so the student may find the Judaism beyond it, without removing all "space" for the student to find themselves?

How Much Code Is Needed?

Internationally renowned theatre designer E. Gordon Craig was famously reported to have asked: "How many trees must be on the stage, in order for there to be a forest?" Here we would seem to be asking ourselves a similar question. How much code must an educator give to the students in order for them to be able to both understand and enter into this piece of art? For both questions, the answer is in the eye of the beholder. The educator needs to carefully assess the piece of art and the students before making the call.

The moment we choose to bring this question to the forefront, we are already on the right track. A few more additions to our glossary might now be of use. In *Gifts of the Muse* (Kevin F. McCarthy), a research paper into the arts commissioned by the Wallace Foundation, the writers are very careful to draw a distinction between what they term the instrumental benefits of the arts, and what they term the intrinsic benefits of the arts. For our purposes in Jewish education we might translate this as art *lo lishma* (for education's sake) and art *lishma* (for art's sake). We are working with art so as to maximize its intrinsic effect as art (for art's sake—*lishma*), and as an instrumental educational tool (for education's sake—*lo lishma*).

It would seem that when we lack code for interpreting art, this lack can affect both aspects of the experience, *lishma* and *lo lishma*. Having said this, we can usefully differentiate between the two different kinds of code required. Generally speaking, the code required to enhance the experience *lishma* needs to be given either before or during the event. The code required to enhance the event *lo lishma*—can wait until afterwards. For example, when contemplating which elements of code would be required for students watching Episode two of the Israeli TV series *A Touch Away* (Ninio, 2006), a group of Greater Washington educators agreed that brief background on the characters and English subtitles were required before and during the screening. Without these essential codes, students would not have "enjoyed" the screening (*lishma*). Only after the screening would the educators have chosen to explore other cultural codes embedded in the film (*lo lishma*), such as the multilayered comment of the secular Russian immigrant actress who remarks that Bnei Brak reminds her of a performance of *The Dybbuk*...

Why are we so concerned about when and how much code should be given? Because the intrinsic values of a piece of art—wonder, imagination, beauty—can too easily be destroyed by "over-teaching." Once we acknowledge that a piece of art, in order for it to be experienced as such, must be presented in "an affecting and sensuous medium," we also acknowledge that we must be careful to do no harm to such qualities.

Skillful...

Here may be a useful juncture to address the key difference between what we might call *kehilla* arts and *kahal* arts. As we mentioned earlier, *Kehilla* arts rate the value of the arts exercise according to the *experience of those doing the arts* (workshops, hands-on crafts, etc.). *Kahal* arts rate the value of the arts experience according to the *experience of the audience*. The artists and the educators are rare, who are able to serve both forms at the expense of neither.

Depending upon which kind of art is foremost, *kahal* or *kehilla*, the educator's search for the "skilful" is affected. The skill involved in Rembrandt's biblical representations is very different from the skill required (and displayed) in the work produced by Jo Milgrom's students, for example. As the introduction to her book *Handmade Midrash* (1992) advertises, many of her *kehilla* exercises assume "no skill ... on the part of the participants, because the goal is not to create fine art but to give visual form to thought."

Without this *kehilla/kahal* differentiation, the difference between the quality of process and the quality of the product is confused. Either too much emphasis is placed on the quality of the product when kids are painting biblical interpretations in order to understand the text or too little attention is paid to the skill of performers of a dance piece, simply because it might be about the book of Ruth....

Affecting and Sensuous Medium

Here we move into dangerous territory. That which is affecting and sensuous may be intangible. It may touch our students beyond their intellect or, in a sense, "bypass" their critical faculties. This is the danger and opportunity of the arts. If we are unwilling to embrace and work with these dangers and opportunities, we should not introduce art into our educational work. It is far cheaper and easier to use well-written textbooks. But if we are working with arts, and wish to take advantage of them, we would do well to enhance the impact of this affecting and sensuous medium.

Practical Reconsiderations

This demands an intellectual and practical reorganization. Practically speaking, in order to maintain the affecting and sensuous qualities of the art, we need to create appropriate conditions. Some educators are notorious for wasting the potential impact of the arts. For instance, an Israeli song may be presented as the translated lyrics on a page without playing the music itself. A film will be screened in a room that is fully lit. When looking at a poem, we must make sure it is read out loud competently by someone who is able to honor the rhythms and sounds. A song needs to be played on a good sound system or sung by a good singer. A film should be screened with a high-quality projector, onto a screen and not a dirty wall. We can all add to this list.

Educators may well bridle at these examples. Surely, these issues might be unavoidable, they may say. They may be caused by the environment or the budget? Yet the same educators would never expect a test to be taken without paper, nor a textbook to be read without a readable text available, nor a lecturer to speak softly. We need to alter the way we assess our "minimal requirements" for working with the arts. Since part of what the arts offers to an educational experience is the quality of enchantment, we educators should take care to provide the conditions for the magic to take place.

The words to Eti Ankri's hit song *Millionim* (Ankri, 2004) read as a searing political poem about the gaps between rich and poor. "And there are millions like me rolling around the streets ... mortal folk/With no money—not worth a dime/Today it's me/tomorrow it's you/No money—not worth a dime."

It is only in listening to the gentle half-reggae rhythms of the song itself, or even watching the video clip as this beautiful woman rides around the streets of Israel on the back of a wagon smiling and strumming her guitar, that students may appreciate how the song is far more than just its words. *It is complex, self-contradictory, full of rage and love. Like life* (Rory McLeod—UK folk hero—would always introduce every one of his seething furious protest songs with: "This is a love song...").

In addition to a practical reorganization, we must also rethink our pedagogy with these qualities of "affecting and sensuous" in mind. The following scenario is familiar to many:

> The movie ends. The credits begin to roll, and the audience is wiping away its tears. Suddenly the fluorescent lighting is turned on, a table and chairs are dragged onto the stage, and the panel discussion begins. The audience is not only blinking at the harsh lighting. It is blinking in shock at the rude awakening from an entire emotional world that has gripped them for more than an hour. The audience stumbles into the academic discussion, as if still shaking off an evocative dream, or nightmare. (Anderson 2004)

There are many logistical reasons why we find ourselves forcing a discussion or a panel immediately after an arts event. Either the lesson is about to end or the audience is likely to go home. We would suggest there are several reasons why this is detrimental to the affecting and sensuous experience the audience has gone through, and then we will question the benefit of such discussion at all.

As Anderson suggests, an art experience is affecting. Its touch can knock an audience off-balance. The more one interferes with this imbalance, the more one interrupts or weakens the enchanting power of the art, the more we help our students gain their feet. In so doing, in reducing the spell-like influence of the art—through poor physical conditions or through halting its reverberations too early—we mistakenly think we are acting as responsible educators. "The questions have been raised," we assure ourselves, "the issues have been exposed," we congratulate ourselves, "and now the learning can begin."

What we have in effect done is to attempt to separate the content from the form. Indeed, in enforcing this separation before the experience has even dimmed, we are attempting to subjugate form to content. We are such faithful servants of ideas and information. We persuade ourselves that *the way* in which these ideas have reached our students is of little significance. In this we may be overestimating our students and underestimating the art experience. It may be precisely the way in which the material has communicated itself, it may be precisely the sublime light, sound, characters that have set fire to the interest of the student. Without allowing these "introductory aesthetics" to play a role, the ideas may not stay with the student as much as we would wish. It is almost as if we have used the arts to engage the student in an issue, and then immediately work to make sure that the arts were not *too* engaging.

We might liken a powerful arts experience to a gust of wind in autumn. A culturally significant, skillfully encoded, affecting and sensuous experience has rushed through us like a swirl of wind in a pile of dry leaves. Our thoughts and emotions are blown about in a whirlwind of confusion and passion. The educator's first instinct will be to rush to offer the student tools to catch the leaves, to offer the student contextual boxes in which to place them, and even encourage the student to disregard some awkward leaves that blew far. Yet, the longer it takes for the "leaves of experience" to settle in our souls, the more the student realizes that a new context, a new understanding is required in order for the settling to begin, the more likelihood there is of a deeper learning to take place. A kind of learning that affects not just the students' knowledge base or tear ducts, but that affects and shifts their identity.

Following this image, it should be in the interests of the educator to encourage the leaves to take their time in settling, to allow the final breeze of the art experience to continue to swirl as long as possible, so that the final settling can have greatest long-term impact on the Jewish identity of the student.

The Downside of Paraphrasing

Another unfortunate by-product of forcing a discussion after a piece of art is that we risk undermining the art through paraphrasing. As Martha Nussbaum comments on literature: "If the writing is well done, a paraphrase in a very different form and style will not, in general, express the same conception" (Nussbaum, 1992). Here once again we see that the affective form of the art is part and parcel of its nature. When stripped of its affective form, when "translated into terms the students can understand," the art is not necessarily an experience understood. It may be only an experience flattened.

Nussbaum expresses more generously what Susan Sonntag suggested: "Interpretation is the revenge of the intellect on art" (Sonntag, 1966). For some with more developed artistic sensibilities, some prosaic plodding discussions of art can feel like an attack.

Answering the Unanswerable

Some might suggest that our desire or need as educators to "follow up" an arts occasion is less because we wish to provide a platform for people to share and respect each others' varied responses, and more because we feel the need to assert some authority over the discourse of meaning. In a sense, we may be feeling that a non-discussed piece of art is one whose interpretation is "out of control."

Yet, what are we to do when we plan to discuss a piece of art that raises questions for which there are no answers, or for which we know no answer?

I once performed my show *About the Oranges* to a mixed group of senior Jewish educators and members of the organization Rabbis for Human Rights (*About the Oranges* is a disturbing comic tragedy about an encounter between a Palestinian suicide bomber and an Aliya Shaliach (Gringras, 2004–2009)). In the discussion following, one of the participants said, "I'm looking at that banner you have at the back of the stage. It's a classic Israeli flag, with words encouraging people to make aliya. But on the stage in front of that message you're presenting us with a picture of the pain and the suffering involved in living the classic Zionist dream. In short," he summed up accurately, "this show is asking a question here. It's a question about the price of Zionism and aliya. And personally," he smiled quietly but without embarrassment, "I'm not sure that's a question I would know how to answer. I don't know whether that's the kind of question I'd be comfortable with, if it arose with my students."

It would seem that many educators are comfortable with the idea that their role is to stimulate questions. But perhaps *only those questions for which they themselves have answers.* Sometimes it has felt that the greatest opponents of *About the Oranges* in the educational world have been immigrants living in Jerusalem. This might be because of all places, Jerusalem and its surroundings paid the highest price of the last Intifada. Living in Jerusalem, one was far more likely to meet people who had lost loved ones, far more likely to fear for one's own safety and that of one's children. Given this daily reality, there are perhaps certain core questions that one's heart asks oneself every moment of the day, but that one's head is desperate not to hear. *Was it worth it?* whispers the heart. *Maybe this was all a terrible mistake?* weeps the soul.

It may be that the value of the arts lies in its ability to give voice to the questions our hearts are asking, but that we have not been able to hear.

Professor Michael Rosenak was once teaching about Mordecai Kaplan, and spent over two hours advocating for Kaplan's philosophy. At the end of his presentation, he was asked how his own philosophy differed from that of Kaplan. Mike said that Kaplan viewed religion as a *solution to a set of problems.* Kaplan's approach had been to assess what problem the religion had tried to solve, and then to look for more contemporary or effective ways of addressing these same problems. "Where I differ from Kaplan," concluded Rosenak, "is that I believe that sometimes life presents problems for which there are no solutions. I believe that *religion's main role is to enable us to live with problems for which there are no solutions.*"

Here Nussbaum suggests that great art can and should do the same.

> There may be views of the world and how one should live in it . . . that emphasize the world's surprising variety, its complexity and mysteriousness, its flawed and imperfect beauty—that cannot be fully and adequately stated in the language of conventional philosophical prose, a style remarkably flat and lacking in wonder—but only in a language and in forms themselves more complex, more allusive, more attentive to particulars. . . (Nussbaum 1992)

Concluding Toward Practice

If art is culturally significant meaning, skillfully encoded in an affecting and sensuous medium, then the educator must aim to work with art that is such. The educator will endeavor to ensure that the students appreciate the art's Jewish significance where the art's codes prevent them doing so. At the same time, the educator will work hard to allow the art to work its magic on the students, without undermining its intrinsic value through prosaic interpretation or poor conditions.

Andrew Taylor points out two aspects of the wonderful moment that is in the aesthetic experience:

> Consider any powerful, transformative moment you've had with an act or artifact of creative expression. That moment required at least *two* lifetimes to form its value—your lifetime to that moment and the artist's. There was a resonance between your experiences or emotions and the expressive voice. The moment required them both. The value was co-constructed. (Taylor, 2006)

As Jewish educators we would add a third "lifetime": that of the Jewish People. For us the ultimate transformative Jewish arts experience would involve the intersection of the piece of art, the life of the student, and the broader narrative of the Jewish People—its wisdom and experiences.

How to Keep the Wind Blowing?

Here we shall refer to work executed by Makōm Israel Engagement Network (Makom) that has extensively addressed the seam-line between arts and Jewish education in general, and Israeli contemporary arts in particular. What pedagogical strategies has Makōm employed that might allow this three-way encounter between self, art, and Judaism, to maintain its resonance? What techniques have been employed to give information without stifling, offer broader context without depersonalizing, and allow for individual interpretation without trivializing?

There is no doubt that Makōm has by no means exhausted the potential answers for such questions, but can perhaps refer to the Hassidic tale of the King lost in the forest:

> The King has wandered off the trail, and is horrified to find himself lost in the thick woods. Whenever he follows a path that would seem to lead out of the forest, it turns out to be a dead end or a full circle. After having returned to the same spot once again, and as the light begins to fade into nighttime, the King begins to despair. Suddenly he hears a whistling. He looks up to see a young man walking by, calm and self-assured.

"I am saved!" cries the King, approaching the young man with a smile, "Surely you can help me find my way home. I am terribly lost!"
The young man smiles at him and nods.
The King begins to walk with him, feeling his despair begin to lift, when he notices that the young man is wearing a pair of shoes that are worn down to the skin. When questioned, the young man replies:
"Ah yes, a pair of shoes can only take so much walking. I have been wandering lost in this forest for the past 3 years."
The King is distraught.
"But you said you could help me! And now it appears you are more lost than I!"
The young man rushes to encourage the King:
"Do not despair, sir! I can indeed help you! Though I do not yet know which path leads us out of the forest, I can tell you from experience which paths definitely do *not* lead out of the forest! And surely that must be worth something..."

It is with the realism and humility of the young man that we may learn from Makōm some directions within the forest.

Interpret Art with Art

It may well be that in order to allow for interpretation to be shared on the one hand, but not fixed down and limited on the other, we might need to strive for a non-prosaic form of sharing interpretations. Instead of building a formal verbal discussion following an art experience, the educator might be better advised to build in an additional artistic genre for the purpose of sharing interpretations. While creating a piece of art allows the participant to conjure a "holding form" (Witkin, 1974) for the whirlwind of emotions left after the art event, it nevertheless does not box them in an analytic and limited way. If, after hearing a song, the class paints their responses, or if after seeing a film, the students write a page in the diary of one of the characters, a form of digesting and processing and sharing takes place without suggesting that the interpretative process has yet ended.

Keep the Discussion Within the World of the Art

By the same token, if a discussion is to be had, make sure that the bulk of it is directed to the art and not its "subject." We have been party to many discussions that have followed a piece of Israeli art that touched on current politics. Whenever general conversation is encouraged, the floor is always commandeered by those with a political axe to grind. Yet whenever discussion is directed toward the creation itself, far more interesting and broadening issues arise. Thus when instead of asking "Do you think Israel's army commits war crimes?" the facilitator asks "Do you think you would have made the same choices as the soldier character?", two things happen. First, everyone is an expert, since they all watched the film or play, and they each have their own levels of empathy. Second, even the most hardened political hacks are forced to express something new, or in a new way: what Anna Deveare Smith calls "authentic speech" (Smith, 2001).

Ask Generative Questions

"Which character did you like?" tends to be an easy yet fruitless question. "Which character did you respect?" leads to far more contemplation. This latter question calls upon the participant to bring together two possibly separate worlds: The play on stage/screen, and their own value system. Makōm's educators' guide (Makom, Cinema Israel, 2007) to the Israeli film Joy (Shles, 2004), for example, worked at combining a scene in the film with personal values systems, and Jewish tradition:

> The real breakthrough in the film is when Simcha confronts her parents' friends. She accuses them of being unfair, of banishing her parents, and making no attempt to repair what was broken. In the Torah such an honest calling of someone to accounts is called *tochacha*. [Leviticus 19:17]
> Can you describe a time in your life when you, like Simcha, did *tochacha*? Or when someone came to do *tochacha* with you?
> Or have you ever felt the need to do *tochacha* but not managed to? What was it that stopped you? (Makom 2007)

Develop Non-intrusive Forms

If, on the one hand, a screening of a film without a discussion would be irresponsible, while, on the other hand, participants will resist any formally facilitated processing, then less intrusive ways of affecting conversation should be attempted. In work for the Eyes Wide Open film production, Makōm created a series of place mats (Makom, Eyes Wide Open, 2008). On these place mats were generative quotations from characters in the film, bits of information, and leading questions. These place mats were printed and placed on tables in the café of the cinema theatre. After the end of the screening, groups of people sat around, drinking their coffee, and relating to the place mat as they saw fit. In this sense we were able to influence the discourse without being seen to be leading it.

Use Jewish Terminology and Structures of Learning

In working to create the three-way encounter between the student's life, the life of the artist, and the life of the Jewish People, an attempt should be made to frame the personal work in a Jewish context. In working with song, for example, PaRDeS can be applied as a hermeneutic tool, while explaining its origins. The study guide Makōm created for the animated documentary *Waltz with Bashir* included a chevruta page that applied Talmudic issues to the subject of the film (Makom, Cinema Israel, 2009).

Conclusion

In his tribute to Yossel Birstein, Haim Beer quotes Yossel's recollection of his father's work as a shoemaker. As he describes the key aspect of finishing the sole of the shoe, one can almost imagine him talking about the stitching together of art and education:

The skill of the stitcher comes into play when the thread breaks off. There's no way of tying it—a knot in the upper part of the shoe would be unsightly, and a knot under the sole hampers walking. And so—either the stitcher has to undo what he's already stitched, or else he has to mend the broken thread in such a way that the knot can't be felt. (Beer, 2004)

It is our job to bring together two different materials—art and education—in such a way as to create a strong, efficient vehicle of meaning. Yet, in so doing, we must take care to make sure that the "knot" that binds the two materials be "mended" in such a way that it cannot be felt.

This "stitching" work requires that we first of all appreciate the different nature of art from education in order to better appreciate the kind of "stitching" required. Through an analysis and application of Anderson's definition of art, we can begin to understand what we are working with, and develop appropriate strategies.

References

Amichai, Y. (n.d.). Retrieved from http://www.poemhunter.com/poem/an-arab-shepherd-is-searching-for-his-goat-on-mo/
Anderson, R. (2004). *Calliope's sisters*. Prentice Hall.
Ankri, E. (2004). Retrieved from http://www.youtube.com/watch?v=CQTIGZ4pzl8
Avidan, A. (n.d.). Retrieved from http://www.myspace.com/findlovenow
Beer, H. (2004). A master craftsman of crossings. In G. Shaked, *Modern Hebrew literature: Lives in discourse*. Toby Press.
Berger, J. (1995). Stories. In J. B. Mohr, *Another way of telling*. Vintage.
Bourdieu, P. (1984). *Distinction*. Harvard University Press.
Chagall, M. (n.d.). Retrieved from http://www.artsfairies.com/Chagall/The Blue Violinist, 1947.jpg
Cohen, L. (n.d.). Retrieved from http://www.youtube.com/watch?v=j2T274bXIxU
Gringras, R. (2004–2009). *About the oranges*. (R. Gringras, Performer) World tour.
Inbari, A. (2004). Retrieved from http://209.85.229.132/search?q=cache:PfrIuwuMgI0J:info.oranim.ac.il/home/home.exe/17547/17551%3Fload%3DT.doc+אסף+ענברי+שלולית+נהר&cd=3&hl=iw&ct=clnk&gl=il
MacIntyre, A. (1981). *After virtue*. University of Notre Dame.
Machinery, S. (n.d.). Retrieved from http://www.swaymachinery.com/
Makom. (2007). *Cinema Israel*. Retrieved from Makom http://www.Makomisrael.org/NR/rdonlyres/FCCD0B54-C16E-422B-B0E9-D25EA8C7B31B/55919/JOY2.pdf
Makom. (2008). *Eyes Wide Open*. Retrieved from Makom http://www.Makomisrael.org/NR/rdonlyres/007F834C-634D-4A72-B019-1C3A76AFCA3D/60502/placematblack.pdf
Makom. (2009). *Cinema Israel*. Retrieved from Makom http://www.Makomisrael.org/NR/rdonlyres/FBB59052-651D-4BF4-A1AE-2F8E2221E232/68708/text_study2.pdf
Makom. (n.d.). Retrieved from Makom http://www.makomisrael.net
Matisyahu. (n.d.). Retrieved from http://www.youtube.com/watch?v=5dorvuCpNug
McCarthy, K. F., & Ondaatje, E. H. (n.d.). *Gifts of the muse: reframing the debate about the use of the arts*. Retrieved from http://www.rand.org/pubs/monographs/2005/RAND_MG218.pdf
Mook, E. (n.d.). Retrieved from http://www.youtube.com/watch?v=QcEPlfGRVqY
Ninio, R. (2006). (Director). *A Touch Away*. Israel: TV Series.
Nussbaum, M. (1992). Form and content, philosophy and literature. In M. Nussbaum, *Love's knowledge: Essays on philosophy and literature*. Oxford University Press.
Paintings, C. (n.d.). Retrieved from http://www.chagallpaintings.org/violonistebleue.html
Shles, J. (2004). (Director). *Joy* [Motion Picture].
Smith, A. D. (2001). *Talk to me: Travels in media and politics*. Anchor.

Sonntag, S. (1966). *Against interpretation*. Farrer, Strous and Giroux.
Taylor, A. (September 19, 2006). *Three short detours back to public value*. Retrieved April 28, 2008, from Arts Journal http://www.artsjournal.com/artfulmanager/thoughtbucket/009101.php
Tradition. (n.d.). Retrieved from http://www.youtube.com/watch?v=ZKHTabTYl_M
Witkin, R. (1974). *Intelligence of feeling*. Heinemann.

Arts and Jewish Day School Education in North America

Ofra A. Backenroth

Introduction

Aesthetic appreciation and creation of works of art have been central to the Jewish experience, linked to the term *hiddur mitzvah* (embellishment of a commandment) and have resulted in an explosion of interest in the arts and Jewish expression in the visual arts and the performing arts. According to Michael Rosenak (1999),

> We are to learn to take the sights, sounds, and forms of the world that are given to us, to cultivate and distill, to reach an understanding of what is beautiful, for what we may be grateful, and to give back this concrete beauty through concrete commandments performed beautifully, with *hiddur* [with embellishments]. (p. 273)

This contemporary interest in the arts, visual arts, music, drama, and dance has made its mark on the Jewish education, even though the traditional view "that presented the written text as the supreme source of knowledge and truth" is deeply established as the ruling paradigm in Jewish education (Cohen, 1988, p. 3).

In this chapter, I will explore how, when, and which of the arts are being taught to middle-school-aged students in North American Jewish day schools. I will begin with investigation of attitudes toward the arts in general education and in Jewish education, continue with an analysis of the various models of teaching the arts in Jewish day schools, and conclude with an examination of the Jewish subjects that are being taught through the arts. The second half of this chapter is focused on a comparison of arts-infused schools and arts-based schools. In contrast to the arts-based school, where the arts permeate all aspects of school life, in the arts-infused schools, the arts are infrequent and integrated or taught according to special interest groups or teachers within the school.

O.A. Backenroth (✉)
Jewish Theological Seminary of America, New York, NY, USA
e-mail: ofbackenroth@jtsa.edu

Context

To date, the arts have received only a mild reception in the contemporary Jewish educational world. One of the reasons for this is that the arts historically do not have a prominent place in the curriculum of general day schools (Hurwitz & Day, 1995). Jewish day schools, overburdened by the requirements of the dual curriculum and in particular the requirements of the Judaic curriculum tend to treat the arts as add-on and frills. The school day at the Jewish day school covers all the secular subjects as well as a wide range of Jewish subjects, including Hebrew and Israeli literature, The Bible, Talmud, Jewish philosophy, Rabbinic literature, and Israeli and Jewish history (Fox & Novak, 1997). Since the curricular requirements are so extensive, the arts, mainly instrumental music, dance, and other forms of performing arts are often neglected and are considered to be extra-curricular activities. Schools generally offer visual arts classes and students might participate in choir and audit for the school play by the end of the year; however, there is a lack of exposure to dance, instrumental music, multimedia, etc. Lack of the arts and experiential teaching is an impediment to what Twersky (1990) defines in *A Time to Act* as the goal of Jewish education.

> Our goal should be to make it possible for every Jewish person, child or adult, to be exposed to the mystery and romance of Jewish history, and to the enthralling insights and special sensitivities of Jewish thought, to the sanctity and symbolism of Jewish existence, and to the power and profundity of Jewish faith. (p. 19)

The arts can play a major role in developing awareness, enhancing Judaism with spirituality, and bringing additional perspectives into Jewish education.

In addition to the time requirements that the dual curriculum presents, day school education is an expensive undertaking for the Jewish community. The high costs are the result, among other reasons, of the requirement to hire two separate teaching staffs for each class; one for Judaic studies and another for general studies (Wertheimer, 2001). Enrichment programs in the arts create an added burden in costs and space requirements for art studios, dance space, and music rooms. Considering the chronic lack of time in the Jewish day school, scheduling planning sessions and faculty meetings becomes a deterrent. As a result, taking into account the expenses "[w]hen it comes to budgets, art is always the first piece that goes" (Wiener, 2002). However, in spite of all these difficulties, there is a deliberate ongoing recognition of the merits of teaching through the arts by some schools. The establishment of various arts organizations such as the Lincoln Center Institute, an arts and education organization founded in 1984 based on Dewey's and Greene's aesthetic approach, and Chicago Arts Partnership which was founded in 1992 as a organization working on school improvement through the arts, lead to a renaissance in arts in education in the public schools system (Burnaford, Aprill, & Weiss, 2001). Jewish schools refused to stay behind, and as Wiener (2002) states, "Jewish education is becoming increasingly inclusive of the arts. [T]he trend is not limited to the visual arts, but also includes newfound interest in using music, filmmaking, dance, and even creative writing as a way to teach Judaism" (p. 63).

For example, a recent edition of *HaYedion*, the RAVSAK'[1] quarterly, is dedicated to the arts and Jewish education. Davis (2008), the editor maintains that the schools experience a "renaissance of creative Jewish exploration of visual and performing arts, as well as new media, as means of increasing students' understanding of the roots of our faith and the many ways in which our faith can be expressed" (2008, p. 2).

Indeed, policy-makers and educators realize that to a large extent progress in schools depend not only on the improvement of the leadership and teaching staff but also on the development of new curricula, textbooks, online learning, the preparation of materials, and the willingness to draw on new methods of teaching (Wertheimer, 2001). Educators have come to believe that teaching through the arts is an effective way of teaching Judaic subjects that texts are only the beginning of Jewish education, and that investing in the arts as a teaching method is a worthwhile enterprise (Backenroth, 2008).

Justifying the Place of the Arts in Education

American educators have long considered the fine and industrial arts an essential part of a well-balanced curriculum. Already in the 1880s, the arts were included in the curriculum of the Park School, the Practice School, and later on at Dewey's Laboratory School (Cremin, 1961). Cremin explains, "Music, drama, hygiene, and physical education: all were seen as vehicles for child expression; all began with what had meaning to the children themselves" (Cremin, 1961, p. 133). Still, it was during the 1920s and 1930s, "as the intellectual avant-garde became fascinated with the arts" (p. 181) that using the arts in education became widespread. Individual teachers, looking to apply innovative pedagogical theories based on the idea of child-centered education (Dewey, 1902/1990, 1915/1990) founded new and innovative schools (Cremin, 1961). Dewey (1915/1990) drew attention to the significance of the arts as an integral part of the way children express themselves. Objecting to education that "appeals for the most part simply to the intellectual aspect of our natures" (p. 26) Dewey believed that children's natural tendency is to learn through activities. Children like to draw, to dance, and to sing, and therefore education should appeal to students' "impulses and tendencies to make, to do, to create, to produce, whether in the form of utility or of art" (Dewey, 1915/1990, p. 26). Since the arts are integral to how children construct their knowledge about the world, Dewey argued for the inclusion of the arts in the curriculum. Cremin (1961) describes the curriculum in Dewey's Laboratory School as including "languages, mathematics, the fine and industrial arts, science, music, history and geography ... in well-planned fashion" (Cremin, 1961, p. 139).

Other educators and researchers advocate for the inclusion of the arts in education. Greene (1997, 2000), the founder of Lincoln Center Institute which promotes

---

[1] The Jewish Community Day School Network.

arts education in public school suggests that immersing oneself in a work of art demands the use of imagination not only as a passageway to empathy and personal meaning-making, but also as the key to teaching the various disciplines and to pluralistic education. Burton, Horowitz, & Abeles (1999) found that "children exposed to strong and varied arts experiences over periods of time, both in and out of school, are more confident and willing to explore and take risks, exert ownership over and pride in their work, and show compassion and empathy towards peers, families, and communities" (Burton et al., 1999, p. 30).

Eisner (1998) argues that the arts are an important part of the curriculum not only because of their ancillary outcomes, but also because of the arts-based outcomes. These outcomes are comprehension of texts, understanding the relationship between form and content in the arts and in texts, contextualizing arts in history, refining aesthetic awareness, and expressing feelings through the arts. Similarly, Smith (1994) maintains that the arts are important in and of themselves. He advocates for the learning of the arts as a source of culture and knowledge in education, and encourages educators to use the arts not only as an expressive tool, but also in a humanities-based curriculum that can inform students about their heritage.

Jensen (2001) underscores cognition and personal development as a result of arts education. Surveying current brain research, Jensen argues that the arts enhance the process of learning. In addition to their effect on the sensory, cognitive, and motor capacities, the arts promote self-discipline and motivation, and improve emotional expression. He further contends that music helps with recall and the ability to retrieve information. Creating artistic representations of texts promotes long-lasting learning, improves retention, and eliminates "fragile knowledge" (Perkins, 1993). Additionally, researchers claim that students' general attitudes toward learning and school improve as a result of a challenging but enjoyable activity, and that learning art skills forces mental 'stretching' useful to other areas of learning (Csikszentmihalyi, 1996). The ideas of these thinkers and educators underscore the importance of including the arts in the school curriculum, not only as separate disciplines, but as a vehicle to teach the entire curriculum of the school.

Research and Arts Education

Integrating the arts in education is grounded in research about human abilities, cognition, and creativity. In 1967, Project Zero was founded by the philosopher Nelson Goodman who believed that arts learning should be studied as a serious cognitive activity. The Project's mission was to understand and enhance learning, thinking, and creativity in the arts, as well as humanistic and scientific disciplines, at the individual and institutional levels. The launching of the project culminated with the publishing of *Frames of Mind* by Gardner (1983) and brought the theory of multiple intelligences to public awareness. Multiple intelligences theory (Gardner, 1983) suggests that there are nine intelligences: linguistic, logical–mathematical, spatial, bodily-kinesthetic, musical, interpersonal, intrapersonal, and naturalist, and the existential intelligence. This theory offers a pluralistic view of competence and suggests that the linguistic and the logical–mathematical abilities cannot be regarded as the only indicators of human intelligence (Gardner, 1983; Perkins, 1991). Consequently, it urges teachers to legitimate the use of alternative methods of teaching and for using art, music, and movement in class (Armstrong, 1994). It encourages teachers to "expand their current teaching repertoire to include a broader range of methods, material, and techniques for teaching an ever wider and more diverse range of learners" (Armstrong, 1994, p. 39).

As the interest in the arts grew, and research in cognitive development and brain research found new evidence to support the value of teaching the arts (Efland, 2002), new experimental programs were established, motivated to use the theory as the foundation for new curricular materials for education. In 1985, Project Zero collaborated with the Educational Testing Service in Pittsburgh to create Art Propel. The project was built on the conviction that arts teach content and that they "exercise not just the hand and heart, but the mind as well" (Wolf, 1987, p. 26). The project's goal was to measure the impact of the arts on assessment in schools. A subsequent program, Project Spectrum, was based on the assumption that every child has the potential to develop strength in one or several content areas and that it is the responsibility of the educational system to discover and nurture these inclinations. Project Spectrum emphasizes identifying children's areas of strength and using this information as the basis for an individualized educational program. Spectrum researchers (Wolf & Piston, 1995) design assessment activities in seven different domains of knowledge: language, math, music, art, social understanding, science, and movement. Blurring the lines between learning and assessment, grounding assessment in engaging real-life situations, applying assessment through different intelligences, and focusing on children's strengths rather than on their weaknesses allow teachers to use hands-on activities in the domains of visual arts, music, dance, and drama, as well as games, machinery, and physical activity.

Jewish Thinkers on the Arts

Many Jewish thinkers are aware of the power of the arts and recognize the importance of the arts in Jewish life, community life, and in worship. For instance, Kaplan (1934/1997) explicitly addresses the issue of the arts, claiming creativity as one of the pillars of civilization. "A civilization cannot endure on a high plane without the preservation and cultivation of its arts. Art creations become part of the social heritage which is the driving force of the civilization" (p. 203). Kaplan argues that artistic creation is the unifying force of a community and therefore "Jews as a group must add to the cultural and spiritual values of the world. They must produce ideas, arts, literature, music" (1937/1997, p. 367). In addition, Kaplan maintains that the arts have the ability to facilitate meaning-making since they demand intensive engagement and personal creation. As the Dean of the Teachers' Institute in the first part of the twentieth century, Kaplan established the arts as part of the education of future teachers (JTS Register, 1918/1919).

A contemporary thinker and educator, Scheindlin (2003), in his research about spirituality, argues that the arts and the emotions bring to consciousness the spiritual aspects of life and urges schools to nurture the emotional lives of students. He encourages Jewish educators to create lessons that "serve as scaffolds to spiritual sensitivity" (p. 190). Through art, music, and creative writing students can represent their emotional lives. Teaching prayers demands as much time and attention as any other discipline. The secret of prayer lies in the sense of awe and wonder, and feelings of religiosity should be expressed in a tangible form of words, gestures, music, art, or dance.

Even the less liberal world that customarily ignored the arts as *bitul Torah* (waste of time that should have been dedicated to the study of Torah), grasps the power of the fine arts. Rabbi Haim Brovender (2003), the head of *Yeshivat HaMivtar*, declared that since the arts play such an important role in young people's lives and are so fundamental to their daily experiences, teachers should use the arts in their teaching. Suggesting that people become spiritual by observing art, Brovender believes that through the arts one can experience *ahavat Hashem* (love of God).

Fox, Scheffler, and Marom (2003) in their study of vision of Jewish education clarify that affect and not only cognition has a legitimate role in Jewish education, and they call for a comprehensive change in the design of the school curriculum. The authors maintain that Jewish education stresses the centrality of texts, and it tends to ignore the arts and use them only sporadically. The authors write that the current curriculum at the Jewish day schools is "[a] mere recapitulation of conventional lessons and past practices, lacking both systematic connections with the depth of Jewish lore and the energy to make such lore come alive convincingly in the hearts of contemporary youth" (Fox et al., 2003, p. 8). They suggest, "Curricula are increasingly understood to require not only recourse to the texts but also to materials drawn from the arts" (p. 7). Exploring the lack of spirituality in education, they state, "For purposes of education, spirituality cannot remain an abstraction" (p. 16). Greenberg and Brinker (in Fox et al., 2003) argue that the character of Jewish education should be religious and spiritual, and as such education should include not only knowledge and values, but also the arts: literature, music, and painting. They state that the arts are not a luxury, but a fundamental requirement.

The Arts in Jewish Day Schools

Research on the place of the arts in Jewish education is sparse; however, lately researchers are looking at school practices and how schools use the arts in the teaching of Judaic studies. Epstein (2003) suggests that Jewish educators often too narrowly define the parameters of what counts as a text within the classroom maintaining that visual images such as a painting or a student-generated tableau can be read as textual commentary upon the Bible. Epstein underscores that teachers who use drama-related activities help students to more fully express themselves in conversations about the text.

Similarly, Miller (1999a/2001) and Milgrom (1992) suggest that teaching art skills in conjunction with text skills enriches the way students interpret the text and helps them make a personal connection with biblical texts. Both researchers demonstrate that art making is a legitimate strategy for traditional Jewish learning. The students are encouraged to work from an intellectual cognitive framework through successive steps in order to develop an understanding of the text through creative activities. To keep students accountable for true understanding of the texts, they are asked to return to the text following the creative activity and re-visit and re-test their interpretations.

Hascal (2001) demonstrates how dance, as a learning-by-doing approach, provides an alternative way to help students recall and sequence events in the Bible. She further suggests that interpreting the events through dance allows the students to visualize the events and therefore gain better understanding. During the discussions that follow, the students demonstrate abstract thinking, renewed interests in the texts, and the ability to ask new questions. The most important finding of the study is the students' ability to engage in hermeneutic methods of text study such as word analysis, juxtaposition, and filling the gaps in the text.

Backenroth (2003b, 2004, 2005a, 2005b) explores day schools that teach the arts as extra-curricular, discrete disciplines, and partially or fully integrate the arts in Judaic studies. She finds that in addition to the arts' contribution to the learning process, the arts fulfill the needs of teachers by giving them a way to express themselves creatively and teach texts in an innovative way. In her study, Backenroth identifies a few models of teaching the arts in Jewish day schools and identifies the domains that are most commonly taught through the arts.

Models of Teaching the Arts in Jewish Day Schools

Most Jewish Day Schools offer a course in visual arts—mostly painting and drawing, and music (mainly choir classes)—to their students. Since Jewish day schools in the United States are members of the independent school system, however, they are not bound by state requirements and standards. Administrations in each school are free to determine the scope, sequence, frequency, and methods of arts education and consequently the distribution of arts varies from school to school and from state to state. It is important to note that the National Standards for Arts Education were developed only in 1994.[2] The standards and benchmarks for arts education describe what every student should know and be able to do at various grade levels in each artistic discipline. However, only half of the states in North America mandate that local districts implement them and in the other states, the standards are voluntary and implementation of teaching methods varies from state to state and district to district. There are no standards and no requirements in regards to teaching of the arts in Jewish day schools.

---

[2] www.Americans for the arts.

Backenroth (2003b, 2004, 2005a) in her study of arts education in day schools in North America identifies a continuum of approaches to teaching the arts in Jewish Day Schools that moves from well-integrated arts-based schools on one edge of the spectrum to teaching the arts as discrete disciplines with very little integration and relationship to the Jewish studies curriculum. The various models of teaching the arts are distinguished by the relationship between the curricular subjects (Beane, 1997; Drake, 1993; Fogarty, 1997; Jacobs, 1989) and the level of cooperation between the different teachers. In some schools, teachers integrate the arts individually in their own classrooms while the arts teachers do their own teaching with no relation to school curriculum (Backenroth, 2004). At arts-based schools, all the teachers integrate the arts into the curriculum in a consistent, coordinated, theme-based method under the supervision of the administration and a specialist for arts-integration (2005b).

According to this continuum, the arts can be taught according to several models:

1. As a distinct discipline—The arts are taught during the school day or after the conclusion of the school day with no connection to the rest of the Judaic studies curriculum.
2. Parallel integration model—The teachers, including the arts teachers, sequence their lessons to correspond to lessons in the same area in other disciplines. Teachers teach each of the disciplines independently, but in consultation with each other or through a curriculum coordinator. The order of the lessons changes but not the content.
3. Integration by an individual teacher—A single teacher who teaches more than one discipline during the same session and creates active connections among the arts and other disciplines.
4. Multi-disciplinary method—The arts teachers and Judaic subject teachers teach together a theme or an issue.
5. Theme-based integration—The entire curriculum revolves around a theme or an issue and thereby breaks down the boundaries of the disciplines. In theme-based integration, the arts are taught as part of the entire curriculum in an integrated method, teaching the same issues or topics as the rest of the curriculum. In this integrated curricular model, the arts not only share a place with the other disciplines, but they also support each other, and they take on the same importance as the other disciplines.

Based on this continuum of integration of the arts, Backenroth (2005a, 2005b) identified two models of teaching the arts in the Jewish day schools:

A. Arts-based schools: The arts are integrated into all aspects of the curriculum in a theme-based integration model and are used across all the disciplines in an integrated curriculum model.
B. Arts-infused schools: The arts are partially infused into the Judaic studies curriculum according to individual teachers' inclinations using integration models from the lower end of the continuum of discipline integration.

The schools share the rationale for using the arts in the curriculum and the belief in the importance of the arts to education. However, there is a philosophical difference in the way the arts are integrated into the curriculum at the arts-based school and the arts-infused school, which affects the way schools function and operate.

The arts-based schools (Backenroth, 2005a, 2005b) are committed to the integration of the arts in all areas of the curriculum by the entire faculty. The arts are represented across the curriculum and their status is equal to the rest of the subjects in the school's curriculum. There is a tight connection between the skills that are taught during the arts classes and the activities that the students perform during their various lessons. Since the curriculum is based on themes, teachers must work together, team-teach, and team-plan their courses. In many occasions, the teachers need to develop their own curriculum and teaching materials. This approach to teaching consciously applies methodology and language from more than one discipline to examine a central theme, issue, or problem. In this model, no subject is taught in isolation (Drake, 1993; Gaudelius & Speirs, 2002; Jacobs, 1989) and it requires intensive planning and cooperation by all the teachers, as well as complete support from the administration, the board, and the parent community.

At the arts-infused schools, Backenroth identifies two models:

1. Self-designed arts curriculum:
   A parallel design of integration in which the teachers re-sequence their lesson plans to correspond to lessons in the same areas in other disciplines. However, the disciplines keep their integrity and often arts specialists work in isolation, rarely interacting with the rest of the faculty. The arts specialists cooperate with the rest of the Judaic curriculum teachers only if there is a school performance that needs musical or choral accompaniment such as a *siddur* (prayer book) ceremony or the *Sukkah* (a temporary dwelling occupied during the festival of *Sukkoth*) needs decoration.
2. Professionally designed arts-integrated curriculum:
   Arts-infused schools that hire professional arts organizations or consultants to introduce the arts into the schools. Hiring companies such as the Lincoln Center Institute, Young Audience Arts, the nation's leading source of arts-in-education services, or inviting individual artists to present a show or work with the teacher on curriculum development can be done on a one-time basis or in a long-term arrangement with an arts consultant who works with the teachers during the school year on creating an arts program. In some cases, the programs brought in from the outside cover the same subjects or themes that are covered in the classroom. In other cases, the arts programs are detached from the school curriculum and function in isolation.

What Is Being Taught Through the Arts in the Jewish Day Schools?

As I stated in the previous sections, the arts are powerful. Research on learning and the arts, and the findings of research on the arts and Jewish education suggest that the arts shape not only the content that is being taught, but also how it is being taught. The arts change the character of the school and its culture, and make it unique (Backenroth, 2005b).

The two models of the schools, the arts-based and the arts-infused schools integrate experiential methods of teaching that include the arts and multisensory teaching approaches. They concentrate on educational experiences and not only on rapid output and coverage of material and espouse child-center philosophy. However, in the arts-based schools, there is an overall commitment by the school community to the arts on all its aspects: arts appreciation, arts skills, teaching through the arts, and teaching with the arts as the locus of the curriculum. Additionally, the teachers at the arts-based school see themselves not only as responsible for imparting knowledge, but also for nurturing abilities and inclinations and developing talents in the arts.

Whereas arts-infused schools treat the arts as add-ons, arts-based schools believe that the arts are imperative and non-negotiable means of education and that integrating the arts in all aspects of the school curriculum is the only way to teach. The arts are considered to be the basic foundation of the teaching methodology and they are taught in conjunction with the rest of the curriculum throughout the school day. The arts are taught and practiced for various reasons including teaching critical thinking, skills, language acquisition, reading skills, problem solving, practicing cognitive skills, making connections with the texts, helping with emotional issues, nurturing spirituality, solidifying knowledge, intensifying memory, and identifying students' strengths. The arts are always integrated with content and are constantly used as a teaching tool in the classrooms, corridors, and public spaces; and they are always part of the many celebrations of a Jewish day school.

Teaching Arts Skills

At arts-based schools, the arts are present in every aspect of the school's life. These schools consider the arts important and believe in the interconnectedness of childhood and the arts. Ruth Belkin, the head teacher of an arts-based school underscores the significance of the arts in the eyes of parents who are searching for schools for their children. She explains, "That was the problem with the Jewish day school that they never used the arts. So people, who would send their children to a Jewish day school, were turned off by the lack of creativity and [lack of] the arts. The school [arts-based] attracts a lot of people who normally would not send their children to a [Jewish] day school" (Backenroth, 2005a, p. 78).

Teaching through the arts happens in all grades and throughout all the disciplines. Visual art, music, and drama have the same importance as other disciplines, and they are integrated into the curriculum as the teachers and the coordinators plan the curriculum. The teachers at arts-based schools understand that to express knowledge and feelings through the arts, there is a need for arts skills (Gardner, 1982). Furthermore, they realize that they cannot impose a love of the arts on students. Knowing that students love the familiar and that knowledge builds on previous knowledge, they design a comprehensive and well-designed arts program that through small steps and experiential activities introduces the student to the arts. Consistent teaching with and through the arts (Goldberg & Phillips, 1995), from the time the students enter the school until graduation, presents the teachers with ample opportunities to teach skills, to provide many creative experiences, and to teach arts appreciation.

The arts-infused schools vary in their commitment to the arts and teaching arts skills is not always at the top of their interest and ability. An interview with one of the teachers in an arts-infused school points to the lack of skills transfer, and to lack of coordination and communication among the various teachers in a school.

> I used to take people on tours of the lower school. Once I took them to a floor where one wall was decorated with artwork done in the classroom and coincidentally, the opposite wall was decorated with art done at the art studio. When you have a good art teacher, I would show people, the same child will produce art in the art room on a completely different level than during Bible class. Use of color, use of form, understanding perspective, they are all different. (Backenroth, 2005a, p. 194)

At the arts-based schools, no dichotomy exists between art in the art or music studio and art in the classroom. The arts teachers and the content teachers plan and implement the curriculum together. Students know that they are accountable for all aspects of learning in each class and that they are expected to apply what they learn in arts classes to the projects done in other classes. This method of teaching encourages responsible learners who can apply learning in one class to another and produces enthusiastic artists and knowledgeable consumers of arts.

Hebrew and the Arts

The teaching of Hebrew is one of the most important issues in the curriculum of Jewish day schools, yet it is one of the most challenging. The shortage of good teachers, appropriate materials for teaching Hebrew as a second language, and confusion about the aims of teaching Hebrew make it difficult to achieve literacy in a language that is the cornerstone of all Jewish texts. Implementing theories of teaching a second language through content (Swain, 1988; Met, 1991) and through the arts (Asher, 1981; Curtain & Pesola, 1994) is efficient, and it maximizes what Jewish day schools can do with the limited time they allocate to language teaching. Jewish day schools pride themselves on teaching Hebrew and teaching the Jewish subjects in Hebrew. However, the time devoted to language lessons is limited. Using Hebrew during arts classes, recess, and lunchtime is an authentic and organic way of teaching the language. As Curtain and Pesola (1994) explain, "Children do not acquire a language primarily by being told about it, but rather through meaningful, communicative experiences with the language" (p. 178). The physical activity helps create patterns that improve memory, aid retention, and facilitate fluency in language acquisition (Asher, 1981). The use of a variety of visuals, music, drama, and dances representing Israel and its culture can help to relate interests of the children to the wider world in which Hebrew plays a major role and instills a deep sense of understanding by involving children emotionally with the content.

A vivid example of teaching Hebrew in an art studio (Backenroth 2005a, 2005b) underscores the complexities of an integrated unit. Preparing for Hanukkah, the students visit the local museum to look at old oil vessels in the Greek and Roman wing, some of which were excavated in Israel. Later on, in the integrated art/Hebrew class, they are learning vocabulary pertaining to sculpture in Hebrew and at the same time learning basic concepts of sculpture. While kneading the clay, they run through a verb conjugation in present tense: *"ani lashah homer," "attah lash homer," "anachnu lashim homer," "attem lashim homer," "atten lashot homer"* (I knead clay, you knead clay, we knead clay, you (masculine) knead clay, you (feminine) knead clay). The jars they produce will be exhibited at the holiday exhibition in which the students will explain how they created the jars. In a history class, students are also preparing for the holiday by creating a live presentation of previously unsung heroines and their contribution to the Zionist dream. "Eventually the students will create a *Hanukkah* lamp of eight heroic Israeli women. Instead of candle lighting, each of the candles represents one heroine" (Backenroth, 2005a, p. 225).

This complex and multi-dimensional structure of learning Hebrew language and the events of the Jewish calendar by using arts, ancient history, and Israel current history helps students make connections between various segments of the curriculum and elicit emotional reaction by having them research, design, create, and finally present their work to the larger school community.

Zionism and the Arts

Creating a knowledgeable and practicing Jew is an overwhelming challenge for the schools. Schools recognize the high expectations of the community, and they realize that they are considered to be the last source of connection to the Jewish community and the last resort for acculturation of Jews (Heilman, 1992). Equally important to most Jewish schools is the nurturing of ties with Israel and the exposure of students to Israeli culture, literature, and the arts.

Ingall (2003) in her portrait of Tziporah Johsberger highlights the power of music and teaching the *halil* (recorder) in creating "musical association to Israeli folkways, natural surroundings, and the towns and the cities, the Shabbat and holidays, and thus bringing children both in Israel in the Diaspora into more intimate contact with these aspects of culture in Israel" (p. 4). Passionate about instilling deep feeling toward Israel, teachers at the Jewish day schools use art forms like poetry, drama, and painting realizing that the arts are a useful tool in deepening experiences. By using Israeli arts such as movies, photographs, visuals, music, and dances teachers want to connect Jewish students with the study of Israel, its land, people, and culture. The arts nurture a sense of belonging, of community, and provide a vehicle for individuals, communities, and cultures to explore their own world and journey to new ones, thus enriching their understanding of the varied peoples and cultures that exist.

Prayer, Spirituality, and the Arts

Spirituality and feelings of closeness to God is the essence of religious education, and at the same time it is one of the most difficult challenges faced by educators in Jewish day schools. Scheindlin (2003), in his research about spirituality, argues that the arts and the emotions bring to consciousness the spiritual aspects of life and urges schools to nurture the emotional lives of students. He encourages Jewish educators to create lessons that "serve as scaffolds to spiritual sensitivity" (p. 190). Through arts, music, and creative writing students can represent their emotional lives.

To instill the sense of spirituality, arts-based schools use the arts to enhance and sanctify the time of prayer. The teachers help their students to explore and understand complex concepts such as creation or the existence of God by moving the students from concrete experiences to reflection and finally creation in the arts.

A moving example of using the arts in prayer sessions is found in the arts-based schools, which nurture spirituality as an outgrowth of their commitment to the arts. Loyal to their mission to teach through the arts, the school teaches the prayers through the arts. Classroom teachers introduce each phrase of the prayers differently, integrating visual arts, songs, and movements. Prayers denote not only words but also "motions" which are used to accompany the words of the prayers, layering words and movements. "Every morning we do a little. It is better that they pray with *kavanah* (feeling) than just do it. We read it slowly, explain it, and we make the movements. The movements add to the *kavanah*" (Backenroth, 2005a, p. 204).

Learning the *parasha*, the weekly portion of the Pentateuch, includes drama, creating visuals, and reflections. Maintaining that young children are not necessarily participating in spiritual life, educators believe that activities that enhance spirituality are a prerequisite for later spiritual activity. By using motions to teach the texts of prayers, the school helps students to achieve emotional memory and to establish the seeds of a spiritual life.

Arts Midrash[3]

The *raison d'être* of teaching Judaic subjects through the arts is the belief that the arts are a valid language of expression and that good teaching involves internalization of the learned material and reproduction of the material in a variety of forms. By using the arts to interpret and re-create biblical texts, the teachers fight against the exclusive use of the written word. They offer students a new way to be re-enchanted by the stories of the Bible and consequently to be able to re-create and re-enact the events of the Bible. Using the visual arts as a language provides teachers with a strategy to relate and to teach every student, even those who are less articulate, and

---

[3] *Midrash* is based on a Hebrew word that means to explore, to interpret, and to find new meaning.

find verbal expression challenging. Teachers create a safe learning environment for students of different backgrounds when they recognize the diversity of the student population in terms of biblical knowledge, analytical ability, and theological convictions. This approach to teaching encourages students to take risks by expressing their own interpretations, and nurtures their confidence by displaying art in front of the school community.

The most prevalent approach, though not the only one being used, is Milgrom's (1992) method of exploring interpretations of biblical texts by looking at visual images and creating torn-paper collages. The method enriches students' understanding of the biblical text and gives them opportunities to concentrate on one verse or on one event in the text. Re-reading the text following the arts activities ensures that the text is the locus of activity and students explore the additional meaning they gleaned from using the arts. A similar method of interpreting Jewish text through dance is practiced by dancers such as Tucker and Freeman (1990). The objective of using movement and dance in teaching texts is not to produce artists but rather to help with content learning. Finding simple methods of using motions, movements, and simple art techniques can help teachers to offer an entry point into the discipline. Teachers' beliefs that the Bible will be understood only by active participation in the learning process echoes Dewey (1934/1977) who claims that the arts need to be experienced by the viewer. Similarly, texts need to be reproduced by the reader.

Teaching biblical texts through the arts emphasizes the importance of students making their own meaning while searching for their own discoveries (Miller 1999b, 2000). The teachers in this case are not the experts who recite the content of the lesson, but rather mediators who facilitate the act of discovery of relevant issues. To reach each student, the teachers choose flexible teaching styles that let the students experiment with the arts, teach themselves, and express their knowledge in a variety of ways. Using the arts as a teaching tool enriches the teachers' repertoire and demonstrates that teachers can have more than one orientation toward teaching and the curriculum. Teachers who stress the cognitive orientation believe that the curriculum is primarily concerned with helping students to solve problems, to develop thinking skills, and with teaching them how to learn. Teachers who emphasize the personal relevance orientation enable the students to find personal meaning in what they study and in that case the curriculum should begin with the students' needs and interests. Given the ability to interpret the biblical text and create their own *midrashim* in their own unique way, the students are actively involved in fulfilling the most essential *mitzvah* (commandment) of Judaism, learning Torah. Thus, the students become a link in the long chain of scholars and commentators engaged in the interpretation and the teaching of the Torah (Holtz, 1984).

Implications of Integrating the Arts in the Jewish Studies Curriculum

Integrating the arts in the Jewish studies curriculum and teaching through the arts create a different environment for studies. Whereas most schools treat the arts as add-ons, arts-based schools[4] are created based on a distinctive vision that the arts should be present throughout the curriculum and have merits on their own and as tools to teach other subjects (Backenroth, 2004, 2005a). The arts are considered to be the basic foundation of the teaching methodology and they are taught in conjunction with the rest of the curriculum throughout the school day. They are taught and practiced for various reasons including teaching critical thinking skills, language acquisition, reading skills, problem solving, practicing cognitive skills, arts skills, making connections with the texts, helping with emotional issues, nurturing spirituality, solidifying knowledge, intensifying memory, and identifying students' strengths. The arts are always integrated with content and are constantly used as a teaching tool in the classrooms, corridors, and public spaces.

To create an arts-based school requires a dramatic shift in the school's philosophy about the arts, about integration, and its place in curriculum design. Integration of the arts in the Judaic curriculum is embedded within a larger commitment to the integration of content areas as a fundamental practice. The underlying premise in an arts-based school is the belief that integration of subjects, including the arts, is crucial to teaching Judaic studies. In addition to being an arts-based school, the school offers other attractive educational features such as small classes, mentoring, minimal frontal teaching, experiential teaching, and many hands-on activities. The arts contribute to the excitement and the creativity that gives the schools their special character. The arts are not a luxury; they are a fundamental requirement.

If Jewish day schools are to transform students' lives, to enhance their spirituality, and to make the study of Jewish subjects more relevant and effective, they need to integrate the arts into the Judaic studies curriculum. Transforming students' lives is the most important task facing Jewish day schools, and the arts can make this possible in a way that can make the Jewish studies curriculum effective and exciting. The arts, which frequently give the impression that they are merely trendy add-ons to education, "might yet prove to be the Psalmist's 'cornerstone'" (Chipkin, 1952, p. 2).

Suggestions for Future Research

Research on Jewish education and the arts provides educators with studies of how the arts shape the curriculum and the teaching of the arts in Jewish schools and how they are being taught and for what reasons. However, there are still many unanswered questions such as what is the effect of arts education on students' achievements. It would be interesting to measure the achievement in Hebrew taught through the arts. Do students achieve more fluency in Hebrew as a result of studying the language through the arts? Does teaching texts through the arts help students to master language skills, acquire richer vocabulary, and provide for richer understanding of texts?

---

[4] Since my research in 2004, two Jewish arts-based schools, "community" and "Orthodox," were founded in North America.

It would be interesting to study whether in striving for depth in knowledge, teaching through the arts shortchanges the students in terms of scope of content. Do students learn fewer chapters in the Bible? Do they learn less of prayer book but reach greater heights of spirituality?

While it is true that arts-based schools do not claim to be art schools, it might be that the students who are enrolled in the school have special inclinations toward the arts. It would be valuable to investigate whether students in arts-based schools have special pre-existing artistic talents or they come from artistic families. What happens to graduates of the schools? Do they continue to pursue interest in the arts? Finally, it would be fascinating to hear the teachers' points of view about what it means to teach in a school that often requires a variety of skills, what are their needs in terms of support and training, and what attracts them to work in a school that believes in integration of the arts.

References

A time to act (1990, June 12). Paper presented at the commission on Jewish Education in North America, New York.
Armstrong, T. (1994). *Multiple intelligences in the classroom*. Alexandria, VA: ASCD.
Asher, J. J. (1981). *Learning another language through actions*. Los Gatos, CA: Sky Oaks Productions.
Backenroth, O. A. (2003b). The arts and the Jewish day school. *Jewish Education News*, 24(2), 60–64.
Backenroth, O. A. (2004). Art and Rashi: A portrait of a Bible teacher. *Journal of Religious Education*, 99(2), 151–166.
Backenroth, O. A. (2005a). *The Blossom School: Teaching Judaism in an arts-Based School*. An unpublished dissertation. The Jewish Theological Seminary, New York.
Backenroth, O. A. (2005b). Weaving the arts into Jewish education. *Journal of Jewish Education*, 70(3), 50–60.
Backenroth, O. (2008). Putting the arts into Jewish education. *Ravsak* (Summer), 8–9.
Beane, J. A. (1997). *Curriculum integration*. New York: Teachers College Press.
Brovender, C. (2003). Towards Ahavat Hashem: Art and the religious experience. In S. Handelman & J. Saks (Eds.), *Wisdom from all my teachers: Issues and challenges in Torah education*. Jerusalem: Atid/Urim Publications.
Burnaford, G., Aprill, A., & Weiss, C. (2001). *Renaissance in the classroom: Arts integration and meaningful learning*. Mahwah, NJ: Lawrence Erlbaum Associates.
Burton, J., Horowitz, R., & Abeles, H. (1999, April). *Learning in and through the arts: The issue of transference*. Paper presented at the AERA national conference, Montreal, Canada.
Chipkin, I. (1952). The role of the Jewish arts in Jewish education. *Jewish Education*, 23, 3.
Cohen, R. (1988). *Jewish icons*. Los Angeles: University of California Press.
Cremin, L. A. (1961). *The transformation of the school: Progressivism in American education*. New York: Knopf.
Csikszentmihalyi, M. (1996). *Flow and the psychology of discovery and invention*. New York: Harper Collins Publishers.
Curtain, H., & Pesola, C. A. (1994). *Language and children: Making the match*. White Plains, NY: Longman.
Davis, B. (2008). A word from the editor. In *Hayedion*. New York: Summer.
Dewey, J. (1902/1990). *The child and the curriculum*. Chicago: University of Chicago Press.
Dewey, J. (1915/1990). *The school and society*. Chicago: The University of Chicago Press.

Dewey, J. (1934/1980). *Art as experience.* New York: Perigee Books.
Drake, S. (1993). *Planning integrated curriculum.* Alexandria, VA: ASCD.
Efland, A. D. (2002). *Art and cognition.* New York: Teachers College Press.
Eisner, E. (1998). *The kind of schools we need.* Portsmouth, NH: Heinemann.
Epstein, S. (2003). *Reimagining literacy practices: Biblical interpretation through tableau in one Jewish supplementary school.* Unpublished dissertation, Columbia University, New York.
Fogarty, R. (1997). *Problem-based learning and other curriculum models for the multiple intelligences classroom.* Arlington Heights, IL: Skylight.
Fox, S., & Novak, W. (1997). *Vision of the heart.* New York: The Mandel Institute.
Fox, S., Scheffler, I., & Marom, D. (Eds.). (2003). *Visions of Jewish education.* Cambridge: Cambridge University Press.
Gardner, H. (1982). *Art, mind, and brain: A cognitive approach to creativity.* New York: Basic Books.
Gardner, H. (1983). *Frames of mind: The theory of multiple intelligence.* New York: Basic Books.
Gaudelius, Y., & Speirs, P. (Eds.). (2002). *Contemporary issues in education.* Upper Saddle River, NJ: Prentice Hall.
Goldberg, M. R., & Phillips, A. (1995). Introduction. In *Arts as education* (Vol. 24, pp. v). Cambridge, MA: Harvard Educational Review.
Greene, M. (1997). The passions of pluralism: Multiculturalism and the expanding community. In S. Cahn (Ed.), *Classic and contemporary readings* (pp. 510–521). Washington, DC: American Educational Research Association.
Greene, M. (2000). *Releasing the imagination.* San Francisco: Jossey-Bass.
Hascal, L. (2001). *Dancing the Torah: The role of performance in extending understanding.* Unpublished Master of Education, York University, Toronto.
Heilman, S. (1992). Inside the Jewish school. In S. Kelman (Ed.), *What we know about the Jewish school* (pp. 305). Los Angeles: Tora Aura.
Holtz, B. (1984). *Back to the sources.* New York: Summit Books.
Hurwitz, A., & Day, M. (1995). *Children and their art.* Fort Worth, TX: Harcourt.
Ingall, C. K. (2003). *Hava N'Halela: Tzipora Jochsberger and the Hebrew Arts School.* Unpublished manuscript.
Jacobs, H. (1989). *Design options for an integrated curriculum. Interdisciplinary curriculum: Design and implementation.* New York: ASCD.
Jensen, E. (2001). *Art with the brain in mind.* Virginia: ASCD.
Kaplan, M. (1934/1997). *Judaism as civilization.* New York: Schocken Books.
Kaplan, M. (1937/1997). *The meaning of God in modern Jewish religion.* Detroit, MI: Wayne State University Press.
Met, M. (1991). Learning language through content: Learning content through language. *Foreign language annals, 24*(4), 281–295.
Milgrom, J. (1992). *Handmade midrash.* Philadelphia: The Jewish Publication Society.
Miller, H. (1999a). *Bezalel's Legacy: Investigating a place for the visual arts within Jewish Studies teaching in Jewish primary schools.* Unpublished Doctoral Dissertation, University of London, London.
Miller, H. (1999b). Visual reflective learning: A new framework for teaching art in Jewish Studies. *The Journal of Progressive Judaism, 13*, 67–78.
Miller, H. (2000). Bezalel's legacy. *Jewish Education News, 21*(1), 36–38.
Perkins, D. (1991). Educating for insight. *Educational Leadership, 49*(2), 4–8.
Perkins, D. (1993). *Smart schools.* New York: Simon and Schuster.
Register (1918/1919). *Art and music.* New York: The Jewish Theological Seminary.
Rosenak, M. (1999). *Roads to the palace.* Providence, RI: Bergahn Books.
Scheindlin, L. (2003). Emotional perception and spirituality development. *International journal of children's spirituality, 8*(2), 179–193.
Smith, R. A. (1994). *General knowledge and arts education.* Chicago: University of Illinois Press.

Swain, M. (1988). Manipulating and complementing content teaching to maximize second language learning. *TESL Canada Journal, 6*, 68–83.
Tucker, J., & Freeman, S. (1990). *Torah in motion: Creating dance midrash.* Denver, CO: A.R.E.
Wertheimer, J. (2001). *Talking dollars and sense about Jewish education.* New York: Avi Chai.
Wiener, J. (2002, June 12). Moving the arts to the head of the school. *The Jewish Week,* 6–7.
Wolf, D. P. (1987). Opening up assessment. *Educational Leadership, 45*(4), 24–29.
Wolf, D., & Piston, N. (1995). *Taking full measure: Rethinking assessment through the arts.* New York: College Entrance Examination Board.

Websites

http://www.capeweb.org/
http://www.lcinstitute.org/
http://www.pz.harvard.edu/research/PROPEL.htm
http://www.pz.harvard.edu/Research/Spectrum.htm
http://www.pz.harvard.edu/index.cfm
http://www.youngaudiences.org/

Bible: Teaching the Bible in Our Times

Barry W. Holtz

Introduction: Teaching the Bible in the Jewish Past

Teaching the Bible surely goes back to the origins of the Jewish people. Yet we do not have a great deal of knowledge about education in biblical times; indeed, the author of the major scholarly work on the subject asks quite baldly, "What do we really know about education in ancient Israel?" And answers, "not very much. The preceding observations are largely conjecture; whether or not they accord with reality can be debated, and undoubtedly will be" (Crenshaw, 1998, pp. 4–5). Even the existence of schools in the biblical world is unproven. We do know that there were schools in *other* cultures of the ancient world and that lends credence to the likelihood of there being schools in Eretz Yisrael, but as Crenshaw states, "Evidence for schools in these areas [Egypt, Mesopotamia] is incontrovertible. The same cannot be said of ancient Israel and much controversy centers on the very existence or non-existence of schools before the second century B.C.E..." (Crenshaw, 1998, p. 86). Inscriptions from ancient Eretz Yisrael point clearly in the direction of the existence of schools "but they do not clarify the nature of these places of learning" (Crenshaw, 1998, p. 112). And, of course, we certainly do not know much about the *pedagogy* of ancient times—who were the students? Who were the teachers? What was the subject matter? All these are hidden in the mists of the past.

Yet, it seems unimaginable that the Bible itself was not part of an ancient Israelite curriculum. The public *reading* of the Torah—mentioned in the Bible itself (e.g., II Chronicles 17: 7, 9; Nehemiah 8:1–10)—has traditionally been understood to be the origin of the practice of *teaching* the Torah, though the texts themselves are not entirely specific about this implication (Fishbane, 2002, p. xx; Sacks, 2009, p. 161). Certainly, however, by the time of the Mishnah (circa 200 CE), the practice of Torah study seems to have been well established. The oft-quoted utterance in Mishnah Avot (Avot 5:21) that Torah study begins at age 5 (with rabbinic literature being introduced in stages as a child gets older) indicates the value of Torah learning. The statement itself, however, is historically problematic. As Marcus shows, the passage

---

B.W. Holtz (✉)
Jewish Theological Seminary of America, New York, NY, USA
e-mail: bholtz@nyc.rr.com

is certainly a later addition to the Mishnah, probably introduced in the early Middle Ages (Marcus, 1996, pp. 43–44; see also Kraemer, 1989, p. 78), but the notion that Torah study begins at an early age is attested in the Babylonian Talmud (Bava Batra 21a). And, as Marcus shows, by the twelfth century, Talmudic interpreters have come to understand the text to mean that fathers are obligated to teach their sons and to find teachers for them as they get older (Marcus, 1996, p. 44).

The passage from Avot, albeit a later addendum, came to have a great influence on the notion of "curriculum" for Jewish education. It indicates an early exposure to learning Torah, but at the same time the statement asserts an important distinction that will come to dominate the course of study in Jewish education for centuries—ultimately the highest value of Jewish study is exploring the great works of *Rabbinic* culture, the Mishnah and even more importantly the Babylonian Talmud. The study of the Bible itself seems to occupy a lower rung on the scale. Moreover, the entire book that we call *Tanakh* or The Bible was not *as a whole* the object of study. When Jews studied the Bible, they focused on the Pentateuch (*Humash*) because of the lexical readings from the Torah that Jews encountered on the Sabbath, the Festivals, and twice weekly on Monday and Thursday mornings.

One way of thinking about the curriculum of ancient times is to look at a large body of literature that in one way may be understood to be the "lecture notes" or lesson plans of the rabbinic schoolhouse (Bregman, 1982). That is, the vast midrashic literature of Torah interpretation that has come down through the ages. If one thinks of Midrash as the mainstream or dominant interpretation of Torah promulgated by rabbinic teachers, it is not unreasonable to argue that the "curriculum" of the Beit Midrash can be mapped onto the books of midrashic writings (*teachings*, as it were) that we have inherited today. By that account, once again, the great preponderance of Midrash deals with the Pentateuchal readings, and although we do have Midrash on books such as Proverbs or Song of Songs, the number of actual textual pages devoted to Midrash on the *Humash* far outstrips that which we find on other books. A not unreasonable conclusion to draw, therefore, is that in rabbinic times the main focus of Bible *teaching* was on the weekly Torah reading and some of the other books of the Bible that were read liturgically (such as Esther, Song of Songs).

But what did this teaching look like? There is a great deal of discussion in the Talmud itself about the nature of the teaching and learning process. Through declarations of pedagogic practices (rarely) and through *aggadot* (legendary tales) about the world of the Beit Midrash itself (frequently), we today do get some insight into the world of the rabbinic study hall. It is hard to be definitive, of course, about the specific pedagogies employed by the teachers of those times and it is even more problematic to judge the practices of the past in the light of current-day values and ideas. It does seem that rabbinic culture, like most traditional cultures of the past, viewed teaching in the mode of what Philip Jackson has termed "the mimetic tradition" (Jackson, 1986). Namely, "transmission of factual and procedural knowledge from one person to another" (p. 117) in which the goal is to reproduce in the student the same knowledge already possessed by the teacher, and hence the term *mimesis*.

But it is certainly also true that rabbinic culture set the tone for a history of Jewish pedagogy that went beyond "soaking up" the wisdom of the wise teacher.

Bible: Teaching the Bible in Our Times

There is, in addition to mimesis, the culture of questioning and analysis that has over time come to characterize the classic Jewish pedagogy (Halbertal & Halbertal, 1998). The culture of the rabbinic schoolhouse is not the culture of memorizing catechisms. It is a world of debate and discussion; challenge and response. We can see this in the plaintive call of Rabbi Yochanan after the death of his opponent and challenger, Reish Lakish (Rabbi Shimon ben Lakish):

> Rabbi Yochanan was very pained by his passing. The Rabbis said: "Who will go and help calm Rabbi Yochanan? Let Rabbi Elazar ben Pedat go, for he is sharp in learning." He went and sat in front of Rabbi Yochanan. Every time Rabbi Yochanan said something, Rabbi Elazar cited a supporting Tannaitic source.
> Rabbi Yochanan said: "Are you like the son of Lakish? When I said something, the son of Lakish would ask me twenty-four questions, and I would respond with twenty-four answers. As a result, learning increased. And you tell me a Tannaitic support. Do I not know that I say good ideas?"
> He walked, and tore his garment, and wept.
> He said: "Where are you, son of Lakish? Where are you, son of Lakish?" He was crying out until he lost his mind.... [Bava Metzia 84a]

Even though this is a tragic tale, this text asserts the positive value in having a culture of questioning and debate (Holzer, 2009). What is clearly indicated is a pedagogic style that strongly resembles the modern perspective that is often called "inquiry" (Bruner, 1979; Schwab, 1978; Shulman & Keislar, 1966; Weinbaum et al., 2004). In "inquiry" the teacher is not the only source of wisdom but students challenge the teacher, examine the evidence (in science it is often experimental data or theory; in the humanities it tends to be documentary or textual evidence), and come to their own conclusions. As we shall see, "inquiry" came to have an important influence on Bible teaching in the twentieth century and into our own times. We can trace its roots back to the values of the rabbinic study hall itself.

Teaching and Learning the Bible Through the Rabbinic Lens

As teachers and learners of the Bible today, we are heirs to a long history in which the dominant approach to understanding the Bible was that given by *rabbinic interpretation*.

The classical interpreters of the Bible operated under certain specific assumptions, most importantly, in James Kugel's words, "the doctrine of 'omnisignificance,' whereby nothing in Scripture is said in vain or for rhetorical flourish: every detail is important, everything is intended to impart some teaching" (Kugel, 1997, p. 21).

Learning the Bible in the schoolhouse from the Middle Ages onward, we may surmise, was a matter of learning the standard rabbinic interpretation of these texts, particularly as preserved in the commentary of Rabbi Shlomo Yitzhaki ("Rashi"), the great French commentator of the late eleventh century. It was Rashi, in large part due to the authority of his commentary on the *Talmud*, who essentially set the way that "we" understand the Torah from his time onward. There were, of course, other commentators and no doubt the more learned among the Jews debated the interpretations of these other figures both in relation to Rashi and independent of him. The famed Mikraot Gedolot ("the great readings" or Rabbinic Bible) edition of the Tanakh lays out the variety of commentators on the page, as if in debate with one another. But for most Jews, the curriculum of "*Humash* with Rashi" was the standard way to understand Torah. And therefore, most certainly, also the standard way to *teach* Torah.

But raising the name of Rashi and the other medieval commentators leads us in another direction as well in which we see that a historical development in the past will lead to important implications about teaching later down the road. As I have stated above, the dominant approach to teaching (i.e., reading) the Bible has been through rabbinic interpretation, the "midrashic" (or *derash*) mode. But in the early Middle Ages, particularly outside the world of Ashkenazi Judaism, a new approach to reading the Bible began to take hold:

> After the rise of Islam in the seventh century, another mode of interpreting Scripture emerged and for several centuries overshadowed *derash* in biblical exegesis. This approach, that of *peshat* [plain meaning], sought to understand the biblical text within the parameters of its historical, literary, and linguistic context. Historical context requires that interpretation must read the text in terms of the world of ancient Israel and the biblical story as a whole. (Greenstein, 1984, p. 217)

As Greenstein and others have noted, *peshat* came into the Jewish world through the encounter of Jewish thought with the intellectual culture of Islam and the approach of Muslim readers to sacred texts. "No longer did the rabbis need to press the midrashic interpretation of the Bible into service as a primary means of learning God's will" (Greenstein, 1984, p. 220). *Peshat*, in its medieval mode, has been seen by scholars to set the stage many centuries later for the growth of modern academic approaches to the study of the Bible. Those approaches, while differing dramatically in their faith assumptions about the nature of the Bible and biblical authorship, nonetheless are focused on using what Greenstein, above, has called the "historical, literary, and linguistic context" to help us understand the text. In the mid-twentieth century, *peshat* in its modern academic guise enters the arena of teaching methods, as we shall see in the next section of this chapter.

Teaching the Bible in the Twentieth Century: Israel

It is not my task here to trace the entire history of biblical *interpretation*, extrapolating from it the history of Jewish *teaching* of the Bible. That is a task that is far too large and fraught with complex historical issues, unrelated to our concerns. These introductory comments are meant to set the stage for a discussion on Bible teaching in the North American context in our times. But before we do so, it is important to spend a brief time talking about the teaching of the Bible in the other major Jewish center of the contemporary period, the Land of Israel.

The issue of the Tanakh in Israeli culture is a complex one that has occasioned a good deal of research from historians, most notably the contemporary scholar Anita Shapira who has written important essays on the topic (most of these have not been translated into English, unfortunately). In one article, "The Tanakh and Israeli Identity," Shapira points out the importance of Bible study in the *secular* consciousness of the early Zionists:

> In Jewish Tradition the Tanakh was considered of lesser importance in comparison to the Talmud—the "oral Torah." The Jewish Enlightenment (Haskalah) raised the status of the Tanakh as part of its return to the ancient sources. Renewal of the Hebrew language, Hebrew grammar, learning Tanakh—all these were elements that were chosen from the Tradition for service in the realization of the new national movement [Zionism], a process of secularizing the Tradition. (Shapira, 1997, pp. 166–167)

Unlike other elements of the Jewish traditional past, Shapira goes on to say, the Tanakh was adopted by the secular Zionist movement as it broke down the traditions of the Jewish past into elements among which the secularists would pick and choose. The first Hebrew Gymnasium in Jaffa gave pride of place to the study of Tanakh, while Talmud "was brought down to 1 hour of study per week" (p. 167).

The major scholarly study of the history of Bible teaching in Israel is that of J. Schoneveld (1976); Schoneveld's work is well summarized and explored in Joel Duman's doctoral dissertation (2005). In the scholarship of Shapira, Schoneveld, Duman, and others, we can see the complex relationship of Bible education to the project of Zionism.

On the one hand, the *religious* Zionists viewed the Bible as a proper object of study in the way it had been studied for millennia, through the lens of rabbinic commentary. And yet at the same time, studying Tanakh in the landscape of Eretz Yisrael—the physical location for most of the Hebrew Bible—added an extra dimension of power to the educational experience. The world of *derash*, one might say, comes face to face with the living reality of *peshat*; so it is no longer sufficient to view the text through the midrashic lens when one can actually walk where the storied characters of biblical times were said to have lived. Religious readers and teachers became more "fundamentalist" or literalist when they could point to a valley and say with pride "here is where David fought Goliath." In a certain sense, an internal tension was inevitable in the religious teacher's mind: are we focusing on the great values and teachings that our rabbis found in these tales or are we worrying about the exact location and terrain in which this or that story took place?

For the vast majority of Israeli society, in the *secular* state school system, the problem was somewhat different. As Duman puts it,

> Rather than being seen as the basis of religious authority and behavior, the Bible became the corner stone of Jewish history and culture, a treasure trove to be valued for its artistic, moral and historical wealth. In this manner modern secular Jewry was able to maintain traditional attachment to the ancient canon, without being committed to the observance of traditional rites, laws and customs. (Duman, 2005, p. 13)

But what about the centuries of traditional commentaries? What role did they now play? For Ahad Ha'am, for example, the Bible teaching that he saw around him in Palestine in the early years of the twentieth century did not emphasize what he called "spiritual education." It was too "archeological"—that is, focused on the specific connection of the biblical text to the physical land of Israel. For Ahad Ha'am, "the

Bible must be studied as part of the chain of Jewish history and culture, linked to the student of today by generations of Jewish thought, interpretation and creativity" (Duman, 2005, p. 15). Over the course of the decades following this debate, many theories about Bible teaching in Israel emerged, rooted in different disciplines—for example, psychology—and competing values (these are all summarized by Duman, pp. 17–33); but in the mid-1980s, a number of studies—culminating in the so-called Shenhar report of 1994—began to document the falling status of Judaic studies among Israeli students. The Bible, which for the Zionist leaders of the twentieth century (Ben Gurion most famously was an ardent student of Tanakh, though a secular man[1]) was so important, no longer became an object of study and veneration for the new generation of Israeli youth, focused so much on technology and economic status. Since the mid-1990s, the Israel Ministry of education has been trying to address these issues, but solutions are not so simple. Some of the root causes of the decline are connected to the nature of Israeli society today and therefore are resistant to easy change.

Teaching the Bible in the Twentieth Century: North America

Educators, literary figures, and philosophers in Israel were faced with the challenge of creating a total Hebrew culture in the actual geographical locale of the biblical world. The revived land required a revived language and set of cultural references. But in North America, the issues were considerably different. Here, the question was the preservation of Jewish life, religion, and culture amidst the allurements of this very welcoming Diaspora. What should be the role of Hebrew in the American landscape? What would be the relationship between this Diaspora and Eretz Yisrael? How should the Bible be viewed in this context—as a religious and authoritative work? As a cultural heritage? As a tool for learning Hebrew language? It is also important to remember that the American context, at least in the first half of the twentieth century, was dominated by a particular educating *institution*, the Talmud Torah, or Hebrew School (Graff, 2008; Rauch, 2004, pp. 41; 57–61). The fact that Jewish education would take place in a part-time institution (unlike, e.g., the Jaffa Gymnasium), conducted in a language that was not a Jewish language like Hebrew or Yiddish[2] was certain to have a huge impact on the way that subjects such as the Bible would be taught.

In the 1950s and early 1960s, the typical approaches to Bible instruction were at two ends of the spectrum. On the one hand, there was the Bible stories approach in

---

[1] See Shapira (1997).

[2] The *lingua franca* of the Eastern European Yeshivah was Yiddish of course. In general (except within parts of the Haredi world) that changed in America and English became the new "mother tongue." That change is not to be underestimated. Although most Jews in Eastern Europe did not *speak* Hebrew, the fact that Yiddish and Hebrew share the same alphabet and that Yiddish has so many Hebrew words and references embedded within it must have had an enormous impact on the experience of young students learning in the European school house.

which simplified versions of narratives from the Bible (mostly *Humash*) were read or told. This approach was found in large measure in the one-day-a-week Sunday schools. On the other hand, in many of the Hebrew schools there was the *ivrit b'ivrit*[3] approach (Hebrew in Hebrew—i.e., biblical texts of a somewhat simplified sort which were then supposed to be "translated" by students into modern Hebrew, while the teacher's instruction was done, or supposed to have been done, in spoken Hebrew). The problem, as Zielenziger (1989) states it well, was the following:

> The emphasis was not on the learning of the values in the Bible but on *Bekiut*, or memorization, the ability to recognize phrases and facts and knowing exactly where in the Bible they occur. This ability to quote and correlate is enriching when the student also understands the ideas and values behind the phrases learned. When, however, *Bekiut* is the final aim of the study of Bible, it becomes a meaningless skill, somewhat reminiscent of the skill of knowing the names of the capitals of the fifty states of the United States without knowing anything about these capitals... (p. 48)

What would it mean to teach the Bible so that students might learn, as Zielenziger puts it "the ideas and values behind the phrases learned"? The great revolution in Bible teaching and Bible curriculum in American Jewish education was spearheaded by the Jewish Theological Seminary's Melton Research Center beginning in the mid-1960s. The Melton Center, conceived by the Jewish educator Seymour Fox and funded by the lay leader Samuel M. Melton, was founded in 1959 as a place of curriculum research, educational theory development, and teacher education. Fox and the Melton advisory board decided early on that it was important to develop new ways of teaching the Bible. This decision flowed out of a number of motivating factors. First, there was the situation in the Hebrew schools, as described in the passage above by Zielenziger. The Bible had become either a tool toward learning Hebrew—in essence, a kind of Hebrew textbook—or the occasion for the dull *Bekiut* exercises that are mentioned above. The Bible in the view of the architects of Melton needed to become a source of values, and in the language of the time, "character education."

But the Melton project was motivated by other factors as well. The age of Sputnik was a time of great reverence and excitement about science and technology. The Bible was seen as an outdated, anti-intellectual work, a book that represented superstition and bad, outmoded science (such as in its depiction of the creation of the world). The Melton design team wanted to counter this attitude and make the case for the Bible in the modern world. Years later, when I asked Fox why Melton had begun with Genesis when in fact they could have focused on any area of Jewish education, such as prayer or the Jewish holidays, he replied bluntly, "because we wanted to show that the Bible wasn't junk."

---

[3] *Ivrit b'ivrit* is a methodology in American Jewish education dating back to the early years of the twentieth century. It was actively promoted by the most extraordinary figure in American Jewish educational history, Samson Benderly and his followers. *Ivrit b'ivrit* was a controversial idea and remained so. It might even be argued that the battle over *ivrit b'ivrit* is *still* being played out in contemporary Jewish education, but the playing field has moved from the supplementary school to the day school. For more on this background, see Graff (2008) and Krasner (2005).

At the same time, interesting developments in the world of general education seemed relevant to new thinking about Jewish education. Bruner's (1960) idea that "the curriculum of a subject should be determined by the most fundamental understanding that can be achieved of the underlying principles that give structure to that subject" (p. 31) had a profound influence on all fields of education. Fox's graduate school adviser at the University of Chicago, Joseph Schwab, though a critic of Bruner, was heavily involved in the new work being done on the "structure of the disciplines." Bruner's memorable phrase that the "schoolboy learning physics *is* a physicist" (p. 14; emphasis his) in essence was translated by the Melton curriculum writers as the "schoolboy learning the Bible *is* the academic Bible scholar!" To show that the Bible wasn't "junk," the Melton Center's curriculum work wanted to highlight the work of Bible *scholars*, not traditional rabbis, but academics in university-type settings whose work was methodologically rigorous and intellectually respectable (Zielenziger, 1989, pp. 70–71).

Thus the Melton Bible project began with two competing ideas: that the Bible should be viewed as a source of values and ideas that aimed toward character education and that the Bible should be viewed through the lens of academic scholarship, "translated," as it were, for children. A leading Bible scholar of the period, Nahum Sarna, was enlisted to write what may very well be the first popular book aimed at presenting the ideas of modern Bible scholarship to a non-professional audience, *Understanding Genesis* (1966). And under the leadership of the Melton Center's first director, Louis Newman, writers were engaged to turn this work into lesson plans. Finally, teachers were recruited for training in the "new method." If the sciences were to have New Math and New Biology, at its heart Melton was the creator of the New Bible.

In retrospect, one can see that the twin goals of teaching the Bible for character education and teaching the Bible in the style of modern biblical scholarship were not fully compatible. After all, university scholars of the Bible—particularly at that period—were very oriented toward seeing the Bible in the context of its ancient setting. They were focused on an historical, contextual approach toward understanding the Bible. Matters of character education and values, though not necessarily at *odds* with the scientific approach, had little in common with it. The approach represented by *Understanding Genesis* was clearly on the side of the university Bible scholars.

Resolving the tension between academic scholarship and values education may well have led to the early introduction of more literary approaches to the biblical lessons being taught in the Melton curriculum. This literary approach was more attuned to a character education pedagogy. Looking at Sarna's *Understanding Genesis* and comparing it to the original Melton teacher's guide by Leonard Gardner (1966), we can see the way that Gardner added a more literary perspective and cut back on the number of ancient Near Eastern comparisons that had appeared in *Understanding Genesis*.

Still one thing that did *not* appear in the Melton work was *rabbinic commentary*. The radical nature of the Melton approach was not only in its adaptation of academic scholarship of the Bible to the world of Jewish education. It also represented a thoroughgoing rejection of the dominant mode of Jewish Bible reading (and hence teaching) throughout the generations—the Bible as seen through eyes of the rabbinic tradition. Melton was the reinvention of the Spanish *peshat* tradition in the new guise of the academic focus on context.

But something else was going on as well and it too had major implications for the future development of Bible pedagogy. Melton strongly rejected the *Bikiut* pedagogy in favor of a very different, one might say, Deweyean approach to classroom teaching and lesson planning. The Melton approach was to be based on an "inquiry" model with teachers leading discussions rather than either giving lectures or examining students on memorized facts. The idea that the Bible could become a focus of investigation and "discovery learning" was revolutionary in its time. And it is, I think, fair to argue that this model of teaching came to have a profound impact on Jewish education in many different venues.

The Melton Bible materials, both in their earliest generations and in the later work done by Zielenziger (1979, 1984) demonstrated the important potential connection between the work of academic scholarship and the practice of education (Holtz, 2006). Hence, the Melton Bible materials more and more came to have a *literary* emphasis (and less of an Ancient Near Eastern focus) not only because of the focus on character education but also as the field of biblical studies itself came to recognize literary analysis as a legitimate academic mode of scholarship (Alter, 1983; Rosenberg, 1984). The influence of scholarship on education could be seen quite clearly in the mid-1980s when Joel Grishaver published his Bible curriculum *Being Torah* (1986), which consciously modeled itself after Robert Alter's work in literary studies of the Bible. Grishaver aimed at giving children the skills and experience related to reading the Bible in a literary way.

Alex Sinclair's doctoral dissertation (2001) further explored the relationship of scholarship for Bible instruction by looking at three Biblical scholars (J. Cheryl Exum, Jeffrey Tigay, and Yair Zakovitch) and exploring the theoretical implications of their work for Bible teaching. Prior to Sinclair, Gail Dorph's doctoral dissertation (1993; see also Dorph, 2002) was another work heavily under the influence of the Schwab tradition. Dorph explored the Schwabian conception of subject matter (syntactic and substantive structures) and did an empirical study of MA students in two different pre-service training programs in Jewish education. She examined the ways in which young teachers' knowledge of the Bible influenced their reactions to certain pedagogic dilemmas, findings that had important implications for the way we prepare teachers for the field. In addition, she added the important element of teachers' *beliefs*—particularly core foundational beliefs—to the picture of how we might improve the practice of teachers. The role of beliefs is underestimated in the Schwab model and Dorph's work put that question on the agenda.

While literary approaches to the teaching of the Bible came to have a larger role in the world of non-Orthodox education, Orthodox educators continued to base their approach on the foundation of classical commentaries (*parshanut*), most importantly Rashi. Within Orthodox education, however, an interesting bifurcation could be discerned in the approach to *parshanut* that various educators employed. On the one hand, Rashi's commentary was viewed as *the* authoritative understanding of the biblical text. To learn *Humash*, one had to learn "*Humash* with Rashi"—the two went hand in hand. For any "problem" posed by the biblical text, Rashi had the "correct" answer. At the same time, another force in Orthodox Bible education was being felt, the enormous power of possibly the most influential Bible educator in the world during the latter part of the twentieth century (and beyond)—Nechama Leibowitz (1905–1997) who taught hundreds (perhaps thousands?) of both Israeli and Diaspora teachers from her post at the Hebrew University. Leibowitz had developed her own particular methodology for the use of classical commentators. Rather than viewing one commentary (Rashi) as providing *the* authoritative reading of any biblical passage, Leibowitz saw the *range* of commentators arrayed over and against one another as the appropriate approach in reading the biblical text. What she aimed at was analyzing the particular commentary's approach and seeing it in relationship to others that she brought to bear on the biblical text. Her pedagogy—influencing all those students whom she taught—was the arrangement of these commentators around key issues in the particular text. She raised certain textual or philosophical questions implicit in the biblical passage and then brought the commentators out to battle over the meaning of the text (see, e.g., Leibowitz, 1963, 1974).

Leibowitz was in many ways an unusual figure in the university. She was not interested in studying the commentators in their historical or geographic context in the mode of academic researchers. She was not interested in the influences upon them from both within and outside Jewish culture. She was trying to discern their readings of the text.[4] And although Leibowitz herself was an Orthodox educator, she aimed at opening up the range of interpretation beyond the Rashi-only approach. And in doing so, Leibowitz suggested that multiplicity of interpretations was the hallmark of a Jewish way of teaching, a view that was not universally accepted among Orthodox educators, though it came to influence a significant number.

Teaching the Bible: Theoretical Considerations

In the mid-1980s, one of Schwab's most distinguished students, Lee S. Shulman, began to publish the results of important research in the field of general education that he and his graduate students were conducting in the area of the relationship between the content knowledge of teachers and the way those teachers conceptualized their teaching. Shulman's influence on Jewish education could be seen in the previously mentioned doctoral dissertations by Dorph (1993) and Sinclair (2001). My own work in this area (Holtz, 2003) was influenced by Shulman and particularly by Shulman's student (later, one of his successors at Stanford) Pamela Grossman (Grossman, 1990, 1991; Grossman, Wilson, & Shulman, 1989). Grossman was working on the way that beginning high school English teachers thought about their subject matter knowledge for teaching purposes. Grossman herself described her project as an exploration of "the nature of pedagogical content

---

[4]The major study of Leibowitz's methodology is Frankel (2007); see also Deitcher (2000), Frankel (1999) and Peerless (2005).

knowledge in English among beginning teachers and the role of subject-specific teacher education coursework in contributing to graduates' knowledge and beliefs about teaching English" (Grossman, 1990, p. x). It was obvious to me at the time that I began reading Grossman's work that her ideas about teaching English "texts" could be applied to Jewish "texts," in particular the Bible, with considerable potential.

Grossman began to describe the teacher's "orientations" to the subject matter that they were teaching. The word "orientation" here is used in a technical sense, a term meant to include aspects of both the knowledge and belief sides of a teacher's relationship to the subject matter. An orientation represents the "English teachers' interpretive stance... toward literature [and] becomes important in understanding their goals for instruction, curricular choices, instructional assignments, and classroom questions. ...More than a casual attitude toward the subject matter, an orientation toward literature represents a basic organizing framework for knowledge about literature" (Grossman, 1991, pp. 247–248). Orientation is a rich and valuable concept in education. It touches not only upon the *practice* of teaching but upon the *philosophy* behind that practice: "An orientation is a description not of a teacher's 'method' in some technical meaning of the word, but in a deeper sense, of a teacher's most powerful conceptions and beliefs about the field he or she is teaching. It is the living expression of the philosophical questions...: What is my view of the aims of education, and how as a teacher do I attain those aims" (Holtz, 2003, pp. 48–49)?

Grossman described three main orientations to a literary text: a text-based approach, a context-based approach, and a reader-response-based approach. Orientations in Grossman's presentation (as I tried to show in *Textual Knowledge*) are rooted in the world of academic scholarship. It is the translation for education of what scholars in the academy do. This is clearly the Schwabian tradition, but "Schwab's description of substantive structures does not take into account the possibility that there may be modes of discourse that do not fit the basic rules of university life. Perhaps, in the context of general education these difficulties would be less likely to appear. But in the realm of Jewish religious education we find ourselves face to face with the reality of multiple approaches to the discipline, some of which are governed by the comfortable rules of university discourse, and others of which are quite different. So different, in fact, that even the word 'discipline' is outside of realm of discourse" (Holtz, 2002, p. 17).

Thus, in conceptualizing the Bible as a subject area, I tried to delineate a more expansive list of orientations that seemed relevant to teachers of this particular text. This is what I called "The Map for Teaching Bible" (Holtz, 2003, pp. 92–95). These orientations are wide-ranging and include classical academic approaches such as what I called "The Contextual Orientation" which tries to teach students an understanding of the Bible based upon the meaning of the biblical texts *within their own times* and "The Literary Criticism Orientation" that reads biblical texts in the spirit of modern literary theory. But the "map" also includes orientations that would not be found in the university world, "The Moralistic–Didactic Orientation" that "aims at discerning the 'message' (or messages) that specific biblical texts offer for our own lives" (p. 93) or "The Personalization Orientation" that tries to find the psychological, spiritual, or political meaning of the Bible, aiming "to see the relationship between text and the life of today" (p. 94).

I have argued (Holtz, 2003, pp. 103–106) that while a knowledge of orientations related to teaching the Bible will give teachers a variety of resources to help address both the differences one finds from one biblical text to the next, such understanding by teachers also helps accommodate the fact that in any given classroom one might find many different kinds of students. One orientation may appeal to certain students more than another, and as teachers of texts we need to be aware of the ways that our teaching reaches a variety of students. A consciousness of the concept of orientations has led some researchers to explore in empirical research the way that orientations might actually be playing out in Jewish classrooms. Most recently, for example, the *Journal of Jewish Education* published a series of articles in which a variety of scholars explored the "contextual" orientation as it was found in different educational settings (Cousens, Morrison, & Fendrick, 2008; Holtz, 2008; Levisohn, 2008; Tanchel, 2008).

Institutional Issues and the Future of Bible Teaching

In the early years of the twenty-first century, it is interesting to see how some of the core issues of Bible teaching in America from the last century continue to persist. The question of "who will do the teaching" that, in various ways, has been a constant in American Jewish education continues to trouble the world of Bible teaching. In the early part of the twentieth century, the battle between the proponents of Benderly's *ivrit b'ivrit* approach and the traditional teachers from Europe was one setting for this same enactment of the "who will teach" question. At the time that the Melton curriculum first appeared in the mid-1960s, the issue revolved around the tension between Israeli teachers who viewed the Bible as a kind of textbook for Hebrew and the curriculum team that wanted the Bible to be taught as a repository of values and scholarly information (Zielenziger, 1989). Later, the question of who was the Bible teacher became connected to the weaker and weaker background in education and Jewish studies of the newer teaching core (Gamoran, Goldring, & Robinson, 1999). It is probable that this is an issue that will not soon disappear. Efforts to improve the preparation of educators at the so-called "training institutions" (schools of higher learning) in North America coupled with ambitious programs for professional development for teachers are likely to be as crucial as they ever were (Dorph & Holtz, 2000; Dorph, 2010).

The nature of the educating institutions themselves also has a profound impact on Bible teaching in the American context. The fundamental institution for the Jewish education of children—the supplementary school (or Hebrew school; now often called the "congregational school")—has, since the latter years of the twentieth century, cut back on the number of hours of instruction and days of the week that it meets. That change had profound implications for Bible study. If schools now only meet 2–4 hours a week, how much of the Bible can actually be taught, especially with all the other items on the school's agenda—especially preparation for bar and bat mitzvah? At the same time, the growth of day schools with (at least in *potential*) more hours for Jewish content instruction offers new opportunities for Bible teaching.

New curriculum materials such as the Melton Research Center's MaToK project, aimed specifically at the day-school setting, offer the possibility of combining a variety of orientations toward the Bible in a single, well-designed curriculum (Miller, 2005; Scheindlin, 2007). The Internet as a resource for both curriculum delivery and teacher education is only beginning to be tapped. And new pedagogic approaches, using techniques that open up the potential of the Bible for personal growth and exploration surely will continue to evolve. Perhaps the most striking in recent years has been the application of approaches from the world of drama and psychodrama to Bible teaching. Recently, the organization Storahtelling has been associated with this approach asserting that "[u]sing an innovative fusion of scholarship, storytelling, performing arts and new media, our programs reclaim the narratives and traditions that define Jewish life yet have failed to adapt to modern times" (http://www.storahtelling.org). Though Storahtelling as an organization has become very popular, its work draws upon earlier experiments in this area, particularly drama as studied by Shira Epstein (2004), Midrash drama as explored by Seymour Epstein (1976), Bibliodrama (http://www.bibliodrama.com) as practiced by Peter Pitzele (1995, 1997), and the work of Samuel Laeuchli and Evelyn Rothchild Laeuchli (1989) in using the exploration of myths in the context of psychodrama.

There is little doubt that the Bible will continue to be the core curriculum content in many settings of Jewish education. The challenges as we face the next century will, in a perhaps unsurprising way, mirror those that Jewish education in America has always faced: in what way is the American setting conducive to the exploration of an ancient literature? In which contexts will Bible education best flourish? And who will be the teachers who carry on the tradition of teaching and learning of this most central text? As for the Bible itself, there is little to worry about. As the Bible scholar Michael Fishbane has written, "…the Bible may become sacred to us insofar as its images and language shape our discourse, stimulate our moral and spiritual growth, and simply bind us to past generations which also took this text seriously" (Fishbane, 1989, p. 132). Future generations, with the benefit of wise and thoughtful teachers, will continue to hear within it the echoes of a people's distant past. And they will find within its language, narrative, and poetry the ways to build a life and map a future.

References

Alter, R. (1983). *The art of biblical narrative*. New York: Basic Books.
Bregman, M. (1982). The darshan: Preacher and teacher of Talmudic times. *The Melton Journal, 14*, Sivan 5742.

Bruner, J. S. (1960). *The process of education*. New York: Vintage Books.
Bruner, J. (1979). *On knowing: Essays for the left hand* (2nd ed.). Cambridge, MA: Belknap Press of Harvard University Press.
Cousens, B., Morrison, D., & Fendrick, S. (2008). Using the contextual orientation to facilitate the study of Bible with generation X. *Journal of Jewish Education, 74*(1), 6–28.
Crenshaw, J. L. (1998). *Education in ancient Israel: Across the deadening silence*. New York: Doubleday.
Deitcher, H. (2000). Between angels and mere mortals: Nechama Leibowitz's approach to the study of biblical characters. *Journal of Jewish Education, 66*(1–2), 8–22 (Spring/Summer).
Dorph, G. Z. (1993). Conceptions and preconceptions: A study of prospective Jewish educators' knowledge and belief about Torah. Unpublished doctoral dissertation, The Jewish Theological Seminary of America, New York.
Dorph, G. Z. (2002). What do teachers need to know to teach Torah? In B. I. Cohen & A. Ofek (Eds.), *Essays in education and Judaism in honor of Joseph S. Lukinsky* (pp. 97–113). New York: Jewish Theological Seminary Press.
Dorph, G. Z. (2010, In press). Investigating prospective Jewish teachers' knowledge and beliefs about Torah: Implications for teacher education. *Religious Education, 105*(1), 63–85.
Dorph, G. Z., & Holtz, B. W. (2000). Professional development for teachers: Why doesn't the model change? *Journal of Jewish Education, 66*(1), 67–76.
Duman, J. (2005). The use of a web site in teaching the cain and abel narrative in an Israeli high school: An action research study of the integration of technology and Bible teaching. Unpublished doctoral dissertation, The Jewish Theological Seminary of America, New York.
Epstein, S. (1976). Models of Jewish Learning. Unpublished EdD thesis. University of Toronto, t OISE: Ontario Institute for Studies in Education.
Epstein, S. D. (2004). Reimagining literacy practices: Creating living Midrash from ancient texts through Tableau. *Journal of Jewish Education, 70*(1–2), 60–73.
Fishbane, M. (1989). *The garments of Torah*. Bloomington, IN: Indiana University Press.
Fishbane, M. (2002). *Haftarot: The traditional Hebrew text with the new JPS translation*. Philadelphia: The Jewish Publication Society.
Frankel, M. (1999). The teacher in the writings of Nehama Leibowitz. In Y. Rich & M. Rosenak (Eds.), *Abiding challenges: Research perspectives on Jewish education* (pp. 359–374). Ramat Gan: Freund Publishing House and Bar-Ilan University Press (Studies in Memory of Mordechai Bar-Lev).
Frankel, M. L. (2007). *Teaching the Bible: The philosophy of Nechama Leibowitz*. Tel Aviv: Miska-Yedioth Ahronoth Books and Chemed books (Hebrew).
Gamoran, A., Goldring, E. B., & Robinson, B. (1999). Towards building a profession: Characteristics of contemporary educators in American Jewish schools. In Y. Rich & M. Rosenak (Eds.), *Abiding challenges: Research perspectives on Jewish education* (pp. 449–475). Ramat Gan: Freund Publishing House and Bar-Ilan University Press (Studies in Memory of Mordechai Bar-Lev).
Gardner, L. (1966). *Genesis: The teacher's guide*. New York: Melton Research Center.
Graff, G. (2008). *"And you shall teach them diligently": A concise history of Jewish education in the United States, 1776–2000*. New York: Jewish Theological Seminary Press.
Greenstein, E. L. (1984). Medieval Bible Commentaries. In B.W. Holtz (Ed.), *Back to the sources: Reading the classic Jewish texts* (pp. 213–260). New York: Simon and Schuster.
Grishaver, J. (1986). *Being Torah*. Los Angeles: Tora Aura books.
Grossman, P. L. (1990). *The making of a teacher: Teacher knowledge and teacher education*. New York: Teachers College Press.
Grossman, P. L. (1991). What are we talking about anyhow: Subject matter knowledge of English teachers? In J. Brophy (Ed.), *Advances in research on teaching* (vol. 2, pp. 245–264). Stamford, CT: JAI Press.
Grossman, P. L., Wilson, S. M., & Shulman, L. S. (1989). Teachers of substance: Subject-matter knowledge for teaching. In M. Reynolds (Ed.), *Knowledge base for the beginning teacher* (pp. 23–36). New York: Pergamon.

Halbertal, M., & Halbertal, T. H. (1998). The Yeshiva. In A. O. Rorty (Ed.), *Philosophers of education: New historical perspectives* (pp. 458–469). London: Routledge.

Holtz, B. (2002). Whose discipline is it anyway? In B. I. Cohen & A. Ofek (Eds.), *Essays in education and Judaism in honor of Joseph S. Lukinsky* (pp. 11–24). New York: Jewish Theological Seminary Press.

Holtz, B. (2003). *Textual knowledge: Teaching the Bible in theory and in practice.* New York: Jewish Theological Seminary Press.

Holtz, B. W. (2006). Across the divide: What might Jewish educators learn from Jewish scholars? *Journal of Jewish Education, 72*(1), 5–28.

Holtz, B. W. (2008). Response to the suite of articles on teaching the Bible. *Journal of Jewish Education, 74*(2), 227–236.

Holzer, E. (2009). "Either a *hevruta* partner or death": A critical view on the interpersonal dimensions of *hevruta* learning. *Journal of Jewish Education, 75*(2), 130–149.

Jackson, P. (1986). The mimetic and the transformative: Alternative outlooks on teaching. In *The practice of teaching* (pp. 115–145). New York: Teachers College Press.

Kraemer, D. (Ed.) (1989). *The Jewish family: Metaphor and memory.* New York: Oxford University Press.

Krasner, J. (2005). Jewish education and American Jewish education, Part I. *Journal of Jewish Education, 71*(2), 121–177.

Kugel, J. L. (1997). *The Bible as it was.* Cambridge, MA: Belknap Press of Harvard University Press.

Laeuchli, S., & Rothchild Laeuchli, E. (1989). Mimesis: The healing play of Myth. *Quadrant, XXII*(2).

Leibowitz, N. (1963). Towards teaching Tanakh in the upper grades. *Maayanot, 1*, 20–26.

Leibowitz, N. (1974). *Studies in Bereshit (Genesis) in the context of ancient and modern Jewish Bible commentary.* Jerusalem: World Zionist Organization.

Levisohn., J. A. (2008). Introducing the contextual orientation to Bible: A comparative study. *Journal of Jewish Education, 74*(1), 53–82.

Marcus, I. G. (1996). *Rituals of childhood: Jewish culture and acculturation in the middle ages.* New Haven, CT: Yale University Press.

Miller, D. U. (2005). What is the impact of a new Bible curriculum on four teachers who use it? Unpublished doctoral dissertation, The Jewish Theological Seminary of America, New York.

Peerless, S. (2005). *To study and to teach: The methodology of Nechama Leibowitz.* Jerusalem: Urim Publications.

Pitzele, P. (1995). *Our fathers' wells: A personal encounter with the myths of Genesis.* New York: Harpercollins.

Pitzele, P. (1997). *Scripture windows: Toward a practice of Bibliodrama.* Los Angeles: Torah Aura.

Rauch, E. (2004). *The education of American Jewry: The past is a prologue.* New York: Liberty Publishing House.

Rosenberg, J. (1984). Biblical narrative. In B. W. Holtz (Ed.), *Back to the sources: Reading the classic Jewish texts* (pp. 31–82). New York: Simon and Schuster.

Sacks, J. (2009). *The Koren Sacks siddur: A Hebrew/English prayer book.* Jerusalem: Koren Publishers.

Sarna, N. M. (1966). *Understanding Genesis.* New York: Melton Research Center and Schocken Books.

Scheindlin, L. (2007). May the study of Torah be as sweet as honey: A critical review of MaToK. *Conservative Judaism, 59*(2), 26–49.

Schoneveld, J. (1976). *The Bible in Israeli education: A study of approaches to the Hebrew Bible and its teaching in Israeli educational literature.* Assen: Van Gorcum.

Schwab, J. (1978). In I. Westbury & N. J. Wilkof (Eds.), *Science, curriculum, and liberal education: Selected essays.* Chicago: University of Chicago Press.

Shapira, A. (1997). Ben Gurion and the Tanakh. In A. Shapira (Ed.), *New Jews, Old Jews* (pp. 217–247). Tel Aviv: Am Oved (Hebrew).

Shulman, L. S., & Keislar, E. R. (Eds.) (1966). *Learning by discovery: A critical appraisal*. Chicago: Rand McNally.

Sinclair, A. (2001). The role of scholarship in education deliberation: The application of Schwabian curricular theory to issues in Bible education in the Conservative movement." Unpublished doctoral dissertation. The Hebrew University, Jerusalem.

Tanchel, S. (2008). A Judaism that does not hide": Teaching the documentary hypothesis in a pluralistic Jewish high school. *Journal of Jewish Education, 74*(1), 29–52.

Weinbaum, A., Allen, D., Blythe, T., Simon, K., Seidel, S., & Rubin, C. (2004). *Teaching as inquiry: Asking hard questions to improve practice and student achievement*. New York: Teachers College Press.

Zielenziger, R. (1979). *Genesis: A new teacher's guide*. New York: Melton Research Center.

Zielenziger, R. (1984). *Exodus: A teacher's guide*. New York: Melton Research Center.

Zielenziger, R. (1989). A History of the Bible Program of the Melton Research Center with Special References to the Curricular Principles on Which It Is Based. Unpublished doctoral dissertation. The Jewish Theological Seminary of America, New York.

Environment: Jewish Education as if the Planet Mattered

Eilon Schwartz

Introduction

Let us be blunt – education as presently practiced has almost categorically ignored the environmental crisis and its educational implications.

Think about just one corner of the environmental crisis: climate change. Experts have painstakingly documented over the past two decades the effects of carbon dioxide emissions on the climate, achieving a rather remarkable consensus uniting widely differing perspectives in the scientific community. They have concluded that the climate is changing and that we are the cause; that its catastrophic consequences are already responsible for significant economic damage, for social and political unrest as a result of large and growing numbers of "environmental refugees", and for rising death tolls from environmentally linked disasters (see, for example, Low, 2009 and Elsayed, 2009). And this is only the tip of the iceberg, so to speak. Whereas worst-case scenarios once hovered around a change of four degrees centigrade worldwide, the newest models are showing that such predictions might be gross underestimates, and that the worst-case scenarios are now the likely scenarios by the end of the century (Sokolov et al., 2009). Most scientists accept that changes above two degrees will have unprecedented effects on life on the planet, and changes of four degrees and higher threatens life as we know it.

Climate change is our most clear and present danger, but the environmental crisis cannot be limited to climate change. Virtually, all of our ecological services – seas, forests, freshwater, productive soil – are rapidly deteriorating. These are not isolated events. They are all the result of a set of cultural, economic, social and political assumptions on which Western society has been built but that are self-evidently no longer tenable. Modernity has brought us many blessings, but the ecological destruction which surrounds us is our most measurable means of asserting that society's current path is unsustainable. Already in 1992, over half of the world's then living Nobel laureates in the sciences signed on to a "Warning to Humanity",

E. Schwartz (✉)
Hebrew University, Jerusalem, Israel; Heschel Center for Environmental Learning and Leadership, Tel Aviv, Israel
e-mail: eilon@heschel.org.il

calling for a radical shift in public policies and personal practices in order to change course and avoid calamity, but the trends have continued to spiral downward (World Scientists' Warning to Humanity 1992).

Given the massive scope of the crisis, it is indeed shocking that our educational systems have until recently barely noticed what was at stake. Even now, one can find only a few ecological science curricula, an occasional Earth Day activity, perhaps a school-wide community project. There is a growing list of success stories, but they continue to be the rare exceptions to the rule, and even in those path-breaking settings the educational challenge has barely been confronted. Let us be clear: It is not simply the absence of any particular curricular component that has created our current state of ecological illiteracy. It is much more perniciously the presence of a certain kind of education which has consciously and subconsciously supported the very trends and ideas which endanger us. David Orr has remarked that far from being part of the solution, education has largely been part of the problem. Orr argues that the environmental crisis is, in fact, a product of the most educated generation in human history (Orr, 1994). The post-Second World War economic and technological revolution, supported by the best and brightest of our students, has led to massive economic growth and unprecedented prosperity. However, the kind of prosperity that has been pursued, and the ways in which it has been achieved, has led to massive disruption and destruction of the ecological infrastructure on which life depends, along with vast and growing inequalities between the rich and the poor. The education that has contributed to getting us into this mess is incapable of being the education that gets us out of it. The environmental crisis is a challenge to education as we know it. Business-as-usual is no longer an option. Environmental education, therefore, is not an addition to a largely successful educational system, but an alternative way of thinking about education, and a call to rethink what we teach, how we teach it and for what ends.

What Does the Environment Got to Do with Jewish Education?

If Jewish education is about adding additional "Jewish" subject matter to our curricular – Bible, Jewish History, Hebrew language, etc. – then clearly the environmental crisis has very little to do with Jewish education. In this view Jewish education is a particularistic component tacked onto the universal curricula that should be in all schools. Ecology is a global issue, not a particularly Jewish one. However, if Jewish education is not parochial subject matter, but rather part of a much larger set of questions about culture, spirit and values, and if, as I have argued, environmental education is likewise more accurately described as a set of questions about culture and values (and as we shall see, about religion and religiosity, as well), then the relevance of Jewish education to the environmental crisis becomes more understandable.

From such a perspective, it is telling that the first attempts to understand the environmental crisis as a crisis of cultural values saw Judaism, and by association Jewish education, as not only relevant to the environmental crisis, but in fact its primary cause. Lynn White's classic essay from the 1960s on the roots of the environmental crisis raised a stir because of his attacks on the monotheistic Judeo-Christian ethos, which he claimed removed holiness from the world by making God transcendent of nature, rather than immanent within it. The result, according to White, was a desanctification of nature, and therefore a license to exploit it for human benefit (White Jr. 1967). In short, a slippery slope led from revelation at Sinai to ecological devastation. From White's perspective, Jewish education can be seen as fueling the crisis. While perhaps teaching ecology in the science classes of the general studies curriculum – learning about the role of the rainforests in protecting biodiversity and their role as a massive carbon sink that absorbs greenhouse gases – White might argue that the hidden curriculum of Jewish studies has nevertheless been nurturing the cultural assumptions which foster and justify ecological destruction.

Over the years the question of Judaism's environmental credentials has been discussed and debated, catalysing a rich and growing literature on the interface between Judaism and the environment. However, while criticism of White exposed his condemnation of the monotheistic traditions as unfounded, White's central point was left unnoticed. White's principle claim was that, fundamentally, the environmental crisis is not a techno-scientific crisis, but rather a crisis of culture and values, and that a proper diagnosis of the environmental crisis demands not only knowing the science, but primarily examining the culture. To understand the crisis, one has to understand the cultural assumptions that make the crisis possible. At its heart, the environmental crisis is a crisis of how we see and relate to the world around us. It is a crisis of culture, society and politics. Jewish education, framed as a cultural endeavour, should therefore be extremely relevant to the questions of the environmental crisis and the ways we are part of the problem, and the ways we can nevertheless become part of the solution.

Hegemony and the Jews

Jewish education, as primarily a cultural project, needs to understand what culture it is in fact passing on, and what are its values. Several years ago I had the pleasure of spending a Sabbatical year in the United States, away from my home in Tel Aviv, and sending my older children, then 12 and 11 years old, to a Jewish day school. The school was in many ways a lovely place – they welcomed us kindly and enthusiastically. The curriculum put strong emphasis on the secular studies of math, science, social studies and language arts, along with Jewish subjects of Bible and Hebrew language. Every day began with morning prayer. I have reason to believe that the school was an example of some of the best Jewish education in North America.

And for all that, I was profoundly aware of the often instrumental, success-driven, individualist nature of the Jewish day school. It struck me that the school was trying to offer a more nurturing version of what is nevertheless essentially a private, prep school education – where academic excellence was the primary value, Ivy League universities were offered as the reward for discipline and hard work (I was fascinated by how elite colleges were at times used as a motivator for kids), and wealthy professionals, making up many of the lay leadership of the school, were symbols of success. The values part of the curricula appeared in the shadows of the school programme – teaching "Jewish values" in Bible class, having a "mitzvah day", trying to have inclusive sports teams where team cooperation rather than individual competition was the norm (although the YMCA was far more successful at that than the Jewish day school).

Most often, Jewish education, like all education, ends up supporting and strengthening the status quo. Schools are agents of socialisation into the values of the larger society, and Jewish education has served as an agent of acculturation to the accepted societal norms. Jewish education, like all education, usually mirrors and recapitulates the values which rule the cultural landscape. Educational interventions that are perceived as pursuing alternative aims, more often than not, are peripheral to the central educational message, barely noticeable at best, and at worst strengthening the very values that they believe to be challenging. I am quite familiar with this phenomenon in environmental education, whose practitioners often believe themselves to be engaged in a subversive activity which is challenging the status quo, and instead are all too often creating only an illusion of critical thinking, with everyone feeling satisfied that schooling is engaged in social change. The core questions about the assumptions on which ecological disaster is based, those questions that would challenge accepted norms and values are seldom addressed.

None of this is surprising. As Antonio Gramsci, the Italian theoretician, argued in his persuasive, although overly pessimistic theory of hegemonic discourse, individuals, often unwittingly, continue to support the values of the ruling class, even when they ostensibly express their opposition to them (Hoare & Nowell-Smith, 1971). The political power of hegemony is in its ability to turn historical, situated notions of society, economics and culture, into ahistorical, transcendent truths. This is the way it has been, is, and forever will be. Without a history, the hegemonic values become a universal that remains unchallenged, since they are, in effect, the only way that is possible. They become "common sense" – much like, for example, "the invisible hand", which we are led to believe tells us a transcendental truth as to the way markets function, rather than a particular economic philosophy with a history, supporting a particular ideology which can be challenged and changed.

Gramsci holds that the only way to challenge the hegemony is to create an alternative culture which nurtures an opposition to the ruling values of the hegemony, and allows one to see them not as "common sense", but in effect as "non-sense". Such a task, however, is not easily achieved. More often than not, our attempts to challenge the hegemonic status quo unsuspectingly accept the "common sense" as the unseen backdrop, leaving attempts at social change to deal with peripheral issues, at best. From the perspective of the environmental world, without challenging the central narrative of economic growth and consumer society which sits at the heart of the environmental crisis, we are largely the decorations' committee on the Titanic, ignoring the core issues which must be addressed, but are rarely noticed, and if noticed, cannot be confronted.

And yet, Gramsci would hold, the task is not insurmountable. There is the possibility of creating, painstakingly, a "second language", which articulates an alternative to the common sense which stifles criticism, and which allows a different story to be told. A second language is a successful metaphor for describing what Gramsci is demanding, for language is not simply a random selection of words. Language needs a cultural background in order to flourish – a community which converses. Historicising the common sense and articulating alternative value assumptions cannot materialise from a collection of disembodied social critiques. It must emerge from a thick cultural milieu, which will give it the intellectual depth and social strength to hold one's ground on an uneven playing field between dominant cultural values and those that try to challenge them. If we frame it this way, Jewish education has at least the theoretical potential to teach us a true second language, rather than a "kosher-style" variety of the first language which more often than not passes for Jewish education today. A second language of cultural alternative can only be built if one is indeed committed to challenging, rather than recapitulating, the dominant assumptions. And to be clear, Jews are no more guilty of the march towards acceptance of the hegemony than any other peoples in the contemporary world. Gramsci's theoretical insights notwithstanding, he could not have imagined the unprecedented power and scale of the globalised neoliberal vision for human society, and its threat to cultural diversity everywhere on the globe. And yet, Jewish education at its best might be part of the solution, and not just another part of the problem. It might, in fact, be one of the best chances we have to challenge the assumptions that allow our ecologically destructive culture to flourish.

Jewish Education as a Second Language

In his book *Caring for Creation*, Max Oeschlaeger confesses that he has come around (Oeschlaeger, 1994). Western religion, contrary to what White had him believe, is in fact part of the solution, not the problem. If the problem is cultural, then only an alternative, living cultural narrative which espouses different values from those of the mainstream culture can possibly challenge the accepted common sense. Oeschlaeger argues that religious cultures, Judaism among them, offer such an alternative – both a cultural language which works according to different assumptions than the dominant one, and concurrently, a community in which the language is alive and, at least in some sense, authoritative. What the tradition "says" matters to its members. In a famous confrontation between environmentalists and business interests who were advocating the clear-cutting of an old-growth forest, the so-called "redwood rabbis" organised and convinced the Jewish owner of the logging company to do *teshuva*, to change his path. They succeeded where others failed in persuading the businessman to spare the old growth from clearing. The combination of language and community persuaded the man and his corporation to act differently (Forum on Religion and Ecology, 2004).

Oeschlaeger's argument is an extension of the work of Bellah and other sociologists, documented in their book *Habits of the Heart* (Bellah et al., 1985). They too wrote of the instrumental, materialist hegemonic discourse of American society. True to Gramsci's analysis, they historicise the discourse, showing its historical roots, and simultaneously identify alternative American cultural values and their histories. According to their findings, one can identify at least four historical narratives that each find expression and define contemporary American culture. Although they claim that the utilitarian one, rooted in Benjamin Franklin's ideas about individual success, has become dominant, religious Biblical narratives and civic secular ones – both of which nurture an alternative set of community values – are still present, but need to be reasserted. Already in the 1960s, Rabbi J.B. Soloveitchik made a similar argument in his "Lonely Man of Faith", claiming that the instrumental values of Adam I have eclipsed the communitarian–religious values of Adam II in modern society, and need to be reasserted within the Jewish community (Soloveitchik, 1965). Bellah's argument, which Oeshlaeger adopts, is that cultural change is a hermeneutic task – identifying suppressed cultural narratives which can be reclaimed, exposing the historic nature of the dominant cultural norms which were assumed to be transcendent and immutable, but are in fact one option among others. Likewise, the historian Simon Schama wrote his opus on the history of nature in the Western tradition in order to uncover alternative traditions, still alive but waiting to be reclaimed, which can serve as an alternative trajectory for Western culture's interface with the environment (Schama, 1995). Reclaiming the past that has never really left us is a central tool for social and cultural change.

From this perspective, Jewish education is more than a process of acculturation to the Jewish tradition. It is part of a multicultural education aimed at exploding the dominance of one particular cultural voice, one which has been particularly damaging to our relationship with the environment, and it allows our students and our culture to learn and participate in other ways of acting in the world. As Bellah argues, it is a second language, and like the difficulty of teaching Hebrew as a second language, it demands immersion and commitment for it to flourish. Otherwise, our attempt to build an alternative cultural voice is trivialised to sentimentalism and nostalgia.

Challenging the Jewish Status Quo

Jewish environmental education, however, does not only challenge the assumptions of the dominant culture and its educational messages. It is also similarly in tension with conventional Jewish education, as it presently is practiced. This is for two reasons, both already mentioned, but worth highlighting. The first is that the Jewish community has largely adopted exactly those values and lifestyles which so many social critics today see as the heart of the problem. As related above, at any given Jewish school one is more likely to find the dominant cultural values than any alternative Jewish voice. The second is that the Jewish community, even when resisting the larger culture's values, often finds that traditional Jewish voices as currently understood have little to offer, or worse, what they have to offer is problematic. Wyschograd was probably the boldest in this regard, given his Orthodox affiliation, arguing that while Judaism had good reasons to resist a natural morality which he saw as sitting at the heart of an ecological worldview, in doing so it had consequently desensitised the Jewish tradition to the glory of the Creation, and that we indeed have what to learn from other, more environmentally aware and sensitive pagan traditions (Wyschograd, 1992).

The idea that "Judaism" teaches us any one lesson, is, however, a mistaken one. There are numerous voices that speak in the name of the tradition, some more dominant than others, but all present (Schwartz, 2002). And these voices are not a self-referential creation emanating from within, but rather have been shaped and moulded by a rich interaction with surrounding cultures. One of the problems with Gramsci's notion of culture is that he suggests that they exist as independent entities. Judaism, like most cultures, has in fact been in constant contact with other cultures, changing as a result. Describing the task as bringing a "Jewish" voice to bear on "contemporary" culture ignores the porous borders which make such essentialist distinctions problematic. Jeremy Benstein, in his beautiful book *The Way Into Judaism and the Environment*, correctly describes the hermeneutical approach needed – accepting that the tradition is a living one, and that our own perspectives and ideas have been shaped by a multitude of influences that in turn influence the ways that we read the tradition, in the same way that those who came before us brought their various cultural traditions to bear on their reading and understanding of "Judaism" (Benstein, 2006).

Similar to the role that Jewish education can play in challenging contemporary culture, perhaps it is most accurate to describe a parallel project that environmental education can play within the Jewish community. Once again building on Bellah, one can argue that Jewish culture is made up a myriad of voices which have developed over the centuries, both internally and in dialogue with voices from other cultures. The task is not only to challenge the dominant culture by allowing alternative cultural voices to assert themselves, but also to challenge contemporary Jewish culture, by allowing alternative Jewish voices to be reclaimed and, at times, reinterpreted.

A Different Voice

Jewish environmental education has many starting points. In Israel, it is historically most associated with the Society for the Protection of Nature in Israel (SPNI). Overseas its history is less well-known, but the first major environmental education initiative familiar to me was that of Shomrei Adama of the late 1980s, founded by Ellen Bernstein, and their wonderful book, *Let the Earth Teach You Torah*, although there were certainly precursors (Bernstein & Fink, 1992). I have my youth movement reader, written by Steve Copeland already in the late 1970s, that contains an activity criticising human hubris as a root cause for the environmental crisis (Copeland, 1978). I am confident, given the growth of environmentalism in the 1970s and 1980s, that similar initiatives sprouted in other countries, as well. Outdoor environmental education activities, at summer camps and as independent initiatives, also were born. The Coalition for the Environment in Jewish Life (COEJL), founded in 1993, gave an organisational home to some of these budding initiatives.

The histories of environmental education in Israel and abroad have different antecedents, different storylines and different motivations. In the Diaspora, similar to the Jewish environmental movement with which Jewish environmental education is affiliated, there has been exponential growth over the last decade since its modest beginnings. Still far from being mainstreamed in the Jewish community, Jewish environmentalism is nevertheless no longer marginalised. Organisations like Hazon, which has eclectically combined biking ("The People of the Bike"), community building and food advocacy, and the Teva Learning Center, which has been training Jewish environmental educators now for a decade, are leading a surge of local and national environmental organisations (see annotated bibliography of websites at end of the chapter). While concentrated primarily on the liberal side of the Jewish community continuum, there are initiatives affiliated with all parts of the Jewish community. These initiatives are making inroads beyond North America as well, as fledgling projects in England and Australia, for example, take root. In Israel, the Heschel Center, inspired by the thought and social activism of Abraham Joshua Heschel, brought an educational approach of social criticism and activism to Israeli environmental education, and its curriculum "Between Human Beings and the World" (Benstein, Samuels, & Schwartz, 1996) along with the environmental education reader "A Place to Ponder" (Benstein, 1998) connected universal environmental messages with the local environmental education that the SPNI had developed for decades. Environmental organisations sprouted throughout the country in the 1990s, growing from a small handful to over 100. The recently established "Hebrew Nature" (Teva Ivri) is an umbrella organisation bringing together the many initiatives throughout Israel now combining Jewish and environmental education, thus creating for the first time in Israel a Jewish environmentalism similar to that which exists abroad, focused on Jewish-environmental identity, and not solely Zionist or Israeli civic identities.

From this growing network of organisations and programmes, an educational philosophy and pedagogy are beginning to emerge. A set of categories and concepts have been mapped out, in which environmentalism and Jewish concerns intersect, creating a unique language which challenges contemporary Jewish and Western cultures at once. If I am right that Jewish environmental education is not simply another discipline, then similarly, its research questions are not simply questions about subject matter. The parallel category to "environmental education" is not "chemistry", or "biology" or "algebra" or even "social studies" and "literature"; it is part of the family of alternative educational models which are rethinking the basic questions of education. As in any grassroots educational movement, there is not yet an intellectual rigorousness to its theory and practice, but its themes are to be the starting point of any reflective academic research in the coming years. What follows is an attempt to categorise those themes, suggesting some of the theoretical questions and educational practices which any (Jewish) environmental educational research agenda should pursue.

Nurturing Wonder

How do we educate towards wonder? Heschel has argued that the central malaise of modern life is the loss of a sense of wonder in the world. "Mankind", as he writes, "will not perish for want of information; but only for want of appreciation" (Heschel, 1956). Rachel Carson, in her moving children's book *A Sense of Wonder* makes a similar point: "A child's world is fresh and new and beautiful, full of wonder and excitement. It is our misfortune that for most of us that clear-eyed vision, that true instinct for what is beautiful and awe-inspiring, is dimmed and even lost before we reach adulthood" (Carson, 1998). Environmental education has correctly made much of creating educational activities that nurture a sense of wonder in the natural world, and Jewish environmental education has linked the practice of berakhot [blessings] to acknowledging the small and great wonders that we witness every day. But if the culture around us, and the educational culture within, are all projecting the antithesis of wonder, what difference does one short educational activity make?

Can wonder be taught? What are its practices? What does a school look like that takes wonder seriously? What does a culture look like that takes wonder seriously? Is it even possible to create an alternative culture, when the rest of society marches to such a different drummer? I have seen classes that go out daily to paint the movement of the clouds; spent nights away from the urban lights that blind the heavens from the earth, to watch the spectacle of stars that moved the ancients and is now all but extinct in our daily experience. And I have seen our educators and our children struggle to see these daily wonders, to change the pace of their lives to be able to hear Nahman of Bratzlav's song of the grasses. We need a better understanding of what wonder is, and whether and how it can be taught in our fast-paced, achievement-oriented world.

Science and Religiosity: Interdisciplinary Education

Ever since Darwin, science and religion have been portrayed as separate realms, at best, clashing worldviews, at worst. The dominant model of Jewish day school education is to divide the day between the secular subjects of general knowledge and the Jewish subjects of values and culture. Jewish environmental education invites us to rethink that divide and its price.

One of the few pedagogic questions about wonder which have been asked, although as yet not researched, is whether scientific understanding enhances our wonder in the world, or retards it. That depends very much upon how science is taught. A reductionist, materialist scientific narrative, as for example that of Richard Dawkins (Dawkins, 1989) and his advocates, is on a collision course with the reverence which sits at the core of a naturalist such as Rachel Carson's worldview (Carson, 1998). Science education is not neutral and cannot be treated as such. It, like any other part of our education, will reflect values and ideas, and it is best that they be attended. We need to explore in a far more sophisticated way the interplay between facts and values, with far more thought given to the ways our values influence how we see the facts, and how information can challenge beliefs that are no longer tenable (Schwartz, 2009). Environmentalists have been leading the way in reconnecting our science with social responsibility, and Jewish environmental education has much to offer in building a dialogue between science and religion. This is not to say that science should be reduced to values education. Notwithstanding the post-modern desire to read ideology into any claim of objectivity, facts and values are different, but are not nearly as separate as the modernists have claimed. Research needs to describe in much more detail the subtle interactions between the two, and how to build educational initiatives which are aware of the ways they can and should interact.

Interdependence

Environmentalists are fond of talking of the web of life, of the ways that all of life is interconnected. And yet, in spite of the core idea that Adam emerges from *Adama*, that human beings are made from the very stuff of the earth, so much of our culture advocates the inherent separateness of human beings from the rest of the natural world, and often enough, the independence of human beings one from another, as well. In one of my favourite quotes of John Dewey, he writes:

> From a social standpoint, dependence denotes a power rather than a weakness; it involves interdependence. There is always a danger that increased personal independence will decrease the social capacity of an individual. In making him more self-reliant, it may make him more self-sufficient; it may lead to aloofness and indifference. It often makes an individual so insensitive in his relations to others as to develop an illusion of being really able to stand and act alone – an unnamed form of insanity which is responsible for a large part of the remediable suffering of the world. (Dewey, 1944, p. 44)

"No man is an island" John Donne wrote, but in the 1600s no one yet knew just how scientifically complex the web is which connects all of life. Although Dewey refers in the above quote to human interdependence, he was well aware of how our interdependence expanded beyond the species barrier (Dewey, 1944). And ecologists have painstakingly documented over the last decades the myriad ways that life is connected, and how that web is fraying at a frightening rate. (See, for example, United Nations Development Programme et al., 2001.)

The Jewish community certainly advocates interconnectedness of the Jewish community – *kol yisrael aravim zeh l'zeh*, all Jews are responsible for one another, but a central question of our times is how do we expand our sense of community beyond the ones closest to us, and how do we recognise and acknowledge the web of attachments which connect us. In a globalised world, where our clothing is made by children in Southeast Asia working under inhuman conditions, taking responsibility for our actions is a complex matter. We buy inexpensive clothing because we are ignorant of, or capable of ignoring, the ways that our actions are intertwined with the well-being of others. Our interconnectedness is not limited to those in other places, either. We are connected in time, as well as in space, and our connections reach back and forward in history. Climate change is our legacy to future generations. Are there examples of education that fosters a sense of our interconnectedness, of uncovering the ways that we are responsible for one another, and of fostering an ethic of care that expands outward into the world?

These connections, we are relearning are not limited to other humans around the world, but to our connections beyond the species barrier. And they are not limited to our material connections to the natural world, on our dependence on its bounty for the food we eat, the water we drink and the air we breathe. Our souls as well as our bodies are dependent on our connections to the world, assuming that it is even possible to consider the human soul and body as separate entities. We are all part of the same creation, share the same evolutionary story, and are intertwined with one another. E.O. Wilson claims that human beings have an innate biophilia – an instinctive bond to the natural world (Wilson, 1986). If that is so, what happens to a generation deprived of the delight of wandering in the woods, and of hearing the sounds of animal life in their native habitats (see, for example, Louv, 2005)? As Midgley says of the existentialists, when life shrinks to a few urban rooms – with no plants, animals or children – no wonder it becomes absurd (Midgley, 1995). Interdependence is dependent on our experience of interdependence. Our education needs to pay attention to what it is teaching and what it is not; what experiences it privileges and what it neglects.

A Sense of Place

I remember the first time I understood the connection between being Jewish and a sense of place. A close friend who had grown up in South Africa was telling me about his youth movement summer camp experiences, and he mentioned how, as opposed to us in the northern hemisphere who turned Tisha B'Av into a central part of the camp's Jewish calendar, they celebrated Hannukah! Hanukkah, not only the festival of freedom, but also the festival of lights, the Jews' winter solstice holiday, was celebrated in the middle of summer. The Jewish calendar memorialises a time when our culture and nature were one.

Environmental educators have recognised that our collective contemporary wanderings – the disconnect of modern culture from land and nature – have damaged our understanding of the natural world, and our sense of connection and responsibility for it. Re-indigenising, however, is an extremely difficult task in our global world. In many ways, the Zionist experiment is exactly that – a noble attempt to reconnect a culture with its natural landscape. Much of Israeli environment education was in fact invested in hiking the land and learning its natural history, although often such education was more centrally about national identity and about political ownership (see, for example, Benvinisti, 1988). There is much to be written on the intersect between national and ecological agendas in Zionism – how questions of local, national and global identities are entwined in the nurture of an ecological identity.

In the Diaspora, a different issue emerges. An agricultural culture found itself outside of its native land. We chose to sacrifice our connection to nature for our connection to the Land of Israel, and by extension to all other Jewish communities. All Jews pray for rain according to the seasons of the Land of Israel, no matter where they live; we bless the agricultural harvest with fruits foreign to the soils of the Diaspora. But Jewish environmental educators will tell you that there is a price to be paid for ignoring the landscape of your home. It means that our Jewishness does not foster a sense of place, and that our rituals, focused on a distant landscape rather than our lived experience in this place, can alienate us from the visceral natural world which surrounds us. What was long ago taken for granted in Jewish life, that our calendar nurtured our relationship with the natural world, and that our religious lives were intimately connected with our natural ones, has been for most of the last 2,000 years far from obvious. One of the great challenges of Jewish environmental education is building a ritual which returns the nature outside of our doors to Jewish culture, while paying attention to the historical reasons why Jews chose to compromise their connection to nature in the name of their connection to the land and people of Israel.

Changing Habits

There is an intentionality about Jewish environmental education – exposing the environmentally damaging beliefs and practices in our lives and nurturing new ways of acting. Eating is perhaps the most dramatic of such acts. The fast-food culture which is so connected to the pace of our lives, the replacement of agriculture with the factory farming of agri-business, and the breakdown of traditional communal practices, is being challenged by educators who pay attention to the hidden curriculum of soda machines and junk food. Jewish practices, like those of any traditional culture, offer different models: whether it is recipes that have been handed down for several generations, the seamless mix of family, tradition and food at any festive meal, blessings over bread and after the meal that bring attention to that which is taken for granted, the many cycles of fast and feast which can fill the Jewish year, all these offer resources from which to resist the mindless and destructive food habits that have become commonplace. Practices that create school and community gardens, as well as community supported agriculture, are attempts to reconnect our lives with the land and its bounty.

Eating is but one of a host of practices that are unreflectively present in our educational culture. Transportation is another – how we move from one place to another is not simply a question of convenience – whether we use public transportation or private cars has moral and social implications. Building a communal culture, which emphasises walking and biking, could transform our communal lives. Similarly, our homes are not simply our castles. Once we accept our interdependence, we recognise that our choice of home and communities is a social, communal and political choice. Jews have traditionally sought out other Jews with whom to live in community. The religious ideas of an eruv [an artificial halachic boundary] and of the need for a minyan [a prayer quorum] in walking distance of one another are a very different kind of community than that of a suburban car-based culture. And the very architecture of our homes embodies social, cultural and political choices. I know an architect who, in planning homes, exposes the electrical wires for all to see. The hidden curriculum is laid bare. Where does our energy come from? How much do we use, and at what price? Where does our water come from? Go to? What materials? The first step in changing habits is exposing what is unsustainable about our present ones, and then creating alternatives. We pay great attention to curricular questions; our education needs to pay far more attention to the hidden curricula of our practices where so much of our education takes place.

Celebrating Physicality

Environmentalists are often called the "gloom and doom" folks. One of the critical questions in contemporary environmental education is whether "gloom and doom" is a motivator, or, more probably, leads to despair and hopelessness. If all environmentalists have to tell us is that the world as we know it is doomed, without any vision of why a different, sustainable world, is not only sustainable in its physical sense, but is also a life worth living – a life that is richer, fuller, compelling, satisfying – in short, sustaining, then the environmental vision will only criticise what is, not celebrate what can be.

Jewish environmental education can focus environmentalism on the spiritual components of the environmental agenda which are too often overlooked, or vaguely articulated. The environmentalists' central thesis, that we are interconnected, means, as Dewey hinted, that living a life of disconnection is in a deep sense, which should be more fully articulated, dehumanising (Dewey & Tufts, 1976). An environmental agenda does not simply protect the ecosphere, it returns values of simplicity, community, and of course, nature, to the centre of human life. Riding a bicycle is not only about reducing our carbon footprint; it is about feeling the wind at our face, reconnecting with our bodies and being alive. When we walk in our towns and cities we get to know our neighbours and our neighbourhood shopkeepers; we create a pace of life that is a more human pace. And when we notice the sight and scent of the flowers we connect ourselves to the larger context of life, which puts our own lives within a setting that gives them meaning. Religious traditions are uniquely positioned to build a language and a pedagogy that can give expression to such intuitions.

Text and Context

And yet, many have argued that Judaism is, in fact, in tension with environmental ideas and concepts, physicality among them. There are those who condemn Judaism's anti-environmental intuitions, and those that praise them, but they both share the supposition that "Judaism" does not sit easily with ecological ideas. For all those who see Judaism as being at odds with environmentalism, the attempts to show the ecological teachings of Jewish culture can be viewed as an apologetic exercise which distorts Jewish culture and its cardinal messages. Against this, a generation has been reclaiming the environmental sentiments of our tradition. From Genesis II and the story of Noah, Talmudic concepts of Bal Tashchit ("not to destroy") and Tzar Baalei Chaim (prevention of animal cruelty), Rabbinic midrash and commentaries, modern Jewish philosophers such as Rav Nachman, Rav Kook, A. D. Gordon and of course Abraham Joshua Heschel, a vibrant alternative textual tradition has been articulated.

Clarifying these issues, of course, is the work of Jewish philosophy, history and sociology. The answers depend on how we read our texts and how our texts intersect with the life around them. Jewish environmentalism is one of the many places of dialogue between traditional text and contemporary society. Feminism is another. But environmentalism is also a place where we recognise our Jewishness as being more than the study of texts. By definition, the text as the canon of Jewish tradition minimises the centrality of the body and the world (see, for example, Biale, 1997; Boyarin, 1995 and Eilberg-Schwartz, 1992). Revelation trumps creation. Jewish environmental education invites our communities to be less text-centred and more life-centred; to find ways of creating a more fruitful dialogue between the people of the book and a people living life.

Responsible Communities

At its core, environmental education is about nurturing responsible citizens engaged in their communities and in their world. Engagement is not simply about acculturation – mimicking the practices of previous generations. It is about identifying as part of the community, and caring enough about its health and well-being to change it for the better. Too much of our Jewish educational practice is focused on belonging, and not enough on engaging.

Engagement demands both belonging and criticism. We need to be part of the community, but we also need to change it. Being part of the community is a necessary condition for any engagement – criticism without a deep sense of belonging often strips criticism of sympathy, an important component in any effective criticism. But belonging without criticism does a profound disservice to the rich, dynamic tradition of which we are part. Jewish environmental education can provide these tools of belonging and criticism, but to be serious, it must be wary of the hegemonic power of dominant cultural values, which always threaten to trivialise or marginalise any attempts to allow a meaningful social critique to flourish. Social criticism cannot simply be empty words. Teaching our children to be citizens – to be active participants in their world, to want to change it and to explore what needs to be changed and how – is the heart and soul of environmental education. Jewish environmental education is uniquely positioned to translate social criticism into social practices for the Jewish community, to allow us to engage sympathetically with our manifold communities, and out of commitment and respect for what was and is, to build a more just, kinder and more sustainable future.

Last Thoughts

There is no academic field of Jewish environmental education today, mirroring the peripheral status of environmentalism within the Jewish educational establishment, and within society in general. For those of us who are conscious of the ecological disaster that has already begun to unfold, and of the chilling consequences that have already been set in motion, we search to find a voice that can shift public consciousness and create political will. Overwhelmed by what is at stake, we struggle to remain hopeful. Optimism is no longer an option.

But young people are way ahead of the curve. I get probably a dozen requests annually, asking where one can go study Jewish environmental education, where one can go to learn – get a masters degree or even a doctorate. This passion is contagious. It contains a large measure of gloom and doom and a pressing sense of the need to create change, but it also is infused with a profound joy in the wonders of the world and a desire to celebrate what we still have and might yet reclaim. Like so many shifts in educational theory and practice, change will not come from the top-down, but from the bottom-up. It will come from a growing field of educational innovators whose central challenge will be to take their intuition as to what needs to change, and transform it into a reflective educational practice that is capable of recreating how we see Jewish education and the Jewish world. Whether the Jewish community will be responsive to their call, whether it will open up its institutions and its budgets to educational innovation that can change the very meaning of Jewish education is an open question – I remain doubtful as to the likelihood of success. But, truth be told, failure really is not an option. The Jewish future – Jewish continuity – depends on our collective ability to re-imagine our educational and communal institutions, and to build a Jewish community where continuity does not begin and end at the Jewish doorstep, as if our Jewish existences live apart from the world of which we are part. It depends on building a Jewish future for which life on the only planet on which we have been created to live actually matters.

References

Bellah, R., Madsen, R., Sullivan, W., Swindler, A., & Tipton, S. (1985). *Habits of the heart*. Berkeley, CA: State University of California Press.
Benstein, J. (1998). *A place to Ponder* (Hebrew: Makom l'Machshava). Tel Aviv: The Heschel Center, The Society for the Protection of Nature in Israel, the Israeli Ministry of the Environment.
Benstein, J. (2006). *The way into Judaism and the environment*. Woodstock, VT: Jewish Lights Publishing.
Benstein, J., Samuels, R., & Schwartz, E. (1996). *Between human beings and the world (Hebrew: Bein Adam l'Olamo)*. Jerusalem: Melitz.
Benvinisti, M. (1988). *Conflicts and contradictions*. Savage, MD: Eshel Books.
Bernstein, E., & Fink, D. (1992). *Let the earth teach you Torah*. Philadelphia, PA: Shomrei Adama.
Biale, D. (1997). *Eros and the Jews*. Berkeley, CA: University of California Press.
Boyarin, D. (1995). *Carnal Israel*. Berkeley, CA: University of California Press.
Carson, R. (1998 [1965]). *A sense of wonder*. New York: Harper and Row.
Copeland, S. (1978). *A modern Jewish history Chinuch and Hadracha source book*. New York: Hadassah Zionist Youth Commission.

Dawkins, R. (1989 [1976]). *The selfish gene*. Oxford: Oxford University Press.
Dewey, J. (1944 [1916]). *Democracy and education*. New York: The Free Press.
Dewey, J., & Tufts, J. (1976 [1908]). *Ethics*. Carbondale, IL: Southern Illinois University Press.
Eilberg-Schwartz, H. (1992). *People of the body*. Albany, NY: State University of New York Press.
Elsayed, S. (2009). Is it Time to Recognize Environmental Refugees? Retrieved December 14, 2009, from http://earthtrends.wri.org/updates/node/342
Forum on Religion and Ecology (2004) Redwood Rabbis. Retrieved December 14, 2009, from http://fore.research.yale.edu/religion/judaism/projects/redwood_rabbis.html
Heschel, A. J. (1956). *God in search of man*. Philadelphia: Jewish Publications Society.
Hoare, Q., & Nowell-Smith, G. (Eds.). (1971). *Selections from the prison notebooks of Antonio Gramsci*. New York: International Publishers.
Louv, R. (2005). *Last child in the woods*. Chapel Hill, NC: Algonquin Books.
Low, P. (2009). Devastating Natural Disasters Continue Steady Rise. Retrieved December 14, 2009, from http://vitalsigns.worldwatch.org/vs-trend/devastating-natural-disasters-continue-steady-rise
Midgley, M. (1995 [1978]). *Beast and man*. London: Routledge Press.
Oeschlaeger, M. (1994). *Caring for creation*. New Haven, CT: Yale University Press.
Orr, D. (1994). *Earth in mind*. Washington, DC: Island Press.
Schama, S. (1995). *Landscape and memory*. New York: Vintage Books.
Schwartz, E. (2002). Mastery and Stewardship, Wonder and Connectedness: A Typology of Relations to Nature in Jewish Text and Tradition. In H. Tirosh-Samuelson (Ed.), *Judaism and ecology*. Cambridge, MA: Harvard University Press, pp. 93–106.
Schwartz, E. (2009). *At home in the world*. Albany, NY: State University of New York Press.
Sokolov, A. P., Stone, P. H., Forest, C. E., Prinn, R., Sarofim, M. C., Webster, M., et al. (2009). Probabilistic Forecast for 21st Century Climate Based on Uncertainties in Emissions. Retrieved December 14, 2009, from http://globalchange.mit.edu/files/document/MITJPSPGC_Rpt169.pdf
Soloveitchik, J. (1965). The lonely man of faith. *Tradition*, 7, 2, pp. 5–67.
United Nations Development Programme, United Nations Environment Programme, World Bank and World Resources Institute (2001). *People and ecosystems: The fraying web of life*. Washington, DC: World Resources Institute.
White, L., Jr. (1967). The historic roots of our ecologic crisis. *Science*, 155, pp. 1203–1207.
Wilson, E. O. (1986). *Biophilia*. Cambridge, MA: Harvard University Press.
World Scientists' Warning to Humanity (1992). Retrieved December 14, 2009, from http://www.worldtrans.org/whole/warning.html
Wyschograd, M. (1992). Judaism and the sanctification of nature. *The Melton Journal*, 24, pp. 289–296.

A Short Bibliography of Judaism, Environment and Education

Benstein, J. (2006). *The way into Judaism and the environment*. Woodstock, Vt: Jewish Lights Publishing.
Eisenberg, E. (1998). *The ecology of Eden*. New York: Knopf.
Elon, A., Hyman, N., & Waskow, A. (Eds.). (1999) *Trees, earth and Torah: A Tu B'Shevat anthology*. New York: Jewish Publications Society.
Nabhan, G. P., & Trimble, S. (1995). *The geography of childhood*. Boston: Beacon Press.
Oeschlaeger, M. (1994). *Caring for creation: An ecumenical approach to the environmental crisis*. New Haven, CT: Yale University Press.
Orr, D. (1992). *Ecological literacy and the transition to a postmodern world*. Albany, NY: SUNY Press.
Sobol, D. (2004). *Place-based education: Connecting classrooms and communities*. Great Barrington, MA: The Orion Society.

Tal, A. (2002). *Pollution in the promised land: An environmental history of Israel*. Berkeley, CA: University of California Press.
Thomashow, M. (1996). *Ecological identity: Becoming a reflective environmentalist*. Cambridge, MA: MIT Press.
Tirosh-Samuelson, H. (Ed.). (2002). *Judaism and ecology: Created world and revealed word*. Cambridge: Harvard University Press.
Waskow, A. (Ed.). (2000). *Torah of the earth: Exploring 4,000 years of ecology in Jewish thought*. Woodstock, VT: Jewish Lights Publishing.
Yaffe, M. (Ed.). (2001). *Judaism and environmental ethics: A Reader*. Lanham, MD: Lexington Books.

Selected Websites

Adama Jewish Environmental Fellowship programme – www.isabellafreedman.org/environment/adamah
Orthodox North American organisation Canfei Nesharim – www.canfeinesharim.org/
The Children and Nature Network – founded as a response to childhood nature deprivation, as documented in the best-selling book *Last Child in the Woods* – www.childrenandnature.org
Coalition on the Environment and Jewish Life (COEJL) Jewish environmental education programme bank
http://www.coejl.org/~coejlor/programbank/viewprog.php
COEJL of Southern California – www.coejlsc.org
Ecological Footprint – Interactive ecological footprint calculator – www.epa.vic.gov.au/ecologicalfootprint/globalfootprint/index.asp
Eden environmental summer camp just north of NYC – www.edenvillagecamp.org
Edible school gardens movement – using school grounds as a food and ecology pedagogic tool: http://www.edibleschoolyard.org/garden http://www.edibleschoolgardens.com.au/; http://www.ediblegardens.org.uk/
The Greening of Jewish Institutions Fellowship – www.isabellafreedman.org/environment/greening
Green Maps – Charting the environmental resources of communities and neighbourhoods – www.greenmap.org
Green Schools Network – largest network of green schools in Israel – www.greennet.org.il/content2.php?cat=73
The Green Teacher – Quarterly magazine on environmental education – www.greenteacher.com
Hazon – pioneers in Jewish outdoor education and leading the Jewish food movement – www.hazon.org
The Heschel Center for Environmental Learning and Leadership – leadership training in sustainability – www.heschel.org.il
The Jewish Ecological Coalition of Australia (JECO) – www.jeco.org.au/
The Jewish Farm School in Philadelphia – www.jewishfarmschool.org
The Jewish Nature Center of Canada – www.torathateva.org
The Kayam Farm outside of Baltimore – www.pearlstonecenter.org/kayam.html
In England, the Noah Project – www.noahproject.org.uk/
The North American Association for Environmental Education – www.naaee.org
Orion Magazine – Placing environmentalism in its cultural, political and educational context – www.oriononline.org
Seviva Yisrael – linking schools in Israel and the Diaspora with joint environmental projects – http://www.svivaisrael.org/programs_en.asp?id=10
The Shalom Center, located in Philadelphia – www.shalomctr.org
The Shalom Institute –West Coast Jewish Environmental Education Center – www.shalominstitute.com

Shomrei Adama of Greater Washington – www.shomreiadamah.org

The Society for Protection of Nature in Israel – one of the pioneers of outdoor education in the world – www.teva.org.il

Teva Ivri – uniting Jewish and environmental identity in Israel – www.tevaivri.org.il

Teva Learning Center – leading Jewish environmental education centre – www.tevalearningcenter.org

Havruta: What Do We Know and What Can We Hope to Learn from Studying in Havruta?

Elie Holzer and Orit Kent

Picture a large room filled with pairs of learners sitting face-to-face, studying a text. Each pair sits at a separate desk, on which a variety of texts, including the Bible, Talmud, medieval literature, and modern Jewish and Israeli literature are placed. Partners read an assigned text together, explain it to each other, and argue about what the text says and means. The room fills with the multiple voices of conversation. All the learners are engaged in the same learning activity—they are conducting conversations with texts and conversations with their learning partner. They are practicing a mode of learning known as Havruta learning, which takes place in a specially designed learning environment, the Beit Midrash, literally the "House of study" or "House of interpretation."

Havruta learning or paired study is a traditional mode of Jewish text study. The term itself captures two simultaneous learning activities in which the Havruta partners engage: the study of a text and learning with a partner. Confined in the past to traditional yeshivot and limited to the study of Talmud, Havruta learning has recently made its way into a variety of professional and lay learning contexts that reflect new social realities in the world of Jewish learning. However, despite its long history and its recent growing popularity, Havruta learning has received little scholarly attention.[1]

We begin this chapter by mapping the current state of Havruta learning in relation to variables such as its structural, situational, and organizational elements. We then present a review of research on Havruta learning, and conclude with a suggested research agenda.

E. Holzer (✉)
Bar Ilan University, Tel Aviv, Israel
e-mail: esholzer@netvision.net.il

[1] According to Stampfer (1995), until the beginning of the twentieth century, Havruta learning was only one among other modes of study, like, for example, studying on one's own which in some contexts was perceived as the more advanced format of learning. In the traditional Lithuanian yeshivot, Havruta learning became a predominant mode of study as a response to the increased number yeshiva students with weak background in Talmudic studies, who needed to be assisted by more experienced learners.

Havruta Learning in the Field

Where is Havruta learning being practiced and in what ways? To date, except for one evaluation study of secular Israeli Batei Midrash (plural form of Beit Midrash) commissioned by the Avi Chai Foundation (Yair, Sagiv, Shimborsky, Akrai, & Lichtman, 2006), there is no research documenting how Havruta learning is being used. In the absence of additional empirical data on this question, we draw on our knowledge of Havruta learning in Israel and the United States in contemporary Jewish-educational settings. First, we present a variety of institutions in which Havruta learning is being used. We then discuss five variables of Havruta learning, each of which has an impact on the way Havruta learning is evolving.

Where Is Havruta Learning Practiced?

Havruta learning has been employed in the past decades in different Jewish learning contexts. It is interesting to note that it prevails across denominations and in non-denominational institutions, involving men and women of all ages. It is found in Jewish day-school classrooms, institutions of Jewish adult learning, and in programs for the training of professionals such as rabbis and teachers. In some of these programs, Havruta learning takes place at the initiative of an individual teacher. In other instances, it is perceived as an official and central element of the program. Havruta learning continues of course to be a predominant mode of study in orthodox/haredi yeshivot, often beginning in middle school.

In addition, with the increasing use of distance learning, some programs have introduced what can be labeled as "remote Havruta learning," which is based on phone or online communications. In remote Havruta learning, Havruta partners do not meet in person but connect via technology to study texts together. Examples of this relatively new type of Havruta learning modality can be found at Oraita, a continuing education program for rabbis, and at the Institute for Jewish Spirituality.[2]

The Structural Organization of Havruta Learning

While different institutions and people may use the same term—Havruta—to refer to paired study, the precise form of Havruta learning may differ across contexts. At the most basic level, some people use the term Havruta to refer to a learning arrangement involving two people and a text. Others use the word more generally to refer to small-group study of texts. These differences in how Havruta learning is set up may affect the type and quality of the dynamics that evolve between the learners, and between the learners and the text.

---

[2]http://www.hebrewcollege.edu/rabbinical-school/rabbi-continuing-education and http://www.ijs-online.org/practices_textstudy.php

Additional elements that shape the Havruta learning experience include the amount of time allocated for Havruta study, the genres of texts that are studied, the Havruta "task," the role of Havruta in the classroom lesson, and the learning environment in which it takes place.

Allocated time: The amount of time allocated to Havruta learning includes a wide range of possibilities. For example, a high school teacher may allocate 15 minutes of his class to Havruta study during which students are told to partner with someone else, study a specific text, and find specific information in the text. This is a very different arrangement than in a Beit Midrash where the same two students study together in Havruta on a regular daily or weekly basis for several hours at a time. In the latter situation, the Havruta has time to develop a learning relationship, which may contribute to the Havruta experience.

Text genre: Traditionally, Havruta learning has been used for the study of rabbinic literature, in particular the Talmud and its commentators. Nowadays, depending on the context, Havruta learning is used for a variety of genres of texts, including biblical texts and medieval commentators, texts of Jewish thinkers, Midrash Aggadah, modern Jewish and Israeli writing, including poetry. This change is interesting not only from a cultural point of view but also from an educational perspective. We may assume that the inherent complexity of the Talmudic text has been a major impetus for learners to seek the help of a Havruta partner. Using Havruta learning for the study of less-complex genres of texts suggests that alternative purposes and needs might lie behind what people expect from Havruta learning today and impact the dynamic of Havruta learning in different ways. For example, when studying a less-complex text in Havruta, students may need to spend less effort or time deciphering the literal meaning of the text and its argument and can devote more time to discussing the broader meaning of the text. An alternative purpose could be the desire to create personal meaning with and from the text with the help of one's Havruta partner.

Open vs. directed Havruta learning tasks: In many traditional settings such as yeshivot, Havruta learning often entails an open-ended inquiry of two learners into one or a series of assigned texts. The learners generally have no more specific task than to study these texts together. There are however contexts in which Havruta learning is directed by explicit guidelines or tasks of various degree of specificity. For example, learners may be invited to focus on particular themes or ideas in the text, or may be given a specific learning task such as comparing different texts or articulating their views about the texts. The guidelines often appear in the form of written worksheets, in some instances inviting the Havruta learners to record their findings in writing.

Role of Havruta in the classroom: Another important factor which may affect the nature of Havruta learning is the purpose(s) it serves in the greater educational context. For example, Havruta learning can serve as the summary of a lesson. In this case, the purpose of the Havruta learning is for students to practice and review together what has been taught in the formal class. Another purpose could be to prepare for an upcoming class by becoming familiar and engaging with the materials that the teacher will be addressing. Havruta learning can also serve as stand-alone activity that has no link to other formal learning activities.

The Havruta learning environment: The learning space in which Havruta learning takes place is another element that affects Havruta learning. In some cases, no specific space is designed for Havruta learning. For example, students simply turn to their nearest classmate without changing the arrangement of the chairs or tables in the formal classroom. This is particularly the case for very brief Havruta study experiences characterized by a very specific learning task such as finding information in the text.

Some institutions allocate a specific space for Havruta learning, which is usually refered to as a Beit Midrash, literally meaning a study house. The Beit Midrash is often designed so that Havruta learners may face each other or sit next to each other in a way that facilitates one-on-one communication despite the presence of many others who share the same space for study. Convenient access to books (and relevant electronic databases) can impact Havruta learning. These additional resources can help encourage learners to be responsible for independently exploring the connections between the text they study and a variety of other texts.

Review of Research

There is limited historical research on Havruta learning. Halbertal and Hartman-Halbertal (1998) briefly discuss Havruta learning in an article on the yeshiva. Havruta learning in its historical perspective, especially in the tradition of the Volozhin yeshiva is discussed in the work of Stampfer (1995) and in Tishby's Hebrew encyclopedia entry (1979), although there is still a great deal that we do not know about when, where, and why Havruta was practiced in different Jewish communities and in different historical periods.

A second line of research is characterized by the attempt to understand and analyze Havruta learning through the prism of theories from the social sciences or the humanities. Segal (2003) briefly reviews the history of Havruta learning and concludes that the practice is not as ancient as we think and that its use in modern contexts should be based around an educational rationale. She then outlines three domains in which Havruta offers potential learning benefits—the affective, the cognitive, and the social—and provides details about each one. Finally, drawing on contemporary educational literature, she compares Havruta to cooperative learning, noting areas of similarity and difference. Feiman-Nemser (2006) offers a rationale for engaging in Havruta learning as part of the professional education of teachers by drawing on a theory of learning to teach, and connecting this theory to the opportunities Havruta study offers prospective teachers to learn about and practice dispositions and skills that are important in teaching. Holzer (2006) draws on philosophical hermeneutics to conceptualize a view of good Havruta learning, conceptualized as engaging in a conversation with text and people, and characterized by the cultivation of specific dispositions such as openness toward another perspective, readiness to revisit one's own preconceptions, attentive listening, and the cultivation of an awareness of one's own limited perspective. Kent (2008) draws on a diverse body of contemporary educational research and video analysis of nine pairs of Havruta learners studying over time to develop a theory of Havruta learning, highlighting six core practices—listening, articulating, wondering, focusing, supporting, and challenging—and their interplay. Kent then explores the use of these practices through four cases in order to illustrate and probe some of the ways in which Havruta has the potential to engage students in generative, textually grounded interpretive discussions of classical Jewish texts, as well as missed opportunities.

There is a range of empirical research that has been conducted on Havruta learning. Tedmon (1991) uses a variety of educational theories to analyze a Havruta between two orthodox teenage boys in a yeshiva high school. Drawing on interviews and two Havruta recordings, she analyzes this Havruta interaction through a socio-cognitive perspective on reading, a sociolinguistic perspective on discourse, a literary perspective of reading, and a cultural perspective of reading. Her dissertation points to the usefulness of analyzing this phenomenon through multiple disciplinary lenses in order to better understand what occurs. Her work also points to the ways in which students can complement each other's learning when they study in Havruta and to the ways in which Havruta learning in the yeshiva high school reflect and reinforce broader orthodox values and beliefs. In her research, Brawer (2002) assesses the advantages of Havruta learning among yeshiva day-school students from the perspective of peer collaboration and critical thinking, and its beneficial impact on the learners. Informed by research on reading and interpreting literary texts and socio-cultural theories of knowledge, Kent (2006) conducts discourse analysis of video footage of adult Havruta learners, focusing on the interactions between Havruta learners and between each Havruta learner and the text. Her article documents and analyzes the social and intellectual moves of Havruta learners in one Havruta discussion. She begins to conceptualize how interpretive conversations in this Havruta unfold and identifies that it includes phases, moves, and norms. In addition, she identifies two different modes of the Havruta partners' engagement with one another, "co-building" and "interpreting through opposition."

In their research, Brown and Malkus (2007) explore how Havruta is organized and experienced in the Rabbinical School of the Jewish Theological Seminary. They interviewed and conducted focus groups with students, the Talmud faculty, the administration, and the Beit Midrash staff. Among other things, they report that students had little guidance about how to pick a Havruta or what to do once they were in a Havruta and that faculty were ambivalent about how much they should intervene. At the same time, many students reported that Havruta helped them form positive bonds with another student, connect to the text, and explore issues of religious meaning. They conclude that Havruta left to itself has enormous benefits and that this "natural" form of Havruta could benefit from research and practice in cooperative learning that points to such issues as the importance of positive interdependence and individual accountability. Raider-Roth and Holzer (2009) study the impact of carefully designed Havruta learning on the quality and the intensity of the relationships that learners establish with the text, with their Havruta partner, and with their own personal beliefs and values.

Two works of research have focused specifically on argumentative discourse patterns in Havruta learning. Schwarz (in press) studies the argumentative rhetoric of highly experienced Havruta partners in a traditional yeshiva. Blum, Kolka, Blondheim, and Hacohen (2008) attend to the characteristics of argumentative discourse that are common to traditional learners of Talmud and to Israeli politicians. Their study is based on a comparative discourse analysis of one Havruta pair with politicians' confrontational rhetoric during a popular Israeli TV show. This research shows a high degree of identity between discourse characteristics in both contexts and suggests a causal connection between the argumentative and non-consensual tradition of Havruta Talmud study and what is often identified as the strong argumentative and non-consensual character of contemporary Israeli culture and political discourse.

Finally, two research articles have applied a hermeneutic methodology to probe rabbinic texts related to peer learning to discuss various aspects of Havruta learning: Ratzersdorfer Rosen (2003) discusses short statements in the Talmud that characterize various learning purposes and modes of interaction between Havruta learners. Holzer (2009) offers an interpretation of a Talmudic legend which emphasizes an ethical dimension of Havruta learning, this being the responsibility that one has for the learning of his Havruta partner.

Currently, we are writing a book which draws on our work designing and teaching in DeLeT's Beit Midrash for Teachers. The book reflects two of our core convictions: that any model of Havruta learning that educators promote should be situated within broader theories of epistemology and learning and that Havruta learning should be treated by educators as composed of practices which can and should be conceptualized and curricularized and into which participants should be inducted. The book offers conceptual and practical tools for Havruta text study design and teaching, as well as a discussion of principles and examples of a Beit Midrash design. Kent is also writing a book which presents a contemporary theory of Havruta learning as composed of six practices and illustrates these practices in concrete cases of people learning in Havruta. This book describes the adaptation and use of her theory in three distinct educational settings: a teacher education program, a third-grade classroom, and a Jewish afternoon school.

An Agenda for Future Research

Mapping

Because of a lack of systematic documentation of Havruta learning, we advocate a mapping agenda to document the uses of Havruta in contemporary times. This documentation process would address a series of questions: Where is Havruta being practiced, with whom, and to study what subject matter(s)? How is it being practiced? What purposes does it serve according to both teachers and students? When and why was it first introduced in various contexts? What are explicit and implicit views about what good Havruta learning entails in these contexts?

In general, we believe that research on Havruta learning should aim to address issues beyond the documentation and the analysis of this phenomenon in contemporary settings of Jewish learning. As with any rich and complex learning practice, educators might benefit from descriptive as well as programmatic research that would turn Havruta learning into a focus of scholarship. For example, educators who promote Havruta learning may gain a more refined understanding of models of what Havruta learning might look like and what purposes it might serve in different contexts and for different learners. The following lines of research illustrate our point.

Studies of the Teaching and Learning of Havruta

Another line of research would focus on Havruta teaching and learning in different contexts. This could include direct classroom studies and experimental studies, such as comparison studies between expert and novice Havruta learners. Comparison studies between novices and experts have been conducted in the area of teaching literature with useful results.[3]

This line of research would explore what Havruta learning requires of teachers as well as a range of learners, how its use can best be supported, and the purposes best served by Havruta learning. Some of the specific questions this line of research could address are as follows: What does Havruta learning require of learners? And, how do educators conceptualize a successful Havruta conversation? Kent's work (2006, 2008), for example, demonstrates a range of practices in which Havruta learners in the DeLeT Beit Midrash engage, some with more success than others. What is the range of skills and dispositions required by these practices? Does Havruta in different contexts entail the same six practices or a different constellation of practices?

Other examples of questions worthy of empirical study are as follows: Are educators in different contexts providing learners with the necessary skills and scaffolding to successfully engage in Havruta and, if so, what characterizes their pedagogies? What are the ways, if any, by which Havruta learning is evaluated and assessed? What are some of the actual effects of Havruta learning on the learners and their learning? How do educators and learners experience the advantages and disadvantages of using Havruta learning and what might this tell us about appropriate and inappropriate applications? And, how, if at all, does the work students do in Havruta contribute to the larger classroom conversation about particular texts?

This type of close study of Havruta learning would benefit from both cultural and gender analysis. Beliefs, assumptions, or preconceptions about Jewish texts in general, and biblical and Talmudic texts in particular are culturally constructed. Such beliefs and assumptions may operate as significant variables in the Havruta learning

---

[3] For example, Earthman (1992), "Creating the Virtual Work: Readers' Processes in Understanding Literary Texts."

dynamic and have an impact, for example, on what is assumed to be representative of a "good" interpretation in different cultural settings.

The participation of both men and women in many contemporary Havruta learning settings also invites interesting research questions. Feminist epistemological and psychological theories present different and new ideas about the connections between knowledge, learning, and relationships which might be the source for generative research questions. For example, according to Gilligan (1982), Coates (1996, 1997), and Sheldon (1992, 1997), women tend to silence their personal views and prefer a consensus when engaging with people with different views. It would be useful to consider the gendered nature of Havruta discourse and whether there are specific norms of discourse, argumentation, negotiation, and support which emerge in these new Batei Midrash.

Conceptual Research

In addition to empirical research, we believe that teachers and students of Havruta learning could benefit from the articulation of various views on what *good* Havruta learning entails. This would have an impact on developing both the textual skills and the interpersonal skills of Havruta learners. Furthermore, images of *good* Havruta learning may be infused by various epistemological or psychological theories, which offer important views of good learning and understanding. For example, Holzer (2006) adopts the concept of conversation developed in philosophical hermeneutics in order to articulate qualities of the relationship both between Havruta learners and between the Havruta learner and the text. One outcome of this analysis is the identification of a set of dispositions such as listening, wholeheartedness, and revising one's prejudices. In this approach, Havruta learning is conceptualized not only as a way of doing, but also as a way of being, from which it is possible to identity a set of essential skills for Havruta learning. Alternative epistemological and psychological theories may help us clarify additional, possibly alternative, elements and skills of what it is that educators are trying to educate for when they promote Havruta learning among their learners.

Sociological Studies of Batei Midrash and Havruta Learning

Sociological work is needed to understand the spread of Havruta learning and its use in non-traditional Batei Midrash. The research should try to understand this phenomenon in relation to other Jewish and societal trends such as people's search for greater community and the renaissance in adult learning, at least in the United States. In addition, the interpersonal nature of Havruta, particularly when used in the context of a collective learning environment such as a Beit Midrash, raises questions about the intersection between learning and identity development. For example, what role might learning in Havruta with peers play in one's own Jewish identity development? Another question pertains to the potential shifts in people's notions of the role of the expert in Jewish learning. Indeed, Havruta learning may indicate as well as cultivate a view in which the individual lay person, rather than the rabbi or the scholar, is entitled to assume and voice ownership of traditional Jewish texts and their meaning.

Finally, given the rise of non-traditional Batei Midrash in Israel and the United States, it would be useful to consider the differences between these new types of study houses and more traditional study houses. For example, Newberg's article on non-traditional Israeli Batai Midrash (Newberg, 2005) and their role in providing a framework for the exploration of Israeli/Jewish identities points to the need for additional research in this area. As noted above, another characteristic of these new Batei Midrash which calls for research is that they include both men and women learners and a variety of Jewish texts, including but not solely focusing on Talmud. One could well imagine that these and other differences could contribute to very different kinds of learning environments, with implications for how teachers teach and how students learn.

Conclusion

Havruta learning, often perceived as a traditional mode of "Jewish learning," has slowly become the object of scholarly interest. One reason for this "late awakening" may be related to the relative lack of scholarship on teaching and learning in Jewish education in general. We believe that research on Havruta learning has important implications beyond simply learning more about this particular phenomenon. As researchers who have made Havruta learning the focus of their work, we are often asked the question if Havruta learning is a peculiarly Jewish form of study. We believe that the meaning of the question itself is not always as straightforward as it may appear. Is the question to be understood to refer to the formal setup of two people engaged in the study of a text? In this case, various forms of collaborative learning in progressive education show that Havruta learning is not peculiar to Jewish learning (Cohen, 1994; Sharan, 1994; Slavin, 1995). Does the question refer to specific features of the Havruta learning dynamic? As implied in our chapter, a formal Havruta learning setting does not necessarily mean specific and pre-defined features of interaction between learners and between learners and text. Rather than answer the question about the peculiarly Jewish aspect of Havruta learning, we prefer to say that in its very essence, Havruta learning creates an intense microcosm of two central activities of Jewish education: the study of Jewish texts and dialogue with contemporary fellow Jews. We believe that scholarship oriented toward both of these learning activities can contribute toward the overall scholarship of Jewish education and the improvement of classroom practice. While Havruta learning admittedly reflects one learning situation among many, we believe that significant progress in documenting, conceptualizing, designing, and teaching the Havruta learning mode will contribute to our attempts to help students learn how to study Jewish texts and to learn together.

References

Blum Kolka, Sh., Blondeim, M., & Hacohen, G. (2008). Traditions of disagreements – from argumentative conversations about talmud texts to political discourse in the media. In M. Neiger, M. Blondeim, & T. Libes (Eds.), *Coverage as story: perspectives on discourse in Israeli media. In honor of Itzhak Roeh* (pp. 245–274). Jerusalem: Magness Press *(Hebrew)*.

Brawer, D. (2002). *Havruta and Talmud Study: Peer interaction in critical thinking*. London: University of London.

Brown, S. & Malkus, M. (2007). Havruta as a form of cooperative learning. *Journal of Jewish Education*, 73(3), 209–226.

Coates, J. (1996). *Women talk*. Cambridge, MA: Blackwell.

Coates, J. (1997). Women's friendship, women's talk. In R. Wodak (Ed.), *Gender and discourse* (pp. 245–262). London, Thousand Oaks, CA and New Delhi: Sage publications.

Cohen, E. (1994). *Designing groupwork, strategies for the heterogeneous classroom* (2nd ed.). New York: Teachers College Press.

Earthman, E. A. (1992). Creating the virtual work: Readers' processes in understanding literary texts. *Research in the Teaching of English*, 26(4), 351–384.

Feiman-Nemser, Sh. (2006). Beit midrash for teachers: An experiment in teacher preparation. *Journal of Jewish Education*, 72, 161–181.

Gilligan, C. (1982). *In a different voice: Women's conceptions of the self and of morality*. Cambridge, MA: Harvard University Press.

Halbertal, M. & Hartman Halbertal, T. (1998). The yeshivah. In A. O. Rorty (Ed.), *Philosophers on education: New historical perspectives* (pp. 458–469). New York: Routledge Stone.

Holzer, E. (2006). What connects "good" teaching, text study and Havruta learning? A conceptual argument. *Journal of Jewish Education*, 72, 183–204.

Holzer, E. (2009). "Either a Havruta partner of death" A critical view on the interpersonal dimensions of Havruta learning. *The Journal of Jewish Education*, 75, 130–149.

Kent, O. (2006). Interactive text study: A case of Havruta learning. *Journal of Jewish Education*, 72, 205–232.

Kent, O. (2008). *Interactive Text Study and the Co-Construction of Meaning: Havruta in the DeLeT Beit Midrash*. Ph.d dissertation submitted at the Mandel Center for Studies in Jewish Education. Brandeis University.

Newberg, A. (2005). Hitchabrut or connecting – liberal houses of study in Israel as political and spiritual expression. *Israel Studies Forum*, 20(2), 97–114.

Raider-Roth, M. & Holzer, E. (2009). Learning to be present: How Havruta learning can activate teachers' relationships to self, other and text. *The Journal of Jewish Education*, 75(3), 216–239.

Ratzersdorfer Rosen, G. (2003). Empathy and aggression in Torah study: Analysis of a Talmudic description of Havruta learning. In J. Sacks & S. Handelman (Eds.), *Wisdom from all my teachers* (pp. 249–263). Jerusalem, New York: Urim.

Schwarz, B. B. (In press). Students' Havruta learning in Lituanian Yeshivot: The case of recurrent learning. In E. Etkes, T. Elor, M. Hed, & B. Schwartz (Eds.), *Education and religion: Between tradition and innovation*. Jerusalem: Magness Press *(Hebrew)*.

Segal, A. (2003). *Havruta study: History benefits and enhancements*. Jerusalem: ATID.

Sharan, S (Ed.) (1994). *Handbook of cooperative learning methods*. Westport, CT: Greenwood Press.

Sheldon, A. (1992). "Conflict talk: Sociolinguistic challenges to self-assertion and how young girls meet them". *Merril-Palmer Quarterly*, 38(1), 95–117.

Sheldon, A. (1997). Talking power: Girls, gender enculturation and discourse. In R. Wodak (Ed.), *Gender and Discourse* (pp. 225–244). London, Thousand Oaks, CA and New Delhi: Sage Publication.

Slavin, R. (1995). *Cooperative learning: Theory, research and practice*. Boston: Allyn and Bacon.

Stampfer, S. (1995). *HaYeshivah haLita'it beHithavutah*. Jerusalem: Shazar *(Hebrew)*.

Tedmon, S. (1991). *Collaborative acts of literacy in traditional Jewish community*. Doctoral dissertation, University of Pennsylvania.
Tishbi, Y. (1979). Yeshivot Lita. In Y. Praver, Y. Gutman (Eds.), *Hebrew encyclopedia* (Vol. 17, p. 689). Jerusalem: Society for encyclopedia Pub (*Hebrew*).
Yair, G., Sagiv, T., Shimborsky, Sh., Akrai, S., & Lichtman, M. (2006). The impact of learning communities and open Batei Midrash in Israel. www.avi-chai.org (*Hebrew*).

Hebrew Language in Israel and the Diaspora

Nava Nevo

Translated by **Daniel Verbov**

This chapter examines the state of Hebrew today, both in Israel and in Diaspora communities, and discusses challenges facing those who are involved with the language. As a first language in Israel, Hebrew is undergoing changes due to globalization processes which cause some to express concern for its fate. As a second language, Hebrew is taught to immigrants and to minority groups with the intent of facilitating their integration into the life of the country; unfortunately, recognition of teaching Hebrew to immigrant students as a particular profession is still needed. In Diaspora communities the status of Hebrew today has changed for demographic, contextual, and pedagogical reasons. Diaspora Hebrew education confronts dilemmas regarding the definition of goals, the language of instruction of Jewish subjects, teaching materials, and human resources for teaching. Given the challenges discussed in this chapter, an in-depth examination of the agenda for Hebrew language education, both in Israel and abroad, is needed to develop and preserve our people's unifying language.

Introduction

Milestones in the History of the Hebrew Language

The name "Ever"[1] and the word "Hebrew" in its masculine and feminine forms appear in the Bible, but there is no reference to the Hebrew language per se. A language called "Judean," as opposed to Aramaic, is mentioned.[2] It is feasible that the implication is what is known as "Hebrew," but we cannot be certain. The name "Hebrew" appears for the first time as the name of a language in an external book,

---

N. Nevo (✉)
Hebrew University of Jerusalem, Jerusalem, Israel
e-mail: msnava@mscc.huji.ac.il

[1] "Ever" has the same root letters as "Ivrit."
[2] "And they cried loudly in Judean to the people of Jerusalem on the wall …," Chronicles 2, 32:18; "And Ravshakeh stood and called out loudly in Judean," Isaiah, 36:13; "half speak in the language of Ashdod and do not know how to speak Judean," Nehemiah, 13:24.

Sefer HaYovlim—"The Book of Jubilees," when God speaks to Abraham: "... and I opened his mouth, and his ears and his lips, and I began to speak with him in Hebrew in the tongue of the creation" (Chapter 12:31).[3]

Hebrew never died out in its written form, neither for public purposes (such as religious and non-religious literature, philosophical treatises, science) nor for private needs (including personal letters and business correspondence). According to Haramati (2000) there were oases of Hebrew speech throughout history, but it was opportune and temporary. Hebrew was spoken by people in Jerusalem and Safed; Torah scholars taught and lectured in Hebrew; Yemenite Jews taught in Hebrew; between the ninth and sixteenth centuries, medical studies in Europe were conducted—inter alia—in Hebrew too; spoken Hebrew was heard among Italian Jews until the end of the sixteenth century, and teaching in Hebrew was also somewhat present during the Enlightenment at the start of the nineteenth century.

The Jewish National Revival Movement sparked the start of the process of making Hebrew the spoken tongue of Jewish settlement in Israel. Thus, Eliezer Ben-Yehuda called for the adoption of Hebrew as the language of instruction: "We should make it (Hebrew) the language of education ... the revival of the language will be a sign that the revival of the nation will also occur without delay" (cited from "Ha-Magid" 1888 in Perlmutter, 2002). In other words, he proposed transforming Hebrew speech into something constant and permanent. A new–old Hebrew was created, written, and spoken, which adapted biblical language, the language of the Sages, medieval speech, and the language of philosophers and writers together with modern innovations (Brosh-Weitz, 2007, p. 68).

Since 1948, Hebrew has been the official language of the State of Israel, together with Arabic. While Hebrew is the dominant language in every sphere in the public domain, Arabic chiefly serves the Arabic-speaking areas.

Representations of the Hebrew Language

In Israel, Hebrew functions in all walks of life just like any other first language in a country: in the education system, academia, the media, in daily life, the world of culture, the Internet, etc. Although Hebrew is expanding and renewing itself, it is noteworthy that the hegemony of Hebrew in Israel and the "melting pot" policy that characterized the first years of the State (the aim of which was to create a homogeneous community of Hebrew speakers) are becoming blurred due to the absorption of immigrants from various countries, with different ethnic backgrounds, and the impact of the era of globalization.

Today, Hebrew is a living, evolving language that can be divided into subcategories: literary Hebrew with high linguistic norms, standard written Hebrew, standard spoken Hebrew, non-standard Hebrew, and the Hebrew spoken by certain

---

[3]The mention of the Hebrew language for the first time in *Sefer HaYovlim* was noted by Professor Rachel Elior at a conference on Hebrew and its Culture, at the Van Leer Institute in Jerusalem, December 31, 2008.

groups in Israeli society, such as soldiers who have developed a military lingo and slang often seeping into "civilian" Hebrew; the language of ultra-Orthodox Jews whose Hebrew contains various Yiddish expressions, interspersed with abbreviations and idioms from the yeshiva world; and the Hebrew spoken by Kibbutz members, which includes unique expressions for daily kibbutz life. Other groups include taxi drivers, sports commentators, tour guides, prisoners, Israeli backpackers, and teenage girls. The language used in post-modern literature is also often a separate category, setting new language norms by combining high Hebrew with foreign words, flouting conventions, sidestepping the rules, using slang, making no commitment to "clean" language, and even making intentional language errors to position protagonists in a particular socio-linguistic and socio-cultural milieu.

Hebrew, apart from its representation as a first language, is also a second language for immigrants and minority groups in Israel. A language defined as "second" is the dominant language in the environment of the non-native speaker, to which he is also exposed in informal frameworks. Immigrants are driven to achieve a command of Hebrew (at various levels) as a second language because of their integrative and/or instrumental motivation. Non-Jewish minority groups are motivated by instrumental needs such as education or employment.

Another representation of Hebrew is as a foreign language. In contrast to a second language, which has contextual support in the student's surroundings, it is studied in a formal framework and is not used in a natural context on an ongoing basis. For example, Hebrew is studied in universities the world over in the framework of Language Studies Departments, in Jewish day schools, and in some cases in public schools, such as "Ben Gamla" in Florida, which includes Hebrew lessons in its curriculum.

In contrast to the clear definitions of the status of Hebrew for native speakers and immigrants, minority groups, or universities outside of Israel, defining its status for Jews in the Diaspora is less obvious. It seems that one cannot link it dichotomously to any one of the above categories. It is not a first language, but is also not a fully second or foreign language. Hebrew in the Diaspora does possess characteristics of a foreign language, for it is not in use in the speaker's macro-world, but at the same time it also has second language attributes related to the speaker's micro-Jewish world and is associated with Jewish belonging, identity, cultural uniqueness, and heritage (Shohamy, 1989). As such, it has been perceived throughout history as a unifying national, social, and cultural value.

The aim of this chapter is to examine the state and status of Hebrew today, both in the Israeli context and in the context of Diaspora communities, and to discuss issues, questions, difficulties, and challenges facing scholars, Hebrew teachers, students, community leaders, and lovers of the Hebrew language.

Hebrew in Israel

The discussion will be conducted on two levels: Hebrew as a first language for native speakers and as a second language for immigrants and the Arab sector.

Changes in Hebrew as a First Language

Like other societies, globalization processes permeate Israeli society. These processes also impact the language and cause it to change. Despite the fact that a body of work has developed in Israel in Hebrew, there are those today who are concerned about the fate of the language and fear a negative attitude change toward it. Schwarzwald notes that Israeli Hebrew speakers display a lack of respect for their language, contempt for careful speech, a detachment from the sources, and self-deprecation when faced with the English (chiefly the American) language and culture, the import of which is not only on a linguistic level, but also on a socio-cultural level. She adds that in contemporary Hebrew, one can see "trends of unification, leveling of systems and finding the lowest and most comfortable common denominator for all speakers" (Schwarzwald Rodrigue, 2007, p. 60). There are others who agree with these claims, for example, Aharon Amir, author and winner of the Israel Prize for Translation: "Things are going beyond purity of language and a zealousness to preserve it. The massive Anglicization of the language contains a certain disrespect which also testifies to ... a feeling of a lack of belonging"(Ma'ariv, 2008).

According to Schwarzwald (2005, 2007), changes in the language originate in a number of causes, including secularization processes and the influence of foreign cultures. I would add social polarization and the "ingathering of the exiles." Social secularization processes have led to a situation in which knowledge of the language of Hebrew sources has declined, and with it a depletion of a rich Hebrew vocabulary. The influence of foreign cultures on Hebrew—particularly the American one—is visible in academia, music, and in ordinary daily life, as speakers tend to slide into English words and expressions. The hi-tech industry has contributed a plethora of English terms, as have the worlds of advertising, entertainment, sport, finance, and commerce. Use of the Internet and exposure to mass communication, cinema, and music have generated a massive English presence in Israeli Hebrew.

There is no doubt that English has a privileged status in Israel and is no longer considered a foreign language. The particular impact of English on Israel can be attributed to the following: Israel's linkage to world globalization processes; its connection to American society and to World Jewry; it being a small country with a language that is rarely understood outside its borders; being a country that seeks resources from the world and whose economic development is linked to international markets and has advanced status in elite technology. As Ben-Rafael puts it, "we are an extreme case of globalization" (Ben-Rafael, 2003, p. 54).

The influence of English is also apparent on other international languages. For example, English has intruded into Spanish and French, but the comparative difference to Hebrew is the level of intrusion and the strength of Hebrew relative to the power of the other languages. French and Spanish are ancient languages whose exclusivity has been zealously preserved for years. In contrast, Hebrew, in its function as a language of communication, is a relatively young language. This arouses concern that the great impact of English is liable to undermine it. Hebrew is not fighting the English influence, but absorbing it within its ranks.

The mass immigration from the Former Soviet Union in the 1990s resulted in Russian also being heard and seen in abundance: in the street, the media, in theater, and on billboards and ads. In the past, new immigrants tried to leave their native languages within the confines of their own narrow surroundings and speak Hebrew in the public sphere. Children would even be embarrassed in front of their native Israeli friends when their parents spoke in a foreign language.[4]

In contrast, today, the spoken foreign languages of various communities are heard in public and are changing the face of the Hebrew language. The trend of borrowed words and expressions slipping directly into Hebrew or translated from other languages is increasing, especially in the spoken language. For example, you made my day (*asita li et ha-yom*), it doesn't make sense (*ze lo ose sechel*)—from English; *achla, sababa*—from Arabic; *kuter, tachles*—from Yiddish; *amigos* from Spanish, and more. This trend is particularly prominent in the gastronomical realm: ice café, noodles, junk food, burekas, chaminados, shtrudel, shnitsel. Similarly, in foreign verbs introduced into the square root structure in Hebrew (e.g., *ledaskes*—to discuss, *lefaxes*—to fax, *leflartet*—to flirt). Furthermore, Hebrew syntactical structure and sentence word order have also undergone transformation, part of which is the fruit of independent creation in Hebrew and part of which is influenced by foreign languages. For example, the order—subject, predicate, complements (widespread in Hebrew)—has been influenced by European languages (such as SVO—subject, verb, object in English), while the dominant word order in a sentence in the classic sources is predicate, subject, and complements (Schwarzwald, 2007).

Like others mentioned above, Rosenthal (2007)—a linguist, author, and journalist—expresses concern for the future of Hebrew as heard in Israel, claiming that the language is becoming increasingly shallow, especially in speech. Rosenthal indicates a number of foci for concern: a distancing from becoming familiar with Judaic sources; a plethora of foreign words in both written and spoken texts threatening the independence of Hebrew; multiple linguistic errors also trickling down into written texts; eliminating words and verbs within the language. I would add the disappearance of the distinction between consonants (*tet* = *tav*, *kuf* = *kaf*, *aleph* = *ayin*, and sometimes *heh*) and the mode of expression in the digital world (text messages, chats, and even e-mail), which youngsters view as legitimate and use quite indiscriminately. Thus, a shriveled language is created, relying heavily on English, accompanied by spelling mistakes, stringing words together (*yom huledet* = *yomuledet*—birthday, *shishi shabbat* = *shishabat*—Friday to Saturday), cutting words and expressions (*ma nishma* = *ma nish*—how are you?), and using "umbrella" verbs instead of specific ones ("brought" instead of "gave," "put on" in the sense of "wore"). Rosenthal notes a gap between what he terms "Israeli Hebrew," spoken by Israelis, and "self-contained Hebrew," in all its historical layers, rules of grammar and syntax, and dictionary entries.

---

[4]See, for example, Shamosh, A. (1979). Vignettes from elementary school, in the story anthology, "Calamus and Cinnamon" (p. 79). Ramat-Gan, Massada Press Ltd. (Heb.).

It should be noted that the trend of linguistic and literacy recession is a transnational phenomenon. Just as there is a recession in literacy skills among Israeli children, one can point to English-speaking children who do not have the necessary skills to read English and American literary classics (Waxman, 1999). What is known as "linguistic deterioration" is characteristic of many languages. Indeed, I would pose the question: Should we relate to the changes occurring in the speakers' languages as regression and deterioration or perhaps as the normal development of a living language?

Hebrew as a First Language—Learning and Teaching

A distinction should be made between acquiring Hebrew as a first language and studying and teaching it. Acquisition occurs naturally from the very fact that the acquirer is part of an environment that functions in Hebrew. Study and teaching occur within the formal framework of the education system. Various arguments have been made in this context, some in a document about the state of Hebrew presented to the Israeli Knesset's Education Committee (Vorgan, 2008). The teaching of Hebrew in high schools is dictated by the demands of the matriculation exam; in essence, the matriculation exam has become the curriculum. Hebrew study and teaching curricula in the education system focus on rules and laws and overemphasize grammatical pedantry at the expense of the richness of the language itself and the analysis of daily spoken discourse. This generates a feeling of revulsion for the subject among students. The result is an insufficient language level, a shallow vocabulary, use of empty words (such as "like"), and primarily no distinction between high and low registers or between written and spoken language. School students often write as they speak, even when faced with a formal academic assignment, and some continue to do so when they progress to institutions of higher education as well. The Hebrew among Israeli school students, argues Schweid (2004), is not only inadequate for reading the Bible or the prayer book, but also for reading modern national classic literature or quality Israeli contemporary literature. Spolsky and Shohamy (1999) further detail problems associated with Hebrew teaching and point out that there is no emphasis on the spoken language in grade schools; many teachers do not use efficient reading instruction methods; and in-service training only reaches a small percentage of the teachers. These two researchers conclude that the education system must rise to the challenge of conducting a comprehensive and in-depth examination of the state of teaching Hebrew as a first language and evaluate its aims.

I would emphasize that garbled and defective language is not only a linguistic problem, but also a perceptual one. Language serves to organize thought and to conceptualize and perceive reality. Language deficiency can have negative ramifications on the thinking or philosophical level. It is imperative that educational frameworks present students with texts representing a range of language registers and point out the distinctions between them. This would raise students' awareness of using an appropriate register in keeping with context and circumstances and ensure that the spoken register does not remain all-exclusive in their consciousness.

A curriculum, "Hebrew Language Education," was developed in 2003 that includes language, literature, and culture, with the aim of addressing the need for developing and nurturing communicative and literacy competence in Hebrew as a first language. The theoretical infrastructure and didactic principles at the root of the program include linguistic knowledge as well as discourse skills. The aim of the curriculum is to cultivate a "literate person," capable of using, understanding, and discussing written and spoken texts (Blum-Kulka, 2007).

Is Hebrew Really in Danger?

In light of the worrying picture described above, the following question arises: Do the influences of globalization, together with the decline in Zionist ideology, have the power to endanger the sustainability of Hebrew? There is no doubting the changes in Israeli Hebrew, but we should also remember that it is hard to avoid the influences of the "global village." Since Hebrew speakers are part of that "village," their language is undergoing natural processes of change.

In contrast to concern for the fate of Hebrew, there are also other opinions, such as that of poet Ronni Somek, advocating Hebrew's natural development: "Hebrew is like a baby whom everybody once protected and nurtured. This baby has now grown up, become independent and he is kicking ... [Hebrew] does not feel any need to fight for its status because its status is assured." There are those who further argue that closing government schools for studying Hebrew (*ulpans*) might even make teaching the language more efficient, because "one can see this as a sign of maturity and self-confidence of a society whose language no longer needs ideological nurturing and is alive and kicking, increasingly acclimatizing to innovations and inventions, some of which are weeds, and some of which are pretty flowers" (Segev, 2007).

I also do not share the fear that foreign languages will subvert Hebrew, or pose a real threat and take control of it (although linguistic cultural "ghettoes" are liable to form): Hebrew is not only an official language of the State of Israel, but a language that is the essence of Israeli identity, bearing a cultural cargo. It is a modern language, in which plays are created, books are written, discussions take place, interviews are conducted, articles are published, and dictionaries are compiled, unafraid to include slang and popular speech as well. In my opinion, these characteristics will preserve balance and cultural identity. Nonetheless, in places where it is possible and logical to do so, it is important to offer alternative forms of expression in Hebrew that will seep into the public discourse. Finding such alternatives in Hebrew is the role of the Academy of the Hebrew Language.

Challenges in Teaching Hebrew as a Second Language to Immigrant Students

Due to the limited scope of this chapter, the following discussion will focus on teaching Hebrew to immigrant students, although teaching Hebrew to other foreign-language-speaking populations, such as immigrant adults or immigrant soldiers, is worthy of attention as well.

The education system is faced with a double challenge in teaching Hebrew as a second language, both regarding students and teachers. In terms of the students, the challenge is to imbue them with the language on four levels: linguistic competence that will enable them to understand and use proper language syntactically and lexically for their various daily needs; communicative competence that will allow them to function appropriately in specific social circumstances; academic competence that includes understanding concepts unique to various study disciplines; and literate competency that will represent Hebrew writing and reading ability.

In contrast to these wide-ranging needs, the basic allocation of the Ministry of Education for an immigrant student in an upper school, for example, is 1 hour a week for learning Hebrew and additional assistance in subjects that are language-dependent. Ethiopian immigrant students are allocated 1.75 weekly hours.[5] Immigrant students have a number of possible study frameworks upon their arrival in Israel. Whichever way, studies examining second language learning among immigrant students in other countries do not support the assumption that so few hours of assistance are sufficient to effectively include the immigrant in a class of native speakers.

Regarding teachers, teaching Hebrew as a second language to immigrant students—in contrast to other teaching professions—is not recognized by the Ministry of Education as a specialization subject area, possibly because waves of immigration are not always foreseeable and the number of immigrant students joining schools changes from time to time. In this situation, the issue of instilling a language is dependent on the needs of a given period, and thus Hebrew teaching is as a transitory profession (Spolsky, Shohamy, & Nevo, 1995). In many cases, teachers teaching Hebrew to immigrant students come from a different field of specialization. At times teachers do receive some training in the principles of teaching Hebrew as a second language, but this is not enough to create expertise in this area, which is different from teaching a first language. Recognition of the field as a particular teaching profession is needed. This will then lead to appropriate formal training and high professional standards, based on a comprehensive and in-depth program. Support for these ideas comes from a study conducted among grades 5, 9, and 11, which compared the level of achievement in the academic language of immigrant students from the Former Soviet Union and Ethiopia, as opposed to native Israelis, in the different subject areas studied at school. The study found that immigrants only equal the academic achievements of native Hebrew speakers after 5–11 years in Israel, depending on age and home country. The researchers' conclusion is that the curriculum must provide support in acquiring language skills and that for this purpose, experts are needed to teach Hebrew as a second language (Levin, Shohamy, & Inbar, 2007).

---

[5]It should be noted that allocation of teaching hours by the Ministry of Education is influenced not only by the student's native country, but also by the number of immigrant students in the school, the time of arrival in Israel and by the preparatory needs of the matriculation exams: http://www.biu.ac.il/hu/lprc/home/HOLSHORT.htm.

The community in Israel is multi-cultural and consists of immigrants speaking a variety of foreign languages alongside speakers of the majority language, Hebrew. In the modern era, it would be fitting to allow space for multi-lingualism and multi-culturalism. A solid and stable status for Hebrew and competence in other languages may facilitate social, communicative, and economic mobility for immigrants. In such a society, it is worth developing a language education model that includes a curriculum ensuring the following: (1) complete command of the majority language skills, both for its native speakers and foreign-language speakers; (2) Hebrew speakers' command of other languages at threshold level. This model will benefit both native Hebrew speakers and foreign-language speakers: Hebrew speakers will nurture and enrich their language alongside the understanding that knowing other languages is of added value in modern society and in the world of the twenty-first century. Speakers of other languages will benefit from the recognition of their right to preserve their language and not to forfeit their ethnic identity together with receiving intensive and extensive support in acquiring Hebrew. This will allow them to integrate into the education system and into Hebrew-speaking society. It would be correct to build Hebrew acquisition on the linguistic and cultural platform that foreign-language students bring with them rather than to destroy what already exists. Their native linguistic and cultural experiences will reinforce the students' confidence and serve as a base for future study (Nevo & Olshtain, 2007).

This linguistic policy, one that recognizes the value of multiple languages and cultural pluralism, is the opposite of what the Zionist enterprise proposed in its time. Immigrants had to forego their language, culture, and identity in favor of Hebrew, and Israeli society relinquished the linguistic and cultural capital that the immigrants brought with them. The principles of the new language policy are at the root of the current curriculum for teaching Hebrew to immigrant children. It acknowledges the importance of preserving first language and cultural continuity, while establishing teaching Hebrew as the overall objective and exposing students to different universes of discourse (Blum-Kulka, 2007).

Hebrew in the Arab Sector

The Arab sector in Israel also acknowledges the need to study Hebrew as an additive second language, because this is the language of official institutions, the media, institutions of higher education, and the street. Acquiring a command of Hebrew allows Arab citizens open communicative access to the Jewish majority group and integration into the life of the country through society, education, and the economy. It also creates a bridging dialogue between the Arab and Jewish cultures. Israeli Arabs, Druze and Circassians cite Hebrew as being most important to them. The recognition of the need to know Hebrew and to be able to use it appropriately in given circumstances led, in 2007, to the development of a new curriculum for teaching Hebrew in Arab schools, from grade 3 through grade 12. This program highlights the communicative aspect of the language. The program stresses linguistic knowledge alongside comprehension and expression of both the written and spoken language, while basing study on texts from the students' world and from various other worlds of discourse that address the needs of Arab adults. These include formal and informal inter-personal communication—interfacing with the immediate environment as well as with official institutions; printed and digital mass communications; theoretical discourse presenting the student with scientific texts from different disciplines studied both in school and outside; and Hebrew literature, enabling the Arab student to encounter the cultural content of the majority society, including a rich vocabulary unfamiliar from daily life (Wated, 2007).

Hebrew in Diaspora Jewish Education

Changes in the Status of the Language

In contrast to other peoples who are masters of their national languages, Hebrew is not the "common possession" of all Jewish people, and it mainly—if not exclusively—lives and breathes in Israel. In the past, Hebrew was perceived as "linguistic capital" with the potential to serve as the common denominator for the Jewish people, connecting various sectors in different communities, and linking them to those living in Israel, to their past, their culture, and heritage; it served as a key to the doors of the Jewish bookcase. The Jewish people's spiritual leadership encouraged study of Hebrew, as well as prayer and Torah study in this language. Today, there is in general a decline in the status of Hebrew in Diaspora communities and in the motivation to study it, which also affects students' perception of Israel's status. While life in Israel demands knowledge of Hebrew as a mutual language that enables the integration and functioning of different parts of the society, Diaspora Jewry needs to adopt local majority languages in order to blend into the surroundings from a social, cultural, economic, and academic perspective. Although there are oases of Hebrew in certain schools, it has not become the Jewish lingua franca and English is rapidly taking its place as the Jewish people's language of communication. Even Hebrew-speaking Israeli representatives tend to use English in their public appearances at international Jewish conventions (Schweid, 2004; Schenker, 1991; Shohamy, 1999). In order not to remain an isolated "nature reserve" unique to Israel or the language of prayer and sacred studies alone, the preservation of Hebrew is one of the most significant challenges facing Jewish education in the Diaspora.

Changes in the status of Hebrew manifest themselves on a number of levels. The role of Hebrew in building Jewish identity is gradually changing; classical Jewish sources are increasingly being translated into foreign languages; there has been a decline in community leaders' positive attitude toward the language (Deitcher, 2007); and most institutions and movements in the Diaspora no longer view the promotion of Hebrew as a major objective (Ganiel, 2007). Thus, for example, in the United States, various Jewish schools feel less committed to the language; Jewish subjects are studied in English; some teachers are lowering expectations for acquiring command of the language and make do with phonetic reading to enable participation in prayers (a goal that could be achieved in a very short time); some children stop learning the language once they finish grade school, and others—once they have the choice—prefer to focus on those subjects that will be of future practical benefit. The use of Hebrew has also become limited in summer camps, many of which traditionally functioned in Hebrew.

Jewish communities do not necessarily perceive Hebrew to be a crucial factor for the existence of Jewish life. There are those who see it as a foreign language in need of revival (Schiff, 1999), whereas others ask: Why Hebrew? After all, it is a minority language, spoken only in Israel, and in the Diaspora there is little to no use for it outside the synagogue. Thus, a new model of the "educated Jew" is created, lacking knowledge of Hebrew. This model, as expressed in the curricula of Jewish schools, does not include training for engagement with Jewish sources using the Hebrew language (Bekerman, 1999; Deitcher, 2008; Steinberg, 1997; Zisenwein, 1997). Mintz (2002), in describing the status of Hebrew within American Jewry, argues that the definition of an educated Jew applies, inter alia, to someone who has access to Jewish sources in the original, since translation—which incorporates the translator's interpretation—cannot be a substitute. Mintz claims that renunciation of the original language and dependence on translated sources not only means that cultural, religious, and national "baggage" is not transmitted as it should be, but that even the future development of Judaism is endangered. Hebrew, he suggests, should be preserved as the key to continuity in all aspects of Jewish and communal life. In a similar vein, Berdichevsky (1998) quotes Mordechai Kaplan who, more than 60 years ago, warned that once Hebrew becomes a foreign language for Jews, they will cease to live Judaism as a culture and no longer experience a sense of intimacy with Jewish life.

There are a number of reasons for the dramatic decline in the status of Hebrew, in the Diaspora in general and in America in particular: According to the Israeli Foreign Ministry, the main causes are the demographic drop in the Jewish people, a weakening of Israel–Diaspora relations, and a leadership crisis in coping with these trends. Furthermore, the Zionist ideology, with Hebrew as one of its dominant symbols, has also become weaker. These factors are bolstered by contextual and pedagogical forces, as indicated by Shohamy (1999).

On the contextual level there are two factors: First, Hebrew was never a heritage language spoken in Jewish homes (unlike Yiddish and Ladino), and, hence, Jewish children today do not identify it with their parents and grandparents. It is detached from their daily reality and does not possess any concrete associations. Second, with most Jews living today in tolerant and welcoming societies, that assist in accelerating assimilation into the dominant society, feelings of Jewish identity have been undermined as has the need to know Hebrew. Bouganim (2007) reports that even among those who are very committed to their Judaism, there are now different symbolic forms of identification that spare the need to learn and speak Hebrew, such as giving children Hebrew names in addition to their regular names, or inserting Hebrew words and (Jewish) concepts in Hebrew in conversation. A holistic approach that advocates knowledge of Hebrew in order to be a Jew is no longer necessary.

On a pedagogic-didactic level, reasons for the poor state of Hebrew in the Diaspora start with the absence of focused, realistic, and measurable goals and objectives in teaching the language. Goals must be defined in accordance with the context in which they are applied and vary from one study framework to another. In one context, teaching Hebrew might be for ritual purposes or for reading classical texts; in another, Hebrew instruction may be for communication purposes in advance of a possible visit to Israel or Aliyah (immigration to Israel); at other times, Hebrew is indeed studied as a ritual language, but with the expectation that the students can use it as a communicative language. Sometimes the aim is to teach Hebrew as a communicative language but without providing the necessary conditions to consolidate it as such. Defining goals and objectives also dictates what study material, contents, emphases, and teaching methods will be, and how the time will be allocated. Lack of clarity in defining the aims of instruction leads not only to a lack of clarity in the style of teaching, but also to confusion about what is expected from graduates of the Jewish educational system. It remains unclear, for example, whether graduates should relate to Hebrew as a national language of the Jewish people or as the language of the Israelis.

Uncertainty is evident also in curriculum choices. In many cases, schools use materials that are not relevant to the student's world; they are often much less attractive than the materials used to teach other languages or the general subjects (lacking color, pictures, illustrations). This ultimately conveys the message that Hebrew studies are less important.

The decline in the status of Hebrew has been exacerbated by a number of factors. First, a trend toward translating classical Jewish texts into local languages, thereby denying students the opportunity to strengthen and enrich their Hebrew. Second, insufficient ongoing evaluation of the curriculum's impact on the students' achievements has a similar effect. Another contributing factor has been rapid teacher turnover and the lack of human resources, that is, people with a good command of Hebrew who are also trained to teach the language professionally. In this context, Deitcher (2008) notes a rise in the number of ultra-Orthodox teachers teaching Jewish subjects in Orthodox schools. These teachers are not experts in Hebrew and do not identify with the Zionist ideal of schools. There is also an increase in the number of young, inexperienced teachers lacking an appropriate knowledge of the language. Furthermore, changes that have occurred over the last decade in educational emissary programs in the Diaspora have influenced the current state of Hebrew: The number of *shlichim* (emissaries) with professional training in Hebrew has declined and their place has been taken by young, untrained *shlichim* who only serve for a short period of time, with limited resulting impact.

One can certainly question whether teaching Hebrew in Diaspora schools and universities must depend on imported teachers. For example, the Argentinean model indicates that Jewish school graduates, who continue their academic studies, can be trained to teach Hebrew locally. The fact that most of the Hebrew teachers in America are Israelis, who acquired the main part of their formal education in Israel, stems, however, from the fact that the American community has not succeeded in generating teachers capable of teaching the language in general and at the university level in particular (Brosh, 1996). In light of the above, it seems that one of the main challenges facing Hebrew education today is how to raise its status and the motivation to study it in the Jewish world.

The Place of Communicative Hebrew

Hebrew's Achilles heel in the Diaspora is the spoken language. Command of spoken Hebrew carries the message that Hebrew is a living, dynamic language. However, research indicates that acquiring even minimal command in schools, even in day schools, is doomed to failure. Different schools relate to Hebrew first and foremost as a symbol of Jewish identity and, in certain cases, as a language of culture; there is almost little to no commitment to teach Hebrew as a spoken language (Bouganim, 2007; Shohamy, 1999). Hence, comments like the following, from parents and students alike are often heard:

– "After 12 years of learning Hebrew, my child is not able to speak the language."
– "What is needed are more spoken Hebrew sessions."
– "I would rather like to concentrate more on practical speech, the Modern Hebrew that I could speak to someone on the street in Tel-Aviv."[6]

Mastery of daily Hebrew for communicative purposes has become almost impossible due to the limited time devoted to teaching and the non-positive attitudes toward it. This reality has been felt recently even in Argentina, where institutions were established to train Hebrew teachers, where Jewish Studies in schools once took place in Hebrew; and where graduates of the Jewish educational system were known for their Hebrew knowledge and motivation to study it. Today, parents believe their children will not use Hebrew anyway, while the science subjects and the English language are perceived as having greater instrumental value. They demand more mathematics, physics, and especially English as a prestigious language that will open the gates to universities and colleges worldwide. This results in a significant reduction in the number of hours devoted to teaching Hebrew. The situation in Mexico is similar.

Following research on the teaching of modern Hebrew in Jewish communities around the world, Rodman (2003, p. 9) found that Russian parents have a similarly negative perception of Hebrew. In the words of one of the participants, "Parents are negative about Hebrew when they feel it is not successful. Some parents ... in Russia think Hebrew is a poor investment of precious time, taking up a large part of the local-option segment of the government-mandated curriculum." Added to this

---

[6]These representative quotes are taken from responses to questionnaires for students and parents, developed as part of an assessment project of Hebrew achievements, conducted by the Melton Centre for Jewish Education of the Hebrew University of Jerusalem. The project was administered in 18 Diaspora Jewish day schools for close to a decade, until 2000.

is the fact that most Jews of the Former Soviet Union have immigrated to Israel or other places and few remain to carry the Hebrew banner.

In light of these circumstances, the question arises: Should Diaspora educational frameworks, particularly supplementary schools, consider completely foregoing the objective of teaching Hebrew as a spoken language in favor of teaching classical texts? Should they invest in teaching biblical Hebrew and Mishnaic language? How this question is answered has significant ramifications since a declared preference for either type of Hebrew means a renunciation of the other. Each of these two types of Hebrew demands different teaching approaches and methods and in turn has implications for resource allocation that not many institutions are prepared to consider.

Dilemmas in Teaching Hebrew in the Diaspora

The Language of Teaching Jewish Subjects

A major dilemma that continues to face teachers and educators in Diaspora Jewish schools relates to the language of teaching Jewish subjects: To teach in the vernacular or in Hebrew? Those who use the vernacular believe that students cannot conduct a serious, comprehensive discussion of the subject matter in a language that is not their native tongue. Others believe that Jewish subjects should be taught in Hebrew due to the added value of a text read in the original language, the loss of cultural impact when translated, as well as the linguistic profit the student derives from the added exposure to Hebrew. However, in-depth elucidation and discussion of the textual content in accurate Hebrew cannot be achieved simultaneously. Involvement in the language will come at the expense of the content and vice versa (Greenberg, 1990). Educational systems need to determine which of these two objectives they seek to advance, while being aware of the implications of this decision. In light of this dilemma some recommend the middle path—reading the text in Hebrew and discussing it in the vernacular.

The Nature of Curricula and Learning Materials

Curricula and learning materials present another serious challenge. Rodman (2003, pp. 13–14), in his survey on the place of modern Hebrew in Jewish education worldwide, found that there is a dearth of curricula with a consolidated approach that have been piloted in the field. Instead, there is "A hodgepodge selection of materials without articulated goals and methods and without careful linguistic gradation" together with students' "frustration at the lack of measurable progress from unit to unit and from year to year."

In recent years, we have witnessed the development of a number of curricula—now widespread—for different age groups: "Chalav Udvash" (Milk and Honey)—Hebrew for ages 3–6; "Nitzanim" (Buds), a program for 5 to 8 year-olds; "TaL

Am" (Teaching Hebrew as a Communicative-Heritage Language) and "Chaverim Be'Ivrit" (Friends in Hebrew), both for elementary school; "Neta" (Youth in Favor of Hebrew) for middle and high schools. Not all of these programs are entirely similar in their approach, but all of them aspire to develop Hebrew as a language of communication, on the one hand, and to cultivate Jewish identity and culture, on the other hand. In this curricula-oriented context, the essential question is whether current innovative curricula will be the key to creating successful change and will lead students in Diaspora Jewish schools to achieve a good command of Hebrew. I will examine a few successful cases and try to identify the responsible factors.

All graduates of the Belgian "Tachkemoni" and "Maimoni" schools speak Hebrew. Is this because of the curricula? In a meeting of the Knesset's Immigration, Absorption and Diaspora Committee on February 24, 2007, Ze'ev Bielski, then Chair of the Jewish Agency, explained that the success in these schools is due to their committed local leadership. Thus, instead of adding hours to other subjects, they increase the number of Hebrew teaching hours, import teachers from Israel, and ensure that every student speaks Hebrew. The importance of leadership commitment is supported by Morhag (1999/2000), who asserts that not even one of the national organizations involved in Jewish education in America places Hebrew at the top of its list of priorities. He suggests establishing a national organization of American-Hebrew teachers that will contribute to professionalization in the field, define professional objectives, and position these objectives high on the national agenda.

It may be assumed that success in Hebrew study is dependent not only on committed leadership but also on supportive parents and family, who believe that studying the language is the right way to preserve the child's link to Judaism and to Israel. In Rodman's survey it was found that the more the members of any given Jewish community perceive themselves to be an ethnic or national minority group—and particularly a minority connected to Israel—the more importance they attribute to the Hebrew language. In his opinion, this can explain the high level of Hebrew language achievement in Antwerp, Belgium.

Another project with ripples of success is "Hebrew in America," an initiative of the Memorial Foundation for Jewish Culture in partnership with the North New Jersey Federation. About 4,000 students in Bergen County have participated in the project since its inception four years ago with early childhood and its current expansion to first and second grades. Here too, the vision and determination of leaders and decision-makers have been critical in increasing awareness of the fact that Hebrew is the agent through which the student can be exposed to Jewish culture.

Despite the respectable position of curricula and their possible impact on achievements and motivation, augmenting the status of Hebrew depends, then, first and foremost upon the will and support of influential bodies such as policy- and decision-makers, community leaders, and parents. As Deitcher (2007, p. 201) argues, Hebrew teaching programs will not generate meaningful change in the Jewish world until Jewish communities make Hebrew acquisition one of their highest priorities.

Human Resources in Hebrew Teaching

Good curricula and learning materials are part of an appropriate design for studying a language. However, it is undoubtedly critical to create a pool of teachers who know both the language and about the language, and who have experience in implementing a range of methods to suit different learning styles. As teacher trainers are accustomed to say, "a good teacher is able to teach even from a telephone directory."

A long-standing debate surrounds the question of whether to prefer native Hebrew-speaking Israelis or local teachers. There are reservations concerning the suitability of Israelis to teach the language. On the one hand, they are indeed native Hebrew speakers with Israeli pronunciation, who bring a living, authentic language spiced with the scent of Israel. On the other hand, they do not always have the training, skills, or qualifications to teach languages in general and Hebrew as a second language in particular. At times they tend to use teaching methods from the Israeli education system, with which they are familiar, but which are not necessarily appropriate for the local student population. Furthermore, Israeli teachers may find it difficult to motivate the students due to an insufficient understanding of the local mentality and culture. According to Ofek (1996), American teachers and principals testify that much time is needed before an Israeli teacher becomes well acquainted with the culture and values of students and their parents, and this often creates tension. She also notes that many Israeli teachers do not come from traditional backgrounds and thus do not feel obliged to conform to the traditional Jewish norms that many schools encourage their students to observe and respect. Local teachers, by virtue of being part of the society in which they function as teachers, are equipped with a good understanding of the local culture and its mores and of the population's needs and world-view. On the other hand, they may not be sufficiently proficient in Hebrew in terms of fluency and functional vocabulary and may lack socio-linguistic competence (Schachter & Ofek, 2008). Supplying resources to expand the local teachers' command of Hebrew for communication and for specific disciplinary purposes could serve well. Having a local Hebrew teacher with good mastery of the language would also have the added advantage of proving to the students that success is possible, something which could generate motivation and confidence in their own ability.

In the Diaspora, there are very few frameworks for training Hebrew teachers. A notable exception is Brandeis University where there is a second-degree program for teaching Hebrew. There are also a few programs in Israel. It is important to consider the character of the training in each framework, as well as its compatibility with the aims and contexts in which Hebrew will be taught as a second language.

What Next?

Given the challenges, issues, and dilemmas discussed above, it is worth asking: What is an appropriate agenda for the development of Hebrew language education in Israel and abroad? What needs improvement? What should be the foci of future research?

Hebrew as a First Language in Israel

In Israel, it is largely the responsibility of the education system to improve the status of Hebrew as a first language (although it is also incumbent on the media to be more pedantic with their language). The main problem in the education system lies in the allocation of teaching hours and the way these are used. Effectively, language learning ends in grade 10; in the last 2 years of upper school, language instruction is not part of the curriculum. Teaching takes place frontally, because of insufficient teaching hours (Vorgan, 2008). In order for a language to develop, especially in the areas of comprehension and expression, frontal teaching, directed to all, is not sufficient. Students need more individualized instruction in writing models based on different genres and for different aims and recipients; in using different reading comprehension strategies to interpret a text; and in practicing good rhetoric. Similarly, the number of teaching hours should be increased and standards raised. It is unacceptable that students are only required to study two units for matriculation in their first language, while at least three are required for foreign languages.[7] This is not only a practical matter, but a question of prestige for Hebrew as an academic subject.

Hebrew as a Second Language in Israel

Regarding teaching Hebrew as a second language, it is worth considering the fact that students come from different backgrounds and have different learning styles. It is important to identify the learning profiles of various groups and to adapt teaching styles accordingly. The smaller the gap between teaching and learning styles, the greater is the chance of success. For example, immigrant students from the Former Soviet Union are accustomed to logical, analytic study and will therefore be better suited to using language rules as a starting point, relating to details and stressing accuracy. In contrast, Ethiopian immigrants who come from an oral culture are accustomed to memorization, repetition, and concretization. Given this, teacher training frameworks should expose trainees to a broad gamut of teaching methodologies.

Teaching Hebrew in the Diaspora

In theoretical terms, there is no shortage of questions to ask, beginning with—Why Hebrew? What are the aims of teaching Hebrew in any given study context and what is the envisioned Hebrew profile of a graduate of that context? Is there a connection between the attitudes of students, teachers, and parents toward the study of Hebrew and the students' achievements? Are these attitudes linked to the size of the community and to its contacts with Israel? Whether and to what extent does

---

[7] As mentioned by the Coordinating Supervisor for Hebrew Teaching at a conference at the Van Leer Institute in Jerusalem on December 31, 2008.

teaching Hebrew have to be part of university Jewish Studies and Jewish identity programs? What is the place of the study of modern Hebrew as compared to Jewish textual study? What, if any, are the implications of having studied Hebrew in childhood and adolescence for the adult Jewish person? Is there a connection between students' attitude to their first language and their achievements in Hebrew? Is it possible to point to a link between students' attitude to Israel and their achievements in Hebrew? What image of Israel does the school's curriculum present? Does teaching the Jewish subjects in Hebrew add or subtract value for these subjects?

In practical terms, teachers sometimes feel professionally isolated, both in their school and in the larger framework of their communities. Professional organizations, frameworks, or supportive networks are needed for those involved in the Hebrew language, providing opportunities for consultation and connection, and for the dissemination of information on what is being done in the field in other places, raising questions, looking for solutions, sharing ideas, successes and failures, and analyzing the reasons for such results. Educational frameworks can serve as "magnets" that expose teaching staff from different places to the experience of different Hebrew realities, so that they may invigorate their own Hebrew frameworks. Upgrading the quality of teaching is essential to the field of Hebrew teaching. Somehow a way must be found to enable schools to be more discriminating in the personnel they appoint. At the same time there is a critical need for pre-service training seminars for new teachers and in-service training courses for the professionalization of existing ones. Teachers must acquire a theoretical and practical knowledge base that will allow them to make informed decisions when selecting learning materials and teaching methods that conform with their schools' aims.

Curriculum development can be based on one of two models: top-down or bottom-up. The first model conceives of a curriculum authority external to the educational system. According to this model, the experts are those who define the aims of the program, determine its characteristics, and develop the materials. The teachers' role is to run the program in line with the program developers' guidelines and expectations. In this constellation, the program developers do not teach in the field and the teachers are unaware of the various considerations of the development team; in fact they may feel that they do not have a say in an issue directly relevant to them. In the second model, the teachers are invited to play an active role in building the curriculum. They are perceived as partners in at least part of the process of shaping the program; they are professionals who know the school reality, are responsible for teaching, and are aware of the students' needs and study conditions. They serve as a starting point for defining problems and objectives in advance of planning considerations, according to Ben-Peretz (1995). The developers of Hebrew teaching curricula will presumably adopt the appropriate paradigm for their own approaches, but I believe that programs built together with teaching staff in the field and tested in "laboratory-like" schools will not only be more efficient, their development may also serve as a learning experience for Hebrew teachers, raising both their status and the status of the language. After developing curricula, it would be appropriate to develop tools to evaluate the students' achievements and their opinions of the curriculum. Assessing students' achievements after using a given program, and updating the curriculum in line with evaluation findings, should be an ongoing process rather than a one-time effort.

Further Research

The themes discussed in this chapter raise a number of questions for further research: First, with regard to Hebrew as a second language in Israel, how do students who studied in formal frameworks integrate into the life of the majority society compared with those who learned "from life?" Is there a connection between the level of immigrants' first language development and their achievements in Hebrew study? What might be the influence of a truly bilingual education model, as opposed to a melting pot model, on immigrants' linguistic, social, economic, and academic success? Second, in relation to the linguistic impact of globalization, the influence of other languages, and particularly English, on Hebrew is well known and has been discussed in this chapter; however, it would be interesting to examine relationships that flow in the opposite direction too: Can we point to the influence of Hebrew on English as an international language, on Arabic as the regional language, or on other minority languages present in Israeli society?

Other topics generating questions for future research relate to Hebrew in the Diaspora: Is there a connection between learning Hebrew and the intensity of Jewish identity and belonging? Is it possible to preserve identity without a unifying language? Similarly, it is worth examining attitudes of students and parents toward the study of Hebrew in general and of specific language skills in particular; the use of Hebrew as the language of prayer and the language of teaching Jewish subjects compared with praying and teaching in the vernacular; the achievements in various aspects of Hebrew of those who learn from native Hebrew-speaking teachers as opposed to those taught by local teachers; the efficiency of Hebrew teaching programs in the Diaspora in relation to the vision of the schools using them and the needs of the students; and what can be done to promote the teaching of Hebrew in supplementary schools, where conditions are different from those in Jewish day schools. The data collected in such studies would shape a more realistic set of expectations in the field and in turn would lead to the development of more appropriate content and methods for each cluster of Hebrew teaching frameworks.

In Conclusion

In this chapter, I have analyzed a variety of issues related to the Hebrew language in both Israel and the Diaspora. Although there are great differences between the goals of Hebrew acquisition in these two contexts, Hebrew nevertheless can provide a cultural bridge between widely different Jewish communities. Just as, in order to be French, one must know French, it is appropriate for Jews to acquire Hebrew as part of their cultural linguistic "baggage." This is true for Jewish school students, members of Jewish communities, community leaders, and even Hebrew speakers who live in Israel whose attitude to their language plays a role in determining its status in the world. Furthermore, in an era of globalization, technology may link those in Israel with Diaspora communities and reduce the gap between Israeli Hebrew and the Hebrew studied in Jewish communities elsewhere. This could create a situation in which Jews in Israel and the Diaspora have equal access to the sources and literature in the language of their people's culture. Let me conclude with the clarion call of Talma Elyagon-Rose (1989, p. 35) in her book *Hebrew: A Language Like That*: "The miracle happened, and there in the mountains, inside the cave, the princess Hebrew opened her eyes, moved her arms and legs, polished up her words and rules, removed the cobwebs from her clothes and went back to being a simple, clear language, our mother-tongue—for we do not have any other—our spoken Hebrew language."

References

Bekerman, Z. (1999). The Hebrew language: A constructive language for Jewishness sometimes private. In D. Zisenwein & D. Schers (Eds.), *Present and future: Jewish culture, identity and language* (pp. 101–124). Tel Aviv: School of Education, Tel Aviv University.

Ben-Peretz, M. (1995). Patterns of teacher intervention in curricula activity. In M. Ben-Peretz (Ed.), *The teacher and the curriculum (Chapter 1)*. Jerusalem: Ministry of Education and Culture, Section for Training Teaching Employees and the Mofet Institute (Heb.).

Ben-Rafael, E. (2003). A national and multilingual language in globalization conditions and a multi-cultural society. *Hed Ha-Ulpan He-Chadash, 85*, 49–56 (Heb.).

Berdichevsky, N. (1998). Why Hebrew? *Hebrew Higher Education, 9*, 37–56.

Blum-Kulka, S. (2007). Teaching Hebrew as first and second language: Two curricula. In N. Nevo & E. Olshtain (Eds.), *The Hebrew language in the era of globalization* (pp. 117–131). Studies in Jewish Education, Vol. XII. Jerusalem: Magnes Press, the Hebrew University (Heb.).

Bouganim, A. (2007). Hebrew in the era of globalization. In N. Nevo & E. Olshtain (Eds.), *The Hebrew language in the era of globalization* (pp. 193–199). Studies in Jewish Education, Vol. XII. Jerusalem: Magnes Press, the Hebrew University (Heb.).

Brosh, H. (1996). Hebrew language diffusion through schools and universities in America. *Journal of Jewish Education, 62*(3), 13–20.

Brosh-Weitz, S. (2007). *The state of literacy in Israel*. Tel-Aviv: Tel-Aviv University Ramot (Heb.).

Deitcher, H. (2007). "We were as dreamers": The impact of the communal milieu on the place of Hebrew in Diaspora Jewish education. In N. Nevo & E. Olshtain (Eds.), *The Hebrew language in the era of globalization* (pp. 105–114, 201 Heb. Abstract). Studies in Jewish Education, Vol. XII. Jerusalem: Magnes Press, the Hebrew University.

Deitcher, H. (2008). Jewish education in a global world: Challenges and opportunities. In S. Della Pergola, A. Bargil, & A. Yovel (Eds.), *The President's study forum on world Jewish affairs* (series C, 2004–2007, pp. 115–130). Jerusalem: Publishing House of the World Zionist Organization and the Institute of Contemporary Jewry at the Hebrew University of Jerusalem (Heb.).

Elyagon-Rose, T. (1989). The sleeping princess. In *Hebrew: A language like that: Stories by Talma Elyagon-Rose* (pp. 32–35). Tel-Aviv: Kinneret Publishing House (Heb.).

Ganiel, D. (2007). Illuminations on difficulties and challenges in teaching Hebrew as an additional language. In N. Nevo & E. Olshtain (Eds.), *The Hebrew language in the era of globalization* (pp. 203–205). Studies in Jewish Education, Vol. XII. Jerusalem: Magnes Press, the Hebrew University (Heb.).

Greenberg, M. (1990). On teaching the Bible. In H. Deitcher & A. J. Tannenbaum (Eds.), *Studies in Jewish education* (Vol. V, pp. 27–34). Jerusalem: The Magnes Press, the Hebrew University.

Haramati, S. (2000). *Hebrew is a spoken language*. Tel-Aviv: Ministry of Defense Publications (Heb.).

Levin, T., Shohamy, E., & Inbar, O. (2007). Achievements in academic Hebrew among immigrant students in Israel. In N. Nevo & E. Olshtain (Eds.), *The Hebrew language in the era of globalization* (pp. 37–66). Studies in Jewish Education, Vol. XII. Jerusalem: Magnes Press, the Hebrew University.

Ma'ariv. (2008, summer). Culture.

Mintz, A. (2002). Hebrew in America: A position paper for the Memorial Foundation for Jewish Culture. Jewish Theological Seminary.

Morhag, G. (1999/2000). Hebrew: A language of identity. *Journal of Jewish Education, 65*(3), 9–16.

Nevo, N., & Olshtain, E. (2007). Bilingualism: Benefits and risks. In N. Nevo & E. Olshtain (Eds.), *The Hebrew language in the era of globalization* (pp. 95–117). Studies in Jewish Education, Vol. XII. Jerusalem: Magnes Press, the Hebrew University (Heb.).

Ofek, A. (1996). The making of a Hebrew teacher: Preparing Hebrew teachers for Jewish schools. *Journal of Jewish Education, 62*(3), 21–28.

Rodman, P. (2003). Israel and the place of modern Hebrew in Jewish education worldwide: A consultation about the possibilities for Hebrew language instruction, report submitted to the Research and Development Unit, Department of Jewish Zionist Education, the Jewish Agency, pp. 1–26.

Rosenthal, R. (2007). On the future of Hebrew: Five areas of concern. In N. Nevo & E. Olshtain (Eds.), *The Hebrew language in the era of globalization* (pp. 179–191). Studies in Jewish Education, Vol. XII. Jerusalem: Magnes Press, the Hebrew University (Heb.).

Schachter, L., & Ofek, A. (2008). Hebrew language instruction. In P. A. Flexner & L. D. Bloomberg (Eds.), *What we now know about Jewish education* (pp. 271–282). Los Angeles: Torah Aura Publications.

Schenker, A. (1991). The Hebrew consciousness amongst the Jewish people in our times. In T. Gur-Arieh (Ed.), *The 8th Hebrew Scientific European Congress*, organized by Universidad de Barcelona facultat de filologia and Brit Ivrit Olamit (pp. 184–187). Jerusalem: Brit Ivrit Olamit (Heb.).

Schiff, A. (1999). Hebrew in the new world: Achievements and obstacles, problems and challenges. *Hed Ha-Ulpan He-Chadash, 78*, 79–85 (Heb.).

Schwarzwald, O. (2005). The language is a reflection of the generation—On the relationship between aspects of society and aspects of the Hebrew language. *Panim, 33*, 4–14 (Heb.).

Schwarzwald, O. (2007). Trends in modern Hebrew. In N. Nevo & E. Olshtain (Eds.), *The Hebrew language in the era of globalization* (pp. 59–81). Studies in Jewish Education, Vol. XII. Jerusalem: Magnes Press, the Hebrew University (Heb.).

Schweid, A. (2004). Culture, community and the continuity of the Jewish people in our times. In S. Della Pergola & A. Yovel (Eds.), *The President's study forum on world Jewish affairs* (Series A, pp. 119–136). Jerusalem: Publishing House of the World Zionist Organization and the Institute of Contemporary Jewry at the Hebrew University of Jerusalem.

Segev, T. (2007, December 21). The essence of the Israeli identity. *Ha'aretz*, p. 10 (Heb.).

Shamosh, A. (1979). Vignettes of elementary school, in the story anthology *Calamus and Cinnamon*. Ramat-Gan: Massada Press Ltd. (Heb.).

Shohamy, E. (1989). The Hebrew curriculum in Jewish schools. In E. Olshtain, D. Zisenwein, & E. Shohamy (Eds.), *Hebrew as a unifying force in Diaspora Jewish education* (pp. 45–54). Tel Aviv: University Enterprises for Publication (Heb.).

Shohamy, E. (1999). Language and identity of Jews in Israel and in the Diaspora. In D. Zisenwein & D. Schers (Eds.), *Present and future: Jewish culture, identity and language* (pp. 79–99). Tel Aviv: School of Education, Tel Aviv University.

Spolsky, B., & Shohamy, E. (1999). *The languages of Israel*. Clevedon, Buffalo, NY, Toronto and Sydney: Multilingual Matters.
Spolsky, B., Shohamy, E., & Nevo, N. (1995). A profile of teaching Hebrew as a second language to adult immigrants. Bar-Ilan University, the Center for Linguistic Policy Research, Reports and Position Papers.
Steinberg, S. (1997). Hebrew: The hallmark of an educated Jew. *Jewish Education News*, *18*(3), 10–11.
Vorgan, Y. (2008, January 6). Document submitted to the Education, Culture and Sport Committee on the state of Hebrew in the education system, pp. 1–9 (Heb.).
Wated, A. (2007). A new educational program: "Hebrew as a second language in Arab schools in Israel". In N. Nevo & E. Olshtain (Eds.), *The Hebrew language in the era of globalization* (pp. 171–177). Studies in Jewish Education, Vol. XII. Jerusalem: Magnes Press, the Hebrew University (Heb.).
Waxman, Ch. I. (1999). Language and identity among America's Jews. In D. Zisenwein & D. Schers (Eds.), *Present and future: Jewish culture, identity and language* (pp. 63–74). Tel Aviv: School of Education, Tel Aviv University.
Zisenwein, D. (1997). Teaching Hebrew: A suggestion for Hebrew educators. *Religious Education*, *92*(1), 55–60.

Websites

Chalav Udvash. Accessed September 13, 2009, from http://www.chalav-udvash.org.il/JewishAgency/Hebrew/Education
Chaverim Be'Ivrit. Accessed September 13, 2009, from http://www.myhebrewbooks.com/prodView.asp?idproduct=146
Ministry of Education (allocation of teaching hours). Accessed August 23, 2009, from http://www.biu.ac.il/hu/lprc/home/HOLSHORT.htm
Neta. Accessed September 13, 2009, from http://www.netahebrew.org/
Nitzanim. Accessed September 13, 2009, from http://melton.huji.ac.il/eng/projects.php?cats=58
Perlmutter, R. (2002). An article in honor of the International Mother-Tongue Day that took place on February 21, 2002 (Heb.). Accessed August 11, 2009, from http://cms.education.gov.il/EducationCMS/Unesco/PeilutUnesco/Taarichon/YamimInt/sfat2003.htm
Tal Am. Accessed September 13, 2009, from http://www.talam.org/talamD.html

History: Issues in the Teaching and Learning of Jewish History

Benjamin M. Jacobs and Yona Shem-Tov

> *For modern Jews, a conception of their past is no mere academic matter. It is vital to their self-definition. Contemporary forms of Jewish identity are all rooted in some view of Jewish history which sustains them and serves as their legitimation.*
>
> (Meyer, 1987, p. xi)

Introduction

Recalling, reviewing, reconsidering, and/or remembering the Jewish past plays a central role in most contemporary preK-12 Jewish schools the world over.[1] In North American Jewish day high schools—the main focus of this chapter—teaching and learning Jewish history normally occurs through formal classroom instruction in Jewish history, Judaics, and/or general history courses, as well as through informal educational experiences including holiday celebrations, commemorations, and historical field trips. When taught chronologically, the course of study typically covers some or all of the following topics: the Hebrew Bible's historical narratives; the ancient Israelite settlements in Palestine; the dispersion of Jews into the diaspora; Jewish life in medieval Europe, North Africa, and the Near East; modernity, enlightenment, and emancipation in western and eastern Europe; Jewish life in North America; the Holocaust; Zionism and the State of Israel; and the contemporary Jewish community. Methods for teaching Jewish history are mostly the same as in any history course, namely primary source analysis, discussion, debate, lecture, roleplay, simulation, and inquiry. Jewish history programs generally emphasize not only Jewish historical facts and figures, but also Jewish thought, civilization, current

---

B.M. Jacobs (✉)
New York University, New York, NY, USA
e-mail: bjacobs@nyu.edu

[1] We acknowledge with appreciation the contributions of Robert Chazan to this chapter, as well as comments on previous drafts from Samuel Kapustin, Shira Lander, and Laura Shaw-Frank.

events, contemporary problems, social service, customs and ceremonies, heroes and holidays, and more.

The objectives for history education identified by researchers in the general education literature include accumulation of factual knowledge and development of intellectual skills; knowledge of the discipline and its methods; illumination of the present in light of the past; and promotion of social awareness and self-knowledge (see, e.g., Barton & Levstik, 2004; Gagnon, 1989; Stearns, Seixas, & Wineburg, 2000). These same objectives also animate Jewish history education in Jewish schools. As a rule, however, Jewish history education is not merely an academic matter; rather, it aims to bolster Jewish identification and commitment among the rising generation. Specifically, the aims of Jewish history education are to develop within Jewish youth an appreciation of the Jewish past and a commitment to Jewish continuity; trust in Jewish culture, values, customs, and community; an understanding of historical and contemporary Jewish issues and problems; and the ability and will to participate actively in Jewish life (see, e.g., Ackerman, 1984; Chazan & Jacobs, 2005; Eisenberg & Segal, 1963; Goldflam, 1989; Golub, 1944; Honor, 1931). Above all, as these objectives intimate, the rationale for Jewish history education—and, perhaps, Jewish education in general—stems from the community's desire to develop in its children a full appreciation of Jewish life, so that the students will cherish the cultural environment and be loyal to it. The main question confronting Jewish educators is how to accomplish this identity-building project appropriately.

Understanding how history is taught and learned effectively entails extensive investigation. The broad field of history education research presently includes analyses of objectives for teaching history; interpretations of curriculum plans and textbooks; descriptions of instructional techniques; studies of how historical thinking is cultivated among teachers and students; assessments of the knowledge-base of history students; critiques of the preparation and competence of history teachers; and much more (Wilson, 2001). The real or perceived role of history education in inculcating notions of national pride; developing among students historical empathy, a sense of cause and effect, and critical thinking; preparing youth for the responsibilities of citizenship; and perpetuating or challenging race, class, gender, and other forms of hegemony are by now well-documented in the scholarly literature as well (Barton, 2008). Increasing attention has been paid to the ways in which teachers' and students' positionality is reflected in their interpretations of historical sources and reconstructions of historical accounts, and the politically laden potential of history education has led scholars to focus much interest on the ways in which debates about history education are emblematic of society's so-called "culture wars" (Nash, Crabtree, & Dunn, 1997; Stearns et al., 2000).

Unfortunately, there is scarce research on how Jewish history education is planned, implemented, and received in Jewish schools in North America or any other diaspora community. Only a handful of scholarly articles, monographs, dissertations, and curriculum guides have been dedicated to issues involving teaching and learning the subject. By contrast, a robust line of inquiry on history education is emerging in Israel and includes analyses of history textbooks, curricula, school-wide commemorations (including those in schools where Jews, Arabs, and Christian students learn together), and student understandings of official historical narratives (see, e.g., Bekerman, 2004; Podeh, 2002; Porat, 2004, 2006). To be sure, this work is particular to the Israeli political, cultural, and religious scene, and, as such, provides valuable insights into the ways research on the teaching and learning of history—and for our purposes, Jewish history—is shaped by context. Jewish history is a state-mandated subject in Israel and includes curriculum standards from a centralized authority; thus, potential research opportunities abound. This is not the case in North America, where Jewish history programs are as disparate as the schools that offer them. For this reason, in part, Jewish history education in North America has eluded any comprehensive research and analysis. It is also the case that scholars of Jewish history, Jewish education, and general education simply have not been interested in the Jewish history education enterprise (Jacobs, 2005b). As a result, we have little concrete, empirical, aggregated data on what actually constitutes the Jewish history curriculum in North American Jewish schools. Indeed, the last formal study of any scale on the aims and practices of Jewish history teachers in North American Jewish day schools was conducted in the late 1980s (Goldflam, 1989).

This chapter seeks to fill a gap in the literature on history education writ-large, and Jewish education specifically, by exploring contemporary perspectives, practices, and prospects for teaching and learning Jewish history in North American Jewish day schools, with a focus on high schools. Our overview of the state of Jewish history education includes a consideration of the origins of Jewish history as a school subject; the purposes and methods of teaching Jewish history today; and prospects for new areas of research in the field. Our scope is necessarily limited to the state of Jewish history education in only one sector of the Jewish education world—namely, the North American Jewish community—and even within this diverse educational network, it is mostly confined to denominational and community sponsored day high schools, the setting in which the most intensive instruction in Jewish history commonly occurs. This chapter is intended as an entry point for new researchers, practitioners, and policymakers in Jewish education who are looking for guidance regarding the essential contours of Jewish history education in North America.

Historical Foundations of Jewish History Education

Any serious discussion of the Jewish history education enterprise must first acknowledge that the teaching of Jewish history, unlike other dimensions of Jewish education (with the exception of teaching modern Hebrew language), is a relatively modern innovation. Its emergence as a school subject is intrinsically linked to the evolution of new ways of conceiving of and reconstructing the Jewish past that began only in the mid-nineteenth century.

"It is the very nature of what and how I study, how I teach and what I write, that represents a radically new venture," writes Yosef Hayim Yerushalmi in *Zakhor:*

Jewish History and Jewish Memory (1982), widely regarded as one of the most important Jewish historiographical works of modern times: "I live within the ironic awareness that the very mode in which I delve into the Jewish past represents a decisive break with that past" (p. 81). The departure Yerushalmi is describing is a break from Jewish history as it was understood in the pre-modern world, where the rabbinical hierarchy governed the way the Jews' past was to be remembered by deliberately culling and appropriating history in the service of Jewish survival and the survival of Judaism. In the pre-modern world, history, even biblical history, was of use to the rabbis only insofar as it could provide concrete support for their own religious and moral considerations. Generally, the rabbis highlighted collective, symbolic religious memories—or myths—without concern for historical details. It was not the subject matter of Jewish history but rather the sentimentalism of Jewish memory that needed to be pondered and preserved. This could be accomplished through commemorative observances such as rituals, festivals, and fasts, rather than through historical investigation or instruction. Formal Jewish education in the pre-modern world consisted almost exclusively of studying the Torah and the Talmud, where the people's theology, wisdom, tradition, norms, and folkways were delineated. Because the subject matter was, according to tradition, derived ultimately from divine sources, Jewish education was seen as a continual process of revelation. Text study was considered the only viable means of preparing for Jewish living and ensuring Jewish continuity.

> Within this scheme, the study of Jewish history as history – that is, the human reconstruction of the Jewish past – was peripheral at best. Instead, Jewish history as gleaned from biblical and rabbinic literature was taught uncritically, buttressed by its obvious truth. The didactic "lessons" of the Jewish past were securely anchored and relatively easy to comprehend (Yerushalmi, 1982).

By contrast, in the modern age, a new historical consciousness emerged largely as a result of Jewish enlightenment and emancipation. Enlightenment thinkers in the Christian majority had come to challenge the traditional religious foundations of their faith, projecting both the Hebrew Bible narratives and the New Testament narratives as the product of human effort rather than divine revelation. For some in the Christian majority and in the Jewish minority, such doubts signaled the end of any belief in Christian or Jewish "Truth." For others, the foundation of faith passed from divine sources (e.g., scripture) and forces (e.g., providence) to the historical creativity of the human community (e.g., culture, politics, etc.). While this shift began in the Christian majority, the new societal openness ensured its rapid passage into Jewish circles as well. "Modern Jewish historiography," explains Yerushalmi (1982), "began precipitously out of that assimilation from without and collapse from within which characterized the sudden emergence of Jews out of the ghetto. It originated, not as scholarly curiosity, but as ideology, one of a gamut of responses to the crisis of Jewish emancipation and the struggle to maintain it" (p. 85). The more traditional Jewish society changed, the more Jews searched for new social, political, and ideological commitments, such as more liberal and humanistic forms of

Judaism. Soon enough, modern scholars rather than traditional rabbis would become the new guardians of Jewish history.

For the nineteenth century founders of *Wissenschaft des Judentums* (the scientific study of Judaism), Jewish history had an entirely new purpose: to bring the Jewish world into harmony with the spirit of the times. For most modern Jewish historians, this meant that Jewish history was to be consciously and necessarily divorced from religious dogmatic considerations. A distinction had to be made between the normative study of Judaism and the critical, academic study of Jewish religion, philosophy, and history. Only when Jewish history was secularized and subjected to the generally accepted tools of historical research could it be considered on an even plane with any other type of history in terms of form and function (Rostenstreich, 1995). It was the historians' task to document the past in detail and to explain historical events and processes as objectively as possible, so that the gaps of historical memory could be filled. In the process, the historians would challenge even those memories that survived intact, debunking old myths, or offering competing views of the Jewish past. In this context, it is not surprising that Jewish memory, with its close ties to religious myth, shared faith, and symbolic meaning, would decay, while Jewish history, with its commitment to humanism, universalism, and rationalism, would gain credibility. Not only was Jewish history now divorced from collective memory, it was often thoroughly at odds with it (Yerushalmi, 1982). For many modern Jews (especially secular intellectuals), the study of Jewish history would supplant observance of Judaism as the primary means of Jewish self-identification.

While the commitment of the new Jewish historians to historical accuracy was sincere, an inevitable tension grew between the objective explication of data and the writing of compelling histories into which these data and explications could be embedded. New, more secular reconstructions of the Jewish past were created to supplant the traditional, theocentric Jewish master narratives. These new narratives were partly intended for non-Jewish readers—an utterly new audience for Jewish historians—and set out to overturn long-nurtured negative stereotypes of Jews and Judaism that had been perpetuated by demeaning Christian authors. At the same time, since the Jewish sense of self-worth also had been adversely affected by negative majority perceptions, these new histories were aimed at Jewish audiences as well, in an effort to convince Jews of the nobility of their heritage. Indeed, the new narratives of Jewish history—works by Abraham Geiger, Heinrich Graetz, Simon Dubnow, and others—often portrayed Jewish experience in a romantic, idealistic, positivistic, and/or nationalistic way that would engender pride in Jewish civilization. It was of course by no means accidental that many of the new Jewish historians were in the forefront of nineteenth century efforts to reform Jewish practices and develop Jewish nationalism, efforts they reinforced through their historical research. Their work often included penetrating criticism of traditional Jewish views alongside arguments for ever-evolving Jewish beliefs, which they claimed were firmly grounded in the ever-evolving historical Jewish experience. The result was a set of rich, informative, and compelling historical narratives that highlighted prior Jewish adaptability and responsiveness to changing external and internal circumstances, as well as divergences and changes in Jewish thought and practice over the ages (Meyer, 1987).

The impact of this shift in Jewish historiography on the teaching and learning of Jewish history in academic and Jewish educational settings was profound. Given that university teaching posts for Jewish studies scholars were virtually nonexistent prior to the mid-twentieth century, many of the *Wissenschaft* and Zionist historians of the late-nineteenth and early-twentieth century earned a living as teachers in Jewish seminaries, historical societies, and primary schools across Europe, America, and the *Yishuv* (the pre-State Jewish community living in Palestine). Their efforts at reconstructing the Jewish past with an emphasis on the wonders of the Jewish heritage were clearly influenced by their teaching experiences and in turn impinged on the educational environment in which they worked. Indeed, their mostly positive Jewish historical message lent itself comfortably to the educational needs of a Jewish community in search of a spiritual, cultural, and political center within the free and open society at-large. An entire generation of Jewish intellectuals and scholars would be initiated into the study of Jewish history by way of national history (Podeh, 2002). They in turn played active roles in the budding communal (America) and national (Israel) Jewish educational enterprises.

As a result, when the teaching and learning of Jewish history became a formal component of the Jewish school curriculum, sometime around the turn of the twentieth century (Ackerman, 1984), its purposes were, on the one hand, to subject Jewish history to the generally accepted scientific tools of historical inquiry (the *Wissenschaft* legacy), and, on the other hand, to employ Jewish history as a means of Jewish cohesion (the Zionist legacy). Pre-modern instruction in Jewish history primarily entailed children memorizing and reciting Bible stories while teachers impressed upon students the moral of every tale (Gold, 2004). Emphasis was placed on biblical heroes and villains, wars and conquests, miraculous events and tragic circumstances, and the rise of the Jewish nation and religion. The overarching theme was God's role in shepherding God's "chosen people" through history. But with the rise of Jewish history as a secular, scientific discipline, it no longer seemed reasonable for Jewish history instruction to rely on the Bible as its sole textbook, or to promote a narrowly providential view of history, or to moralize excessively about the dictates of tradition. Instead, many Jewish educators strove to teach the expanding corpus and emergent methods of Jewish historical scholarship, adapted for pedagogical purposes (Jacobs, 2005a; Krasner, 2004). As noted, this did not necessarily mean abandoning history as a vehicle for Jewish identification. Rather, the challenge for Jewish history educators was to seek a proper balance between teaching academic Jewish history and cultivating collective Jewish memory (Honor, 1953; Pomson, 1994).

Gerson Cohen (1977) describes this challenge in one of the few essays written by an academic Jewish historian on the subject of Jewish history education.

> In the study and teaching of Jewish history ... scholars of our time have harped on the need for a critical approach, so that ... the orientation of Jewish education should not be totally out of line with the universe of discourse in which Jews are educated for life as a whole. Great stress has been laid on the need to alert the student to an understanding of

Jewish history not reflected in dogmatic texts, and, accordingly, to the need of bringing him to see uncensored data and to appraising Jewish political, economic, social, intellectual, and religious development in the light of the general milieu in which the Jews lived . . . .

Since [however] our concern with Jewish education and a Jewish curriculum implies the desirability in our eyes of a corporate Jewish identity in the United States, of a relationship of American Jews with other Jewries, past as well as present . . . the history of the Jews must be related to American Jewish life and experience; that is, this history must suggest some continuing thread, some constant Jewish quest for corporate expression. (pp. 35, 37)

For Cohen, there is a profound distinction between academic and classroom Jewish history. The former concerns itself, foremost, with normalizing the Jewish historical experience by subjecting it to the same spirit and standards of all other fields of historical inquiry. The latter concerns itself foremost with maintaining a sense of Jewish historical exceptionality by claiming that the Jewish community is a part of a perpetual "Jewish quest for corporate expression." In an attempt at synthesis, Cohen (1977) claims, "if Jewish education is to produce any significant yield in this country [i.e., the United States]," it "will require the rewriting of Jewish history to bring its relevance home to the Jewish student and to achieve for the American Jew what we feel the study of history in our society seeks to achieve generally" (pp. 38–39). If Jewish educators expose students to the ways that Jews and Judaism have adapted to their time and place through history, the students will come to understand how they came to be as Jews in their own time and place; ultimately, this will lead to a positive, deeper Jewish identification. Cohen suggests that students ought to analyze sources critically, using the tools of the historian, and then evaluate the evidence for themselves.

This approach to Jewish history education holds in tension the objectives of critical inquiry and positive Jewish identification—a longstanding tension in the field of Jewish studies. The historian Lucy Dawidowicz (1994) argues for the "uniqueness" of Jewish history and rejects the stark distinctions historians like Yerushalmi (1982) draw between history and memory, arguing instead that a historian's subjectivity could potentially enrich historical writing. "Some people think that the professional historian's commitments – to his people, his country, his, religion, his language – undermine his professional objectivity. Not so," writes Dawidowicz (1994), "as long as historians respect the integrity of their sources and adhere strictly to the principles of sound scholarship. Personal commitments do not distort, but instead they enrich historical writing" (p. 19). For Dawidowicz (1994), the study of Jewish history is about Jewish survival: "For if interest in the Jewish past is not sustained by concern for the future, then Jewish history loses its animating power, its very life" (p. 17). *Ahavat yirsrael*, "that distinctive Jewish concept of love of one's people," is essential in transmitting a significant and meaningful account of Jewish history, she argues (Dawidowicz, 1994, p. 16). This concept of *ahavat yisrael* "entails not only a sense of identity with the Jewish past and an involvement in its present, but also a commitment to a Jewish future" (Dawidowicz, 1994, p. 16).

While Dawidowicz's approach, with its blurred distinctions between historical integrity and Jewish identification, would not go without serious critique in the mostly dispassionate university setting, it offers a potentially useful paradigm for Jewish history education in North American Jewish schools: one that complicates Yerushalmi's dichotomous approach between history and memory and instead allows for teaching critical historical inquiry *and* positive Jewish identification at once. As we shall see in the remainder of this chapter, it is but one of several different approaches to the teaching and learning of Jewish history found in Jewish education classrooms today.

Orientations to Jewish History Education

In this section, we outline a variety of orientations toward Jewish history education that over time have gained legitimacy in North American Jewish schools. The orientations, which build on Keith Barton and Linda Levstik's (2004) categorization of stances toward the teaching of history generally, include (a) identification, (b) group citizenship, (c) moral response, (d) integration and adjustment, and (e) Jewish history as an intellectual and disciplinary pursuit. These orientations encompass an array of educational objectives, subject matter, instructional methods, and organizational modes, oftentimes simultaneously, depending on how much weight certain educational ideas, activities, and approaches carry relative to others in a given educational setting. Indeed, the values inhering in the aims, content, methods, and/or intended outcomes of a particular Jewish history curriculum may not always be consistent. Ideological ambitions may be tempered by practical constraints, such as the structural limitations of schooling (e.g., time and space, administrative policies, access to materials and resources, teacher preparation and competence, teacher and student buy-in, school culture), while practical ambitions may be tempered by ideological constraints, such as the inconsistent purposes ascribed to Jewish education at-large (e.g., mastery of basic Judaic skills, intellectual development, enculturation, interpersonal relations, moral and ethical character, communal continuity). A balance therefore must be negotiated between the desirable and the possible in designing and implementing the Jewish history curriculum. Our hope is that a better sense of the multiple objectives that may be realized through the teaching and learning of Jewish history can help improve the curricular decision-making processes that might bring about the realization of these objectives in Jewish schools.

An important methodological caveat is in order. The following orientations *typify* what transpires in Jewish history classrooms in most North American denominational and community Jewish day and supplementary schools today. We say "typify" because, as noted previously, we have virtually no empirical data on what actually transpires in these Jewish history programs. Nonetheless, the past experience of this chapter's authors as Jewish history teachers in North American Jewish day high schools as well as professional development workshops we have facilitated over the last few years with a growing network of Jewish history educators representing diverse schools and communities throughout North America (The Network for the Teaching of Jewish History) have made us well-acquainted with the types of

Jewish history curricula that are currently in place.[2] In addition, there is a small but rich body of literature that addresses in considerable detail some important conceptual questions related to Jewish history education—Why study Jewish history in Jewish schools? What are the aims of Jewish history education, and how can these aims be met? What impact does Jewish religious and historical consciousness have on Jewish history education? In what ways are children expected to think, feel, and behave after having gained a Jewish historical education? (see, e.g., Ackerman, 1984; Chazan & Jacobs, 2005; Eisenberg & Segal, 1956, 1963; Gereboff, 1997; Jacobs, 2005a; Krasner, 2002; Levisohn, 2004)—much of which we attempt to synthesize in our discussion of orientations. All the same, we are adamant that evidence-based research in the field of Jewish history education is significantly lacking at this point and would enhance further conceptual work substantially.

Jewish History and Memory as Keys to Jewish Identification

Traditionally, the aims of Jewish history education have been to give students the ability to interpret contemporary Jewish life in light of Jewish history; to develop within students an emotional appreciation of Jewish values, ideals, hopes, and struggles through history; and to inspire within students identification with Judaism and the Jewish people. Affective, behavioral, and attitudinal goals take precedence over cognitive goals in this type of pedagogical scheme (Barton & Levstik, 2004). Indeed, within this program of Jewish socialization, *knowing* Jewish history is often not as important an outcome as *feeling* Jewish, *sensing* Jewishness, or *identifying* with Jewish peoplehood (Ackerman, 1984; Gereboff, 1995; Jacobs, 2002; Krasner, 2003).

The identification stance toward Jewish history education commonly sees the ends as outweighing the means. As a result, in many cases, rather than presenting critical, scholarly versions of Jewish history, the curricula instead emphasize mythical historical constructs and collective memories, based on the assumption that celebratory narratives have the power to instill pride in Jewish students. [By "collective memory," we mean those remnants of past experience—such as formative events, traditions, customs, texts, and values—that are remembered, repeated, and reinforced by a contemporary group for the sake of bolstering its collective identity (Gedi & Elam, 1996).] Jewish heroes and holidays play a central role in

---

[2] The professional development workshop, "Re/Presenting the Jewish Past," is a joint project between RAVSAK: The Jewish Community Day School Network and The Network for the Teaching of Jewish History at New York University, and is funded by the Avi Chai Foundation. To date, we have worked with more than 50 teachers from over 20 day and supplementary schools across the United States and Canada. The workshops are focused entirely on issues regarding teaching and learning Jewish history. The teachers spend 5 days in intensive workshop meetings—guided by scholars of Jewish history and education—revising their schools' Jewish history curricula, working to incorporate primary and secondary historical sources into the teaching of the Jewish past, and devising new modes of organization, instruction, and assessment.

this curriculum, as do stories of Jewish triumph and cohesiveness. Jews are depicted as resilient in the face of adversity, owing in part to their faith and in part to their exceptionality as the "chosen" ones. Nationalistic elements predominate as well, with the rebirth of Israel portrayed as the epitome of the Jewish spirit. At the same time, North America is seen as the *"goldene medine"* (golden land) where Jews not only have succeeded, but have in fact thrived and in some cases dominated. Heady triumphalism is the stuff of Jewish pride and identification, according to this perspective. (See, e.g., Solomon Grayzel's popular, triumphalist *A History of the Jews* (1968), which has long been a standard textbook in North American Jewish history classrooms.) Such identification brings with it an optimistic assessment of the Jewish present and prospects for the Jewish future (Ackerman, 1984; Gereboff, 1997; Levisohn, 2004; Pomson, 1994).

Critics of the identification approach to history education—which, it should be noted, is equally prevalent in the teaching of American history, society, and culture in public schools—draw an important distinction between teaching *history* and teaching *heritage*. David Lowenthal (1998) writes: "History is the past that actually happened, heritage a partisan perversion, the past manipulated for some present aim. Substituting an image of the past for its reality . . . heritage effaces history's intricate coherence with piecemeal and mendacious celebration" (p. 102). To be sure, there is a genuine distinction to be drawn between what might be termed dispassionate, scientific, critical history, and tendentious, affected, self-serving heritage. But for Lowenthal and many other like-minded scholars, the distinction between history as truth and heritage as faith, or history as impartial and heritage as chauvinistic, is specious. William McNeill (1986) coined the term "mythistory" to suggest that "the same words that constitute truth for some are, and always will be, myth for others, who inherit or embrace different assumptions and organizing concepts about the world" (p. 19). In other words, in the end, history is what the individual and/or community makes of it and takes from it, despite what the historians or mythmakers might say. Thus, both history and heritage have their place in the recounting, recollection, commemoration, memorialization, and teaching of the past.

With reference to the teaching of Jewish history specifically, Levisohn (2004) suggests that teachers "need not be ethnic cheerleaders, and [they] need not abandon [their] critical perspectives" (p. 14). Rather, Levinsohn argues that teaching students Jewish history warts and all, but with an eye toward asking "what is best" in the community (i.e., what aspects of history are most worthy of being remembered), can allow students to be empowered to create their own thoughtful narratives of the Jewish past. Thus, they will achieve personal ownership of their past—perhaps the most lasting form of identification.

Jewish History as the Basis for Jewish Citizenship

Jewish history has been assured a central place in the contemporary Jewish school curriculum partly because of its parallel role as a core subject of the general school curriculum (Jacobs, 2004). Why then does history occupy the place that it does in public schools? There are, of course, a number of possible responses to this question, but the primary answer lies with the notion of promoting citizenship. American schools have adopted the position that studying the past will ultimately promote good citizenship in the present (Gagnon, 1989; Nash et al., 1997; Thornton, 1994).

In a similar vein, some Jewish schools hope that teaching the Jewish past will help inspire and orient young Jews toward active participation in the contemporary Jewish community. Indeed, learning the Jewish past—it is hoped and anticipated—will encourage the rising generation to be concerned with and see themselves as part of the Jewish present and future (à la Dawidowicz's *"ahavat yisrael"* approach to historical study). In this scheme, emphasis often is placed on interrogating the evolution of present-day Jewish issues and problems. For example, Beth T'filoh Dahan Community School in Baltimore recently refashioned its ninth-grade Jewish history curriculum as a "Jewish social studies" course, intended as a complement to public school civics courses. The Jewish social studies course addresses major contemporary Jewish issues as defined by the Jewish history department, including the demographics of contemporary Jewish society, interdenominational differences, and the role of Israel in American Jewish life. The Tanenbaum Community Hebrew Academy of Toronto has a similar course for ninth graders which is also intended to initiate students into an understanding of contemporary Jewish life while providing foundations for inquiry into the Jewish past.

Jonathan Golden, chair of the history department at the Gann Academy–New Jewish High School outside Boston, articulates the goals of history education at his school thusly: "I describe it as a John Dewey-inspired experiment in democratic education. So what that means is, I think, that the most important thing for me to teach students is [how] to prepare them to participate in American democracy" (personal communication, July 11, 2007). What is more, "I would expand that definition beyond American democracy to be civically minded within the Jewish community, [asking], What are some contemporary Jewish issues and problems?, and looking at the past and history and choices that Jews had in the past, and asking, How does that shape current Jewish choices and American choices that our students make?" (personal communication, July 11, 2007). At Gann Academy, the teaching of Jewish history is meant to provide historical context for contemporary Jewish problems with the hope that doing so will empower students to make informed choices about Jewish life. One method they use is what Golden terms the "debate *midrash.*"

> You literally sit if you're "pro" the question, you sit on one side, if you're "con" you sit on another side; if you're unsure, you sit in the middle and you can't speak, you have to be in one of those places. But during the course of the debate you can move, and people can move from "pro" to "con" if they want to, if their mind changes, and we do this in all sorts of subjects and scenarios.
> And the question there we ask is: "Should there be active efforts to revive Jewish life in Europe today?" So this is an example of a modern Jewish choice in terms of resources, priorities and so we have them debate that before they go, while they're there and after, when

they come back, being reflective upon it . . . . So this is an example of history, the experience learning about it, but also the modern choices of the community. (personal communication, July 11, 2007)

This method illustrates one way in which Jewish history education can be utilized to encourage students to deliberate how Jews ought to respond individually and/or collectively to the challenges confronting the community.

This kind of history teaching and learning is potentially less authoritarian than what might be found in the identification orientation, in that it allows opportunities for questioning and disagreement (although the range of these disagreements is admittedly quite limited, depending on the mores of the school setting). There is no divinely revealed or humanly unfolded essence of Judaism, the Jewish community, or the Jewish past and future to contend with. Rather, contingencies and differences are recognized and honored in the hope that students capable of tackling today's problems will be well prepared to confront new challenges going forward. The general idea is that studying the Jewish past and contemplating its complexities will enable Jewish children to become intelligent, engaged, active, and effective citizens of the Jewish community in the future (Chazan & Jacobs, 2005; Levisohn, 2004).

Jewish History as Motivation for Moral Response

The study of Jewish history has the capacity to stir up a host of emotions, ranging from the pain of abject loss (the Holocaust) to the thrill of existential victory (Six-Day War). Taught this way, Jewish history also inspires intense moral responses, such as admiration for things good, right, and just, and condemnation for the bad and unjust. It is expected that students will emerge from their studies believing that Hitler was reprehensible and the Holocaust was tragic, while Herzl was a visionary and the establishment of the State of Israel was a triumph. The Holocaust has commonly been taught with a specific moral imperative in mind, such as Emil Fackenheim's famous "614th Commandment," through which it is hoped that students will not give Hitler a posthumous victory by abandoning Judaism, and, likewise, they will regard discrimination of any sort as abhorrent and social justice as a desideratum (Sheramy, 2000). The history of the State of Israel has typically been taught with a heavy dose of faultless Zionist mythology and Israel advocacy, intended to inspire North American Jewish youth to go to Israel and get their hands dirty just like the young *chalutzim* (pioneers) did before them (Ackerman, 1986). It is hoped that Jewish students will grow to be *mensches* in the course of their Jewish education, in part by developing "proper" and "desirable" moral responses to the events of Jewish history. A Jewish history program that raises and leaves unresolved too many moral ambiguities would be anathema to the Jewish education enterprise (Chazan, 1978).

However, teaching Israel's history has become, for many schools, one of the most challenging aspects of Jewish history education, given the rising prominence of the work of critical "new"/"post-Zionist" Israeli historians and the seemingly intractable nature of conflict in the region (see chapter on teaching Israel, this volume.) Barbara Kirschenblatt-Gimblett (2002) points out the irony of mythologizing Israel in North American Jewish classrooms, as it necessitates employing "idealizations that are being contested in what has been called a post-Zionist Israel to anchor the identity of American Jewish youth" (p. 281). Teaching politically loaded subject matter has long been one of the great challenges for social studies educators in general. Compounding the complication for North American teachers of Israel's history is the simple reality that Israel is different and distant from their students' lived experiences. Thus, while some diaspora versions of Israel education, such as teen tours to Israel, seek to drop the anchor of "Jewish identity in contemporary Israel, the Israel to which it anchors the youngsters is [today] elsewhere – historically and existentially," argues Kirschenblatt-Gimblett (2002, p. 281). Indeed, the moral imperative messages traditionally tied to Israel education may be missing their mark these days.

The moral response orientation toward history instruction is generally unacknowledged, in part because it appears to be more suggestive of a program of indoctrination than an effort to cultivate critical thinking. It also seems to run against the idea of history as a scientific area of inquiry that is subject to open interpretation (Barton & Levstik, 2004). Moral compasses and social conventions (not to mention laws in some nations) dictate that Hitler was the embodiment of evil—there is no other possible or at least acceptable interpretation of his actions, in the final analysis. But moral decisions related to other subject matter, such as the actions of controversial Jewish historical characters, may not be as clear-cut. A further complication is the developmental consideration regarding when students are ready to tackle moral ambiguity in the first place. In her study of teaching the documentary hypothesis to high school students in a TaNaKH (Hebrew Bible) class, Susan Tanchel (2008) argues, "late adolescence (ages 16–20) . . . is precisely the appropriate time for learning the documentary hypothesis and source criticism" (p. 48). Developmentally, at this stage, students are in a position to reexamine their beliefs and explore provocative ideas, holding in tension contradictory versions of "Truth." In her view, "it is invaluable for this faith questioning to happen when the students are still in a supportive Jewish environment" (ibid., p. 48). Given that the vast majority of students in North American Jewish high schools will attend universities where critical theories of the Jewish experience are accepted and espoused, it is "not only unrealistic, but also potentially counterproductive" to shield students from such provocative material while in late adolescence, claims Tanchel (2008, p. 49).

For these reasons, Jewish schools would benefit from contemplating what aspects of Jewish history are to be considered foregone conclusions within the life of the school and which are more nuanced and contentious. A critical examination of difficult history may not necessarily come at the expense of certain ideological, ethnic, national, religious, or moral commitments, but it does not come without its challenges to those inclinations, either (Levisohn, 2003). In the end, the question regards how passionate or dispassionate Jewish history instruction ought to be and what moral outcomes are expected from it.

Jewish History as a Paradigm of Integration and Adjustment

In many Jewish day schools, Jewish history is not taught as a separate core subject of the curriculum; rather, Jewish history content is integrated into general history courses. A number of considerations motivate this curricular decision (Levisohn, 2008). First, teaching one history course is simply more efficient than teaching two courses—and by efficient we mean not only more expeditious vis-à-vis the scope and sequence of the curriculum, but also more economical vis-à-vis personnel, materials, resources, space, and scheduling. Second, presenting Jewish history alongside and within general history reinforces the notion that Jewish history cannot be understood in a vacuum, that is, without its inextricable link to general history. Jewish history is dependent on external developments. In many times and places, general history is dependent on developments in the Jewish world as well. The integrated history curriculum demonstrates literally and symbolically that Jews are "normal" actors in history, rather than exceptional. Last, interweaving Jewish and general history validates the notion that Jewish life is compatible with North American life, and the ideas and experiences of the Jewish people are a part of, not apart from, the broader North American society. As Jonathan Sarna (1998) puts it, Jewish schools "are the primary setting, along with the home, where American Jews confront the most fundamental question of American Jewish life: how to live in two worlds at once, how to be both American and Jewish, part of the larger American society and apart from it" (p. 9). In this sense, the integrated Jewish general-history course serves as a paradigm of adjustment—the full adjustment of Jews to their surrounding society, and more generally to the modern, secular world.

Another version of curriculum integration entails the fusion of Jewish history with other branches of Judaic studies, creating a total program of Jewish social education in the school (this is the type of Jewish history education once commonly found in part-time supplementary schools). Conceptually speaking, almost everything that happens in the Jewish school curriculum—be it studying Biblical and Rabbinic texts, speaking Hebrew, singing songs and dancing to Jewish music, praying, celebrating holidays, etc.—can be considered an aspect of Jewish social education, for it is related to the development of Jewish identity and the cultivation of Jewish citizenship. The broad-based Jewish studies course helps model for students the intricate connections of various facets of Jewish thought, culture, and life (Jacobs, 2005a).

At the same time, ironically, the integrated Judaic studies approach has the capacity to marginalize the value of teaching and learning Jewish history as well. In many ultra-orthodox schools, Jewish history—in the critical, modern sense discussed earlier in this chapter—is essentially not taught at all. In omitting Jewish history from their curricula, these schools are, first of all, remaining true to their heritage. As noted above, pre-modern Jewish schools had no place for Jewish history in their teaching. The essence of Judaism was—in this traditional view—transmitted clearly by God to the Jewish people in the written Torah that God had graciously bequeathed, and clarified further through the oral Torah that had the imprimatur of the rabbis. The written and oral Torahs provided all the historical knowledge a Jew might need, in two senses. First, the narratives described the crucial phases of the Jewish past, the phases in which Judaism emerged and Jews were properly located in their promised homeland. Equally important, these narratives identified clearly the crucial dynamic of Jewish history that needed to be pondered: namely the system of divine reward and punishment that was intended to govern Jewish fate over the ages (Bernstein, 1986; Bloomberg, 1992). This understanding of Jewish history continues to hold sway among certain segments of Jewry who feel that history primarily unfolds according to a divine plan that is unknowable. The study of Jewish history as a social science is seen as secular in nature; it is therefore regarded, at best, as a theft of time that could better be used studying sacred texts, and, at worst, as a threat to sacred education altogether. Hence, in these settings, there is little support for teaching and learning Jewish history—as we presently conceive of it—extensively or rigorously.

Jewish History as an Intellectual and Disciplinary Pursuit

History educators and curriculum reformers on the general North American schooling scene frequently have asserted that teaching history should introduce students to problems in reconstructing the past and, by extension, to the uncertainties in assessing information available on the present and future as well (Barton & Levstik, 2004). Some have referred to this model as the "student-as-historian" approach to history education (Kobrin, 1996). Here the key is a direct student encounter with the data of the past: the artifacts and texts that historians utilize in their reconstructions of history. Students are encouraged to confront these data directly, to draw their conclusions, and to assess the reliability of their conclusions. This can be a potentially exciting intellectual exercise. Development of these critical skills is deemed useful for students as they engage the challenge of encountering complex data and assessing the meaning of these data, whether they involve issues of the economy, American political life, and/or foreign affairs. In a sense, this type of history teaching might well be viewed as an extension of the notion of training for citizenship. Here, however, the citizenship training does not involve the content of the past, but rather the methodology of studying past events systematically and critically, which then becomes available for engaging and assessing present-day issues as well.

A few Jewish schools have begun to gravitate in this direction (Graff, 2000). There is now a considerable corpus of data available—much of it on the Internet—for confronting students with the raw materials of the Jewish past (among them, texts, artifacts, maps, art, architecture, photographs, audio recordings, and video footage), encouraging them to the stimulating task of assessing and drawing conclusions from these materials and using these honed skills to tackle historical and contemporary issues. Pre-conceived results are usually eschewed in such teaching, with students exercising considerable independence in reaching meaningful personal conclusions from their study of the Jewish past. The teacher plays essentially the role of coach in overseeing independent student effort. Students, in constructing their own histories of the Jewish experience, become critical thinkers about Jewish history. This pedagogical approach necessitates a teacher who is highly familiar with the content of Jewish history and the methods of doing historical research (anecdotally, our work with Jewish history educators suggests that many are expert in one or the other but not always both). It also often entails a significant time commitment, both in planning for and engaging in instructional activities. When carefully developed and guided by a skillful teacher, this kind of teaching and learning can have great success in engaging students in the process of historical inquiry (VanSledright, 2002; Wineburg, 2001). Students may thereby devise creative solutions to the religious, social, political, and cultural challenges that Jews have faced in any given time and place, including the world today.

Prospects for Future Research in Jewish History Education

In this chapter, we traced the origins of Jewish history as a school subject and laid out a variety of orientations toward Jewish history education that may be found in North American Jewish schools today. In this final section, we consider prospective new directions for research in the teaching and learning of Jewish history. It is our hope that researchers, practitioners, and policymakers alike will find this a useful departure point for work in a rich, yet largely untapped, field.

As previously noted, current research on how Jewish history education is planned, implemented, and received in North American Jewish schools is limited, at best. The modest numbers of scholarly works that have focused on the study of Jewish history in schools have enriched the field in important ways—mostly in terms of explicating the history and purposes of Jewish history education (hence the focus of this chapter)—yet, we know remarkably little about the what actually goes on in Jewish history classrooms and programs these days. What constitutes the Jewish history curriculum and how is it organized? What time periods, events, and themes are most emphasized, and why? What instructional methods, learning activities, and materials are utilized, and to what effect? Who teaches Jewish history in Jewish schools, and what kinds of formal preparation have Jewish history teachers had, if any? What is the place of Jewish history education in the overall Jewish school curriculum, vis-à-vis other Judaic studies and general studies subjects as well as curricular activities outside the classroom? Finally, and perhaps most important, how do students make sense of the Jewish past they encounter in schools? These and other subjects have eluded scholarly pursuit up till now but are certainly worthy of investigation.

Of particular interest to us are questions that address the problematics of teaching Jewish history. What are the sacred cows of Jewish history education? For example, what is the status of the identity-building project? How are Jewish history educators and students wrestling with the tension between promoting critical thinking while upholding positive Jewish identification? Much has been written about the possibilities in this regard (see, e.g., Chazan & Jacobs, 2005; Gereboff, 1997; Levisohn, 2004). But how does this tension actually play out in Jewish history classrooms? What about the numbers of non-Jewish teachers who teach Jewish history, particularly in settings where Jewish history is integrated into the general history curriculum? Can a teacher who lacks a personal connection to Jewish history and culture be as effective as an "insider" to the community? How are non-Jews (Christians, Moslems, others) treated in the Jewish history curriculum? What about groups that historically have been marginalized in general history, such as women, people of color, gays and lesbians, and poor people, not to mention those marginalized in certain Jewish history circles, such as Sephardic, Oriental, and Persian Jews? What issues are educators and students grappling with personally, and how do they manifest in the Jewish history classroom? This list of potential avenues for research is only a start. Clearly, there is much work to be done.

Fortunately, the prospects for growth in the field of Jewish history education research are encouraging. Academic interest in the teaching of Jewish history in North America has burgeoned since the start of the twenty-first century (see works by Gold, Jacobs, Krasner, Levisohn, and Sheramy cited in this chapter) and continues to expand in Israel (see works by Bekerman, Podeh, Porat, and others). The progress is due in part to (a) the proliferation of research-based graduate programs in Jewish education in the United States and Canada; (b) new initiatives focused on bridging research and practice in various spheres of the Jewish education world (e.g., collaborations between historians and veteran educators have emerged, such as *Understanding Second Temple and Rabbinic Judaism* (2003), a secondary school-level adaptation of Lawrence H. Schiffman's scholarly work on late antiquity, edited by Jon Bloomberg [Maimonides Jewish Day School] and Samuel Kapustin [Tannenbaum Community Hebrew Academy of Toronto]); (c) a surge of scholarly interest in history and social studies education in K-12 schools writ-large; and (d) continuing concern in the Jewish community about the role of Jewish schools in fostering Jewish identification and maintaining communal continuity, both of which have been attributed in part to Jewish history education. We hope that as the scope of research in history education and Jewish education grows, so too will interest in Jewish history education widen and deepen.

We are especially excited by the growing range of methodologies being utilized to investigate history education and their potential application to Jewish education. The works of Sam Wineburg, Keith Barton, Linda Levstik, Bruce VanSledright, and others in the field of general history education have deepened our understanding of how students think about and understand historical texts. Wineburg's method of probing students' historical thinking through read-aloud exercises and other techniques has generated comparable research in Israel (Porat, 2004). Ethnographic, classroom-based (or other context-based) studies that profile in detail the ways Jewish history is organized, presented, and mediated by both students and teachers can enrich our understanding of history education and Jewish education more broadly. While historical and philosophical works on Jewish history education are essential foundations for further investigation, empirical and qualitative research in this field can take us beyond "official knowledge" and enable us to peer into how students and teachers are actively constructing meaning from Jewish history in schools.

References

Ackerman, W. I. (1984). 'Let us now praise famous men and our fathers in their generations': History books for Jewish schools in America. In *Dor ledor: Studies in the history of Jewish education in Israel and the Diaspora* (Vol. 2, pp. 82–116). Tel Aviv: Ramot Publishing Company.

Ackerman, W. I. (1986). "The land of our fathers' in the 'land of the free'": Textbooks on Israel in American Jewish schools. *Jewish Education*, 54(4), 4–14.

Barton, K. C. (2008). Research on students' ideas about history. In L. S. Levstik & C. A. Tyson (Eds.), *Handbook of research in social studies education* (pp. 239–258). New York: Routledge.

Barton, K. C. & Levstik, L. S. (2004). *Teaching history for the common good*. Mahwah, NJ: Lawrence Erlbaum Associates.

Bekerman, Z. (2004). Potential and limitations of multicultural education in conflict-ridden areas: Bilingual Palestinian-Jewish schools in Israel. *Teachers College Record*, 106(3), 574–610.

Bernstein, D. (1986). Two approaches to the teaching of Jewish history in orthodox yeshiva schools. Unpublished Ph.D., New York University, New York.

Bloomberg, J. (1992). The study of Jewish history in the Jewish day school. *Ten Da'at*, 6(1), 31–32.

Chazan, B. (1978). *The language of Jewish education: Crisis and hope in the Jewish school*. Bridgeport, CT: Hartmore House.

Chazan, R. & Jacobs, B. M. (2005). Jewish history from the academy to the schools: Bridging the gap. In M. Nisan & O. Schermer (Eds.), *Educational deliberations: Studies in education in honor of Shlomo (Seymour) Fox* (pp. 157–180). Jerusalem: Keter Publishers.

Cohen, G. D. (1977). Translating Jewish history into curriculum: From scholarship to paideia—A case study. In S. Fox & G. Rosenfeld (Eds.), *From the scholar to the classroom* (pp. 31–58). New York: Melton Research Center for Jewish Education, Jewish Theological Seminary of America.

Dawidowicz, L. S. (1994). In N. Kozodoy (Ed.), *What is the use of Jewish history?* New York: Schocken.

Eisenberg, A., & Segal, A. (Eds.). (1956). *Readings in the teaching of Jewish history*. New York: Jewish Education Committee Press.

Eisenberg, A. & Segal, A. (1963). *Teaching Jewish history: A handbook* (3rd ed.). New York: Jewish Education Committee Press.

Gagnon, P.(Eds.) The Bradley Commission on History in the Schools (1989). *Historical literacy: The case for history in American education*. Boston: Houghton Mifflin Company.

Gedi, N. & Elam, Y. (1996). Collective memory—what is it? *History and Memory*, 8(1), 30–50.

Gereboff, J. (1995). Heroes and history in American Jewish education. In M. Mor (Ed.), *Crisis & reaction: The hero in Jewish history* (pp. 105–150). Omana, NE: Creighton University Press.

Gereboff, J. (1997). Can the teaching of Jewish history be anything but the teaching of myth? In S. D. Breslauer (Ed.), *The seductiveness of Jewish myth: Challenge or response* (pp. 43–69). Albany, NY: SUNY Press.

Gold, P. S. (2004). *Making the Bible modern: Children's Bibles and Jewish education in twentieth-century America*. Ithaca, NY: Cornell University Press.

Goldflam, D. (1989). *Survey of current practices and attitudes of Jewish history teachers in the high Jewish day schools in the United States*. Unpublished Ph.D., University of Miami.

Golub, J. S. (1944). Goals in teaching Jewish history. *Jewish Education*, 25(2), 90–95.

Graff, G. (2000). Primary sources revisited: Methodology in the study of Jewish history in Jewish secondary schools. In Z. Garber (Ed.), *Academic approaches to teaching Jewish studies* (pp. 297–315). Lanham, MD: University Press of America.

Grayzel, S. (1968). *A history of the Jews: From the Babylonian exile to the present.* Philadelphia: Jewish Publication Society.

Honor, L. (1931, November 26). Guiding principles for writing and teaching Jewish history. *The American Israelite.*

Honor, L. (1953). The role of memory in biblical history. In M. Davis (Ed.), *Mordecai M. Kaplan jubilee volume: On the occasion of his seventieth birthday. English section* (pp. 417–435). New York: Jewish Theological Seminary of America.

Jacobs, B. M. (2002). Where the personal and pedagogical meet: A portrait of a master teacher of Jewish history. *Journal of Jewish Education, 68*(1), 73–86.

Jacobs, B. M. (2004). Jewish education for intelligent citizenship in the American Jewish community, 1910–1940. In C. Woyshner, J. Watras, & M. S. Crocco (Eds.), *Social education in the twentieth century: Curriculum and context for citizenship* (pp. 76–92). New York: Peter Lang.

Jacobs, B. M. (2005a). *The (trans)formation of American Jews: Jewish social studies in progressive American Jewish schools, 1910–1940.* Unpublished Ph.D., Columbia University.

Jacobs, B. M. (2005b). What's wrong with the history of American Jewish education? *Journal of Jewish Education, 71*(1), 33–52.

Kirschenblatt-Gimblett, B. (2002). Learning from ethnography: Reflections on the nature and efficacy of youth tours to Israel. In H. Goldberg, S. Heilman, & B. Kirschenblatt-Gimblett (Eds.), *The Israel experience: Studies in youth travel and Jewish identity* (pp. 267–311). Jerusalem: Studio Kavraph, Andrea and Charles Bronfman Philanthropies.

Kobrin, D. (1996). *Beyond the textbook: Teaching history using documents and primary sources.* Portsmouth, NH: Heinemann.

Krasner, J. (2002). *Representations of self and other in American Jewish history and social studies schoolbooks: An exploration of the changing shape of American Jewish identity.* Unpublished Ph.D., Brandeis University.

Krasner, J. (2003). "New Jews" in an old-new land: Images in American Jewish textbooks prior to 1948. *Journal of Jewish Education, 69*(2), 7–22.

Krasner, J. (2004). When the present took precedence over the past: Social adjustment and the mainstreaming of American Jewish history in the supplementary school. *Journal of Jewish Education, 70*(3), 27–39.

Levisohn, J. A. (2003). Young patriots or junior historians? An epistemological defense of critical patriotic education. *Philosophy of Education Yearbook, 2003,* 94–102.

Levisohn, J. A. (2004). Patriotism and parochialism: Why teach American Jewish history, and how? *Journal of Jewish Education, 70*(3), 2–15.

Levisohn, J. A. (2008). From integration of curricula to the pedagogy of integrity. *Journal of Jewish Education, 74*(3), 264–294.

Lowenthal, D. (1998). *The heritage crusade and the spoils of history.* Cambridge: Cambridge University Press.

McNeill, W. H. (1986). *Mythistory and other essays.* Chicago: University of Chicago Press.

Meyer, M. A. (1987). *Ideas of Jewish history.* Detroit, MI: Wayne State University Press.

Nash, G. B., Crabtree, C., & Dunn, R. E. (1997). *History on trial: Culture wars and the teaching of the past.* New York: Alfred A. Knopf.

Podeh, E. (2002). *The Arab-Israeli conflict in Israeli history textbooks.* Westport, CT: Bergin and Garvey.

Pomson, A. (1994). *Critical history and collective memory: A problem in Jewish education.* Unpublished Ph.D., University of London.

Porat, D. (2004). It's not written here, but this is what happened: Students' cultural comprehension of textbook narratives on the Israeli–Arab conflict. *American Educational Research Journal, 41*(4), 963–996.

Porat, D. (2006). The nation revised: Teaching the Jewish past in the Zionist present (1890–1913). *Jewish Social Studies, 13*(1), 59–86.

Rostenstreich, N. (1995). The 'science of Judaism' and its transformation. In M. Davis (Ed.), *Teaching Jewish civilization: A global approach to higher education* (pp. 11–15). New York: New York University Press.

Sarna, J. D. (1998). American Jewish education in historical perspective. *Journal of Jewish Education, 64*(1), 8–21.

Schiffman, L. H. (2003). In J. Bloomberg & S. Kapustin (Eds.), *Understanding second temple and Rabbinic Judaism*. New York: Ktav.

Sheramy, R. (2000). *Defining lessons: Holocaust education and American Jewish youth from World War II to the present*. Unpublished Ph.D., Brandeis University.

Stearns, P., Seixas, P., & Wineburg, S. (Eds.). (2000). *Knowing, teaching, and learning history: National and international perspectives*. New York: New York University Press.

Tanchel, S. E. (2008). "A Judaism that does not hide": Teaching the documentary hypothesis in a pluralistic Jewish high school. *Journal of Jewish Education, 74*(1), 29–52.

Thornton, S. J. (1994). The social studies near century's end: Reconsidering patterns of curriculum and instruction. In L. Darling-Hammond (Ed.), *Review of research in education* (Vol. 20, pp. 223–254). Washington, DC: AERA.

VanSledright, B. (2002). *In search of America's past: Learning to read history in elementary school*. New York: Teachers College Press.

Wilson, S. (2001). Research on history teaching. In V. Richardson (Ed.), *The handbook on research on teaching* (4th ed., pp. 527–544). New York: Macmillan.

Wineburg, S. (2001). *Historical thinking and other unnatural acts: Charting the future of teaching the past*. Philadelphia: Temple University Press.

Yerushalmi, Y. H. (1982). *Zakhor: Jewish history and Jewish memory*. Seattle, WA: University of Washington Press.

Holocaust Education

Simone Schweber

Introduction

Although there are literally tomes of writing concerning teaching and learning about the Holocaust, it is only since the 1990s that rigorous research in these domains emerged. Prior to that period, there were heated arguments about the nature and aims of Holocaust education, who ought to receive it, under what conditions, in what contexts, and with what intended results. While often well-argued and highly readable, most of that literature was philosophical in nature; it was based on ideas and commitments rather than research or investigation. And while much of that body presented powerful insights and masterful argumentation, very little examined the lived world of Holocaust education. In other words, most of this writing dealt instead in the realm of ideas about Holocaust education rather than experiences with it. Or, when that literature did delve into Holocaust education as practiced in specific contexts, the data were typically anecdotally seized rather than systematically generated.

Arguably, the field is so recent that it is in some way itself to blame for the lack of experiential evidence on which to base current practices. As Thomas D. Fallace (2008) explains, the treatment of the Holocaust as a curricular topic in US public schools dates back only to the 1970s. Though it was taught about in Jewish congregational schools prior to that period (Sheramy, 2003), research on Holocaust education commenced only some 20 years later. Holocaust education in Israel has taken many different ideological forms from the 1950s onward, corresponding precisely to which political parties are in power. In Germany, the history of Holocaust education is likewise multilayered, as it took decidedly divergent routes in each of the former States of East and West Germany and as Germans remain committed to understanding the Holocaust's various legacies. What it means to teach about the Holocaust in Germany is thus very different from what it means to teach about the Holocaust in Israel or in the United States "after Auschwitz," as teaching is

S. Schweber (✉)
University of Wisconsin, Madison, WI, USA
e-mail: sschweber@wisc.edu

inevitably connected to national ideas about the state, citizenship, morality, and history. As such, research on Holocaust education, indeed wherever it is carried out, has a wide range of contexts to consider. Conceived of as a scholarly enterprise and a sub-field of Holocaust studies more broadly, Holocaust educational research has been slow in developing. In reviewing the education literature published in the last decades, it becomes clear that the literature on Holocaust education has grown slowly, if steadily, unlike related domains such as Holocaust memory studies or Holocaust historical works that have expanded exponentially over the same period. Though the field is small, there are broad philosophical divides that characterize it. A review of some of these divides follows. It is limited to publications in English, which regrettably excludes the works produced in other languages and gives this chapter a decidedly Anglo-centric bias.

Philosophical Divides

Much early education work delimited the pedagogical implications of the historiographical debate between the universality and the uniqueness of the Holocaust. Put simply, educators and educational researchers early on tended to align themselves either with the position advocating for the Holocaust's uniqueness or with the position claiming its universality. Thus, writing in 1979, Henry Friedlander already advocated for the Holocaust's universality, hoping that the study of the Holocaust might serve as a basis for civic participation. Not long thereafter, in 1982, Chaim Schatzker lamented that much universalistic Holocaust education seemed to him to deny the Holocaust's singular status. Schatzker explained that with such educational efforts, "there is the danger that [the Holocaust] will be dwarfed, diminished and will lose its... significance... instead of making students sensitive to [its] abnormalities" (Schatzker, 1982: p. 80). As this brief juxtaposition implies, the unique/universal divide tends to play out among educational researchers in discussions involving curriculum, student learning, and teacher preparation. Like Schatzker, those who lean toward the "unique" pole of the continuum tend to caution teachers about the limits involved in teaching about the Holocaust, given the unintelligibility of the event itself. They thus tend to advocate for the use of particular pedagogical formats over others, and they sometimes argue against drawing comparisons between the Holocaust and other genocidal events. In a famous essay that reiterates this position from a data-rich standpoint, the historian Lucy Dawidowicz railed against "How *they* teach the Holocaust." Most American curricula that she examined at the time of her writing (1992), she claimed misrepresented the Holocaust, glossing over its sources, evading its horror, and universalizing its main victims.

Samuel Totten, a prolific writer in this first generation of Holocaust education scholars, shared Dawidowicz's commitment to historical specificity and helped shape the field from that standpoint (Totten, 2002). Following Elie Wiesel's particularist approach to Holocaust representation, Totten has avidly delimited the pedagogical choices he deems appropriate. Teaching about the Holocaust, he has argued, demands specialized knowledge and careful handling—beyond that which might be involved in teaching about other events. Thus, Totten has argued that children in the early grades should not be exposed to the Holocaust, that teachers should never engage Holocaust simulations and that the curriculum materials used to teach about the Holocaust should be realistic. Along with William Parsons, Samuel Totten wrote the US Holocaust Memorial Museum's (heretofore USHMM) *Guidelines for Teaching about the Holocaust*, which were published in 1993 to correspond to the opening of the museum. These guidelines showcase Totten and Parsons' ideological commitment to the Holocaust's "uniqueness," albeit in a somewhat understated manner, as the officially sanctioned position of the US Holocaust authority, a position that museum administrators have begun to revisit as the institution continues to develop.

Other educators within what might be considered this "unique" school of thought proposed strategies for patrolling the boundaries of representation. Karen Shawn, for example, suggested that teachers ought to be specially "certified" to teach about the Holocaust before being enabled to do so (Shawn, 1995). Like Totten, Shawn objected to the oversimplification of the Holocaust in many curricula and classrooms, the watering down of its content such that it becomes trivialized. Shawn worked for many years as an education specialist at Yad Vashem, the Israeli Holocaust Memorial, whose educational philosophies coalesce at a similar point along the unique/universal continuum, though in an Israeli context, the stance serves different socio-political purposes than it does elsewhere. For critics like Ruth Firer, the ideological position of uniqueness supports Israeli prejudices and racism, shrouded beneath Israelis' national "siege mentality" (1998), all of which appear in her review of Israeli textbooks. For supporters, however, the Holocaust's "uniqueness" is authentically justified such that its implications for that country's national security interests are legitimate. Dan Porat's (2004) careful research on debates over the Holocaust among officials in the Israeli Ministry of Education and the resulting textbook treatments of the topic from the early 1950s to the late 1990s demonstrates the complexities of educational uniqueness, including Israel's relationships to Zionism, state-building, post-Zionism, and militarism.

German debates over the Holocaust's uniqueness translate into educational orientations as well, though they have utterly different implications in that national context. As the German educational philosopher Micha Brumlik maintains, the project of "education after Auschwitz" is necessarily vexed, and a denial of its uniqueness implies a denial of responsibility, which is morally repugnant. As Friedrich Schweitzer writes, following Brumlik's logic, "there are at least two different ways of not doing justice to the Shoah in education," the first being a simple "forgetting" of it in the curriculum, the second being "treating the Shoah as if it were like any other topic in the curriculum" (2000: p. 371), a structural relativising that might position study of the Holocaust "after biology and right before the test in math" (Schweitzer, 2000: p. 371). On even a cursory comparison of Holocaust education debates in the US, Germany, and Israel, what surfaces is the importance of national contexts in framing curricular issues.

In the US context, a second generation of educational researchers tends to disparage the unique/universal divide itself as falsely dichotomous, paradoxically aligning with the latter pole. These researchers argue against Holocaust uniqueness out of commitments to democratic, socially just, anti-racist, and humanistic education. The purpose of teaching about the Holocaust is precisely to learn from it, no matter how difficult, not to hold it in abeyance as impossibly non-educative, no matter how appealing such a theoretical position may be. Thus, Geoffrey Short, whose empirical and theoretical work spans multiple decades in England, demonstrates repeatedly that the Holocaust may provide useful lessons, not only for students as individuals, but "for the educational system as a whole" (Short, 2003: p. 285). As he writes in the introduction to a study he co-authored with Bruce Carrington, "If taught properly, [the Holocaust] can make an invaluable contribution to the general development of the skills, attitudes and dispositions usually associated with 'maximalist' notions of citizenship in a participatory democracy" (Carrington & Short, 1997: p. 271). Like Short, researchers in this contingent question the morality of a rigid boundary cordoning the Holocaust off from other atrocities. The sacralization such categorization enacts prevents its being learned from morally and learned about in historical detail. Rather than treating the Holocaust with reverence, its artificial seclusion renders it trivialized.

Within this group of researchers are those who turned to empirical studies as a mode of questioning some normative assumptions about Holocaust education in the USA. Beth Aviv Greenbaum's discussion of six works she assigns in her semester-long, public high-school Holocaust elective is a good example of this genre. Her book *Bearing Witness* (2001) considers her literature choices and her students' readings of them, thereby usefully straddling the line between guidebook for educators and research on Holocaust education. I (Schweber, 2004) studied what teachers who were highly regarded within their communities taught *as* the Holocaust and what students in their classrooms learned from the experience. Melinda Fine (1995) had written a polished case study of a class engaged with the still-exceedingly popular curriculum, *Facing History and Ourselves,* and I wanted to see how very experienced teachers adapted this curriculum and others. I purposefully observed a teacher who designed and ran an elaborate, semester-long Holocaust simulation, a masterful storyteller, and a third teacher who was a powerful dramaturge. The pedagogical practices and student impacts upended notions that were commonsensical on the "unique" end of the ideological spectrum. It turned out, for example, that simulations can teach students important lessons, despite the reality that they are problematic formats that can go awry in practice. In this study, the teachers' home-grown, classroom-based practices butted up against the prescriptive institutional directives aimed at constraining their choices. It is worth noting that Dawidowicz's assessment of official Holocaust curricula applied to the enacted curricula in these school rooms, too; anti-Semitism tended to be ignored as an explanatory framework for atrocity and Jewishness as a category tended to be oversimplified.

What might be considered a third generation of US researchers has emerged. Karen Riley's (Totten & Riley, 2005) work exemplifies the continuity of the "unique" position—as when she finds a pronounced absence in US state standards documents of language that treats the Holocaust as a historically specific event.

By contrast, Karen Spector's and Mary Juzwik's careful studies of classroom discourse illustrate the widening of "universalist" research. Spector's study followed students whose fundamentalist Christian eschatology funneled their interpretations of the Holocaust into particular pathways. Some of the middle-school students she observed, for example, thought that the Holocaust was preordained by God, not unlike the sacrifice of Jesus for the salvation of humanity. Other students, after reading Elie Wiesel's memoir, considered his faith to have grown during his incarceration in the concentration camps. Like Spector's work, Juzwik's research focuses on classroom narratives, but Juzwik employs an almost microscopic lens to examine discourse (2009). Juzwik examines the grammar of Holocaust teaching, finding, for example, that even at the syntactic level of middle-school students' talk, Jews within Holocaust narratives end up being literally "objectified." Within the structure of the sentences explaining their treatment, Jews are discussed as the receivers rather than the generators of action; their position grammatically reflects their persecution historically.

While the aforementioned researchers' work may be positioned in different spaces along the unique/universalist continuum, all of the examples above might be grouped together in regard to conceptual orientations toward research. The studies above may be classified generally as either post-positivistic or constructionist works; that is, in all of these studies, "reality" is assumed to exist outside of individual experience or discursive performance. History exists regardless of its narration as such. Post-modernists have also considered Holocaust education, however, and have incorporated the concepts of trauma, the theorization of pedagogy, and the role of testimony in the body of Holocaust education literature. Proponents of this school of thought have tended to rely heavily on literary theories of the Holocaust as when, for example, Michael Bernard-Donals and Richard R. Glejzer (2001) discuss what testimony "teaches," or when Marla Morris (2001) considers the generation of a "dystopic curriculum" in the wake of the Holocaust—that is, a curriculum that reveals the practices of "othering" in order to pursue a non-utopian world. Given their indebtedness to literary concepts and methodologies, post-modern researchers tend to give preference to the generation of high theory over the gathering of empirical data. There are, nonetheless, researchers whose work bridges both worlds.

Shoshana Felman's groundbreaking work, "Education and crisis, or the vicissitudes of teaching" may well be considered a scholarly first-generation work within this post-modern school of thought (Caruth, 1995). Interpreting her own post-secondary teaching through a psychoanalytic lens, Felman positions the hardship of learning about the Holocaust as an opportunity to revisit and re-envision the act of teaching as a whole. Her students, she writes, experienced a terrible crisis in learning about this topic, an experience that left them with an absence of speech and an overabundance of talk; that is, her students could talk, but in the midst of learning about the Holocaust, they could not generate meaning. She concludes with the speculation that all teaching ought to be risky, writing, "if teaching does not hit upon some sort of crisis, if it does not encounter either the vulnerability or the explosiveness of an (explicit or implicit) critical and unpredictable dimension, it has perhaps not truly taught" (p. 55).

Deborah Britzman is another active participant in the development of psychoanalytic approaches to Holocaust education. Britzman (1998) proposes a theory of "difficult knowledge"—that kind of knowledge which challenges people's notions of themselves and humanity, inducing a type of Freudian melancholia. Expanding on these ideas, Elisabeth Ellsworth examines the ways in which the Holocaust necessarily exceeds the conventional boundaries of language. Education about the Holocaust, Ellsworth explains, cannot be contained in dialogue, communication, or representation. Instead, education must be about "the necessity, the right, the responsibility of participating in the ongoing, never-completed historical, social, and political labor of memory construction" (2005, pp. 177–78). In later work, Ellsworth examines how the Permanent Exhibit of the US Holocaust Memorial Museum positions viewers pedagogically. She asks what it is that viewers are positioned to know, feel, and be able to do. Fracturing staid notions of identity and psychoanalytic notions of agency, Ellsworth attends to how the "pedagogical address" of the Museum (re)produces power relations (2005).

The two ideological divides I have used to characterize research on Holocaust education—both the unique/universal debates that grew out of early historiographical disputes and the epistemological domains that punctuate all academic inquiry—are of course not the only bases for categorizing work in this field. There are many other important divides ideologically and historically. In this regard, for example, the Eichmann trials initiated a particular era of education reform in dealing with the Holocaust in Israel, just as the anti-Semitic wave of 1959–1960 ushered in a new era of education reform in Germany. The list of ways to section the field is dauntingly long given its short history, and none of the options is blatantly the best. The remainder of this essay summarizes what is known about where the Holocaust is taught, in what kinds of venues, how, by whom, and with what effects. In each section, significant issues are raised, but what we do not yet know is also highlighted in the hopes of inspiring further study in exactly those domains.

Educational Venues

Educational venues can be classified along a number of axes, among them: grade-level (elementary to university), regional setting (where in the world people are learning about the Holocaust), and venue type (whether the institution provides formal or informal educational opportunities, whether it is a private Jewish setting, for example, or a public one). In light of their interpenetration as categories, grade-level has been prioritized in the hope that it provides some measure of analytic clarity.

In terms of schooling level, in the USA, it appears that the Holocaust has drifted from upper to lower grades over time. That is, whereas the Holocaust was initially only taught about in the high-school curriculum, it has been absorbed into the middle school, and in recent years, has entered the elementary school, a trend I have labeled "curricular creep" (Schweber, 2008b: p. 2075). Because the USA has neither a standardized curriculum nor even intra-state content consistency, the scope and rapidity of "curricular creep" is impossible to assess nationally. In Scotland,

Henry Maitles and Paula Cowan interviewed five teachers who taught the Holocaust to 9-year-olds, and all five, perhaps not surprisingly, considered their units a success (1999). Geoffrey Short and Carole Reed interviewed young children in England, ascertaining that "8- and 9-year-olds have almost no conception of a Jew" (2004: 126), which prompts them to argue for "substantial preparatory work" (2004: p. 127) before teaching the Holocaust as part of the formal curriculum to youngsters. In a study I conducted of a third-grade classroom in which children learned about the Holocaust in-depth through picture books, the parents of the children all thought the unit was a success, and many of the children valued their learning. Only a few students and I felt that they were too young for the subject, given the nightmares some students experienced and the general lack of comprehension other students reported (Schweber, 2008b). That single, small-scale study, while theoretically generalizable, proposes too limited an answer to the question of when children are old enough to learn about the Holocaust. Moreover, because the study-setting was a nonsectarian public rather than a private Jewish school, the transferability of its results to Jewish school settings is questionable. Only one student in that classroom was Jewish, and she experienced a depression directly related to her strong identification with Holocaust victims; such a reaction implies that schools with large numbers of Jewish students need to be especially vigilant about not teaching children directly about the Holocaust until at least the 4th grade. Cowan and Maitles' survey research in Scotland assesses students' reactions to learning about the Holocaust in "upper primary school," where students are aged 10–12, and it strongly indicates that their learning carried positive short-term effects on their civic engagement (2007). Taken together, these studies seem to suggest that students ought to begin learning about the Holocaust formally in school only when they reach double-digit ages.

Children in Israel typically learn about the Holocaust much earlier since the country officially commemorates the Shoah as a nation and because the Holocaust so saturates public discourse. German children, too, often encounter the Holocaust long before they learn about it officially as part of the school curriculum. Does this heightened awareness mean that Israeli and German children *should* learn about the Holocaust at earlier ages? Both more and more nuanced research ought to be conducted in answer to the questions involved in what children actually learn from study of the Holocaust, at various young ages, given the complex facets of their identities (e.g., social class, religious identities, gender identification, ethnic heritages, psychological development, national and local affiliations). This dearth of research is especially problematic for Jewish school principals and teachers, where Yom Hashoah commemorations or the Tenth of Tevet[1] rituals frequently expose children to the Holocaust at young ages. What such commemorations look like and how young children interpret them is an area ripe for investigation.

The Holocaust is frequently taught about in middle schools, wherein adolescents are roughly 12–15 years old. However, what this schooling level endows students

---

[1] Because Yom HaShoah falls within the month of Nisan, a month when mourning is prohibited, many orthodox Jews say kaddish for the murdered of the Holocaust on the Tenth of Tevet.

with specifically is also not well documented. How students understand the material they learn, and how such learning affects their moral, intellectual, and spiritual lives are only beginning to be examined. Veronica Boix Mansilla explored how Canadian adolescents understood the Holocaust cognitively, focusing in particular on how the students were able to perform their acquired knowledge (1998). Research on how the Holocaust was taught and learned about in two religious 8th-grade classrooms, one at an evangelical, Charismatic, fundamentalist Christian school, and the other at an ultra-orthodox Jewish, Chabad/Lubavitch girls' *yeshivah*, strikingly revealed teaching strategies meant to enhance students' identification with very narrowly defined groups of victims: fundamentalist Christians in the first case (Schweber & Irwin, 2003) and ultra-orthodox Jews in the second (Schweber, 2008a). The Lubavitch case in particular illustrates how the Shoah can be taught about from the perspective that it is historically incomparable and fundamentally incomprehensible, "unique" not only in history but of particular importance in Jewish history. In both of these studies, the students' religious identities shaped their learning of the material, which had already been narrowed by the ideological biases of the institutional settings. No studies as yet compare Holocaust learning between schooling levels, that is, between upper-elementary, early middle-school, or late high-school students. Moreover, none compare the Holocaust learning that occurs at different religious settings, between, say Lubavitch and Satmar yeshivahs or between liberal Jewish congregational schools and the more conservative ones. Given individuals' differential growth and development trajectories, such study might be especially illuminating and helpful in scaffolding a developmentally appropriate, systemic Holocaust education curriculum.

Because the Holocaust has been positioned within the high-school curriculum historically, most studies of Holocaust education have situated research at the secondary level. In one of the few comprehensive US-based surveys, Jeffrey Ellison established that in Illinois high schools, teachers spent 8 days of instruction on the Holocaust on average, usually "… during students' junior year" of high school. Ellison also found that most teachers tended "to subsume the topic of the Holocaust within the topic of tolerance and stereotyping" rather than within the specific history of anti-Semitism. The United States Holocaust Memorial Museum sponsored a survey in 2003–2004, which found that "the vast majority of teachers (72%) reported that the Holocaust was addressed in one of more of their [English and social studies] courses" (Donnelly, 2006: p. 51). Students in England and Wales are taught about the Holocaust in history classes of Year 9, when students are roughly ages 14–15. Britain's national curriculum includes the Holocaust, but its positioning within the standardized content implies that it has lower status than other subject areas (Brown & Davies, 1998). The Council for Cultural Cooperation (CDCC), the Council of Europe's educational arm, perhaps in the hopes of spurring greater coverage, published a range of small guides on Holocaust education available to all 40 of its member nations.

While it has been a mainstay curricular presence in Germany and Israel, in many places where the Holocaust took place, education about it is just beginning to be broached. As Ruchniewicz (2000) has shown, Poland only initiated Holocaust education in 1996, and in "the Ukraine, Byelorussia, Hungary, and Slovakia, Holocaust education remains in its infancy" (Crawford & Foster, 2007b: p. 22). In 2006, the South African province of KwaZulu-Natal initiated Holocaust education (Schneider, 2006). Such reports indicate an increase in Holocaust education in certain regions of the world. Nonetheless, reports have indicated that in specific locales, the Holocaust is being excised from the curriculum. In certain Parisian suburbs that house large populations of North African immigrants, teachers gave up trying to teach about the Holocaust because it was presumed by students that such teaching symbolically supported the existence of Israel as a state. During an interview about his report on anti-Semitic events and attitudes in French schools, Georges Bensoussan shared that he "[knew] of cases in which the teacher mentioned Auschwitz and Treblinka, and students clapped," which presumably prompted teachers to refrain from teaching hostile learners (2004). In 2007, a rumor that the Holocaust was being removed from the United Kingdom's national curriculum prompted multiple organizations to clarify its falsity. Interestingly, the power of Internet communication in the twenty-first century ended up pressuring the University of Kentucky to host Holocaust teacher training programs (since the "UK" was widely perceived among US e-mail recipients to refer to that institution rather than the United Kingdom).

In those countries with national curricula, the venues for Holocaust education are documented in policy. Whether increasingly or decreasingly covered, in these locales, the need for research on the experiential dimensions of such curricula looms large. One might well ask how subject area context affects instruction and learning; how might it be different to learn about the Holocaust through mandatory religious studies classes, through citizenship classes, or in English classes, the three main venues in England? Tom Misco has studied how the Holocaust is being treated in Romanian classes and what institutional supports exist to further that education (Misco, 2008), and he has found that continued anti-Semitism has impeded progress. A qualitative study of Eastern Ukrainian high-school students' writings illuminates their multiple and competing discourses with regard to anti-Semitism, Jews, Nazis, and responsibility (Ivanova, 2004). The two studies beg for more and broader comparative research across national borders, as when Shamai et al. compare Israeli and German teenagers' conceptions of National Socialism and the Shoah. Interestingly, that study determined that the greater the level of students' Holocaust knowledge, regardless of whether they were German or Israeli, the more they hoped to interact with students from the other country (Shamai, Yardeni, & Klages, 2004). A few, very carefully designed, large-scale, international studies could be exceedingly fruitful in mapping Holocaust education worldwide. Such studies, thoughtfully done, could help to answer the questions that revolve around how different it is to learn about the Holocaust within a context where genocide lingers in lived memory vs. where it exists only as learned history. Moreover, such a study could help answer the important questions involved in how Jewish students in different national contexts are taught about the Holocaust and with what results.

At the college and university levels, the Holocaust is a common offering, and yet very little research has been undertaken to assess the results of such courses. In his survey of Holocaust courses offered at US institutions, Stephen Haynes (1998) found tremendous diversity among professors as to curricular materials, historical scope, and pedagogic activities. Moreover, those who chose to teach about the Holocaust tended to be untrained in the subject area and thus "neither their perspective on the subject matter nor their pedagogical style [was] necessarily informed by any coherent philosophy of Holocaust education" (1998: p. 282). In attempt perhaps to develop such philosophies, however, many college-level instructors write about their experiences teaching and their perceptions of its impact. As an example, Wink discusses how she teaches about the Holocaust in the hopes that her students reject apathy and examine the "tension between obedience and critical thinking" (2006: p. 84) in her English class at the US Coast Guard Academy. Marion Faber (1996) writes informatively about teaching a Holocaust course that highlights the role of German culture, and Judith Tydor Baumel (2002) considers the potential intersections of Holocaust and gender studies. Other authors discuss other kinds of subject areas through which to teach the Holocaust, as well as different kinds of institutional settings and what their students learned within them, including community colleges, the US Air Force Academy (Westermann, 1996), and both Catholic (Braiterman, 1999; Farnham, 1983) and state-affiliated (Berlak, 1999; Friedrichs, 1996; Halperin, 1986) universities. In an especially compelling essay, Tinberg (2005) grapples with the dilemmas of designing a Holocaust course as the child of Holocaust survivors, sharing his sense of entitlement to "regard the Shoah as a family matter" (73). For numerous other essays on the perspectives of college and university teachers, see Marion Hirsch and Irene Kacandes' (2007) engaging edited volume. Self-studies of post-secondary teaching are, on the one hand, a valuable resource revealing of the beliefs and practices of academics. On the other hand, the number of such studies alone highlights the need for other kinds of research on this important schooling level as well.

In addition to grade level, another important categorical distinction is type of venue, whether the educational institution offers formal education—in the form of classroom instruction, for example—or informal education—in the form of trauma tourism, museum excursions, or online learning. A number of studies have considered Israeli youth pilgrimages to Poland, examining how the sponsoring institutions' ideological orientations shape the trips' programmatic dimensions and in turn, affect travelers' experiences, for better and worse (Feldman, 1997; Kugelmass, 1993, Hazan 2001). When Lazar, Chaitin, Gross, and Bar-On (2004) studied Israeli students' pre- and post-trip reactions to their state-sponsored trip, they found that adolescents' conceptions were unstable. The Poland trips tended to emphasize Zionist goals rather than humanistic ones, a trend that some have argued supports Israeli militarism, which critics refer to as the " 'new Israeli religion,' based on the notion that since the Jews were weak during the Holocaust, there is a need to ensure that Israel remains strong" (Lazar et al., p. 190). When Shlomo Romi and Michal Lev (2007) studied students who had participated in a pilgrimage tour 5 years earlier, they determined some of the long-term consequences for students'

Jewish identities, specifically the participants' greater conviction of the importance of supporting Israeli military might. It is worth noting, though, that "peak experiences" like these trips are available for a wide range of educators and students, and that ideologically, some trips can cement general humanitarian values, too, which Elizabeth Spalding and her research collaborators found to be the impact of one such trip for multi-ethnic pre-service education professionals (2007). This is to say that informal educational experiences, even if they cover similar geographical territory (Auschwitz and Birkenau concentration camps, for example), may convey radically different messages about the Holocaust.

Holocaust-based trips specifically geared toward American Jewish youth constitute a burgeoning market, which has been little studied. How, for example, do Birthright tours cover "Holocaust content" as opposed to denominationally specific Jewish tours that cover similar content? And, how do students' receptions of that content differ? Just as classrooms in Jewish institutional settings will necessarily differ from classrooms in diverse public school settings, so tours directed at Jewish participants will necessarily focus on what is deemed important for Jews. Such efforts necessarily reveal the contours of collective memory as it is being forged, an exceedingly fruitful domain for inquiry into how Jewishness itself is represented, constituted, and continued.

Another area that remains understudied is museum excursions. Few researchers have examined the educative and non-educative dimensions of exhibits, even if much literature is devoted to analyzing displays. Fewer studies consider the actual reception of museum exhibits among visitors. Though not technically a research project, the trenchant article by Philip Gourevitch, entitled "Behold now behemoth—the Holocaust Memorial Museum: One More American Theme Park" (1993) remains one of the most gripping examinations of how museums are necessarily interpreted through audiences' pre-existing conceptions. In the religious eschatology of certain believing Christians, Jews were fated to be murdered during the Holocaust as divine punishment for their rejection of Jesus as the messiah. In riveting prose, Gourevitch points to the inevitability of any museum exhibit—and by implication, most educational materials—inadvertently reinforcing such religious notions by not engaging them directly. Researchers have yet to devote attention to the question of how students' experiences with authentic sites of tragedy compare with their visits to museums designed to evoke such tragedies.

Commemorative activities, sometimes referred to as "Holocaust days" or weeks, are another informal education venue rarely studied in terms of reception. What is it organizers hope to accomplish educationally? What do participants and observers learn from the commemorative events? What do college-based, student-organized commemorative activities look like, what do they teach, and how are they received? In Britain, Holocaust Memorial Days have been annually marked in schools since January 27, 2001. Neil Burtonwood (2002) usefully describes the research literature to support the relatively new ritual, and Cowan and Maitles (2002) carefully dissect the kinds of supports and efforts that converged to make its first instantiation in a Scottish locale highly effective among a wide circle of stakeholders. To date, very little research has looked into how summer camps for Jewish youth commemorate the Holocaust and with what effects. Researchers could well ask how Jewish youth camps in different parts of the country, with different religious interpretations of the Holocaust, and with different denominational affiliations commemorate the Holocaust. How do insiders and outsiders understand the importance of such commemorations and how do they experience such programs? A carefully designed, international comparative research study on the educational dimensions of Holocaust commemorations could be enormously informative, especially in light of the widening discourse of global education. For many involved in Holocaust education, however, the most pressing questions do not concern its venues only, but its curriculum and pedagogy as well. What students learn from study of the Holocaust is not only a product of where they encounter it, but how.

Curriculum

This section focuses first on traditional materials that guide teachers' classroom choices: textbooks, educational literature, and packaged curricula. It then briefly considers alternative educational media forms like films, websites, and emerging technologies. For the sake of brevity, the discussion of curricula includes pedagogy, though the two are conceptually separable. The little that is known about student learning is also incorporated.

According to most educational literature, the majority of history teachers still rely on textbooks as their primary source of information despite the fact that textbooks are never neutral documents. Though written in a narrative voice to imply that they are balanced, textbooks are always value-laden. A sensitively rendered and methodologically impeccable comparison of textbook treatments appeared in 2007 in the form of Keith Crawford and Stuart Foster's study, *War, Nation, Memory: International Perspectives on World War II in School History Textbooks*. Having compared German and British textbook selections on the Holocaust, Crawford and Foster analyzed major themes represented in each. "It is not surprising," they write, "that in both England and Germany the content base for teaching the Holocaust is broadly similar as are the generic educational objectives couched in the all too often cliché-ridden language of democracy, freedom, and human rights" (26). Their analytic constructs encompass many of the dilemmas that all Holocaust educators face, for example: whether Hitler's agency should be overstated or understated, whether personal accounts that students read should include perpetrators' testimonies or only victims', how resistance and rescue are included, and whether the Holocaust is compared, explicitly or implicitly, to other genocides or historical events. In regards to this last point, Crawford and Foster find that the legacies of different post-war commitments appear in textbook treatments of the Holocaust, such that German textbooks explicitly make contemporary connections to the event whereas British textbooks tend not to. Their examinations of the massacre of Nanjing within Chinese textbooks, "responsibility and victimhood" in Japanese textbooks, and resistance and collaboration in French textbooks are not only important on their own terms but also for what they suggest about the imprints of nationhood on Holocaust education writ large. The study of textbook treatments is unquestionably important, and much more needs to be done, but more research on the reception of such treatments is also necessary given that we know that the complexities of students' identities influence their textual interpretations.

The Diary of Anne Frank and Elie Wiesel's *Night* are popularly believed to be the most widely read and consistently assigned texts for teaching about the Holocaust through literature. Given the worldwide popularity of these books, Sam Wineburg has cleverly labeled a Holocaust education phenomenon, "Victim as Curriculum," by which he means that the major works used to teach about this atrocity have been and remain memoirs that focus on survivors' perspectives exclusively. In this formulation, the survivor is the teacher, and the readers, the students. In high school classrooms, the most frequently shown educational film about the Holocaust, certainly since the Shoah Foundation distributed copies to all American high schools free of charge, is *Schindler's List*. By focusing mainly on the oversized character of Oskar Schindler, the film encourages identification with him as a rescuer. This conjunction of materials is not misplaced, but it may well be worth questioning. Some have referred to this tri-partite constellation of larger-than-life iconic figures as a trinity (of sorts): with Schindler cast as the father-figure, Elie Wiesel in the position of the son, and Anne Frank as the ghostly victim. The array importantly leaves out sympathetic representations of perpetrators, bystanders, or collaborators, which when coupled with the typical neglect of anti-Semitism and the glossing over of Jewish complexity, turns out to be a consistent theme in teaching and learning about the Holocaust outside of Germany.

As "curricular creep" has moved the Holocaust into lower and lower grade levels, a host of new materials for young audiences has emerged in the form of a "literature of atrocity" (Baer, 2000). Lydia Kokkola (2003) and Adrienne Kertzer (2002) have reviewed many of the literature choices in this body, considering what it is that these texts teach. Among the incisive questions both ask are why victims in Holocaust fiction for young people are so often girls. As Kertzer explains, "if we persist in thinking that children need hope and happy endings... then we will need to consider narrative strategies... that give child[ren] a double narrative, one that simultaneously respects our need for hope and happy endings even as it teaches a different lesson about history" (2002, pp. 74–75). While insightful readings of literature and films designed for young audiences are beginning to find authors (Baron, 2003), more educational research is needed to investigate students' understandings and teachers' uses of these materials. Which texts are typically used in Jewish settings versus non-Jewish settings and why? Which materials tend to generate which kinds of reactions among children of different denominations? Jeremy Stoddard's (2007) analysis of teachers' uses of Hollywood films as tools for teaching history is here the exception, as it demonstrates teachers' beliefs in films as projected truth-tellings. The expansion of Holocaust-themed graphic novels alone begs for comparative research across genres and geographic contexts, asking for example, whether students' repeated study of the Holocaust alone can lead to "Holocaust fatigue" (Short & Reed, 2004: p. 67) or whether it is the repeated viewing of filmic materials that produces this phenomenon.

Official curricular packages comprise a third major source of teacher knowledge and know-how, and many have been thoroughly critiqued and evaluated. In the USA, *Facing History and Ourselves* (FHAO) will provide schools with an entire comprehensive Holocaust curriculum that includes audio-visual materials, testimonies, specialized textbooks, and workbooks. FHAO has been critiqued variously for its universalistic orientation and its drawing of inapplicable comparisons (Lipstadt, 1995), but teachers report satisfaction in using their materials, being well supported by FHAO staff, and being impressed by their students' learning. FHAO, however, is a costly program, which makes it inaccessible to poorly funded schools. The Shoah Foundation's sales of more than 14,000 interactive CD-ROMs designed to teach about the Holocaust are in the process of being evaluated. Most US states that mandate Holocaust education provide state-based Holocaust curricula as well, which vary in quality. The US Holocaust Museum and many smaller, city-based Holocaust centers also provide curricular materials and educational services. Thus, the Houston Holocaust Museum designed "teaching trunks" that contain Spanish-language materials to be shipped to Latin American countries where such resources on the Holocaust are scarce. How such materials are used, how they contribute to (or detract from) student learning, and what they include and exclude all deserve to be researched, and not only in the USA. Moreover, curricula specifically designed for Jewish school settings deserve devoted scrutiny in terms of what they include and exclude, and what coverage patterns symbolically convey about Jews, non-Jews, and their relationships in history and the present.

Dan Magilow (2007) has labeled "a new trend in Holocaust education... memorial collecting, whereby groups, often student groups, accumulate six million of a particular object (such as paper clips, buttons, or shoes) to symbolize the murdered" (23). Magilow has postulated that these projects, though well-intentioned teachers design them with the aim of fostering empathy, can become symbolically problematic, fetishistically pursued accounting exercises, empty of educative import. As Magilow argues, however, even when they are overly commercialized and somewhat obsessive, the efforts themselves may be worth celebrating as kitsch.

The richness of online environments has enabled new forms of educational materials on the Holocaust to proliferate, which, as with most new technologies, have as yet to be fully investigated by social scientists. Researchers and graduate students at the University of South Florida designed a web-based instructional site for in-service and pre-service teachers (Calandra, Fitzpatrick, & Barron, 2002: p. 78). Utilizing an experimental methodology, these researchers found the site to wield only a small impact on teachers' ideas and practice, after which they concluded that sustained engagement with new technology would be required to change teachers' habits in any significant way (Kern, 2001; Lincoln, 2003). Other technologies that may be used to study the Holocaust, such as interactive geographic maps, streamed testimony excerpts, online discussion, social-networking and social action sites (Manfra & Stoddard, 2008), online groups, and GPS-based interactive technologies have all emerged in the last few years. Such new forms require the development of new research methods to study them. At the time of this writing, the vast majority of Holocaust-based video games feature anti-Semitic plotlines and contrivances, but when interactive video environments are designed to educate toward worthwhile goals, these will merit research as well.

Reflections

As a new field, Holocaust education research is still in its infancy, and much more work remains, preferably research that includes the reception of Holocaust teaching among students rather than solely its production by teachers or curriculum writers. Preferably, too, the new generation of researchers will pursue comparative research agendas that broaden the national contexts and ideological locales of Holocaust education. Much more work needs to be done on what Holocaust education looks like in Jewish school settings in particular. In terms of teacher training and practices, curricular materials and usage, and student learning and impact, it seems as though there are consistent themes across venues. The history of anti-Semitism tends to be avoided, the range of pre- and post-Shoah Jewish life tends to be underplayed, and Germans, Nazis, collaborators, and other perpetrators and bystanders tend to be vilified rather than treated with nuance, empathy, or understanding. Most Holocaust education efforts have also focused on victims' experiences rather than aiming to understand perpetrators' choices to the detriment of students' great potential for learning. Of course, these biases function within particular regional frames; Holocaust education efforts taking place in Rwanda vs. those which occur in the former Yugoslavia, for example, are necessarily very different projects, bound up with very different political aims, cultural goals, and beliefs about learning. Given that the new millennium did not see the end of genocidal violence, it seems worth asking what Holocaust education should and can do, and then to build research on its effects. What might Holocaust education do if conceptualized not within the frame of building nations but as a project of global citizenship and human understanding? What might students of the Holocaust learn if the goal is not to understand themselves but others? What might Holocaust education accomplish if, in Jewish contexts, it was not about creating Jewish identity in any narrow sense but rather Jewish coexistence in its most radically expansive form? More research holds out the hope of finding a shorter path to a more humane world.

References

Baer, E. (2000). A new algorithm in evil: Children's literature in a post-holocaust world. *The Lion and the Unicorn, 24*, 378–401.
Baron, L. (2003). Not in Kansas anymore: Holocaust films for children. *The Lion and the Unicorn, 27*, 394–409.
Baumel, J. T. (2002). 'Can two walk together if they do not agree?' Reflections on Holocaust studies and gender studies. *Women: a cultural review, 13*(2), 195–206.

Bensoussan, G.. Dec. 13 (2004). "It Began with Students Denying the Holocaust", *The Jerusalem Report*.
Berlak, A. (1999). Teaching and testimony: Witnessing and bearing witness to racisms in culturally diverse classrooms. *Curriculum Inquiry*, 29(1), 99–127.
Bernard-Donals, M., & Glejzer, R. (2001). *Between witness and testimony: The Holocaust and the limits of representation*. Albany, NY: State University of New York Press.
Braiterman, Z. (1999). Teaching jewish studies in a radically gentile space: Some personal reflections. *Religious Education*, 94(4), 396–409.
Britzman, D. (1998). *Lost subjects, contested objects: Toward a psychoanalytic inquiry of learning*. Albany, NY: State University Press of New York.
Brown, M., & Davies, I. (1998). The Holocaust and education for citizenship: The teaching of history, religion and human rights in England. *Educational Review*, 50(1), 75–83.
Burtonwood, N. (2002). Holocaust memorial day in schools– context process and content: A review of research into Holocaust education. *Educational Research*, 44(1), 69–82.
Calandra, B., Fitzpatrick, J., & Barron, A. E. (2002). A Holocaust website: Effects on preservice teachers' factual knowledge and attitudes toward traditionally marginalized groups. *Journal of Technology and Teacher Education*, 10(1), 75–93.
Carrington, B., & Short, G. (1997). Holocaust education, anti-racism and citizenship. *Educational Research*, 49(3), 271–282.
Caruth, C. (Ed.) (1995). *Trauma: Explorations in memory*. Baltimore: The John Hopkins University Press.
Cowan, P., & Maitles, H. (2002). Developing positive values: A case study of Holocaust memorial day in the primary schools of one local authority in Scotland. *Educational Review*, 54(3), 219–229.
Cowan, P., & Maitles, H. (2007). Does addressing prejudice and discrimination through Holocaust education produce better citizens? *Educational Review*, 59(2), 115–130.
Crawford, K. A., & Foster, S. J. (2007). *War, nation, memory: International perspectives on World War II in school history textbooks*. Charlotte, NC: Information Age Publishing, Inc.
Dawidowicz, L. (1992). How They Teach the Holocaust. In L. Dawidowicz (Ed.), *What is the use of jewish history?* (pp. 65–83). New York: Schocken Books.
Donnelly, M. B. (2006). Educating students about the Holocaust: A survey of teaching practices. *Social Education*, 70(1), 51–54.
Ellsworth, E. A. (2005). *Places of learning: media, architecture, Pedagogy*. New York: Routledge Falmer.
Faber, M. (1996). Teaching a multidisciplinary course on the Holocaust and German culture. *Annals of the American Academy of Political and Social Science*, 548, 105–115.
Fallace, T. D. (2008). *The emergence of Holocaust education in American schools*. New York: Palgrave Macmillan.
Farnham, J. (1983). Ethical ambiguity and the teaching of the Holocaust. *The English Journal*, 72(4), 63–68.
Feldman, J. (1997). 'Above the death-pits and with the flag of Israel waving on high'– the structure and meaning of Israeli youth missions to Poland of the Shoah. In H. Schreier & H. Matthais (Eds.), *Never again!: The holocaust's challenge for educators* (pp. 117–132). Hamburg: Kramer.
Fine, M. (1995). *Habits of mind: Struggling over values in America's classrooms*. San Francisco: Jossey-Bass.
Firer, R. (1998). Human rights in history and civics textbooks: The case of Israel. *Curriculum Inquiry*, 28(2), 195–208.
Friedlander, H. (1979). Toward a methodology of teaching about the Holocaust. *Teacher's College Record*, 81(3), 519–542.
Friedrichs, C. R. (1996). Teaching the unteachable: A Canadian perspective. *Annals of the American Academy of Political and Social Science*, 548, 94–104.

Gourevitch, P.. (1993, July). *Behold now behemoth– the Holocaust Memorial Museum: One More American Theme Park*.

Greenbaum, B. A. (2001). *Bearing witness: Teaching about the Holocaust*. Portsmouth, NH: Boynton/Cook.

Halperin, I. (1986). Teaching the Holocaust by indirection. *Judaism, 35*, 441–446.

Haynes, S. (1998). Holocaust education at American colleges and universities: A report on the current situation. *Holocaust and Genocide Studies, 12*(2), 282–307.

Hazan, H. (2001). The three faces of the Holocaust: A comparative discussion on the preparation of students of different schools for the Voyages to Poland. *Panim, 11*, 66–75.

Hirsch, M., Kacandes, I. (Eds.) (2007). *Teaching the representation of the Holocaust*. New York: Modern Languages Association Publishers.

Ivanova, E. (2004). Ukrainian high school students' understanding of the Holocaust. *Holocaust and Genocide Studies, 18*(3), 402–420.

Juzwik, M. (2009). *A rhetoric of teaching: Performing Holocaust narratives in a literacy classroom*. Cresskill, NJ: Hampton Press.

Kern, H. (2001). An end to intolerance: Exploring the Holocaust and Genocide. *The English Journal, 91*(2), 100–103.

Kertzer, A. (2002). *My mother's voice: Children, literature, and the Holocaust*. Peterborough, ON: Broadview Press.

Kokkola, L. (2003). *Representing the Holocaust in children's literature*. New York: Routledge.

Kugelmass, J. (1993). The rites of the tribe: The meaning of Poland for American Jewish tourists. In *YIVO annual, going home (*Vol. 10). Evanston, IL: Northwestern University Press.

Lazar, A., Chaitlin, J., Gross, T., & Bar-On, D. (2004). Jewish Israeli teenagers, national identity, and the lessons of the Holocaust. *Holocaust and Genocide Studies, 18*(2), 188–204.

Lincoln, M. (2003). The Holocaust project: A media specialist's success story in online resource use, staff collaboration, and community outreach. *MultiMedia Schools, 10*(4), 32–36.

Lipstadt, D. (1995). Not facing history. *The New Republic, 212*(26).

Magilow, D. H. (2007). Counting to six million: Collecting projects and Holocaust memorialization. *Jewish Social Studies, 14*(1), 23–40.

Maitles, H., & Cowan, P. (1999). Teaching the Holocaust in primary schools in Scotland: Modes, methodology and content. *Educational Review, 51*(3), 263–272.

Manfra, M., & Stoddard, J. (2008). Powerful and authentic digital media and strategies for teaching about Genocide and the Holocaust. *The Social Studies, 99*(6), 260–264.

Mansilla, V. B. (1998). Beyond the lessons from the cognitive revolution. *Canadian Social Studies, 32*, 49–51.

Misco, T. (2008). 'We did also save people': A Study of Holocaust education in Romania after decades of historical silence. *Theory and Research in Social Education, 36*(2), 61–94.

Morris, M. (2001). *Curriculum and the Holocaust: Competing sites of memory and representation*. Mahwah, NJ: Lawrence Erlbaum.

Parsons, W. S., & Totten, S. (1993). *Guidelines or Teaching about the Holocaust*, United States Holocaust Memorial Museum, Washington, D.C.

Porat, D. (2004). From the scandal to the Holocaust in Israeli education. *Journal of Contemporary History, 39*(4), 619–636.

Romi, S., & Lev, M. (2007). Experiential learning of history through youth journeys to Poland: Israeli Jewish youth and the Holocaust. *Research in Education, 78*, 88–102.

Ruchniewicz, K. (2000). "Die Darstellung des Holocausts in polnischen Schulbuchern fur die Oberschulen in nen 90er Jahren," International Conference in Buchenwald (Weimer), September 24–26. As noted in Crawford & Foster 2007b, p. 38.

Schatzker, C. (1982). The Holocaust in Israeli education. *International Journal of Political Education, 5*(1), 75–82.

Schneider, M.. (2006, October 11). *South African province makes teaching of Holocaust*.

Schweber, S. (2004). *Making sense of the Holocaust: Lessons from classroom practice*. New York: Teacher's College Press.

Schweber, S. (2008a). 'Here there is no why': Holocaust education at a Lubavitch girls' Yeshivah. *Jewish Social Studies, 14*(2), 156–185.

Schweber, S. (2008b). 'What happened to their pets?': Third graders encounter the Holocaust. *Teacher's College Record, 110*(10), 2073–2115.

Schweber, S., & Irwin, R. (2003). 'Especially special': Learning about Jews in a fundamentalist christian school. *Teacher's College Record, 105*(9), 1693–1719.

Schweitzer, F. (2000). 'Education after Auschwitz'– perspectives from Germany. *Religious Education, 95*(4), 360–370.

Shamai, S., Yardeni, E., & Klages, B. (2004). Multicultural education: Israeli and German adolescents' knowledge and views regarding the Holocaust. *Adolescence, 39*(156), 765–778.

Shawn, K. (1995). Current issues in Holocaust education. *Dimensions: A Journal of Holocaust Studies, 9*(2), 15–18.

Sheramy, R. (2003). "Resistance and war": The Holocaust in American Jewish education, 1945–1960. *American Jewish History, 91*(2), 287–313.

Short, G. (2003). Lessons of the Holocaust: A response to the critics. *Educational Review, 55*(3), 277–287.

Short, G., & Reed, C. A. (2004). *Issues in Holocaust Education*. Hampshire: Ashgate.

Stoddard, J. (2007). Attempting to understand the lives of others: Film as a tool for developing historical empathy. In A. Marcus (Ed.), *Celluloid blackboard: Teaching history with film* (pp. 187–214). Charlotte, NC: Information Age Publishing.

Tinberg, H. (2005). Taking (and teaching) the Shoah personally. *College English, 68*(1), 72–89.

Totten, S. (2002). *Holocaust education: Issues and approaches*. Boston, MA: Allyn & Bacon Publishers.

Totten, S. & Riley, K. (2005). Authentic Pedagogy and the Holocaust: A critical review of state sponsored Holocaust curricula. *Theory and Research in Social Education, 33*, 120–141.

Westermann, E. (1996). The Holocaust course at the united states air force academy. *Annals of the American Academy of Political and Social Science, 548*, 116–122.

Wink, K. (2006). A lesson from the Holocaust: From bystander to advocate in the classroom. *English Journal, 96*(1), 84–89.

Israel Education: Purposes and Practices

Alick Isaacs

The Need for Theory

Like the State of Israel itself "Israel Education" seems to have evolved as an area of practice that desperately needs a clearer sense of direction and purpose. Again, like Israel itself, the teaching of Israel seems to generate more questions than it does answers. The result is that many educators are deeply committed to the idea that Israel must feature in their curricula while they are often hard put to explain why and to what ends.

It perhaps seems clear to an older generation of educators that Israel programming is just one of the ways Jewish education is done. (This is particularly true in informal Jewish education where young *madrichim shlichim* from Israel have played a central role in making ad hoc curricular decisions for decades.) But, as much of the recent sociological research shows, the firm and central place of Israel in the future of Jewish education should not be taken for granted.[1] Many feel alienated and distant from Israel – if not even put off by it – and choose to avoid teaching about it in both formal and informal Jewish educational settings. It is in these circumstances that the lack of a rich theoretical conversation about the purposes of Israel education is starting to show.

A. Isaacs (✉)
Hebrew University, Jerusalem, Israel
e-mail: msaliki@mscc.huji.ac.il

[1] This has been widely demonstrated in studies with a particular focus on the United States. See for example (Cohen, 2008; Cohen & Kelman, 2007a), also (Chazan & Cohen, 2000, pp. 76–82). From these studies the picture emerges that less than 25% of North American Jews younger than 35 define themselves as Zionists. More than 60% of North American Jewry has never visited Israel and furthermore, a very large portion of them no longer considers Israel to be a major component in their Jewish identity. Having said this it is important to mention that there is some debate about the social reality. See for example (Saxe, Phillips, Sasson, Hecht, Shain, Wright, and Kadushin, 2009) who argue that the Birthright trips to Israel have a profound effect of deepening attachment to Israel among its alumni. Given that this study is confined to Birthright alumni, it is hard to determine how significant the widespread ripple effect of these findings might be.

The absence of theoretical clarity in Israel education is perhaps most acutely felt where a teacher or principal must overcome either estrangement from or opposition to Israel in a Jewish educational setting. But indifference and ideological opposition to Israel are by no means the only obstacles that theoretical clarity might help overcome. Even in institutions where commitment to the importance of Israel is high, a clear sense of exact purpose is still required to justify the allocation of time to Israel at the expense of the other disciplines. Finally, even in an institution where Israel's place in the curricular pecking order is firm, a clear vision of the educational goals for the teaching of Israel is still essential for making informed choices about *which* aspects of Israel to teach, how to teach them, and how to measure educational success.

The subject matter of Israel education is both extremely varied and extraordinarily hard to define. A cursory list of academic disciplines that might come under the rubric of Israel Education could easily include History, Political Science, Geography, Bible, Talmud, Jewish Thought, Jewish Law, Economics, Sociology, Law, Folklore, Food, Group Dynamics (e.g., *mifgash*), Music, Dancing, Song, Environmental Studies, Archeology, and many more. In addition to this remarkable spread of subject matter choices, the complexity of the questions in the field is quite an imposition on the teacher's capacity to make informed curricular choices.

Practitioners in the field of Israel education ultimately need theoretical debate because the practice of Israel education brings them face to face with some of the most confusing and confounding questions in contemporary Jewish life: What is the meaning of Israel today? How has this meaning changed in recent times and how does this change affect Jewish life, culture, and education today? Is Zionism still ideologically viable? Can it be compelling in Diaspora Jewish education? How is Israel education affected by such issues as the rights and wrongs of the Arab–Israel conflict, the Jewishness of the Jewish State, the secular/religious tensions in Israel, and the socioeconomic justice of Israeli society? The list goes on. All of these questions require immensely rich theoretical treatment.

There is a noticeable gap between the frequency with which Israel appears in the practice of Jewish education around the world and the theoretical sophistication with which the questions raised by this field are discussed in the academy. Israel educators need theory because so many of the issues that we know as part and parcel of the seemingly intractable complexity of the social, religious, and political debates in Israel today are also the unavoidable questions of Israel education. Bridging this gap by addressing the real questions of Israel's meaningful purpose today is the primary theoretical challenge that the field of Israel education must face.

Asking the Right Questions

As we move in to take a closer look at how Israel education is discussed theoretically today, it seems quite clear (though regrettably so) that the field is dominated by an overwhelming tendency to define the problems of Israel education in primarily pedagogical terms. Teachers have tended to assume that the difficulties they encounter engaging their students with Israel-related subject matter can be countered by the use of more exciting and stimulating teaching aids. Despite all the games, videos, and creative use of interactive websites, the confusion has not subsided and the crisis of teaching about Israel has not been alleviated. It is my view that persistent and repeated attention to the "wrong" questions (i.e., the exclusively pedagogical ones) has led the field astray. One of the purposes of a renewed theoretical debate about Israel education must be to redirect the attention of educators back to the "right" questions. These *are* the philosophical, historical, sociological, political, religious, and ideological issues that Israel's complex reality raises and *are not* those that emerge from the difficulties teachers encounter making Israel appealing or meaningful for kids in the classroom. When I say this I am basically agreeing with Barry Chazan who argues that,

> ... the core of the problem is not about instructional materials, pedagogy or didactics... You cannot "do" Jewish education very well without clear content and stances. Education generally – and certainly Jewish education – demands normative content, values, and "meaning making." In no way have these requirements been met with regard to teaching Israel. Until this is changed, we are doomed to decades more of one-day pedagogic seminars on "how to teach about the kibbutz "or the like. (Chazan, Schechter's Lament, 2004)

According to Chazan, the emphasis on instructional materials has led the field to ask the wrong questions about its own problems. The answers to these questions have produced a bundle of misguided assumptions that are the root cause of (what Chazan sees as) an entirely inadequate range of educational responses. Examples of *wrong* questions that took hold of the field include the following: "How do we get our students to love/support/care about Israel?" or "How can we equip our students with the answers they will need when forced to defend Israel on campus?" or "How can we use Israel effectively as a weapon in the fight against assimilation?" None of these is up to the task of what Chazan calls "meaning-making." None of these questions takes our students any further along the road toward making sense of Israel herself.

A brief contrast of Israel education with its predecessor – Zionist education – might help illustrate how a clearer broad conception of the field helps articulate the questions that can crystallize an educational sense of purpose. A glance back at Israel education's history will reveal an age of relative clarity (though not one of conformity and agreement) that coincided more or less with the plain equation of Israel's meaning with Zionist ideology. As long as Israel's ideological significance was self-evidently cast in Zionist terms the traditional Zionist alternatives that presented themselves to Israel educators were obvious. More importantly, they were also engaging for educators and students alike. Israel was taught within a context of larger meanings that were clear to everyone in the field. Different attitudes to Israel's purpose and meaning could be neatly divided into group identities and even youth movement affiliations. Each approach had its own literature, songs, folklore, and ideological heritage – each of which represented a different "mythical" or "romantic" vision of the Zionist State. From these clear ideological visions, clear educational practices, traditions, and pedagogical approaches ensued.

But, what kind of meaning-making will help give clarity to Israel education today? How can we talk about "meaning" when both educators and students are confronted with so much less than a normative understanding of Israel everywhere they turn? In an era of dramatic disenchantment with ideology in the West, what system of meaning-making is broad enough and deep enough to replace Zionism? In an age when Israel education is deeply affected by the accessibility of information – where the *so-called* real Israel is in everybody's reach (via the Internet, electronic media, and 'Israel Experience' educational travel to Israel) – how can a meaningful, ideal or mythical vision of Israel ever take hold?

My purpose in raising these questions is twofold:

a. to suggest that Israel education is difficult because the subject matter in the field has moved beyond its era of simplistic idealism and into an age of complex realism
b. to state my opinion that ideology – which we must remember can be both complex and realistic – is still essential to the successful practice of Israel education.

Let's briefly consider each of these:

a. Israel education is such a particularly difficult practice to theorize precisely because the primary issues that need to be addressed today are the same as the fundamental "ideological" questions that the Jewish world as a whole needs to explore in terms of its relationship with Israel. Israel poses very real challenges to educators as thinking people and not just pedagogical questions they must deal with in their teaching. Israel generates the most complex, important, and radical shifts in Jewish thought that the Jewish people face today at a time when teaching about it is sometimes very awkward.
b. In the absence of a broad ideological system that explains the necessity of Israel – its moral and ethical standing, its purpose in the world, its consistency with the Jewish tradition, and its promise for the Jewish future – how can the story of a small conflicted island of Jewish life in the Middle East that faces existential challenges from within and from without ever be made compelling? This pedagogical question that is so often asked in the field is really an ideological one. In order to answer it, we must imagine that our concern is not simply with teaching about Israel but with the challenge of replacing or rejuvenating Zionism. The ultimate obstacle to success in Israel education is predicated upon what I see as the indispensability of ideology to the telling of Israel's story. The State of Israel owes its existence to an ideology. Ideology is so central to its genealogy that anything less than an ideological message from "Israel education" strikes me as inadequate to the task of giving Israel a clear meaning and purpose in the Jewish lives of the next generation.

Working with these assumptions, I propose that *the right question* that demands rich theoretical attention and practical implementation in Israel education is this: *What ideas about Israel today are compelling enough to excite ideological commitment to it in a time when the complexities of its realities are so well-known?*

Theory Catching Up with Practice

This question has not been answered well by anyone writing theoretically about Israel Education. I shall return to it later in this discussion. But first I think it is important to point out that practitioners in the field are already responsible for significant shifts in the field that need to be noticed and conceptualized. This is what I mean by "theory catching up with practice."

With all the unresolved issues that plague Jewish life in Israel and Israel–Diaspora relations, it is hardly a surprise that educators have just pushed ahead developing curricula and building upon the well-tested practices of Israel education – such as the Israel trip, army day, Zionist history course, Yom Hazikaron/Ha'atzmaut ceremonies, falafel night, Israeli movie night, Israeli dancing, "Israel" and "Me" identity seminar – to try and make them better, more interesting, more relevant, and more fun. They have pushed on, adapting the old to suit the new without waiting for more contemporary theoretical frameworks to emerge. And who can blame them? They have programs to run and classes to teach each morning at school or camp, while the theoretical conversation about Israel education in the wider context of Israel's meaning today has hardly started and – even when it does get underway – will surely take a long time to yield educationally useful results.

It seems especially appropriate in a field where so much is already being done to think of the theoretical debate as one that must catch up with the work of practitioners. In this spirit, I believe it is worthwhile – before briefly suggesting a new ideological framework of my own – to give careful consideration to the possible ideological and theoretical directions implied by current practices in Israel education.

I would like to present a brief taxonomy that describes and critiques some of the dominant paradigms of Israel Education in theoretical and even ideological terms. I submit that this exercise will offer insights into the implicit intuitions of many educators about the new purposes of Israel Education and that these will help mark the starting point of the ideological discussions that I believe must ensue. As taxonomies go, the point of this one is a little unusual in that it seeks to work "backwards" gleaning "purposes" from "practices" and not the other way round.[2] The categories below have been assembled because the pedagogical choices

---

[2] The taxonomy depicting common pedagogical strategies used in the field of Israel Education that I shall present in this section is hypothetical. The list is illustrative, not exhaustive. While it does reflect actual curricula and observed practices, it is not the product of a systematic survey done in the field. As a result, I shall make no attempt to describe educational practices and pedagogies in detail.

made in each one reflect distinct visions of Israel's ideological meaning. After discussing each category separately, I shall attempt to draw general conclusions about them all.

I propose dividing up the "purposes and practices" of Israel Education into six models:

1. The Classical Zionist model
2. The Israel Engagement Model
3. The Jewish Peoplehood Model
4. The Romantic/Realist Model
5. The Classical Jewish Text Model
6. The Comparative Model

1. The Classical Zionist Model – In this model, the State of Israel is understood as the culmination of Jewish History and the solution to the Jewish problem. The advantage of this approach is its clarity of purpose that we have already discussed above. This model builds upon an educational tradition that has been well established during more than 100 years of Zionist educational activity. The totality and centrality that it extends toward the meaning of Israel in every aspect of Jewish life, past, present, and future is perhaps unparalleled in its scope by any other theoretical or ideological position articulated in modern Jewish life. However, within the context of this discussion it is important to distinguish a naïve approach to Israel education – that embraces classical Zionism as its organizing principle – and one that seeks to *reassert* the validity of Zionism within a context in which it has come under attack.

Significant questions have been raised about the validity of the classical Zionist vision. In particular the ethical plausibility of Zionism's totality has been challenged. Oppositional voices have called into question the ethics of Zionism's exclusive approach to the "Jewish" right of settlement in the Holy land.[3] Similar, but more subtle claims have been made for the colonialist nature of the Zionist aspiration, as well as its Ashkenazi ethnocentrism. Finally, though by no means least significantly, pro-Diaspora (and perhaps also assimilationist) voices have criticized Zionism's totality on the grounds that it is blind to and intolerant of the different forms of Jewish life evolving outside of Israel.[4] The "Classical Zionist" model seeks to combat these critiques with renewed efforts to diagnose them as the cultural

---

[3]The discussion of the ethics of Zionism's totality was particularly precipitated by Edward Said's *Orientalism* that provoked a striking Israeli response. See for example Kalmar and Penslar (2005). This ideological position was championed by the so-called New Historians whose reanalysis of the events of 1948 underlined the inability of the founders of the state to identify the claims of the Palestinian people to both national identity and self-determination in the land of Israel as morally viable. See for example, Morris (1995, 1999, 2004) and Pappe (1992)

[4]Some of the most prolific critiques of this "blindness" are carefully analyzed by Laurence Silberstein (1999). For a detailed critique of the Zionist negation of the exiles and its implications for the questions of Israel's internal culture see (Raz-Krakotzkin, 2005)

"problem" that Israel education must help overcome.[5] In other words, the classical Zionist model comes to combat a weakening of Zionist conviction by reasserting its own validity as the answer to the critiques that it itself must face. In this sense the uninhibited reproduction of classical Zionist educational practices promotes a "tight"[6] social identity designed to withstand adversity and generate a "masculine" ethos of cultural (but also military) heroism.[7]

2. The Israel Engagement Model – The shift from the Classical Zionist to the Israel Engagement model is perhaps the most obvious and visible development in the field of Israel education as practised in the past two or three decades. In many ways, this model reconstitutes the claims of classical Zionism in terms that are understood by its proponents as more complex, nuanced, and indeed realistic. According to this model, the Zionist movement must retract its claims against the viability of the Diaspora and acknowledge the vitality of the new forms of Jewish life that are generated outside the State of Israel. Similarly, the Israel Engagement model seeks to retract the over-ambitious claims of the Zionist movement to solve the problems of assimilation and anti-Semitism. However, within the more realistic context that these two retractions create, the Israel Engagement model seeks to reclaim ground lost on precisely these two issues by reasserting the centrality of the educational encounter with Israel to the formulation of Diaspora Jewish identity and to the struggle against both spiritual and physical adversity in contemporary Jewish life (Gringras, 2006). In this model, "Israel" is a quintessential resource for Jewish education. It is in Israel that communal Jewish life and contemporary Jewish culture are most publicly on display. In Israel Judaism is most significantly pushed, tested and challenged, and most compellingly connected to claims of authenticity about the Jewish past (Margolis, 2005).

The Israel Engagement model is often criticized for its "instrumentalization" of Israel.[8] Israel as it appears in contemporary Jewish life as well as in history, literature, etc., is turned into an educational playground for Jewish exploration. While this approach is perhaps not the most conducive one to gaining a rich, mature, and sophisticated grasp of all that Israel's contemporary and historical reality might

---

[5]One of the more outspoken proponents of this approach is Gil Troy. See for example Zionist Dreams (2002)

[6]My use of "tight" in this context echoes Erving Goffman's (1971) xiii.

[7]An example of this is Tuvia Book's curriculum, *For the Sake of Zion* (2004). The curriculum emphasizes Zionist Jewish heroism with a particularly striking emphasis on male and military role models.

[8]Lisa Grant voiced this criticism in an unpublished paper submitted to the Think Tank on Israel Education that I organized at the Melton Centre for Jewish Education in the Hebrew University in January 2008. Grant writes, "I hardly mean to suggest that using Israel as a means of building and reinforcing Jewish identity is a bad thing. Neither do I mean to belittle or diminish the impact that Israel experiences have had on participants. Nonetheless, from an educational perspective, this instrumental focus on Jewish identity seems incomplete, not to mention the fact that in congregational schools, day schools, and Jewish summer camps Israel education seems to have had little or no impact on how American Jews' attitudes towards Israel are shaped."

stand for, the overwhelming critique of this approach is not directed at its reductionism. From an educational point of view it seems to tackle some of the most direct problems in Diaspora Jewish life in a convoluted way. It seems far-fetched to imagine that identification with a distant and foreign complex reality is the key to Jewish continuity within the context of local Jewish life. As a result, proponents of this model are perennially challenged by the question, "Why Israel?" If the objective is to engage students with their own Jewish identities through powerful meaning-making experiences, why must these engage with the distance and ambivalence attached to Israel? Surely, more accessible alternatives could be found. It is perhaps for this reason that the Israel Engagement model might be perceived as disingenuous and manipulative in that its accommodating retractions are perhaps nothing more than tactical compromises that ultimately conceal ulterior – classically Zionist – educational objectives.

3. The Jewish Peoplehood Model – This approach to Israel education seeks to stitch the uniqueness and centrality of collective Jewish life in Israel into a broader fabric of globalized Jewish nationalism.[9] Ideologically, it might be compared to models of pre-Zionist nationalism proposed by thinkers such as Pinsker, Dubnov, and Kaplan. However, within the contemporary context, after the fact of the Jewish State's establishment, the peoplehood model must accommodate what is unique and special about the Jewish State without overemphasizing its privileged status. (Ariel, 2007; Brown & Galperin, 2009)

The peoplehood model of Israel education suggests that the State of Israel should be conceptualized as one of many possible frameworks of collective Jewish identity. In this sense Israel's status as a unique center of Jewish life is understood against the backdrop of all other collective forms of Jewish existence that are found elsewhere in the world. This construction is responsible for the tendency to give special attention to the North American and Israeli Jewish communities which sometimes comes at the expense of the other Jewish centers around the world. Most importantly, from the classical Zionist point of view, the peoplehood model tends to downplay the unique importance of Jewish sovereignty in the Holy Land.[10] Israel is generally recognized by most advocates of this model as a uniquely full and rich expression of the collectivist and nationalist impulses of the Jewish people. Like the Israel Engagement model, proponents of peoplehood hope to redress the undemocratic imbalances of classical Zionism's attitudes to the communities of the Diaspora and articulate a non-ideological vision for embracing the present realities of Jewish demography (as far as the international spread of Jewish life is concerned). The offshoot of this approach is that its proponents must depend very heavily upon the leadership and guidance of sociologists whose surveys and studies monitor the heartbeat of the Jewish people. Since the emphasis of this approach is upon the Jewish people, the realities of how Jews actually live their lives lead

---

[9] A curricular example of this is a curriculum sponsored by the Jewish Agency (Israel, 2003).
[10] Dan Ehrenkrantz, "The Primacy of Peoplehood" *Contact* (Spring 2008). See also Brown and Galperin's discussion of Mordechai Kaplan's role in generating this model in ibid. 13–16

the way while values, ideals, and possibilities for the future are inappropriately marginalized.

It is hard to ignore the red squiggly line that Microsoft Word puts under the word "peoplehood" every time you type it. The option of removing the offensive squiggle by adding "peoplehood" to the dictionary is always there, but I confess that this is a temptation I have thus far chosen to resist. My point is that despite "peoplehood" being a term that has attracted a great deal of philosophical and legal attention (both inside and beyond Jewish circles), in my view proponents of peoplehood have not yet made a compelling case for its "authenticity" in Jewish culture. The idea that the Jewish people must take their lead from what Jewish people happen to think today (and not from Jewish values, texts, traditions, and ideas) is not one that I can easily recommend in this age of confusion, Jewish ignorance, and disillusion. Difficulties of translation into Hebrew (*ami'ut* being the best option available) only reinforce the irony of the general point.

4. The Romantic/Realist Model – The tension between mythology and realism is inherent to the history of Israel education (as it is indeed to the history of Israel herself). In its essence the history of the State of Israel is the story of an ancient mythological-utopian vision for the future taking the form of a concrete political reality in the present. Ultimately, much of the early opposition to the idea of building the Jewish State came from those who understood Zionism's realism as a pollution of Israel's ancient messianic heritage.

The practitioners of the Romantic/Realist model of Israel education understand that both mythology and realism are essential to the understanding of Israel's meaning and purpose. They seek to explore the tensions between the realm of the ideal and the world in which this realm is necessarily implemented imperfectly.[11] The educational strategy employed by the practitioners of this model seeks to forge a simultaneously ironic and sentimental relationship with Israel in which ideological convictions can be perpetuated without naïveté. An awareness of Israel's accomplishments that is accompanied by deep recognition of its flaws is essential to a healthy and balanced relationship with the idea of Israel in an age in which that ideal is no longer pure and unadulterated by political realism. This ironic awareness is seen as the key to maintaining a sense of ideological commitment to Israel that is robust enough to withstand the confusing experiences that many encounter as they come to know the real Israel better.

By the same token, in this approach Israel's flaws are to be treated with the same irony when these are presented in the context of a grand effort to do better and to improve the quality of Jewish collective existence in our time. (For example, Sarna, 1996, pp. 41–59.) The desired product of this educational approach is often referred to as a consciousness of "critical engagement" with Israel. Israel is presented as "a work in progress" desperately in need of both loyalty and sincere vehement criticism.

---

[11] The implementation of this model in American community day schools has been studied by Ezra Kopelowitz (2005)

5. *The Jewish Text Model* – This is an approach that is most commonly practised (though not exclusively so) in religious educational settings. Israel is (perhaps naively) understood as integral to the Jewish studies curriculum in ways that echo the treatment of Mitzvot, Breishit, or the laws of Shabbat. In this model Israel deserves attention in the Jewish studies curriculum simply because it is one of the classical foundations of Jewish belief and thought. The Land of Israel is one of the pillars of the Biblical covenant between God and the Jewish people. The land was promised to the Jewish people and it is therefore their religious and historical right to reclaim it today. The settlement of the Jewish people in the land is the primary point of overlap between the proponents of this approach and the Zionist idea. The state and the realities of statehood take a second place to the fulfillment of Judaism's historical role in the holy land. As such, the curricular content presented by the proponents of this approach pays little attention to the "on the ground" realities of the modern State of Israel. Instead, the subject matter that is emphasized is connected with the concept of Israel as it appears in Biblical and Classical Rabbinic texts. Israel is dealt with as the land of covenant and prophecy, the home of Jewish life in the times of the First and Second Temples, the site of the composition of the Mishna, the early Midrashic literature, and the Jerusalem Talmud. Such issues as the comparative importance of the centers of Torah learning in ancient Israel and Babylon might be explored with special reference to such themes as the exclusive right of scholars in Israel to determine the final form of the Jewish calendar. Israel is a land of pilgrimage and the home to such holy sites as the western wall and Mount Carmel.

In many cases this approach to Israel education is adapted to meet the challenge of facing Israel's recent secular political history. Israel is studied as a historical phenomenon in courses that deal with the precursors of Zionism such as Kallischer, early Zionist thinkers such as Ahad Ha'am and Herzl, the first Zionist congress, the Uganda debate, the waves of immigration (aliyot), the foundation of the state, the wars, the social map of Israeli society, and the Oslo peace process. While this kind of curriculum seems to be addressing contemporary Israel, it does so through a kind of historicism that absolves the teacher from engaging in the fundamental questions of Israel's meaning. In this sense, though the subject matter is modern history, it is similar to the mode of teaching about Israel that relies on more classical religious source material.

The primary challenge that this approach must face is how to contextualize the reading of classical and modern texts about Israel in contemporary Diaspora reality. This is an issue that is easily avoided, perhaps in the hope that no more than a deep religious or historical commitment to the land and to God's promise of Israel to the Jewish people is sufficient to the challenge of breeding a deep commitment to the modern Jewish State. Some variations of this approach stimulate discussion that invites comparisons between classical biblical rabbinic ideas about Israel and modern life. For example, the teaching of Joshua's conquest of the land might be taught in tandem along with the history of the aliyot and the War of Independence in 1948. Similarly, questions dealt with in rabbinic texts that touch upon the tension between the Jews of Babylon and the Jews of Israel might be considered in the context of contemporary Israel/Diaspora relations. But the question of how these comparisons might be incorporated in a compelling contemporary belief system is avoided through the conversion of "Israel" into a (recent or ancient) piece of historical subject matter.

6. The Comparative Model – This approach seeks to treat the State of Israel and the contemporary realities of Jewish political sovereignty as a resource for exploring "essential questions" in Jewish life. As in the "Jewish Text Model of Israel Education," this approach is characterized by its treatment of contemporary Israel as "subject matter." However, in the comparative model, subject matter associated with Israel is integrated into a broader discussion that is not exclusively focused upon "Israel" itself. For example an "essential question" in ethics about the correct distribution of charity may be examined through the study of certain biblical or rabbinic passages along with an analysis of a particular event or phenomenon in contemporary Israel. As such, the living breathing Judaism that is the public culture of the Jewish State is placed beside the classic texts of the Jewish tradition and is made open to analysis and discussion. However, in this approach, contemporary Israel emerges as one of the piecemeal resources that Jews look at when they want to think about issues in the world. Israel becomes a reference point for formulating contemporary Jewish thought in the Diaspora in the same way as the Talmud. This approach utilizes the richness of Jewish life in a sovereign state to allow Israel to emerge as an integral part of the exploration of contemporary Jewish identity.

By way of extension this approach may be used to introduce Israel related subject matter into discussions that address ethical or political dilemmas elsewhere. For example, a significant local question raised in an American, English, Argentinean, or Australian classroom might concern the environment, racism, road rage, conflict, or government. The question might be explored drawing upon local examples alone. It might also be explored in the context of Jewish studies through the analysis of pertinent Jewish texts. Similarly, contemporary examples of how the same environmental, political, social, or military issues are dealt with in Israel allow for a comparative exploration that establishes connections between the local context of the students' lives and the wider experience of Jewish culture in our time. In this approach, the State of Israel is the primary arena in the Jewish world today that raises pressing questions that motivate and contextualize the contemporary challenge of (re) interpreting the Jewish tradition. As such it is both the source of essential questions and a resource of their explication.

The primary challenge that this approach faces is the degree of abstraction that is necessary for its implementation. The questions raised are often hard to clarify while the pertinence of Israel to engaging with them is as challenging an issue here as it is in all of the non-ideological approaches to Israel education.

As I said earlier, this taxonomy is not the result of a broad survey. Rather, it is an attempt at conceptualization that both theoreticians and practitioners in the field might find helpful. It allows for the clear categorization of the dominant articulations of purpose that can be found in the field of Israel education. Though, it is often the case that a single curriculum might adopt two or more of these models and combine them.

If this taxonomy is in any way reflective of the most common practices in the field (and I believe it is) then it allows us to draw one clear and striking conclusion. The overwhelming characteristic that each of the models described here seems to share is that educators have implicitly recognized and adapted themselves to a reality in which they must teach about Israel in a post-ideological atmosphere. The six models outlined here can be understood as six answers to the question of why Israel still deserves educational attention. This question is tackled in one of two ways: The first of these – exemplified by the Classical Zionist model/the Israel Engagement Model/the Jewish Peoplehood Model/the Romantic-Realist Model – attempts to justify the importance of Israel by reconstituting components of classical Zionist ideology in the context of post-ideological Israel education. As such, these approaches argue respectively that "in spite of everything" (a) Zionism is still relevant, (b) Zionism today need not be offensive to Diaspora Jewish life, (c) Zionism should be seen as merely a special but not unique form of collective Jewish life, and (d) Zionism is a historical movement in need of post-ideologically ironic (but not cynical) review.

The second overall approach to the dissonance between Israel education's ideological charge and the current climate – exemplified by the Classical Jewish Text Model and the Comparative Model – seeks to justify Israel education in predominantly professional terms that bypass the challenge of reconstituting Zionism altogether. Thus it is appropriate to engage with Israel in Jewish education because the complexity and the richness of this area of Jewish subject matter allows for the acquisition of such skills as textual analysis, historical analysis, complex thought, ethical engagement, and complex abstract thinking. All of these are merits that might be evaluated in purely professional educational or developmental terms. It is these considerations that account for the curricular decisions in the field as in other fields such as general history, physics, or social science. In these two models the decision to dedicate time to the teaching of Israel is defensible without ideology.

The Gap Between Theory and Practice

Again, while we must remember that this discussion is analytical and theoretical (i.e., not empirical), this taxonomy seems to suggest a way of thinking about one of the more puzzling "empirical" questions in the field of Israel education. While it seems clear that there is a significant decline of interest in Israel (not to mention commitment to Israel) most particularly in the American Jewish communities (though not only), this decline is coming at a time when the field of Israel education is enjoying an unprecedented period of growth. The resources of time and money that are being dedicated to this field are consistently on the rise at a time when the problem that these resources are trying to tackle is not being alleviated.

I would like to suggest that the widespread evasion of Israel's ideological meaning for the future is not healthy and that passionate commitment to Israel will only be possible when the reasons for it are more apparent to educators and students alike. As such, the field of Israel education has a great deal of work to do in gaining this clarity. A rich and informative process of discussion and debate conducted at the Melton Centre for Jewish education in the Hebrew University during the course of 2007–2009 has facilitated what I believe is a useful articulation of how this work should be conducted. The academic study of Israel education needs to bridge the gap between theory and practice in three distinctive areas of research:

1. Israel Education Studies
2. Philosophy of Israel Education
3. Israel Education Design

1. Israel Education Studies addresses practices in Israel Education in a wide variety of educational settings (formal and informal for example, teaching of Israel in schools, university-level Israel Studies courses, informal activities in schools, camps, community events, adult education, synagogues, etc.,) as well as attitudes to Israel and its contemporary meaning fostered by educators, teachers, lay leaders, youth, graduates, and participants in Israel trips (such as Birthright, March of the Living, Youth Movement, and Israel Experience programs), among Jews of different denominations, in the media, etc. This is work that must rely heavily upon the academic disciplines of the social sciences such as sociology, anthropology, and ethnography and must engage in both qualitative and quantitative research in as many educational settings around the world as possible.
2. Philosophy of Israel Education addresses conceptualizations of Israel's meaning as expressed in classical and modern texts. The research in this field must attempt to conceptualize the different approaches to Israel's meaning as these appear in a variety of contemporary scholarly debates about the Jewish past while considering their implications for the present and the future. Understandings of Israel's meaning are also implicit in contemporary Israeli and international politics, media, contemporary literature, art, music, theatre, etc. In each of these fields, questions of political sovereignty, the establishment of Jewish public space, territorial conflict, religious and national conflict, human rights, minority rights, environmental responsibility, Israel and Diaspora relations, Jewish–Gentile relations, Hebrew language, contemporary (secular and religious) Zionism, Nationalism, Messianism, Jewish law, and Jewish philosophy are dealt with in thoughtful depth that could provide the practice of Israel education with a host of fresh ideas. A systematic conceptual analysis of the educational/ideological implications of this cultural/political/social activity is therefore essential to Israel Education's quest for future direction.
3. Israel Education Design addresses, proposes, or describes curricular models and taxonomies for implementing theories and philosophies of Israel Education in practical educational settings. It also evaluates the boundaries of the field vis-a-vis Bible education, Jewish history, Israel Advocacy etc., and proposes theoretical meanings and purposes for the practices of Israel education.

These categorizations help organize the potential contributions of academia to Israel education in ways that mirror the academic disciplines and expand our sense of which forms of study – which questions – are indeed applicable to the challenge of enriching the discussion about the teaching of Israel in the world today.

Renewing Ideological Commitment to Israel – Where Zionism and Peace Meet

Finally, I would like to return to the issue of tackling the "right" questions when attempting to give clarity to the field of Israel education. My proposal is that the "right" question is, what ideas about Israel today are compelling enough to excite ideological commitment to it in a time when the complexities of its realities are so well known? I believe that this is a question that should stimulate a great deal of discussion. This question invites many different answers each of which might subdivide into multiple points of view. My intention in beginning to discuss it here is therefore not to close down or negate alternative answers to my own, but to open up a debate by providing *an* answer that I find personally compelling and meaningful.

If an ideological discussion is still possible in the twenty-first century's post-ideological environment, it seems clear that the reasons for the rejection of ideological thinking as a mode of discourse must first be acknowledged and not ignored. The primary criticism leveled against ideology concerns the ethically questionable nature of a point of view that is either blinkered or unswerving in its commitments. By insisting that an ideological perspective must have something to say about the past, the present, and the future, it must encounter the challenges of articulating a method of interpretation, a critique, and a vision. It is this multidimensional approach to ideology that enforces a regime of hermeneutic accountability on any given perspective. It must have the capacity to support a varied and compelling interpretive analysis if it is going to compete, not only with other causes, but with other ways of understanding the world.

This chapter is not the place to expand upon this in too much detail, but I will say – perhaps cryptically – that I believe that the return to ideology is made possible by the post-modern critique of positivism (and its pseudo-scientific notion of a single truth) and by the possibilities that this critique creates for subjectivist understandings of phenomena to compete on an even field. In many ways, the successes of Zionism in the nineteenth and early twentieth centuries might be evaluated in terms of the Zionist movements capacity to articulate a clear methodology for interpreting the Jewish past, for critiquing vigorously the Jewish present, and for envisioning a better Jewish future. The same may be said for other ideological movements such as socialism and feminism. Zionism's fundamental flaw – which I suggest is connected to positivist ideas – is that its notion of the truth was necessarily exclusive of other understandings. Thus the idea of negating the Diaspora was of such decisive importance. That said, it is possible today to retract the absolute truth claims that ideologies necessitated in the context of positivist discourse without discrediting the validity of a given point of view. As a rule of thumb, I would suggest that these ideologies go wrong – or are indeed abused – when they function without self-criticism as a means of justifying an absolute truth claim especially if that focuses most particularly on the present and the recent past. However, when an ideology or a cause invites a broad interpretive vision that spans past, present, and future and indeed contains within it spheres of internal debate, ideology strikes me as a source of meaning, motivation, and purpose that should be celebrated and not feared.

In the context of contemporary Israel, I would like to propose here – very briefly – that the idea of making peace in the Middle East is one that can be developed into a rich ideological perspective in which the value of peace in Israel or Judaism as it appears in biblical rabbinic, kabalistic, and philosophical texts might be considered richly in ways that interpret the past, critique the present, and envision the future. The value of "peace" can be taken as the foundation of an interpretive prism that yields understandings of the entire Jewish religious heritage, as well as Zionist thought while at the same time proposing a vision for the future of Israel. The ideology of peace that I have in mind would understand Judaism and Zionism as oriented toward the accomplishment of peace in Israel, for Israel, and perhaps for the world.[12] The notion that the purpose of the Jewish State is "the up-building of peace" in the whole world was central to Buber's understanding of the Zionist movement's ideological purpose.[13] Like many other Zionist thinkers, Buber believed that normalcy was not a worthy objective for Jewish Statehood. He hoped that Zionism would allow for the implementation of Jewish ideas in politics. For Buber as indeed for Rav Kook and others, the Zionist vision was not one that could be accomplished through the establishment of the state alone. Indeed, a certain sense of ulterior purpose that echoes the messianic dimension of Zionist thought as it is seen in the writings of Ahad Ha'am Moshe Hess, Rav Kook, Gershom Scholem, Ernst Simon, and even Ben Gurion is easily connected with the prophetic visions of the Bible that epitomize the "politics of messianism" in ultimately peaceful terms.

Within the context of a richer discussion of Zionism's ultimate purpose as peace, the question of how to critique both the internal and external dimensions of the State of Israel's recent history becomes much clearer. The question is not simply one of right and wrong – land and compromise. The yardstick of "peace" as a Jewish concept is rich enough to contain a varied and nuanced debate about both the internal and external conflicts that Israel is connected to within the Jewish world and beyond it. The internal conflict over the Oslo agreements is a case in point. It exemplifies how a narrow understanding of peace became the subject of a violent existential debate. What I propose is a deep investigation into the richness of peace as a Jewish concept that might fuel a values debate similar to the one that took place 100 years ago over competing understandings about the meaning of Jewish Statehood.

---

[12]This idea echoes Immanuel Kant's conception of the modern state as a peacemaker. For a fascinating critique of the assumption, made most explicit in the writings of Thomas Hobbes, that secular nationalism can bring war to an end see William T. Cavenaugh (2009), pp. 314–337

[13]Martin Buber, wrote in his (1976) article, "The Spirit of Israel and the World of Today" 186, "Our purpose is the upbuilding of peace.... for only an entire nation, which comprehends peoples of all kinds, can demonstrate a life of unity and peace, of righteousness and justice to the human race..."

It is important to be clear here that the ideological debate I am proposing is not one that correlates simply with the contemporary political debate in Israeli politics over the conflict with the Palestinians. It is an ideological debate about how the State of Israel best fulfills the biblical, rabbinic, and indeed Zionist understanding of peace as a core Jewish concept. One might hope that such a debate would create a positive ideological energy for resolving conflict. But, this is not its exclusive purpose. Rather, it is connected to the ideological vision that the State of Israel might fulfill something very fundamental to Jewish values. "What does peace mean in classical Jewish texts?" is a core contemporary ideological question that might echo the nineteenth century question "Are the Jewish people a nation?" But, in the same way as one can easily distinguish between the answers given to that question and the political strategies that led to the foundation of the state, one may also distinguish between the ideological debate about the implementation of peace as a collective Jewish value and the political debate about settlements, security, refugees, and Jerusalem in a final status agreement. Answers to the ideological question of peace's meaning must tackle both the classical usages of the word and the phenomena associated with it (such as the biblical lying together of wolves and lambs) before engaging the visionary question, "how can the Jewish State give public meaning to this value?"

This discussion is only a sketch of something much more elaborate that I have begun proposing in a separate context. However, I think that this sketch is sufficient to the task of illustrating here how a contemporary idea about Israel might be developed into a full-blown ideological perspective that is both rich and varied as well as capable of generating criteria for clear curricular decision making and educational practice.

Concluding Remarks

In my view, the genuine confusion in the field of Israel education is only compounded by the widespread instrumentalization of Israel in Jewish education as part of the overwhelming effort to keep the next generation of Jews Jewish. "How can we use Israel to connect the next generations of Jews to their heritage?" is the wrong question to put to Israel in this time of confusion. The reverse effects of this strategy – the ones we tend to blame on CNN – are surely obvious. We invite the young generation to identify with a concrete reality that they have every opportunity to evaluate negatively for themselves and expect them to embrace it as if it were an unequivocally optimistic dream come true.

It is ironic, but the foundational idealism that made the establishment of the State of Israel possible is responsible for a general confusion between ideology and blind loyalism. Today's Zionists (and I count myself among them) are forced to stand alone against a hostile world convinced that nothing has really changed since the dark days of crusades and blood libels because it is a law of nature that "Esau will always hate Jacob." The alternative to this is seen as flaky and perhaps even a threat to the firm conservation of the Jewish future. This is ideology gone wrong. Ideology is abused when an establishment uses it to justify – rather than to change – its ways.

Ideology is only plausible when it broadens our view of the future not when it narrows our understanding of the recent past.

The challenge of Israel education as I see it is therefore the challenge of unraveling the confusion between ideology and reality in order to begin the search for a new ideological purpose that Israel's future can realistically "stand" for. I propose we start by thinking ideologically and educationally about peace. By this I mean peace as a dream that we seek to fill with Jewish content and reinvigorate with Zionist Jewish meaning. Today's "Jewish question" is, what does peace mean in Judaism? What did peace mean in the unfulfilled dreams of the great prophets, rabbis, and Zionist thinkers of the past? What should it mean across the Jewish world today? How can we – as educators – ensure that our heritage yields as rich an answer to these questions today as it once did to such classical Zionist questions as "What is Jewish sovereignty? How does Jewish history look if we tell it as the story of a nation?"

The educational coherence of teaching about Israel's present reality in a curriculum for Jewish education will come from a clearer sense of purpose about our ideological dreams for Israel's future. We need not fear criticizing Israeli society's part in its internal and external conflicts any more than classical Zionist education feared its critical evaluations of Diaspora Jewish life. But these critiques must leverage a hopeful imagining of a future in which our tradition's commitment to peace – like its dreams of self-determination 100 years ago – are finally given their day in history.

References

Ariel, J. (2007). Your people shall be my people: Notes on nurturing Jewish peoplehood. In *The peoplehood papers*. New York: UJC.
Book, T. (2004). *For the Sake of Zion: Pride and Strength Through Knowledge* published by the board of Jewish education in New York and the Jewish Agency.
Brown, E., & Galperin, M. (2009). *The case for Jewish peoplehood: Can we be one?* Woodstock, VT: Jewish Lights Publishing.
Buber, M. (1976). *Israel and the world: Essays in a time of crisis*. New York: Schocken Books.
Cavenaugh William, T. (2009). The wars of religion and the rise of national state. In J. Milbank & S. Oliver (Eds.), *The radical orthodox reader*. London and New York: Routledge.
Chazan, B. (2004). "Schechter's Lament: Israel and Jewish Education Once Again" in, *Agenda: Jewish Education* 18 (Winter 2004) 4–6
Chazan, B., & Cohen, S. M. (2000). What we know about American Jewish youth: Some implications for birthright Israel. *Journal of Jewish Communal Service*, 77(2).
Cohen, S. M. (2008). *The Uncontestable, Incontrovertible, & Absolutely Convincing Case for the Distancing from Israel Hypothesis*. Paper presented at the Association for Jewish Studies.
Cohen, S. M., & Kelman, A. Y. (2007a). *Beyond distancing: Young adult American Jews and their alienation from Israel*. New York: Andrea and Charles Bronfman Philanthropies.
Cohen, S. M., & Kelman, A. Y. (2007b). *The Continuity of Discontinuity: How Young Jews Are Connecting, Creating, and Organizing Their Own Jewish Lives*. www.rebooters.net.
Goffman, E. (1971). *Relations in public: Micro studies of the public order*. New York: Basic books.
Gringras, R. (2006). "Wrestling and Hugging: Alternative Paradigms for the Diaspora-Israel Relationship," Paper written for Ma-kom, Israel Engagement Network. www.makomisrael.net.

Israel, S. (2003). *Connecting to Community: Jewish Peoplehood – Belonging and Commitment*. The composition of this curriculum was sponsored by the Jewish Agency and published by the Maor Wallach Press

Kalmar, I. & Penslar, D. (Eds.). (2005). Orientalism and the Jews, Tauber Institute for the Study of European Jewry Series

Kopelowitz, E. (2005). "Towards What Ideal Do We Strive? A Portrait of Social and Symbolic Israel Engagement in Community Day Schools" *RAVSAK Report*.

Margolis, D. (2005). "Towards A Vision of Educational Re-engagement with Israel", *Agenda: Jewish Education* 18

Morris, B. (1995). "The New Historiography: Israel Confronts its Past," *Tikkun*, November 1995

Morris, B. (1999). *Righteous victims: A history of the Zionist-Arab conflict 1881–2001*. New York: Vintage Books.

Morris, B. (2004). *The Birth of the Palestinian Refugee Problem Revisited* (Cambridge Middle East Studies), Press Syndicate of the University of Cambridge.

Pappé, I. (1992). *The making of the Arab-Israeli conflict, 1947–1951*. London: Tauris.

Raz-Krakotzkin, A. (2005). The Zionist return to the west. In *Orientalism and the Jews*. Brandeis University Press Lebanon New Hampshire 2005.

Said, E. W. (1979). *Orientalism*. New York: Vintage Books.

Sarna, J. (1996). A projection of America as it Ought to be: Zion in the mind's eye of American Jews. In A. Gal (Ed.), *Envisioning Israel – the changing ideals and images of North American Jews*. Detroit, MI: Wayne State University Press.

Saxe, L., Kadushin, C., Hecht, S., Rosen, M., Phillips, B., & Kelner, S. (2004). Evaluating Birthright Israel: Long-Term Impact and Research Findings. Maurice and Marilyn Cohen Center for Modern Jewish Studies, Brandeis University, November 2004. http://www.cmjs.org/files/evaluatingbri.04.pdf

Silberstein, L. J. (1999). *The Postzionism debates: Knowledge and power in Israeli culture* (pp. 69–82). New York and London esp: Routledge.

Troy, G. (2002). "Zionist Dreams as North American Dreams", *Why I am a Zionist: Israel, Jewish Identity, and the Challenges of Today*. The Bronfman Jewish Education Center, Montreal.

Israel Travel Education

Scott Copeland

Introduction

Israel travel has deep cultural roots as a central element of the practised memory of the Jewish people. The repeated yearly cycle of Torah reading, from the story of Abraham to the Exodus from Egypt, is a story of virtual travel: of wandering and transformation and homecoming. Already in the dawn of Jewish beginnings, where myth, memory, and history have no clear borders, the family tribe emerges bearing the name 'Israel' long before it took on the name 'Jew'. The story of Israel – the people – is a story whose *locus* – the place – provides a compass point for Israel's *mythos* – the community's foundational stories. The constantly shifting interplay between *locus*, *mythos*, and *ethos* (a community's vision of its most cherished values core) is shaped and reshaped as a community contends with tensions of time and place, with the responsibilities of ideas consummated in meeting with the real world. For many centuries, the realities of politics, the shortcomings of transportation technologies and the trepidations of Jewish ideological-religious tradition largely consigned Israel to an other-worldly status, rather than a living geographic territory (Ravitzky, 2006).

After 60 years of Israeli independence, in a world where physical distances seem to shrink as transportation and communication technologies constantly improve has Israel travel become a fundamental educational practice in Jewish life?

Israeli tourism, although a small slice of the international pie, has grown tremendously since the 1950s (World Tourism Organization, 2008). In the period 1950–1954, the Israeli Central Bureau of Statistics recorded 169,940 tourist arrivals. For 2006, tourist arrivals to Israel numbered 1,825,200 (Israel Central Bureau of Statistics, 2008). In 2005, approximately 43% of Israel's tourists were Jews (as compared to 20% of all incoming tourists to Israel in 2000) (Israel Central Bureau of Statistics, 2006). Among American Jews specifically, slightly more than one-third have visited Israel, and in most of these cases, such visits are once in a lifetime events most commonly lasting for a week to 2 weeks. An additional

S. Copeland (✉)
Makom, Jerusalem, Israel
e-mail: scottc@jafi.org

20% reported having participated in two or more Israel visits (Kotler-Berkowitz et al., 2004).

In considering Israel travel as an emerging field of practice for Jewish education, and not solely as a branch of the business of tourism, it is my contention that education – the attempt to expose learners to meaningful experiences for imagining their lives in relation to others – needs educators whose practice is part of a reflective tradition and creative community. In the context of Jewish education as an attempt to expose learners to experiences for imagining their lives as part of a Jewish community, Israel travel has a central role to play in the bolstering of an expanded sense of self that marks the individual's recognition of his/her memberships and allegiances. Rather than promoting a dichotomy between the self and community, Jewish education needs to be able to cultivate the inter-relationship between self and community. Jewish education ought to be able to articulate and offer the ways that individual growth depends on intense contact with cultural-communal models, the ways through which particular lenses embody real-life interpretations of humanness, and the possibilities for choice as learners imagine, try on, and adopt their own paths towards becoming. Israel travel, like camp experiences, provides thick Jewish living environments. Unlike the Jewish virtual microcosm of camp life, however, with all of its transformative potentials, Israel travel, at its best, is about the celebration of, and confrontation with the challenges of a Jewish majority under conditions of sovereignty in the Land of Israel. As Michael Rosenak offers,

> The restoration of Eretz Yisrael to a prominent place in Jewish life actually makes the struggle and the search more complex and even frustrating, but, for those who persevere, more interesting and promising. (Rosenak, 1985)

Too much of Jewish education accepts the seldom-articulated assumption that at best Jewishness is a kind of hobby, a part-time affair, and that real life is lived in acquiescence to the majority culture. The Zionist experiment[1] is, at its best, an attempt to participate vigorously in a communal conversation about the meanings of Jewishness as one expression of the human, through confronting the responsibilities of life in a sovereign Jewish democracy. Israel travel education and Israel engagement ought to be an ongoing attempt to contend with the beautiful and the ugly, the successes and flaws, the triumphs and challenges of Israeli life for Jews wherever they live. In preferring the term 'Israel engagement' to 'Israel education', there is a de-emphasis on Israel as a formal subject matter, and an emphasis on the ways in which the encounter with Israel may become an elemental part of a learner's choices regarding his/her own Jewishness. My hope is that Israel travel education can contribute to the position of Israel as a prime instigator for a rich exploration towards notions of Jewish flourishing.[2]

---

[1] Martin Buber spoke about the Kibbutz movement, and perhaps by extension, the Zionist movement, as 'an experiment that did not fail' (Buber, 1958).

[2] I thank Daniel Gordis for the phrase – 'notions of Jewish flourishing'. A person who cites a source in the name of its speaker brings redemption to the world (Ethics of the Fathers 6:6).

Building for Organization

Especially since the late 1990s, the organizational capacities for Israel travel, primarily for Jewish students and young adults (roughly ages 16–30)[3] have developed substantially. The establishment of Birthright Israel, *Masa*, and most recently *Lapid* all aim to provide umbrella organizations for increasing participation of Jewish students and young adults in Israel travel. Birthright Israel provides a 10-day Israel tour for young adults who have not previously participated in an educational tour of Israel. (Hazan & Saxe, 2008) Participation is free. *Masa* operates as the umbrella for long-term Israel programmes (between a semester to a year) and provides scholarship monies to participants and development funds to potential programme operators. In both the case of Birthright Israel and MASA, the funding is jointly provided by major philanthropists, by the State of Israel, and by Jewish public organizations like the United Jewish Communities, the Jewish Agency for Israel, and the Keren HaYesod. Lapid, an initiative to provide a similar organizational and economic umbrella for summer and semester programmes for high-school-age Israel travellers, has begun its efforts towards recognition in 2008–2009.

Have Birthright Israel, MASA, and Lapid succeeded in bolstering educational travel to Israel? One measure is numerical. As of December 2007, following 8 years of Birthright Israel activity, over 150,000 young Jews from 52 countries have participated in these intense, short Israel-travel experiences (Rosenbloom, 2007). The Birthright Israel web site (birthrightisrael.com) counts 230,000 program participants over their first decade of operations. In comparison, similar programmes sponsored by the now defunct 'Youth and HeHalutz' department of the Jewish Agency brought to Israel approximately half of that number in the decade between 1987 and 1997, previous to Birthright Israel's establishment (Cohen & Cohen, 2000). There is no doubt that the financial enticement of a free trip is an important element in the marketing strategy and numerical success of the Birthright trips.

With regard to MASA, organizational statements set a target of 20,000 high-school graduates from Jewish communities around the world coming to Israel for semester- and year-long programmes annually.[4] During the period from 2006 to 2009, MASA brought to Israel 23,700 Jewish students and young adults.[5]

---

[3] The websites of the two largest umbrella organizations dealing with Jewish student and young adult educational travel to Israel define the age parameters for participant eligibility as ages 18–26 for Birthright Israel, and ages 18–30 for MASA. See http://www.birthrightisrael.com/site/PageServer?pagename=trip_faq and http://www.Masaisrael.org/Masa/English/About+MASA/MASA+Definitions/respectively.

[4] See the use of 20,000 participants annually as an organizational benchmark on the MASA website – http://www.jewishagency.org/JewishAgency/English/Home/About/Masa – and in Hoffman (2005).

[5] Data regarding MASA participation was provided by the MASA offices (April 2009).

Year	Number of participants
2008–2009	8,303
2007–2008	8,230
2006–2007	7,167

Although the 20,000 annual mark remains an aspiration, MASA has impacted on young Jews deciding to choose Israel as a destination for long-term educational and volunteer experiences. With that said, the increase over the last couple of years is slight. Based on the financial circumstances in 2008–2009, it may be that, at least in the short term, numbers may decline. For all of the organizations looking to bring more Jewish travellers to Israel for more meaningful experiences, the demographic realities of a shrinking Diaspora, and a concurrent decline in numbers of Jewish youth in the age group eligible for Israel travel programmes through Birthright, MASA, and Lapid, suggests that the margin for significant numerical growth beyond current participation numbers may be limited by general trends in twenty-first century Jewish demography.[6]

The move towards the creation of Israel travel umbrella organizations like *Masa*, Birthright, and *Lapid* – towards more centralized organization and attention to more highly professionalized marketing/public relations strategies – are significant. However, the focus on bureaucratic solutions based on models from the business world largely disregards detailed concern for developing the foundational visions – in conception and practice – that are necessary for transforming Israel travel into a meaningful arena for Jewish learning and life. Part of the lack of emphasis on constructing Israel travel education as a sub-field within Jewish education is based on a widespread assumption that the encounter between Jewish travellers and Israel has a transformative power in and of itself, almost regardless of the quality and content of the specific experience. If the potential transformative power of the Israel experience is to be taken seriously, organizers, policy makers, and educators would do well to examine more closely how to strengthen the potential impact through deliberate practice in order to serve the visions of Jewishness and Israel that they seek to advance.

Challenges from the Literature

Attempts to define Israel travel as Jewish education and to set standards for excellence are not new. Within the organizational contexts of Birthright and MASA, standard documents attempt to provide a common denominator for the wide range of interests and organizations that enjoy their broader umbrellas. Because these broader organizational umbrellas provide cover for a broad spectrum of Jewish organizations – from ultra orthodox religious seminaries to secular Zionist youth movements,

---

[6]For a recent discussion of trends in Jewish demography, see Della Pergola, 2008.

from committed Reform Jews to frameworks for the so-called 'unaffiliated' – standards documents have little impact beyond perhaps so-called 'standards of delivery'. Their attempt to be all inclusive ends up producing the kinds of slogans about Jewish identity, continuity, and peoplehood that prove thin beyond initial examination. A lowest common denominator approach to standards for Israel travel encourages the inclusion of a wide spectrum of programme organizers and supporting agencies. With that said, without ongoing, facilitated professional forums where programme organizers, developers, and educators can share professional-educational best practices and challenges, standards documents run the risk of becoming fossilized rhetoric. Organizers and educators desperately need forums where they can articulate the vision hidden in their practice, be challenged by colleagues, and respond thoughtfully to the gauntlets thrown down in the dynamic and complex realities that Israel travel education operates.

An additional problem of the attempt to standardize Israel travel education stems from the volunteer nature of contemporary Jewish life. Unlike a state apparatus that for good and bad can enforce educational policy as it enforces economic, or health, or military policy, Jewish communal life is built on persuasion and consensus, not enforcement. In such a situation, if standards of excellence in Israel travel education are to be advanced in actual educational practice, the umbrella organizations need to construct educational teams and resource centres that because of their proven educational expertise can engage Israel travel operators in a meaningful conversation about the whys, hows, and whats of their practice. Israel travel education suffers from inflated attention to enrollment/participation and a distinct lack of attention to research and development for improving practice. The work needed to transform Israel travel from a tourism enterprise to an educational project is, to paraphrase Deuteronomy 30:11, 'not beyond you, nor is it far away...' In fact, as I relate below, already in the late 1980s and early 1990s, several researchers and reflective practitioners attempted to point to the kinds of innovative development needed to lay solid ground for Israel travel as a key practice of Jewish education.

Calls for Innovative Development

In 1988, Annette Hochstein prepared a report for the Jewish Education Committee of the Jewish Agency's Board of Governors – 'The Israel Experience Project' (Hochstein, 1988). Three key areas of development are pointed to by Hochstein and her team as vital for instigating the kinds of strategic upgrade to increase the number of participants and the quality of programs. Hochstein proposes the following:

1. Recruiting and training appropriate educational personnel to serve as planners, counsellors, and programme directors. Such personnel would introduce the changes necessary in curriculum, training, and recreation to ensure that the programmes meet the needs and expectations of today's participants.
2. Improving logistics. Current logistical arrangements often fail the educational goals of the programme instead of serving them. Logistics and administration

should, where necessary, be reorganized to become an integral part of the programme and be regarded as educational administration.
3. In order to increase participation (assuming that the crisis of the current year will not continue),[7] recruitment and marketing of programmes should make use of professional marketing techniques. Recruitment networks can and should be expanded. (Hochstein, 1988)

The report points to several pilot programmes carried out within the Jewish Agency, in cooperation with the Kibbutz Institute's for Jewish Experience seminars (connected with the Hebrew instruction seminars once widely popular on kibbutzim throughout Israel – *ulpanim*), and with the Alexander Muss High School in Israel.

Cohen and Wall (1994) in a report examining a wide range of Israel experience programmes in the early 1990s summarize their sense of the constituent ingredients that together form a meaningful standard of excellence for Israel travel education:

> [...] some trips are indeed qualitatively superior to others. In varying degrees, trips are characterized by: participants who are more thoroughly prepared and more cohesive; staff members who are more enthusiastic, capable, trained, and supervised; Judaic and educational philosophies that permeate every aspect of the trip; a well-designed curriculum; and extraordinary activities. (Cohen & Wall, 1994)

In a comparison that seems obvious, but is not typically considered because much of the field is dominated by a paradigm of Jewish youth and student travel to Israel as tourism, Cohen and Wall make reference to Lawrence-Lightfoot's 'Good High School' as a point of contrast.

> Good high schools provide safe and regulated environments... A strong sense of authority is reinforced by an explicit ideological vision, a clear articulation of the purposes and goals of education. Ideology, authority, and order combine to produce a coherent institution that supports human interaction and growth. These institutional frameworks and structures are critical for adolescents, whose uncertainty and vulnerability call for external boundary setting. In their abrupt shifts from childishness to maturity, they need settings that are rooted in tradition, that will give them clear signals of certainty and continuity. *[Sara Lawrence Lightfoot, The Good High School, p. 350.]* (Cohen & Wall, 1994)

Even among the best Israel programmes, and there are many, time and energy need to be devoted to articulating a vision of success, of 'the good' that is embodied in practice and can be evaluated through qualitative evaluation of Israel programmes' staff and participants.

Paul Liptz, writing at around the same time as both Hochstein and Cohen and Wall, echoes concerns regarding programme quality and the educational goals for Israel travel education:

> The Israeli experience must surely be more than just a tour. It has to include both cognitive and affective elements. It should encourage the highest level of participatory learning and also be flexible in design. The term "learning *Kehillah*" (learning community) should be

---

[7] Hochstein refers to the Palestinian uprising against the Israeli occupation of the West Bank and Gaza that became known as the *Intifada*. There is no doubt that the security/political situation in Israel at any given time has an impact on tourism and Israel travel education.

used to refer to a group on tour, indicating that the participants are not only gaining information about Israel but are also experiencing a meaningful dialogue with other participants. (Liptz, 1993)

The three examples above, all written between 1988 and 1994, point to a range of programmatic/educational moves needed to transform the Israel travel experience into a meaningful arena for Jewish education, into as Liptz suggests, 'a learning Kehillah'. The creation over the last decade of umbrella frameworks like Birthright Israel, *Masa*, and *Lapid*, as discussed earlier on, provide partial answers to some of the challenges already raised in the late 1980s and early 1990s. From the writing of Hochstein's 'The Israel Experience Project', 20 years have passed. What are the practices that might advance the Israel travel experience as a fundamental arena for Jewish education and Israel engagement?

Research for Improved Practice

A central tool in the research on Israel travel has been the questionnaires evaluating participant satisfaction with programme experiences. Although the opinions of programme participants regarding the value of programme components and their overall experience are important both in educational terms and as a marketing tool, such tools are insufficient in considering the extent to which a programme's practice embodies its oft-times unspoken vision, and consequently the educational success of the program beyond 'customer satisfaction'.

Research work of a different kind has been conducted over the last number of years along two main themes – impact and significance. In studies like 'Building Jewish Identity: A Study of Young Judaea Alumni' (Cohen & Ganapol, 1988) or in the more recent 'Tourists, Travelers, and Citizens: Jewish Engagement of Young Adults in Four Centers of North American Jewish Life' (Chertok, Sasson, & Saxe, 2009), sponsoring bodies measure the significance of the Israel experience based on the ways that programme participants articulate and exhibit increased Jewish involvement following participation in some Israel travel experience. In these studies, Israel travel as an educational practice is rooted in a vision that sees the travel experience as a method and means for increasing the Jewish involvement of young people in organized communal life.

With regard to significance, at least two pertinent questions are typically addressed in the research:

1. What are the interpreted meanings of Israel and Jewishness that are embodied in the educational programming included in Israel programmes?
2. And how do Israel experience travellers/learners begin to make sense of the meanings of their Israel experience in their ongoing identity building?

Claire Goldwater's reading of the ways that Israel tour-guide-educators present and discuss the meanings of Israeli-Jewish historical sites (as signifiers for their understandings of broader ideological issues of Jewish meaning and life) provides an important lens on the stated and unstated connections between practice and vision, and the centrality of place as a category of meaning in Israel travel education (Goldwater, 2002). Sasson and Kelner add another piece to the exploration of the ways that place, and notions of the remembered past, play themselves out in the explicit narratives and implicit self-understandings of Israeli tour-guide-educators at Masada (Sasson & Kelner, 2008). Kelner, in other work, focuses not on the educator, but on the learner, and on the ways that the learner contends with Israel, with the place of Jewishness in his/her life, and with the important experimental Jewish community that the Israel experience offers learners/travellers (Kelner, 1988).

Research for improved practice focusing on questions of negotiated significance – both of Israel educators and of learners/travellers – is both sorely needed and under-represented. Research by Goldwater, Sasson, and Kelner provide the kinds of portraits of real-life learning experiences that give voice to educators and learners, and to the questions of the complex ongoing dialogue between vision and practice. If educational work is a craft it will be most readily understood through activity, work, presentation, and action. Research for improved practice has the potential to act as a mirror in which educators can see the reflection of their practice. Based on that reflection of practice, educators can challenge themselves to reconsider and hone both the 'whys' and the 'whats' of their work. As such, a more concerted effort is needed to produce a series of Israel travel education portraits that could become a centrepiece for analysis and discussion about the signature pedagogies of Israel travel education and the visions that grow out of and nurture them.

Training for Israel Travel Education as a Profession

Israel travel education suffers from a lack of forums for professional training and development. In a basic way, the lack of such forums is a symptom suggesting that Israel travel education has not been able to establish itself as a recognized professional branch on the Jewish educational tree. For example, one of the most significant roles in the work done during Israel travel experiences is that of the tour guide. Like in a number of other countries, Israeli tour guides are trained and licensed by the state through the ministry of tourism. The Israeli tour guide course includes between 18 and 24 months of study, and 450–500 contact hours. Study includes both classroom time and extensive field visits to sites (between 50 and 70 field days) throughout Israel. The syllabus includes a wide variety of brief, survey courses – botany and zoology, archaeology and history, religion and religious communities, climatology and geology – from the prehistoric until contemporary times. Students vary widely in ages and backgrounds, but must all possess a high school diploma and not possess a criminal record. A portion of the course is devoted to methodology and includes such topics as typology of incoming tourism to Israel and Israeli tourism, tools and aids for guiding, experience in guiding, administration and organization of a tour, methodology of guiding by target public and subjects, workshops in leadership and activation of a group, manners and conduct, security and safety, and the tour guide and his connection with tourism sectors. As compared with tour guide courses in other countries, the Israeli tour guide course is extensive and serious.

With that said, the tour guide is not trained as an educator. Beyond methodological issues of public speaking and basic presentation techniques, there is no attempt to introduce the tour guide-in-training to educational theory, to relevant topics in informal education, or to educational thinking regarding, for example, dilemmas of history and memory, and possibilities of competing narratives. Issues concerning contemporary Jewish identity and the relationships between Jewish communities outside of Israel and Israel are not included in the course, even for those who will work with groups of Jewish learners/travellers.

Even if Israeli tour guides were trained in a way that heightened their professional sense of self as educators, which planted them firmly in the tradition of education, and that, helped them gather and use a richer tool box for both their thought and work, it would be a mistake to perpetuate an Israeli monopoly over Israel travel education. There is no doubt that Israeli educators with the appropriate training, background, and sensitivities do bring to their teaching a tremendous amount of authenticity and commitment when working with Jewish groups from the Diaspora. Especially for Jewish youth and student travellers to Israel, the personal model offered by a successful guide/educator offers the traveller/learner a gateway to enhanced identification with Israeli life. With that said, the lack of trained educators from the Diaspora communities, who have made an existential or practical decision to remain in the Diaspora as community leaders and educators, and who at the same time embody an ongoing intimacy and engagement with Israel, limits the possibility that learners will be able to imagine paths for their own lives that entail both vigorous involvement in Jewish life in their home communities and at the same time, ongoing, intensive engagement with Israel. An over-reliance on Israeli guides/educators, and the failure to develop educational leadership in Diaspora communities – whether in Bible, or Hebrew language and literature, or in Israel engagement – weakens the ability of the communities to demonstrate, through modelling, the relevance of Jewishness and Judaism in the lives of potential Jewish learners. Training programmes for Jewish educational leadership need to develop paths for developing cadres of professional educators from the Diaspora communities and from Israel who can jointly take on the challenge of developing sophisticated, compelling approaches to Israel engagement. The cultivation of reflective practitioners for Israel engagement can encourage a situation where Israel is met repeatedly by the learner in a wide variety of Jewish settings, including a richer palette of long- and short-term Israel travel options. An expanded palette of Israel travel options for a wider variety of learners, available at various developmental junctures and rooted in the kinds of follow-through programming (before an Israel journey and after it) offers a framework for a kind of lifelong Israel engagement cycle.

Israel experience organizers who construct themselves as educational institutions have, in many cases, built training units for their own staff. The Alexander Muss High School, Young Judaea, NIFTY, and the Canada Israel Experience all take upon themselves to provide seminars to enrich the work of their educators. Much of this training focuses on sharpening basic logistic and pedagogical skills, and on deepening the allegiances of the staff to the specific organization.

The distinct lack of institutions to provide educational training for tour-guide-educators, for programme directors, and for Israel experience logistical staff perpetuates a situation where participants in Israel travel education settings do not receive the quality of faculty expected at Jewish day schools, in general public and private education, and in the colleges and universities that the graduates of Israel experience programmes are exposed to throughout their lives. As long as staff development and training for Israel travel education fails to take seriously the development of a cadre of Israel travel professionals who can measure up to the level of the best educational professionals that students will encounter in their long learning careers, Israel travel education will not be able to achieve the kind of impact and success that are its potential.

Lee Shulman, in describing the kind of 'signature pedagogies' needed to induct novices into their professional lives, raises the following challenge for the training of educators:

> I would respectfully propose that a major challenge for the education of teachers and the professional development of veteran teachers for this next generation will be to recognize that what we desperately need is a suite of signature pedagogies that are routine, that teach people to think like, act like, and be like an educator. We need signature pedagogies that respectfully recognize the difference between pedagogical thinking associated with promoting deep understanding in mathematics, and doing it deeply in English literature, or in history. And that we build our programs of teacher education around these kinds of signature pedagogies. (Shulman, 2006)

What would be involved in taking up Shulman's challenge for Israel travel educators? What would be the 'suite of signature pedagogies... that teach people to think like, act like and be like' an Israel travel educator?

Towards Israel Travel Experiences as 'Attentive Travel'

Travel experiences by their very nature entail a level of deliberate disconnect with home, and with travellers' usual routines. Beyond the small inconveniences that are part of arriving in and adapting to a new place where people may speak a different language, use a different currency, or drive on the opposite side of the road, travel is by its nature a kind of escape, a 'getting away from it all'. Travel as 'escape from' frames the place visited as an episodic adventure, or temporary refuge. If the destination is episodic or temporary, the experience of the traveller while away from home has little chance to impact the life of the traveller after returning home. In the case of Israel travel in Jewish communal and educational settings, Israel ought not to be framed as a distant 'island' separated from the 'mainland' of Jewish communal life. Rather, Israel travel education needs to be seen as an experience rooted in and growing out of Jewish communal life and that community's educational agendas. Israel travel needs to be practised as part of the ongoing series of milestone events in the life of the Jew towards vigorous engagement with the meanings of Jewish life, and cultivating expanded Jewish involvements.

Building Jewish communal capacity for an Israel experience cycle that would encourage Jews to visit Israel repeatedly at different points in their lives within appropriate educational programmes would involve building the conceptual and practical scaffolding to turn Israel travel education from tourism – from episodic and temporary – to a kind of contemporary pilgrimage[8], to 'attentive travel'. Huston Smith suggests

> The object of pilgrimage is not rest and relaxation – to get away from it all. To set out on a pilgrimage is to throw down a challenge to everyday life. (Cousineau, 2000)

Although central trends in both general Western and Jewish education are dominated by models borrowed from the business world, a more serious appreciation of traditional pilgrimage models has the potential to significantly enhance the ways in which we think about and implement Israel travel education. I want to highlight one aspect of the pilgrimage experience that is suggestive for our work in Jewish educational travel.

A traditional pilgrim does not arrive at a site of meaning without initiation and preparation, without having been introduced to the communal story that frames the significance of the journey, the centrality of the destination, and the role of the traveller as an actor in both bearing and forging anew the community's most cherished values. For example, the Babylonian Talmud describes a paradigmatic example of Jewish travel in describing a visit to Mount Scopus, looking from the east onto the ruins of the Temple Mount in the generations after the Roman destruction of Jerusalem in 70 C.E.

> Rabbi Elazar teaches – one who sees the cities of Judah in their ruined state recites the verse, "Your holy cities have become a desert, Jerusalem a desolation." (Isa. 64:9) and tears his garment... One who sees Jerusalem in its ruined state, recites the verse, "Our holy temple, our pride, where our ancestors praised you... all that was dear to us is ruined." (Isa 64:10) As soon as one reaches Mt. Scopus they tear their garments; one tear for the Temple and one tear for Jerusalem... (Babylonian Talmud, Tractate Moed Katan 26a.)

For a modern-day traveller to perform a visit to Mount Scopus in the way suggested by Rabbi Elazar, an entire educative process would have to have been put in place by the community before the journey. First and foremost, the traveller would need to be familiar with the above text. He/she would need to be familiar with why the cities of Judah and Jerusalem are in ruins; why the verses chosen to be read at Scopus are from Isaiah, Chapter They would need to be familiar with why the cities of Judah and Jerusalem are in ruins; why the verses chosen to be read at Scopus are from Isaiah, Chapter 64, and what is the meaning of tearing one's clothing as a Jewish ritual act, and what is the meaning of tearing one's clothing as a Jewish ritual act. They would need to have a sense of the historical contexts of the importance of the

---

[8]See Lisa Grant's dissertation on the opportunities and problems of the use of the pilgrimage metaphor in Israel travel education (Grant, 2000).

Temple and Jerusalem in Jewish civilization, and the significance of their destruction for the Jewish experience. On a cultural level, the power of Rabbi Elazar's suggestion emanates from what Paul Connerton (1989) might call the reinforcing linkage between the inscriptive (reading, writing, drawing) and incorporative practices (embodied activities). Significant communal memories (in the case above, the destruction of Jerusalem in 70 C.E.) are able to remain significant with the eroding passage of time because the event is captured both in text, and is re-enacted on some level through physical place, sacred text, and ritual activity.

It would be difficult for most Jewish travellers today to carry out Rabbi Elazar's suggestion in their own visits to Jerusalem and Mount Scopus. Shaul Kelner highlights our difficulty and the realities of the lives and attitudes of contemporary Jewish 'pilgrims' by quoting a Birthright Israel participant's reaction to his first visit to the Western Wall:

> With expectations raised for the visit to the Temple Mount, Judaism's holiest site, participants were easily underwhelmed. 'Are the mountains here all so small?' one disappointed participant asked semi rhetorically. To the guffaws of those who heard, another responded by poking fun at the holy site and at the goals of Birthright: 'I hope Mount Sinai isn't such a piece of shit, or it might really shake my Jewish identity!' (Kelner, 2004)

Obviously a galaxy's length separates the historical realities of the world that produced the text from the Talmud from the world that produced the Birthright Israel participant quoted above. However, the educator can not afford to be dismissive of the voice brought by Kelner. Educationally, the challenge is to take both the learner seriously and to ask what communities ought to do to transform the Israel experience from an exotic episode largely disconnected from the life of the learner/traveller to Jewish-attentive travel.

Planning for Israel educational travel needs to take into account the wider placement of Israel engagement in Jewish communal life. If Israel is not woven in and out of the Jewish story that is encountered at holidays, at life events, on the family bookshelf, at the family dinner table, in camping, etc., Israel will remain a foreign country with a vague connection to an even vaguer notion of Jewish flourishing.

Visions of the Purposes of Israel Travel, and of Israel Engagement for Flourishing Jewish Life

In order to plan effectively, before the funding, before building the right staff, there needs to be an idea – a vision that maps the purposes of the specific venture and that like a map is a basis for continued reference, analysis, and exploration. With regard to Israel travel education, the outstanding question whose answer is a prerequisite for 'how', is 'why'. Why is Israel travel education crucial not only to Israel engagement, but to a Jewish education whose main goal is to help Jews to employ the wide-ranging tapestries of the Jewish experience as a central inspiration for the ways that they choose to build their lives?

Travel has long been recognized as a mode of experiential learning that is laden with potential transformative power. One need not look far for foundational stories from many cultures about travellers discovering the world, the other, and hence themselves, along the road far from home. Abraham, Jesus, Muhammed, and the Buddha all take part in transformative journeys, in life-changing challenges that prepare them for their life's work. Michel De Montaigne (De Montaigne, 2009), heralding the age of exploration and the place of 'The Grand Tour' in European education, extols the importance of travel education. For Montaigne, leaving home and the opportunity to see new places and meet new people is a means to testing the limitations and foibles of our own home culture. Travel becomes a lesson in humility – 'that we may whet and sharpen our wits by rubbing them against those of others' (De Montaigne, 2009) – as it offers the traveller alternative models of the meanings of being human, and the possibility that the way we live is not the only way to live. Here, travel becomes a deliberate quest for enhanced meaning – a journey rather than a tourist jaunt (Cohen, 2001). In recent years, major universities like Princeton and Harvard, in the United States, are reprioritizing study abroad both in their admission policies and in their study programmes. In a world where technology seems to bring people closer together and where, at the same time, there is no wane in inter-communal, cultural, and religious conflict, travel is receiving new attention in promoting citizens who are 'culturally competent and globally aware' (Mohn, 2006).

For the purposes of Jewish education, cultural competence can be understood as a number of concentric circles, each one seeking to expand the experience of the learner beyond the familiar circles of 'I', 'family', and 'local community' to more expansive encounters with Jews in other localities, with Jews in other historical times, and with the State of Israel. Through the encouragement of an expanded sense of self – a sense of self linked to an 'imagined community' – the learner has the opportunity to imagine himself or herself as part of a larger 'we' linked to the larger Jewish people and human family. The travel experience, not built as a bus tour 'seeing there' but constructed as a diverse array of encounters that challenge the learner's own notions of the meanings of Jewishness and the human can become a 'being there'. Such a 'being there' has enormous potential in making Jewish education not only about texts on paper, but about real-life questions of who do I want to be and how is my own Jewish community a microcosm of the image of the world that I want to inhabit.

What is the vision of a decent Jewish communal life that is worth championing? Although contemporary Israel as a majority Jewish, sovereign, and democratic state is very different from the Jewish communities of the Diaspora, Israeli life holds out the educational opportunity to explore visions in action, and the ways that competing visions for the Jewish future play themselves out in polity and society. Israel, with all of its differences from the Jewish communities of the Diaspora offers a potentially challenging mirror for Jewish life in the twenty-first century. Issues like environmental consciousness and responsibility, social justice, internal Jewish diversity and pluralism, and Jewish-non-Jewish relations – with all of their successes and failures and future challenges – can be explored through the Israeli reality. Values, confined to the realm of fine sermons and well-intentioned statements, cannot be taken seriously as promoting any vision for the Jewish future. Israel travel education holds out the possibility of exploring the dilemmas of a unique sovereign Jewish community as it debates in real life and real time its understandings of the Jewish past, present, and future through its necessity to act in the world.

Michael Rosenak reworks Oakeshott's (1962) terms 'language' and 'literature' as central categories for Jewish educational exploration.[9] Rosenak defines language and literature as two separate, yet interdependent concepts. Language is 'a basic world picture', 'a set of paradigms', 'a basic explanation of reality' (Rosenak, 2001). However, language is only activated through literature and becomes meaningful only through interpretation. He writes,

> Language becomes a social and spiritual reality only when literature is initially made in it, when it is first 'spoken'. A language comes alive when what it means is interpreted... when it 'speaks' to the circumstances of those addressed by it. (Rosenak, 2001)

In other words, language is transformed in to meaningful, relevant literature through the encounter with life. Based on its unique position as a Jewish community possessing national sovereignty, the State of Israel represents an arena where the debate between the various literatures over the meanings of Jewish language, over the significance and meanings of Jewish stories takes place at a greater level of intensity, and with a wider range of responsibility because it is rooted in a historically unique 'social and spiritual reality'. For Jewish students and teachers coming to Israel, exposure to the tough issues facing Israeli society, with all of their complexities and heterogeneity, is a challenge towards engagement with the possibilities of unfolding Jewish and non-Jewish literatures in debate. Discussions of social justice, of peace, and of community are forced to develop a thicker aspect as the concepts themselves are fired, forged, and reformed between the sparks of living people acting within a living community. Michael Walzer, in his *Exodus and Revolution* (1986), like Rosenak, suggests that argument and interpretation are facilitated and enriched by a thick cultural context, a rich cultural range that can offer a variety of interpretative possibilities. Interpretation and the debate between interpretations, in this sense, is an essential expression of cultural commitment.

> Cultural patterns shape perception and analysis too. They would not endure for long, of course, if they did not accommodate a range of perceptions and analyses, if it were not possible to carry on arguments inside the structures they provide... Within the framework of the Exodus story one can plausibly emphasize the mighty arm of God or the slow march of the people, the land of milk and honey or the holy nation, the purging of the counterrevolutionaries or the schooling of a new generation. One can describe Egyptian bondage in terms of corruption or tyranny or exploitation. One can defend the authority of the Levites or of the tribal elders or of the rulers of tens and fifties. I would only suggest that these alternatives are themselves paradigmatic; they are *our* alternatives. In other cultures, men and women read other books, tell different stories, confront different choices. (Walzer, 1986)

Israel travel education ought to become an initiation into the creative challenges surrounding the ways a sovereign Jewish community debates and acts on its worldly

---

[9] See Michael Rosenak, 2001, p. 4.

responsibilities, and the ways that notions of Jewishness impact on that debate and action. The more time a traveller/learner spends in Israel encountering the nuance of day to day life in all of its glorious complexity, greater is the chance that initiation will move to identification and action.

Israel travel education offers an arena not limited by four classroom walls where learners/travellers have the opportunity to become engaged interpreters of the possibilities of Jewish life through an honest wrestling with who they are, and who they want to become. "For what must be interpreted in a text is a proposed world which I could inhabit and wherein I could project one of my own most possibilities" (Ricouer, 1981).

For Jews, visiting Israel, at once holy land and homeland, at once foreign and familiar, offers possibilities of not only of imagining literary or historic models, but of new possibilities as Jews confront the challenges and opportunities of responsibility.

Closing Thoughts

Israel travel education is a field still in the making. Enormous organizational strides have been taken since the late 1990s towards marketing, enrolment, and financing. And yet, to encourage more Jews to have a wider range of educational opportunities to encounter Israel for varying lengths of time, on a number of journeys throughout their lives, is not only an issue of organization and logistics. Cultivating Israel travel education as a unique branch of Jewish experiential learning, and as a dynamic, sophisticated meeting with the challenges of Israel, calls for moving beyond the organizational to constructive work of articulating vision for practice. In building on existing achievements, Israel travel education would do well to renew emphasis on providing definitions for qualitative excellence, and develop compelling educational expressions of Israel's foundational place in Jewish life – with all the celebration and challenges entailed.

In traditional pilgrimage models, travellers/learners return from their journeys as messengers and emissaries. They bring from the sites they have seen, from the people they have met, and from the challenges of the journey a renewed meaning for the values and ideals cherished by their community (Shutz, 1945). It is through those renewed meanings carried home from the road that a community has the opportunity to consider its inspirations and aspirations. At its best, Israel travel education ought to be a kind of cultural mapping for a discussion about where we have been, and where we want to go.

References

Buber, M. (1958). *Paths in utopia*. Boston: Beacon Press.
Chertok, F., Sasson, T., & Saxe, L. (2009). *Tourists, travelers, and citizens: Jewish engagement of young adults in four centers of North American Jewish life*. Waltham, MA: Cohen Center for Modern Jewish Studies: Brandeis University.

Cohen, E. (2001). A Phenomenology of tourist experiences. In S. L. Robertson (Ed.), *Defining travel: Diverse visions* (pp. 29–55). Jackson: University of Mississippi Press.
Cohen, E. H., & Cohen, E. (2000). *The Israel experience*. Jerusalem: The Jerusalem Institute for Israel Studies.
Cohen, S. M., & Ganapol, A. (1988). *Building Jewish identity: A study of young Judaea alumni*. New York: Hadassah.
Cohen, S. M., & Wall, S. (1994). *Excellence in youth trips to Israel*. New York: CRB Foundation & JESNA.
Connerton, P. (1989). *How societies remember*. Cambridge: Cambridge University Press.
Cousineau, P. (2000). *The art of pilgrimage: The seeker's guide to making travel sacred*. Berkeley, CA: Conari Press.
De Montaigne, M. (2009). *On education*. Retrieved from http://oregonstate.edu/instruct/phl302/texts/montaigne/montaigne-essays-1.html#II
Della Pergola, S. (2008). Jewish demography and peoplehood 2008. In R. Tal & B. Geltman (Eds.), *Facing tomorrow: Background policy documents* (pp. 231–250). Jerusalem: The Jewish Peoplehood Policy Planning Institute.
Goldwater, C. (2002). *Constructing the narrative of authenticity: Tour educators at work in the Israel experience*. Unpublished master's thesis, Hebrew University, Jerusalem.
Grant, L. (2000). *Paradoxical pilgrimage: American Jewish adults on a congregational Israel trip*. Unpublished doctoral dissertation, The Jewish Theological Seminary, New York.
Hazan, B., & Saxe, L. (2008). *Ten days of birthright Israel: A journey in young adult identity*. Waltham, MA: Brandeis University Press.
Hochstein, A. (1988). *The Israel experience project*. Jerusalem: Native Policy and Planning Consultants for the Jewish Agency.
Hoffman, A. (2005). Israel for Jewish education and Jewish education for Israel. *The Journal for Jewish Communal Service*, 81(1/2), 53–58.
Israel Central Bureau of Statistics. (2006). *Tourism in Israel 2005 – statistilite 58*. Retrieved from http://www.cbs.gov.il/statistical/touris2005e.pdf
Israel Central Bureau of Statistics. (2008, November). *Entrances and exits of Israelis and tourists*. Retrieved from http://www1.cbs.gov.il/shnaton58/st23_01.pdf
Kelner, S.1988. (Spring 1988). Birthright Israel and the creation of ritual. *Contact – Jewish Life Network/Steinhardt Foundation*.
Kelner, S. (2004). The Impact of Israel experience programs on Israel's symbolic significance. *Contemporary Jewry*, 24, 124–154.
Kotler-Berkowitz, L., Cohen, S. M., Ament, J., Klaff, V., Mott, F., & Peckerman-Neuman, D. (2004). *The National Jewish Population Survey 2000–2001: Strength, Challenge and Diversity in the American Jewish Population*. New York: United Jewish Communities.
Liptz, P. (1993). The Jew on a short-term visit to Israel. *Journal of Jewish Communal Service*, 69(4), Retrieved from https://www.policyarchive.org/bitstream/handle/10207/10596/JJCS69-4-03.pdf?sequence=1
Mohn, T. (2006, September 6). How to become a World citizen before going to college. *The New York Times*, Retrieved from http://www.nytimes.com/2006/09/03/college/coll03gap.html
Oakeshott, M. (1962). The Study of politics in a university. In *Rationalism in politics and other essays* (pp. 184–218). London: Methuen & Co. Ltd.
Ravitzky, A. (2006). The land of Israel: Desire and dread in Jewish literature. In G. Glas (Ed.), *Hearing visions and seeing voices: Psychological aspects of biblical concepts and personalities* (pp. 193–213). Amsterdam: Kluwer Academic Press.
Ricouer, P. (1981). *Hermeneutics and the human sciences*. Cambridge: Cambridge University Press.
Rosenak, M. (1985). The land of Israel. In S. T. Katz (Ed.), *Frontiers of Jewish thought* (pp. 13–32). Washington, DC: Bnai Brith Books.
Rosenak, M. (2001). *Tree of life, tree of knowledge: Conversations with the torah*. Boulder, CO: Westview Press.

Rosenbloom, I. (2007, December 14). Record number of students to take part in birthright Israel this year. *Haaretz*, Retrieved from http://www.haaretz.com/hasen/spages/934475.html

Sasson, T., & Kelner, S. (2008). From Shrine to forum: Masada and the politics of Jewish extremism. *Israel Studies, 13*(2), 146–163.

Shulman, L. (2006, February). *The Signature pedagogies of the professions of law, medicine, engineering, and the clergy: potential lessons for the training of teachers.* Retrieved from http://www.taylorprograms.com/images/Shulman_Signature_Pedagogies.pdf

Shutz, A. (1945). The homecomer. *American Journal of Sociology, 50*(5), 369–376.

Walzer, M. (1986). *Exodus and revolution.* New York: Basic Books.

World Tourism Organization, (2008, November). *Historical perspective of world tourism.* Retrieved from http://www.unwto.org/facts/eng/historical.htm

Jewish Peoplehood Education

David Mittelberg

Introduction

Recent studies sponsored by the American Jewish Committee (Ukeles, Miller, & Beck, 2006; Shimoni and Shaltiel, 2006) and Cohen et al. (2008), indicate that the next generation of American and Israeli youth are relatively ignorant of, uneducated about, and unaffected by each other, suggesting that the goal of global solidarity of the Jewish people is constantly challenged. Increasingly, the paradigm of Jewish peoplehood is being offered as a framework to address this problem. Before reviewing some of the educational models that currently exist and addressing the question of what a useful paradigm of Jewish peoplehood might look like, it is important to consider the larger question of the very need for peoplehood education. Is there even such a need and why? This chapter will argue that (1) in both Israel and the Diaspora, Jewish youth seem to feel little existential need to belong to a Jewish collective (local or global), (2) The Jewish people has an existential and urgent need to instill a sense of belonging in its next generation if it wishes to survive, (3) the paradigm of Jewish peoplehood and the practice of Jewish peoplehood education, can respond effectively to the task of instilling a need to belong that can be shared by both Israeli and Diaspora young Jews.

The need shared by Israeli and Diaspora Jewry as collectives, is their common incapacity to awaken in their youth a sense of strong belonging to their Jewish community. While in the Diaspora the tension between the non-Jewish universal and the Jewish particular is emphasized by, and reflected in part by increasing rates of out-marriage, in Israel the tension between being universal and being Jewish manifests itself quite differently, specifically between being Jewish and being democratic. Sometimes, it is also reflected between being Jewish and being Israeli, or between staying in Israel and leaving the nation. All of these are serious tensions and pose in fact a threat not only to the connections and commonalities between Israeli Jews and Jews in the Diaspora, but perhaps even to the Jewish continuity of each community.

D. Mittelberg (✉)
Oranim, Academic College of Education, Tivon, Israel
e-mail: davidm@oranim.ac.il

One of the universal but non-ideological factors that differentiates between being Jewish in Israel and being Jewish in the Diaspora, is that in the Diaspora *no one* can take being Jewish for granted. One has to make the effort to be Jewish. One must create Jewish space in the non-Jewish world within which we live. Thus, in the modern world where personal identity is a matter of a choice among multiple choices, the challenge is to promote the choice to be Jewish where the prevailing majority status quo is non-Jewish.

In Israel, the reverse side of the same problem is prevalent. In Israel, *everyone* takes being Jewish for granted. Since Jewishness is ubiquitous in the public domain, Israeli Jews are not compelled to affirm it. Indeed, it is precisely because being Jewish is taken for granted that it becomes the problem. Because Israeli Jews take their Jewishness for granted, Israeli Jewish adolescents have to go to European sites; for example, the death camp of Majdanek, in State-sponsored visits, in order to begin to understand Jewish tradition and pre-State history. Of course, there is an additional problem in that the Israeli educational system does not teach contemporary Jewish history to its pupils, certainly not about Jewish life in the Diaspora today, or the last 60 years for that matter.

Despite the wide-ranging plurality of its forms (albeit without an ideology of pluralism), Israeli Jewishness lacks its flexibility and portability. One cannot take Israeli Judaism when leaving Israel, unless one is a practicing religious Jew. So while Diaspora Judaism has the fundamental weakness of not being situated within a sovereign Jewish state, it has the powerful advantage of being portable and adaptable through multiple mutations and permutations of external society. These are very fundamental, existential differences between Israeli and Diaspora Judaism that I do not think can be transformed by *any* ideology. Moreover, they both represent critical flaws to a thriving Jewish existence. It is possible that Jewish peoplehood might offer a reasonable, responsible response to these existential challenges facing both Israeli and Diaspora Judaism.

Philosophical Underpinnings of the Discourse

Michael Rosenak (2008) suggests that the discourse of peoplehood provides a constructive answer. He claims that the search for commonalities offered by the paradigm of Jewish peoplehood is both useful and meaningful, for it offers "…Jewish self-identification without shared religiosity, or a cultivation of a national culture. . . . . it does not even require a common language: and it does not insist that all Jews come on Aliya…" (ibid., 13). By neither mandating a common language nor insisting on normative immigration to Israel, and, moreover, by blurring the differences between Jews, rather than accentuating antagonistic differences, Jewish peoplehood fuels the continuing search for shared meaning within the current ambiguity and ambivalence that face Jews in both Israel and abroad.

Unlike Soloveitchik, for Rosenak the choice is not between 'mere' fate and essential destiny, but rather is a question of whether there can be found a new foundation for Jewish peoplehood that all Jews can share. Rosenak is searching for

"... a prescriptive Jewishness that... involves fostering a community identity that leaves questions of belief, behavior and commitment as open, yet important issues." (ibid., 16).

Citing the religious philosopher Eliezer Goldman and the philosopher Martin Buber, Rosenak offers the prescription that "...the concept Am Yisrael as including those who do not observe the (religious) norm" (ibid., 28). This inclusion of those who do not define themselves as "religious" is quite pertinent today; institutionalized Jewish religion, rather than serving as a unifying force for the larger proportion of Jews who are not Orthodox, increasingly appears to divide different groups of Jews worldwide. The inclusiveness of Jewish peoplehood could well provide a meaningful remedy.

Arnold Eisen has already decided it is so. In his words, "... peoplehood is probably the *only* concept that suits the present situation and meets present needs. "Nation" and "religion" are each in their own way too all-encompassing. They demand more than many Jews are willing to identify with in terms of belief or behavior, and thus render significant portions of the population outsiders to a group which they know belongs to them and which they want very much to claim as their own. On the other hand, ethnicity and heritage are too narrow. They miss out on much of what makes Jewish identity attractive and even compelling to many Jews—a part of the self for which they are profoundly grateful and that many are profoundly disappointed not to transmit to the next generation. Only *peoplehood* seems just right." (Eisen, 2008, p. 2) for it blurs the divisive differences between the contrasting modalities of Jewish existence today, namely nationality and faith, or nationhood versus ethnicity. Peoplehood, argues Eisen, stands between these dualisms and authentically reflects Jewish biblical and historical heritage in and of itself. Moreover, the utility and robustness of peoplehood derives from what Eisen chooses to call its sociological constituents, akin to the term *civilization* as coined by Mordecai Kaplan. In Kaplan's own words,

> Judaism as otherness is thus something far more comprehensive than Jewish religion. It includes that nexus of a history, literature, language, social organization, folk sanctions, standards of conduct, social and spiritual ideals, esthetic values, which in their totality form a civilization.... (Kaplan, 1967, p. 178)

Indeed, what is referred to here is the social structure on which peoplehood can rest.

Ami Bouganim has pointed out that in 1954, Kaplan adopted the term *peoplehood* instead of *civilization* articulating a transnational vision when referring to "a new type of nation—an international nation, with a national home to give them cultural and spiritual unity" (Kaplan cited in Bouganim, 2008, p. 84). Thus, while *civilization* was coined to avoid the contraction of Judaism to a religion, *peoplehood* was coined by Kaplan to avoid the contraction of Judaism to a State. But if so, what would be the basis of the new contract between all Jews?

For Eisen, the tool of conversation and dialogue is the agency of peoplehood building. This dialogue will require a framework within which to live and breathe. We will consider below, through the examination of certain educational ventures, whether this project can indeed be undertaken, and what conditions would be necessary to do so.

While Mordecai Kaplan offered us a groundbreaking formula to resist the reduction of contemporary Judaism to a religion or State alone, Simon Rawidowicz pioneered a language of dialogue that was ahead of its time and rejected by his peers. In his "Ever Dying People," Rawidowicz writes that as early as in 1948 he called in Hebrew for a partnership relation between Israel and the Diaspora.

> "Twenty years ago, I began to speak about a "partnership" between the Land of Israel and the Diaspora of Israel. Instead of Ahad Ha-Am's prevailing conception of a center and circumference, of a circle with one focus, I attempted to develop a conception of the people of Israel as a whole, as an ellipse with two foci, the Land of Israel and the Diaspora of Israel. Later, I tried to develop this system further under the symbolic title of "Israel is One": the Land of Israel and the Diaspora of Israel, two that are one." (Rawidowicz, 1986, p. 151)

Thus, Rawidowicz referred directly to the transnational component of Jewish collective life, presaging current Jewish Agency for Israel (JAFI) terminology by calling for a *partnership* between Israel and the Diaspora.

Rawidowicz's call was unheeded because it was framed or perceived in normative contested language; when understood as sociological imperative of partnership, however, as in Eisen's terms, it may be that what was rejected 60 years ago can now become a center piece of global Jewish life.

The Jewish Peoplehood Discourse

A wide-ranging discussion on Jewish peoplehood exists, as reported in part by Kopelowitz and Engelberg (2007). It seems, however, that for the most part, this is an internal discourse between Israelis, mostly of Anglo origin, with primarily, North American Diaspora Jews. This lack of symmetry belies the attractive inclusiveness of the term 'peoplehood' and undermines its capacity to serve as a shared paradigm for Jews both in Israel and the Diaspora.

Fishman (2007) succinctly defines "*peoplehood* as an ethnic group sharing a common descent, language, culture and homeland" (2007, p. 44). These four components may become subjective, compelling constructs of individual life, through the engagement of Jews with each other, through value-driven local and transnational, reciprocal, social networks, generating the individual and group resource of ethnic social capital. They too must be emphasized and nurtured in order to achieve a more mutual, shared discourse than currently exists.

Thus, Jewish peoplehood may be conceived as the dimension of Jewishness that 'thickens' the lines of engagement between Jews. Jewish peoplehood, furthermore, *crosses* the divides that exist between religious – secular and Israel – Diaspora. In this regard, Jewish peoplehood cannot be reduced to a particular constituent of either of these two antinomies, but rather contains them both—and maybe even others. We adopt Shulman's conviction (2009) that a multiple identity is a *virtue* for the modern person, and add that the Jewish peoplehood paradigm provides the quintessential framework within which may be situated the multiple identity of the global Jewish modern. In actuality, neither Israeli Jewry nor Diaspora Jewry can, *on its own*, generate global Jewish peoplehood; both are dependent on each other to utilize the transnational platform for transcendent goals.

The goal for Jewish peoplehood education, therefore, is to build *interdependence, reciprocity,* and *mutuality* while accepting multiplicity of identity. In the emerging field of Jewish peoplehood education, there is a range of different educational programs (see Kopelowitz and Engelberg, 2007). This chapter will review only those programs that include core practices engaging both Israeli and Diaspora Jews with the goal of enhancing the Jewishness *of* each other, through the connectivity *with* each other (see below).

This discourse on Jewish peoplehood has been propelled by a number of recent initiatives and institutions. Kopelowitz and Ravivi (2008) report on a conference convened by the UJA-Federation of New York and JAFI in 2005, where the Jewish peoplehood discourse received an important, intellectual contemporary articulation.

In the following years, Oranim Academic College of Education, the Department of Jewish Peoplehood—Oren convened two conferences on Jewish peoplehood. In June 2006, with the support of the Department of Education at JAFI, a conference summarizing the work of a year-long think-tank on the subject of Jewish peoplehood education for *Israeli* Jews, was convened. Two years later in June 2008, Oranim hosted a second conference dealing with Global Jewish peoplehood education.

Philanthropic foundations have also exercised initiative in building institutions to address this issue. Efforts by the Nadav Fund led to the establishment of the International School for Jewish Peoplehood Studies at Beth Hatefutsoth (since November 2006). This school has pursued critical strategic initiatives with UJA-Federation of NY and JAFI, as well as with important practitioner educational institutions in Israel and the Diaspora (see below). In the second half of 2009, the School has shifted to developing programs for the renewed *Museum of the Jewish People,* and in response in November 2009, the Partnership of NADAV, UJA- Federation of NY and JAFI will launch the *Jewish Peoplehood Hub.* This new entity will function as a strategic catalyst and incubator in the Jewish world, aspiring to nurture Jewish Peoplehood globally (including the continuation of projects originally launched by the SJPS).

The field of *research* on Jewish peoplehood was advanced with the establishment of the Jewish People Policy Planning Institute in 2002, (see www.jpppi.org.il). Cohen and Yaar (forthcoming) reported at the Herzliya Conference in April 2009 on their work developing a Jewish peoplehood index, based on a first-ever, bi-national survey conducted in Israel and in North America.

At the time of writing this chapter, the Israeli government had launched a global 'consultative process' designed by JPPPI, to generate policy recommendations for the Israeli government on how to strengthen Jewish identity and connection to Israel. The questions still to be addressed are whose identity needs to be strengthened and the purposes of the connections.

Just as the above process has unfolded *top-down,* so educational practitioners working on the transnational interface between Jewish communities in Israel and the Diaspora, have pioneered bottom-up initiatives in Jewish peoplehood education. Here, too, support of private foundations, major Jewish Federations such as New York, Boston, and San Francisco as well as JAFI, have been critical in this process. Inductively and at first, perhaps somewhat intuitively, over the last decade, as Kopelowitz and Engelberg report, select institutions such as Oranim Academic College of Education, have developed a structure and content of Jewish peoplehood education. Oranim, in fact, has maintained uninterrupted, in-house evaluation of this process over the entire decade. When taken together, all of these processes present us with an opportunity to review both the intellectual discourse and the practice of Jewish peoplehood education and to seek the possible sources of synergy between them. Finally, an attempt will be made to develop an agenda of the many research questions that remain unasked and/or unanswered despite the intensive activity reported above.

The Jewish Peoplehood Discourse and Educational Practice

Kopelowitz and Engelberg (2007) review the renaissance of the discourse on Jewish peoplehood since Kaplan and the degree to which this intellectual discourse guides Jewish educators today. They point out how the very term is contested by Jewish scholars worldwide who are divided into two broad schools, with at least one Israeli institution in denial over the very term (*Amiut* = peoplehood in Hebrew), (See also Kopelowitz & Ravivi, 2008).

The two schools of thought, 'communitarian' on the one hand and 'liberal' on the other, bear some correlation to Rosenak's understanding of Soloveitchik's distinction between the "covenant of destiny" and "covenant of fate," respectively. (Rosenak, 2008, p. 15). The communitarian scholars emphasize normative prescriptions of peoplehood including: Covenant, Tikkun Olam/repairing the world, mutual responsibility, commandments/obligations; the liberal notion of peoplehood, recognizing the power of individual choice, is characterized as seeking a pluralistic content within a shared framework or common public. This latter notion is envisaged as a cross-cultural conversation transcending Jewish cultural and religious diversity while building the social capital required for the networks and institutional structure of Jewish community.

Kopelowitz and Engelberg offer three core principles common to both schools, which define Jewish peoplehood as:

1. A multi-dimensional experience
2. Rejection of a strong ideology
3. Connections between Jews, not Jewish identity
   To their three categories, I would offer a fourth:
4. Connections between communities and their local institutions

My fourth category refers of course, to the platform on which Jewish peoplehood must stand if it is not to be reduced to an idea or an image, namely the "glocal." I define glocal as "the global and the local simultaneously and contend that glocal relationships must exist between Jewish communities qua communities. The *transnational* School-to-School Connections Program (see below) is one example of this dimension.

Further developing these ideas, Kopelowitz and Engelberg (2009) articulate three levels of [*an individual's*] (my emphasis) connection to the Jewish people. These are (1) the emotional (2) the intellectual and (3) holding a consciousness of belonging to the Jewish people (ibid., 14).

While these are critical elements required to evaluate change in a participant's sense of belonging to the Jewish people following Jewish peoplehood programming, this subjective domain of the *participant* does not exhaust the theoretical field of Jewish peoplehood, and hence, the addition of my fourth objective element above.

In both papers, Kopelowitz and Engelberg explain the post-2000 peoplehood renaissance as a consequence of an ideological vacuum that derives from the loss of a centrist ideology that is compelling for a majority of Jews worldwide. While this absence may explain the openness of Jewish leadership to an alternative framework, it does nothing to sustain Jewish peoplehood in the long term. What might add to this analysis by Kopelowitz and Engelberg? Scholarship in the areas of Jewish philosophy and sociology, for all its historical breadth and depth, begins its analysis understandably from within, moving outward from there. Strengths and weaknesses are sought and found within the Jewish sphere. Peoplehood has developed vitality not just because of what has changed within the Jews, but rather due to what has changed in the world at large.

Just as Zionism arose within the larger project of European and then global nation building, so too peoplehood will thrive in the global world of transnational peoples. It is not, as some post-modernists might claim, that the nation-state has declined, but rather that we are witnessing the demise of the culturally *homogenous* nation-state, everywhere. That type of nation-state is being replaced by multicultural societies; they will be followed by multicultural regimes. Hundreds of millions of human beings today live *outside* the country in which they themselves were born. The phenomenon of transnational peoples is growing and expanding. While the Jews may well have been the FIRST transnational people with homeland and diasporas, today they are only one among a growing number of peoples in this situation.

The time has come for mainstream global Jewish scholarship to take these changes seriously and to look beyond the often self-serving, dyadic, quasi mutually-exclusive relationships that have characterized the Israel – Diaspora discourse and existence. The historical possibilities and opportunities exist now for the Jewish people to continue to thrive and actually to develop a transnational civilization not very different from that imagined by Kaplan and Rawidowicz. Through the reconstruction of innovative multilateral global Jewish scholarship can be generated a new discourse on Jewish peoplehood that can recommend policy change for Jewish leadership.

The normative call for a glocal (both global *and* local) relationship of all Jews with each other, implied by the fourth domain I referred to above, has already been made by Deborah Dash Moore (2005), who critiques the current model of Jewish citizenship, particularly of Israeli and American Jews, as being essentially binary: Israel *versus* the Diaspora (ibid., 38).

Moore argues that transnationalism is a state encompassing both the identity and practices of individuals and groups that "assumes multiple social relationships – familial, economic, social, organizational, religious, and political – that link together" (ibid.) different societies. Moore believes that a transnational Jewish citizenship characterized by "cultural exchange, mutual support, political engagement, religious dialogue, social interchange, economic cooperation, [and] educational fellowship" (ibid.) is the "best way to support and sustain Israel" (ibid.). The transnationalism Moore envisions involves several important elements: the active participation of both the Diaspora and Israeli Jews in Jewish societies, the expression of a variety of different (Jewish) perspectives in Jewish societies (ibid., 37), the encouragement of "multiplicity rather than uniformity" (ibid., 38), and finally, the encouragement of "cooperation rather than competition [in response to] changing circumstances" (ibid.).

Moore believes that increasing interaction and transcending binary roles—and thereby "moving to a new type of transnationalism that could reconfigure what is implied in the term 'Jewish State'" (ibid., 37)—is the best strategy for sustaining Israel. A first step for Israel might be to "redefine its understanding of a 'Jewish state [by] re-examining the Zionist belief in the negation of the Diaspora" (ibid., 38); while increasing interaction with Israel "would allow American Jews to identify with sectors of the Israeli population rather than with the state... help[ing] to move American Jews away from an idealized understanding of Israel" (ibid., 37). In addition, by sharing in a transnational Jewish citizenship, Israelis would forge "multiple ties of involvement that would broaden and deepen their understanding of Jewish peoplehood" (ibid., 38), invigorating the Israeli experience of Judaism. Through the above-described transnationalism, Jews would develop a form of "ethical peoplehood" that would "re-imagine the possibilities of religious community and responsibility" (ibid.).

Measures of Jewish Peoplehood

Can one offer any social scientific basis that such a transnational strategy would have any popular support? In order to explore the potential for this re-imagination of Jewish peoplehood among Diaspora Jews, I report below briefly part of my own analysis of the American NJPS2001 data, followed by a brief contrast with data from British and Australian Jewry.

(A) Collective Definition of American Jews
The 2001-2002 National Jewish Population Study explored several different definitions of what Jews in America consider themselves to be, i.e., a religious group, an ethnic group, a cultural group, a nationality, a part of a worldwide people. While variations exist across denominations and between respondents who have or have not visited Israel, 70–80% of Jews in America see themselves as a religious, cultural, and ethnic group (Mittelberg, 2007). The percentage of Jews in America who agree that Jews are a nationality drops significantly;

Jewish Peoplehood Education

Jews in America: A Part of a Worldwide People

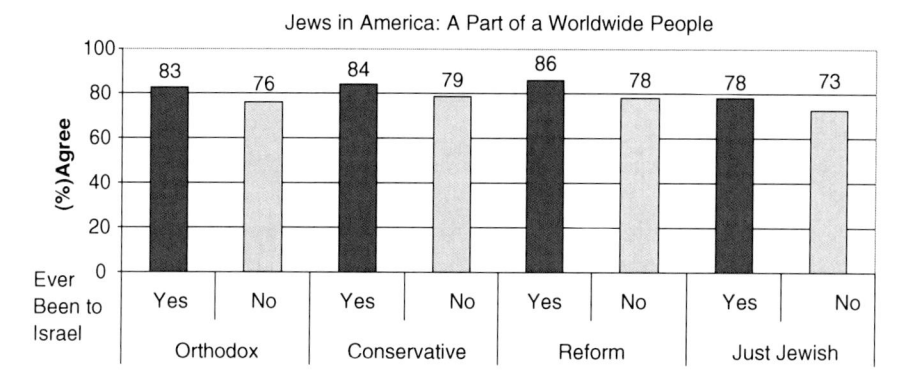

	Orthodox		Conservative		Reform		Just Jewish	
Ever Been to Israel	Yes	No	Yes	No	Yes	No	Yes	No
(%) Agree	83	76	84	79	86	78	78	73

Fig. 1 Jews in America: A part of worldwide people (NJPS 2001 data)

Orthodox Jews are the only denomination with a majority (around 60%) agreeing with this statement. Despite the widespread rejection of the collective identity of nationality, we find across-the-board acceptance (again, 70–80%) of the collective identity of American Jews as being part of a worldwide Jewish People (see Fig. 1).

(B) How American Jews Define Themselves as Jews

The 2001–2002 NJPS also asked respondents whether they themselves have a strong sense of belonging to the Jewish People (see Fig. 2). While these personal rates were far lower than the group definitions, generally, respondents under 30, in all denominations, who had visited Israel, expressed a stronger sense of belonging to the Jewish people than their age and denomination peers and often the adult denominational peers who had not visited Israel (see also Mittelberg, 2007).

Strong Sense Of Belonging to the Jewish People

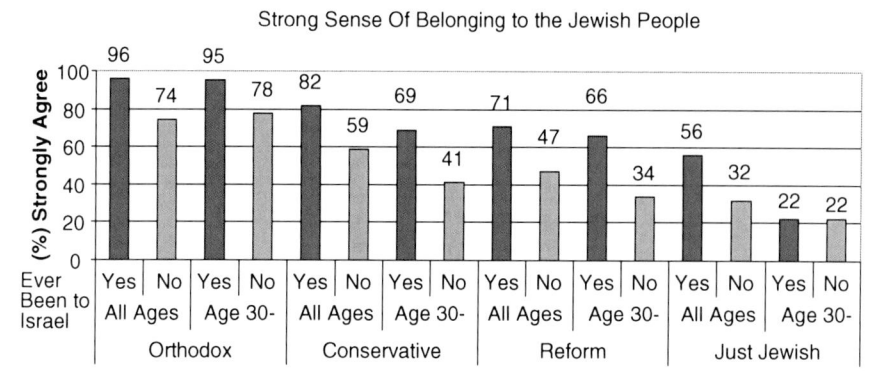

	Orthodox				Conservative				Reform				Just Jewish			
	All Ages		Age 30-		All Ages		Age 30-		All Ages		Age 30-		All Ages		Age 30-	
Ever Been to Israel	Yes	No	Yes	No	Yes	No	Yes	No	Yes	No	Yes	No	Yes	No	Yes	No
(%) Strongly Agree	96	74	95	78	82	59	69	41	71	47	66	34	56	32	22	22

Fig. 2 Jews in America: A strong sense of belonging to the Jewish people

(C) British and Australian Jewry
It is important to note, however, that not all the Jewish diasporas follow the American mould. On the contrary, Sinclair and Milner report that

> "88% of young British Jews aged 16–30 years old agreed somewhat or strongly with the following statement: 'I have a strong sense of belonging to the Jewish people." (ibid., 2005:100)

Moreover in Australia, the notion of Jewish Peoplehood is so un-problematical it requires no unique language and is expressed in the notion of being a Zionist. This is so in the majority of the Jewish day schools and also in the wider community. So much so, that in the current nationwide survey, not a single question was asked concerning Jewish peoplehood. Instead, all respondents were asked

> "Do you regard yourself as a Zionist? By the term Zionist we mean that you feel connected to the Jewish people, to Jewish history, culture and beliefs, the Hebrew language and the Jewish homeland, Israel"

To which 82%, of a national sample of 2,758 respondents replied yes (Markus, 2009).

Toward an Index of Jewish Peoplehood

I have written elsewhere that what is methodologically called for today is deliberative, transnational Jewish social research (Mittelberg, 2007). This methodology is not neutral. It calls for an end to Jewish social research that is provincial by demand and habit and suggests a restatement of the Jewish question so that it can be referenced by a priori, worldwide Jewish inclusiveness and reciprocity. Cohen and Yaar's work conducting a bi-national survey with the goal of developing a Jewish peoplehood index (2009, forthcoming), presented at the Herzliya Conference (February 2009) adopts my position.

Even before the presentation of the full report of these two surveys, including 1,000 Israeli Jewish adults and 1,161 American Jewish adults, it is useful to note their measures of Jewish peoplehood which include: a sense of belonging to the Jewish people, a sense of pride in being Jewish, the importance of Israel and America as spiritual centers of the Jewish people, emotional attachment to Israel and American Jews. In addition, the index included measures of transnational social networks including personal family relations abroad, as well as willingness to support activities that would promote inter-community (Israel – America) relationships.

Cohen and Yaar's (2009, forthcoming) preliminary findings may be summarized in the following four key points:

1. Large majorities of both American and Israeli Jews affirm a sense of belonging and emotional attachment to the Jewish people and to Israel.
2. Despite the researchers' own expectations, younger Americans shared these views no less than the older members of the population.

3. Both communities score far lower on indices of reciprocal knowledge or sharing relationships. In our terms, they lack transnational social capital.
4. Reciprocal visits are associated with higher scores on Jewish peoplehood measures; however, few Israelis or American Jews actually engage in activities that might foster these relationships. The researchers did not find any sort of ideological abyss, reciprocal negation, or age-related distancing. However, intimate knowledge and familiarity with the other, or any activity designed to create transnational relationships, is decidedly missing. What is lacking is an organizational infrastructure for global Jewish peoplehood.

Over a decade ago, I posited that a way to ensure the Jewish future was through purposeful and programmatic *Jewish People Building* built on engagement and interaction through reciprocal relationships.

> "Thus the Jewish communities in the Diaspora today could assume a *new* historic role of *partner* with Israel, to ensure the Jewish future of Israel in the Diaspora and the Diaspora in Israel – the Jewish future of the Jewish people. It would pursue this goal by engaging intentionally, purposefully, and programmatically in *Jewish People Building* through lateral Israel-Diaspora Jewish programming, of social engagement and interaction between different Jews from different communities who mean something personal to each other and who live out existential commonalities in partially shared communities, even if only for segments of their daily lives, or at important stages in their biographies." (Mittelberg, 1999, p. 135)

Since then, the research mentioned above has shed light on such possibilities and has fueled the hypothesis. Indeed, now we would claim that initiated, educational, reciprocal visits ought to enhance the sense of belonging to the Jewish people. We would argue that this would be true for all ideologies and ages, and, moreover, that it would work for Jews both from Israel and from the Diaspora. Through the lens of this hypothesis, we will now examine several practical interventions.

Top-Down Programming, Jewish Peoplehood Formal Education: Beth Hatefutsoth—International School for Jewish Peoplehood Studies

Beth Hatefutsoth, the Nahum Goldmann Museum of the Jewish Diaspora, is an institution dedicated to telling the story of the Jewish People and describing the special bond between the Jewish People and Israel. Education is central to the work of Beth Hatefutsoth, which in November 2006 (through the support of the Nadav Fund), established the International School for Jewish Peoplehood Studies (SJPS) (http://www.bh.org.il/about-us.aspx).

Often working in cooperation with other institutions, SJPS functioned as a "headquarters" producing learning and teaching guides, as well as educational curricula and activities for distribution. In addition, SJPS invited diverse audiences to events it hosted including enrichment programs, conferences, think-tanks, etc.; the following are descriptions of some of the main projects launched by the SJPS.

My Family Story

This curriculum encourages students to investigate their personal family histories, stimulating and reinforcing family ties. It is designed to strengthen students' identity, convey an appreciation and understanding of the connection between different individual histories, Jewish people's history and global events. Those who use this curriculum are eligible to enter for the "My Family Story" International Competition. SJPS has created an accompanying curricular unit to support teachers and students preparing projects for the competition.

The Educational Kit: Israel—the Vision and the Venture of the Jewish People. Developed in partnership with the Center for Educational Technology (CET), this curriculum includes an assortment of classroom resources: materials, sources, disk, facilitator's guide book, project cards, video, access to the interactive website (www.israventure.com), and ideas for engaging students in the account of international Jewish complex partnership and cooperation in establishing the State of Israel.

Peoplehood Papers

This collection of essays deals with philosophical aspects of Jewish peoplehood, covering subjects of thinking about and creating new understandings and action plans around Jewish peoplehood. Created in collaboration with KolDor and The United Jewish Communities, The Peoplehood Papers feature articles from a diverse group of Jewish leaders and thinkers.

Global Task Force of Jewish Peoplehood Education

With the support of UJA-Federation of New York, SJPS established The Global Task Force of Jewish Peoplehood Education. Over 30 leading practitioners in formal, informal, and adult Jewish education from around the world were invited by SJPS to construct a platform for conceptualizing, strategizing, and educating for Jewish peoplehood. The Task Force projects are presently being collated into a book on Jewish peoplehood education.

Top-Down Programming, Jewish Peoplehood Informal Education: The Taglit-Birthright Israel *Mifgash*

A quarter of a century of extensive research on the *Israel Experience* focused almost exclusively on the Jewish visitors from the Diaspora, showing unequivocally the significant and long-lasting impact that a visit to Israel can have on the Jewish identity and behavior of participants (Mittelberg, 1994, 1999, Chazan and Koriansky, 1997, Cohen, E.H. 2008; Saxe & Chazan, 2008). Increasingly, however, Israel Experience trips—and Taglit-Birthright Israel trips in particular—include a *mifgash*—an "encounter" between the Diaspora Jewish visitors and Israeli peers. Recently, there has been some research dedicated specifically to this element of *mifgash*. On a typical Taglit trip, six to eight Israelis, usually soldiers, join the tour group for half or more of the 10-day experience. For a comprehensive account of the Taglit-Birthright experience, see Saxe and Chazan (2008), who highlight not only the dynamics of the *mifgash*, but also the meanings attached to the experience by Diaspora and Israeli participants. Sasson, Mittelberg, Saxe and Hecht (2008) conducted research on the *mifgash* itself. The study conducted in 2007 consisted of qualitative research on 20 tour groups and post-trip surveys of more than 400 Israeli participants, and approximately 6,300 North American participants. The data indicate not only that individuals who participate in Taglit-Birthright, experience significant post-trip impact on a personal level, but also that the cross-cultural, transnational encounter provided by the *mifgash* serves to promote in them a hybrid sense of belonging to the same Jewish people.

The *mifgash* is a structured encounter between individuals; it is at the same time, an encounter between Jewish worlds. The *mifgash* challenges the cultural identity of all its participants, enhancing their sense of collective belonging to the global Jewish people. Both groups recognize commonalities in Jewish background and practice, and this recognition serves as a basis of their sense of common belonging to the Jewish people. During the encounters, participants examine previously taken-for-granted assumptions regarding religion, nationality, and peoplehood. In so doing, they reject antagonistic dualisms of either/or religious or non-religious, Israeli Jew and Diaspora Jew. By creating a common framework of identification, participants come to better understand not only their counterparts—but themselves as well. Thus, the *mifgash* promotes not only Jewish identity, but also builds a sense of belonging to the Jewish people in participants.

Bottom-Up Jewish Peoplehood Informal Education Within Schools: Israel–Diaspora Jewish School-to-School Connections Program

The school-to-school programs discussed below are designed not only to impact the participants involved and to build a sense of Jewish peoplehood, as in the Taglit mifgash, but also to impact the infrastructure culture of the participating school *communities,* through the creation of meaningful and mutual people-to-people connections between the administrators, teachers, parents, and students of the partnered schools.

Methodology

The following is based on a secondary analysis of several interim evaluation reports for the School-to-School Connections Program, in two separate regional partnerships, that has been ongoing for a total of 7 years (2003–2009). In School Twinning

Table 1 School-to-school connections program survey database, 2008

Israeli educators—partnership A December 2007 ($N = 10$) Post-questionnaire only	*American educators—partnership A* Two groups (2007, 2008), $N = 14$ Post-questionnaire only
Israeli students—partnership A Two groups (2007, 2008), $N = 49$ Pre- and post-questionnaires	*American students—partnership A* Three groups (2008), $N = 76$ Pre- and post-questionnaires
Israeli students—partnership B Three groups (2004–2006), $N = 82$ Pre- and post-questionnaires	*American students—partnership B* Three groups (2004–2006), $N = 66$ Pre- and post-questionnaires

Partnership A, evaluations were conducted among three delegations of teachers and school administrators (24 educators in total), and among five delegations of Israeli and American students (numbering 125 in total). In School Twinning Partnership B evaluations included student data only from six delegations, totaling 148 American and Israeli students (see Table 1).

The educator data is retrospective, administered to the participants who traveled either to the United States or to Israel, following their *mifgash*. All of the student data are longitudinal, collected from the same students at the following three stages: at the outset of the program or just prior to the first *mifgash* (Stage 1); following the trip and *mifgash* either in the United States or Israel, completed by those who traveled (Stage 2); and following each hosting experience, either in the United States or in Israel, completed by those who hosted (Stage 3).

The survey instrument consisted of a written questionnaire composed of "closed" questions with multiple-choice answers as well as a qualitative component of "open" questions to which participants responded in their own words.

The School-to-School Connections Program reported below is the flagship program of the Department for Jewish Peoplehood—Oren, at Oranim College. Pairing schools in Israel and around the world, these programs include building personal and professional relationships between the teachers of each school, developing a joint curriculum, visiting the respective communities, and experiencing "*mifgashim*" or facilitated encounters during these visits. Below are two concrete examples of such programming, where Partnership A, connects American day schools with Israeli state schools, Partnership B connects American day and afternoon schools with Israeli State schools.

School Twinning Partnership A

Together with the local Bureau of Jewish Education and the Jewish Federation, Oren has connected two schools (one school having two campuses) in one geographic area of the United States with four schools in Israel (referred to here as 'School Twinning Partnership A'). Oren's work focuses on (1) creating connections between the educators of the partnered schools through exchanges of educator delegations and articulating a shared vision, goals, and programs for joint study; (2) building a joint curriculum for student study; and (3) carrying out student delegations.

School Twinning Partnership B

Oren currently coordinates and supervises a major School-to-School Partnership, linking 19 schools in another region of the United States with their partner schools in one city in Israel (referred to here as 'School Twinning Partnership B'). Oren provides the educational curriculum and teacher training, bridging the two communities, with positive impact on thousands of students. This large-scale effort demonstrates the ability, capacity, and efficacy of people-to-people programs, using existing school frameworks, matching communities, and leadership, thus reaching dozens of schools.

With respect to school change, in both partnerships, the impact on administrators, educators, students, parents, families, and entire communities grows each year. In addition to the participant-level questionnaire data to be reported below, participating faculty have formally reported the following impacts on school life:

1. Video conferences on topics determined by the educators, with prepared lesson plans. Parents often attend these video conferences as observers.
2. Beit Midrash via video conference, involving preparation of sacred texts for study with questions for discussion.
3. Award-winning Eighth Grade Science curriculum developed and implemented by both the Israeli and American partner schools. While not a Jewish content program, it is powerful in its basis of connections and indirect impact on families and parents, especially after shared success and recognition of successful enterprise, resulting from reciprocal visits and hosting.
4. Exchange of joint curriculum on Jewish subjects for high-school students, noticeably strengthened Jewish component of the curriculum in an Israeli school.
5. Exchange of maps with the partner class, indicating birthplaces and homes of students in each class. Exchange of "identity cards" between partnered classes, indicating essential elements of students' personalities, identities, and lives.
6. Development of website accessible only to the members of the twinned classes and available for the purpose of sustaining formal and informal communications between the students. Establishment of other e-mail and Internet forums to facilitate communication between students.
7. Multilateral school partnerships with classes in various countries besides Israel and the United States. Such relationships exist with schools in Turkey, Germany, and England.

Basic Survey Findings

The following analysis will investigate the impact of Jewish peoplehood education, within four separate sub-groups: Israeli students, Israeli Educators, American students, and American Educators. However, the central finding across all of the schools is related to the *mifgash* (facilitated encounter) *between* these four different sub-groups.

Israeli Students

In order to ascertain whether the goal of building Jewish peoplehood was met, the questionnaires included a variety of questions about the strength of the bond that participants feel toward Jews across the world and toward Israel. Figure 3a–c report pre- and post-*mifgash* student responses from the same Israeli school, which report a meaningful change in Israeli students' sense of belonging to Israel and the Jewish people. Following their hosting experience, the Israeli students recorded significant, positive changes in their strengthened bond with Jews of the United States and all over the world, their view of Israel as the homeland as well as a national, cultural, and religious center for the Jewish people, all together indicate a heightened subjective sense of Jewish peoplehood.

The Israeli students exhibit another equally important response to the *mifgash*. The data show that they were unequivocally proud to be Israeli both before and after their travel. In the United States, they encountered a strikingly different model for being Jewish and for relating to Israel and the Jewish people. The data suggest that they realized that Jews living in other lands hold alternative views both of Israel as the Jewish homeland and of the place of Israel in the Jewish world. Their previous ideas were challenged and re-examined, and the Israelis arrived at new, nuanced understandings, resulting in decreases in their view of Israel as the homeland of the Jewish people and as a national, cultural, and religious center of the Jewish people. (These decreases from Stage 1 to Stage 2 are illustrated in Fig. 3c.) At the same time, the Israeli students did express a heightened connection to Jews of the United States and to Jews around the world. Thus, despite their realization that Jewish life and attitudes outside of Israel are quite different from what they are accustomed to, the Israeli students did not feel alienated from the "other." Rather, they felt closer and more connected to American Jews after meeting them and learning first-hand about their different and new ways. Students were also asked to respond to the statement, "Israel is a national, cultural, and religious center of the Jewish world." Figure 4 reveals that over several years, both Israeli and American students generally agreed more with this statement following the *mifgash*.

Many students internalized the idea of Jewish peoplehood, and some were able to extrapolate from the personal to the global, and vice versa, from the global to the personal.

> ... before the trip I related to myself as a Jew without any questions. After the trip I understood that I am Jewish, and this is not self-evident. (Israeli student, November 2008)

Comments by two different groups of Israeli students following the *mifgashim*, also indicate that they grasped the importance of the Diaspora and the vitality of Jewish life outside of Israel.

- I have a greater awareness of being Jewish, and I understood things about Judaism in the Diaspora that it's not important where you're Jewish; it's important how much you feel Jewish. (Israeli student, November 2008).

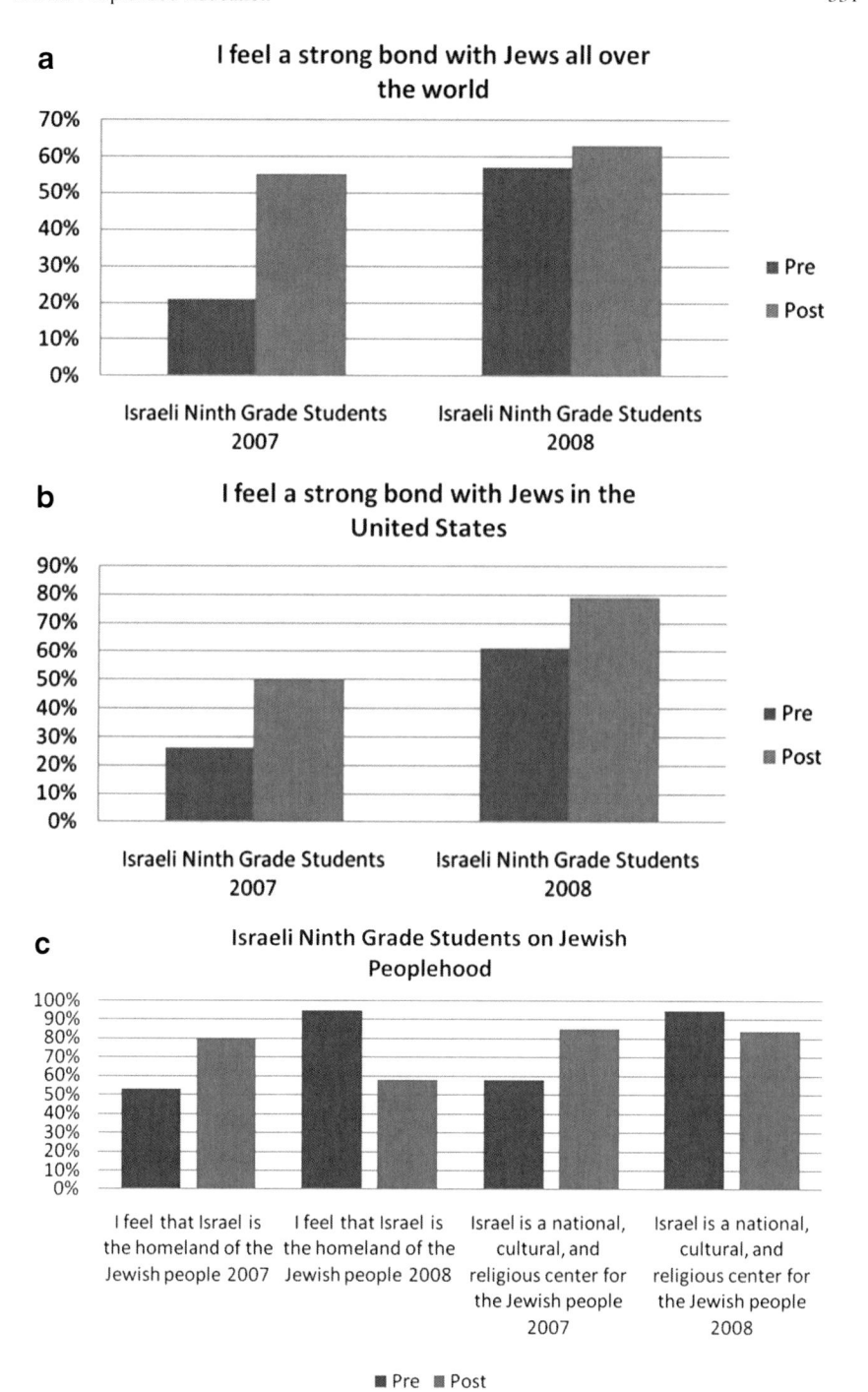

Fig. 3 Examples of impact of *Mifgashim* on Israeli Jewish students' sense of Jewish peoplehood (school twinning partnership A, ninth graders, percentage of responses for the two highest categories, "strongly agree" and "very strongly agree")

Israel serves as a national, cultural and religious center for the Jewish people

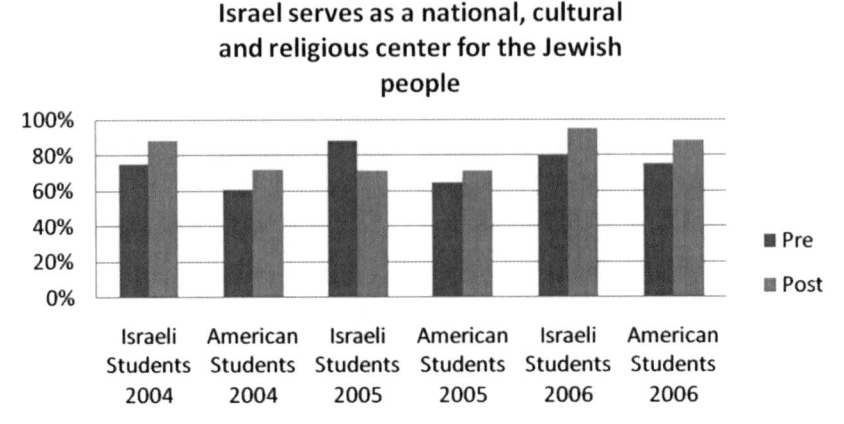

Fig. 4 Israeli and American student response rates to the statement, "Israeli serves as a national, cultural, and religious center for the Jewish people." (school twinning partnership B, tenth graders, percentage of responses for the two highest categories, "strongly agree" and "very strongly agree")

- What changed is that I will think again about maybe going to a synagogue, lighting Shabbat candles, etc. I saw the Judaism of the Americans, and I was surprised that I wasn't connected that way to Judaism. (Israeli student, November 2008).

Israeli Educators

When asked why they chose to participate in the School-to-School Connections Program, Israeli educators pointed to the importance which their *school* places on this program, as well as their own desire to contribute to the relationships.

- My participation in the group was for me a direct continuation of Jewish programming that exists at the school. [It also came] from an ability to contribute to strengthening the connection between teachers in Israel and in the Diaspora. (Israeli educator, June 2008)

Israeli educators, likewise, commented on changes in their sense of Jewish peoplehood following the *mifgash*, in response to questions about the impact of the *mifgash* on their lives.

- A huge influence! It opened a greater exposure in terms of being Jewish, in the State of Israel, being a principal, and what the role is regarding peoplehood, etc. (Israeli principal, December 2007)

Israeli educators were asked how the *mifgash* affected them personally. Again, the transnational, mutual, Jewish connections figured prominently in these educators' reflections.

- Personally, the experiences shaped within me a renewed and deep connection to the land. (Israeli educator, June 2008)

- Absolutely, I am already [experiencing] changes in [my own level] of acceptance and tolerance. (Israeli educator, June 2008)

Israeli educators foresaw that this experience would impact their entire school community through their relationship to Judaism and to each other:

- I will act to strengthen the connection between the [American] students and Israeli students with a focus on Judaism and Eretz Yisrael. (Israeli educator, June 2008)
- I believe that we are the pioneers and from here we can spread out to families, friends, the community, and more. (Israeli educator, June 2008)

American Students

The American students' comments also reflect a heightened sense of Jewish peoplehood and connection to Israelis and Israel, following their hosting experience. Remarks about the highlights of their hosting experience included positive reflections on meeting Jews from around the world; on learning about the Israelis' lives; about showing them their lives in the United States, and/or about similarities and differences with their own; on their mutual connection via Shabbat, being Jewish, or the Hebrew language; and on enjoying these "amazing" people and the process of becoming friends. Among students, a growing sense of Jewish peoplehood seems to begin with an appreciation of the different lives that each group leads and of the commonalities and connections between them.

- As a result of this program, I am more... attached to kids from the [Israeli] School. (American student, June 2008)
- As a result of this program, I am more... interested in visiting Israel and meeting Israeli kids. (American student, June 2008)

The American students also became more aware of their relationship with Israel and Israelis. When asked to complete this statement, "As a result of the Twinning Program you are more....," they responded that they are more "informed about the situation in Israel;" "more connected with kids/people in Israel;" "understanding toward Israel;" "aware of how life is in Israel;" and "interested in visiting Israel and meeting Israeli kids." Their sense of Jewish peoplehood was enhanced through their mutual relationship with their Israeli partners.

American Educators

American educators also experienced meaningful transformations as a result of their *mifgash* in Israel and their relationships with their Israeli counterparts. When asked if any of their attitudes or beliefs about Israel had been impacted by this visit to Israel, they responded as shown in Table 2. As can be seen from the data, following their Israel experience, 80% of the participants feel an increased sense of emotional attachment to Israel as well as an increased sense of attachment to Israeli

Table 2 Impact of the American Jewish educators' *Mifgash* in Israel on their relationship to Israel, June 2008

Statement	Less than before (%)	Same as before (%)	More than before (%)
Your sense of attachment to Israeli culture	0	20	80
How emotionally attached are you to Israel?	0	20	80
Your familiarity with Israel-related groups and organizations in your community	0	40	60
To what extent do you think that Israel serves as a national, cultural, and religious center for the Jewish people?	0	40	60
Your level of participation in Israel-related social activities	0	80	20
To what extent do you feel that your fate and future is bound up with the fate and future of the Jewish people?	0	100	0
To what extent do you see Israel as a source of pride and self-respect for Diaspora Jewry?	0	100	0

culture. Sixty percent are more familiar with Israel-related groups and organizations in their community; and the same percentage feel more strongly that Israel serves as a national, cultural, and religious center for the Jewish people, as did their students (see Fig. 3c).

American Educators relate how this will in turn affect their educational practice:

- Deeper connections to Israel through our friendships and classroom partnerships, and a chance to use the window and mirror of our relationship with the Israeli schools to peer into their lives and re-examine our own. (American educator, June 2007)

American educators were asked why they were interested in participating in this program. The highest rated responses were (a) strengthening ties between Israel and the Diaspora, (b) developing a joint project with a Jewish-Israeli colleague, and (c) being a part of a community of professionals. In their comments regarding their own motivation, they focus on the partnership and on the Jewish and Israeli connections.

- My colleagues and I are embarking on a remarkable partnership with an established Israeli school to deepen and expand our students' connections with and love for Israel. (American educator, June 2008)

Framing the motivation in this way gives structure to future work, both in terms of the content of future programming and also in terms of research.

- I have gained colleagues abroad but more than this, I have close friends, family with the [Israeli] teachers whom, I feel, can work with me on a common goal. (American educator, June 2008)

- I definitely feel more connected to [the Israeli partner school] and have a clearer understanding of the complex situation in Israel. Personally, I can now say that I have friends in Israel. (American educator, June 2008)

In reflecting on how this experience will affect them personally, the American educators commented as follows:

- I have a dee*per* sense of Israel, culture, people... as an educator in this time of my life... and will bring this back with me on a personal level. (American educator, June 2008)

Professionally, the impact of this experience on the American educators and potentially on their school appears to be profound:

- It will indeed help me in my work. It has given me the passion to continue my studies in both Hebrew language and "Jewish studies." (American educator, June 2007)
- This program... will strengthen the connection between youth in US and in Israel, hopefully laying the foundation for a lifetime of connection and community involvement. (American educator, June 2008)

Echoing the findings of Pomson and Grant (2004, p. 67), these educators report that their encounter in Israel allowed them to build powerful personal connections to Israel and with fellow teachers, though we add here, that the teachers involved are not only those from their home school but also their partnered *Israeli* teachers. This experience also served to impact their educational vision and practice, perhaps even to structure the way they now know Israel and its educational promise.

This research, methodologically pairing Israeli and American students as well as Israeli and American educators, all from the very same schools, demonstrates that there is tremendous opportunity in an educational encounter between Jews from different parts of the world. This central element of the program, the *mifgash* is a powerful tool for impacting participants' Jewish identity and sense of Jewish peoplehood. This finding holds regardless of the locale of the particular *mifgash,* whether in Israel or North America. Participants in the *mifgash* discover common beliefs and ideas regarding important aspects of Jewish history and life. In the process of beginning to understand "the other" comes the realization that both American and Israeli Jews essentially share a common Jewish cultural language. Particularly powerful are the opportunities to glimpse into others' lives through home hospitality and sustained contact. The outcome is an enhanced Jewish identity and sense of Jewish peoplehood, i.e., sense of belonging to the Jewish community.

Oren's baseline expectations were that the schools and their communities in North America would be the primary beneficiaries of the connection to Israel. That was, in fact, the case. Nonetheless, we have offered here concrete evidence of impacts on students, educators, schools, and parents in Israel as well, so that the impact on the Israeli side *is as significant* as it is on the North American participants. Connecting Israelis to their Jewish counterparts overseas (a global connection) has led to a dramatic new understanding of their own local Jewish identity. It is eminently clear that the mutuality of the process is a unique and critical element of this model for building Jewish peoplehood.

The model is driven by the communities with support and facilitation by Oren as an outside educational provider by creating concentric circles of engagement between communities. It begins by matching communities and schools. It expands outward to encompass interaction and dialogues between leadership, administrators, and educators, and then to the students, parents, and others involved in the educational life of the communities. Finally, the findings offered here both quantitative and qualitative, indicate the potential that a school twinning program with a well-structured *mifgash* may have, not only the individual participant (as seen in Taglit), but also on the schools (Israeli and American) and the wider communities within which they lodge.

Summing Up: Some Essential Components of Jewish Peoplehood Education

Recalling that the goal for Jewish peoplehood education is to build *interdependence*, *reciprocity*, and *mutuality* while accepting multiplicity of identity, what are the essential components of such an education?

Jewish peoplehood education enhances the identity of Jews by virtue of the connectivity between different types of Jews.

Jewish peoplehood education seeks to discover commonalities among Jews from different countries out of respect for differences between them.

Jewish peoplehood education is propelled by soft ideology and seeks to build bonding social capital between Jews of different ideological persuasions and different backgrounds.

Jewish peoplehood education recognizes the importance of the Hebrew language and culture, but engages Jews in a multi-lingual framework. Hebrew cannot be a sine qua non for Jewish literacy and peoplehood engagement.

Jewish peoplehood education flattens (Friedman, 2006) the educational institutions of the Jewish world (Mittelberg, 2007).

Thus, Jewish peoplehood education is symmetrical, reciprocal, and mutual, thereby laying the groundwork for synergy within the global Jewish community.

Jewish peoplehood education strives to establish transnational frameworks of activity amongst school populations that include students, teachers, parents, and community institutions, thereby striving to generate communities that are infused with a strong sense of belonging to a global Jewish people.

Pedagogic goals of Jewish peoplehood education for participants include emotional commitment, reciprocal knowledge, caring, and engagement based on global Jewish literacy.

Jewish peoplehood education occurs in an environment where multiple identities are valued as a virtue, constituting recurrent transnational personal Jewish relationships, embedded in institutionalized school-to-school partnership relationships.

Future Research Questions

Some of the research questions that need to be answered in order to develop further the emerging field of Jewish peoplehood education would include the following:

- How can we articulate a clear vision of Jewish peoplehood education, shared by Israeli and Diaspora Jewish communities and their educators, which will drive the field forward?
- What are the educational processes, both top-down and bottom-up, that might transform a local, segmented, sectarian provincial Jewish identity of any intensity, into a glocal transcendent sense of belonging to a worldwide Jewish people?
- How does Jewish identity located within the paradigm of the Jewish State (without a synagogue) become connected to a Jewish identity located within the paradigm of the synagogue (without the Jewish State), and what binds the adherents of each with the other?
- What can we learn from the best practices of the *mifgash* and its pedagogy in developing the conversation and dialogue necessary to build a common Jewish cultural language for Jews worldwide?
- What is required to systematically and consistently translate the demonstrated impact of peoplehood programming on *individuals*, into sustained change in the *school culture* of Israeli and Diaspora schools, so that we may say that the schools are infused with Jewish peoplehood education?
- How are we to reconstruct institutions of Jewish education that will facilitate and sustain long-term transnational institutional relationships between Israel and Diaspora educational institutions, both high schools and Institutions of Higher education?
- What would then be required to translate the impact of the emerging transnational relationships on schools into impact on their wider host communities?
- How can we develop a methodology and practice of transnational Jewish research teams, building common core research instruments in multicultural environment based on the partnership model of EU research?

Acknowledgements The author would like to acknowledge with thanks the support of the following: Lori Abramson, in charge of evaluation at Oren, prepared the original interim reports and was very helpful in preparing the data on which was based the secondary analysis reported here. Tally Gur from Oren and MeLena Hassel from the Cohen Center at Brandeis University assisted with different parts of background research for this chapter. Elana Sztokman from Beit Hatfutzoth assisted with the materials from The International School for Jewish Peoplehood Studies. Roberta Bell Kligler read the entire manuscript and offered invaluable comments that enriched the chapter. My thanks to the anonymous reviewers who helped to sharpen many of the points made here. Finally, I wish to thank all the educators in the field who gave of their time to respond to my many questions, we all owe them a debt of gratitude for their innovative work.

References

Bouganim, A. (2008). Jewish sectarianism and Jewish peoplehood. In E. Kopelowitz & M. Ravivi (Eds.), *Jewish peoplehood change and challenge*. Boston: Academic Studies Press.

Chazan, B., & Koriansky, A. (1997). *Does the teen Israel experience make a difference?* New York: Israel Experience Inc.

Cohen, E. H. (2008). *Youth tourism to Israel: Educational experiences of the Diaspora*. Clevedon: Channel View publications.

Cohen, E. H., Auron, A., Cohen, Y., Gross, Z., Margolin, R., Shkedi, A., & Shur, P. (2008) *Jewish Identity, Values and Liesure. Some explorations amongst Israeli General State Schools 15–16 year old students*. Kelman Center for Jewish Education, Tel Aviv University. (Hebrew).

Cohen, S. M., & Yaar, E. (2009). *Peoplehood papers: Vol. 4*. Tel Aviv: Beth Hatefutsoth.

Eisen, A. (2008). Four questions concerning peoplehood –and just as many answers. In E. Kopelowitz & M. Ravivi (Eds.), *Jewish peoplehood change and challenge*. Boston: Academic Studies Press.

Fishman, S. B. (2007). *The way in to the varieties of Jewishness*. Woodstock, VT: Jewish Lights Publishing.

Friedman, T. (2006). *The world is flat [Updated and Expanded]: A brief history of the twenty-first century*. New York: Farar, Straus and Giroux.

Kaplan, M. (1967). *Judaism as a civilization*. New York: Schocken Books.

Kopelowitz, E., & Engelberg, A. (2007) *A framework for strategic thinking about Jewish peoplehood*. Position Paper Commissioned by the Nadav Fund

Kopelowitz, E., & Engelberg, A. (2009) *Jewish peoplehood criteria for the development and evaluation of peoplehood programming*. Position paper commissioned by the UJA Federation of New York and The International School for Jewish Peoplehood Studies. Beth Hatefutsoth, Tel Aviv.

Kopelowitz, E., & Ravivi, M. (Eds.) (2008). *Jewish peoplehood change and challenge*. Boston: Academic Studies Press.

Markus, A. (2009) *Australian Centre for Jewish Civilization*, School of Historical Studies Monash University. Private Communication.

Mittelberg, D. (1994) *"The Israel Visit and Jewish Identification,"* The Institute on American Jewish-Israeli Relations, Issues Series No. 4, American Jewish Committee, New York.

Mittelberg, D. (1999). *The Israel connection and American Jews*. Connecticut and London: Praeger, Westport.

Mittelberg, D. (2007) Convergent and Divergent Dimensions of Jewish Peoplehood. Paper presented at the 2007 WCJCS Quadrennial, Jerualem, June 24–26, 2007 http://www.wcjcs.org/QC2007/Materials/Mittelberg%20David-%20Convergent%20and%20Divergent%20 Dimensions%20of%20Jewish%20Peoplehood.pdf

Moore, D. D. (2005) *Reimagining Transnationalism* in *Israel on My Mind. Israel's Role in World Jewish Identity*. Dorothy and Julius Koppelman Iinstitute on American Jewish-Israeli Relations, American Jewish Committee, New York.

Pomson, A., & Grant, L. D. (2004). Getting personal with professional development: The case of short-term trips to Israel for Diaspora teachers. In J. Bashi, M. B. Peretz, & A. Bouganim (Eds.), *Education and professional training*. Jerusalem: Jewish Agency.

Rawidowicz, S. (1986). *State of Israel, Diaspora, and Jewish continuity*. New England: Brandeis University Press.

Rosenak, M. (2008). The problem of Jewish peoplehood. In E. Kopelowitz & M. Ravivi (Eds.), *Jewish peoplehood change and challenge*. Boston: Academic Studies Press.

Sasson, T., Mittelberg, D., Saxe, L., & Hecht, S. (2008) *Encountering the Other-Finding Oneself. A Study of the Taglit-Birthright Israel Mifgash*. Maurice and Marilyn Cohen Center for Modern Jewish Studies. Brandeis University. www.brandeis.edu/cmjs

Saxe, L., & Chazan, B. (2008). *Ten days of birthright Israel: A journey in young adult identity brandeis series in American Jewish history, culture, and life*. Lebanon, NH: Brandeis University Press, University Press of New England.

Shimoni, S., & Shaltiel, S. (2006) *The place of American Judaism in high school education in Israel*. American Jewish Committee. Jerusalem, New York. (Hebrew)

Shulman, L. (2009). Keynote address multiple identities in Jewish education, The 5th International Conference of The Israel Association of Research in Jewish Education January 7–8, 2009, Oranim and Jerusalem. http://mandel.mli.org.il/MandelCMS/News/5th+International+Conference+on+Research+in+Jewish+Education.htm

Sinclair, J., & Milner, D. (2005). On being Jewish: A qualitative study of identity among British Jews in emerging adulthood. *Journal of Adolescent Research, 20*(1), 91–117.

Ukeles, J. B., Miller, R., & Beck, P. (2006) *Young Jewish Adults in the United States Today.* American Jewish Committee. New York

Life Cycle Education: The Power of Tradition, Ritual, and Transition

Howard Deitcher

The power of rites of passage to shape, impact, and alter human life has been documented in a host of social, anthropological, psychological, and religious studies (Driver, 1998; Grimes, 2000; Marcus, 2004; Turner, 1967; Van Gennep, 1960; Marcus, 1996). The primary purpose of these rites is to ensure that individuals mark these transitions in meaningful ways that address spiritual, religious, psychological, and social needs. These rites can serve to either facilitate or obstruct critical passages in human life. As Driver claims, "they inscribe images into the memories of participants, and they etch values into the cornerstones of social institutions" (1998, p. 5).

In Jewish life responsibility for this education was traditionally subsumed within the family structure as young Jewish children were full participants in the various rites of passage (Marcus, 1996). With dramatic changes in Jewish family and communal structures arose the need to design educational programs that would prepare Jews of all ages to understand, appreciate, and acquire the necessary knowledge that would enable them to perform these rites. In attempting to address these critical educational challenges in a relevant and purposeful way, numerous educational programs have chosen to focus on life-cycle education as a means to integrate the realms of history, *halakhah* (law), sociology, and psychology, and thereby link the individual Jew's life passages with the rich array of rituals and ceremonies that have been practised throughout Jewish history.

The current study will include four main foci: (a) The factors that have secured the prominent role of life-cycle rituals in Jewish life; (b) The place of life-cycle education in Jewish education programs; (c) Research studies that have addressed educational issues related to the Jewish life cycle; (d) Suggestions for future studies that will expand and deepen our knowledge about the central role of life-cycle education in Jewish life.

Until the latter half of the twentieth century there was a limited number of books that addressed the Jewish life-cycle in a comprehensive way; since that time and over the past two decades in particular, there has been an unprecedented proliferation of

---

H. Deitcher (✉)
Hebrew University, Jerusalem, Israel
e-mail: mshoward@mscc.huji.ac.il

popular and scholarly materials that have examined these life passages through a host of different religious, cultural, anthropological, and social lenses.[1] In direct contrast to the ever-growing number of popular volumes on Jewish life-cycle education, one is struck by the limited research-based projects on this topic. This phenomenon will be discussed more extensively at a later point.

The recent upsurge in interest has not only been noted in the proliferation of books and the significant increase of courses and programs, but is also reflected in the observance of life-cycle rituals by a growing number of moderately affiliated Jews around the world (Cohen & Eisen, 2000; Milburn & Seidman, 1999; Levi & Katz, 2000).

Four explanations for this growing phenomenon shed light on various social, religious, and psychological dimensions of these rituals. In their seminal work on the lives of contemporary American Jews, Cohen and Eisen (2000) highlight the critical role that ritual observance plays in the lives of these Jews. As these individuals mature, the importance of family takes on new meaning, and life-cycle events assume a renewed sense of purposefulness as they serve to bond the individuals to their past and forge new ties for the future. The rites of passage fill a critical vacuum that allow young Jewish families to add meaning to their newly acquired status, and concurrently, establish a link with their historical roots.

A second explanation is offered by Jeffrey Salkin (1991) who maintains that the recent proliferation of life-cycle rituals represents a paradigm shift in Jewish liturgical spirituality from celebration of festivals to commemorating life-cycle events. He argues that two recent developments in Jewish life have triggered a renewed interest in life-cycle rituals: first, from a theological perspective, there has been a loss of sacred meaning that interprets commandments like celebrating festivals as a divine obligation, and concurrently, from a sociological perspective, there has been a loss of the organic worshipping community that would have commonly celebrated these festivals in a communal setting. In celebrating the Brit Milah (male circumcision), baby namings, Bar/Bat Mitzvah, weddings and funerals, Jews experience a more compelling theological sense of *kedusha* (holiness) than in the traditional festival paradigm which is far less meaningful and appealing. The personal meaning of life-cycle passages buttresses their status and drives individuals to search for public arenas in which they can celebrate these events. A supporting argument for this claim is Salkin's belief that many American Jews consider Yom Kippur's *yizkor* (memorial) service to be the holiest component of not only the sacred season, but the entire Jewish year. Consequently, the holiest component of the festival cycle is, in fact, a life-cycle ritual that is marked by Jews around the world.

A third school of thought posits that this renewed interest in life-cycle rituals can best be understood from a social-historical perspective. Historically, ritual knowledge in general, and life-cycle ritual in particular, was acquired through observation and active participation within the confines of the family, synagogue, or various communal settings. Young Jewish children actively participated in these rituals on

---

[1] For an annotated bibliography see Marcus, 2004, pp. 20–29.

a regular basis and there was no need to devote precious study time to learn about these practices (Marcus, 2000; Kanarfogel, 1992).

In attempting to explain the dramatic changes in twentieth-century American Jewish life, Sarna (1998) employs the Deweyian distinction between *intentional* education that is provided in schools from *incidental* education, where education is absorbed from the world around. Incidental education clearly dominated early American Jewish life, where the explicit priority was to initiate children into the world of Jewish ritual and practice. Only at a later period did incidental education decline in importance and was replaced by a structured form of intentional education that continues to dominate Jewish life to the present time. "This represents a sea change in Jewish life. Where once Jews learned to negotiate the challenge of living Jewishly in America incidentally, informally, and largely by example, today many of these same lessons are provided intentionally through formal educators and curricula" (p. 11). This paradigmatic shift was explained by Isa Aron (1989) as a move from "enculturation" to "instruction." Borrowing the terms from the Christian theologian, John Westerhoff, Aron contends that *enculturation* constitutes the broadly conceived task of introducing children into a set of values and norms, and thereby initiating them into a particular culture and its commitments. *Instruction* is a more narrowly conceived task that assumes the child's pre-existing commitment to a culture and its norms; it is concerned with assisting children to acquire knowledge of the ideas and skills that society values. Instruction typically takes place within the walls of a classroom, while enculturation is less structured, experienced by direct exposure to the culture and its norms, and leans heavily on the affective. The emerging shifts in Jewish family structures and communal life has created a new set of circumstances which in turn has given over this responsibility to a host of formal educational frameworks (Dash-Moore, 1987).

A fourth thesis is discussed by Taylor (1992) and focuses on the central role of radical individualism in modern society. In modern society, the social environment of each individual is transformed, individual self-awareness is enhanced, and individual choice assumes a new sense of urgency. This newly defined sense of individualism challenges traditional understanding about religious belief and ritual behavior (Berger et al., 1973). Cohen and Eisen labeled this change as a move from an emphasis on "public Judaism" to "private Judaism," whereby contemporary Jews discover and construct Jewish meaning in the private sphere through prayer, study, and ritual and are much less engaged in organizational life, including philanthropy, support for Israel, or the fight against anti-Semitism. In sociological terms, the shift from the group experience to the individual Jew has heightened the popularity and prominence of life-cycle rituals across all denominations.

The Place of Life-Cycle Education in Jewish Education Programs

Over the past two decades the celebration of rites of passage has assumed a more prominent and influential role in the lives of Jewish families around the world. This dramatic change is reflected in the increasingly dominant role that life-cycle education plays in school curricula, adult education programs, as well as a host of different family education programs (Moskowitz, 2003).[2] In non-Orthodox circles life-cycle education serves as one of the key building blocks in both congregational schools as well as day-school settings.

Israeli middle-school syllabi include extensive programs on personal and group celebrations of Bar and Bat Mitzvah as a means to bolster the Jewish identity of these youngsters (www.daat.ac.il). A similar trend emerges from the new CHAI curriculum that is currently being taught in American Reform congregational schools (see Avodah section in www.urj.org). In browsing some of the book publishers for American Jewish schools, one is struck by the disproportionate number of publications on life cycle (www.torahaura.com; www.behrman.powerwebbook.com). In Orthodox schools the role of life-cycle education is less dominant; at the same time one notes a significant emphasis on celebrating new and emerging rituals that have recently secured a place in Orthodox circles. In reviewing the curricular programs of Torah U'Mesorah, for example, it is intriguing to note that the bat mitzvah rite is the most prominent rite of passage, overshadowing the other rites in a pronounced and significant way (www.chinuch.org). This is a curious development, as it illustrates the use of life-cycle education as a means to addressing new social developments in the Orthodox world, a phenomenon that to date was most closely identified with the non-Orthodox.

Adult education programs also devote a significant amount of time to exploring the Jewish life cycle. In most cases these programs weave together the values and conceptual underpinnings of the various rites of passage with practical information about how to best commemorate these ceremonies in a meaningful and personal way (Florence Melton Adult Mini school curriculum; Israel, Steve, "The Jewish Life Cycle," www.jewishagency.org; www.judaism.about.com/od/lifeevents/Life_Events.htm). The opportunity to contemplate rituals that are rich in ideas, values, and psychological wisdom, and at the same time invite the adult learner to perform these ceremonies at transitional points in their lives has generated a flurry of new programs that have caught the imagination of many Jews and succeeded in changing the face of ritual observance.

Research Review

After determining the inherent need for life-cycle education and the wealth of educational opportunities that this topic holds for large numbers of Jews around the world, one is struck by the dearth of research that has been conducted to date.

In summarizing the current state of educational research on life-cycle education several points of interest emerge: (a) the vast majority of research has been conducted in non-Orthodox circles and focuses on issues of identity, psychological

---

[2] For Israeli education see http://www.daat.ac.il/daat/mishpach/index.htm

development, and issues of policy planning. (b) Few studies have examined curricular issues or challenges of professional development. This observation is even more pronounced when one compares this area of study to parallel studies of other content areas such as Bible education or Hebrew language instruction. (c) Finally, in reviewing the range of studies on the various rites of passage the over-representation of Bar/Bat Mitzvah ceremonies is arresting.

In the 1980s a single doctoral dissertation examined the need for and potential impact of life-cycle education in Orthodox day schools (Deitcher, 1985). The study presented a theoretical argument for the need and critical role that a course on life cycle might fill in Orthodox high schools and then provided guidelines for the implementation of such a program. The suggested program was piloted in eight educational settings worldwide and the findings reflected different contextual nuances and influences. Educators from these communities were invited to respond to the following two questions: (a) Is there a perceived need to address the rites of passage in your educational program? (b) If so, does the cited project serve as a viable model for achieving this goal? Both questions elicited positive responses and demonstrated the need for ongoing research as well as the preparation of additional educational materials for use in various settings.

As noted above, rites of passage meet a host of psychological, social, and religious needs that deeply impact human development. In the following section I will review some of the most salient research projects that have explored these issues, highlight those areas that have not received adequate attention, and suggest new research projects that can further our understanding of the field and thereby impact educational practice.

The Power of Ritual

Durkheim's 1912 book, *The Elementary Forms of Religious Life*, is oftentimes identified as the classic guide to understanding the power of life-cycle rituals on human development. This study argues that ritual performance is an essential mechanism in helping individuals deal with the chaos of human experience and in creating a coherent framework that introduces a sense of order and regularity into people's everyday lives (Kertzer, 1988). In describing this process, Durkheim and his followers identified three functions that rituals fulfill in the construction of self: (a) ritual creates a sense of *sacredness* (although the meaning of sacred often radically differs from one theorist to another); (b) ritual contributes to feelings of *social solidarity*; (c) ritual works to *maintain the social order*. Drawing on these concepts, Schoenfeld (1997) describes a Bar Mitzvah as a socially structured ritual occasion that takes humans out of the world and focuses our attention on what is really valuable. It generally evokes a powerful emotional response in both child and parent as it touches on a host of different inner struggles: it formalizes the transition into new stages and the accompanying sense of responsibility, it makes onerous demands on both the child and parents, and usually triggers positive forms of growth and maturation.

A second point about the primacy of life-cycle ritual refers to the deep sense of order that these rites contribute during a turbulent period of one's life which is oftentimes filled with a sense of instability and fear of the unknown. In many cases, these rituals serve as the glue that binds individuals to each other and to modes of living that have stood the test of time. At the same time, many of these well-anchored rituals invite the participants to imagine innovative ways to find meaning and relevance in their particular cultural, social, and historical context (Grimes, 2000).

These rituals also reflect the way individuals assemble together as a community and celebrate the various stages of life in a dynamic and innovative way. Victor Turner (1969) has labeled this modality of celebration as "communitas," and argues that this is not only a matter of providing a general stamp of legitimacy to a society's structure, but rather gives recognition to an essential and generic human bond, without which there would be no society. Examples of how Jewish life-cycle rituals embody this value have been the focus of numerous educational programs across different age levels and denominations (Musleah, 1997; Ichnold, 2007; Grant, 2007).

Furthermore, all efficacious rituals are pregnant with symbols and symbolism that provide special opportunities for the participants to engage in a process of interpretation and wonder (Marcus, 2004; Rubin, 1995). The multiple interpretive meanings of these symbols reflect different social contextual frameworks and hermeneutics.

Finally, rites of passage presuppose a mystical or supernatural dimension that is oftentimes sought by the individual Jew during periods of liminality and transition. Under these circumstances many individuals seek communion with a transcendent being that provides them with a new sense of time, space, and destiny beyond their finite experience. This alleviates some of the uncertainty and instills a sense of hope and confidence about the impending challenges that lie ahead (Salkin, 1993).

Impact on Identity

A number of American researchers have studied the critical role of the Bar/Bat Mitzvah ritual on the personal, religious, and ethnic identity of the young person and its impact on the family system. In 1979, Zegans and Zegans interviewed nine boys who had celebrated their bar mitzvah ceremony in a Reform synagogue in order to explore how this process impacted their lives. The results were arresting as all of the boys reported that it enhanced their self-image and perceived image within their larger community. In addition the boys felt a deeper connection to other Jews and a sense of rootedness and attachment to the Jewish people and its values. A later and much larger study by Kosmin (2000) surveyed 1400 families who had celebrated a Bar/Bat Mitzvah in Conservative synagogues in order to learn how the ceremony impacted the lives of the youngsters and their families. Over 90% of the youngsters reported that the ceremony was the most important part of the event, in contrast to 8% who stated that the party was, and 2% who felt that the gifts were. Four years later, Kosmin and Keysar (2004) revisited these families and learned that the Bar/Bat Mitzvah experience was still regarded as having been a formative and significant experience. Nearly half of the sample (49%) reported that the Bar/Bat Mitzvah ceremony continued to be the most important component for shaping the Jewish identity of adolescents and their families, while 29% of the respondents pointed to the training period as a critical part of the experience.

Impact on Family Structure and Identity

Judith Davis (1987) studied the impact of the Bar Mitzvah ceremony on families celebrating this ritual for the first time. She observed four diverse Jewish families, including a blended Conservative family, an intact Reform family, a Russian immigrant family, and a Hassidic family, and reported on how they planned, participated in, and reflected on their first child's Bar Mitzvah. In summarizing the results of her study, Davis suggested that the Bar Mitzvah process is a natural coping mechanism for contemporary Jewish families facing the normative crisis of adolescent transition. More specifically, the Bar Mitzvah process impacts the family system in two distinct ways: on the one hand it introduces new forms of stress and anxiety into the family, and at the same time, it provides a way for dealing with these challenges by drawing on the family's inherent resources to enact change and focus on the road ahead. Vogel's study (2002) demonstrated similar results in Israeli families.

In a related study, Schoenfeld (1993) examined the impact of the Bar/Bat Mitzvah ceremony on Jewish families from a social-psychological perspective, invoking the term "reflexitivity and its discontents" as a means to describe the family's approach to this celebration. These families expressed a sense of ambivalence about what it meant to continue a traditional practice in contemporary society. The social celebrations acted as a counterpoint to synagogue ritual, a kind of "hedging one's bets" by building the event around meanings which contrasted with those being expressed in the synagogue. The second theme was uncertainty about the meaning of transition into early adolescence as it occurs in contemporary society. Schoenfeld (1997) pursued this line of thinking in a later article that focused on sociological theory of identity as it emerges in studying family celebrations of Bar/Bat Mitzvah and its implications for family education. The study adopted a research model that is borrowed from the field of contemporary identity and probed its meaning for Jewish families' celebration of the Bar/Bat Mitzvah ceremony.

Impact on Social Integration

A different body of research has probed the critical role that religious rituals play in cultivating social integration. This work claims that while in the past, religious and political myths provided members of a community with a sense of their origins and destiny, in today's society, synagogues and other Jewish communal organizations serve as sources for communal identity and affinity. Synagogue rituals thus provide participants with an opportunity to voluntarily identify with the community and thereby affirm their commitment to its ideals, values, and norms (Cohen & Eisen, 2000). Through song, dress, liturgy, and food, Jews identify with their community. At the same time, the synagogue provides an immediate and unmediated sense of involvement with the "sacred," confirming the world view and indeed the very being of the participant (Durkheim, 1965).

All of these studies underscore the crucial role of life-cycle rituals in general, and Bar/Bat Mitzvah in particular, in shaping and strengthening the personal identity of Jewish adolescents, their families, and the impact of these rituals in forging meaningful bonds with the larger Jewish community. This research also sheds light on the dominant role that life-cycle education continues to play in Jewish educational frameworks worldwide.

Emerging Trends in Bar/Bat Mitzvah Celebrations

Competing Agendas

In attempting to exploit the potential impact of Bar/Bat Mitzvah celebrations, Jewish communities seek to create rituals that on the one hand are anchored in traditional customs and at the same time meet the diverse needs of celebrants and their families. Attempts to reach this goal are outlined in Schoenfeld's (1988) discussion about the ongoing tension between two competing groups about the essential message of the Bar/Bat Mitzvah celebration in contemporary North American Jewish life. Rabbis and educators have championed the "elite religion of Judaism" whereby study and active participation in Jewish ritual will entitle the Jewish child to become a Bar/Bat Mitzvah. At the same time, parents have assumed responsibility for the "folk religion of Judaism," which emphasizes the importance of the *simcha* (joy and celebration) as imbedded in the traditional party. Both groups continue to pull in opposite directions and the gap between them has grown exponentially, thereby fueling feelings of alienation and mutual feelings of irrelevance. Various attempts have been made to bridge the gap between the competing agendas, but this knotty issue demands more extensive research if it is to be addressed in a constructive and thoughtful way (Schein & Wyner, 1996).

In further considering how to make the Bar/Bat Mitzvah ceremony relevant for modern Jews, Salkin (1991) probed the impact of changing the liturgical service to meet the theological needs of the celebrating family and their community. He suggested conceiving of Bar/Bat Mitzvah as theater and changing the liturgy of the ceremony to meet the evolving needs of modern Jews. His research involved interviewing families who attended the ceremonies in order to determine the extent to which they assimilated new meanings. In addition questionnaires were distributed to 160 guests who participated in the ceremonies and their responses were tabulated. Salkin discovered that the changes in the ceremony positively altered people's perceptions of the meaning of Bar/Bat Mitzvah; in particular these changes impacted the immediate family's perception and attitude. Furthermore, for those people who were active in the synagogue and in Jewish life, the new ceremony tended to affirm their commitment to the ritual. For those who were more on the periphery of Jewish life, the changes had greater potential to "upgrade" their spirituality. In other words, Salkin's experiment showed that the further one is from the center of Jewish life, the more effective the ceremony can be in strengthening one's Jewish identity and sense of spirituality. At the same time, as Salkin cautions his readers, the longevity of this "spiritual high" remains to be seen, requiring additional research.

Re-riting Life-Cycle Rituals

A key feature of rites of passage is their ability to impact, mirror, and be shaped by various social, cultural, and historical conditions. Rituals that don't reinvent themselves become stagnant and risk becoming extinct or irrelevant. Historically, the process of re-riting Jewish rites of passage has continued to flourish since the Talmudic period (Marcus, 2004). In recent times we have witnessed a growing and significant trend to "re-rite" these ceremonies by a host of groups including feminists, converts, gays and lesbians, spiritual seekers, intermarried couples, adults returning to Judaism, etc. (Friedland-Arza, 2002; Gefen, 2005; Ichnold, 2007; Orenstein, 1994). Reflecting on significant changes in American Jewish life in the twentieth century, Charles Liebman (1999) distinguishes between *ritual* and *ceremony*, whereby ritual is defined as explicit religious behavior that is based on tradition and steeped in the sources, while ceremony is driven by a perceived need to adapt the tradition to meet the evolving needs of the larger group. While the former leans on the authority of the tradition, the latter is more flexible and invites the individual Jew to actively identify with the community and thereby assume his/her place in the larger collective. Liebman notes a dramatic drop in ritual behavior among young Jews that corresponds with the larger American trend of distancing from the formal institutionally based traditions. Concurrently, we witness a flourishing of custom-based ceremonies that cater to the particular needs of Jews who choose to celebrate life-cycle events that are meaningful to them, and are less bound to the inherited ceremonies.

During the past half century new rites have been created and existing ones have been modified and these clearly reflect changes in life styles, gender roles, personal and collective identity, and other social developments (Gefen, 2005). The power and potency of these changes have clearly impacted the teaching of life-cycle programs. One of the most significant and momentous examples of this phenomenon is the emerging trend of adult women and men to celebrating their adult Bar and Bat Mitzvah ceremonies at an advanced age. In fact, there appears to be a far larger number of adult women celebrating Bat Mitzvah ceremonies than there are adult men. The phenomenon is more prevalent today and has generated the creation of new rituals and ceremonies that respond to this expressed need (Adelman, 1990; Levine, 1991; Umansky & Ashton, 1992; Grant, 2000, 2003; Cousens, 2002). As the level of women's Jewish education has risen and their knowledge base expanded, the desire to celebrate personal milestones has increased dramatically. The surge of interest in

Jewish feminism and Jewish Studies has fueled the creation of academic and popular literature on new rituals and ceremonies for Jewish women. This phenomenon cuts across all streams of Jewish life and is truly recognized as a watershed development in Jewish life and ritology.

Traditionally women felt excluded from the mainstay of Jewish ritual observance and as a result they have seized the opportunity to reclaim their part of the tradition (Vergon, 2006). Furthermore, public celebrations of rites of passage allow women to identify with the larger Jewish community and provide a "safe space" to share these life-transition moments. Thus, celebrating a Bat Mitzvah in a synagogue lends legitimacy and offers public acknowledgement that the woman's place in Jewish life has been transformed in the most dramatic ways (Friedland-Arza, 2002; Goldberg, 1998; Grant, 2007). This new sense of elevated stature is reflected in an interview that Grant (2000) conducted with a woman named Audrey who had never felt comfortable with her Judaism: "There is also no question that being able to read the Torah and Haftarah gives me a stronger sense of identity and of my membership within the community, my synagogue family" (p. 289).

In addition, celebrating the Bat Mitzvah ceremony oftentimes encourages Jewish women to embark upon an ongoing program of Jewish learning that carries serious implications for their religious development (Cousens, 2002; Grant, 2007). It is interesting to observe how these experiences shape the lives of the participants over an extended period of time, including their perceived sense of empowerment, a deeper sense of meaning in worship and religious practice, and intensification of their relationship to the synagogue community (Grant, 2003a, 2000).

A striking characteristic of these new rituals is the attempt to reclaim traditional ceremonies and infuse them with a new-found sense of meaning and relevance that speaks to mature adults. This phenomenon is most evident when one examines the features of older-women Bat Mitzvah ceremonies, where the prevailing practice is to adopt an existing Jewish ritual rather than attempting to create a totally new one. This practice helps older people navigate the aging process and to create a "wise elder" role for themselves within their family, synagogue, and larger Jewish community.

In attempting to delve deeper into this phenomenon, Vergon (2006) considered how Erikson's classic theory of human development may explain the desire of older Jewish women to celebrate a Bat Mitzvah ceremony. She discovered that during their Bat Mitzvah experience, the majority of women were dealing with issues that were consistent with the Erikson stage they were in, and were also revisiting earlier life stages, a point suggested by the Eriksonian concept of epigenesis as a key stage of human development.

A different sort of change and innovation in Jewish ritology appears in studies that were conducted by Schoenfeld (1986) on how the Bar/Bat Mitzvah ceremony functions as a catalyst for social change in various Jewish ideological groups. Schoenfeld posits that because the Bar/Bat Mitzvah is a ritual of identification, various ideological groups modified or transformed the ceremony in order to meet evolving social needs. A particular area of interest examines how these rituals were transformed in order to address questions of pluralism that took on immediate urgency in North American Jewish life. An evolving trend adopts the Bar/Bat Mitzvah ceremony as a means of promoting social networking and philanthropy among young North American Jews (www.jchoice.org; www.globaljsam.ning.com).

In surveying the multitude of new rituals and modification of existing ones that have emerged in the past two decades, it seems imperative that ongoing research focus on the impact of these changes and their educational implications. Potential questions include the following: Who assumes responsibility for creating new rituals and what is the process of conceptualizing as well as introducing these new rites into Jewish communities? How are these new rites presented in the various life-cycle educational programs? How do communities respond to these new developments? What factors contribute to the successful integration of certain new rites and distinguish them from those that never seem to take root?

The Impact of Bar/Bat Mitzvah on Policy Planning for Jewish Education

An area of acute concern to the field of Jewish education relates to the severe drop of Jewish involvement beyond the Bar/Bat Mitzvah period. Two research projects address this issue from a social and policy planning perspective, by interviewing a group of congregation school students and their parents. Bragar Weinglass (1995) conducted a quantitative study of policy and program characteristics that explain enrollment of post-Bar/Bat Mitzvah Jewish students in synagogue school-education programs. The study considered the following characteristics: accessibility to school, synagogue and school costs, and types of communication with parents and students. The characteristics also included indicators relating to the structure and content of classes, recruiting activities, and school-sponsored youth activities. These findings help inform policy makers about the needs and concerns of congregation school students and their families, and can help determine the goals, structures, and educational programs of these institutions.

A later study focused on the motives of teenagers from interfaith families as they weigh the possibility of continuing their formal Jewish education in the post-Bar/Bat Mitzvah years. Levy-Rotstein (2006) conducted a narrative analysis of interviews with students and their families in order to deepen our understanding of the most salient factors that influenced the decision of these teens to continue their Jewish education beyond the Bar/Bat Mitzvah. The study examined five case studies and identified the following three factors as firmly impacting the decision-making process: the family context, present and prior religious school experience, and the personal motivation to learn. In summarizing the results of her study, Rotstein claims that teenagers from interfaith families, unlike many of their peers have had successful religious school experiences that have served a key role in their deciding to continue their Jewish education. When questioned about what specific influences were most powerful, the interviewees cited the influence of caring teachers, rabbis, and youth advisors who succeeded in engaging the whole child, and did not focus only on the cognitive parts of the program.

Analyzing Teaching Approaches to Life-Cycle Education

As noted above, few studies have analyzed curricular materials or professional development programs on life-cycle education. The dearth of research in this area is most unfortunate as this knowledge could enrich our understanding about some of the most significant challenges facing Jewish life-cycle education today. Cultural norms, ideas, and values shape, modify, and impact curricular Jewish educational programs in general and life-cycle programs in particular. Barry Holtz (2003) as well as Michael Rosenak (1986) addressed this issue in the context of teaching Bible in contemporary American society, and argued that in attempting to wrestle with competing values between the larger American society and Biblical texts, teachers oftentimes "rewrite" these narratives in ways that seek to bridge the two worlds. This form of "rewriting" is highlighted in two separate studies that examined Bar/Bat Mitzvah programs in Israel and in North America.

Sochachevsky-Bacon's (2008) recent article compared and contrasted three curricular programs that are currently being taught in different educational streams of the Israeli public-school system. The study analyzed attitudes toward gender, theology, and autobiographical texts, and demonstrated how each educational stream interprets these themes in starkly different ways. An earlier project was undertaken by Schoenfeld (1994) in which he reviewed two popular books on the role of Bar/Bat Mitzvah in the North American Jewish context. Schoenfeld's content analysis of these books sought to uncover the historical and social role of the Bar/Bat Mitzvah rituals in North American Jewish life. Both studies point to the profound role of the Bar/Bat Mitzvah in Jewish life and the significant impact of the underlying social, religious, and psychological assumptions of the curriculum writers on the various programs.

Over-Representation of Bar/Bat Mitzvah Programs

In reviewing and analyzing curricular programs on life cycle, one is struck by the over-representation of Bar/Bat Mitzvah programs and the glaring absence of other life-cycle passages. This phenomenon begs the question about the unique role of Bar/Bat Mitzvah celebrations in modern Jewish life, and the implications for educational practice.

Several theses shed light on the inherent appeal of the Bar/Bat Mitzvah ritual, and concurrently, explain the over-representation of educational materials that address this rite of passage. In attempting to understand this phenomenon one is struck by the claim that over the past two decades there has been a steady decline in the number of registered Jewish weddings and synagogue-based funerals (Kosmin, 2000). By contrast, the Bar/Bat Mitzvah ritual has weathered the storm of erosion, and in point of fact, the number of Bat Mitzvah celebrations has increased exponentially over the last decades. Furthermore, as discussed above, the significant increase of adult Bar/Bat Mitzvah celebrations underscore this rite's prominence in contemporary Jewish life.

A second explanation maintains that the vast majority of North American formal Jewish education takes place in congregation schools and culminates with the Bar/Bat Mitzvah ritual. Consequently, congregation schools oftentimes target families who wish to celebrate their children's Bar/Bat Mitzvah ceremony in the synagogue and require parents to enroll their youngsters in these schools for a minimum number of years prior to the celebration. This results in a situation where the Bar/Bat Mitzvah ceremony is viewed as the climax of the child's education and thereby becomes a key focal point in the curriculum. This helps create a sense of synergy between the goals of the synagogue and their sponsored schools as synagogues understand that the Bar/Bat Mitzvah is a critical hook to involve the child and her family in the lives of the congregations. "If one is looking for ways to engage Jewish families in the synagogue, this (the bar/bat mitzvah celebration) is one that obviously works" (p. 234). The power of Bar/Bat mitzvah celebrations to mobilize the family and engage them in a panoply of educational programs has been documented and fuels the synagogues' attempts to promote these rites (Kosmin, 2000).

A third theory argues that schools around the world have grasped the extraordinary potential of extensive Bar/Bat Mitzvah educational programs as a means to engage youngsters in a rigorous and meaningful educational experience on identity formation, and at the same time allowing them to forge meaningful bonds with the larger Jewish community. Bar/Bat Mitzvah year-long study programs are a central educational component in Israeli national schools, and include a battery of group and individual tasks that engage the students for a significant portion of their middle school studies (http://www.daat.ac.il/daat/mishpach/index.htm).

The Emerging Role of Death Education and Laws of Bereavement

Aside from Bar/Bat Mitzvah the only other rite of passage that has been researched to date is death and bereavement. In the 1980s two dissertations focused on the need to introduce death education into formal Jewish settings, and both of them included an analysis of existing programs.

In 1979 Wolowelsky conducted a study on the goals and curricula of selected New York City religious high schools in the area of death education and contrasted them with those prepared for public schools. In the course of his research, Wolowelsky discovered that serious discussion of death and bereavement is all but omitted from the public school not because of an oversight, but because it is considered to be a cultural taboo. This is an inversion of the situation in religious schools where serious discussion of issues related to death was considered to be an integral part of the religious system and is afforded a prominent role in the overall educational program. In cases where death education was omitted from the religious schools' program, it was usually the result of an oversight or caused by the rigid structure of the course offerings. On the whole religious schools felt strongly that high-school students should have the opportunity to clarify their values and express their fears about death, as the principals of these schools argued that their educational mandate was to teach and develop values rather than simply help students clarify their own value systems.

Elkin's study (1980) presents research, data, and insights concerning an educational program on death, dying, and bereavement for Jewish adolescents. The stated purpose of this study was to examine death-education programs for Jewish adolescents from Conservative and Reform families. Elkin echoes Wolowelsky's claim about the critical role of death-education programs in helping these adolescents develop healthy and positive understandings about the final stage of life, and concurrently deepen their understanding and appreciation about the laws of bereavement.

It is a curious fact that since the 1980s, only one doctoral dissertation has addressed issues of death instruction in Jewish educational settings. Rich (2001) presented a case study that analyzed a process used to create a death-education curriculum for use in American liberal-congregation schools. In presenting his findings, Rich repeatedly underscores the critical importance of death education in the congregation school curriculum, and the need for teachers to confront the range of emotions that can be triggered by engaging in this topic. Furthermore, this study points to the crucial need for keeping parents informed about the implementation of death-education programs and their ongoing involvement throughout the process.

An additional and particularly insightful piece of research on death education examined the dynamics of cultural performance and social dramas at a Reform congregational school in the United States (Reimer, 1997). This study focused on a death education lesson for a group of sixth-grade students and their families, where many of these children were accompanied by their parents and siblings. In reflecting on the educational impact of studying the laws of mourning in this framework, Joseph Reimer claims: "Sitting with these parents and children as they came alive with a heightened level of interest and engagement, I felt as if an electric current were running this group. I could feel the current running through me as well leading me to wonder: what makes the educational moment so alive?" (p. 26). One could argue that a key factor that guaranteed the success of this program was the selection of a unit on death education that met the diverse needs of the students and their families, and thereby highlighted the educational potential of this subject matter for a wide range of Jewish students. As stated above each of these studies emphasized the critical need to teach about death and bereavement in a systematic and candid way; unfortunately, to date the impact of this plea has been minimal.

An Agenda for Future Research

As argued above, the stunning contrast between the number of available life-cycle educational programs and related research studies is most telling. There is an urgent need to conduct research on topics of life-cycle education that will enhance our understanding of current educational practice and concurrently provide new vistas for introducing this topic in novel and creative ways that criss-cross educational frameworks and new target populations. Herewith is a sample of such topics:

Evaluating the Goals, Content, and Underlying Assumptions of Life-Cycle Programs

In attempting to understand the underlying philosophical, hermeneutic, and educational assumptions of any educational program it behooves the researcher to analyze the content of the particular program and reflect on the variety of ways in which it approaches the subject matter and makes the subsequent "educational translation" (Rosenak, 1987). This examination is not only concerned with the level of difficulty or sophistication of the material, its factual accuracy, its aesthetic presentation, or the assumed background of the student and teacher. Perhaps most importantly, this exercise allows the reader to uncover the program's tacit beliefs about the central purposes of education, the way people learn, preferred teaching styles, the assumptions about the particular subject matter, and the social milieu in which the material will be studied and taught.

Efficacy of Life-Cycle Programs

Our current knowledge about how life-cycle education impacts the lives of students is sporadic, anecdotal, and lacking in depth. This knowledge would prove invaluable in helping us conceptualize a variety of educational programs for Jewish adolescents, adults, families, and the larger community. We recommend interviewing students who have completed a life-cycle course and exploring with them the place that these formative issues played in their studies and their ongoing development. A model for evaluating this impact might focus on the following three areas: knowledge (Dorph, 1993; Grossman, 1990), practice (Marcus, 2004; Rubin, 1995), and the affective realm (Marcus, 2004). Viable evaluation instruments to gauge these indices have been prepared for other areas of Jewish studies, and could be easily adapted for life-cycle education.

Integration of Jewish and General Studies

One of the most promising and innovative ways to introduce Jewish life-cycle education into the lives of Jewish day schools could involve the process of curricular integration. Over the past three decades this approach has attracted much attention in the areas of research and practice in Jewish education and has sparked much debate and deliberation (Holtz, 1980; Malkus, 2001; Pomson, 2001; Solomon, 1984; Zeldin, 1998).

To date, several innovative educational programs have adopted the integration model to educate about life-cycle events. In attempting to highlight the evolution of the Bat Mitzvah ritual, Regina Stein (2001) traces a host of social, political, and historical forces in the larger American context that shaped and impacted this ceremony. In so doing, she adopts Solomon's use of integration of Judaism and Americanism, and thereby provides students with an engaging and dynamic example of curriculum integration. Similarly, Davis (1987) analyzes how the ongoing search for new adult rituals in the larger American social context has impacted the celebration of adult Bar Mitzvahs. Research projects on curriculum integration for life-cycle education need to explore the inherent match between the subject matter and the stated educational goals and its programmatic implications. In addition, the field would greatly benefit from an evaluative study about the impact of these integrated programs and the challenges they present for large-scale adaptation.

A Standards and Benchmarks Project

The issue of accountability for student achievement stands at the forefront of American education (Malone & Nelson, 2006). Parents, politicians, community leaders, and educators have joined forces to support efforts that will help children attain the types of knowledge, develop the skills, and acquire the ability to become productive citizens. The underlying assumption behind this campaign is that without a firm grasp of projected goals and clear outcomes, our educational efforts will be futile and our students will flounder.

The standards and benchmarks approach carries a series of core implications for Jewish education. A hallmark feature of Jewish schools is their commitment to mission-driven goals that attempt to infuse the learners with a sense of love, commitment to, and knowledge of Jewish life, that criss-crosses the cognitive, affective, spiritual, and normative realms. It seems only natural that Jewish schools would be keen to engage in an educational process that would set benchmarks and standards for their work in Jewish Studies. In 2004, the Avi Chai Foundation supported a project by the Melton Research Center of the Jewish Theological Seminary of America to introduce a set of standards and benchmarks into the study of Bible at Solomon Schechter, Community, and Reform day schools across North America (www.jtsa.edu/davidson/melton/standards).

This project holds much promise for the teaching of life-cycle education. One of the recurring themes that surfaces in educational circles about the role and efficacy of life-cycle programs in the Jewish studies curriculum is their lack of clarity, a defined role, and purposefulness (Wertheimer, 2007). The Melton Research Center project directly addresses this challenge by seeking to "create mechanisms to map the terrain of the relationship between subject matter (curricular content) and Jewish belief and practice, the common freight of most day schools vision and mission statements." An accessible standards and benchmarks project for life-cycle education would fill a critical role in curriculum development, and carry implications for school self-study, professional development, learner achievement, and lifelong Jewish study.

Over the past two decades life-cycle education has assumed a more prominent and influential role in Jewish life. Recent studies on the power of ritual in general and life-cycle rites in particular, have demonstrated the unique role that life-cycle education can play for contemporary Jews. Social, historical, and cultural trends have helped modify and shape existing rituals and fueled new ceremonies that have caught the imagination of Jewish communities worldwide. As these changes continue to penetrate Jewish life, new issues and challenges will emerge that spawn empirical and qualitative research for scores of researchers in Jewish education.

References

Adelman, P. V. (1990). *Miriam's well: Rituals for Jewish women around the year*. New York: Biblio Press.

Aron, I. Instruction and Enculturation in Jewish Education, An unpublished paper presented at the First Conference of the Network for Research in Jewish Education, Jerusalem, (1989).

Bacon, B. S. (2008). Reading three Israeli Bat/Bar Mitzvah curricula as gender, theological and autobiographical texts. *Journal of Jewish Education, 74*(2), 144–180.

Berger, P., Berger, B., & Kellner, H. (1973). *The homeless mind: Modernization and consciousness*. New York: Random House.

Cohen, S. M., & Eisen, A. M. (2000). *The Jew within*. Bloomington, IN: Indiana University Press.

Cousens, B. (2002). Adult Bat Mitzvah as Entrée into Jewish Life for North American Jewish Women. Working paper for Hadassah International Research Institute on Jewish Women, (2002).

Dash Moore, D. (1987). The construction of community: Jewish migration and ethnicity in the United States. In M. Rischin (Ed.), *The Jews of North America* (pp. 105–117). Detroit, MI: Wayne State University Press.

Davis, J. *Mazel Tov: A Systems Exploration of Bar Mitzvah as a Multigenerational Ritual of Change and Continuity,* an unpublished doctoral dissertation, Ann Arbor: UMI, 1987.

Deitcher, H. *The Rites of Passage: An Instructional Guide for Yeshiva High School Teachers,* an unpublished doctoral dissertation, Yeshiva University, New York, 1985.

Dorph, G. Z., *Conceptions and Preconceptions: A Study of Prospective Jewish Educators Knowledge and Beliefs About Torah,* an unpublished doctoral dissertation, New York: Jewish Theological Seminary, 1993.

Driver, T. F. (1998). *Liberating rites: Understanding the transformative power of ritual*. Boulder, CO: Westview.

Durkheim, E. (1965). *The elementary forms of religious life: A study in religious sociology* (trans. Joseph Ward Swain). New York: The Free Press.

Elkin, J. C. *An Exploration of Alternatives for Educating Jewish Adolescents to dying, death, and bereavement: A Pre-deliberation Research Project,* an unpublished doctoral dissertation, Columbia University, New York, 1980.

Friedland-Arza, S. (2002). *Bat Mitzvah* (Hebrew). Jerusalem: MATAN, 2002, appears also in English as *Bat Mitzvah Book: Traditions and Celebrations for the Bat Mitzvah;* Ahituv, Ronen. *Y'mai Adam* (Hebrew). Tel Aviv: Yediot Sefarim.

Gefen, R. M. (2005). Life cycle rituals: Rites of passage in American Judaism. In D. E. Kaplan (Ed.), *The Cambridge companion to American Judaism*. Cambridge: Cambridge University Press.

Goldberg, P. (1998). Minyan of crones: New rituals for Jewish women. In S. S. Swartz & M. Wolfe (Eds.), *From memory to transformation: Jewish women's voices*. Toronto, ON: Second Story Press.

Grant, L. Adult Bat Mitzvah – An American Rite of Continuity', Courtyard I, Winter, 2000 pp. 142–168.
Grant, L. (2003a). Restorying Jewish lives post adult bat Mitzvah. *Journal of Jewish Education,* 69(2), 44, Winter.
Grant, L. D. (2003b). Transitions and Trajectories post Adult Bat Mitzvah. *Journal of Jewish Education,* 69(3), Fall.
Grant, L. D. (2007). Finding her right place in the Synagogue: The rite of Adult Bat Mitzvah. In R. E. Prell (Ed.), *Women remaking American Judaism.* Detroit, MI: Wayne State University Press.
Grimes, R. (2000). *Deeply into the bone: Reinventing rites of passage.* Los Angeles: University of California Press.
Grossman, P. L. (1990). *The making of a teacher: Teacher knowledge and teacher education.* New York: Teachers College Press.
Holtz, B. (1980). Towards an integrated curriculum for the Jewish day school. *Religious Education,* 75(3).
Holtz, B. W. *Textual Knowledge: Teaching the Bible in Theory and in Practice. New York:* Jewish Theological Seminary, 2003.
Ichnold, D. (Ed.) (2007). *Life's cycles: Ceremonies of Jewish life.* Tel Aviv: Yedioth Aharonoth Books (Hebrew).
Israel, S., The Jewish Life Cycle, www.jewishagency.org
Kanarfogel, E. (1992). *Jewish education and society in the high middle ages.* Detroit, MI: Wayne State University Press.
Kertzer, D. I. (1988). *Ritual, politics, and power.* New Haven, CT: Yale University Press.
Kosmin, B. A. (2000). Coming of age in the conservative Synagogue. In *Jews in the center: Conservative Synagogues and their members.* New Brunswick, NJ: Rutgers University Press.
Kosmin, B. A., & Keysar, A. (2004). *The college years: The Jewish engagement of young adults raised in conservative Synagogues, 1995-2003.* New York: JTS.
Levi, S., & Katz, E. (Eds.) (2000). *Jewish Israelis: A portrait.* Jerusalem: AviChai.
Levine, E. R. (1991). *A ceremonies sampler: New rites, celebrations, and observances of Jewish women.* San Diego, CA: Women's Institute for Continuing Jewish Education.
Liebman, C. (1999). Ritual, ceremony and the reconstruction of Judaism in the United States. In R. R. Farber & C. I. Waxman (Eds.), *Jews in America: A contemporary reader.* Hanover: Brandeis University Press.
Malkus, M. (2001), Portraits of curriculum integration in Jewish day schools, an unpublished doctoral dissertation, UMI.
Malone, B. G., & Nelson, J. (2006). Standards based reform: Panacea for the twenty-first century? *Educational Horizons,* 84(2), Winter.
Marcus, I. G. (2004). *The Jewish life cycle.* Seattle, WA: University of Washington Press.
Marcus, I. G. (1996). *Rituals of childhood: Jewish acculturation in Medieval Europe.* New Haven, CT: Yale University Press.
Milburn, S., & Seidman, L. (1999). Which comes First Jewish values or Jewish education. *Journal of Jewish Education,* 65(1).
Moskowitz, N. S. (2003). *The ultimate Jewish teacher's handbook.* Denver, CO: A.R.E.
Musleah, R. (1997). *Journey of a lifetime: The Jewish life cycle book.* Springfield: Behrman House.
Orenstein, D. (1994). *Lifecycles: Jewish women on life passages and personal milestones* (edited). Woodstock: Jewish Lights.
Pomson, A. (2001). Knowledge that just doesn't sit there: Considering a reconception of the curriculum integration of Jewish and general studies. *Religious Education,* 96(4), 528–545.
Reimer, J. (1997). *Succeeding at Jewish education.* Philadelphia: Jewish Publication Society.
Rich, C. J. *A Case Study for Developing a Death Education Curriculum for use in Hebrew Schools,* an unpublished doctoral dissertation, Ann Arbor: UMI, 2001.
Rosenak, M. (1986). *Teaching Jewish values: A conceptual guide.* Jerusalem: Hebrew University of Jerusalem.

Rosenak, M. (1987). *Commandments and concerns.* Philadelphia: Jewish Publication Society.

Rotstein, E. L., *Connection, Commitment and Community: What Motivates Teenagers from Interfaith Families to Continue Post Bar/Bat Mitzvah Jewish Education?,* an unpublished doctoral dissertation, Ann Arbor: UMI, 2006.

Rubin, N. (1995). *Reishit Ha'Chayim: Tiksei Leidah, Milah, U'Pidyon Haben B'mekorot Hazal* (Hebrew).

Salkin, J. K. (1991) *Appropriating a Liturgical Context for Bar/Bat Mitzvah,* an unpublished doctoral dissertation, Ann Arbor: UMI.

Salkin, J. K. (1993). *Putting God on the guest list: How to reclaim the spiritual meaning your child's bar or bat mitzvah.* Woodstock, VT: Jewish Lights.

Sarna, J. (1998). American Jewish education in historical perspective. *Jewish Education,* 64(1&2), Winter/Spring.

Schein, J., & Wyner, S. (Spring 1996). Mediating the tensions of Bar/Bat Mitzvah: The Cleveland experience. *Journal of Jewish Communal Service,* 72.

Schoenfeld, S. "Theoretical Approaches to the Study of Bar and Bat Mitzvah", *Proceedings of the Ninth World Congress of Jewish Studies,* 1986.

Schoenfeld, S. (1988). Folk Judaism, Elite Judaism, and the role of Bar Mitzvah in the development of Synagogue and school in American Jewish life. *Contemporary Judaism,* 9, 67–85.

Schoenfeld, S. (1993). Some aspects of the social significance of Bar/bat Mitzvah celebrations. In *The Bar/Bat Mitzvah handbook.* Denver, CO: Alternatives in Religious Education.

Schoenfeld, S. (1994). Recent Publications on Bar/Bat Mitzvah: Their implications for Jewish education research and practice. *Religious Education,* 89(4).

Schoenfeld, S. (1997). Late modernity, self identity, and Bar/Bat Mitzvah: Implications for family education. *Journal of Jewish Education,* 63(3).

Solomon, B. (1984). *Curricular integration in the Jewish all-day school in the United States* (p. 2). Jerusalem: Studies in Jewish Education.

Stein, R. (2001). The road to Bat Mitzvah in America. In P. S. Nadell & J. D. Sarna (Eds.), *Women and American Judaism: Historical perspectives.* Hanover: Brandeis University Press.

Taylor, C. (1992). *The ethics of authenticity.* Cambridge, MA: Harvard University Press.

Turner, V. (1967). *The forest of symbols: Aspects of Ndembu Ritual.* Ithaca, NY: Cornell University Press.

Turner, V. (1969). Liminality and communitas. In *Ritual process, structure, and anti structure.* Chicago: Adline Publishers.

Umansky, E. M., & Ashton, D. (Eds.) (1992). *Four Centuries of Jewish* Orenstein, D. (Ed.) *Lifecycles: Jewish Women on life Passages and Personal Milestones, Women's Spirituality: A Sourcebook,* Boston: Beacon Press.

Van Gennep, A. (1960). *The rites of passage.* Chicago: University of Chicago Press (translated M. Vizedom).

Vergon, K. S. (2006). *An Exploration of Middle Aged and Older Women's Experiences of Bat Mitzvah Within the Framework of Erikson's Theory of Human Development,* an unpublished doctoral dissertation, University of South Florida.

Vogel, G. (2002). *Shehehiyanu V'kiy'manu Laz'man Hazeh: The Significance of a Bar/Bat Mitzvah Ceremony for Children with Developmental Disabilities and Their Parents,* an unpublished doctoral dissertation, University of Haifa.

Weinglass, E. B. (1995). *Policies and Programs Related to Retention in Jewish Education after the Bar/Bat Mitzvah,* Ann Arbor: UMI.

Wertheimer, J. (2007). *Recent trends in supplementary Jewish education.* New York: AVI CHAI.

Wolowelsky, J. (1979). *Death Education in Religious High Schools,* an unpublished doctoral dissertation, New York University, New York.

Zegans, S., & Zegans, L. S. (1979). Bar Mitzvah: A rite for a transitional age. *Psychoanalytic Review,* 16, 115–132.

Zeldin, M. (1998). Integration and interaction in the Jewish day school. In R. Tornberg (Ed.), *The Jewish educational leader's handbook.* Denver, CO: A.R.E.

Other Religions in Jewish Education

Michael Gillis

In many countries the reality of plurality has given rise to rethinking the role of teaching religion in general education. The different approaches taken in the United Sates, Israel and Britain are reviewed in the chapter. The case maintained here is that there is a rationale for teaching about other religious traditions as a dimension of the Jewish mandate of the school beyond any expectation, legally imposed or otherwise, to include such learning as part of the general education offered. Not only need there be no incompatibility between learning about other religions and Jewish education but, it will be argued, such learning can be viewed as a necessary part of a Jewish education.

A Rationale

The case for cultivating an understanding of other religions within Jewish education may be highlighted by some incidents in the past few years. The first is the controversy over Mel Gibson's film "The Passion of the Christ" (2004), which purported to be a truthful and accurate representation of the events surrounding the death of Jesus. The film gave rise to protests from both Jews and Christians who took the view that it perpetuated belief in a continuing Jewish responsibility for the death of Jesus. It is not possible to make sense of this controversy without some knowledge and understanding of the gospel narratives; the way in which alleged Jewish guilt has been a focus for anti-Judaism and anti-Semitism; changes in recent decades in Christian attitudes to Jews and Judaism, and the ways in which recent scholarship has shed new light upon the events portrayed in the film. With regard to Islam it is impossible to avoid the increasing prominence of the religious dimension of the conflict between Israelis and Palestinians. So for example the charter of Hamas notoriously cites a Hadith (an ex-Qur'anic tradition of a saying or action of Mohammed) in which Jews are portrayed as treacherous who at some end time will

---

M. Gillis (✉)
Hebrew University, Jerusalem, Israel
e-mail: msgillis@huji.ac.il

be handed over by the very trees behind which they hide. Is this tradition authoritative for all Muslims? Can it be taken as representative of Muslim attitudes towards Jews? Answers to these questions can only be arrived at by some knowledge and understanding of Islam and the history of its relationship to other religions.

Beyond this pragmatic argument lies a deeper rationale that recognizes the cardinal role of plurality in modern life, including in the religious sphere. This plurality is a social fact independent of what value is attached to it. Religious communities live alongside one another on the local level and, through modern means of communication, they relate to one another globally. An understanding of religious traditions is an essential element for understanding our world that education must address. Students need to be prepared to contribute to a cohesive society that includes a variety of religious commitments. They need to know how to react knowledgeably, with understanding and respect to the questions and challenges they will encounter throughout a lifetime of interactions with members of other faith communities.

This general imperative applies also in the context of Jewish education but, it will be argued, simply tacking on a subject to the curriculum without integrating it into the overall Jewish educational goals of the school is an inadequate response.

If many other religions have enjoyed long periods of hegemony in which a particular religion was seen as universal, taken for granted, and the basis for a shared culture, Judaism has for the most part functioned as a minority religion. Interaction with the dominant religions is a cardinal factor in Jewish history, not only in the form of persecution but also through the subtle play of religious and cultural influence (Yuval, 2006). Learning something of other religions is thus also necessary for a proper understanding of Judaism itself.

For many young people Jewish identity is to an extent defined by negative factors – to be Jewish is not to be a Christian or not to be a Muslim. The building of a positive identity requires some positive understanding of difference rather than crudely conceived dichotomies.

Modernity, Pluralism, and Secularization

One possible response to the fact of plurality is the denial of its value. Plurality can give rise to a reactive assertion of exclusive truth that is a feature of religious fundamentalism. At the other extreme is a full-blown pluralism that embraces plurality as a primary value denying the validity of all exclusive claims to truth. Yet another position uses the ideology of multiculturalism to assert the right of communities to maintain distinct beliefs, practices, and social norms, against the demands of the liberal state for shared core values held alongside a tolerance of difference.

Religious educators who seek to assert the privilege of their own tradition without denying the legitimacy of other religious traditions need to confront the inherent tensions in this position. Judaism is, in principle, well placed to cope with this tension as it does not assert universal validity. Other religions can be accepted as approved spiritual paths, provided they meet certain basic conditions (Sacks, 2002).

This understanding of Judaism as a particularistic tradition has important implications for the potential of Jewish education to look outwards to the significance of other religions.

Contrary to the expectations of secularism theorists, religion remains a potent social force alongside, and not despite, modernity. Secularization theory postulated that as modernization progresses religion will lose its plausibility and attempts to reach an accommodation between modernity and traditional belief will be fragile and unstable (Berger, 1967). Secularization theory posited that a prime cause of the erosion of religion by modernity is pluralism (Berger, 1979). Modern societies are inherently pluralistic, valuing personal choice over imposed group obligations. Modern people come to see their religious commitments as a choice rather than a self-evident set of truths. Peter Berger, himself a leading secularization theorist, has led the way in drastically revising this theory in the light of the persistence of religion in its most traditional forms in the midst of modern societies (Berger, 1996; Berger, Woodhead, Heelas & Martin, 2001). Religion, not necessarily in its accommodating and compromising forms, is alive and well and is frequently a formative influence on the lives of individuals (Berger, 1979), on whole societies and indeed on the world in general, as can be seen in the influence of resurgent Islam, thriving ultra-Orthodox Jewish communities, and the impact of evangelistic Christianity (Stark, 2000).

Some religious groups are likely to be suspicious of educational efforts to develop a respectful and empathetic understanding of other religions because of a fear that the consequence will be a relativization of religious commitment. It is not possible, therefore, to divorce the approach to other religions from the ideological commitments of the particular educational setting.

Educational Traditions Regarding Religious Education

There are also significant variations of educational tradition in different countries with respect to religious education. In the United States, for example, public schools are prevented by the constitution from engaging in religious education or mandating any religious practice. The Supreme Court decision in *Engel versus Vitale* (1962) gave force to a strict interpretation of the constitution's separation of church and state and outlawed all forms of prayer and religious instruction in public schools (Gash & Gonzales, 2008). Recognizing the importance of learning about religion, curricula have been devised that rest upon a sharp distinction between teaching for religion and teaching about religion.

Other countries have quite different traditions with respect to religious education. In Britain, the 1944 Education Act required that there be a daily act of worship and that religious instruction be provided. It seemed clear in 1944 that while religious instruction was not to be in a particular denomination it was to be in the Christian faith. The word "instruction" also implied that this was not only a matter of learning about Christianity but that belief in Christianity was to be inculcated. Under the 1988 Education Act "instruction" was replaced by "education", but this law, like the subsequent 1996 Education Act, continued to maintain that religious education was part of the legislated basic curriculum for all government-maintained schools. The common school was still expected to privilege Christianity and to mandate a daily act of worship. Much had changed in British society since 1944 including a rise in secularism and mass immigration. These changes led to a degree of multiculturalism; the notion that "religion" meant Christianity could no longer be taken for granted, even though the new legislation continued its privileged position in religious education. The 1988 Act, therefore, opened the possibility of consultation with non-Christian religious groups in devising curriculum (Jackson, 2004).

In the United States, Jewish schools, which, by definition, are not state schools, are free to educate for Jewish belief and practice. In Britain, where many Jewish schools are government funded, like other faith-based schools, they are free to devise their religious-education curriculum in line with their particular religious orientation. Because of a concern that faith-based schools may cultivate cultural separatism and even conflict, the 2006 Education and Inspections Act provides that all British schools, including government-funded faith-based schools, be appraised for their education for "community cohesion". This is interpreted to include an expectation that pupils learn about the faith and religious practices of others.[1] Jewish government-funded schools may thus find themselves required to teach about other religions. The willingness of Jewish schools to respond to this requirement is closely correlated with the religious orientation of the school (Short & Lenga, 2002).

Other countries reflect distinct traditions and policies of religious education. In Finland, for example, religious education is also part of the core curriculum. The Finnish system, however, provides for separate religious education within the common school, according to the religious affiliation of the students. Even a small number of students of faiths other than the dominant Lutheranism are entitled to separate classes. Jewish children receive Jewish religious education but the curriculum is nevertheless endorsed by the state and needs to conform to the general requirement to include knowledge of other faiths (Honkaheimo, 2007). In European countries where religious education continues to be mandatory, there is a process of negotiating a path from the assumed privilege of Christianity to an approach that acknowledges the multiplicity of religions within each society including secular humanist orientations (Felderhof, 1985; Hobson & Edwards, 1999; Jackson, 2004).

In some countries the requirement to teach about the religions of the world is a requirement within social studies. In the State of Victoria, Australia, the curriculum requires teaching about religion, looking at how religion operates as a social force, and also a study of the origins of religions (VCAA, 2009). In Jewish schools other religions are likely to be taught but quite separately from Jewish studies. While this separation solves a difficult problem for many Jewish educators – how to deal appropriately with other faiths within the Jewish studies lesson – it also seems anomalous

---

[1] These matters are discussed more fully in Helena Miller's contribution to this volume, "Community Engagement: The Challenge of Connecting Jewish Schools to the Wider Community".

to teach, for example, about the origins of Christianity without a Jewish context and without a Jewish point of view.

In the cases of Christianity and Islam we are concerned with two religions that have an intimate connection with Judaism. They each make explicit assertions about the status of Judaism and there are Jewish sources that make assertions about them in return. They are part of the Jewish story and this could fruitfully find expression in the way they are taught in Jewish educational contexts.

Judaism, Christianity, and Education

Historically, the relationship between Judaism and Christianity has been troubled, with episodes of cruel violence erupting against the background of a view of Judaism as the religion of a people once-chosen and now rejected because of their own rejection of Christ. The image of the two statues, Ecclesia and Synagoga that adorn the façade of Strasbourg cathedral makes this relationship graphically vivid. Ecclesia stands erect and proud holding a staff adorned by a cross in one hand and the chalice of the Eucharist in the other. By contrast, Synagoga is blindfold, her staff broken, and the book of the Law is held facing downwards. The image represents the idea of supersession – the Church is the New Israel that sits in the place of honour once held by the rightly deposed Old Israel of the flesh.

The authority of St. Augustine had previously established the teaching that conversion was not to be forced and that the Jews were to be tolerated if only as witness, in their humbled state, to the truth of Christianity (Fredriksen, 1995b). During the Middle Ages the balance shifted towards a demonization of Jews and Judaism. The unleashing of the Crusades, the violence against Jewish communities of Northern Europe, the emergence of the blood-libel and other accusations led to a perception of the Jew as satanic compelled by his very nature to be the enemy of Christ and Christians. In recent years Jewish historians have turned to focus upon resulting Jewish attitudes towards Christianity during this period. They discover that a fierce hostility towards Christianity became a significant force in Jewish life shaping Jewish images of the Christian and influencing Jewish culture and religious practice.

It should be noted, however, that the attitude of traditional Jewish sources to Christianity and Islam is not necessarily negative. Maimonides (1135–1204), the towering figure of rationalist Jewish thought refers in his great code of Jewish law the Mishneh Torah (Laws of Kings and Their Wars, Chapter 11), to the positive role of Christianity and Islam in the Divine plan for the redemption of the world, despite his general evaluation of Christianity as a form of idolatry. In his philosophical work, Guide of the Perplexed (Part 1 Chapter 71), he refers to the commonly held theological fundamentals of the three religions. Likewise the philosopher and poet Yehudah Halevi (c.1075–1141) regards the other monotheistic religions as having a positive and redemptive role in the spreading of monotheistic belief (Kuzari 4:23). Rabbi Jacob Emden (1697–1776), the controversial but traditionalist rabbi of Altona, had a favourable view of Christianity: His interpretation of the teachings of

Jesus and St. Paul as in no way undermining Judaism, in as much as they are directed to gentiles, anticipates the direction of much recent scholarship on the foundation figures of Christianity. (Letter published in his edition of Seder Olam Raba v'Zuta, Hamburg, 1757.) Among more recent Jewish thinkers there are many who have adopted a positive orientation towards Christianity (Berger, 2002; Heschel, 1966; Lévinas, 1990; Rosenzweig & Glatzer, 1961) while others continue to maintain traditional reservations (Berger, 2002; Soloveitchik, 1964).[2]

In many Jewish educational settings, however, Christianity is only encountered as a negative force in Jewish history. This image does not match the present relationship with Christianity given such developments as the dramatic reorientation of Catholicism towards Judaism since the Second World War. It is not even adequate for an understanding of the complex realities of Jewish Christian interaction in different periods in history. This is not to suggest that the painful episodes in this history be overlooked. A reorientation of the educational approach can not simply be the replacing of one narrative with another.

Changing realities, as well as developments in scholarship, lead to the need for a fresh approach. Such a reorientation can be illustrated by consideration of approaches to the historical figure of Jesus.

The Historical Jesus

Traditional Jewish sources, which are often folkloric in character, have been characterized as embodying "counter-history" (Cohen, 1999). Counter-history is a version of history that feeds off the history of another but subverts that history by reversing its values. There is a Jewish tradition of narrative about Jesus that essentially derives its basis from the Gospel narratives but subverts them. This is the tendency of the fragments in the Talmud that discuss the life of Jesus and the various versions of the "Toldot Yeshu" parts of which some scholars trace back to before the tenth century.

These portrayals would seem to have no basis in historical reality. They are the product of an interaction with a hostile and derisive Christianity. In Christianity, Jesus, as Christ, is the focus of faith. His rejection by the Jews was understood by Christians as an act of obstinate and evil perversity resulting in the rejection of the Jews as God's people. Not surprisingly, Jews needed an account for themselves of this central personality that would explain their rejection of him.

The Christian search for the historical Jesus is an essentially Protestant enlightenment project. Jewish scholars have joined in this search and their approach is distinguished by their tendency to tie Jesus to his Jewish origins and context

---

[2]The controversy over the pronouncement "Dabru Emet" which sets out a call by a group of Jewish scholars and rabbis for a reorientation of Jewish attitudes to Christianity exemplifies the diversity of views in the present day (http://www.jcrelations.net/en/?item=1014) and for a critique see Levenson, J. D. (2001).

(Flusser & Notley, 1997; Fredriksen, 1999; Klausner & Danby, 1925; Vermes, 1973). The various conflicts and controversies in which Jesus engaged were no more than internal Jewish arguments about the way in which to serve God. The gospel writers, writing after the destruction of the Temple, have an interest in framing these controversies in terms of an outright confrontation between Jesus and the religious authorities of Judaism, but the historian can see through this tendency to the essentially Jewish teacher.

For example, the Sermon on the Mount contains what are known as the "antitheses" in which the Ten Commandments are contrasted with Jesus's own teaching. On the surface, this contrast, "You have heard it said – but I say to you", may seem like a critique of the commandments of the Torah but it is clear on closer reading that Jesus's teaching is not against the commandments but a call for a going beyond the commandments (Flusser, 1979). This going beyond the call of the law (*lifnim mishurat hadin*) is the attribute the rabbis ascribe to the "Hasid" – the pious one who is not satisfied with the bare requirements of the Torah.

Jesus's teaching in the Sermon on the Mount that one should return goodness to those who do wrong and give love to those who hate is often taken as a teaching which shows up a contrast between Judaism and Christianity. This view was popularized by the Zionist thinker Ahad Ha'am who identified a distinctive Jewish ethics in contrast to what he considered to be the "inverted egoism" of Christian ethics (Ahad Ha'am, 1992). Jesus's demand is indeed extreme but David Flusser has shown that it is not alien to at least some teachings within the rabbinic tradition (Flusser, 1988). Reading the Sermon on the Mount this way we find a Jewish text, distinctive in its coherence and its demands for supererogatory standards, but not by virtue of this at odds with ideas that find expression in rabbinic literature.

Does this amount to an argument for teaching the New Testament text as a Jewish text? Here we need to advance with care. At one level the text is a Jewish text but one that is embedded within the sacred texts of another faith for which the speaker is not merely a Jewish sage with an identifiably Jewish, if radical message, but a divine and messianic being of cosmic theological significance. Nevertheless, the Jewish educator should be aware of the text's Jewish context in order to avoid false dichotomies and distortions. A significant issue for Jewish educators is the development of an awareness that religious traditions are not necessarily sharply defined entities, just as Judaism itself cannot be reduced to a single clear-cut set of doctrines or ideas.

The emphasis on the Judaism of the historical Jesus is not without its challengers among scholars some of whom emphasise Jesus's identity as a somewhat Hellenized Galilean, influenced by the outlook of Cynicism, preaching an anti-establishment, radically egalitarian, and subversive doctrine (Crossan, 1994). Such views are usually rejected by Jewish scholars who are almost affronted by any tendency to deny the essential Jewishness of Jesus. We thus arrive at a position, rich with irony, in which Jewish scholars resist the attempt to take Jesus from Judaism while some Christian scholars resist the attempt by Jews to appropriate Jesus by subsuming him under the existing currents of first-century Judaism (Fredriksen, 1995a).

A Counter-View

The Israeli scientist and philosopher Yeshayahu Leibowitz provides a radical counter-view to what has been said here about an approach to the historical Jesus as a way of reorienting Jewish attitudes to Christianity. Leibowitz argues that Christianity is essentially defined by its hostility to Judaism. Its claim to supersession is essential to Christianity. The two faiths are locked in a theological conflict that cannot be resolved except at the cost of the renunciation of the core identity of one of the religions.

Leibowitz is skeptical of any possibility of recovering the historical Jesus based on firm knowledge. What matters is the Jesus of the Church – the Jesus as constructed by Christology – the son of God, God incarnate, the unique path to redemption.

The educational implications of this view are clear. Knowledge of Christianity is important precisely to understand the unbridgeable gap between the two religions which are locked in eternal conflict over the claim of election. In this conflict there can be no compromise. In Leibowitz's view, in as much as a Jew or a Christian blurs this divide, they lose their authenticity as Jew or Christian (Leibowitz & Goldman, 1992).

Rabbi Joseph B. Soloveitchik, whose essay on interfaith dialogue, "Confrontation", expresses strong reservations about interreligious contacts, held a more nuanced view (Soloveitchik, 1964). This largely philosophical essay continues to carry great weight with many Modern-Orthodox rabbis in shaping their attitudes on this question. There are two major reservations about interfaith dialogue. First, ultimate religious beliefs cannot be shared and communicated. Each religious tradition has its own core beliefs and eschatological hopes which cannot be argued or negotiated. Second, dialogue can lead to an expectation for reciprocal theological or religious change. There is a risk of a blurring of difference in the name of brotherly dialogue leading to loss of faith and religious identity. The meaning and applicability of Rabbi Soloveitchik's argument has been much discussed.[3]

The present discussion is of education not of interfaith dialogue. Indeed it is important to distinguish clearly between these two areas of activity. Dialogue is a complex process requiring not only theological and historical expertise but also an awareness of the political dimension in such contacts. Dialogue is motivated by a desire not only for mutual understanding but also for harmony and reconciliation. The educational discussion should focus on learning and understanding which may foster attitudes of tolerance and respect. It is a recipe for likely confusion if Jewish education attempts go beyond this brief and become a vehicle for reconciliation when basic issues of identity and difference are still being worked out by students.

---

[3] See the symposium published online at http://www.bc.edu/research/cjl/meta-elements/texts/center/conferences/soloveitchik/

There are nevertheless educational implications raised by Rabbi Soloveitchik's essay. The first is the avoidance of a stance of disputation. Teaching of other religions is not a matter of proving the falsehood of their beliefs or the truth of those of Judaism. A believing Jew does not accept the Christian idea of incarnation or accept the Christhood of Jesus. In a sense, she cannot even understand these ideas. Similarly a Jew does not accept the status of Mohammed as the ultimate prophet or the Qur'an as the supreme revelation. These are not matters for negotiation but there is no need to seek arguments to undermine these beliefs on the part of the adherents of other religions. An avenue is opened up for education on other faiths which does not compromise faith and identity on the one hand, while avoiding triumphalism and polemic on the other hand.

Islam

Islam offers fewer challenges and difficulties for Jewish belief than Christianity. Jewish authorities consider Islam pure monotheism; there is no Islamic doctrine of supersession, nor is there the same record of murderous persecution. At the same time while Jews and Christians have largely made their peace, Jews are seen, largely because of the Middle-East conflict, as being in conflict with the Muslim world. This sense of conflict is deepened by the perception of a wider clash between Islam and the Western world. There are representatives of both Judaism and Islam at various levels engaged in activity aimed at discovering other understandings of the relationship between Judaism and Islam in order to subvert the view, convenient to extremists, of unrelenting conflict.

There are some striking points of similarity between the two religious traditions. Islam like Judaism resists being defined in Western terms as a religion rather than an all-encompassing way of life. Islam, like Judaism, has a highly elaborated system of law governing all aspects of life with traditions of interpretation and precedent. In Islam, at least in principle, religious authority stems from the religious and scholarly standing of individuals rather than fixed hierarchies.

While the relationship between Judaism and Christianity is problematic, its drama offers didactic opportunities lacking in the case of Islam. Furthermore, almost all Jewish education in the Diaspora is conducted in contexts which are, at least at the cultural level, Christian. Islam is a fellow minority religion. One reason for learning about Christianity is the ineluctable reality of living in a Christian environment. Islam does not pose this challenge. At the same time, as the reality of the Muslim presence in these societies is increasingly felt, the need for an understanding of Islam is more pressing.

In the State of Israel familiarity with Islam would seem to be an even more urgent necessity. About one-fifth of the population of Israel is Muslim. The surrounding population both in the territories and in the bordering countries is overwhelmingly Muslim. Most Jews are, however, almost totally ignorant of the beliefs and practices of Islam and their ideas are shaped by the way Islam is depicted in the mass media.

Islamic sources do not relate to Judaism as a "mother" religion or as an "elder brother".[4] In Islam the Qur'an is the perfect revealed word of God. The differences between it and the Hebrew Bible are to be explained by the failure of the Jews to preserve the true revelation once entrusted to them. Instead of preserving this revelation, the Jews distorted and altered it (Sura 2:79).[5] On this point there would seem to be an equivalent to the issue of supersession in Christianity (Lazarus-Yafeh, 1992). Two important distinctions should be pointed out. First there is a difference between the rejection of a people and the rejection of a book; the former would seem to have more dangerous implications. The second distinction is that the claim is not that a previously valid revelation has been replaced but that distortions in the transmission of the revelation have been corrected.

To teach about Islam in its own terms requires that the teacher suspend judgment on the question of who influenced whom and to teach what Muslims believe. In his "An Introduction of Islam for Jews", Reuven Firestone adopts just this approach of non-engagement in the question: "Because this book is an introduction to Islam, we are less concerned with what actually happened than we are with what Muslims believe happened" (Firestone, 2008). In his praise, printed on the cover of the book, the historian of Islam, Marc Cohen writes that the book avoids "succumbing to the temptation to say who took what from whom".

A second focus for considering Islam from a Jewish point of view is the history of the relationship between the two faiths. Marc Cohen has judiciously weighed two alternative readings of this history which he calls the "myth" and "counter-myth" (Cohen, 1994). The myth is that of the Golden Age of medieval Islam represented as a multireligious paradise. The counter-myth denies the myth and highlights periods of persecution and the existence of Islamic legislation that discriminated against Judaism often in humiliating ways. Cohen shows that neither myth nor counter-myth provides an adequate account. His comparison of how Jews fared under Islam and Christianity shows, and tries to explain, how Jews generally fared better under Islam than under Christianity. At the same time, an adequate educational approach will not attempt to overlook the more painful aspects of the relationship between Jews and Islam, such as the inconsistently applied terms of the Covenant of Omar that delineates the terms of the disadvantages Jews and Christians must endure in return for their protection.

Educators concerned about softening the prevailing picture of Islam as intrinsically hostile to Jews and Judaism will look to alternative Islamic voices, often drowned out in the tumult of international conflict, who offer an alternative vision of the relationship between Islam and other religions. A crucial educational imperative here is the avoidance of developing a monolithic view of other traditions. Such views

---

[4] This latter formulation was used by Pope John Paul II in describing the relationship of Judaism to Christianity

[5] Maimonides, who considered Christianity to be idolatrous and Islam as a pure form of monotheism, nevertheless ruled that it is possible to explain the Torah to a Christian but not to a Muslim because the Christian and the Jew both regard a shared text as sacred and revealed (Maimonides responsum: Blau 148).

can be convenient for polemic purposes and they offer a simple and clear-cut division of the world but it is obvious that a religious civilization as old, as diverse, and as complex as Islam cannot be reduced to a set of simple propositions (Lovat, 2005).

As our analysis of curriculum examples shows, teaching about Islam presents few difficulties for Jewish education. The doctrinal closeness to Judaism combined with the absence of a tradition of rivalry makes the case quite different from that of Christianity. At the same time the present climate of Jewish-Muslim relations in many sectors makes for difficulties of a different kind that are intensified by a general ignorance about Islam.

Theories of Religious Education

Before analysing some curriculum examples I will review some of the central trends and approaches in religious education and their possible relevance to Jewish education.

Much of this theorizing has taken place in the United Kingdom and other European countries in which religious education is mandatory. The central question that faces religious educators is the reality of religiously pluralistic societies. How should religion be taught in classrooms where students of different religious backgrounds (and students of no religion) are to be found? How are children to be prepared for life in a society in which they are to live peacefully and respectfully side-by-side with believers in a variety of faiths (Hobson & Edwards, 1999; Jackson, 2004)?

Traditionally religious education was confessional in nature; it sought to inculcate in the young of a particular faith community the beliefs of that faith and to provide the knowledge necessary for adequate participation in the life of the community (Thompson, 2004). Such education is open to the charge of indoctrination with the assumption of defined religious truth that the young are to be taught to accept. Confessional religious education can take a variety of forms and may attempt to combine education for religious adherence to a particular faith with learning about and respect for, other religious traditions (Yu-Phelps, 2006). In the current ecumenical climate of interfaith dialogue this has come to be an expectation of Christian education with respect to Judaism. A policy document of the Catholic Church on the presentation of Jews and Judaism states:

> We should aim, in this field, that Catholic teaching at its different levels, in catechesis to children and young people, presents Jews and Judaism not only in an honest and objective manner, free from prejudices and without any offenses, but also with full awareness of the heritage common to Jews and Christians.[6]

There is more than just a liberal religious sensibility at work here. There is a claim that to properly understand their own Christianity, Christians need to learn about

---

[6]"Notes on the Correct Way to Present the Jews and Judaism in Preaching and Catechesis in the Roman Catholic Church", http://www.ewtn.com/library/CURIA/RRJJEWS.htm

Judaism. There is also a consciousness of the dire consequences of the "teaching of contempt" over the centuries. There is recognition that Judaism needs to be addressed as a living religious tradition and not as the backdrop against which Christ and Christianity redeemed the world. Much recent non-Jewish scholarship has been directed at counteracting this view (Gager, 1983, Sanders, 1977). While the Catholic approach emphasizes a "common heritage" and the need to be "free from prejudices", this does not mean that the Catholic Church has abandoned its beliefs in the centrality of Christ as redeemer or that at some end-time Christian belief will be vindicated in the eyes of all.

A second approach to religious education is phenomenological in emphasis. Many educators adopting this approach worked under the influence of Ninian Smart (1989) and his approach to the study of world religions. Smart approaches religion from a neutral stance, avoiding any element of theological commitment. In studying religions he identified what he called "dimensions" of religions. All religions express themselves in these various dimensions albeit in quite diverse ways. The seven dimensions are:

1. Doctrinal
2. Mythological
3. Ethical
4. Ritual
5. Experiential
6. Institutional
7. Material.

These dimensions provide a basis for comparison between religious traditions and, in curriculum terms, a structure for teaching about different religious traditions. The approach requires at least a methodological agnosticism about the truth claims of all the religions.

The appeal of the approach is obvious as a response to the reality of religious and cultural pluralism. Each tradition is afforded equal respect and status (O'Grady, 2005). Although it is not an explicit claim of the approach, in practice it generally assumes that all religions are equally true (or untrue) or that ultimately they aim at the same thing. The problematic nature of such an approach for an educational setting committed to a particular religious tradition is evident. In multifaith environments also the approach has been criticised for a lack of sensitivity to the actual religious beliefs and affiliations of students. The approach has also been criticised for an emphasis on external structures and behaviours rather than issues of meaning and spirituality (Barnes, 2009).

A third approach flows from a critique of the neutral methodology of the "world religions" approach. The critique notes that by adopting a neutral stance – the view from nowhere – the learner is able to learn a great deal about religion but is unlikely to learn from it. Hence a third approach is advocated that may be labeled philosophical. Here, students study religion and religions as an opportunity to build their own worldview and scheme of meaning. As opposed to the confessional approach, students are regarded as individuals who can be empowered to develop their own philosophy and worldview, and the study of the ideas of diverse religious traditions can play an important part in this process (Carr, 2007). In recent years there has emerged a rich theoretical literature suggesting different ways in which religious education can make a contribution to children's spiritual development in environments of diversity without undermining their identity and beliefs as members of a particular community (Jackson, 2004). Religious-education theorists grapple with the tensions between respect for students' beliefs and religious affiliations on the one hand and the educational imperative to cultivate autonomy on the other.

This approach is likely to have little appeal for Jewish educational settings of all ideological stripes whose main aim is to inculcate a sense of belonging to the Jewish people and tradition. At the same time it may be that amid the urgent work of inculcation of identity and group norms, the spiritual growth of the individual does not get the attention it deserves. Within the sources of Judaism the approach provides a rationale for the teaching of Jewish thought by exposing young people to the rich diversity of philosophies of Judaism so that they have the means to shape their own orientation from them. In this way Jewish education can go some way in satisfying autonomy as an educational value.

Extending the approach to other religions risks confusion at best and a corrosive syncretism at worst. It is, however, possible to conceive of adult education for those with a mature and settled identity and Jewish worldview being able to engage with other religions and finding in this engagement learning and even inspiration that has an impact on their Jewish self-understanding. This is, however, a sophisticated level of thinking, conscious of boundaries while being aware of their porosity. The ground can be prepared at earlier stages by avoiding the dichotomous approach referred to above with regard to other religions.

An Analysis of Curricula

This section will review some examples of curricular materials relevant to the teaching of other religions in the contexts of Jewish education. Here, curricular materials will serve as proxies for investigating actual educational practice. The examples do not constitute a comprehensive survey of existing materials but rather a sampling that represents distinctive approaches.

A Religious-Thought Approach

One of the most interesting attempts to teach about Christianity in the context of Jewish education is an experimental unit, "To be a Jew in a Christian World", that was part of a curriculum project "Teaching Jewish Values" developed in the 1980s at the Melton Centre for Jewish Education at the Hebrew University (Cohen, 1983). As the title suggests, this unit is ultimately about what it means to be Jewish for students who live in a context where the majority religion and culture is Christian. In such contexts to be a Jew means "not being a Christian". The presenting problem is that many Jewish young people cannot give positive substantial content to this essentially negative identity. This approach requires learning about the majority religion.

The curriculum clearly belongs to a mode of religious education that seeks to deepen the existing religious affiliation of the learners. The writers explicitly distance themselves from the neutral approach of comparative religion. The aim of the unit is to help students develop their distinctive Jewish worldview. In this respect the curriculum contains elements of the philosophical approach to religious education with the reservation that learners are expected to work out their personal worldview from within the intellectual and spiritual resources of Judaism.

The writers are sensitive to the danger that teaching about Christianity from a Jewish point of view can lapse into polemic, triumphalism, and chauvinism. They declare their intention to avoid a dichotomous presentation in which Judaism is the negation of Christianity presented in an extreme or one-dimensional fashion. The unit includes Christian texts and viewpoints that can be correlated with Jewish texts as well as modern Christian expressions of a positive orientation towards Judaism. At the same time the material also deals with points of conflict, particularly those from the past such as the charge of deicide.

To illustrate the nature of the curriculum I will focus on the section comparing Jewish and Christian ideas about morality. The material avoids setting up a dichotomy with Jewish morality based upon justice opposed to a Christian morality of self-effacement. Instead the writers do two things. First they show how in modern Christianity there is a movement to review distorted traditional Christian images of Judaism as legalistic, loveless, and tied to the flesh. To do this they use an anti-Jewish text from John of Damascus (c.676–749). This is preceded by an extract from the 1973 "Statement by the French Bishops' Committee for Relations with Jews" which calls for the need for a deeper understanding of Judaism: "It is wrong to oppose Judaism as a religion of fear to Christianity as one of love." The use of texts, both Jewish and Christian, give students direct access to the ideas in question, and it is significant that the modern text sympathetic to Judaism is brought before the text from John of Damascus.

The rest of the section compares teachings of Jesus with rabbinic texts on such questions as supererogatory behaviours (*lifnim mishurat hadin*), attitudes to wealth and the material world, and love of the enemy. The Jewish texts present a range of viewpoints some of which are quite similar to Jesus's teaching while others are quite different. There is, therefore, no monolithic Judaism that can be opposed to Christianity.

It is, however, problematic to present a text like the Sermon on the Mount as a Christian text as it is problematic to present Jesus as a Christian. If this text is seen primarily as a Jewish text to be viewed against the context of streams in first-century Judaism (themselves reflected in subsequent rabbinic texts) we need not be surprised to find a degree of overlap with Jewish texts.

Over and above these minor criticisms the curriculum is an important attempt to teach about Christianity from within the context of Jewish education while avoiding false dichotomies and self-serving caricatures of the other religion.

A World-Religions Approach in Israeli Schools

The curriculum "Living in the Holy Land: Knowing and Respecting the Other, One God – Three Religions", is written from within the phenomenological "world-religions", approach to religious education (Schoneveld, 2008).[7] The curriculum was developed in Israel by the Centre for Educational Technology with support from the European Union and UNESCO. The approach is that of the study of "world religions" but the context for learning is the coexistence of the three Abrahamic religions in Israel. The curriculum was published in three languages, Hebrew, Arabic, and English and is intended as a contribution to both religious education and peace education.

The material is structured around topics which constitute something like Smart's dimensions of religion: origins of life; origins of monotheistic belief; beginnings of religious community; sacred texts; authoritative, traditional, and interpretation literature; beliefs; obligations; religious leadership.

The curriculum is aimed at students in Israel from the three religions but it is not adapted in any way, apart from language, to the needs and interests of the particular communities within which it will be taught. Muslim students will learn about their own faith with the same measure of neutrality with which they approach Judaism and Christianity. Given the aim of cultivating respect for the other faiths in the context of rivalry and conflict, this approach has certain advantages. It is the combination of looking with respect at other traditions and looking with a certain detachment at one's own tradition that is likely to cultivate greater tolerance and openness. All the same, there is something artificial about teaching in this way to those rooted in their own religious tradition.

While each section concludes with an invitation to compare the traditions, the curriculum is careful to present each tradition independently without reference or comparison to the others. The concluding discussion relates to comparisons with a particular focus on similarities which fits the irenic tendency of the whole project.

The materials avoid the points at which the rivalries and conflicts between the traditions arise, for example, the central Christian beliefs in the divinity of Jesus and that belief in Jesus-as-Christ is a condition for salvation. These beliefs, which are rejected by Jews and Muslims, are mentioned in the text but are not given any particular emphasis.

A Historical Approach

The curricula discussed so far are essentially ahistorical in their approach. Their purpose is to help the student understand the current moment as their present-tense titles indicate: "Being Jewish", "Living in the Holy Land". The final group of materials is essentially historical in character. One practical advantage of this approach

---

[7] See also http://lib.cet.ac.il/pages/item.asp?item=12439

is that Jewish history is already part of the curriculum in Israeli schools and in most Jewish schools in the Diaspora and so the learning slots into an existing curriculum framework.

Living as a religious and ethnic minority amid a Christian or Muslim majority was the defining fact of Jewish history for almost two millennia. Any course in Jewish history will inevitably explore this condition. The question is, therefore, not whether to touch upon Christianity and Islam but how. Salo Baron wrote of the need to recover from the "lachrymose theory" of Jewish history according to which this history is a catalogue of persecution and oppression (Baron, 1937). The question to ask of the treatment of other religions in Jewish history textbooks is, to what extent these books present a nuanced view? To what extent do other religions emerge as traditions with a life of their own or merely as agents of anti-Jewish activity?

This is not to suggest that teaching Jewish history can or should avoid the facts of persecution, expulsion, crusade, and pogrom. Even in the Middle Ages, however, as Baron emphasized, Jews enjoyed certain privileges as well as disabilities and they had more opportunities economically and culturally than feudal serfs who made up the bulk of the population.

The two major areas in which the teaching of Jewish history needs to deal with other religions are, first, the continuing unfolding of the relationship with the dominant religion and its effect on Jewish life, and second, the story of the birth and emergence of Christianity and Islam. I will focus on the second by looking at some text books in use in the Israeli education system in secular and religious schools.

A standard text used in many Israel middle schools is "In the Days of the Crescent and the Cross" (Kleinberg & Bar-Navi, 1997). The authors are academic historians with a specialization in Christianity and Islam respectively. As the title of the book suggests, Jewish history in the Middle Ages is to be understood primarily in terms of minority existence alongside the two dominant religions.

When describing the beginnings of Islam the textbook gives a neutral description of the beginnings of Islam and the career of Mohammed as the prophet of the new religion. The book sets aside considerable space not only to historical events but also to explain the principal beliefs, institutions, and practices of Islam. There is a general reference to Christian and Jewish influences on Mohammed but the book states that it is unknown exactly how this influence came about.

The teacher's guide, but not the student text, devotes a page to a discussion of the "Jihad", noting that it is not included among the "pillars of Islam". The term is explained as "effort taken on behalf of Allah". The sense of Jihad as war undertaken to spread Islam is joined by subsequent interpretations that include other forms of effort including financial and spiritual as under the category of Jihad.

The student text includes a section, "Mohammed and the Jews", that refers to Mohammed's disappointment with the rejection by the Jews of the Arabian Peninsula of his revelation and mission. Mention is made of the expulsion of two Jewish tribes and the slaughter of yet a third, the Qurayt tribe.

The text characterizes the attitude of the Qur'an and the Hadith to Jews as "alienated and contemptuous", arising from a desire "to remove all Jewish influence on faithful Muslims". The text goes on to describe the establishment of the status of Jews and Christians as inferior but protected under Islamic religious law.

The text is mainly concerned with describing the rise of Islam and the character of Islam as a religion. The small space allotted to the relationship with Judaism presents a somewhat harsh view of the position of the Jews during the life of Mohammed and early Islam.

I now turn to the parallel section of the textbook "From Generation to Generation" which was written for religious schools (Doron, 1994). The textbook devotes considerable space to a description of Arab culture before Mohammed. The textbook describes the beginning of Islam and Mohammed in entirely neutral terms presenting the events and personalities as they are represented in Islamic tradition. The text continues to describe the basic beliefs and practices of Islam. It is striking that in this text prepared for Orthodox schools there is no element of criticism or reservation in describing these facts and events (Bartal, 2002).

Following chapters on the early conquests and spread of Islam and on "The Islamic World and its Culture", comes an extended section on "The Jews in the Shadow of Islam", the first chapter of which is entitled "Under the Protection of the Muslims". There is an account of Mohammed's attitude to the Jews beginning with his hopes that they would accept his mission, then his disappointment and anger at their rejection, and, finally, once his rule became established, his adoption of a policy of tolerance and protection. The attitude to the Jews is portrayed in a nuanced way that explains tensions and contradictions within the texts.

Both the textbooks described here show how it is possible to teach about other religions in the context of the teaching of history in a manner which is balanced, neutral, and nuanced. Crucial in this respect is the input of academic historians either as writers or advisers. History can easily degenerate in this area to a polemical narrative if it becomes a tool for the purpose of religious education rather than an academic field with its own canons of evidence and balance.

Conclusion

The study of other religions within Jewish education remains an undeveloped field with important potential as well as attendant risks. It will be argued by some that such study is a luxury for Jewish education with its limited time and resources. In response, I suggest that such study is not only important for understanding the contemporary world but is also an important way to achieve a deeper Jewish self-understanding.

The manner and spirit of the learning is all-important. We tend to rejoice in the many-faceted nature of our own tradition and take pride in the power and subtlety of interpretation and development within the tradition but with regard to others it is all too easy to lapse into a perception of them as monolithic, and to portray other traditions in a manner that is self-serving. An opposing risk is that in the desire to demonstrate understanding and cultivate tolerance the historical record is distorted, and differences and boundaries are blurred. Scholarship in the relevant fields is a crucial resource for the development of new approaches to the teaching of other religions. This scholarship needs to be considered alongside developments in the theory of religious education together with what can be learned from significant examples of educational practice.

References

Ahad Ha'am. (1962). *Nationalism and the Jewish ethic: Basic writings of Ahad Ha'am*. New York: Herzl Press.
Barnes, P. L. (2009). An honest appraisal of phenomenological religious education and a final, honest reply to Kevin O'Grady. *British Journal of Religious Education, 31*(1), 69–72.
Baron, S. W. (1937). *A social and religious history of the Jews, by Salo Wittmayer Baron*. New York: Columbia University Press.
Bartal, I. (2002). The history of the Jewish people in textbooks of the state-religious school sector: A different story? In A. Ben-Amos (Ed.), *History, identity and memory: Images of the past in Israeli education*. Tel Aviv: Ramot (Hebrew).
Berger, P. L. (1967). *The sacred canopy; elements of a sociological theory of religion*. Garden City, NY: Doubleday.
Berger, P. L. (1979). *The heretical imperative: Contemporary possibilities of religious affirmation*. Garden City, NY: Anchor Press.
Berger, P. L. (1996). Secularism in retreat. *National Interest, 46*, 3–12.
Berger, D.. (2002). "Dabru Emet: Some Reservations about a Jewish Statement on Christians and Christianity." from http://www.ccjr.us/dialogika-resources/documents-and-statements/analysis/286-dabru-emet-berger.
Berger, P. L., Woodhead, L., Heelas, P., & Martin, D. (2001). *Peter Berger and the study of religion*. London, New York: Routledge.
Carr, D. (2007). Religious education, religious literacy and common schooling: A philosophy and history of skewed reflection. *Journal of Philosophy of Education, 41*(4), 659–673.
Cohen, J. (1983). *Being a Jew in a Christian world (Hebrew)*. Jerusalem: Melton Centre for Jewish Education.
Cohen, M. R. (1994). *Under crescent and cross: The Jews in the middle ages*. Princeton, NJ: Princeton University Press.
Cohen, J. (1999). Jesus crucified: Jewish memory and counter-history (Hebrew). *Zmanim, 68–69*, 12–27.
Crossan, J. D. (1994). *Jesus: A revolutionary biography*. San Francisco: HarperSanFrancisco.
Doron, A. (1994). *Midor L'dor: lessons in history for the state religious school (Hebrew)*. Jerusalem: Maalot.
Felderhof, M. C. (1985). *Religious education in a pluralistic society: Papers from a consultation on theology and education held at Westhill College, Selly Oak (an affiliated college of the University of Birmingham)*. London: Hodder and Stoughton.
Firestone, R. (2008). *An introduction to Islam for Jews*. Philadelphia: Jewish Publication Society.
Flusser, D. (1979). The Torah in the Sermon on the Mount (Hebrew) in Judaism and the sources of Christianity. In *Judaism and the sources of Christianity* (pp. 226–234). Tel Aviv: Sifriyat Hapoalim.
Flusser, D. (1988). *Judaism and the origins of Christianity*. Jerusalem: Magnes Press, Hebrew University.
Flusser, D., & Notley, R. S. (1997). *Jesus*. Jerusalem: Magnes Press.
Fredriksen, P. (1995a). What you see is what you get: Context and content in current research on the historical Jesus. *Theology Today, 52*(1), 75–97.
Fredriksen, P. (1995b). *excaecati occulta justitia dei*: Augustine on Jews and Judaism. *Journal of Early Christian Studies, 3*(3), 299–324.

Fredriksen, P. (1999). *Jesus of Nazareth, king of the Jews: A Jewish life and the emergence of Christianity.* New York: Knopf.

Gager, J. G. (1983). *The origins of antisemitism: Attitudes toward Judaism in pagan and Christian antiquity.* New York: Oxfor University Press.

Gash, A., & Gonzales, A. (2008). School prayer. In N. Persily, J. Citrin, & P. J. Egan (Eds.), *Public opinion and constitutional controversy* (pp. 62–79). New York and Oxford: Oxford University Press.

Heschel, A. J.. (1966). No religion is an island. Union Theological Seminary Quarterly. Review 21(2): 117 (reprinted in Jewish Perspectives on Christianity edited by Fritz A. Rothschild, Crossroad, New York, 1990, 309–324).

Hobson, P. R., & Edwards, J. S. (1999). *Religious education in a pluralist society: The key philosophical issues.* London: Woburn Press.

Honkaheimo, M.. (2007). From http://www.mmiweb.org.uk/eftre/reeurope/finland_2009.html.

Jackson, R. (2004). *Rethinking religious education and plurality: Issues in diversity and pedagogy.* London: RoutledgeFalmer.

Klausner, J., & Danby, H. (1925). *Jesus of Nazareth; His life, times, and teaching.* New York: The Macmillan company.

Kleinberg, A., & Bar-NavI, E. (1997). *In the days of the crescent and the cross (Hebrew).* Tel Aviv: Sifrei Tel Aviv.

Lazarus-Yafeh, H. (1992). *Intertwined worlds: Medieval Islam and Bible criticism.* Princeton, NJ and Oxford: Princeton University Press.

Leibowitz, Y., & Goldman, E. (1992). *Judaism, human values, and the Jewish state.* Cambridge, MA: Harvard University Press.

Levenson, J. D. (2001). How not to conduct Jewish-Christian dialogue. *Commentary, 112*(5), 31–37.

Lévinas, E. (1990). *Difficult freedom: Essays on Judaism.* Baltimore: Johns Hopkins University Press.

Lovat, T. J. (2005). Educating about Islam and learning about self: An approach for our times. *Religious Education, 100*(1), 38–51.

O'Grady, K. (2005). Professor Ninian Smart, phenomenology and religious education. *British Journal of Religious Education, 27*(3), 227–237.

Rosenzweig, F., & Glatzer, N. N. (1961). *Franz Rosenzweig: His life and thought.* New York: Schocken Books.

Sacks, J. R. (2002). *The dignity of difference: How to avoid the clash of civilizations.* London: Continuum.

Sanders, E. P. (1977). *Paul and Palestinian Judaism: A comparison of patterns of religion.* Philadelphia: Fortress Press.

Schoneveld, J. (2008). *Living in the holy land: Knowing and respecting the other, one god – three religions.* Tel Aviv: Center for Educational Technology.

Short, G., & Lenga, R.-A. (2002). Jewish primary schools in a multicultural society: Responding to diversity? *Journal of Beliefs & Values, 23*(1), 43–54.

Smart, N. (1989). *The world's religions,* Cambridge: University Press.

Soloveitchik, J. B. (1964). Confrontation. *Tradition: A Journal of Orthodox Thought, 6*(2), 5–29.

Stark, R. (2000). Secularization. R.I.P *Sociology of Religion, 60*(3), 249–273.

Thompson, P. (2004). *Whatever happened to religious education?* Cambridge: Lutterworth.

VCAA. (2009). 2009, from http://vels.vcaa.vic.edu.au/support/progression/history.html#lev5.

Vermes, G. (1973). *Jesus the Jew. A historian's reading of the Gospels.* London: Collins.

Yu-Phelps, J. (2006). *Teaching about other religions: Ideas and strategies for use in the Catholic high school.* Winona, MN: Saint Mary's Press.

Yuval, I. J. (2006). *Two nations in your womb: Perceptions of Jews and Christians in late antiquity and the middle ages.* Berkeley, CA and London: University of California Press.

Talmud: Making a Case for Talmud Pedagogy—The Talmud as an Educational Model

Marjorie Lehman and Jane Kanarek

Introduction

The Babylonian Talmud (Bavli) stands at the canonical center of Jewish tradition. Composed between the third and seventh centuries C.E., the Bavli has been and continues to be studied in a variety of contexts, ranging from religious academies (*yeshivot*) to modern secular universities. Its study has resulted in a long chain of commentaries, including the almost line-by-line commentary of Rabbi Solomon Yitzḥaki (Rashi, 1040/1–1105) and the medieval dialogical commentaries of the Tosafists. Legal codification was also an outgrowth of Talmudic analysis and interpretation and resulted in Isaac Alfasi's (Rif, 1013–1103) *Hilkhot Ha-rif* and Moses Maimonides' (Rambam, 1135–1204) *Mishneh Torah*, to cite two examples. More recently, contemporary scholars in the field of Talmud have utilized a number of methodologies, including, but not limited to, legal, literary, and philological analysis (Ben-Menahem, 1991; Epstein, 1962; Rubenstein, 1999; Saiman, 2006). However, despite the significant attention given to the study of the Talmud, it has largely been overlooked as an educational model. Since, at its core, Judaism is a tradition defined by pedagogical concerns, this omission is particularly striking. Furthermore, despite the many institutions in which Talmud is studied today, it is surprising that the development of curricular models for how to study this work is still in its infancy (Friedman (internet file), Hayman, 1997; Kanarek, 2010; Kraemer, 1981; Kress & Lehman, 2003; Lehman, 2002, 2006, Mandel Center for Studies in Jewish Education 2007).

This chapter represents a first step in framing the field of Talmud pedagogy. Our goal is to discuss why Talmud study matters as a model for teachers, regardless of whether they teach Talmud. In this regard, our initial foray into the world of Talmud pedagogy will focus on "why" the Talmud is such an important component in the education of teachers, rather than on "how" we should approach these texts when teaching them in our classrooms. We will approach the issue of "why" Talmud study

M. Lehman (✉)
Jewish Theological Seminary of America, New York, NY, USA
e-mail: malehman@jtsa.edu

matters through an examination of one sugya (or Talmudic unit), Bavli Bava Metzia 33a. This sugya presents the rabbis as men who were engaged in reflecting on their own teaching practice and prompts us to look at them for what they can teach us about pedagogy.

Why Studying Talmud Matters

The relationship between liberal education and responsible citizenship has sparked debates about the components of an education that creates good citizens. Most would agree that irrespective of how one defines the "canon" of liberal education, one of the overarching goals of such an education is to raise reflective citizens who possess the capacity for critical examination of one's self, one's traditions, and the traditions of others (Shulman, 2004a, p. 401). As Martha Nussbaum argues, drawing on the Stoics and Socrates, "the central task of education ... is to confront the passivity of the pupil, challenging the mind to take charge of its own thought" (Nussbaum, 1997, p. 28). Liberal education does not aim to teach its students to defer to authority, be it person or text, or to accept a particular belief as authoritative, whether through tradition or habit. Rather, it, "... requires developing the capacity to reason logically, to test what one reads or says for consistency of reasoning, correctness of fact, and accuracy of judgment" (Nussbaum, 1997, p. 10). To produce responsible citizens, liberal education aims to develop the capacity to question, to examine issues from multiple perspectives, and to explore a variety of cultures.

For those of us, however, who are committed to the continuity of religious traditions, these goals of liberal education may appear in conflict with a primary goal of Jewish education: the desire to cultivate in our students a sense of embeddedness in an ancient and ongoing tradition. We seek to teach our students to be open-minded citizens of a democratic world who pose thoughtful questions because we want them to be people who are poised to shape and even transform society. Yet, we also seek to teach the importance of sustaining Jewish tradition and to respect that tradition's authority (Rosenak, 1987, pp. 9–10, p. 28). How can our students both learn to respect the authority of tradition and, at the same time, question and criticize that authority, as the liberal educational model demands?

Judaism is a tradition defined by pedagogical concerns. Due to the fact that the acquisition of knowledge is ontologically and historically a core component of Jewish identity, Jews have continuously cultivated methods of teaching and learning (Twersky, 2003, p. 47). In fact, many of the works that comprise Judaism's library exemplify types of pedagogical approaches that grapple in varying ways with the very issue we posed above—the tension between the development of critical thought and the preservation of authority. This characteristic makes Jewish texts fitting models for teachers. In our possession we have a set of texts that comprise ancient case studies useful for exploring the question of how pedagogues interested in religious education should educate in the twenty-first century.

The literary structure of the Bavli makes it a fitting exemplar from the Jewish library through which to pursue this model of liberal education. The redactors of the

Babylonian Talmud adopted a style in which ideational stasis was rejected in favor of a style of argumentation that promotes ever-deeper analysis of already stated laws and narratives. In place of blind acceptance of principles and concepts, multiple angles are considered in an argumentative schema where one rabbi is comfortable undermining the logic of another's ideas. Rabbis are presented as possessing the capacity to reason logically, to evaluate ideas for their consistency, and to justify their views. Literal readings of Toraitic material are overturned, verses from different books in the Tanakh are put into conversation with one another, passages from the Mishnah are reinterpreted, arguments are decided in favor of one authority over another, disputes are left unresolved, and new ideas are proposed. The Talmud thus reveals itself as a book whose style evinces that it is the creation of a citizenry steeped in the tenets that define a liberal education. Yet, within this culture of questioning and dispute, the voices of the Talmud also reveal themselves as acutely aware and reverently wedded to the concept of religious authority. The Talmud juggles both dispute and authority in a manner that needs to be studied carefully for what it can teach us today about how to grapple with these competing ideals.

Talmud study therefore matters as an educational practice for all teachers of Jewish studies, regardless of whether or not they actually teach Talmudic texts themselves. Jewish studies instructors should study the Talmud for what it conveys about how we can teach our students to be simultaneously critical thinkers and embedded within a particular tradition. The Bavli is important not only because of its content, but also because of how it expresses that content. While it never explicitly resolves this anxiety or tension between the privilege to challenge and the value of religious authority, it does not place the two in a dichotomous relationship with one another. Reading the Bavli can help teachers to see the ways in which sustained and close discussion of a topic can open new understandings of that subject within a Jewish educational framework. In addition, because arguments are often not resolved, it can push readers to add their own voices into the discussion, critically examining the Bavli's statements to see which they consider the best position. The Bavli does not force us to choose between critical thinking and authority. Instead, the two speak to one another.

Making a Case for Case Methods: Getting Inside the Text

The challenge, however, is to figure out a way to present the Talmud's texts to teachers so that they see them as pedagogical tools capable of serving as the building blocks for professional reasoning and discourse in their development as teachers. We do not want the Talmud to be defined by a set of vague general principles and maxims that apply broadly to a group of men we call the rabbis. Our teachers need to get inside the heads of these rabbis as they think about teaching. For this reason, we have adopted a model articulated by Lee Shulman, among others (Shulman, 2004b; Shulman & Sato, 2006; Holzer, 2002; Merseth, 1991; Richert, 1991; Wasserman, 1994). Shulman has proposed that learning to provide a liberal education emerges most effectively from the study of case-like segments that bracket specific dilemmas (Shulman, 2004b, pp. 464–465). Teachers who are presented with individual experiential "chunks" of discourse that are context specific are better able to visualize and grapple with the uncertainty and unpredictability that defines the art of teaching (Shulman, 2004b, p. 465). They are given a means through which they can "store, exchange, and organize their own experiences" (Shulman, 2004b, p. 465). In order to use the Talmud as a means for the pedagogical development of teachers while working within the Jewish tradition, we need to re-present these Talmudic texts as accounts of human experience, that is, as accounts of teaching dilemmas and strategies, each situated in their own time, place, and subject matter (Shulman, 2004b, p. 464). Like our own observations about pedagogy and our inability to generalize about one's experience as a teacher, the Talmud does not speak in general terms about its concepts and ideas about pedagogy. It does not have one uniform approach to the dilemmas of teaching and learning. And, since liberal education entails understanding that ideas develop in particular contexts and at particular moments, case-models drawn from the Talmud help us to cultivate that understanding within the context of the Jewish tradition. The case study is, therefore, a means of translating the sugyot of the Talmud into usable material for teacher education and for bridging the gap between liberal education and Jewish education.

The case study is also an attempt, as Elie Holzer has argued, to think about "what kind of [text] study leads to good teaching" (Holzer, 2002, p. 385). In recommending that we utilize Jewish texts to develop case-models in the training of teachers Holzer correctly challenges the belief that what makes teachers better is either a deeper knowledge of their subject matter or a better understanding of the meta-goals of text study (Holzer, 2002, pp. 378–379). Instead, we argue that the texts of the Talmud, when molded into usable case studies, not only provide teachers with necessary content knowledge, but also enhance the pedagogy of learning how to become more effective in the classroom (Holzer, 2002, p. 385).

That said it is important to note that the Talmud's cases are not actual records of what transpired in the academy. They are images constructed by a set of redactors who may or may not have experienced the events as they are described in a particular text. However, the fact remains that the redactors have left us a document rooted in the cultivation of the value of ongoing study. Although the events they describe and the conversations they record may not be rooted in real-life events and may not have our twenty-first century educational tensions in mind, one can still view the Bavli as testing, analyzing, and grappling with "what is" good pedagogy. Moshe Berger reports that in an introductory Talmud course designed for Jewish educators at the Cleveland College of Jewish Studies, the Talmud quite naturally and unexpectedly became a "gateway" to the students' development as Jewish educators. This happened despite Berger's initial objective, which was merely to introduce his students to the world of the rabbis (Berger, 1998, p. 109). As Elie Holzer argues, we can "narrow the cultural gap that separates us from these sources" so that they can speak to our teachers on the level of teacher development (Holzer, 2002, p. 388; Berger, 1998, pp. 109–110, 120).

Yet, while we seek to narrow that gap we do not want to close it entirely. Since teaching often involves negotiating the unfamiliar and operating in multiple cultural worlds (Kleinfeld, 1988, p. 5), a case study that emerges from an unfamiliar context can also be particularly useful. The very strangeness of Talmudic cases can provoke constructive conversation as teachers try to compare the Talmud's pedagogy with their own. For example, recognition of the differences between ancient and modern constructions of societal hierarchies may result in reflections on contemporary social class and gender. Difference as well as similarity can aid teachers in their formation. Furthermore, while teachers think about their own teaching, they become embedded in a cultural world that has always been about a value-laden commitment to pedagogy despite its transformations over time.

Making a Case for a Case Studies' Methodology

In the next stage of this chapter we will bring you inside the world of the Bavli by translating one sugya from Bava Metzia into two teaching case studies. The first will bring us face-to-face with the rabbis as they comfortably read the Mishnah, the canonical text on which the Talmud is constructed, through the lens of other texts. Despite the fact that such a reading practice complicates the issues presented in the Mishnah, the Bavli presents the rabbis as men governed both by the authority of the Mishnah and by the notion that textual complexity is generative and thus a positive force in the development of understanding. The rabbis model the advantages of resisting a more simplistic type of learning where one text has sole authority. Such a case study offers the modern-day teacher an example of what can occur when material that complicates the main subject or topic under discussion is brought comfortably into the flow of classroom discussion.

The second case moves us away from the issue of textual authority and focuses our attention on the issue of human authority. In a culture so strongly identified with preserving tradition and fostering argumentation, the issue of the teacher's authority in the face of his students' questions emerged as a source of anxiety for the rabbis. What was the extent of rabbinic authority? How were the rabbis supposed to view their students and, in turn, how were their students supposed to view them? The challenge is a familiar one as we too consider how to confront our students' questions.

These cases are only two among the many that remain to be developed from the Bavli. They offer examples of how the Talmud can provide teachers with the resources to guide students toward a much-needed sense of humanity as they find ancient Jewish evidence of the conflicts that they themselves confront in the modern world of education. These case studies provide accounts of how the tension between the development of critical thinking skills and the commitment to the authority of a tradition can be generative and constructive rather than destructive. They inform us that it is possible to cultivate a sense of skepticism while, at the same time, build a sense of reverence for tradition that is crucial to strong Jewish identity.

Bavli Bava Metzia 33a (bBM 33a):[1] The Ideational Background

The biblical commandment found in Exodus 23:4 and Deuteronomy 22:1–3 requiring the return of lost objects to their owners becomes the central focus of the second chapter of tractate Bava Metzia. Within a religious universe where one's relationship to God plays a definitive role, this chapter focuses on the material (rather than the spiritual) realm by exploring issues raised by situations involving the loss and return of one's material possessions. Repeatedly, the rabbis attempt to balance their religious need to observe the biblical commandment regarding the return of lost objects with the realities of everyday life that challenge its implementation. What happens if the object has no identifying mark on it and therefore the finder cannot locate the owner? Without an identifying mark will the finder know whether the claimant is the rightful owner? What occurs if the finder does not have the financial means to care for the object during the length of time it takes him to locate the owner? To what extent should he incur financial loss in order to fulfill the biblical command? Do the same responsibilities to return lost objects apply to cases where one finds objects belonging to non-Jews? As the rabbis grapple with these legal issues about the lost objects of individuals, we find that their discussions also become an opportunity for them (and therefore for us) to think about how to grapple with loss on a larger scale. Their conversations about material loss are also discussions about spiritual and religious loss. In the cases that we will bring below the effects of the potential loss of rabbinic, parental, and textual authority are explored in terms of their ability to endanger the acquisition of Torah knowledge.

Case 1: Confronting Textual Authority

From the Talmud's self-presentation it appears that learning began with one small unit of material drawn from the rabbinic canon, the Mishnah. As teachers, we are no different. We also begin with a central body of material, a core text or idea. When we meet the rabbis in the final sugya of the second chapter of Bava Metzia we find them, within the context of discussing the return of lost objects, proposing guidelines with respect to which individuals take precedence in cases of retrieving these lost things.

Mishnah Bava Metzia 2:11[2]

> His own lost object and his father's lost object—
> [retrieving] his own lost object takes precedence.
> His own lost object and his teacher's lost object—

---

[1] Throughout the remainder of this chapter Bavli Bava Metzia 33a will be referred to as bBM 33a.
[2] For ease of reference we have listed and referenced this mishnah in accordance with printed editions of the Mishnah (Albeck, 1988). However, in MS Kaufman this mishnah appears as 2:13–14. From now on Mishnah Bava Metzia 2:11 will be referred to as mBM 2:11.

[retrieving] his own [lost object] takes precedence.
His father's lost object and his teacher's lost object—
[returning] his teacher's [lost object] takes precedence;
[this is] because his father brought him into this world,
but his teacher who taught him wisdom brings him into the world to come.
But if his father is wise,
[retrieving] his father's [lost object] takes precedence.
If his father and his teacher are [each] carrying a burden,
he removes that of his teacher, and afterwards removes that of his father.
If his father and his teacher are taken captive,
he redeems his teacher, and afterwards redeems his father.
But if his father is wise,
he redeems his father, and afterwards redeems his teacher.

Mishnah Bava Metzia 2:11[3] imagines a specific circumstance where a person can retrieve only one object and needs to choose between retrieving his teacher's object or that of his father. In such a scenario, his teacher takes precedence. mBM 2:11 then uses this case as a jumping off point to reinforce the value that teachers take precedence over fathers, unless one's father is himself a scholar, by citing other situations. For example, in the event that a teacher and a father are carrying heavy burdens and need assistance, his teacher's needs take precedence. In a case where both a person's teacher and his father are taken captive, he is to redeem his teacher before his father. The value is clearly stated: in rabbinic society teachers, or individuals who possess knowledge of Torah, are valued more highly than one's parents. Status is determined by knowledge.

While the rules as laid out by this mishnah seem quite clear and teachable, the redactors of the Talmudic sugya that follows undermine this clarity. They introduce a source chronologically parallel to mBM 2:11, a baraita (a rabbinic source contemporaneous with the mishnah), that has nothing to do with lost objects, or carrying burdens, or redeeming captives. This text raises new questions and expands upon the initial reading of the mishnah. The baraita reads as follows:

> The Rabbis taught: "His teacher" that the rabbis spoke of [mBM 2:11] is the teacher that taught him wisdom [that is: how to analyze with great insight the collection of rabbinic material found in the Mishnah] and not the rabbi who taught him [rote forms of learning as would be used to teach] Scripture or the [literal sense of the] Mishnah. These are the words of Rabbi Meir.[4]
>
> Rabbi Yehudah says: ["His teacher" is] the [person from] whom one learned the majority of his wisdom.
>
> Rabbi Yossi says: Even if he clarified for [a person the teaching] of one [individual] mishnah [not previously understood] he is considered "his teacher."

The baraita indicates that in order for a person to prioritize "teacher" versus "parent" properly, the term "teacher" needs further definition. It is not, as one might expect,

---

[3] When we refer to an individual mishnah in a chapter we will refer to it as "mishnah," with a lower case "m." When we refer to the entire collection of Mishnah, we will refer to it as "Mishnah," with a capital "M."

[4] Our translation reflects the interpretation of Rashi.

a straightforward term with an agreed upon definition. The baraita forces us to consider the possibility that there are many different types of teachers and not all types achieve a degree of societal power strong enough to trump one's parent. In Rabbi Meir's estimation, the "teacher" capable of overriding one's parent is only the one who teaches "wisdom." In this context "wisdom" refers to the teaching of a particular method of Mishnaic analysis. It is a methodology that results in the production of the analytical give-and-take of Talmudic discourse. This is not the teaching of the actual text of the Talmud, but rather the clarification, unpacking, and explication of the Mishnah (Rashi bBM 33a). The text of the Talmud as we have it did not exist until many years later. In Rabbi Meir's opinion, the rote teaching of the texts themselves, that is, of Scripture and Mishnah does not give a teacher the power to trump one's parent. The teacher of Scripture or Mishnah, in this view, is valued less than a teacher capable of imparting an analytical ability to one's students. The rabbi-teacher who helps his students to produce new insights from the words of older texts trumps one's parent.

The remaining two opinions presented in the baraita consider the possibility that what defines a "teacher" is the quantity of material imparted to his students. As Rabbi Yehudah argues, the label "teacher" is bestowed only on the person from whom one learns most of what he knows. Read back into the mishnah, only a teacher from whom one has learned a sizable amount of material can override one's parents in the matter of who takes precedence. In this view, what defines a teacher is less the method of learning he imparts and more the quantity of knowledge he teaches. A teacher trumps the parent when he has become the main conveyer of knowledge to the student. In place of the parent, the teacher has become the chief pedagogue in the child/student's life.

The third position in the baraita stands in stark contrast to that of Rabbi Yehudah. Rabbi Yossi claims that within the framework of rabbinic society a teacher capable of overriding one's parent is anyone who enlightens another person with respect to even one detail of a mishnah. Taking a far more minimalist approach with respect to the quantity of teaching content necessary for a teacher to trump a parent, Rabbi Yossi widens the scope of who, in fact, can be termed a teacher. The baraita raises the possibility that teaching happens in small ways as well as large, and that these small moments of teaching may be of equal significance.

By placing the text of mBM 2:11 in conversation with the baraita, the redactors problematize the mishnah and distance their students from any notion that learning this mishnah is somehow a simple and straightforward endeavor. In their view, the Mishnah is not a stand-alone text. More importantly, they model pedagogical fearlessness in the face of new information. The redactors are comfortable acknowledging that such information makes the learning process better. They convey the idea that teachers can be more effective when they are not afraid to introduce information that makes their lessons more complex.

The baraita challenges the clarity of mBM 2:11 and exposes the fact that unless we have a clear understanding of what defines "his teacher," we cannot implement the mishnah's injunctions. By quoting this baraita the sugya freely and comfortably reveals a terminological problem that affects the law. If the term "teacher" is defined minimally to refer only to the person who serves as a student's central teacher there are not many people that supersede one's father. If, however, the term teacher can refer maximally to anyone who taught another a small amount of information, then parents more commonly assume a secondary position in the teacher/parent hierarchy.

Interestingly, while the sugya seems to resolve the debate of the baraita by defining a teacher as the person from whom one derives the majority of his wisdom, it also strives to support and defend the opinion of Rabbi Yossi. The sugya goes on to refer us to several amoraic[5] examples where the teaching of minutiae earns one the ability to be considered a significant teacher. For example, the amora, Rava, cites the case of Rav Seḥorah who did no more than clarify an obscure type of utensil to which a mishnah in tractate Kelim refers (mKelim 13:2, 25:3). This terminological elucidation alone earned him the title, "teacher." The amora, Shmuel, was known to tear his garments, a display of mourning normally reserved for teachers and family members, upon the death of someone who explained the meaning of a difficult Mishnaic phrase about opening doors in the Temple precincts (mTamid 3:6). And, according to the amora, Ulla, Talmud scholars in Babylonia would tear their garments for their peers because they were continuously engaged in learning from one other; in this regard, each was considered a teacher.

The sugya's extended discussion indicates that the rabbis were not only trying to open the text of the mishnah for further conversation, but they were also concerned about their very identity as teachers. When the Bavli introduces these examples of teachers it is expressing its unease about rabbinic self-definition and status. In other words, at what point did rabbinic teachers cross the boundary line that divided them from everybody else, even parents? And, what was the cost of acquiring the type of knowledge that earned one the title "teacher?" Did it diminish the importance of the parental role or maybe equate "good parenting" with the acquisition of Torah wisdom? The baraita enables us to recognize that the idea stated so distinctly in the mishnah—that rabbi-teachers can ultimately trump even the honor due one's parents—while desirable, is also profoundly problematic. Once the "teacher" referred to in the mishnah can even be the person who does no more than clarify a difficult term or unclear concept, the societal axis shifts to an even greater degree away from that of family. The tension between the rabbi–student relationship and that of father–son is exposed for what it is: a conflict of competing values whereby the attainment of Torah knowledge that weds someone to a rabbi-teacher does not comfortably coexist with the cultivation of a familial bond that connects a son to his father. The three opinions found within the baraita show us that this conflict is not, even for the rabbis, easily resolved.

The rabbis, therefore, are engaged in a struggle over the values that the system they embrace and produce generates. While they begin with a mishnah (mBM

---

[5]Amoraic material is attributed to rabbis who lived after the close of the Mishnah, that is, approximately between the years 200 and 500. Amoraim in Babylonia as well as in the land of Israel analyzed earlier, tannaitic material found in the Mishnah and in various baraitot.

2:11) and do not reject its authority outright, they comfortably introduce additional material in order to bring more issues and problems to the fore. The rabbis' embeddedness in a textual tradition leads them to place these multiple texts in conversation with one another, expanding their knowledge as they expose questions, conflicts, and doubts. In their estimation, while teaching can be defined many ways, deeper understanding comes only from fearlessly admitting more information into discussions. Certainly, this is a pedagogical tactic not easily welcomed by teachers who may wish to engender more control over their material in the classroom or are fearful that clarity is sacrificed when the subject of a lesson becomes more complicated. But, as the Bavli enables us to see, critical thinking arises out of a commitment to a conversation that is generated by the admission of additional material that problematizes issues more than it resolves them. Ironically, this admission of material brings issues of concern more clearly into focus generating larger questions about what is at stake when one's teacher comes before one's parent. The fact that the questions emerge as a result of a baraita, a contemporaneous source to that of the mishnah with an equal level of authority, indicates that challenges were rooted in authoritative material. The rabbis' sugya establishes the authority of its texts as it questions their very definition.

Indeed, the fact that Talmudic discussions often reach no straightforward conclusion parallels the observations made by those, including Selma Wasserman, who advocate for the case-study method in training teachers. As Wasserman argues, cases heighten ambiguities. Through them teachers become "more distrustful of certainty and increasingly comfortable in a world where there are no easy answers." They learn never to be "satisfied with simple answers to complex problems" and, as a result, develop "habits of thinking" that enable them to behave "maturely and wisely in dealing with the far reaching choices of modern society" (Wasserman, 1994, p. 6; Kleinfeld, 1988, p. 29).

Case 2: Challenges to Human Authority

In bBM 33a we also find the rabbis confronting one of the greatest challenges that we face as teachers: the extent of our own authority in the classroom. Is good teaching about knowing more than one's students? Or, is it about laying the groundwork so that our students, in turn, teach us? Possibly, it is even about knowing how to revel in the challenge that comes in the teaching moment when our students feel enough confidence to introduce an idea about which we, their teachers, know nothing. Thus, we learn from them. In a hierarchical system such as rabbinic Judaism, challenges of any sort to authority might be considered dangerous. When a student teaches his teacher, it implies that a chain of tradition whereby knowledge is imparted from teacher to student has gone awry. Yet, the rabbis of this sugya, albeit with a great deal of anxiety, acknowledge that it is acceptable pedagogical practice for students to teach their teachers. Students can and do offer insights that enlighten their teachers.

This sugya wonders how the law of mBM 2:11 concerning who takes precedence—one's teacher or one's father—plays out when a student assumes the role of teacher to his teacher. Would this student retrieve a lost object for, or pick up a burden for, or concern himself with the redemption of—his father or his teacher—in a case where he taught his teacher something his teacher did not know? Does "his teacher," as referred to in mBM 2:11, always remain the teacher who trumps his father irrespective of the type of pedagogical interchange that occurs between them? Or, alternatively, does teaching his teacher diminish the authority of this teacher and enable his father to supersede him? With the help of the following short Talmudic story, the rabbis of the Bavli invite us to explore the issue of students teaching teachers.

Bava Metzia 33a

> Rav Hisda asked him [his teacher Rav Huna]: What is the ruling about the case of a student [where] his teacher needs him [in order to understand a matter]? [How would we then understand the mishnah with regard to whether the teacher takes precedence or the father?]
>
> He [Rav Huna, thinking Rav Hisda was referring specifically to the student–teacher relationship that existed between them] said to him: "Hisda, Hisda! I do not need you. You need me for 40 years [in order to acquire the knowledge necessary to become a teacher]."[6]
>
> They were angry at one another and they did not visit one another.
>
> Rav Hisda fasted forty fasts [as a sign of repentance] because [his actions caused] Rav Huna to feel dejected.
>
> Rav Huna fasted forty fasts because he [mistakenly] suspected Rav Hisda [of acting disrespectfully].

We can imagine that the subject of the day in the academy was mBM 2:11 and that the rabbis were operating within a world of their own making where the most prized relationships were those of teacher–student and parent–son. Upon hearing the mishnah and the baraita the amora, Rav Hisda, pushed his teacher, Rav Huna, to consider redefining what the mishnah meant when it stated, "his teacher." He presumed correctly that defining the term "his teacher" would have serious legal consequences for how the mishnah would be implemented in the cases that it cited. And so he asked what if a teacher needs his student for knowledge? What if that student is the son referred to in our mishnah? What if in choosing between his teacher and his father with regard to retrieving their lost objects he needs to consider that he successfully enlightened his teacher and his teacher learned from him? Does his teacher still take precedence over his father in such a case or does his father now supersede his teacher because his teacher relied on the aid of his student? In other words, what breaks down if the teacher needs his student for understanding a given matter? Does the fact that a student is capable of teaching his teacher diminish his

---

[6]There are two ways to read the phrase "for 40 years." We have chosen to read it in accordance with Rabbeinu Hananel's commentary on bBM 33a. However, it could also be read in connection with the next sentence. In other words, it could be read as follows: "For 40 years they [Rav Huna and Rav Hisda] were angry at one another and did not visit one another."

teacher's authority and make his father more deserving of the honor of superseding a teacher? Is the goal of being a teacher to know more than everybody else or, at least, to know more than those whom one is charged with teaching?

The Bavli does not give us a clear answer. Instead, the Talmudic story exposes all of the anxiety so well known to us when students challenge us, or attempt to overturn our insights, or pose new ideas, or simply teach us something we do not know (Wasserman, 1994, p. 4). Rav Huna's response is familiar. He shudders upon hearing Rav Hisda's question. He immediately presumes that Rav Hisda is trying to outdo him. His insecurities and desire for authority prompt him to dismiss readily the notion that his student has the ability to teach him anything. For Rav Huna, the question posed by Rav Hisda is not a question whose answer is necessary for understanding the mishnah. The question is a personal attack; this student simply wishes to convey that he knows more than his teacher. Rav Huna quickly puts Rav Hisda in his place by informing him that the student always needs the teacher and not the other way around. Knowledge flows in one direction—from the teacher to the student. He also reminds him that the teacher maintains his role as teacher for 40 years. Such a time span must pass before the student acquires enough knowledge to become a teacher himself.

Eventually, Rav Huna and Rav Hisda realize their own failings and each undertakes days of fasting as a sign to themselves and to the other that they regret their interchange. Rav Hisda laments that he caused his teacher pain by asking him an inappropriate question. Rav Huna, in turn, realizes that he mistook Rav Hisda's intentions as a sign of disrespect. Their regret signals the danger of a teacher's unconsidered response to a student who poses a challenging question or adds information to a classroom discussion about which the teacher is unaware. It also signals the way in which a student needs to be trained to pose questions so that the teacher will (correctly) understand his query as a respectful and well-intentioned desire to learn more. We learn from this interchange between a teacher and his student that a student's question can easily be misinterpreted and that such misinterpretation can end pedagogical dialogue.

This Talmudic story conveys all too well that the relationship between a teacher and a student is tenuous. It is a relationship that preys on the insecurities of both teacher and student in a manner that threatens to destroy the learning process altogether. As such, knowledge gets lost. Had Rav Huna been slower to react he might have learned that part of what defines a teacher as a teacher is his ability to learn from a student. He might have found that instead of fasting 40 fasts the two together could have uncovered even more interpretive possibilities about teachers, students, and lost objects. Therefore, as Rav Huna and Rav Hisda point out, it is in the best interest of both teacher and student to maintain the delicate balance that exists between them, just as Mary Haywood Metz argues when she discusses the teacher–student relationship through her real-life teacher–student cases (Haywood Metz, 1993, pp. 108–113). In fact, we infer from our case study that one model of successful teaching occurs when teachers explicitly define for their students the parameters of their relationship and how they understand the meaning of being a teacher. They guide their students in the art of critical thinking by asking questions of the texts that they introduce into the classroom. They also commend those students who model an acceptable form of questioning by describing the types of questions that are generative and pinpointing those that are destructive. Critical thinking, the continuous discussion and creation of knowledge old and new, emerges when the maintenance of authority is not an end in itself.

In fact, later commentators on this sugya offer two different interpretations of what it means to be a student who teaches his teacher. Rabbi Hananel ben Hushiel of Kairouan (Rabbeinu Hananel, d. 1055/6) suggests that the sugya refers to an intellectually sharp student whose probing questions enable the teacher to gain knowledge. In this model, the student is not necessarily in possession of factual knowledge that the teacher does not have. Instead, the student's intellectual prowess refines what the teacher already knows and helps him to understand the material in a new way. In this light, Rabbeinu Hananel quotes the Talmudic passage found in bTa'anit 7a, "Rabbi Hanina said, 'I have learned a lot from my teachers, and from my peers even more than from my teachers, and from my students more than them all.'"[7] In contrast, Rashi suggests that this student has learned "traditions" (שמועות)—that is, teachings from others about which the current teacher is unaware. Rashi's comment focuses on the student's content knowledge, implicitly recognizing that a teacher's knowledge is not absolute. Students often add material that they have learned in other contexts to their teacher's presentations. Unless there is only one central teacher through which all learning happens such a situation would be impossible to avoid.

While we are not taking sides in the debate between Rabbeinu Hananel and Rashi, we raise their views to highlight the fact these two Talmudic commentators struggle with pedagogical issues that parallel our own. What do we want our students to teach us? What are constructive teaching moments? Are we looking for our students to guide us toward refined understandings of the material that we present or are we hoping that our students will introduce facts and ideas that are unknown to us? Possibly, the answer is both. Either way, as teachers we need to be prepared for how to receive the questions, comments, and ideas that are posed by our students so as not to thwart the effectiveness of the teacher–student interchange.

When we think about the rabbis as teachers and the texts of the Bavli as exploring the dimensions of pedagogy, we find that they do not value passivity in their imaginary classrooms. The Bavli's own terminology conveys its preference for questions and answers, challenges and rebuttals. As we have seen, our Talmudic story about Rav Huna and Rav Hisda opens with the words, "Rav Hisda asked [his teacher Rav Huna]." The Aramaic verb ב.ע.י. (ask), signals a legal question and is a common Talmudic term. Indeed, asking is a necessity for a student who wishes to learn from his teacher. Through the very act of "asking," Rav Hisda models the kind of student–teacher behavior necessary for developing students who are not passive recipients of their teacher's teachings. It makes us wonder why Rav Huna was taken

---

[7] Also see bMakkot 10a where Rabbi Yehudah Ha-nasi makes the same point.

by surprise at all when Rav Hisda posed his question. Should he have not expected, even encouraged, the query?

This interchange between teacher and student on bBM 33a introduces us to the humanity of even the greatest rabbinic figures. Although the rabbis of the Bavli are committed to the notion that learning involves the ability to reason logically and to test ideas for their consistency, echoing for us Nussbaum's argument about the aims of a liberal education (Nussbaum, 1997, p. 19), they struggle with the very pedagogy that they wish to nurture. The interchange between Rav Huna and Rav Hisda allows us to observe a teaching moment that is familiar to many of us. We often regret the times when we have dismissed or not listened to our students' questions and ideas in the name of preserving a desired hierarchy. We are surprised at how difficult it is to relinquish our intellectual authority in the classroom. However, we can find comfort in the fact that the Bavli's anxiety parallels our own. We can learn from Rav Huna and Rav Hisda's feelings of regret that it is important to keep our fundamental goal of developing active and critical thinkers at the center of our teaching mission and put our students before ourselves. In enabling and encouraging our students to expand the arena of classroom knowledge we give up a degree of personal authority in the classroom. However, through this two-way movement we grant authority to our texts and to the process that keeps them alive. This was a goal of the rabbis of the Talmud, albeit not easily achieved. It should be ours as well.

Conclusion and Future Implications

The development of both critical thinking and a sense of "reflective skepticism" can dovetail with our commitment to the authority of an inherited tradition (Brookfield, 1988). Within Judaism, and more specifically within the texts of the Babylonian Talmud, Jewish educators can find a disciplinary logic regarding what constitutes critical thinking that preserves older ideas as it critiques and even transforms them. By translating Talmudic texts into case studies teachers can locate a variety of different types of critical–reflective moments. Talmudic texts can provide them with an array of opportunities to assess the manner in which they can develop critical thinking while immersing themselves within a religious tradition. Such texts and the rabbinic pedagogies that they present marshal a type of critical thinking that is both reverent and rooted (Goleman, 2008, p. 1). Much as one can utilize Socratic techniques to criticize Socrates' thought (Nussbaum, 1997, p. 41), one can utilize Talmudic modes to critique Talmudic concepts.

The ideas presented in the above two cases were rooted in a Mishnaic conversation about the return of lost objects. The Mishnaic conversation, in turn, emerged out of a concern for the meaning of a set of biblical verses regarding the requirement to return the lost objects that one finds. The twists and turns of the Babylonian sugya kept these authoritative texts front and center while bringing additional issues to the fore. Using the Bavli as a model for how to encourage critical thinking instructs students that such a mode is internal to Jewish tradition. Earlier texts are interrogated, contemporaneous texts are put into conversation with one another, and students question their teachers. Questions provoke anxiety and debate fosters intellectual growth. But, at the root of this inquiry is a desire to embed rabbinic tradition in the hearts and minds of its participants. These are not empty rhetorical forms; these are the ways in which the Bavli builds knowledge. When we follow this model, whereby conversations are rooted in a set of authoritative texts, we ask students to learn to speak a specific language and to think along with a particular tradition.

More time needs to be spent studying the Bavli for its pedagogical lessons. It is important to push the boundaries of the discipline of Talmud to include Talmud pedagogy in a more serious way. We need to think about how the rabbis defined pedagogy and to explore the models of teaching and learning that they set up for us. Therefore, our future research will focus on the pedagogy of the rabbis and their definitions of teaching. In addition, our commitment to turning Talmudic material into usable cases reflects our commitment to finding answers to Elie Holzer's question, "what kind of [text] study... lead[s] to good teaching [in the training of teachers]?" (Holzer, 2002, p. 385).

In addition, because teaching and learning have always been integral to Jewish tradition, the task is set before us to explore the pedagogies embedded in other Jewish texts and to think about the degree to which they foster and/or critique Talmudic pedagogy. There are other models of Jewish pedagogy that we can find outside of the Bavli that offer different insights on Jews' attitudes toward teaching and learning. For example, midrashic texts, Jewish code literature, works of medieval scriptural exegesis, and philosophical treatises, to name a few genres, serve as additional resources in our quest to define "what is" Jewish pedagogy. It is then up to us to translate this material into useful teacher case studies that will not only contribute to teacher education, but will also help us to develop a better understanding of the nature of Jewish thought and culture. As such, within the field of Talmud lies a burgeoning field of Jewish pedagogy that bridges the scholarly worlds of Jewish literature and Jewish education.

References

Albeck, H. (Ed.). (1988). *Shishah Sidre Mishnah: With new commentary, introductions, additions, and completions* (Vol. 6). Jerusalem: Mossad Bialik.

Ben-Menahem, H. (1991). *Judicial deviation in Talmudic law: Governed by men, not by rules*, Jewish Law in Context V. 1. Chur Switzerland. New York: Harwood Academic Publishers.

Berger, M. (1998). Towards the development of a Jewish Pedagogy: Rav Chiya's vision of Torah education. In M. Haim (Ed.), *Judaism and education: Essays in honor of Walter I. Ackerman* (pp. 109–120). Beer-Sheva: Ben-Gurion University of the Negev Press.

Brookfield, S. (1988). *Developing critical thinkers: Challenging adults to explore alternative ways of thinking and acting*, Jossey-Bass Higher Education Series (1st ed.). San Francisco: Jossey-Bass.

Epstein, J. N. (1962). In E. Z. Melamed (Ed.), *Introduction to Amoraitic literature: Babylonian Talmud and Yerushalmi*. Jerusalem: Magnes Press.

Friedman, S. "Benjamin and Minna Revees Chair Lecture." http://www.atranet.co.il/sf/revees_chair.pdf.

Goleman, L. (2008). Spotlight on theological education. *American Academy of Religion Newsletter*, 1.

Hayman, P. (1997). On the teaching of Talmud: Toward a methodological basis for a curriculum in oral-tradition studies. *Religious Education, 92*(1), 61–76.

Holzer, E. (2002). Conceptions of the study of Jewish texts in teachers' professional development. *Religious Education, 97*(4), 377–403.

Kanarek, J. (2010). The pedagogy of slowing down: Teaching Talmud in a summer Kollel. *Teaching Theology and Religion, 13*(2), 15–34.

Kleinfeld, J. (1988). "Learning to think like a teacher: The study of cases." *Alaska University, Fairbanks. Center for Cross-Cultural Studies*. 2–36.

Kraemer, D. C. (1981). Critical aids to teaching Talmud. *Jewish Education*, Spring, 37–40.

Kress, J. S., & Lehman, M. (2003). The Babylonian Talmud in cognitive perspective: Reflections on the nature of the Bavli and Its pedagogical implications. *Journal of Jewish Education, 69*(2), 58–78.

Lehman, M. (2002). For the love of Talmud: Reflections on the teaching of Bava Metzia, Perek 2. *Journal of Jewish Education, 68*(1), 87–103.

Lehman, M. (2006). Examining the role of gender studies in teaching Talmudic literature. *Journal of Jewish Education, 72*(21), 109–121.

Mandel Center for Studies in Jewish Education. 2007. "Bibliography on Pedagogy of Jewish Studies," Bridging Scholarship and Pedagogy in Jewish Studies. http://www.brandeis.edu/mandel/pdfs/Bridging_Initiative_Bibliography_6_07.pdf.

Merseth, K. K. (1991). The early history of case-based instruction: Insights for teacher education today. *Journal of Teacher Education, 42*(4), 243–249.

Metz, M. H. (1993). Teachers' ultimate dependence on their students. In J. W. Little & M. W. McLaughlin (Eds.), *Teachers' work: Individuals, colleagues, and contexts* (pp. 104–136). New York: Teachers College Press.

Nussbaum, M. C. (1997). *Cultivating humanity: A classical defense of reform in liberal education*. Cambridge, MA: Harvard University Press.

Richert, A. E. (1991). Using teacher cases for reflection and understanding. In A. Lieberman & L. Miller (Eds.), *Staff development for education in the '90s: New demands, new realities, new perspectives* (pp. 113–132). New York: Teachers College Press.

Rosenak, M. (1987). *Commandments and concerns: Jewish religious education in secular society*. Philadelphia, PA: Jewish Publication Society.

Rubenstein, J. L. (1999). *Talmudic stories: Narrative art, composition, and culture*. Baltimore, MD: Johns Hopkins University Press.

Saiman, C. (2006). Legal theology: The Turn to conceptualism in nineteenth-century Jewish Law. *Journal of Law and Religion, 21*(1), 39–100.

Shulman, L. S. (2004a). Aristotle had it right: On knowledge and pedagogy. In *The wisdom of practice: Essays on teaching, learning, and learning to teach* (pp. 399–415). San Francisco: Jossey-Bass.

Shulman, L. S. (2004b). Just in case: reflections on learning from experience. In *The wisdom of practice: Essays on teaching, learning, and learning to teach* (pp. 461–482). San Francisco: Jossey-Bass.

Shulman, J., & Sato, M. (2006). *Mentoring teachers toward excellence: Supporting and developing highly qualified teachers*, Jossey-Bass Education Series (1st ed.). San Francisco: Jossey-Bass published in partnership with WestEd.

Twersky, I. (2003). What must a Jews study-and why. In S. Fox, I. Scheffler, & D. Marom (Eds.), *Visions of Jewish education* (pp. 47–76). Cambridge: Cambridge University Press.

Wasserman, S. (1994). Using cases to study teaching. *Phi Delta Kappan, 75*(8), 602–610.

Technology: The Digital Revolution That Is Shaping Twenty-First-Century Jewish Education—A Fleeting Snapshot from the First Decade

Brian Amkraut

Introduction

The socio-cultural environment of the early twenty-first century reflects a watershed moment in modern civilization. Rapid developments in technology and communication have transformed not merely how business, governments, and other institutions operate, but also challenge our understanding of the individual's role in society and his or her relationship to the surrounding world. These changes reflect an accelerated process of modernization that has been unfolding for many generations, with unprecedented recent developments. We find ourselves amid the ongoing digital revolution, in which information is easily accessible in seemingly limitless quantities. The individual can connect interactively with unlimited points of access in the virtual universe, constantly defining and redefining the terms of his or her association with other individuals and institutions to suit his or her unique needs. These seminal shifts in contemporary culture profoundly influence an increasingly individualized society and indeed may be transforming Jewish life. The impact of these most significant developments will shape the face of Jewish education as it engages the future.[1]

The Revolution

Assessing the technological landscape at any given moment in the digital age provides what can perhaps best be described as a fleeting snapshot. With respect to judging accurately technology's role in our world, we can only confidently assert that the changes come so fast and furiously that we cannot truly have a sense of

---

B. Amkraut (✉)
Laura and Alvin Siegal College of Judaic Studies, Cleveland, OH, USA
e-mail: Amkraut@siegalcollege.edu

[1] This study focuses on Jewish life in North America but the pervasiveness of digital culture in an age of globalization makes the analysis applicable to Jewish education on an international level even in Israel with its unique Jewish educational environment. Sherlick and Hong (2008) directly address the issue of technology's influence in Israeli schools.

what the next wave of change may herald, and that each technological "generation" is shorter than that which precedes it, in accordance with "Moore's law."[2] Nevertheless, this chapter attempts to present an analysis of overarching trends and influences related to the broadest application of digital culture as it can be apprehended in late 2009. It proposes a hypothesis as to how those patterns may influence the world of Jewish education, rather than focusing on specific innovations in software or hardware. A concise formulation: digital culture is a way of thinking, not tied to a specific technology or industry, to paraphrase a 2001 review of the peer-to-peer file sharing phenomenon (Truelove, Shirky, Gonze, & Dornfest, 2001). Trying to list the websites and networks that best demonstrate how Jewish life flourishes in cyberspace or ways that Jewish educators have taken advantage of these developments, both in their classrooms and in the development of the field as a whole, is a Sisyphean endeavor. In the preparation of a scholarly publication on the subject, the landscape can (and usually does) change substantially between the time of composition and appearance in print (Amkraut, 2008). A subsequent lag between the time the work is read broadly by professional peers will likely result in significant digital developments absent from the initial scholarship. If the work in question generates substantial feedback with a computer-mediated discussion group, subsequently allowing for updating the original findings, the work can remain consistently relevant with respect to specific applications. So too the research can stagnate unless the dialogue is sustained. (Therein lies the attraction of electronic publication or simply blogging, as opposed to traditional print media, but migrating to a purely digital environment would be a radical step for conventionally trained academics, where the profession has been defined and evaluated by the criteria of peer-reviewed print publication.)

In fact, the most salient means by which the digital revolution impacts Jewish education are by-products of technology, rather than the technology itself. The fact that the most profound transformations will be seen in the area of social culture—relationships between people, communities, and ideas as opposed to cyberspace in its own right—creates challenges for communal leadership as a whole and Jewish educators in particular. This approach to the twenty-first-century contemporary Jewish life emerges from a widely held axiom among Jewish historians which forms the basic premise of this analysis (Meyer, 1987): In any given era and at any given point on the globe, the realities of Jewish life can only be understood in the context of, and as a reflection of, the surrounding culture in which Jews find themselves. Based on that hypothesis, an accurate assessment of what Jewish life looks like in the early twenty-first century, and perhaps a prediction of where it is headed, depends on appropriately apprehending the milieu in which Jewish life is unfolding. Hence much of the research cited in this overview emerges from the realm of general social observation and not from the Jewish environment per se. The future of Jewish

---

[2]The theory first posited by Intel co-founder Gordon Moore in 1965 holds that the cost of developing integrated circuitry decreases exponentially nearly every 18 months, thereby improving computing capacity in consumer products in a geometric progression.

education perhaps can help shape, but will undoubtedly be shaped by, the revolutionary forces in communication and technology that are profoundly redefining our social culture.

Educator Responses

The first decade of the twenty-first century has seen a fair amount of attention given to the dramatic changes in the worlds of communication and information technology, and the Jewish education community of course has taken note of these changes, even if it has assimilated these developments less rapidly than the surrounding environment. The overwhelming focus of these efforts has been placed on addressing the so-called "digital divide," that is the enormous generation gap between the "digital natives," or so-called "Millennials" (Howe & Strauss, 2000), who constitute the K-16 student population (and slowly but surely some of their parents) and the "digital immigrants" who comprise the overwhelming majority of Jewish education professionals, be they classroom teachers, school administrators, congregational rabbis, or even lay leaders (Levine, 2006).[3] Indeed, this focus has deserved attention since pedagogues do need to be versed in the discourse of the student population.

One can easily argue that on the whole educational practitioners (as is true of their age cohorts in general) have at least developed some basic literacy in computer technology and do increasingly attempt to integrate technology into their educational planning. An earlier concern that older teachers would be hesitant in utilizing email or their school's websites and electronic educational resources has proven unfounded and indeed a small industry has grown up around the development of Jewish educational tools for the digital age.[4] Furthermore, a cadre of digitally astute Jewish educators and scholars has actively and effectively advocated for incorporating the latest technology and communication developments into the landscape of Jewish educational activity (Grishaver, 2008; Margolis, 2008; Woocher, 2008). In reality most of the professional development activity geared toward bridging this knowledge gap has been skills-oriented: teaching Jewish educators how to make effective power point presentations; how to surf the web for useful Jewish resources; how to educate parents regarding the dangers of internet predators; how to teach courses on-line; and, of course, how to submit grades and communicate with students and parents electronically. Even much of the Jewish education research agenda

---

[3] A related issue to the developments addressed in this analysis is the demography of Jewish educators which remains heavily skewed toward educators over the age of 40 (Ben-Avie & Kress, 2008, pp. 18–19).

[4] A significant related question, however, is the sustainability of those efforts as an important element of the digital age, and the development of sustainable business models in the midst of the current paradigm shift (see below on Freeconomics). Even as some of the educational resources attempt to shift their services to on-line only models, their longevity remains unclear without sustained philanthropic support (Berkman, 2009).

has been focused on this generation gap, highlighting those initiatives that are working toward bridging the divide and lamenting the fact that the field as a whole seems to operate at least a step behind the broader education community's efforts to incorporate the latest technologies into the classroom (Berger, 2003; Woocher, 2008).

Arguably, these efforts have succeeded in at least ensuring that the older educator population is not entirely ignorant of the computer-generated language of today's students. As important as they may be, such steps often miss the larger more significant cultural shift. In this respect Jewish education hardly stands alone; religious education in general is slower to adapt, reflecting, perhaps, the conservative nature of the field. Thus, in a relatively recent assessment of the field, Goldburg noted the importance of incorporating creative arts for today's students with a focus on the visual, but basically ignored the path-breaking interactive capabilities of the digital age. (2006, p. 1241)

Jewish family educator, Vicky Kelman (2009) has referred to the incursion of technology on day-to-day living by stating explicitly that technology is "invading our lives." Kelman was not advocating that we eliminate technology from our daily routines, but rather was, in her own way, applying one of Melvin Kranzberg's six "Laws of Technology," "Technology is neither good nor bad; nor is it neutral" (1986). As a challenge to conventional modes of interpersonal communication, Kelman's assertion hits the mark, and educators struggle between co-opting technology effectively to further pedagogical aims on the one hand and achieving those goals through limiting the use of technology in the educational environment on the other. Duke University's Alex Roland frames the power of technology in the following way: "It can be what military people call a force multiplier, but humans can decide if that force is used for good or ill" (2009).

Why Revolution?

Adjusting to the latest technologies as they emerge, while necessary, only partly responds to the enormously significant changes in the broader cultural landscape. Undertaking such piecemeal activities without recognizing the tectonic sociocultural shift unfolding around us is analogous to a physician treating a patient's symptoms with blatant disregard for the underlying causes of an illness, although this metaphor should not be seen as portraying digital culture as a disease to be cured. A historian does not employ the notion of revolution lightly, but indeed the characterization is apt. The *Oxford English Dictionary* defines revolution as "an instance of great change or alteration in affairs or in some particular thing" (1971, p. 2533). And applying this term to the digital landscape suggests an intellectual leap that recognizes early twenty-first-century computer technology as not merely the latest electronic communication device to follow telephones, radio, and television in their various incarnations, but rather sees the current moment of the information age as having totally rearranged fundamental social institutions such as community, authority, and identity. Media analyst Clay Shirky asserts that even a development that we can take for granted and that in and of itself seems modest can have profound implications when viewed within the framework of systemic change.[5] "Email is nice," Shirky writes, "but how big a deal can it be in the grand scheme of things? The answer is 'not such a big deal considered by itself.' The trick is not to consider it by itself... We now have communications tools that are flexible enough to match our social capabilities, and we are witnessing the rise of new ways of coordinating action that take advantage of that change" (2008, p. 20). When digital communication proliferates on a massive scale, to its fully interactive multimedia potential, it can make conventional broadcast and telephonic communication appear primitive.

The technology itself is so radically different from that of the previous communications revolution that it will likely be some time before most of us will truly appreciate the nature of that change. In *Blown to Bits*, technology experts Abelson, Ledeen, and Lewis place the differences between digital technology and its precursors in stark contrast. In their attempt to explain the impact of what they term the "digital explosion," they identify a whole host of areas in which society as a whole, and not merely the arena of information access, is being reshaped by this brave new world (2008, pp. 1–17).

This revolutionary transformation impacts the field of Jewish education on two fronts: (1) In the rapidly changing nature of classroom instruction, both in terms of educational technologies and the evolving relationship between students and teachers as a reflection of digital culture. (2) In the dynamic impact that the social culture produced by our digital environment has had on religious life in general and in the challenges these changes have already posed to our understandings of Judaism. No doubt the latter helps shape the former.

The educational landscape is already adapting. Just one example should demonstrate the potential. The Jewish Publication Society, a vestige of a pre-digital era, has sponsored the construction of what is being called a *Tagged Tanach*, still in development as of late 2009. Yonatan Gordis advocates: "*The Tagged Tanach* is a natural next step in the ongoing Jewish tradition of creative biblical exegesis. This is essentially what we have been doing for generations, revealing layers upon layers of interpretation and understanding. When Web 2.0 meets the Tanakh, the result should be a text that includes everyone and creates a shared sense of ownership and vision for the future" (Gordis, 2009). Stretching one's imagination gives rise to extrapolating beyond the limitations of the *Tagged Tanach* to a totally interactive user generated multimedia *midrash* (commentary on or interpretation of biblical text). Standing one of the basic precepts of Jewish textual interpretation on its head, and reflecting a basic element of digital culture, this development will allow the broad Jewish public an active role in an arena that had consistently been the purview of a limited number of experts.

---

[5] For a 15-min video presentation from 2009 by Shirky on the revolutionary impact of social media, see http://www.ted.com/talks/lang/eng/clay_shirky_how_cellphones_twitter_facebook_can_make_history.html

To some extent, the question is whether or not these changes in communication technology are indeed of a revolutionary rather than evolutionary nature. And while one is not confident in applying such terminology to a process that is still unfolding and whose course is unpredictable, nevertheless it would seem to be appropriate. The myriad examples that already populate the landscape of contemporary Jewish life, as well as the more immediate evidence from the general society in which we live, demonstrate how radical the changes can be and how fast they will come. Some well-known examples include harnessing the internet to develop grass roots political enthusiasm, "bystanders" using mobile technology to quickly and broadly disseminate news, including audio and video, and bloggers utilizing their own public forums to comment, thereby challenging the whole business model of print and broadcast journalism. Once the notion of a communications revolution is accepted, it stands to reason that such a transformation will profoundly impact the nature of society at large, religious life in general, and the Jewish experience in particular.

A number of social commentators have compared the digital revolution to the era that followed the advent of the printing press, often noting the important correlation between the innovations in media that Gutenberg represented with the radical change in religious life associated with Martin Luther. Luther was not the first cleric to dissent from the Catholic Church's monopoly on Christian authority, but he was the first dissenter to take advantage of "broadcast media" in one of its earliest forms. So too in Jewish life both the *Zohar* and the *Shulchan Aruch*[6] enjoyed wide distribution in the century following the advent of the Gutenberg press, thereby changing the nature of what counted for religious authority in subsequent generations (Brasher, 2004, pp. 14–15; Seltzer, 1980, p. 460).

Over 35 years ago Donis Dondis embraced the notion of contemporary cultural literacy with respect to the visual arts and highlighted a significant historical parallel when he wrote "if the invention of moveable type created a mandate for universal visual literacy, surely the invention of the camera and all its collateral and continually developing forms makes the achievement of universal visual literacy as an educational necessity long overdue" (1973, p. ix). How much more so is such advice an imperative for our society with respect to digital literacy?

Again, educational professionals must recognize that such literacy demands not merely facility with the technology but also a comprehension of the radical shift in communication from the norms of the late twentieth century. While it is true that the field of educational technology is not all that new, and indeed scholars have long recognized the profound impact that popular culture has in shaping students' perceptions of knowledge and their surroundings, "popular culture remains as a teacher who competes with the classroom teacher for students from pre-school through college, whether educators care to acknowledge it or not" (DeVaney, 1994,

---

[6] The *Zohar* is the primary text of Medieval Jewish mysticism (compiled in the thirteenth-century Spain) and the *Shulchan Aruch* serves as the definitive late Medieval code of Jewish law (compiled in sixteenth-century Palestine).

pp. 356–357). The dramatic change in the current environment is that students themselves play a significant part in helping to shape the very popular culture that, in turn, defines social norms. Perhaps most importantly for educators to internalize, the students themselves know the powerful role they play.

Digital Judaism

From its earliest incarnations, even before the advent of the World Wide Web, internet applications accessible to the general public have been utilized to explore issues of religious identity. Subsequently, they have been harnessed both in the service of organized religion and to enable individuals to challenge the authoritative nature of most religious movements. Quite often the framework for such exploration is the rapid and mass communication of news to a specific group, or the ever-present jokes appropriate for the "in-crowd." And, indeed, for some religious groups, the ongoing opportunities afforded by on-line religious experience as opposed to conventional real-world traditions result in changes that can even transform the character of religion itself (Brasher, 2004, p. 13, and Helland, 2007). For example, do the massively circulated viral communications constitute "Jewish texts"?

Ironically, a hallmark of the digital age, and of software applications in particular, is their innovative quality, and their ability to push the envelope with respect to what can be accomplished via computer. While one can certainly argue that organized monotheism was in and of itself quite revolutionary, typically Judaism as it has been practiced and organized has not been a way of life geared toward experimentation. With the exception of various significant moments in the course of its thousands of years history (such as the advent of rabbinic Judaism, or the emergence of Reform and other denominations), Jewish life has been conservative. Indeed, the most radical innovations to emerge from within the Jewish mainstream (Christianity, e.g., as well as the lesser known Karaism, and Sabbateanism) were generally dismissed as heretical and beyond the realm of normative Jewish life. As Jews take a page from the digital notebook and view innovation not merely as episodic but as central to the twenty-first century, will rapid regular change be tolerated within the bounds of communal legitimacy? Attempts to block innovation in the digital realm, whether due to legal concerns or economic interests, are often viewed by the most active community of on-line entrepreneurs as stifling the very essence of the digital age (Abelson et al., 2008, pp. 218). In an environment where digital footprints have potentially infinite life spans, attempts at digital censorship will probably prove futile.

Twentieth-century marketing organizations, not to mention powerful forces in the conventional media arena, have been slow to adapt to this new reality in which the rules of the game have so drastically changed. The tools of digital networking have empowered end-users, be they members of a tribe, consumers of products, or citizens of a state, to share their voices with one another independent of the forces that have shaped the marketplace for the last few centuries (Shirky, 2008, p. 47).

Not surprisingly, some substantial innovative communal engagement is, in fact, visible on the Jewish landscape, be it in the form of "independent *minyanim*" (Jewish prayer quorums, also refers to congregations not affiliated with established synagogues) (Musleah, 2009) or "cultural events" (Cohen & Kelman, 2005) that emerge from the grass roots—in digital terminology these phenomena demonstrate user-generated expressions of Jewish commitment. Significantly, these examples challenge the hegemony of Jewish establishment institutions, be they synagogues, JCCs, or community federations and they depend on what I have called a "define-it-yourself" Judaism which could be seen as representing a progression from the "do-it-yourself" approach that characterized the *havurah* movement of the 1970s and 1980s (Amkraut, 2007). These innovative approaches challenge not only notions of authority but also conceptions of community, an issue of great significance for Jewish education (Bloomberg, 2007; Wertheimer, 2009)

One could argue for an evolutionary rather than revolutionary progression with respect to individual control over Jewish expression, with contemporary developments merely representing the latest incarnation of deep-seated trends dating back to the pre-modern era (see Figs. 1 and 2). These grass roots developments engender optimism among advocates of Jewish continuity as the tools empower a new generation of engaged leadership. However, the model of end-user creativity raises questions for educators with respect to what will be the consequences of their constituencies in utilizing the power of networks. Consider the dilemma of the modern synagogue and its educational programs: Can education professionals legitimately

Simple version of Evolving Expressions of Jewish Life

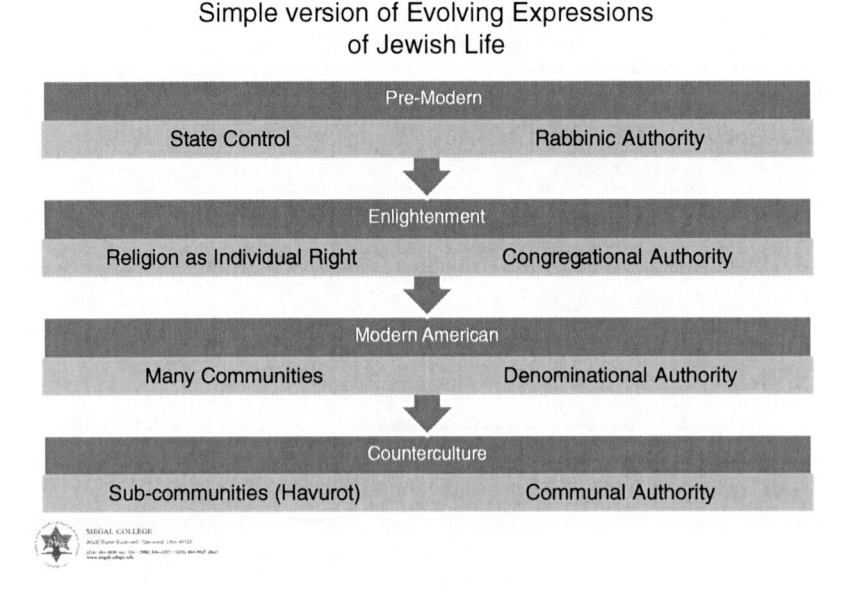

Pre-Modern	
State Control	Rabbinic Authority

Enlightenment	
Religion as Individual Right	Congregational Authority

Modern American	
Many Communities	Denominational Authority

Counterculture	
Sub-communities (Havurot)	Communal Authority

Fig. 1 Jewish authority and historical/cultural context

```
                    Individualized Judaism


    Define-it-                        Personal
    yourself                          Authority
```

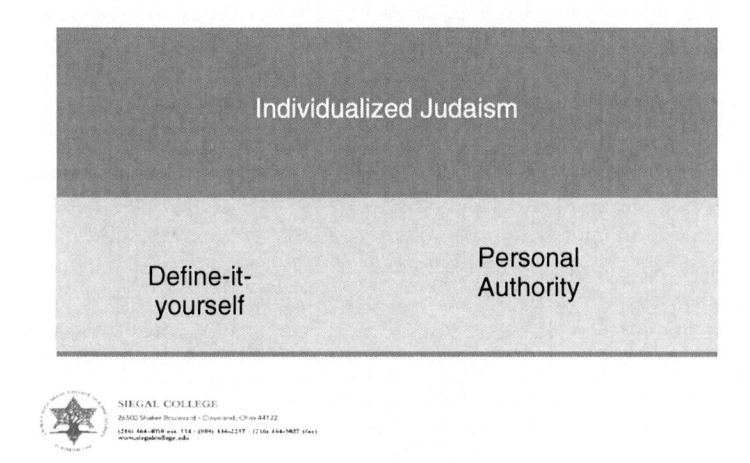

Fig. 2 Authority in the era of individualization

advocate for engagement that may very well obviate the need for the institution itself (Musleah, 2009, pp. 36–38)?

Media analyst Douglas Rushkoff sees the cultural shift as a great opportunity, and argues for the transformation of conventional Jewish life as an imperative.

> Just as the definition of social justice had to evolve over time, so must the definition of what it means to be Jewish... Jews who pursued careers in social justice, or who dedicated their lives to the most universally progressive ideals, became known as "lapsed" Jews... Though they had merely followed the same path as Moses toward unbiased compassion and selfless activism, they had seemingly abandoned all that was nominally Jewish. Now, Jewish "outreach" efforts are spending millions of dollars each year in a misguided effort [to] get them "back."

Rushkoff continues, "This so-called lapsed constituency might actually comprise Judaism's most devoutly practicing members. It is not these people, but what is considered "Jewish" that needs to change" (2003, pp. 42–43).

One need not agree with Rushkoff regarding the essential core of Jewish life and the Jewish establishment's rejection of these values. But his assertion that grassroots efforts by unaffiliated or previously alienated Jews can redefine the terms of communal engagement does reflect the social culture indicative of the digital revolution.

Community

The power of the network is such that it can and perhaps should be understood by those seeking to nurture Jewish continuity as an unprecedented opportunity to cultivate a sense of Jewish unity and belonging. The phenomenon of social networking allows (whether in a virtual environment or physical reality) for otherwise isolated individuals or small disconnected networks, often tied only marginally to larger entities, to take advantage of those nodes which happen to overlap, thereby linking many networks, large and small, and subsequently creating, perhaps, a meta-network serving to tie the disparate pieces together (Singh, 2007). Jewish educators and/or educational institutions have the opportunity to serve as strategic nodes or to encourage individual students to step into these roles.

To be sure, one can hardly blame communal leadership for lack of imagination in this respect as even many of the most astute business and political leaders have had difficulty grasping the totality of this change. As noted above, the digital era can be perceived as evolutionary rather than revolutionary—as merely the next link in a chain, albeit one whose progressions of late have been increasing at a geometric pace, along the lines of Moore's Law, as mentioned above. Misreading the digital landscape can have dire economic consequences. In Shirky's words, "When a profession has been created as a result of some scarcity, as with librarians or television programmers, the professionals are often the last ones to see it when that scarcity goes away. It is easier to understand that you face competition than obsolescence" (2008, pp. 58–59). In some respects contemporary technology has merely enabled individuals to express themselves in ways consistent with a process that had already been unfolding over the course of the twentieth century and had been shaped by various episodes of significant change during that time. Jeane Twenge, for example, links the individualism so often characteristic of today's teens and young adults to the impact of the social attitudes and parenting styles of the baby-boomer generation who have raised their children and grandchildren with continuous messages of personal empowerment and boundless individual ambition (2006).

There is no doubt a tendency among those in authority to view these developments with trepidation. Quite often the language of concern is overly critical. Take, for example, the pejorative connotation of "individualist," "self-centered," and "narcissistic," terms that could easily describe the cultural orientation of the young generation. But just because the technology and culture permit greater individualization, the changes they usher in need not rupture the social fabric. The ability to construct one's own identity and the fact that these identities are generally not monolithic simply reflects the complexity of human psychology and behavior. But the fact that individuals today grow accustomed to defining themselves on their own terms does not mean they lack the capability of serving the greater good or acting communally. Rather they will demand the opportunity to determine both what exactly that greater good will be and how they will interact at the communal level. In the digital age the very concept of community is continually redefined, just as within the individual multiple parts directly contribute to the greater whole.

Personal Identity

The centrality of identity questions for Jewish education professionals cannot be understated. Indeed, one could argue that Jewish education as an endeavor is a misnomer if by "educate" one means "give intellectual, moral, and social instruction" (Compact Oxford English Dictionary, 2009). While these realms do concern Jewish educators, the reality of the profession, at least in North America, is that the vast majority of Jewish education could be more aptly defined as "Jewish identity construction." This moniker would be appropriate for most synagogue schools, day schools, and informal educational settings in which the key outcome from the perspective of parents and practitioners is the creation or reinforcement of a strong Jewish identity promoting cultural and/or biological continuity.

Thus, the question of how the digital revolution impacts questions of identity is extremely relevant, and not surprisingly the early twenty-first century has seen a re-examination of this issue. Whether due to inertia, their own ideological sensibilities, or some other factor, most analysts of Jewish life simply cannot break free from attempts to classify Jews according to religious markers. Perhaps this approach is rooted in Will Herberg's claim over 50 years ago, in his seminal *Protestant–Catholic–Jew*, that the age of the secular Jew was past and that Judaism must be perceived in purely religious terms (1955). Even in *Modern Judaism: An Oxford Guide* published in 2005—the chapter titled "Jewish identities" employs a system based on religious denomination or level of observance when classifying Israeli and American Jews (Kopelowitz, 2005, p. 208). Strikingly, the same author in a 2008 study argues for using the term "peoplehood," with all its complexity as the appropriate approach to understanding Jewish identity (Kopelowitz and Engelberg, 2009, pp. 4–10).

With respect to Jewish identification there are at least two related realms in which the digital era poses new challenges. First, the hyper-individualization characteristic of this era allows both for increasingly narrow identity definitions and multiple-identity expressions in line with broader cultural trends such as multiracialism. On-line anonymity allows individuals opportunities to experiment with identity in what may be a protected environment, in which there are few (if any) real-life consequences to adopting innovative religious identities. On the other hand, the request (or demand) to assert one's religious identity for the purposes of an on-line profile in a social network challenges the user either to identify with one or more "accepted" terms of religiousness or to define religious identity on his or her own individualized terms. For many people who are typically comfortable in digitally profiling themselves without much cause for introspection the question of religious identity gives pause. And while the topic is easily avoided or ignored, at least one example of a large social network shows that more than half of the users did choose to claim a religious identity (Wan, 2009).

In the Jewish on-line world the issue of religious identity has been present from an early stage with respect to one of the internet's most popular Jewish spaces, that of on-line dating. JDate ("the premier Jewish singles community online" 8/30/2009) is the most ubiquitous, but there are lesser known variations, particularly for the Orthodox community, such as frumster.com (boasting "5 weddings *every* week" 08/30/2009) and dosidate.com (promoted as "the online dating site exclusively for Orthodox Jewish singles" 8/30/2009). To further complicate matters, among the hundreds of thousands registered with JDate, maybe as many as 10% do not identify as Jewish, but are nevertheless interested in meeting and perhaps marrying someone who is. For many of JDate's Jewish members, the presence of large numbers of gentiles, some of whom contact them, may defeat the purpose of a Jewish singles network. Yet this issue cannot be all that problematic if so many Jews nevertheless remain active on the site.

In December 2004, David Siminoff, the head of JDate's parent company MatchNet, defended the site's unrestrictive policy: "'I'm not going to tell someone who wants to be part of Jewish culture you can't come online," he said, though he noted that JDate clearly targets Jews. Since that time the company has added a "willing to convert" option in the religion category, and, as of August 2009, allows for the following options in the religious background category: "Reform, Conservative, Orthodox (Frum), Orthodox (Baal Teshuva), Modern Orthodox, Traditional, Conservadox, Hassidic, Reconstructionist, Another Stream of Judaism, Culturally Jewish but not Practising, Willing to Convert, Not Sure if I'm Willing to Convert, Not Willing to Convert." Over the last few years other labels such as secular and unaffiliated have been on the list, but those no longer appear. Why non-Jews would be interested in pursuing romantic relationships with Jews remains an open question. Some non-Jews on JDate claim to believe that Jews simply make good spouses or offer an unexplained fascination with and attraction to Judaism and Jewish people (Richards, 2004).

Attempts to place Judaism in mainstream American religious life, or gentile participation in JDate and fascination with things Jewish, pose significant questions regarding Jewish identity and the redefinition of community. Where does one draw the line? Do you support JDate's Siminoff who refuses to reject those who may be attracted to Jews and Judaism, and perhaps even embrace that position as potentially bringing in "new blood," in an era when Jewish population in the United States is waning? Do you accept the Jew for Jesus student who wants a free trip to Israel on the Birthright program? Perhaps the Israel experience will impact so powerfully that she will revert to the Judaism of her birth. Or do you reject JDate's "unrestrictive policy" because it not only allows non-Jews to participate but conceivably allows anyone to claim Jewishness and join the community on his or her own terms. This position helps explain the ultra-orthodox alternatives to JDate at dosidate.com and frumster.com.

The identity formation question resonated in late twentieth-century Jewish circles as a byproduct of a social culture deeply in touch with so-called identity politics. Various talking points have been proffered to American Jews to promote strong identification with their Jewish heritages: These approaches range from support for an embattled Israel, through nostalgia for the insular life of the European shtetl, the Jewish victimization represented by the Holocaust, to the mystical components of Jewish spirituality. A popular approach in informal Jewish educational settings in 1970s and 1980s was to pose a simple question: "Do you define yourself as an American-Jew or a Jewish-American?" The cultural pluralism of the era saw the return of the hyphen (Lang, 2005). But framing the question as Jewish leadership often did, "which are you?" suggested only two possibilities when it came to identity construction. This approach reflected an expectation that every American identify with his or her singular ethnic background in order to properly fulfill his or her role in the symphony that comprised American society. But this exclusivism does not translate to an environment shaped by digital culture on the one hand and models of multiracialism on the other. More appropriate is the use of multiple-identity theory or what Robert Jay Lifton called "the protean self" to explain contemporary trends (1999).

On-line behavior reflects this multiple identity phenomenon. An individual conceivably possesses an infinite number of email addresses, screen names, etc., each indicating a different identity, but every one of them authentically representing the same individual. The multiple identity reality of the digital era does not necessitate conflict among the constituent parts, but rather each piece, shaped by the individual to serve his or her needs, contributes to the whole, in a phenomenon Dan Mendelsohn Aviv has called *protean tribalism* (2009, p. 17). Current social psychological theory on identity construction recognizes these changes and puts less emphasis on the group in producing identity and shifts primary focus onto the individual (*The Hedgehog Review: Critical Reflections on Contemporary Culture*, 2002, 1999; and Sula, 2002). Of course, the process of technological progress possesses pitfalls in addition to advantages. Critics have recognized, for example, the dangers inherent in unregulated on-line behavior, ranging from student plagiarism and cyberbullying, identity and financial data theft, to sexual predators trawling the internet in search of victims and using untraceable email addresses to coordinate terrorist activity.

The complications and anxieties of identity construction in the digital era, including multiracialism, simply reflect the complexity of humanity. While these complexities have always been present, the digital revolution both provides a means for expressing multiple identities and engenders a social culture that encourages those expressions. Imagine the challenge faced by the supplementary school instructor who must navigate this terrain with only 2 hours of face-time per week with her or her students.

Just as one may reformulate the concept of identity in general to include the possibility of multiple identities, the role that Jewishness plays in such identity construction is also in flux. Instead of posing a "yes or no" question, the complexity of twenty-first century identities demands a reassessment in more sophisticated terms. One should not ask whether the individual has Jewish identity or not, but rather how are the different Jewish identities defined and how often do they come to the forefront of the individual in question? The question could be posed in the awkwardly phrased, "How Jewish are you?" but should not be understood either in conventional religious terms ("well, I don't go to synagogue too often") or biological terms (I'm one half or one quarter Jewish), though these factors contribute greatly to the construction of Jewish identities. Reflecting digital sensibilities, the question seeks to determine how the different elements of Jewishness (religion, ethnicity, culture, nationality, biology, etc.) shape individuals' various identities, and the ratio need not be fixed but can fluctuate depending on the specific environment.

As Jews marry into non-Jewish families, and as non-Jews choose to identify as Jews through formal conversion or some other process, the identity permutations of successive generations only increase—complicating the question, "Who are your people?" Thus, on numerous campuses, young Jews, whether of mixed or "purebred" ancestry, while not hiding their religious and ethnic backgrounds, appear as primary movers in student organizations supporting Palestinian national movements and protesting Israeli injustice. Many Jewish communal leaders bemoan the fact that such activism is wasted on the wrong side, and criticize the Palestinian sympathizers as "self-hating" Jews. Yet many Jews, young and old, engaged in such activity see their support of Palestinian refugees as a humanitarian cause, a direct outgrowth of a Jewish component of their identities. Putting all the pieces together consistently is quite often an arduous task, replete with contradictions and confusion.

And while most Jewish education professionals need not concern themselves with student profiles on Jewish dating websites, the issues raised are nevertheless relevant and present in their teaching environments. Teenagers in particular are not merely web savvy but active in accessing Jewish resources and conversations to address questions related to Jewish identity. It is not difficult to imagine a seemingly innocuous student assignment to map the demography of contemporary Jewry. Almost certainly, the web research related to this assignment (and where else is the student likely to turn but Wikipedia and Google) will lead to questions of who is a Jew, various related debates among Jewish leadership in the United States and Israel, and tensions between the concepts of Jew-by-Choice and *halachic* (Jewish religious law) definitions of Jewishness.

Key Issues

The impact of the digital revolution is most apparent in a number of specific areas. The following critical issues highlight ways that changes in communication technology radically alter the landscape in which Jewish education professionals operate.

Anarchy—Virtual environments are not only borderless but often leaderless, in some respects they are the ultimate level playing field or a "flat" world to use Tom Friedman's phrase (2006). Can Jewish education adapt effectively to the "wild west" on-line landscape without losing a sense of direction? Is the field amenable to this anarchic grass roots model?

Authority—How does Jewish education (or any other facet of organized Jewish life) respond to a world in which respect for authority, or consensus surrounding the notion of authority, is increasingly challenged. The world of Wikipedia allows individual users to assert their expertise regardless of any bona fide credentials. Rabbinic Judaism evolved on the basis of authoritative leadership sanctioned on the credential of knowledge, duly recognized by an established body of scholars. Authorities with respect to information on-line are data-driven or crowdsourced (Howe, 2006), rather than sanctioned by the "experts."

The Infinite Marketplace—The language of free market economics has been applied not merely to the exchange of goods and services but also to ideas. Jewish educators have had to grapple with this concept and have often attempted to keep Jewish learners engaged by utilizing the market analogy hoping to "sell" a vision of Jewish life that can attract students and parents even in the face of stiff competition. One prominent North American Jewish educator has recently spun this approach away from the market model of trend spotting and issued a call for "relevance" in a way that encourages personal engagement by students and families (Simhai, 2009).

Freeconomics—In a world where consumers' expectations for certain goods, particularly anything associated with information, is a price continually dropping toward zero, how can the product be scaled to the point that it is economically viable (Anderson, 2008). This challenge is particularly acute in industries whose business models have been predicated on access to information or expertise. To be sure even such sacred cows as the university model of higher education are unlikely to be immune to the digital revolution. Not only must faculty accommodate to a student body that was reared in the global environment of cyberspace, but the very existence of such institutions, the ultimate voices of wisdom and authority throughout the second millennium, are likely to be challenged in the near future (Kamenetz, 2009).

As Rosenberg notes, even as the "business" of publishing faces increasing challenges, more and more people continue to publish on-line. Citing blogging pioneer Justin Hall, he notes the power of emotional commitment in redefining the economics of information access. The result is a potential total paradigm shift away from a model in which the profit motive explained every action in the business world. On the digital landscape "the best content comes from people who love what they are doing," even if there is no money in it. (Rosenberg, 2009)

Redefining the locus for community: Cyberspace versus Physical Space—Since traditional Jewish communal activity depends heavily on physical presence, specifically with respect to religiously oriented activities, the migration to virtual territory enabled by the digital revolution challenges the demand for real-life proximity. The on-line virtual world *Second Life* has hosted prayer meetings, boasts a number of synagogues, and has witnessed the lighting of chabad-size *chanukkiyot* during the festive season. As early as 1996 Temple Emanu-El in New York hosted a Cyber-Seder allowing participants to connect from around the globe, not only passively receiving "broadcasts" of the ritual meal, but enabling them to interact via chatrooms. At one time the cyber-seder had the potential to be the largest on-line broadcast event of its time (Brasher, 2004; Kushner, 1998, p. 76).

Conclusions

Professionals in the field of Jewish education should be cautious in recognizing that technology and the tools it provides are neither good nor bad, but neither are they neutral, so says Kranzberg (1986). The purpose of this analysis is not to pass judgment on what might be called user-generated Judaism. These phenomena and a whole host of Jewish-related content already exist on-line and the broader digital revolution is willy-nilly redefining our social culture. But during revolutionary times the ultimate impact can take a very long time to emerge. As one professor of English language notes with respect to the lack of observable changes in reading/writing skills among digital natives, "this doesn't mean that a revolution isn't going on, only that its effects are indeterminate" (Bauerlein, 2009). The general education community continues to grapple with the broader meaning of technology in and out of the classroom and its impact on student learning (Bielaczyz, 2006). To the chagrin of some professionals, in the Jewish education realm there seems to be a gap between the hypothesis that the digital environment is reshaping the landscape of Jewish life and the need for measurable data testifying to the return on investment in digital educational resources. As *Tagged Tanach* pioneer JT Waldman noted on his blog,

> Foundations and donors often wait for hard evidence before making large investments. But time is a precious resource too. I understand the need to invest in products and services that have proven revenue streams and measurable impact, but there are more perils for the Jewish community if we continue to lag behind the education and technology trends evolving around us. Maybe losing money isn't as bad as losing the imagination and attention of the youngest members of our community?! The longer we wait in investing in the digital future of Judaism the greater the risk of losing our most treasured members. (Waldman, 2009)

Although many Jewish educators have invested an appropriate sense of urgency in trying to understand the digital language of the next generation, most practitioners remain only tangentially connected to the interactive mass producer culture that proliferates; many Jewish education professionals are only connected to Jewishness in cyberspace through professional listservs or conventional content providers such as www.myjewishlearning.com. In late 2009 there are a number of innovative, technologically astute resources that inhabit the landscape, including but in no way limited to Darim Online (www.darimonline.org), Babaganewz (www.babaganewz.com), PresenTense (www.presentense.org) or Jlearn2.0 (www.etheoreal.com/jlearn2.0/), in addition to the constantly evolving blogosphere; the websites of conventional Jewish education organizations also serve to bridge the gap. While a vital cadre of Jewish educators are actively committing their time and energy to confronting this new reality, ultimately a generational shift may be needed, in that the profession may only truly comes to grips with the revolutionary nature of digital culture when a critical mass of digital natives engages the field of Jewish education whether on a professional or voluntary basis.

References

Abelson, H., Ledeen, K., & Lewish, H. (2008). *Blown to bits: Your life, liberty, and happiness after the digital explosion*. Boston: Addison-Wesley.

Amkraut, B. (2007), "21st Century Jewish Life: Judaism, Identity, and Community in the age of Hyper-Individualization," Keynote Address delivered at the Coalition for the Advancement of Jewish Education Conference, St. Louis, August 2007.

Amkraut, B. (2008). Jewish education in the world of web 2.0. In R. L. Goodman, P. A. Flexner, & L. D. Bloomberg (Eds.), *What we now know about Jewish education: Perspective on research for practice* (pp. 39–44). Los Angeles: Torah Aura.

Anderson, C. (2008). "Free! Why $0.00 is the Future of Business," *Wired Magazine* 16. 3. Accessed August 28, 2009, from http://www.wired.com/pring/techbiz/it/magazine/16-03/ff_free

Bauerlein, M. (2009, August 29), "Technology and the Seduction of Revolution," *Chronicle of Higher Education.* Accessed August 31, 2009, from http://chronicle.com/blogPost/Technologythe-Seduction/7859/?sid=at&utm_source=at&utm_medium=en

Ben-Avie, M., & Kress, J. (2008), "A North American Study of Educators in Jewish Day and Congregational Schools: Technical Report of the Educators in Jewish Schools Study". Accessed August 26, 2009, from http://www.jewisheducationalchange.org/docs/Ben-Avie%20and%20Kress%20EJSS%20Technical%20Report%20(FINAL).pdf

Berger, S. (2003). Teachers' use of computers in the North American Jewish day school: A research study. *Jewish Educational Leadership, 1*(1). Accessed December 8, 2010, from http://www.lookstein.org/online_journal.php?id=63

Berkman, J. (2009, August 26), "J-Vibe to Shut Print Publication and Maybe Online Mag, as JFL Sunsets". Accessed August 27, 2009, from http://blogs.jta.org/philanthropy

Bielaczyz, K. (2006). Designing social infrastructure: Critical issues in creating learning environments with technology. *The Journal of the Learning Sciences, 15*(3), 301–329.

Bloomberg, L. D. (2007). Culture and community: Case study of a video-conferenced graduate distance education program. *The Journal of Distance Education, 22*(1), 41–58.

Brasher, B. (2004). *Give me that online religion.* Piscataway, NJ: Rutgers University Press.

Cohen, S. M., & Kelman, A. (2005) *Cultural Events and Jewish Identities: Young Adult Jews in New York.* Accessed August 29, 2009, from http://www.jewishculture.org/content/pdf/CultureStudy.PDF

Compact Oxford English Dictionary. (2009) "Educate". Accessed August 30, 2009, from http://www.askoxford.com/concise_oed/educate?view=uk

DeVaney, A. (1994). Ethical considerations of visuals in the classroom: African-Americans and Hollywood film. In D. M. Moore & F. M. Dwyer (Eds.), *Visual literacy* (pp. 355–368). Englewood Cliffs, NJ: Educational Technology Publications.

Friedman, T. (2006). *The world is flat: A brief history of the twenty-first century.* New York: Farrar, Straus and Giroux.

Goldburg, P. (2006). Approaching the teaching of religious education through the creative arts. In M. de Souza, et al. (Eds.), *International handbook of the religious, moral and spiritual dimensions in education* (pp. 1237–1252). London: Springer.

Gordis, Y. (2009) Accessed August 31, 2009, from http://jpsinteractive.org/projects/tagged_tanakh/testimonials

Grishaver, J. L. (2008). The Jewish message as medium: Jewish education in the information age. In R. L. Goodman, P. A. Flexner, & L. D. Bloomberg (Eds.), *What we now know about Jewish education: Perspective on research for practice* (pp. 51–56). Los Angeles: Torah Aura.

Helland, C. (2007). Diaspora on the electronic frontier: Developing virtual connections with sacred homelands. *Journal of Computer-Mediated Communication, 12*(3). Accessed December 8, 2010, from http://jcmc.indiana.edu/vol12/issue3/helland.html

Herberg, W. (1955). *Protestant-Catholic-Jew: An essay in American religious sociology.* Garden City, NY: Doubleday.

Howe, J. (2006, June). "The Rise of Crowdsourcing". Accessed August 31, 2009, from http://www.wired.com/wired/archive/14.06/crowds_pr.html

Howe, N., & Strauss, W. (2000). *Millennials rising: The next great generation.* New York: Vintage.

Kamenetz, A. (2009, September 1), "How Web-Savvy Edupunks are Transforming American Higher Education". Accessed August 25, 2009, from http://www.fastcompany.com/magazine/138/who-needs-harvard.html

Kelman, V. (2009), Remarks at Siegal College Summer Institue, August 11, 2009.

Kopelowitz, E. (2005). Jewish identities. In N. de Lange & M. Freud-Kandel (Eds.), *Modern Judaism: An oxford guide* (pp. 205–215). Oxford: Oxford University Press.

Kopelowitz, E., & Engleberg, A. (2009). A guide to Jewish peoplehood. *Jewish Educational Leadership, 7*(2), 4–10.

Kranzberg, M. (1986). Technology and history: 'Kranzberg's Laws'. *Technology and Culture, 27*(3), 544–560.

Kushner, D. (1998), "Cyberseder to Bring Out Musical All-Stars," *Wired Magazine*. Accessed August 30, 2009, from http://www.wired.com/culture/lifestyle/news/1998/04/11605

Lang, B. (2005). Hyphenated Jews and the anxiety of identity. *Jewish Social Studies, 12*(1), 1–15.

Levine, C. (2006). *White paper: Jewish learning in the digital age.* New York: Board of Jewish Education of Greater New York.

Lifton, R. J. (1999). *The protean self: Human resilience in the age of fragmentation.* Chicago: University of Chicago Press.

Margolis, P. (2008). Technology and distance learning. In R. L. Goodman, P. A. Flexner, & L. D. Bloomberg (Eds.), *What we now know about Jewish education: Perspective on research for practice* (pp. 317–326). Los Angeles: Torah Aura.

Mendelsohn Aviv, D. (2009). You have 600,000 friends' Jewish identity and community in the age of social networking sites and computer-mediated communication. *Jewish Educational Leadership, 7*(2), 15–20.

Meyer, M. A. (1987). Introduction. In M. A. Meyer (Ed.), *Ideas of Jewish history* (pp. 1–42). Detroit, MI: Wayne State University Press.

Musleah, R. (2009). Individualism and community. *Hadassah Magazine, 91*(1), 30–38.

Richards, S. (2004, December 5). You don't have to be Jewish to love JDate. *New York Times*. Accessed August 29, 2009, from http://www.nytimes.com/2004/12/05/fashion/05DATE.html?_r=1&scp=1&sq=you%20don't%20have%20to%20be%20jewish%20to%20love%20jdate&st=cse

Roland, A. (2009). Letters to the editor. *Wilson Quarterly, 33*(2), 9.

Rosenberg, S. (2009). *Say everything: How blogging began, what it's becoming and why it matters.* New York: Crown.

Rushkoff, D. (2003). *Nothing sacred: The truth about Judaism.* New York: Crown.

Seltzer, R. (1980). *Jewish people, Jewish thought: The Jewish experience in history.* Upper Saddle River, NJ: Prentice-Hall.

Sherlick, L., & Hong, J. (2008). *Internet popular culture and Jewish values: The influence of technology on religion in Israeli schools.* Amherst, NY: Cambria.

Shirky, C. (2008). *Here comes everybody: The power of organizing without organizations.* New York: Penguin.

Simhai, N. (2009), Remarks at the Siegal College Summer Institute. August 11, 2009.

Singh, S. (2007), "Social Networks and Group Formation: Theoretical Concepts to Leverage". Accessed August 30, 2009, from http://www.boxesandarrows.com/view/social-networks

Sula, J. R. (2002). Identity management in cyberspace. *Journal of Applied Psychoanalytic Studies, 4*, 455–460.

Onions, C. T. (Ed.) (1971). *The Compact Edition of the Oxford English Dictionary: Complete Text Reproduced Micrographically* Oxford: Oxford University Press.

The Hedgehog Review: Critical Reflections on Contemporary Culture, (Fall 1999), Identity.

The Hedgehog Review: Critical Reflections on Contemporary Culture, (Fall 2002), Technology and the Human Person.

Truelove, K., Shirky, C., Gonze, L., & Dornfest, R. (2001). *2001 P2P networking overview: The emergent p2p platform of presence, identity, and edge resources.* Sebastopol, CA: O'Reilly Research.

Waldman, J. T. (2009, August 21). "Validating the Tagged Tanakh's Mission and Goals". Accessed August 31, 2009, from http://jpsinteractive.org/blog/jt/validating-tagged-tanakhs-mission-and-goals

Wan, W. (2009, August 30), "Soul-Searching on Facebook: For Many Users, Religion Question Is Not Easy to Answer," *Washington Post*. Accessed August 30, 2009, from http://www.washingtonpost.com/wp-dyn/content/article/2009/08/29/AR2009082902400.html

Wertheimer, J. (Ed.) (2009). *Learning and community: Jewish supplementary schools in the twenty-first century.* Waltham, MA: Brandeis University Press.

Woocher, J. S. (2008). Jewish education in the age of Google. In R. L. Goodman, P. A. Flexner, & L. D. Bloomberg (Eds.), *What we now know about Jewish education: Perspective on research for practice* (pp. 31–38). Los Angeles: Torah Aura.

Travel as a Jewish Educational Tool

Erik H. Cohen

Introduction

There is a growing awareness among researchers, educators, and students, of the educational value of travel. In the realm of religious education, the traditional concept of pilgrimage has been expanded to include various forms of religious-educational tourism (Senn, 2002; Tomasi, 2002; Cohen, 2006). The identity-affirming nature of travel and pilgrimage has been well documented particularly among minorities and those with "hyphenated identities" (see, for example, Mazumbar and Mazumbar, 2004; Singh, 2006; Timothy and Olsen, 2006). In Jewish education, the benefit of travel is widely recognized (see, for example, Cohen and Kotler-Berkowitz, 2004; Cohen, 2008a; Saxe and Chazan, 2008). According to Ioannides and Ioannides (2004, p. 101) "One way in which Jews in America and elsewhere seek to reaffirm and strengthen their affiliation to Judaism is demonstrated through their travel patterns."

This chapter briefly outlines some of the major sociological trends in the general field of educational travel, and then explores in depth the use of travel as an educational tool in contemporary Jewish education. Key challenges and issues in Jewish educational travel are discussed, including shifting Israel–Diaspora relations; preconceived destination images among various sub-populations; differing motivations and goals among travelers and program organizers; and guiding and interpretation at sites. Many parameters of the subject will be addressed, including the impact of age, nationality, previous educational background, level of religiosity, the framework of the tour, and the role of the staff and guides. Each of these is a rich subject in itself and it is not possible in the scope of this chapter to delve into each of these in-depth.[1]

E.H. Cohen (✉)
Bar-Ilan University, Ramat Gan, Israel
e-mail: ehcohen@mail.biu.ac.il; msaharon@mscc.huji.ac.il

[1] See, for example, among the numerous articles on the impact on educational travel of these subjects: age (Cohen, 2005; Desforges, 1998; Gibson and Yiannakis, 2002; Reisman, 1993) nationality (Boniface and Fowler 1993; Burns 2005; Reisinger and Turner, 2003); previous education (Cohen, 1999, 2004); level of religiosity (Jutla, 2006); the framework of the tour (Anderson, Lawton,

Nevertheless, it is important to note this wide range of factors which impact the educational travel experience. The chapter draws on empirical research conducted by experts in the field of educational tourism, including recent research on specific educational tour programs (i.e., Israel Experience, Taglit-birthright, Shoah tourism, and Jewish summer camps). Directions for future research in the field will be indicated.

Travel as a Metaphor for Education

Travel can be a powerful metaphor for education. The teacher acts as a guide, leading the learner through unfamiliar territory. Language invoking images of journeys and exploration has long been used to describe the educational process. The Torah includes numerous stories of personal growth and lessons learned through travel from the journeys of the patriarchs through the wanderings of the Children of Israel in the desert. Maimonides considers the patriarch Avraham's first test by God to be the commandment *lekh lekha*—to leave his homeland.[2] The kabbalistic teacher the Arizal suggested that the purpose of the Exile or Diaspora was educational—enabling the Jews to gather the "sparks of enlightenment" scattered throughout the various cultures of the world. The core prayer, the *Shema*, dictates teaching one's children the laws of the Torah "while sitting in the house and while walking on the way." This approach may in some ways interfere with or block experiential encounter with the natural, physical landscape. At the same time, travel is indicated as a time for learning. Travel is a key concept in the Jewish world, expressed variously in the traditional texts, folklore, and literature and popular culture (Ioannides and Ioannides, 2006).

Travel as an Educational Tool

Travel offers a holistic educational experience. Being taken into a new environment opens the mind to new information and ideas, challenging travelers to integrate new information, concepts, and patterns of understanding. International travel helps develop a cross-cultural perspective. Travel enables, even demands, exploration of a subject with all the senses and with the three modes of cognition, emotion, and behavior. MacCannell (1976, 1992) describes tourism as a cognitive activity through which the traveler seeks authenticity and holism. Cohen's typology of tourism (1979, 1984, 2007) describes a range of travel experiences from the recreational through the existential. Each of these various types of travel experiences may be included within a single tour.

Rexeisen, & Hubbard, 2006; Richards and Wilson, 2003) and the role of the guide and staff (Fine and Speer, 1985; Katz, 1985; Reisinger and Steiner, 2006).

[2]This refers to a comment of Maimonides on the Chapter 5 item 4 in Pirkei Avot (Sayings of the Fathers): "Our forefather Abraham was tested with ten trials...."

Although it may be argued that travel is inherently educational and that education is inherently a "journey," an effective educational tour must be intentionally planned. If the program intends to transmit certain ideas and values, these must be addressed during the tour clearly and explicitly (Shulman, 2009[3]). However, it is not possible to plan every detail of the trip, nor is it desirable to do so. The experience should be authentic so that the traveler does not encounter only staged "pseudo-events" (Boorstin, 1964). As Jewish philosopher Martin Buber said, "All journeys have secret destinations of which the traveler is unaware." A chance encounter may be a pivotal experience for the traveler—a conversation with the bus driver about a site being visited, a meeting in the marketplace, an unanticipated event (Dr. Zeev Mankovitz, personal communication, 2008; Laubscher, 1994). If the trip is too tightly controlled and exploration of the environment is not possible, the educational value of the tour suffers.

To plan an effective yet authentic educational tour, many parameters must be taken into account. These include factors related to the target population, the destination, and the framework of the tour. Important factors related to the population of student-travelers include demographics such as age, gender, nationality, and religion; their previous knowledge and attitudes about the destination and the subjects to be addressed and their expectations for the tour.

Some researchers have looked at gender differences in terms of motivations, expectations, and interpretations of the trip (Carr, 1999; Kinnaird and Hall, 1994; Pritchard and Morgan, 2000; Sered, 1999) and differences in the educational experience of male and female students (Blair, Holland and Sheldon, 1994; Grossman and Grossman, 1994). National origin has been found to have a significant impact on travelers' motivations and expectations. Previous knowledge and attitudes of participants must be considered, so that the itinerary and curriculum of the tour program will be understandable and interesting to participants. Another parameter is the site itself. Jewish educational travel may take visitors to museums, historical and cultural sites, memorialized cites related to the Shoah, pilgrimages to cemeteries, and visits to parents' or grandparents' pre-migration homes (for instance, in Poland or Morocco).

The framework in which the travel is carried out also impacts the nature of the educational experience. Does the traveler go alone or with a group? If with a group, what is the nature of the group? It may consist of strangers recruited by a travel agent, which, in turn, may be either predominantly Jewish (as in "kosher" tour packages) or heterogeneous. The group traveling together may be an extended family, members of the same youth group, schoolmates, etc. The experience, clearly, will be different in each of these circumstances. Educational travel spans a wide range of options including: an educational event as part of a vacation (for example, visiting a museum or attending a lecture); short-term educational tours; semester or year-long programs at Israeli educational institutions (high school, college, university,

---

[3] Lee Shulman's presentation (during the closing session of the Multiple Identities Conference in Jerusalem, January 8, 2008) referred to Jewish identities. But his remarks are equally relevant to the issue of Jewish educational travel.

yeshiva); internships with Israeli programs; earning a full degree at an Israeli college or university; and Hebrew language study.

Each of these parameters affects the overall educational travel experience, and must be considered by researchers and Jewish educators attempting to understand this sociological phenomenon.

Jewish Educational Travel: Israel and the Diaspora

The journey has been a foundational element of Jewish identity since its inception. The tension between homeland and Diaspora or exile has been similarly fundamental. For centuries, Diaspora – Israel relations were essentially spiritual and symbolic. Jewish travel to Israel was almost entirely limited to pilgrimages of a very few, devoted individuals. Since the founding of the State, travel to Israel has become a widespread phenomenon. Dynamic and varied Diaspora–Israel relations affect patterns of Jewish travel to Israel and the role Israel plays in Jewish education. Steinberg (1984, p. 103) noted that with few exceptions, "... Diaspora Jewish education in its aims and its content is inherently Israel-oriented..." It has become common in some Diaspora communities for a trip to Israel to be included as a part of the Jewish educational process (although it is worth noting that only a minority of American Jews, the largest Diaspora population has ever traveled to Israel, even taking into account the tens of thousands who came in the framework of initiatives such as Israel Experience and Taglit birthright). The impact of educational travel to Israel is expanded to those who do not travel themselves, in that by now the majority of educators in Jewish educational settings in the Diaspora have spent at least some time in Israel.

Although travel to Israel is a widespread and important phenomenon, it is far from the only type of Jewish travel. Diaspora Jews undertake travel to destinations in their own home countries and other countries which may be strong educational experiences. There are now over a hundred specifically Jewish museums in the world, and many more general museums with exhibits related to Jewish history and culture (Grossman, 2003). Travel to European sites related to the Shoah or to pre-Shoah Jewish communities has grown dramatically in recent years. "Dark tourism" to sites such as former death camps has its own logic and its own educational value, and may be considered types of heritage tourism and pilgrimage (Ashworth, 2002; Beech, 2000; Kugelmass, 1994). The issue of the Shoah is to be presented and perceived differently during a tour of Auschwitz, a visit to Yad Vashem in Jerusalem, or a visit to the Holocaust museum in Washington, DC. Holocaust tourism in Europe tends to focus on the destruction of the local Jewish communities (Kugelmass, 1994), visits to Yad Vashem highlights the link between the Holocaust and the creation of the State of Israel (Auron, 2008, 1994), while the Holocaust museum in DC underscores the fight against racism and the triumph of American ideals over Nazism (Rosenfeld, 1997).

Jewish summer camps are another important example of Jewish travel. During the weeks of the camp, young Jews are immersed in an all-Jewish environment, allowing for every moment to be incorporated in the educational approach (Levinas,

1963, [1997]). For some, particularly those who live outside of Jewish population centers, the camp may be one of the only Jewish milieu in which they have the opportunity to participate (Sales and Saxe, 2002, 2004; Cohen and Kotler-Berkowitz, 2004; Lorge and Zola, 2006).

Israeli Jews also learn from their travel experiences within Israel and throughout the Diaspora. The post-army tour has become a rite of passage for many young Israelis, and its import in broadening the travelers' understandings of self, home, and the world has been documented (Noy and Cohen, 2006). Israeli schools, youth groups, and other institutions organize educational trips to museums, nature reserves, and historical sites in Israel. Israelis participate in the growing phenomenon of travel/pilgrimage to sites related to Europe to learn about the Shoah in the lands in which it took place. Israeli travel to Diaspora countries to broaden their perspective on Judaism has become more common in recent years. For example, bringing Israeli teachers and counselors to work in Diaspora Jewish schools and summer camps was once considered beneficial primarily for the Diaspora participants. Today the educational benefit to Israeli counselors and *shlichim* (educational emissaries) is also considered (Ezrachi, 1994; Wolf & Kopelowitz, 2003). Israeli teachers reported that a tour of US Jewish educational settings impacted them as individual Jews, as members of Israeli society, and as educators (Grant, Kelman and Regev, 2001).

Many tours for Diaspora youth include structured meetings with Israeli peers (*mifgashim*). Although the emphasis of organizers has been on the educational value for the visitors, the meetings have been found to be powerful and fruitful learning experiences for the Israeli youth as well (Cohen, 2000, 2008a). Following mifgashim between Israelis and Taglit-birthright participants, Sasson, Mittelberg, Hecht, and Saxe (2008) found that the Israeli participants "... indicated that the program made them feel pride—pride in service to the IDF, pride in country, and pride in being Jews. To a significant but lesser extent, the program also made them feel connected to the Jewish people worldwide and cultivated a desire to learn more about Judaism."

Another growing phenomenon in Jewish travel, in which both Israelis and Diaspora Jews take part, involves travel to the various "Old Countries" from which Jews have migrated, particularly in Europe and North Africa. While these are most often organized as family vacations or pilgrimages to holy sites and graves, this type of travel has educational value in terms of historical knowledge of Jewish communities that may no longer exist, and in learning about how Jews lived in different times and places.

Jewish Educational Travel and "Destination Image"

The images travelers have of their destination prior to the trip have been found to have a profound impact on the trip (Baloglu & McCleary, 1999; Walmsley & Young, 1998). In educational travel organized through schools, youth groups or other community institutions, there is a valuable opportunity to direct the formation of destination image. During orientation programs prior to the trip, participants may be given information about the destination and helped to form realistic images of it. Participants also receive "structural preparation" for the trip through their larger educational and community environment.

The images Jewish tourists have of Israel are deeply affected by the assumption of a primordial connection between them and the Land. However, these images are not homogenous across the Diaspora. Young Jews from various countries and affiliated with different sub-communities in each country (Orthodox, Conservative/traditional, Reform/liberal) hold different images of Israel, reflecting the prevailing views in their educational systems and communities (Cohen, 2003a, 2008a). Jewish Israelis' images of *aretz* (the land of Israel) and *hutz l'aretz* (outside the land of Israel) affect the educational value of their travels within and outside their country. Domestically, a spiritualized connection with the land and its sites, transforms hikes in Israel into secular pilgrimages (Katriel, 1995). India and the Far East are perceived as exotic locales for spiritual seeking by many young Israelis, even if their knowledge and expectations of Indian spirituality are superficial (Maoz, 2006).

Motivations and Goals for Jewish Educational Travel

Strengthening Jewish identity, a sense of Jewish Peoplehood and connection to Israel are among the strongest and most widely cited objectives in Diaspora travel to Israel (Cohen, 2008a) and Jewish summer camps (Cohen and Kotler-Berkowitz, 2004; Lorge & Zola, 2006; Sales & Saxe, 2004). It should be noted that participants, particularly young travelers, may consider having a good time with a group of peers a more important goal. Nevertheless, the emphasis on enjoyment does not preclude educational benefits of the travel experience, and in fact may enhance them (Cohen, 2008a; Cohen and Bar Shalom, 2010). While in the early days of the State of Israel it was hoped and expected that Diaspora travel to Israel would lead to *aliyah* (immigration to Israel as a citizen), today there is greater emphasis on the ways in which travel may enhance Jewish identification and participation in the traveler's home Jewish community (Ari, Mansfeld & Mittelberg, 2003; Cohen, 2008a). "Tours to these Jewish places of death [Eastern Europe] and life [Israel] are used to consider how participants might translate their memories of travel into action at home, that is, in America or other communities around the world..." (Aviv & Shneer, 2007, p. 67).

The goals of Shoah tourism include keeping alive the memory of those who were killed and enhancing feelings of common fate among the Jewish People. For organizers of group tours for Israeli youth to Auschwitz, instilling a strengthened sense of the importance of the State of Israel as a refuge and homeland for Jews is another primary goal.

The Impact of Age

Travel experiences undertaken at different ages necessarily have different educational impacts. Travel undertaken at various ages may complement the development of the individual's perspective, gradually expanding from one's self to parents, friends, community, country, and the world at large (Erikson, 1959, 1963; Piaget, 1972). Educational travel may benefit learners of all ages, and some of the basic factors in a successful educational tour are the same regardless of the traveler's age. For example, the importance of the group among teenaged participants in tours to Israel has been established: Similarly, a study of Elderhostel educational tours found that "Being with like-minded people with common special interests" was important to most seniors who joined the group tours (Ritchie, Carr, & Cooper, 2003: 91 citing research by Arsenault, 2001). Nevertheless, the tour program must be adapted for the age range of the participants. Age appropriateness touches on participants' abilities, needs, and preferences in the cognitive, emotional and behavioral realms. Motivations for international study change with age; younger visiting students tend to emphasize tourism and socialization, while older students tend to emphasize educational and professional goals (Cohen, 2003b). Professional goals are further emphasized by those traveling to conferences, seminars or on sabbatical, although tourism and personal development are also important (Griffith, 2008; Cohen, 2008b). Retired tourists on educational tours seek personal fulfillment through new experiences (Ritchie et al., 2003).

The Impact of Nationality

Nationality has been found to have a major impact on Jewish identity, related to differences in the Jewish educational systems of various Diaspora countries and Israel (Cohen & Horenczyk, 1999; Cohen, 2008a; Gitelman, Kosmin and Kovács, 2003; Wettstein, 2002). As noted by Moscardo (1996, p. 376), "... interpretation is the key to ensuring the quality of the tourism experience," and interpretation is impacted by cultural values, assumptions, and habitus, which are formed in the travelers' home society. Tourists often travel within enclaves of co-travelers from the same home country, thus extending the impact of the home society into the tour destination(s).

In a survey of Israel Experience participants, nationality was the most discriminate variable for virtually every questionnaire item, including motivations for joining the tour, educational background, attitudes, and values toward Judaism and Israel, and evaluation of the tour (Cohen, 2008a). Groups traveling together are often from the same home country and interaction with locals tends to be limited. Often interaction within the group of co-travelers is more important than interaction with "locals" (Urry, 2002). For example, Israel Experience is groups are almost always homogenous in terms of the participants' home country, and since participants spend virtually all their time with the group. Thus, a tour to Israel may reinforce participants' identity as *American* Jews, *French* Jews, etc., and their commitment to participate in their home Jewish community, in addition to strengthening their attachment to Israel (Comet, 1965; Shapiro, 2001). Indeed, the goal of most Diaspora Jewish educational institutions in organizing tours to Israel is not to encourage aliyah, but rather to expand the knowledge of Israel and Judaism and to strengthen the Jewish identity of Jews in the home country (Cohen, 2008a).

Following MacCannell's (1976, 1992) assertion that the modern tourist is seeking a sense of holism and authenticity, I have noted that Jewish tourists to Israel are seeking a holistic and authentic Jewish identity. Diaspora Jews may seek that which is difficult to achieve in their home countries. For example, French Jews, raised in a political culture limiting the expression of an ethnically particular community, seek out the experience of the Jewish political culture in Israel. American Jewish youth, living in a culture which stresses individuality and in which the community and extended family have largely broken down, seek out the experience of solidarity offered in group tours and camps. Jewish-American adults may seek religiously meaningful experiences (Grant, 2000).

In a parallel phenomenon, Israelis on the post-army backpack tour, "... spend most of their time with other Israelis, and their conversations revolve to a considerable extent on their military experiences and the complexities of the Israeli society. The trip thus offers them an opportunity to reflect upon their recent past and re-evaluate at a distance their perceptions and attitudes regarding their society and their own place and future within it" (Cohen, 2004, p. 56).

The Impact of Previous Knowledge

Another major feature which may be used to differentiate between educational tourist experiences is the level of previous knowledge of the sites visited and the subjects addressed during the tour. Previous knowledge includes how much visitors know and what they know, think, believe, and feel about the sites and subjects at hand. Tour programs can offer specific orientation sessions to help give participants necessary information to make the tour comfortable and comprehensible. However, long-term "structural" preparation, conveyed through years of community involvement, education and even previous trips, has a greater impact on the educational experience of a tour.

Participants in youth tours to Israel who received extensive formal and informal Jewish education were able to understand and appreciate the tours more than those who came with little or no background (Cohen, 1999, 2004, 2008a). Further, not all structural preparation yields the same type of interpretation. Studies of group tours to Israel and Jewish summer camps found significant differences in attitudes and previous knowledge regarding Zionism and Judaism among participants from Orthodox, Conservative/Traditional and Reform/Liberal families. Structural preparation provides cognitive knowledge and emotionally powerful symbols which serve as keys for accessing the travel experience. For example, a trip to the Kotel,[4] no matter how well planned and guided, would not hold the same meaning for tourists with no previous understanding of or connection to the site as it does for visitors who have for their whole lives been familiar with its symbolic and religious significance for the Jewish People. Studies at pilgrimage sites worldwide have also noted the difference in impact of the trip on believer-participants and non-believer-observers (Coles & Timothy, 2004; Timothy & Olsen, 2006).

---

[4]The Western Wall or Wailing Wall, the only remnant of the Jews' Temple built during the era of the Israelite kingdom in Jerusalem and destroyed by the Romans in 60 C.E.

Jews of all levels of religiosity participate in travel to Israel (Kelner, 2002; Cohen, 1992; Grant, 2000), to sites of the Holocaust (Feldman, 2001; Greenblum, 1995; Kugelmass, 1994), and to graves of tzaddikim or relatives in "the Old Country" (Kosansky, 2002; Levy, 1997). Such trips may be deeply spiritual experiences for the secular and the religious alike. Nevertheless, the tourists' level of religiosity affects the nature of the experience and the symbolic-affective ways in which the experience is constructed. Activities or sites which may be moving to one group may be uncomfortable or incomprehensible to another. The goals and motivations for study in Israel were found to differ between students in a religious study program and a university program (Ohayon, 2004). Thus the level of religiosity of the group members must be taken into consideration by organizers and guides.

To the extent that all tourism is staged and that tourism may be understood as a type of performance, "... the effect of performance is contingent upon an audience that understands the message" (Edensor, 2000, p. 327). In heritage tourism, visitors who identify with the heritage presented and share the outlook of the interpretation given are more likely to enjoy and to learn from the experience (Katriel, 1993). Jewish summer camp participants who share the religious affiliation of the camp they attend were found to better able to receive its messages (Cohen, in press).

Travelers may also be more or less competent in the act of travel itself. Some travel skills may be refined with age and experience, although in some cases young travelers may be more open, more willing, and able to adapt to new situations. Moscardo (1996) found that the success of heritage tourism is greatly improved if tourists are "mindful." Also important is the extent to which the travelers try to interact with the local culture and to what extent they remain in their tourist enclave. Among visitors who worked or volunteered on kibbutzim or with community projects in Israel, those who had intense social interactions with their hosts were more satisfied with their experience and were more likely to report that their feelings toward Israel and Israelis improved compared with those who had minimal interactions with their Israeli hosts (Pizam, Uriely and Reichel, 2000).

Educational tours tend to be more successful at strengthening and intensifying pre-existing attitudes toward Judaism and Israel than in radically changing them or creating nonexistent ones. Thus, program organizers and guides must know the depth and nature of the background of their audience. Educational travel programs attempting to recruit participants with varying degrees of background must find ways to make the program interesting for those with more previous knowledge yet understandable for those with less.

The Impact of the Framework of the Tour

The case of the working tourists points to yet another parameter of travel as an educational tool, namely, the framework of the tour. Tourists may travel alone, with family and friends, as part of group tours, and on various types of "working vacations." Educational tours offering opportunities to volunteer with local projects have gained popularity (Wearing, 2001). These may include extended, intensive programs such as the Peace Corps, or shorter volunteer work incorporated into a larger tour itinerary. Even if family tours and outings are not intentionally planned as educational trips, they may yield numerous important lessons, particularly when they are related to Jewish holidays or life-cycle events. Each of the different frameworks of tours may be superficial or existentially meaningful, purely recreational or deeply educational, depending on the intention of the organizers and the participants.

Regardless of the framework, educational travel is primarily an informal educational experience. A number of characteristics of informal learning are crucial to its application as a tool for Jewish education, including: a balance between cognitive, affective, and instrumental dimensions of learning; the experiential and interactive nature of the "lessons"; and the emphasis on group dynamics and the social component (Cohen, 2006). The balance between various modes of learning yield changes in participants' knowledge, attitudes, feelings, and behaviors regarding the place visited, the hosts, and the subjects covered. A director of a network of Jewish Day Schools in South Africa (1990, personal communication) found that sending students to overnight camps helped achieve the affective and behavioral parts of the syllabus which are difficult to achieve in the classroom, by offering experiential and interactive activities. For example, the student-campers were more willing and able to learn to pray when away from their daily routine and close to nature. School-sponsored travel links formal and informal educational settings. Recreation and socialization do not simply make the learning more enjoyable, they are an integral part of the educational experience. Various frameworks and types of tours may be more or less "informal" and may manifest different aspects of informality (for an in-depth exploration of this issue, see Kahane, 1997).

One of the most common types of educational travel program is the group tour. In this case, the group functions as a sort of temporary "total institution" (Goffman, 1961), within which all the co-travelers' movements and activities take place. This framework has certain educational benefits, as the itinerary-curriculum may be carefully planned and tailored to the specific group's needs and goals. Additionally, the group itself is important in reinforcing the messages of the tour, providing mutual support during an intense experience, and allowing for a combination of learning and socialization.

Educational travel may also take place independently. In this case, travelers may benefit from educational resources such as guidebooks, museums, and guided tours at specific sites. The experiences of other travelers, often passed on by word-of-mouth at meeting places such as youth hostels, may be important sources of information (Cohen, 2004; Jack & Phipps, 2005; Noy, 2002). It requires significant resourcefulness and competence to effectively plan one's own educational itinerary. Some independent travelers may work, volunteer, or study at various institutions during their journey. Agencies promoting the use of travel as a Jewish educational tool may facilitate this type of educational tourism by promoting avenues for participating in study or work programs. For example, the MASA project helps direct Diaspora Jews to the various opportunities for long-term programs in Israel.

Visiting students represent a distinct type of educational tourists. While in many cases students may study overseas primarily for educational purposes or to broaden their experiences in a general way, Jewish students in Israel are almost always motivated, at least in part, by a desire to explore their Jewish identity (Herman, 1962, 1970; Cohen, 2003b). Visiting students are also interested in touring the country, making social contacts with Israelis and with other Diaspora Jews, with expanding their personal development, and with furthering their academic and professional goals (Cohen, 2003b; Richards & Wilson, 2003).

Taking a wide view of the phenomenon of Jewish travel, organizers may strive to offer a range of frameworks, each of which may be utilized as an educational experience. Some individuals may prefer one type of travel over another. Travelers also may choose different frameworks at different times. For example, someone may come to Israel first as part of a group tour and then return to explore the country with friends in a less structured way. Alternatively, someone may first come informally with family and then return to volunteer on a kibbutz or join a long-term educational program. Diaspora Jews (and other supporters) volunteering in Israel during times of war has been an important phenomenon in travel to Israel, offering a unique type of educational experience (Cohen, 1986; Horowitz et al., 1971) as has the kibbutz volunteer experience (Mittelberg, 1985). A wide range of educational tourism opportunities allow potential travelers to find the framework most appropriate for their evolving needs and interests.

The Role of the Guide

Related to the framework of the tour are the staff and the type of guiding provided. The guide may act as a pathfinder, coordinator, teacher, role model, and cultural interpreter (Cohen, 1985; Cohen, Ifergan, & Cohen, 2002). The recruitment of staff, which may include Israelis, home community members, professionals, rabbis, teachers, and counselors, is an important aspect of planning a Jewish educational tour. Training the staff in various educational techniques also affects the nature of the educational tour. Teacher-guides may mirror the passive and frontal type of lecturing common in classrooms, or they may encourage tourists to question, discuss, and draw their own conclusions about the sites and subjects. In Jewish summer camps, for example, there has been a movement away from seminar-style lessons toward discussions integrated into other activities (Cohen and Bar Shalom, 2010). Also, during some activity units during Israel Experience tours, the counselors engaged participants in open-ended discussions about issues related to Jewish religion and contemporary Israeli society (Cohen, 2008a). The skill of the counselor-guide is of the utmost importance in order to cover a subject adequately while allowing for discussion. At some controversial sites (for example, in Shoah-related tourism), guides may find it necessary to limit the range of discussion in order to preserve the group integrity and to stay in line with the educational goals of the organizing institution (MacDonald, 2006).

Conclusion: The Opportunities and Challenges of Educational Travel

In this chapter, I have endeavored to define the concept of educational tourism, and specifically Jewish educational tourism, as it has been understood until now by researchers and those involved in the field. There already exists quite a significant body of academic literature on the issue, including both strong empirical data and insightful theoretical discussion. Case studies and theoretical contributions in the social research on tourism, ethnicity, and education are valuable in understanding Jewish educational and heritage travel. It may be seen that Jewish travel is part of a global phenomenon in which tourists seek, to varying degrees, emotional connection with their own roots, exploration of the self through encounter with the exotic "other," intellectual stimulation, and an enjoyable break from daily routine. The Jewish case has greatly enriched the study of these phenomena, as much Jewish educational travel is organized by community institutions and is particularly well documented. The Jewish case shows how tours to heritage sites may be used to enhance ethnic-religious identity and encourage changes in related attitudes and behaviors. Jewish educational travel has been found to impact the tourists' relationship to the Jewish community at home, as well as to the site visited. As these are stated goals of many group tours, the depth and persistence of these changes should be tracked longitudinally.

This provides a solid basis for strategizing research and activity in this field in the next decades. What are the major strengths of educational travel? How can it be improved? How can we understand it more fully? And what are the challenges presented?

One aspect which could be further explored is the link between communal Jewish education (day schools, extra-curricular learning, youth organizations) and educational travel. How can travel enhance and advance the educational goals of a school? For example, how can travel organized through a school further an aim such as enhancing Jewish identity? What is the interaction between the school and the tour in terms of staff and curriculum? How can educational tours for teachers impact the school? These questions have yet to be systematically surveyed.

It is clear that travel is an important and widely used tool in the field of Jewish education. Effective school-sponsored travel necessitates the design of a holistic educational strategy. In designing this strategy, the many inter-connected facets of educational strategy outlined in this chapter must be considered including: the role of the staff, the balance between cognitive, affective, and behavioral modes of learning, previous knowledge and attitudes of the travelers, the importance of the social element, and balance between intentional planning and allowing for authentic, spontaneous "teachable moments" (Cohen and Bar Shalom, 2010).

Additionally, there is a need for further study of the educational value of travel undertaken by individuals who do not join groups or programs organized through any institution. Independent travel is particularly common among young adults (ages 18–26). Some study has been done on independent travelers as a sub-group of educational tourists (Ritchie et al., 2003) and Israeli backpackers traveling abroad (Noy & Cohen, 2006, as discussed above), but virtually no empirical studies have been conducted on the Jewish Diaspora youth who travel to Israel or to Jewish sites in other countries outside the framework of a group tour. These travelers may take part in educational activities such as guided tours, museums, day-long seminars or may volunteer with community projects during their travelers, thus creating their own educational tour. Surveying independent travelers poses logistical challenges, as they are not as easily reached as participants in group tours. Nevertheless, studies of this sub-population would contribute to a fuller picture of Jewish educational travel.

Yet another sub-population which deserves further attention is ultra-Orthodox or *haredi* Jews. Only in recent years have *haredi* Jews begun to participate in educational travel, for example, programs offered through yeshivot or seminaries or field trips for students in haredi schools. One of the first systematic studies is being conducted by Bar Ilan MA student Ety Rehimi (2010), who is investigating the motivations for travel by haredi families and how their travels correspond to their educational and value priorities.

The ways in which Israelis learn from Jewish-Diaspora visitors deserve more research. Stronza's recommendation (2001, p. 261), that "The goal of future research should be to explore incentives and impacts for both tourists and locals throughout all stages of tourism," applies also to research on educational tourism.

Longitudinal research carried out in a variety of settings and with a variety of populations, linked by a "… viable theoretical and conceptual framework and a systematic methodological scheme," (Steinberg, 1984, p. 93) can go far in providing the data and analysis necessary to evaluate and understand what is happening in the field. It is hoped that this chapter offers some useful directions toward this cumulative goal.

Acknowledgments I would like to thank Allison Ofanansky for helping me to organize and edit this manuscript.

References

Anderson, P., Lawton, L., Rexeisen, R., & Hubbard, A. (2006). Short-term study abroad and intercultural sensitivity: A pilot study. *International Journal of Intercultural Relations, 30*(4), 457–469.

Ari, L., Mansfeld, Y., & Mittelberg, D. (2003). Globalization and the role of educational travel to Israel in the ethnification of American Jews. *Tourism Recreation Research, 28*(3), 15–24.

Arsenault, N. (2001). *Learning travel: Canadian Ed-ventures: Learning vacations in Canada: An overview* (Vol. 1). Vancouver, BC: Canadian Tourism Commission.

Ashworth, G. J. (2002). Holocaust tourism: The experience of Kraków-Kazimierz. *International Research in Geographical and Environmental Education, 11*(4), 363–367.

Auron, Y. (1994). The Holocaust and the Israeli teacher. *Holocaust and Genocide Studies, 8*(2), 225–257.

Auron, Y. (2008). *The Shoah: Central factor in Jewish-Israeli identity*. Jerusalem: The Open University Press.

Aviv, C., & Shneer, D. (2007). Traveling Jews, creating memory: Eastern Europe, Israel and the Diaspora business. In J. Gerson & D. Wolf (Eds.), *Sociology confronts the Holocaust: Memories and Identities in Jewish Diasporas* (pp. 67–83). Durham, NC: Duke University Press.

Baloglu, S., & McCleary, K. (1999). A model of destination image formation. *Annals of Tourism Research, 26*(4), 868–897.

Beech, J. (2000). The enigma of holocaust sites as tourist attractions: The case of Buchenwald. *Managing Leisure, 5*(1), 29–41.

Blair, M., Holland, J., & Sheldon, S. (Eds.). (1994). *Identity and diversity: Gender and the experience of education*. Clevedon: Multilingual Matters.

Boniface, P., & Fowler, P. (1993). *Heritage and tourism in the global village*. London: Routledge.

Boorstin, D. (1964). *The image: A guide to pseudo-events in America*. New York: Harper & Row.

Burns, P. (2005). Social identities, globalization and the cultural politics of tourism. In W. Theobald (Ed.), *Global tourism* (3rd ed., pp. 390–406). Amsterdam: Elsevier, Butterworth-Heinemann.

Carr, N. (1999). A study of gender differences: Young tourist behavior in a UK coastal resort. *Tourism Management, 20*(2), 223–228.

Cohen, E. (1979). A phenomenology of tourist experiences. *Sociology, 13*, 179–201.

Cohen, E. (1984). The sociology of tourism. *Annual Reviews in Anthropology, 10*, 373–392.

Cohen, E. (1985). The tourist guide: The origins, structure and dynamics of a role. *Annals of Tourism Research, 12*, 5–29.

Cohen, E. H. (1986). *Les volontaires Juifs de France vers Israel durant la Guerre de Kippour, contribution à l'étude des relations Israel–Diaspora*. PhD dissertation, Université de Nanterre.

Cohen, E. (1992). Pilgrimage and tourism: Convergence and divergence. In A. Morinis (Ed.), *Sacred Journeys: The anthropology of pilgrimage* (pp. 47–61). Westport, CT: Greenwood Press.

Cohen, E. H. (1999). Prior community involvement and "Israel Experience" educational tours. *Evaluation and Research in Education, 13*(2), 76–91.

Cohen, E. H. (2000). Mifgashim: A meeting of minds and hearts. *Journal of Jewish Education, 66*(1–2), 23–37.

Cohen, E. H. (2003a). Images of Israel: A structural comparison along gender, ethnic, denominational and national lines. *Tourist Studies, 3*(3), 253–280.

Cohen, E. H. (2003b). Tourism and religion: A case study—Visiting students in Israeli universities. *Journal of Travel Research, 42*(1), 36–47.

Cohen, E. H. (2004). Preparation, simulation and the creation of community: Exodus and the case of diaspora education tourism. In T. E. Coles & D. J. Timothy (Eds.), *Tourism, diasporas and space* (pp. 124–138). London: Routledge.

Cohen, E. H. (2005). *Touristes Juifs de France en 2004*. Paris and Jérusalem: AMI.

Cohen, E. H. (2006). Religious tourism as an educational experience. In D. Timothy & D. Olsen (Eds.), *Tourism, religion and spiritual journeys* (pp. 78–93). London and New York: Routledge.

Cohen, E. (2007). Authenticity in tourism studies: Aprés la lutte. *Tourism Recreation Research, 32*(2), 75–82.

Cohen, E. H. (2008a). *Youth tourism to Israel: Educational experiences of the Diaspora*. Clevedon: Channel View Publications.

Cohen, E. H. (2008b). *Educational Dark Tourism at an "In Populo" Memorial: The Case of a Seminar at the Yad Vashem Holocaust Museum in Jerusalem*. Paper presented at conference on "Heritage and Cultural Tourism: The Present and Future of the Past" at BYU Jerusalem Center for Near Eastern Studies, Jerusalem. June 19, 2008.

Cohen, E. H., & Bar Shalom, Y. (2010). Teachable moments in Jewish education: An informal approach in a reform summer camp. *Religious Education, 105*(1), 26–44.

Cohen, S. M., & Horenczyk, G. (Eds.). (1999). *National variations in Jewish identity: Implications for Jewish education*. New York: State University of New York Press.

Cohen, E. H., Ifergan, M., & Cohen, E. (2002). The *madrich*: A new paradigm in tour guiding: Youth, identity and informal education. *Annals of Tourism Research, 29*(4), 919–932.

Cohen, E. H. (in press). *Towards the development of a new scale of Jewish identity: A case study in reform, conservative and Orthodox Jewish summer camps in the US.* Ramat Gan: Lookstein Center, Bar-Ilan University.

Cohen, S., & Kotler-Berkowitz, L. (2004). *The Impact of Childhood Jewish Education on Adults' Jewish Identity: Schooling, Israel Travel, Camping and Youth Groups.* United Jewish Communities Report Series on the National Jewish Population Survey 2000–01.

Coles, T., & Timothy, D. (Eds.). (2004). *Tourism Diasporas and space: Travels to promised lands.* London: Routledge.

Comet, T. (1965). *Research findings on the effect of a summer experience in Israel on American Jewish youth.* Philadelphia, PA: AZYF.

Desforges, L. (1998). Checking out the planet: Global representations/local identities and youth travel. In T. Skelton & G. Valentine (Eds.), *Cool places: Geographies of youth cultures* (pp. 175–192). London: Routledge.

Edensor, T. (2000). Staging tourism: Tourists as performers. *Annals of Tourism Research, 27*(2), 322–344.

Erikson, E. (1959). Identity and the life cycle. *Psychological Issues, 1*(1), 1–32.

Erikson, E. (1963). *Childhood and society.* New York: W.W. Norton.

Ezrachi, E. (1994). *Encounters between American Jews and Israelis: Israelis in American Jewish Summer Camps.* Doctoral dissertation, Jewish Theological Seminary.

Feldman, J. (2001). In the footsteps of the Israeli Holocaust Survivor: Israeli youth pilgrimages to Poland, Shoah memory and national identity. In P. Daly, et al. (Eds.), *Building history: The Shoah in art, memory, and myth*, McGill European Studies Series (Vol. 4, pp. 35–63). New York: Peter Lang.

Fine, E., & Speer, J. (1985). Tour guide performances as sight sacralization. *Annals of Tourism Research, 12,* 73–95.

Gibson, H., & Yiannakis, A. (2002). Tourist roles: Needs and the lifecourse. *Annals of Tourism Research, 29,* 358–383.

Gitelman, Z., Kosmin, B., & Kovács, A. (Eds.). (2003). *New Jewish identities: Contemporary Europe and beyond* (pp. 139–158). New York: Central European University Press.

Goffman, E. (1961). *Asylums: essays on the social situation of mental patients and other inmates.* Garden City, NY: Anchor Books.

Grant, L., Kelman, N., & Regev, H. (2001). Traveling toward the self while visiting the other: Israeli TALI school educators on a US study tour. *Journal of Jewish Communal Service, 77*(3–4) 172–181.

Grant, L. (2000). *Paradoxical Pilgrimage: American Jewish Adults on a Congregational Israel Trip.* Unpublished PhD Dissertation, The Jewish Theological Seminary of America.

Greenblum, J. (1995). A pilgrimage to Germany. *Judaism, 44*(4), 478–485.

Griffith, S. (2008). *Gap years for grown-ups.* Surrey: Crimson Publishing.

Grossman, G. (2003). *Jewish museums of the world.* New York: Hugh Lauter Levin Associates.

Grossman, H., & Grossman, S. H. (1994). *Gender issues in education.* Boston: Allyn & Bacon.

Herman, S. (1962). American Jewish students in Israel: A social psychological study in cross-cultural education. *Jewish Social Studies, 34,* 3–29.

Herman, S. (1970). *American students in Israel.* Ithaca, NY: Cornell University Press.

Horowitz, T., Cialic, M., & Hodara, J. (1971). Volunteers for Israel during the six day war: Their motives and careers. *Dispersion and Unity, 13–14,* 68–115.

Ioannides, D., & Ioannides, M. (2004). Jewish past as a "foreign country": The travel experiences of American Jews. In T. Coles & D. Timothy (Eds.), *Tourism Diasporas and space: Travels to promised lands* (pp. 95–109). London: Routledge.

Ioannides, M., & Ioannides, D. (2006). Global Jewish tourism: Pilgrimages and remembrance. In D. Timothy & D. Olsen (Eds.), *Tourism, religion and spiritual journeys* (pp. 157–171). London: Routledge.

Jack, G., & Phipps, A. (2005). *Tourism and intercultural exchange: Why tourism matters.* Clevedon and Buffalo, NY: Multilingual Matters.

Jutla, R. (2006). Pilgrimage in Sikh tradition. In D. Timothy & D. Olsen (Eds.), *Tourism, religion and spiritual journeys* (pp. 206–219). London: Routledge.

Kahane, R. (1997). *The origins of postmodern youth: Informal youth movements in a comparative perspective*. New York and Berlin: Walter de Gruyter.

Katriel, T. (1993). "Our future is where our past is": Studying heritage museums as a performative and ideological arena. *Communication Monographs, 60*(1), 69–75.

Katriel, T. (1995). Touring the land: Trips and hiking as secular pilgrimages in Israeli culture. *Jewish Folklore and Ethnology Review, 17*(1/2), 6–13.

Katz, S. (1985). The Israeli teacher-guide: The emergence and perpetuation of a role. *Annals of Tourism Research, 12*, 49–72.

Kelner, S. (2002). Almost pilgrims: Authenticity, identity and the extra-ordinary on a Jewish tour of Israel. PhD dissertation, City University of New York.

Kinnaird, V., & Hall, D. (1994). *Tourism: A gender analysis*. West Sussex: Wiley.

Kosansky, O. (2002). Tourism, charity, and profit: The movement of money in Moroccan Jewish pilgrimage. *Cultural Anthropology, 17*(3), 359–400.

Kugelmass, J. (1994). Why we go to Poland—Holocaust tourism as secular ritual. In J. E. Young (Ed.), *The art of memory holocaust memorials in history* (pp. 174–184). Washington, DC: Prestel.

Laubscher, M. (1994). *Encounters with difference: Student perceptions of the role of out-of-class experiences in education abroad*. Westport, CT: Greenwood Press.

Levinas, E. (1963). *Difficile liberté, essais sur le Judaïsme*, Albin Michel. [English translation (1997). *Difficult Freedom: Essays on Judaism,* translator Seán Hand. Johns Hopkins University Press.]

Levy, A. (1997). To Morocco and back: Tourism and pilgrimage among Moroccan-born Israelis. In E. Ben-Ari & Y. Bilu (Eds.), *Grasping land: Space and Place in contemporary Israeli discourse and experience* (pp. 25–46). Albany, NY: State University of New York Press.

Lorge, M., & Zola, G. (Eds.). (2006). *A place of our own: The rise of reform Jewish camping*. Tuscaloosa, AL: University of Alabama Press.

MacCannell, D. (1976). *The tourist: A new theory of the Leisure class*. New York: Schoken Books.

MacCannell, D. (1992). *Empty meeting grounds: The tourist papers*. London: Routledge.

MacDonald, S. (2006). Mediating heritage: Tour guides at the former Nazi party rally grounds, Nuremberg. *Tourist Studies, 6*(2), 119–138.

Maoz, D. (2006). The mutual gaze. *Annals of Tourism Research, 33*(1), 221–239.

Mazumbar, S., & Mazumbar, S. (2004). Religion and place attachment: A study of sacred places. *Journal of Environmental Psychology, 24*, 385–397.

Mittelberg, D. (1985). *Volunteers in Kibbutz: Their Motives, Integration Process and Social Consequences*. Jerusalem: Ph.D. Dissertation, Hebrew University.

Moscardo, G. (1996). Mindful visitors: Heritage and tourism. *Annals of Tourism Research, 23*(2), 376–397.

Noy, C. (2002). You must go trek there—The persuasive genre of narration among Israeli *tarmila'im*. *Narrative Inquiry, 12*, 261–290.

Noy, C., & Cohen, E. (2006). *Israeli backpackers: A view from Afar*. New York: State University of New York Press.

Ohayon, S. (2004). *Students from North America in Israel: The Machon gold one-year program compared to university program*. Philadelphia, PA: Schechter Institute.

Piaget, J. (1972). Intellectual evolution from adolescence to adulthood. *Human Development, 15*(1), 1–12.

Pizam, A., Uriely, N., & Reichel, A. (2000). The intensity of tourist-host social relationship and its effects on satisfaction and change of attitudes: The case of working tourists in Israel. *Tourism Management, 21*, 395–406.

Pritchard, A., & Morgan, N. (2000). Privileging the male gaze: Gendered tourism landscapes. *Annals of Tourism Research, 27*(4), 884–905.

Rehimi, E. (2010). *Educational tourism among Sefardi Ultra-Orthodox families*, MA Thesis, School of Education, Bar Ilan University.

Reisinger, Y., & Steiner, C. (2006). Reconceptualising interpretation: The role of tour guides in authentic tourism. *Current Issues in Tourism, 9*(6), 481–498.

Reisinger, Y., & Turner, L. (2003). *Cross-cultural behaviour in tourism: Concepts and analysis*. Oxford and Boston: Butterworth-Heinemann.

Reisman, B. (1993) *Adult Education Trips to Israel, A Transforming Experience*. Jerusalem: JCC, Melitz, Melton Center for Jewish-Zionist Education in the Diaspora.

Richards, G., & Wilson, J. (2003) *New Horizons in Independent Youth and Student Travel: Summary Report*. International Student Travel Confederation (ISTC) and the Association of Tourism and Leisure Education (ATLAS).

Ritchie, B., Carr, N., & Cooper, C. (2003). *Managing educational tourism*. Clevedon and Buffalo, NY: Multilingual Matters.

Rosenfeld, A. (1997). The Americanization of the Holocaust. In A. Rosenfeld (Ed.), *Thinking about the holocaust after half a century* (pp. 119–150). Bloomington, IN: Indiana University Press.

Sales, A., & Saxe, L. (2004). *"How Goodly are Thy Tents": Summer camps as Jewish socializing experiences*. Hanover, NH: Brandeis University Press.

Sales, A. L., Saxe, L., Boxer, M., & Rosen, M. I. (2002). *"How goodly are thy tents, O Israel": Summer camps as Jewish socializing experiences*. Waltham, MA: Cohen Center for Modern Jewish Studies, Brandeis University.

Sasson, T., Mittelberg, D., Hecht, S., & Saxe, L. (2008). *Encountering the other, finding oneself: The Taglit-birthright Israel Mifgash*. Waltham, MA: Brandeis University, Cohen Center for Modern Jewish Studies.

Saxe, L., & Chazan, B. (2008). *Ten days of birthright Israel: A journey in young adult identity*. Hanover, NH: Brandeis University Press.

Senn, C. (2002). Journeying as religious education: The shaman, the hero, the pilgrim and the labyrinth walker. *Religious Education, 97*(2), 124–140.

Sered, S. (1999). Women pilgrims and woman saints: Gendered icons and the iconization of gender at Israeli Shrines. *NWSA Journal, 11*(2), 48.

Shapiro, F. (2001). Learning to be a diaspora Jew through the Israel experience. *Studies in Religion, 30*(1), 23–34.

Shulman, L. (2009). Closing remarks to the multiple identities in Jewish education conference, Jerusalem.

Singh, R. (2006). Pilgrimage in Hinduism: Historical context and modern perspectives. In D. Timothy & D. Olsen (Eds.), *Tourism, religion and spiritual journeys* (pp. 220–236). London: Routledge.

Steinberg, B. (1984). The present era in Jewish education: A global comparative perspective. *The Jewish Journal of Sociology, 26*(2), 93–109.

Stronza, A. (2001). Anthropology of tourism: Forging new ground for ecotourism and other alternatives. *Annual Review of Anthropology, 30*, 261–283.

Timothy, D., & Olsen, D. (Eds.). (2006). *Tourism, religion and spiritual journeys*. London: Routledge.

Tomasi, L. (2002). Homo Viator: From pilgrimage to religious tourism via the journey. In W. H. Swatos, Jr. & L. Tomasi (Eds.), *From medieval pilgrimage to religious tourism: The social and cultural economics of piety* (pp. 1–24). Westport, CT: Praeger.

Urry, J. (2002). *Consuming places*. London: Routledge.

Walmsley, D., & Young, M. (1998). Evaluative images and tourism: The use of personal constructs to describe the structure of destination images. *Journal of Travel Research, 36*, 65–69.

Wearing, S. (2001). *Volunteer tourism: Experiences that make a difference*. Oxon: CABI Publishing.

Wettstein, H. (Ed.). (2002). *Diasporas and exiles: Varieties of Jewish identity*. Berkeley, CA: University of California Press.

Wolf, M., & Kopelowitz, E. (2003). *Israeli staff in American Jewish summer camps: The view of the camp director*. Jerusalem: Jewish Agency for Israel.

Travel: 'Location Location Location' – A Practitioner's Perspectives on Diaspora Jewish Travel

Jeremy Leigh

Introduction

In the dark years of the recent Intifada in Israel, I was asked by a Zionist educational organization in the UK to assemble a Diaspora – based equivalent of Israel teen tours, for those unwilling or unable (due to parental opposition) to travel to Israel itself. The purpose was both simple and complex: on the one hand, to ensure that 16-year-old Jews would not lose out on the crucial summer tour experience, an accepted rites of passage for Anglo Jewish youth (simple); and, at the same time, to strive as hard as possible to fill the experience with as many of the same value messages about the Jewish People and their connection to Israel, whilst travelling in Europe and not Israel (complex). The idea of somehow 'visiting' Israel educationally, without actually physically going there may not be dissimilar to the challenges of Israel education in the Diaspora, but what complicated matters was the travel element which, in most cases, carries an expectation of actually seeing something tangible, something 'authentic'. Furthermore, this was not to be old style, unreconstructed Zionist negation of the Diaspora, with its fixation on the dangers of Jewish life in the Diaspora. Without being too vulgar, Israel was still to come out on top, the central focus of the Jewish world.

In essence, the planned 'non-Israel–Israel tours' represented a battle between the authority of the narrative versus that of the location. Such was the importance of the narrative that the sites played second fiddle to it since the story somehow had to be told. There were certainly some interesting locations to be utilised: Spain to look at successes and failures of Diaspora life, as well as the crucial component of 'exile'; a cluster of Herzl and early Zionist sites such as Paris (Dreyfus), Vienna (anti-Semitism) and Basle (First Zionist Congress) were also entertained as possibilities. It was agreed that all programmes were to finish by a port, symbolically

---

J. Leigh (✉)
Hebrew Union College, Jerusalem, Israel
e-mail: nikgem@netvision.net.il

In memory of Elly Dlin z"l (1953–2010), my teacher, colleague and friend who inspired many of the ideas in this article.

looking to board the ship we could not take to Israel. Collectively, we were to be Moses, looking out to the land, 'seeing' it from afar but unable to enter.

The complicated guidelines set for this unusual programme notwithstanding, the project as a whole was not without merit. It provided yet further proof of just how deeply travel and 'educational journeys' have penetrated educational practice, to the extent that it was worth twisting sites to match the story. It would have been intriguing to contrast the presentation of the same sites with the approach employed on 'hybrid' tours that combine both Diaspora and Israel travel. In these models, the stopover in Europe en route to Israel offers the chance for a similarly constructed Israel-centred narrative. Yet, in actual fact, educators on such programmes tend to skirt the controversies of the Israel–Diaspora relationship, preferring to concentrate a seamless description of history.

Personally, the true value of the 'non-Israel'–Israel tour episode was the prompt it gave to confront core issues that form the basis of this chapter: (1) In what ways can focussed travel to Diaspora Jewish sites draw on or inspire connections to feelings of Jewish interconnectedness and Peoplehood? (2) What other aspects of the identity matrix are most easily visible and accessible through travel to sites of Jewish interest?

Narrative: Peoplehood

In visiting the sites of Jewish past and present, Jews allow themselves the opportunity to connect with the large and powerful story of Peoplehood. This idea is described in more poetic terms by the contemporary Israeli educator Ari Elon in his attempt to connect history and identity. 'Who is a Jew?' asks Elon, 'A Jew is anyone who looks at himself or herself in the mirror of history and sees a Jew' ('From Jerusalem to the Edge of Heaven', JPS, 1996). This simple statement is a powerful building block of the Peoplehood narrative and can be extended in so many ways. In travel terms, the 'mirror of history' is the site, and the act of looking is the 'tourist gaze'.

Tourism too can be an exercise in *self*-recognition, whereby the visitor is able to recognise and even identify with the Jewish drama contained in the site. To a certain type of Ashkenazi traveller, a German synagogue is easily recognisable, reflecting the familiar idea of a synagogue and all that it represents, from back home. The further afield one goes with the sites, the greater the challenge for recognition – what of a Moroccan synagogue, a small Polish *shtiebel*, or simply a stone cellar, as in the case of the excavated medieval synagogue below the streets of Barcelona? For some, brought up in Moroccan synagogues or tiny *shtielblekh*, the cathedral-sized synagogues of Central Europe are no less challenging. Yet throughout, s/he is seeking of a reflection in the familiar mirror of the site.

Needless to say, nothing is that straightforward. Issues of recognition stir up the thorny problem of non-recognition as well. On the one hand, the educator is offering the chance to 'meet' or encounter the personalities and events of the past, by visiting the sites that represent them. However, do they genuinely recognise each other?

I may take a group to visit the sites of Rashi in Mainz and Worms, to somehow 'bring him to life'. However, what if we knew that the same Rashi would struggle to recognise me, the teller of his story, a Reform Jew of the twenty-first century? What if the tourist sees neither her own reflection in the life, character or outlook of Rashi? How do we create a dialogue? Acknowledging the potential for Jewish travel to emphasise the broad notion of Jewish Peoplehood is not sufficient. More useful is to ask what are some of the sub-elements of the Peoplehood narrative that can be supported by travel journeys? Furthermore, what pedagogic strategies are necessary to make the project work? I offer this question as an entry point to the following reflections from the field, all of which are illustrated by reference to case studies (locations).

History/The Past

More than anything else, Jewish travel programmes traverse the pathways of 'history', visiting locations that seamlessly move participant and guide alike up and down the Jewish historical timeline. For better or worse, in most cases sites mean 'where something once happened', and even present tense locations, such as contemporary communities, are often seen as add-ons to assist connectivity between the present and the past. For educators this is anything but straightforward since the past is not an easy domain to navigate. For one thing, history is not necessarily a subject that excites and inspires contemporary younger generations in the way it did previous generations. I am aware, for instance, that visits to former Communist countries speak differently to adults than to teenagers, for whom the Cold War is school book history and not personal life history. The fact is that the past is not all it used to be, so to speak. Post-modernism has successfully managed to deconstruct and relativise most things to the point that history is a battleground for competing versions of constructed narratives.

In many ways, the notion of 'history' and the interest in the past was always an outgrowth of ideology, where the reading and construction of history provided a necessary validation for present-day understandings and actions. So much of Israel tourism, for instance, was founded on the projection of Zionist values – 'our' connection to the land, the projection of a Jewish history that has the Land of Israel as a central pivot with the inevitable journey homewards.

To deepen the understanding of the significance and potential for educational travel, I offer three possible models for presenting the past:, for talking at the sites where the story of our People is seen: (1) documentary and informational ('this arch is from the Roman Period'); (2) collective memory ('here we all stand where our ancestors stood'); and (3) dialogical ('in what way does this building connect with who we are?').

Documentary/Informational

The standard practice of many (most?) travel programmes I have observed is to emphasise vast quantities of knowledge. Guides, including the most accomplished, entertaining and engaging, invest energy in conveying quantities of information deemed necessary for the experience to be complete. This need not be dry facts and certainly does not preclude the telling of stories, but the purpose is to increase the body of knowledge conveyed. This is the 'great books' approach in which students are required to have acquired the canonised volumes and remembered their contents.

I mention this mode specifically, since as a practitioner I am aware that many participants are convinced that this is what they seek in travel journeys – to be shown things that are interesting, the sorts of things for which guide book are written. I recall the anger of a woman who complained after a lengthy discussion by the site of the non-existent Berlin Wall that she was fed up with discussion, with hearing other participants talk, 'when are you (the guide) going to tell us something? When is the sightseeing going to begin?'.

At its most mundane, this approach is witnessed in the faces of dazed tourist herded around archaeological ruins or museums as gallons of raw unfiltered information about things they neither understand nor care about are poured over them. At its most impressive this is the picture of eagerly attentive tourists walking around the same site, with a different guide alert to the thrilling knowledge being revealed to them at each stone and every exhibit. Again, whether requested or not, the information is valued. This approach is supported via the 'official' interpreters of sites, graduates of guiding courses whose exams test the degree to which future site – professionals have swallowed the library.

Collective Memory/'Standing Before the over Powering Edifice of History'

In this mode, the past is not merely a body of knowledge but a real and living memorial. The mere telling of the story is a type of living monument, replete with meanings and demands on the visitor from the present. Attention should be drawn to the 'collective' as much as the 'memory'. In this mode, the visitor is not alone but part of a great collective or community, connecting past and present. Significantly, however, it is not a democratic collective, since the 'we' of the present is being looked down upon from the 'they' of the past. It is as if to say, 'we' live in 'their' shadow, of all that has gone before us.

This approach has strong relationship to the world of ideologies, which similarly imagines the accumulated collective past experiences as the proof of the ideology. Typically, national movements venerate sites of collective dramas such as political struggle (Dublin's 1916 Post Office Uprising Monument), catastrophes (battle sites) and the significant sites of ideological heroes (Lenin's mausoleum in Moscow; Chmielnicki's statue in Kiev). The visitors, assuming they are members of the tribe, the agreed communities of belief or meaning, become pilgrims joining the project of communal national memory.

In some cases the narrative of collective memory is confused, exposing dissonances between competing collective communities. James E. Young draws our attention to this in his classic work on Holocaust memorials and in particular the convoluted approaches of the Auschwitz curators in choosing a monument to stand at the end of the railway tracks in Birkenau (Young, 1993). The clash between the communities of Polish state-sponsored socialism, the 'survivors', and an assumed humanity all made for a confused but nevertheless theoretical collective memory. Far more successful is the powerful edifice of Nathan Rapaport's statue that stands at the centre of Yad Vashem. The contrast between powerless Jews of the Diaspora is contrasted with the heroism of the fighting Jew thus acting as an inspiration for present-day Israelis.

The primary example of this mode in action as a full-blown travel programme can be seen in the thousands of people who march through Auschwitz in the annual March of the Living parade. They are not necessarily offered a chance for talking back, but they are most definitely being invited to feel the drama of the historical site. Speeches are delivered, poems are recited and ceremonies completed. Indeed, they ritualise the moment by re-enactment. Standing beneath the shadow of history they are asked to accept its full weight as an act of national responsibility.

Dialogue

Finally, in this mode, we recognise that the site is but one, albeit crucial element in the educational moment of travel. It is joined by the participants and the guide to develop a conversation of meaning and interpretation. In place of the received truth, the participant may seek a truth through their own investigations, by listening, talking and reading. It is possible that some elements may indeed remain sacred but this is not guaranteed. For example, Jewish visitors to Auschwitz are not asked to judge the Jews who were once inmates, or indeed anyone from that time. However, in discussing the thorny question of meaning and interpretation, participants must be able to speak, offer opinions and interpretations of what took place in the camp. The visitor is not obliged to only listen passively to details of the site and its working, nor to recite a pre-written credo of the significance of the site and its message for the future, but to engage in a conversation. Let me offer two examples of this in action drawn from two different parts of the Jewish world.

Volubilis

Sitting in the shade of a tree by the elaborate Roman archaeological site at Volubilis, Morocco, we wished to draw attention to the discovery of a Hebrew shard found many years ago, establishing a second-century connection with the site. A bare mountain, Roman columns and richly preserved mosaics, whilst theoretically impressive only go so far in sparking the imagination. The activity thus focussed on the dilemmas of the second-century Diaspora Jew who may have passed through Volubilis, seeking to understand their mental world and by extension, to find some points of connectivity. The site itself was the perfect expression of 'walking in the footsteps of history' but what if the walk was boring, too distant or meaningless?

We experimented with two activities, both focussing on the period, 50 years after the destruction of the Second Temple. The first activity simply posed one question to be considered by participants, namely 'what advice would you give from the vantage of point of the present to the Jews of second-century Volubilis?' (regarding how to live their lives). In so doing, we wished to establish a dialogue across time, and, at the same time, humanise the face of the historical interlocutor. Inevitably, the advice tended to focus on issues of cultural identity, strategies for survival, suggestions for religious development and warnings about political relationships with the ruling powers.

The second activity offered specific principles to be prioritised and debated as the survival plan for Jewish life in light of the circumstances of second-century Diaspora life. These were all familiar ideas designed to illustrate commonalities across time, including: developing dietary laws to encourage social segregation; investment in Jewish education; prioritising projects to remember the Temple; building strong bonds with Jews in others' Diaspora communities, etc. In short, neither activity may be regarded as site-specific and yet both brought the present-day dilemma to a specific time and place. Most crucially, however, the subsequent tour of Roman mosaics and columns took on a different context entirely. The miracle of surviving colourful patterns in stone and architectural fashions of the Roman empire could be contrasted with their own appreciation of the site, now as 'insiders', modern-day Jews visiting Volubilis, sharing in the discussion of the legacy contained therein.

Kiev

In the August 2006, as Hizbollah katyusha rockets rained down on the north of Israel, we travelled to Kiev and St. Petersburg. Standing in the square in the old Jewish suburb of Podol, we recalled the famous pogrom that had occurred in the early years of the twentieth century. The appropriate text chosen was the powerful and iconic poem by Chaim Nachman Bialik, 'In the City of Slaughter', not because it was composed in Kiev but because its ideas were as relevant to Podol as they were to Kishinev, from where Bialik had taken his inspiration. In the poem, Bialik famously rounded on the passivity of the Jews in the face of a murderous enemy. The participants listened as the poem was read and one by one, to the last person, related it to its contemporary message – how does one deal with vilification and attack in present times. What conclusions can one draw about history when Jews are still attacked? What if the Jews are vilified by western liberals and not pogromists? Are the rules different now that the Jews have their own state? Indeed, are there limits to the powerful Jew that Bialik so sought? The implicit conclusion throughout was that whilst Kiev and Podol were important and atmospheric, from the visitors point of view, they were also necessary backdrops for a conversation about issues more immediate.

Concluding this focus on the core issue of the past and its variant models of expression, I wish to emphasise that these modes for visiting sites and recalling the story of the Jews need not be mutually exclusive. It can be argued that without a significant knowledge, without information, there can be no intelligent dialogue. Similarly, not every site is about the 'I', the subject of many dialogues, but the 'we' of collective memory.

Furthermore, the concentration on the past is only one of the building blocks for discussing Peoplehood. Beyond mediating the past (through any of the above approaches) there are other key values that equally comprise core elements arising from the Jewish travel experience: 'sense of place', 'community', 'culture', 'mutuality' and 'self-awareness'.

Place

Yehuda Amichai writes,

> That's why they [Jews] are so dead, and why they call their God *Makom,* 'Place'.
> And now that they have returned to their place, the Lord has taken up wandering to different places, and His name will no longer be Place but Places, Lord of the Places.
> (From 'Jewish Travel', Yehuda Amichai, 'Open Closed Open' Harcourt 2002)

There could be no greater encounter with the Jewish People's complex understanding of place than through travel since, by definition, the educational conversation questions the rootedness of any community, very often offsetting it against an imagined or real Jewish homeland. Indeed, 'Peoplehood' terms such as 'homeland' and 'Diaspora' represent values as much as they do locations. Therefore, the more Jews visit the locations of Jewish history, the greater the confrontation with the meaning of this term. Are the Jews a static people, defined by and always aspiring to be part of a particular place? Or are they wanderers, always seeking a place but never believing it is permanent? In what way does the search for a place change the persona of the Jews themselves?

Venice

There are probably few places so well defined as 'the place of the Jews' as the late medieval Ghetto in Venice. Complicated explanations of its founding notwithstanding, it is the example par excellence of 'place'. But how does one keep finding sites when there are only two streets, a square and five synagogues all of which are closed to the public except when on the 45-min guided tour provided by the museum?

Our entry point for the Venetian Jewish journey was the pier by the Palazzo Ducale and St. Marks overlooking the lagoon and out to sea. We begin this Jewish journey in Venice by consciously choosing a 'non-Jewish site' that seems to sum up the complex meanings of the place. We recall the following local Venetian custom – every year on the second Sunday of May, Venetians gather opposite the church of San Nicolo on the Lido to witness the throwing of a gold ring into the seas around them. In so doing, they continue a ceremony begun on Ascension Day in the year 1000 when Doge Pietro Orseolo II set sail to defeat the Dalmatian pirates who had harried the merchants of Venice. Formalised in 1177, the ceremony became known as 'sposalizio del mare', or the 'Marriage [of Venice] to the Sea' and provides an important starting point in the presentation and discussion of this unique city. Perched precariously on the edge of the sea, Venice is a place defined by insecurity.

What then, we ask, of the Jews and their ghetto perched precariously on the edge of someone else's society, relying on goodwill and partial utility to stop themselves from being thrown out into the sea of wandering? It would seem that Jews, like Venetians have insecurities about where they belong and how they can put down roots. It is interesting therefore that the inhabitants of the ghetto were divided into 'schools' defined by 'place' – the Italian, the Spanish, the Levantine, the 'Canton' and the German.

In the collective memory mode, the ghetto of Venice is a story of exclusion, a special place for Jews which seems to reinforce the yearning to be somewhere else. Yet the 'dialogical' offers a more complex reading wherein it is apt to question notions of 'inside' and 'outside'. At the ghetto's entrance, the crossing point separating being in and out we read Chad Gadya, the short story by Israel Zangwill telling of the first generation of Jews after the gates were torn down and Jews allowed to live where they wish. The modern and emancipated Jew of the outside returns to see his father on the evening of Pesach and is haunted by the patriarch's stubborn refusal to leave the psychological and cultural ghetto. Torn between the two seemingly irreconcilable worlds, he drowns himself in the waters of the Grand Canal. We achieved two goals, one pedagogic, the use of a story relating directly to where we physically stood, and, at the same time, a text that commented on the wider symbolic value of place that we are all part, i.e. where do we survive better, in the rooted and exclusively 'Jewish' quarter or to navigate the complex waters of modernity outside?

The group of 25 adults showed genuine interest in understanding the fortunes of Venetian Jewry and why its ghettoisation was not, initially at least, a hardship. Its place in the collective memory seemed straightforward as the symbolism of exclusion par excellence. Yet we sought to open this conversation about the true meaning of being somewhere; inevitably, the real discussion became one about the relative comfort and warmth found in the many informal ghettos of today. Venice quickly became a discussion of everywhere but Venice.

Community

Tourists on the highways of Jewish history may ask themselves what are the commonalities that unite the people across time and place? Faith? Culture? Yearning for another place? Community?

By drawing attention to the value of community, we see a micro version of the Peoplehood ideal, namely, that Jews bind themselves to each other for the purpose of self-expression, to share the travails of life and to support and share – they discover themselves as a group and in relation to each other. Community seems the most identifiable connecting point between all periods and locations, since without community, there is no Jewish People, only Jewish people.

Larissa (Greece)

I offer the example of Larissa, making no claim for its exclusive ability to represent the idea of 'community', but simply because it was a highlight – a deep and visceral expression of a community in action. Our Greek Jewish journey went from Salonika to Athens via Veria, Volos, Chalkis stopping in Larissa for Shabbat. Three of those communities have roots going back at least 2,000 years but the marvel was found in Larissa, a community of the present, noticeably decimated by the Holocaust and more recently by inter-marriage. Yet, we witnessed scenes of thriving and interconnected community life

The scene is easily recognisable, beginning in synagogue with fully vocal prayer (with no special illusions about the meaning of prayer except as a 'communal activity that we do' as it was explained); a communal meal with more singing; complete with a special table set aside for the 20 excitable younger members of the community; and the obvious sense of pride contained within this community. There was lots of *spanakopita* and ouzo, much enthusiasm for our company despite almost no common language. The hosts were impressed that we could offer someone to chant a chapter of Song of Songs and the visitors were impressed that they knew almost none of the melodies yet managed to join in. No-one seemed bothered by the laxer than lax approach to gender separated seating. Consistently, it seemed, the Larissa Jewish story was one of interconnectedness and community solidarity. People were proud of their insider-ship. The visitors were impressed that with a community no bigger than a few hundred it managed to express such strong bonds of interconnectedness. In the mirror of Larissa they tried to see themselves.

Leeds

In a totally different frame altogether, I was asked to lead a Jewish tour of Leeds, in the north of England, which was advertised to the Leeds Jewish community. I had been to Leeds twice in my life and so set about reading furiously of its roots, historical past and sociological present, the ups and downs of its relations with the local community and with itself. I learnt about the story of its Jewish schools, its leaders, youth movements, social clubs and sports teams. In a short time, I was an 'expert' in Leeds Jewry!

Throughout the tour, I was in 'knowledge' mode, after all it is the members of the community who share collective memory, not I. Against the backdrop of my faulty commentary, the participants conversed with each other, recalling the past and arguing passionately about the present. Few wished to address the thorny issue of the future. As well as being a case book example of dialogical education through travel, it was also a full-throated discussion of the meaning of community. Everyone was an insider (except me) and the conversation was largely about the sense of 'us'. This brief tour was quite different from the conventional 'journey', never quite leaving home. Yet in 3 h, the community discussed itself.

Culture

I recall the bizarre moment when, standing by a glass case containing 'tallitot' (prayer shawls) in the exhibition in Auschwitz I, one guide asked the group of attentive blue-shirted Israeli youth-movement members, if they all knew what they were looking at. There were not an insignificant number of embarrassed shrugs. The fact that the journey to Poland, to a death camp of all places is what draws a keen and committed member of the Jewish People to recognise or even simply learn about what many would argue are basic symbols of Jewish religious or cultural life is not something to be taken lightly.

In a different context, I recall the enthusiastic desire by a group of solidly Ashkenazi adults determined to go all out to learn a Ladino rendition of 'Ein Keloheinu' in order that their journey to Salonika be made more authentic.

In both cases, the travel journey presented examples and opportunities for confronting core, even profound moments of cultural experience. In one, the awkwardness of cultural unfamiliarity was the catalyst for change. In the second, there was no embarrassment only a thirst for something more, something intrinsically Jewish but outside their own cultural experience. Ultimately, both were important experiences that reinforced expressions of Peoplehood.

Morocco

We assemble around the site, the grave of one of the Abuhatzera rabbis near the desert town of Erfoud and begin the process of explaining the meaning of Moroccan Jewish veneration of saints and the Hiloula (pilgrimage). We begin by performing some of the rituals. I recite a selection of 'qasida' poem-prayers in honour of the saint whose grave we stand by. A glass of 'mahia' is produced to be auctioned to the highest bidder who will thereby receive the blessing of the saint. The group erupts into righteous indignation at the thought that this custom, central to Moroccan Jewish culture, should be taken seriously by 'people like us'.

Nearby, other Jews are praying furiously with pictures of those whose illness may be cured by the intervention of the saint concerned. The chief prayer is a man dressed exactly like 'people like us', and his commitment to restoring the health of his loved ones is impressive. The group is confused and disturbed, although unsure if they are displaying an unacceptable level of western/Ashkenazi/middle class/cultural superiority or if they still wish to associate with a Judaism that allows the veneration of saints.

The conclusion of this encounter is that travel showcases the world of culture and exposes all who come in its path. What really is Jewish culture? What is Jewish about Jewish culture?

Prague

The Jewish Museum offers an all inclusive ticket gaining entry to a variety of synagogues and the famous Old Cemetery. As one moves from site to site, the museum shares its displays of artefacts saved and preserved from the turbulent past. The museum attempts to present the totality of Jewish Prague via its exhibits. I am loathe to 'guide' museums since they speak well enough for themselves and are best simply discussed at the end. Discussion comes to rest, ironically on the least 'Prague' exhibit, namely, the open text of a seventeenth-century Tanach printed in the city. Its significance lies in the fact that it is the most recognisable of all Jewish artefacts – the layout of the page, the Hebrew letters, commentaries, and of course, the meaning of the text itself. This 'site' epitomises the culture of Peoplehood. Its very familiarity reinforces the point all the more powerfully since in theory one does not need to be in Prague to see the text. The text is, as others have pointed out, the 'portable homeland' of the Jewish People, and by definition its cultural hallmark. I wonder how that would go down with the 'non-Israel–Israel tour'? It suggests that a battle exists between the physical currency of places versus the spiritual currency of language and text.

Mutuality

In the simplest of forms, the question in this Peoplehood value centres around the oft-quoted adage, *Kol Yisrael Areivim Ze Baze* (all Israel is responsible for one another). I am intrigued to discover if there is a way of representing this through sites and discussion?

Budapest

We are by the site of the medieval synagogue on Tanhacs Mihaly Street on the Castle Hill in Budapest, and tell the story of the community caught on the Turkish side of the Austrian siege of the city in 1686. We are back in history, in the 'knowledge' mode and explaining how the Jews found life under Muslim Turkish rule preferable to that under Christianity. This explains their willingness to take up arms for the Turks to keep the Austrian Catholics out. Yet, as the Austrians broke through, a massacre took place in the synagogue and very quickly our re-telling shifts to the mode of collective memory – the possibility of reciting prayers for the dead and linking this tragedy to many other similar ones from the past. What room is there for the dialogue? In what way does the site invite a conversation? The answer is to be found in the far less famous story of Sender Tausk, an Austrian Jew who was present at the time and intervened with the victorious Austrian authorities after the massacre was over. Seeing the scores of dead Jews in the synagogue and the several hundred in hiding, Tausk stepped up to the plate of history, seeking permission to bury the dead and gain a release for the newly captured Jews. Agreeing upon a price with the Austrians and offering himself and his family as a deposit, he sought to raise the necessary money from around the Jewish world to redeem the captives of Buda. Thus we open the dialogue.

We have the commitment to the mitzvah of 'pidyon shvuim' offered up at this site as a primary case of Jewish solidarity and mutuality. What of its contemporary relevance? The conversation easily picks up steam as participants pose the tough questions: What are the limits of Jewish mutual solidarity? How reactive or able are communities to respond to similar calls? (the example offered is of the 13 Iranian Jews sentenced to death for alleged espionage charges for Israel). How has the passing of time and the emergence of modern Jewish identities altered the basic terms of mutuality? The site establishes a dialogue with another cluster of sites, in Paris, that tell the story of Napoleon's questions to the Assembly of Notables, how does Jewish inter – responsibility contradict other responsibilities such as to fellow citizens?

The last example leads to a re-run of an oft-repeated conversation on the Jewish tourist trail, the limits of identity – it parallels questions of the responsibility of Jews to recall other victims of oppression, as well as the responsibility of Jews to fight for the countries of their citizenship. Indeed, the very same conversation re-emerges later the next day by the Heroes Synagogue built as a memorial to Budapest Jews who fought for the Empire in the First World War. We recall the account by Ansky of the Jews who emerge from their trenches on the eastern front firing at the enemy only to discover at the moment of death, they have killed a fellow Jew. They die in each other's arms declaring 'Shema Yisrael'.

The ability of Jewish travel sites to stir up deep emotions of mutual solidarity is a likely consequence of Diaspora-based travel where issues of identity are so much to the fore. The flip side of the Peoplehood – mutuality narrative is the charge of dual loyalty. The final discussion at the Heroes Synagogue turns to the story of Jonathan Pollard, an American Jew accused and imprisoned for spying for Israel and the 'dialogue' soon disintegrates into a shouting match.

Self-awareness: Looking Inwards/Outwards

In purely theoretical terms, this concept is not really a sub-value of Peoplehood or a narrative; however, the point I wish to emphasise is that self-awareness and relationship with the outside world is about as pivotal for group identity as anything else mentioned here. If there is one overriding experience of travel common to almost every tourist, it is awareness that 'who I am' is happening continuously throughout the journey. Food, manners, conversation, body language, etc. almost everything that the locals do reminds the traveller of how they do it differently and who 'they' are in relation to 'us'.

Berlin: (Siegersauller)

This towering edifice is a powerful emblem of Prussian militarism, a symbol of late nineteenth-century nationalism and national conflict. Constructed largely out of French cannons, and pock marked with bullet hole from the 1945 Battle of Berlin, the monument seems ironic given the turbulent fortunes of German nationalism in the twentieth century. Theoretically, it is a classic German collective memory site – for Jews it is an opportunity to reflect on the subject of nationalism, citizenship and identity.

Participants arrive at the site via one of the four dark subways that go underneath the busy road. As we walk in half darkness, I play music from a portable CD player, selected specifically to expose the national identity of the group – Land of Hope and Glory/Three Lions/Vindaloo (British), Star Spangled Banner (the USA); Hatikvah (Israeli), etc. The purpose is to engage participants with a variety of familiar and yet powerful symbols of identity. As the participants reach the bottom of the underground stairs leading to the monument, they look directly up at the towering monument above them. On one occasion we set up national flags to welcome them as they emerge into the light so that all that could be seen was a line of bunting, the towering Siegersauler and the sky.

Why put the participants through this ordeal? First to generate a dialogue with the site before we fully experience it. Second, in order to offer the site as an expression of 'our' exclusion and by definition as a trigger to an array of related questions: Why are nationalist monuments so powerful? Could this have 'worked' for Berlin Jews in the late nineteenth century? Is there a model of national identity that nevertheless seeks out inclusivity instead of exclusivity?

Predictably, certain participants are bothered by the activity for, matters of politeness aside, they fear how it is perceived by other visitors to the site.

Sites

I was once party to a conversation discussing the possibility of replacing actual visits to Israel, summer teen tours that would simply drive around the Ring Road around London. Madrichim would lead the participants in games and songs, hormones would successfully express themselves; there could be time to get off for the occasional swimming trip, campfire, shopping mall or night activity. The centre of gravity on such tours is so inward-looking, it was argued, that the reality of actually being in Israel is often disregarded and the primary site was the group itself. Ridiculous though this idea was, it focuses attention on the significance of sites themselves. What is the nature of the site and how does it work alongside the experience?

Frustratingly, the standard international Jewish travel guides and most local or single country volumes all seem to be involved in a conspiracy to define Jewish sites in the narrowest of terms. Constructing interesting and engaging journeys using the standard 'synagogue, cemetery and memorial' approach seem a guaranteed strategy for an uncreative experience. A better understanding is needed of the nature of sites themselves. For this I offer four models described below.

Sites Where 'It' Happened

This ought to be the easiest category since who will argue with history that 'it' took place there. If Ferrant Martinez did eventually incite against the Jews from the pulpit of Seville's Cathedral then surely, it is a site of great value. In a parallel category are the great rivers of Europe, the Rhine, Vistula, Tiber, etc. all of which have their Jewish stories. The Rhine transported the pioneers of early Ashkenaz to their new homes in Mainz and Worms. Such was the Jewish trade on the Vistula that Sholem Asch described it as the 'river that sang in Yiddish'. Jewish slaves disembarked from the Tiber after their exile in the first century. This category is probably longer than the sum of all the synagogues and cemeteries and it is the task of the creative educator to find them.

People as Sites

The programme in Larissa illustrated a compelling truth regarding travel as an educational instrument, namely, that some of the most powerful sites are in fact people. 'People as site' is a powerful expression of the dialogical potential of Jewish travel, since the one thing you can do with a person better than with a building or memorial is to talk to them! The spontaneous encounters with people are the essence of a truly educational travel since they demand openness and the immediate ability to squeeze until a good story comes out. In Larissa, an elderly man hobbled his way over to us from across the streets, recognising us as Jews. Within seconds we had learned that he had hidden a few local Jews in the war and that his brother had been executed for that crime. Our tears were rolling before his and the encounter was indelibly etched in the mind of all. Similarly, there is no-one in Sarajevo that does not have a story to tell about ethnic identity and the horrors of war; no-one over the age of 25 in St. Petersburg that cannot say something about life under Communism; no-one in Paris that does not have an opinion about multiculturalism, religious apparel in schools and the implication for identity.

Blindingly obvious it may be, but 'people as sites' is a principle more often honoured in the breach. For many years, groups visiting Jewish Poland rarely approached the tiny Polish-Jewish community for fear of upsetting the narrative of total and utter destruction. The voice of those trying to reconstruct something amidst the ruins did not seem to fit with the 'destruction to redemption' messages of most trips since 'redemption' was supposed to take place elsewhere, not in Poland. Equally insidious was the antipathy towards meeting local Poles, since for many programme organisers and guides, there was a startling inability to distinguish between 1940s German or Austrian murderers and 1990s inquisitive Poles. With the passing of time, some attitudes have changed and Poles, Jew and gentile have come into focus, at least for some.

Invisible Sites

The great conundrum of Jewish travel, must surely be to assess what is the permissible ratio of visible sites to invisible ones? For some this is at its greatest in Holocaust sites – the seven streets of the Vilna Jewish quarter that mean nothing now that there are no Jews. For others the great challenge must surely be Spain where the story is so much larger than the sites available to show it. Five hundred years of not being there inevitably takes its toll on the visibility of Jewish sites, leaving a handful of buildings and some street plaques saying 'Juderia'.

Symbolically, Jewish travel involves much virtual archaeology, which, in educational terms, means creating a picture in the mind or convincing the audience that even though it may not feel that way, the land they are standing on really is 'sacred'. Stripping away the layers of an outwardly mundane appearance and replacing it with jewels of intrigue. In other cases the invisibility is the story itself. The gall that allows the Aristotle University of Salonika to stand on the remains of the largest Jewish cemetery in Europe, destroyed by the Nazis and built over by modern Greeks, is impressive in a macabre sort of way. The absence of a sign or plaque only adds to the drama of the site.

'Jewish' and 'Non-Jewish' Sites/Looking Through Jewish Eyes

It is not post-modernism gone mad to assert that the boundaries that separate Jewish sites and non-Jewish ones need not be defined by formal and standardised definitions. Few would argue with the idea of synagogues and cemeteries as solidly Jewish sites. What then of churches (in general or specific churches in particular) or indeed any site that has implications for the Jews? The Sistine Chapel, for instance, maybe the high point of renaissance art, but it is also a theological manifesto in which Jews cannot really be neutral on.

Conclusion: Modelling an Alternative Narrative

By way of conclusion I offer an alternative model for Jewish travel, one not fixated on Peoplehood yet no less Jewish.

In the searing heat of a Bosnian summer, I had the opportunity to open a Jewish travel programme on the slopes of a Jewish cemetery overlooking the beautiful city of Sarajevo. I drew attention to how this cemetery built by Spanish Jewish refugees in the sixteenth century had been the front line in the recent Balkan war. My story continued by explaining how, in 1992, Serbian militia had fired down onto the city from one side of the cemetery wall whilst Bosnian Muslims returned fire from the other. Caught in the crossfire, Hebrew inscribed tombstones were left pockmarked from bullets, whilst small holes in the ground showed where landmines had recently been cleared. Some of the graves were those of long deceased Sabbateans, who had died centuries ago still believing that the Messiah had in fact come to banish conflict and restore the light of God to the world. It was, by any stretch of the imagination a powerful site, bursting with symbolism with a rich seam of educational possibilities: the parallel Jewish and gentile experience of displacement and war; the timeless nature of conflict; the ambiguous position of Jews and their story in the memory landscape of Europe; the role of present-day visitors/witnesses in the search for ethnic reconciliation ... etc. And this was only the first site of what was to be a 9-day journey.

Later that evening we met with Tzisko, the cook from the small Sarajevo Jewish community centre who recalled how during the recent war local Jews joined together with international Jewish aid agencies to activate La Benevolencia, a non-partisan humanitarian aid programme to assist people of all national and religious identities. By the war's end, tens of thousands had been fed, cared for or evacuated by the efforts of the Jews. Significantly, La Benevolencia had swung into action in 1992, the year that Sarajevo Jewry joined together with world wide Jewry to commemorate 500 years since their ancestors, together with Muslims were expelled from Catholic Spain.

Sarajevo, its Jews, sites and stories were brimming over with symbolism; just waiting it seemed for an educational interpreter or filter. What was the narrative? On the one hand, it seemed this was the story of a community whose historical experience as refugees and immigrants contrasted so powerfully with its success integrating into the multi-ethnic landscape of the Balkans. In specific terms, it was an illustration of the powerful sense of Jewish ethnos that became so visible in the terrible days of the ethnic conflict that overwhelmed the area in the early 1990s. In short, a narrative of Jewish history, identity, and Jewish–Gentile relations. On the other hand, maybe there was something more, not merely a story of Jews against an overpowering backdrop of ethnic violence? Maybe this was emblematic of 'history' itself, and the inexhaustible impact of conflict

Over 9 days, the group travelled to Mostar, Dubrovnik and onto Zagreb, via the ancient Jewish centre in Split/Soline and the former Croatian death camp at Jasenovac. Site after site, it became clearer that the Sarajevo cemetery experience had merely been an overture for a longer and deeper journey that continually collided with those meta themes of 'history' and 'conflict'. Sarajevo was after all the city where the 'history' of the twentieth century began, by the bridge where Gavrillio Princip shot Archduke Ferdinand in 1914, triggering the First World War. Through this small expression of conflict, the history of the world was changed forever. We took a few minutes to discuss the forbidden question, 'what if it had not happened...?' Or put differently, what history has changed as a result of the First World War?

Site after site, the narrative explained itself. In Sarajevo's National Museum we peered through the protective glass shielding the famous Sarajevo Hagaddah, an original manuscript brought over by Spanish exiles, from the harmful and unfiltered light of the present. The Hagaddah, having escaped Spain, had to be hidden by local Muslims, in bank vaults and other such adventures, to ensure its survival through the Nazi occupation and the recent Serbian siege. The artefact was itself the story of slavery to freedom.

In Mostar, we sat with the head of the community whose grandson and husband were both victims of the recent war and who in spite of everything, and the fact that there are no more than 40 Jews in Mostar, was determined to look optimistically to the future. Despite having the highest level of intermarriage between Serbs, Croats and Bosniaks, Mostar endured total war and mass death. In pedagogic terms, it was here that we studied powerful *midrashim* concerning Cain and Abel, seated by the rebuilt bridge that had once united the different sides of the community.

In Split, the group visited the Jewish cemetery whose prayer hall is now a trendy café whose owners look after the key. It was here that we were on the receiving end of not so latent Croatian anti-Semitism, a series of insults hurled freely and without embarrassment by a middle-aged and respectable-looking man in his fifties. The following day, we were unable to visit the museum at the death camp of Jasenovac where over one hundred thousand Serbs were murdered by Croats since it was a national holiday in Croatia, commemorating with pride, the far more recent expulsion of Serbs from Croatia in the 1990s. The flag of present-day Croatia, containing amongst other things the emblem of the murderous Ustasha party of the 1940s, fluttered above us as we sat in the killing fields, studying our text.

On the last day, the group engaged in conversation with the director of the Zagreb Jewish Old Age Home on the challenge of working with so many Holocaust Jews who, in the light of own their experience of history and conflict, chose to abandon their distinctive identity and become the most Yugoslavian of all Yugoslavs. Again and again we returned to the role of conflict as the ubiquitous force fuelling history. And, so we concluded the programme with a study of two versions of a text we had seen in the Sarajevo Hadggadah, Had Gadya – in both traditional and modern form.

Why suddenly do you sing *Chad Gadya*
When spring hasn't yet arrived and Passover hasn't come?
...That on all nights, all other nights I asked only Four Questions
This night I have another question:
'How long will the cycle of violence continue?'
Chase and be chased, beat and be beaten,
When will this madness end?
How have you changed, how are you different?
...I was once a sheep and a tranquil kid
Today I'm a tiger and a ravening wolf
I was once a dove and I was a deer.
Today I don't know who I am.
Dizavin abba bitrei zuzim, chad gadya, chad gadya.

(Chava Alberstein, 1989)

Reflecting on the journey, I am struck at how the core conversations were not defined by traditional subject matter of Jewish travel. Unlike Poland travel, for instance, this was not about the persecution of the Jews, although issues of anti-Semitism and displacement were certainly present. Unlike Israel travel, there was no thesis supporting the need for a Jewish homeland, closer ties to the land, or even the centrality of Israel etc., even though most if not all participants were committed Israel supporters. This was travel in the service of a very broad agenda, large universal issues all of which were being interpreted through particularistic eyes.

What made this journey Jewish? If the themes were so universal and the sites and stories drawn from across the board, what defined this as a Jewish journey? Primarily, the answer was the eyes, experiences and texts through which it was filtered: 'Looking at the Balkans through Jewish eyes'. This powerful, albeit for some, controversial notion is most challenging for the educator – developing a tourist experience that sharpens the ability to look with Jewish eyes.

Bibliography

Alberstein, C. (1989). On 'London', NMC, Tel Aviv.
Cohen, E. (1979). A phenomenology of tourist experiences. *Sociology, 13*, 179–201.
Connerton, P. (1989). *How societies remember*. New York: Cambridge University Press.
Kugelmass, J. (1994). Why we go to Poland: Holocaust tourism as secular ritual. In: J. Young (Ed.), *The art of memory: Holocaust memorials in history* (pp. 175–183). Munich and New York: Prestel.
Lowenthal, D. (1999). *The past is a foreign country*. Cambridge: Cambridge University Press.
Reisinger, Y., & Steiner, C. (2006). Reconceptualising interpretation: The role of tour guides in authentic tourism. *Current Issues in Tourism, 9*, 6.
Savenor, C. (1996). Encounters abroad: Travel as a Jewish educational tool. *Jewish Education News, 17*, 3.
Urry, J. (1990). *The tourist gaze: Leisure and travel in contemporary studies*. London: Sage.
Young, J. E. (1993). *The texture of memory*. New Haven, CT: Yale University Press.